The Wine Roads of Spain

The Wine Roads
of
SPAIN

MARC AND KIM MILLON

Photographs by Kim Millon

HarperCollins*Publishers*

HarperCollins*Publishers*
77–85 Fulham Palace Road,
Hammersmith, London W6 8JB

Published by HarperCollins*Publishers* 1993
9 8 7 6 5 4 3 2

Distributed in the United States by
HarperCollins*Publishers*,
10 East 53rd Street,
New York 10022

A catalogue record for this book is
available from the British Library

ISBN 0 246 13871 8

Set in Century Schoolbook by
Rowland Phototypesetting Ltd, Bury St Edmunds, Suffolk

Printed in Hong Kong

For Tiny and Jean

The Wine Roads of Spain

CONTENTS

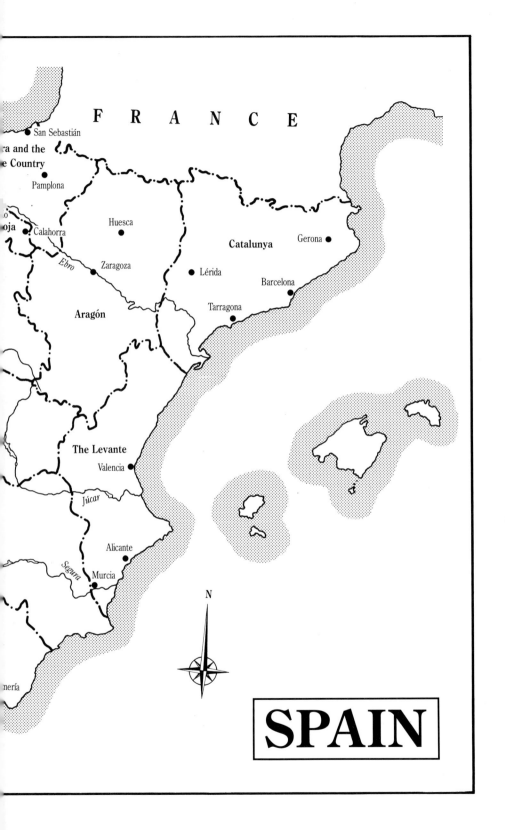

FRANCE

San Sebastián

ra and the
e Country

Pamplona

oja   Calahorra

Huesca

Catalunya

Gerona

Ebro

Zaragoza

Lérida

Barcelona

Aragón

Tarragona

The Levante

Valencia

Júcar

Alicante

Segura

Murcia

nería

N

SPAIN

Plaza de Toros, El Puerto de Santa María.

INTRODUCTION

Spain, a Catholic Country for Wine Lovers

When Ferdinand of Aragón and Isabel of Castile married in 1469 and subsequently united Spanish Iberia for the first time, they called themselves '*Los Reyes Católicos de las Españas*' – The Catholic Kings of the Spains, a recognition that the peninsula was not a single entity but comprised many different and separate kingdoms and countries, each with its own history, culture and traditions.

Today, wine lovers with catholic tastes will discover most enjoyably that from a vinous point of view Spain remains a collection of very different countries and separate autonomous regions. Imagine for a moment the briefest journey through some of Spain's varied wine country. Castilla y León, the heart of Catholic Spain, is a hard, uncompromising land, and the source today of the country's most manly and austere wines, the great aged reds of Ribero del Duero, as well as the immense, dense *caldos* of Toro. By contrast, in the far north-west corner of the peninsula there is Galicia, the wettest, greenest region of Spain, where fragrant delicate Albariño wines are served in white china cups to accompany wooden platters of boiled, spicy *pulpo* (octopus).

The Costers del Segre in Catalunya's inland Lérida province, on the other hand, is a near-desert wasteland that has been transformed into an oasis through the virtual sole efforts of the Raventós family, whose highly advanced and innovative Raimat estate is considered something of a model not only for Spain but for all of Europe. Nearby, the Penedés, with its sparkling Cava and superlative red and white table wines, has emerged as one of the country's leading and most forward-looking wine zones. Yet if Catalunya represents the new modern face of Spain's wine industry, the country's vast central interior, Castilla-La Mancha, remains on the whole timeless and little changed, its endless flat plains topped by white windmills, an ancient land where wines are still made today as in the days of the Romans, fermented in immense terracotta urns known as *tinajas*.

To the south, what region could be more quintessentially Spanish than Andalucía, land of *flamenco*, the bullfight and *mañana*? Here, in great whitewashed, low-lying *bodegas*, wines continue to be produced by an age-old, patient system of fractional blending and ageing in *soleras*: the resulting sherries are vivid, fresh, above all bone dry in their native country, dramatically fine, especially when sampled in the cool of the *bodega* itself, dashed from on high with a flick of the whalebone-and-silver *venencia* into a waiting handful of *copitas*.

Even areas not primarily noted for wines may yield some unexpected surprises. In the Alicante hinterland behind the ghastly concrete sprawl of Benidorm, for example, an old-fashioned, rarely encountered *vino rancio* is still produced, Fondillón, which by any standard must be considered among the great wines of the world, regardless of the fact that such heady, powerful and sweet aged dessert wines are hardly fashionable today. Yet what a total contrast Fondillón presents with the slightly fizzy, sometimes turbid, usually home-made 'green' wine, Txakolì, produced in the northern Basque Country and drunk in prodigious quantity in its bars and male-only gastronomic societies.

Medieval pilgrims who crossed the Pyrenees via the high, historic Roncesvalles Pass on the long road to Saint James's shrine in far-off Galicia historically slaked their thirst with the wines of Navarra and Rioja. Today wine pilgrims may choose to follow this same route: Navarra has emerged in recent years as one of Spain's most dynamic wine regions and the source of robust *rosados* as well as excellent oak-aged 'new wave' reds produced from blends of classic Spanish grapes together with international interlopers such as Cabernet Sauvignon and Merlot. Rioja, meanwhile, with its great

How to Get There

By Air   Iberia (071-437 5622) and British Airways (081-897 4000) operate daily scheduled flights to Spain, with services to Madrid, Barcelona, Seville, Valencia, Santiago de Compostela and other regional capitals. Furthermore, there are numerous charter airlines that operate flights to a large variety of coastal holiday destinations. For independent touring, there are numerous fly/drive options available.

From North America, there are direct flights to Spain on Iberia, TWA, American Airlines and AeroMexico.

By Ferry   Touring Spain's wine country is without doubt an activity for independent travellers; for this, the use of a car is essential, so many visitors from Britain may choose to travel to Spain with their own car, either by passage across the Channel then on by way of France, or else directly from Britain to Spain on Brittany Ferries' Plymouth–Santander service (0752-221321). The crossing takes 24 hours; the ships are extremely well fitted and comfortable (weather permitting) and there are excellent restaurants on board.

collection of internationally known *bodegas* where thousands of oak barrels of fine red wines lie ageing, remains (in spite of increased competition from other emerging zones) the country's premier table wine region, and a wonderful place to visit to sample those great wines at source, together with feasts of baby lamb cooked in wood-fired baker's ovens, or *chuletas* grilled over a fire of vineshoots by the *bodeguero* himself.

The wine roads of Spain lead you to all of these places and to many more.

The Wine Roads of Spain: Something Different

Some years ago, the Spanish came up with an advertising campaign to promote their country, noting the obvious: Spain is different. Separated from the rest of Europe by the physical barrier of the Pyrenees and for much of this century by its political isolation during the years of dictatorship, Spain has long stood apart. It has probably always been so, since at least the days when the Moors held sway over most of the Iberian peninsula;

even after they departed, they left behind considerable remnants of their unique culture that still colour life in Spain today.

Over the last decades, thousands and millions of tourists may have visited Spain yet experienced little more than the 'delights' of Lloret del Mar, Benidorm, Torremolinos and other such popular hot spots along the Spanish *costas*, gaining little or no true insight into what a peculiarly individual and different country Spain is. It may be a truism to state that one need only travel a few kilometres inland, away from the usually disappointing beaches, the concrete *paseos* and high-rise blocks of flats and hotels, to find something of the real Spain; but true it remains.

Touring the wine roads of Spain is

The Alhambra, Granada.

one particularly enjoyable means of experiencing the country and its people. In some cases, excursions can be made into the heart of classic wine zones as a diversion from more traditional holiday pursuits. The resorts of Catalunya provide easy access into that region's great wine zones, especially the Penedés and Cava country. Visitors to Galicia should not miss touring the vineyards of the Rias Baixas near the Portuguese border in the intervals of enjoying the clean Atlantic beaches and superlative feasts of seafood and shellfish. In Andalucía, the historic vineyards of Málaga are actually located along or just inland from the Costa del Sol, while the great sherry towns of Jerez de la Frontera, El Puerto de Santa María and Sanlúcar de Barrameda form an inland triangle above the still mainly unspoiled Costa de la Luz. The wine country of Montilla-Moriles lies just to the south of one of the greatest Moorish cities of Spain, Córdoba.

Inland Spain, with its vast and endless central *meseta*, provides rewarding wine travel, too, if to less obvious destinations. Castilla y León, the historic region of Old Castile, boasts the great cities of the central interior: Salamanca, León, Burgos, Valladolid, Segovia, Avila and Zamora. The region makes up a full fifth of the Spanish mainland and is traversed by the great Duero river, which, across the national frontier with Portugal, becomes the mighty Douro of port wine fame. This is without doubt one of the great wine rivers of the world.

Castilla-La Mancha to the south, an interminable and wide plateau covered with stumpy, low-yielding Airén vines, fields of wheat, or scrubby grazing lands for sheep and goats, is the spiritual homeland of Cervantes' Don Quixote. In this endless and lonely country, with its thin, rarefied atmosphere, it is perhaps no wonder that the knight errant hallucinated so vividly, seeing windmills as giants or a barber's basin as the precious helmet of Mambrino. Today, outside small *pueblos* and larger wine towns alike, immense outdoor fermentation vessels appear like similar incongruous mirages, shimmering in the relentless midday sun.

Even as remote a region as Extremadura deserves to be visited from a wine point of view. Land-locked, located above Andalucía and adjacent to the Portuguese frontier, Extremadura is Spain's forgotten region, poor, underdeveloped, little visited. Yet this harsh land sent forth into the world native sons who were to become Spain's greatest *conquistadores*. On their voyages of discovery, they took the wines of Extremadura with them to present to the native kings they encountered as one of their most prized gifts, and later missionaries took the vine and so planted the New World's first *Vitis vinifera* vineyards. Today Extremadura is a wine region of only minor importance; none the less, it is the source of isolated wines that deserve to be better known, as well as local wines that will serve to slake the thirst of adventurous explorers who happen to bushwhack their way to this remote but still fascinating region.

If the regions of Spain demonstrate the great variety of a vast land, its wines are also evidence of a similar expansive ingenuity. Indeed, no other country on earth – not even France or Italy – produces such a wide variety of classic styles and types of wine as Spain. Sherry, of course, is one of the world's most famous fortified wines, a benchmark type imitated widely throughout the world, even its rightful name blatantly and shamelessly plagiarized. Yet authentic sherry, which comes only from the delimited triangle of vineyards in south-west Andalucía centred on Jerez de la Frontera, is wholly unique and one of the great classic wines of the world. Sherry itself comes in a remarkable variety and range of styles, from the lightest, tangy and sea-fresh *manzanillas* through elegant, bone-dry *finos*, nutty *amontillados* and fuller *olorosos*, to dark, sweet creams and black-and-raisiny Pedro Ximénez wines.

Spain is a land that produces fine and prestigious red wines from Rioja, Ribera del Duero, Navarra, Penedés and Valdepeñas. Fine, modern fresh white wines that combine fruit, acidity and moderate levels of alcohol are being produced in Rueda, Penedés, Alella, Valencia, Galicia, Somontano and elsewhere, while traditional oak-aged white wines are still made in Rioja, and new style *barrica*-fermented Chardonnays come from Costers del Segre, Somontano and Penedés. Navarra is the source of superlative *rosados*, at once fruity, bone dry and robust. Cava without doubt ranks among the best mid-range sparkling wines of the world.

These – and many others – are the classic as well as the new wines of Spain. Yet the old, traditional, timeless wines of Spain still exist, too, and for the curious wine traveller they may prove just as fascinating. The Levante, for example is still the source of vast quantities of dense, anonymous, hugely tannic *vinos de doble pasta*, produced by a unique system of maceration on a double '*sombrero*' of skins, so imparting deep colour and extract to wines destined mainly for blending (but which in their zones of production are actually enjoyed as beverages in their own right – try them, if you dare, at your own peril). Old-style traditional *vinos rancios* continue to be produced in Alicante, Huelva, Rueda, Tarragona, Ampurdán-Costa Brava and elsewhere. In Rueda and parts of Catalunya, such wines are put into loosely-stoppered 16-litre glass *bombas* then left outside to bake in the hot summer sun and freeze in the bitter cold of winter. The wines that

INTRODUCTION

In Galicia local wines are served in white china *tazitas*.

emerge from such brutal treatment may not be wholly to our taste, but beyond dispute they are unique!

For the visitor – the curious wine traveller – Spain furthermore provides classic wine-drinking experiences that are uniquely Spanish and which should not be missed.

I am thinking about sitting out at Sanlúcar's Bajo de Guía *paseo* as the sun sets over the Coto de Doñana, lingering over straight-sided *cañas* of sea-fresh *manzanilla* together with a plate of freshly boiled *langostinos de Sanlúcar*; of relaxing in a pavement restaurant in Sitges, enjoying *flûtes* of elegant, artisan-made Cava while watching that particularly crazy corner of the world stroll by; of the *taberna* in Ribadavia where we sat with old Gallegan men around the wooden barrels, sipping home-made Ribeiro wines out of white china *tazitas* as if time did not exist; of holding a *porrón* at arm's length, the red wine passing most pleasantly into our mouths in a fluid parabolic arc, but spattering our white shirt fronts most embarrassingly when we tried to finish the drink; and of the time we shared wine from a *bota* with a cheesemaker in La Mancha on a hellishly hot summer's day, the white Manchegan wine, squeezed from a pitch-lined leather goatskin, hissing into the back of our parched throats and combining so well with the salty Manchegan cheese (the cheesemaker even insisted on giving our three-year-old son, Guy, a squirt of the cave-cool wine).

These are wines and wine experiences unlike those you will encounter anywhere else in Europe or the world. Spain and its wines and wine roads, it is true, are nothing if not different.

La Movida: Feel It, Enjoy It!

It is less than twenty years since the death of Franco liberated Spain from four decades of arch-conservative and authoritarian dictatorship. In the ensuing brief period, Spain has shed outdated images of torpor to emerge as one of the most exciting, vibrant and dynamic countries in Europe. This, one senses, is above all a young country that is on the move and enjoying itself greatly in the process.

'*La movida*' is the name given to Spain's post-Franco renaissance, a virtually total – almost overnight – transformation in values, mores, lifestyle and material aspirations that has taken hold certainly in Madrid, Barcelona and Seville, as well as throughout the Iberian peninsula, even in the most unlikely and out-of-the-way outposts. At its heart is the belief that the country, for so long on the fringe of European affairs, is now ready to take its rightful place at the centre of where the action is. Since joining the European Community as a full member state in 1986, Spain's commitment to Europe has been positive and wholly enthusiastic. Today, its economy is strong and everywhere there is a feeling of boundless confidence and optimism, an excitement perhaps unlike anything the country has experienced

since an intrepid Genoese sailor set sail from Palos de la Frontera in Andalucía some five centuries ago and returned seven months later having discovered a new world.

Certainly Spain today is emerging as something of a 'new world' wine country. That is not to say that this country's previously unwieldy, at times dinosaur-like wine industry has yet been completely transformed. It has not. But change is happening, and fast.

Take Alejandro Fernandez's now famous wine, Pesquera, produced in Ribero del Duero and a worthy representative of the new wines of Spain. As recently as fifteen years ago, this wine was produced in a primitive peasant *bodega* adjacent to the modern one that has since been built,

The older generation have time to observe and reflect on a rapidly changing country.

INTRODUCTION

fermented in the timeless traditional manner, on the stalks and skins in an open-topped stone *lagar*. Yet so rapid has been the rise from obscurity to international stardom that today the new winery is full of gleaming stainless steel and banks of sweet-smelling new American oak *barricas*, and the resulting wine has been dubbed by the American wine guru Robert Parker the 'Pétrus of Spain'.

In Spain itself, few may have heard of either Parker or Pétrus, but there have been notable changes of attitude and outlook here, too. For if until recently the Spaniards themselves hardly appreciated the worth of their own wines (with the exception of sherry and Rioja), today there is a growing awareness of and pride in the wealth of wines now being produced throughout the country. Wine previously was viewed as little more than a basic and everyday commodity – as ordinary, as indispensable, as noteworthy and as taken for granted as bread or water.

Miguel Augustín Torres, a genius of a winemaker as well as a leading representative of Spain's youthful dynamism, helped bring about profound changes by pioneering a range of both modern, young fruity everyday wines, and serious wines of the highest quality. Indeed, when Torres' Gran Coronas Reserva 'Black Label' 1970 took top honours at the so-called 'Wine Olympiad' organized by the French gourmet publishers Gault-Millau in 1979 (beating even the *premier grand cru classé* Château Latour), it awoke Spaniards and the world to the country's immense and as yet still not fully tapped potential.

Spain's wine *movida* has since gathered pace and there is no shortage of youthful energy and ideas in *bodegas* throughout the country. The profession has attracted a large number of highly motivated and intelligent young people who will no doubt take Spain and Spanish wine to the very top as we approach the next millennium.

The Wine Roads of Spain: Visiting *Bodegas*

Spain's wine regions still remain very much uncharted country. There is a signposted *ruta del vino* in the sherry zone, a *ruta del sol y del vino* in the Axarquía zone of Málaga, and a projected plan for a signposted *ruta del vino* in La Rioja. Tiny Somontano in Aragón has a wine route with producers along the way happy to receive visitors, offer tastings and sell their wines direct. Some region's tourist organizations suggest itineraries into the wine country (Valladolid's '*ruta del vino blanco*' and '*ruta del vino tinto*' or Vilafranca del Penedés' suggested itineraries into the Penedés and Cava country). But these are isolated or as yet incipient projects.

Indeed, the concept of wine as a precious commodity, as an object or source of intrinsic interest for the foreign tourist, is still something of a novelty in a country that has traditionally viewed the growing of grapes as little different from the growing of oranges, tomatoes, or any other agricultural cash crop.

There is, for example, little tradition of estate winemaking in Spain. Small growers have traditionally chosen to sell their grapes to co-operative wineries, or else to larger private concerns who vinify, blend and finally market the finished wines. This remains broadly the case even today. Even those *bodegas* that have their own vineyards may usually also purchase grapes, pressed but unfermented grape must, or fermented but unaged wines to supplement their production.

Visiting vineyards and wineries in Spain is thus somewhat different from pursuing the same activities in either France or Italy. In those countries, there is no shortage of small growers anxious to receive visitors, proud to show off their wines and talk about them over copious and extended tastings, and, naturally, eager to sell their wines by the bottle or case to passers-by. Though such opportunities do exist in Spain, they are fewer and further between.

On the other hand, many of the great sherry houses in south-west Andalucía, the famous sparkling wine concerns in San Sadurní de Noya, Torres in Vilafranca del Penedés, and some of the internationally known Rioja *bodegas* do keep open house for the wine tourist, conduct informative tours of winemaking installations, and offer generous free tastings.

There is, moreover, a long-standing tradition of purchasing wine direct from the *bodega* or *bodega cooperativa* that still exists today, so visitors who turn up prepared to purchase a few bottles may often be able to taste the wines and tour the winemaking installations if time permits.

We have visited, corresponded with or spoken over the telephone with all the *bodegas* included in this book. They have been selected above all for the excellence of their wines, as well as for their willingness to receive visitors. This selection, however, makes no claim to be comprehensive: many of those included are the producers of wines that are world famous; others may not yet be well-known internationally but perhaps will be in the near future. Others again may simply be good local producers whose wines are delicious to encounter and enjoy on the spot. On the other hand, some well-known producers may be notable absentees simply because they have not responded to our queries, letters or faxes, or because we are not familiar with them.

The *bodegas* themselves have supplied their own practical visiting details. Most state that it is necessary to make an appointment. This means generally that you should write or telephone in advance before turning up on the doorstep, if possible. If you are staying in the zone, ask your hotel to telephone ahead for you. On the other hand, if this is not possible, it never hurts simply to turn up and take pot-luck. If there is someone on hand to show you around, you will probably be well received. Spaniards are above all hospitable: it has certainly been our experience that they are more than happy to receive foreign visitors and serious, interested wine lovers.

We have indicated whether or not English or other foreign languages are spoken; however this does not necessarily mean that someone will always be on hand at all times. Most of the younger generation will have studied at least a little English at school, and few Spaniards will actually expect you to speak their own language. None the less, as always, a little Spanish goes a long way and will invariably be well appreciated.

Do bear in mind that most *bodegas* – like most of the rest of the country – close for the entire month of August.

Purchasing Wine and the EC Single Market: Minimum Indicative Levels

As of 1 January 1993 and the completion of the EC Single Market, private individuals are permitted, in theory, to buy unlimited quantities of excisable goods on which duty has been paid in another Member State. The term 'allowance' is no longer applicable; however, persons bringing into the UK goods in excess of any minimum indicative level may be required to provide evidence, to the satisfaction of HM Customs and Excise, that they are not transporting such goods for commercial purposes. EC Directive COM (90) 432, article 8a, gives the following guide to minimum indicative levels:

Spirits	10 litres
Fortified wine	20 litres
Wine	90 litres (of which 60 may be sparkling)
Beers	110 litres

The directive also allows for duty-free allowances for intra-Community travellers to continue until 30 June 1999.

An Abundant Table is Laid

Travel anywhere in Spain, enter virtually any bar in the country, and you will invariably find that an abundant table is laid. This is the land, above all, where the variety and quantity of drinking snacks – *pinchos, tapas, banderillas*, call them what you will – has been raised virtually to an art form, the tasty titbits and morsels serving one principal aim: to encourage and promote a healthy thirst and the liberal consumption of wine. In San Sebastián's old quarter, whole streets lined with little else but bars compete for custom by offering amazing arrays of bite-size *bocadillos, tortillas*, stuffed eggs, fried fish, spicy meatballs, stewed spider crab and much else. In Galicia, bars invariably tempt with sea-fresh arrays of superlative shellfish: *mejillones* (mussels), *pulpo* (boiled, spicy octopus), *navajas* (razor-shell clams), *almejas* (clams), quickly prepared and usually served piping hot to accompany fresh, cold white wines. In Extremadura, on the other hand, *pinchos* – hot *cazuelitas* of *pruebas de morcilla* (spicy blood sausage) or home-made *chorizo* or *longaniza* – accompany tumblers of gutsy home-made *pitarra* wines. Meanwhile, way down in Andalucía, especially in that region's famous sherry triangle, bars offer a simply staggering choice of fried fish and shellfish, together with boiled *gambas* and *langostinos*, as well as more elaborate *raciones* of *salpicón* or seafood *guisos* to accompany half-bottles of *bodega*-fresh *fino* and *manzanilla*.

As this wonderful custom demonstrates, drinking and eating are two activities that are wholly inseparable in Spain.

Strictly speaking, *tapas* should serve to whet the appetite, not satiate it. Obviously, if they are varied enough, they may more often than not form a virtual meal in themselves; indeed, 'cruising' from one *tapas* bar to the next is one of the most popular and enjoyable activities in Spain, almost, it could be said, the national sport.

For the Spaniards, though, *tapas* usually serve to fill in lengthy gaps between mealtimes that are at variance with the rest of the world. In Spain, it is essential to remember that it is rare to go out to lunch much before 1.30 or 2 P.M., and not unusual to begin as late as 4 P.M. In the evening, no one would consider going to a restaurant any earlier than 9 or 9.30 P.M.; it is by no means uncommon to sit down at 11 o'clock or later. The Spaniards are great and gregarious night owls, and a weekday's evening might well continue into the wee hours of the next morning.

If Spain as a nation is made up of separate historical entities, with their own histories, traditions and culture, so does each also demonstrate its own proud gastronomic traditions. Indeed, one of the most enjoyable aspects of touring the country is that it is virtually impossible *not* to eat well regionally. The *freidurías* – fried fish stands or shops – of Andalucía producing the lightest floured-and-fried hake, squid, or *gambas* exist nowhere else. In Old Castile, the great *hornos de asar* – wood-fired baker's ovens for the cooking of *lechazo* (milk-fed baby lamb), *cochinillo* (sucking pig), or *cabrito* (kid) – are similarly unique institutions that should not be missed. True, *paella a la valenciana*, it could be argued, is one Spanish dish that has transcended regional, even national borders: yet to enjoy real *paella*, as served only in the Levante and preferably in Valencia's Albufera rice-growing zone, is one of the great gastronomic highlights of a trip to Spain, the special short-grain rice cooked to perfection in the traditional steel pan, preferably over a wood fire, and containing most classically not great arrays of shellfish, but simply chicken, rabbit, a particular type of fresh bean known as *garrafon*, and always *caracoles* – snails.

It is impossible for a journey along the wine roads of Spain not to become at the same time something of a culinary adventure, and the curious traveller with an open mind will rarely be disappointed. Based on the successful formula followed in the other volumes in the 'wine roads' series, we have asked the wine producers themselves to nominate their favourite local restaurants since they know their own areas best, and most have been more than happy to oblige. We then visited, ate at, corresponded with, or telephoned these restaurants, and, together with scores of other restaurants that we have encountered in the course of our travels, they form the core of our recommended restaurant sections. They range from the most humble and basic *fondas* to elegant and sophisticated temples of Spanish gastronomy. Most serve local or locally-inspired dishes and regional foods, and should have at the very least a reasonable selection of local wines.

The brief of this book does not intend it to be either a comprehensive restaurant or hotel guide. However, travel in inland Spain in particular remains something of an adventure, and many of the wine regions covered are well off the beaten track. We have therefore also included where relevant a brief selection of good hotels that may serve as bases for exploration of the wine country. We have also included details of *paradores* in the wine country, as well as a selection of recommended campsites.

Since prices always rise, we have used the following simple guide to indicate the approximate price range for a full 3- or 4-course meal and local wine based on Spanish restaurant prices current in 1992 (at the time of writing, the pound is equivalent to about 180 pesetas; the US dollar is equivalent to about 100 pesetas).

Very Inexpensive	Less than 2000 *pesetas*
Inexpensive	2000–3500 *pesetas*
Moderate	3000–4500 *pesetas*
Expensive	4500–6500 *pesetas*
Very Expensive	Over 6500 *pesetas*

Paradores

Spain's network of state *paradores* is one of the world's great chains of hotels. Located in castles, monasteries, restored medieval hospitals, Moorish palaces, royal hunting lodges and the like, as well as in modern buildings usually sited to take advantage of a particularly fine position or view, they enable the visitor to experience the flavour and history of Spain in a wholly unique way. They all have reasonable to excellent restaurants that serve a selection of local foods and regional specialities, together with a more than adequate choice of local, regional and national wines.

We have highlighted all those *paradores* in or near the wine country. Even if you are not staying in a *parador*, don't hesitate to drop in for a drink or *tapa*, or to eat in the restaurant. They are part of Spain's national heritage and they are there for everyone to enjoy.

Paradores can be booked in the UK prior to departure, or you can use the central booking office in Madrid. Alternatively, telephone the individual *paradores* direct, or simply take pot-luck and turn up.

Keytel International
402 Edgware Rd
London W2 1ED
tel: 071-402 8182; fax: 071-724 9503

Paradores de Turismo de España, SA
Velázquez 18
28001 Madrid
tel: (91) 435 97 00; fax: (91) 435 99 44

INTRODUCTION

Denominaciónes de Origen

Spain has a long history of laws issued to maintain the quality of its wines and to preserve their reputation, as well as to protect them from unwanted outside competition. As early as 1102, for example, King Sancho of Navarra drew up *fueros* to protect the wines of Rioja and Navarra after entreaties from local growers.

Today, Spain's system of *denominación de origen* (DO) serves the same essential purpose. There are now nearly 40 zones entitled to DO status, a designation that brings regional, national and even international recognition, and which lays down strictures relating to the delimited zone itself, types of grape varieties that are authorized, methods of production, styles of wine, minimum alcohol levels, and other quality-control factors.

There has been some vociferous criticism in the international press at the granting of DO to some zones that are tiny or whose wines will rarely be encountered outside the zone or region of production. I don't necessarily agree, however. Just a decade ago, virtually the only wine regions in Spain that were known internationally were Jerez and Rioja. Today, through the great improvements made in the Spanish wine industry in the intervening years, quality wines are emerging from many different wine zones and regions, some of which only a few years ago were unlikely and virtually unheard of (Costers del Segre, Rias Baixas, Somontano, for example). I believe that as Spain's wine revolution gathers pace, better and better wines will continue to emerge in the future, even from zones or regions not yet even demarcated.

Furthermore, a new tier of superior quality has recently been created, *denominación de origen calificada* (DOCa). At present, only Rioja is entitled to this new, select status, which imposes even stricter controls on viticulture and vinification, and demands, for example, mandatory bottling in the zone of origin. However, it is certain that other quality wine zones will soon be granted DOCa and this will serve as a further guarantee of quality for the consumer.

May You Have Much Thirst

Spain, the real Spain, is not a country for the fainthearted or overly timid. Like its wines, Spain is, above all, authentic and genuine, with its own inimitable and unmistakable personality and soul. The wine roads of Spain take you to the very heart of the country, the myriad and diverse regions that collectively make up this immense nation, stretched out like a tawny bull-hide tacked on to the very edge of Europe.

Distances are vast, the roads often dusty, and along the way, it is likely that you will work up an immense and healthy thirst. The well of Spanish wines is abundant and overflowing: drink deeply and enjoy.

April 1992
Topsham, Devon, England

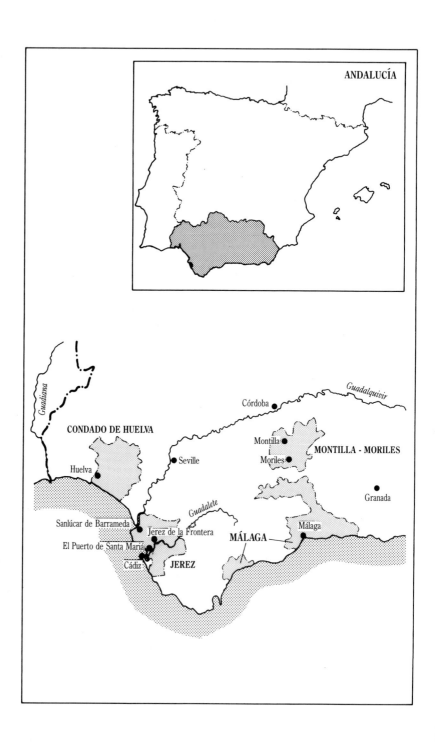

ANDALUCÍA

Guadiana

Guadalquivir

Córdoba

CONDADO DE HUELVA

Montilla

MONTILLA - MORILES

Moriles

Huelva

Seville

Granada

Guadalete

Sanlúcar de Barrameda

Jerez de la Frontera

El Puerto de Santa María

Málaga

MÁLAGA

Cádiz

JEREZ

ANDALUCÍA

oro, the *'bodega* of the bull', Antonio adillo, Sanlúcar de Barameda.

Andalucía is the Spain of our dreams. All those Iberian associations – images, sounds and smells – that we from northern Europe or North America harbour in the cold of winter, originate here, shimmering under an intense, almost African sun that shines some 300 days of the year: the blinding, whitewashed villages – *los pueblos blancos* – and endless parched-brown *campos* where bulls are raised to fight and die in the afternoon; hooded penitents, winding their way through city and village *barrios* during Semana Santa; the frenetic clack of castanets, the manic strum of the guitar to counterpoint the arrogance and sensuality of the *flamenco*; the mosques, minarets and pleasure palaces built by emirs and caliphs a thousand years ago when the Moors held court and made the region one of Europe's most enlightened centres of learning, art and culture; and mosques, marinas and pleasure palaces built only decades ago by petrol-rich kings and princes from the Gulf.

Yet Andalucía is not simply a land of southern stereotypes. Tourism has undoubtedly brought prosperity to coastal zones but the region remains on the whole poor and underdeveloped, with the highest percentage of unemployment in Spain. The movement of young people from rural outlying *pueblos* to cities continues, while the realities of *latifundio* – the feudal system of land ownership whereby immense tracts are owned mainly by aristocratic absentee landlords – adds to the general lack of prosperity and initiative, the heat-sapping torpor that gives rise to the cult of *mañana*.

It is too hot, you may think, in this southern land of *sol* and not much *sombra*, too arid, brown and parched for the fruitful cultivation of the vine. And yet, for centuries if not millennia, the blazingly white chalk soil around the town known today as Jerez de la Frontera – frontier between Moor and Christian – has proved a most propitious habitat for the Palomino grape, destined, when fermented and dynamically matured in *soleras*, to yield one of the world's great classic wines, sherry.

Elsewhere, vines grow as they do throughout the Mediterranean, here, there, everywhere, mixed among the olive groves, citrus orchards and

Orientation

Andalucía, the southernmost mainland region of Spain, comprises eight provinces: Seville, Málaga, Cádiz, Huelva, Córdoba, Jaén, Granada and Almería. Encompassing the Costa del Sol (which extends from Almería in the east to Tarifa in the west), and including such important cities as Seville, Córdoba and Granada, it remains undoubtedly the most popular of all Spain's regions and is extremely well served by air, rail and road.

There are international airports at Málaga, Seville and Jerez de la Frontera. By train, the main rail routes connect the principal cities: Madrid–Córdoba–Seville–Jerez–Cádiz, Madrid–Málaga, and Madrid–Granada. The fastest new 'super-train', when up and running, will connect the capital with Seville in only three hours. There are numerous local trains and buses connecting Seville and Cádiz with Jerez, El Puerto de Santa María and Sanlúcar de Barrameda.

The region is well served by roads, though driving times should be adjusted to take account of the mountainous nature of the terrain. Jerez de la Frontera, the region's foremost wine zone, is located about 84 km south of Seville, off the A4 *autopista* between the regional capital and Cádiz. Jerez can also be reached from the Costa del Sol via Ronda and is also within a day's drive of the Portuguese Algarve.

Those visiting Córdoba can enjoy Montilla in the bars and restaurants of that great Moorish city, as well as visiting nearby Montilla itself to taste those magnificent *tinaja*-fermented wines at the source.

Málaga, its wines and *bodegas*, makes an unusual interlude away from the more obvious attractions of the Costa del Sol, while the vineyards of Condado de Huelva can be dipped into by any heading either to the Coto de Doñana or further west to the Portuguese Algarve.

Maps: Michelin No. 446 (Southern); Firestone Hispania C-9, T-30.

almond plantations. The steep slopes above Málaga, for example, are the source of a sweet wine much loved by the Victorians who knew it as 'Mountain'. South of the old Moorish capital Córdoba, the vine is cultivated extensively in the zone of Montilla-Moriles to produce an extensive and impressive range of wines that deserve to be better known, and which would

The *Reconquista*

In 711 AD, the Berber Tariq Ben Zeyad crossed the Straits of Gibraltar from northern Africa and at the Battle of the Guadalete near present-day Jerez de la Frontera routed the Visigothic King Roderic. Within three years, the Berbers swept north and overran almost the entire peninsula, so beginning the occupation of Spain that was to last nearly 800 years until they were pushed out of Granada in 1492 and finally expelled from Spain in 1568.

The *Reconquista*, or Reconquest of Spain by the Christians, began with a historic victory by Pelayo, a Visigothic ruler of Asturias, at Covadonga in 722. In 844, on the field of battle at Clavijo, the Christian cause was further aided considerably through the apparent supernatural intervention of Santiago Matamoros, Saint James the Moorslayer. And so the struggle continued, virtually without pause throughout the history of the Moors' occupation of the peninsula. Little by little, lands and cities were reclaimed, the frontier between Christian and Moor was redrawn, and the border moved ever further south.

Córdoba, the Moors' fabled capital, fell in 1236; Seville in 1237. Jerez was finally brought under Christian rule by King Alfonso X in 1264. But this did not mean that the Moors relinquished control of all their precious Al-Andalus, for they retreated and regrouped in the Kingdom of Granada, in the splendour of the fabled Alhambra palace. The wars and struggles were to continue for a further 200 years, and thus Jerez de la Frontera together with Vejer de la Frontera, Chiclana de la Frontera and Arcos de la Frontera, continued to stand for long as the final frontier between Christian and Moor.

After his victory at Jerez, Alfonso X divided the lands he had expropriated from the Moors into '*aranzadas*' of 4000 square metres each (one hectare equals 2.25 *aranzadas*), and distributed these among his loyal followers and soldiers, the so-called Knights of the Fief. Great tracts of vineyards were planted and the descendants of some of these medieval *caballeros* remain even today the heads of some of the great sherry dynasties.

ANDALUCÍA

be if they had not hidden for so long in the shadow of their more famous neighbours at Jerez (indeed the sherry term *amontillado* means 'in the style of Montilla'). The province of Huelva, too, has long supplied wines to Jerez, though it is now increasingly producing them under its own *denominación*, both in the old, maderized traditional style, and in fresher, lighter styles of young table wines.

Notwithstanding the fact that Jerez de la Frontera is one of the great wine towns of Europe (and indeed, one of the most welcoming and enjoyable to visit), few who come to Andalucía will be here solely in search of wine. There are too many other vivid attractions that vie for our attention. Yet, none the less, wine, whether dashed dramatically from the *venencia* into a waiting handful of *copitas*, or served in beaded bottles or *jarras* at any number of inviting shellfish bars up and down this considerable southern coastline, remains one of the region's principal pleasures, and a means of connecting us with a way of life that is never less than flamboyant and always compellingly intoxicating.

LOS VINOS: THE WINES OF ANDALUCÍA

Jerez-Xères-Sherry DO The *denominación* for sherry lays down specific rules relating to the demarcated zone of cultivation, authorized grape varieties, yields and minimum alcohol levels, and production methods and ageing disciplines.

The delimited vineyard extends over some 19,000 hectares mainly in the province of Cádiz in municipalities including Jerez de la Frontera, El Puerto de Santa María, Sanlúcar de Barrameda, Trebujena, Rota, Chipiona, Puerto Real and Chiclana de la Frontera; Lebrija lies in the province of Seville. The *bodegas* for the maturing of sherry must be located in Jerez de la Frontera, El Puerto de Santa María and Sanlúcar de Barrameda. The three authorized grape varieties are Palomino, Pedro Ximénez (PX) and Moscatel, though in practice, PX and Moscatel are used primarily for sweetening blends.

Sherry is a fortified wine aged by a unique dynamic method known as the *solera* system. Wines of varying ages but of essentially similar character (*fino*, *amontillado*, *oloroso*) are constantly refreshed with quantities of older wines, the rationale being that the character of the older will gradually be absorbed by the younger. Each firm's various *soleras* maintain a unique character, thus enabling the skilled blender to produce consistent house brands year after year.

A range of different styles and types of sherry is produced, the principal types of which are:

Fino   Bone-dry, pale, light sherry, considered by many to be the finest apéritif in the world. *Fino* is produced from wines with the propensity to grow *flor*, a beneficial yeast growth which appears on the surface of the wine, both protecting it from oxidation and imparting inimitable bouquet, flavour and elegance. Alcohol 15.5–17°.

Manzanilla   Type of *fino* produced only in *bodegas* located in the seafront town of Sanlúcar de Barrameda; such wine is prized foremost for its extremely pale colour, bone-dry finish, and a characteristic salty tang. The cooler temperature and moister atmosphere of Sanlúcar results in an even thicker, more luxuriant growth of *flor* here, thus enabling the unique production of this special wine. While *manzanilla* is most usually the most delicate and freshest of all *finos*, there are also aged styles: *manzanilla pasada*, for example, is a type of aged *manzanilla* that approaches the style of an *amontillado*. Alcohol 15.5–17°.

Amontillado   True *amontillado* is an aged *fino* whose *flor* has eventually died off; the result is a bone-dry wine with a characteristic pungent and nutty flavour. However, the term has come to be used by blenders of branded wines to indicate any type of medium-dry to medium-sweet sherry. True dry *amontillados* are rare and unique wines that should be sought and tried. Alcohol 15.5–18°.

Oloroso   Broad class of wines which, unlike those of the *fino* family, have not been brought up under the beneficial influence of *flor*. At an early stage of the wine's life, it is decided to fortify it above the level at which the *flor* yeast can survive. *Oloroso* wine generally has bolder, rounder, fuller flavours than *fino*. In its natural state it is bone dry: a magnificently pungent and powerful wine. Usually, however, it forms the base for the great, dark, sweet blends of medium and cream sherries very popular not so much in Spain but internationally. Alcohol 18–20°.

Palo Cortado   A rare aberration: a sherry from the *oloroso* family that displays the elegance and bouquet of a *fino*.

Cream   Cream sherry is a blended wine produced usually from *oloroso* together with the addition of Pedro Ximénez or Moscatel wines that

ANDALUCÍA

add not only intense sweetness but also the rich mahogany colour that is its hallmark.

Pale Cream Sweet sherry produced from a pale base of either *fino* or *amontillado* to which is added colourless rectified sweet must or wine.

Pedro Ximénez Pedro Ximénez grapes are usually laid out on *esparto* mats to dry and shrivel in the sun, thereby concentrating their sugars to make super-sweet, dark wines that are used primarily for sweetening blends. However, some producers bottle straight PX wines in their own right: thick and black as *espresso*, and hugely concentrated in rich, raisiny sweetness.

Table Wines Increasingly in the Jerez zone, producers are using their modern winemaking installations to produce light fruity table wines from early-harvested Palomino grapes. Such wines can be excellent and make a change for those who tire of drinking fortified sherries while in the zone. However, as they are prone to early oxidation, they must always be drunk as young as possible, definitely within their year of production.

Montilla-Moriles DO Range of wines broadly similar in type and style to sherry produced from grapes grown in delimited vineyards in the southern half of the province of Córdoba, centred primarily on the towns of Montilla and Moriles. The Pedro Ximénez grape accounts for almost the total production; grown in a hot, dry inland climate, it is picked when fully ripe and ferments to about 14–16° alcohol naturally. Montilla is produced in a similar range of styles to sherry: *fino* (15.5–17°), *amontillado* (16–22°), *oloroso* (16–20°), *cream, pale cream, Pedro Ximénez*. One significant difference between sherry and Montilla is that because the grapes ripen to a higher degree in Montilla-Moriles, the *fino* wines do not need to be fortified, and in some cases even the *amontillado* and *oloroso* wines are not fortified. In the UK market, the wines are sold as Montilla Dry (corresponding to *fino*), Montilla Medium and Montilla Cream or Pale Cream.

Málaga DO 'Mountain' wine made primarily from grapes grown in demarcated vineyards around Málaga, in two main sub-zones: the rocky hills of Axarquía to the east of Málaga itself, and the Antequera plateau in the mountains above Málaga. Grape varieties authorized under the DO regulations are Moscatel and Pedro Ximénez.

Málaga is a fortified wine and can appear in a variety of bewildering guises, ranging from bone dry to extremely sweet, and with an alcohol level of between 15 and 23°. Some of the styles of Málaga that may be encountered include:

Trasañejo   Indicates a superior wine that has undergone a lengthy ageing process. Can be dry or sweet. Sometimes sold direct from the barrel in Málaga bars.

Dry Málaga   Produced usually from totally fermented must of Pedro Ximénez grape, and varies in colour from pale yellow to deep amber depending on age. Excellent as an apéritif.

Málaga Lágrima   Produced from the *lágrima* or free run juice, that is, the must that has percolated freely without the additional use of mechanical pressure. *Lágrimas* are generally considered fine or superior wines and can range in colour from golden to dark amber. They are generally sweet.

Málaga Pedro Ximénez   Málaga wine produced entirely from Pedro Ximénez grapes grown on the Antequera plateau. Rich, dark and intensely sweet.

Málaga Moscatel   Produced entirely from Moscatel grapes, usually grown in the sub-zone of Axarquía. Finely scented, with the distinctive grapey bouquet of this delicious table grape, gold to dark amber in colour, and lusciously sweet.

Málaga Dulce Color   The most popular type of Málaga, produced with the addition of *arrope* (grape must boiled down to form a thick syrup); dark, treacly and raisiny.

Málaga Paxarette   Rare semi-sweet tawny-coloured Málaga. Old aged Paxarette wine is called 'Pajarete'.

Condado de Huelva DO   Large delimited vineyard extending over 13,000 hectares planted across some 17 communities located in the south-western province of Huelva. Principal grapes cultivated include Zalema, Palomino, Listan and Garrido Fino. Three styles of wine are produced:

Vino blanco joven   Young, fruity white wines produced from early harvested Zalema grapes, fermented at low temperatures. Alcohol 11–14°.

Condado Pálido   Fino-style wine produced from Listan, Palomino and Garrido Fino grapes, matured dynamically in *soleras* under a veil of *flor*. Alcohol 15–17°.

Condado Viejo   Oloroso-style wine matured in *soleras* and produced in *seco*, *semi-seco*, and *dulce* versions.

Brandy de Jerez DE

One of many great legacies of the Moors was the development and perfection of the art of distillation – perhaps surprisingly, given the Koranic ban on alcohol. Yet even the word 'alcohol' points to Arabic derivation, as do the words alembic and *alquitara*, both indicating the still, that is the vessel in which grapes or other fruit are vaporized into spirit, the latter a term still used by brandy producers in Jerez today.

Though undoubtedly made by the Arabs during their centuries-long occupation, the first documentation of brandy from Jerez dates from the sixteenth century. Today brandy remains a hugely important part of the sherry industry. The quality and distinction of Jerez brandy was recently recognized through the granting of the Brandy de Jerez *denominación específica*.

Interestingly, it is not the base wine itself that gives its character to Jerez brandy. Indeed, so great are the demands on production that most of the requisite wines come from Airén grapes grown in La Mancha, vinified and processed into *holandas* (grape spirit under 70% alcohol) in the great distilling centre of Tomelloso, self-proclaimed world leader in grape distillation. Rather, it is the process of maturation that makes Jerez brandy unique. For after distillation, the raw colourless spirit is transported to the Jerez region, and there begins a process of dynamic maturation in oak casks which have previously, for several years, contained sherry, using the same distinctive *solera* system of fractional blending.

As with other classic spirits, Jerez brandy is produced in a range of different qualities, styles and ages, from the youngest (Solera Brandy de Jerez) to the oldest and most prestigious (Solera Gran Reserva Brandy de Jerez). Generally speaking, ageing in casks by the *solera* system results in rounder, richer and apparently sweeter styles of brandy than, say, Cognac.

LA GASTRONOMÍA: FOODS OF ANDALUCÍA

The foods of Andalucía, like the region itself, are nothing if not vivid, direct and colourful. Here in this harshly-lit land of dazzling brightness and intense summer heat, what could be more refreshing or inviting to the eye than a colourful bowl or glass of cold *gazpacho*? Or what could be more delicious with a chilled *copita* of *fino* or *manzanilla* than to pick at a shimmering counter-top array of shellfish *tapas* as displayed in any number of the region's famous seafood and waterfront bars?

Of course, Andalucía is the land of *tapas*. These favourite Spanish bar-top snacks and nibbles may now be found all over the country, but it is claimed that they originated here. The word means 'cover' because apparently in this dusty and insect-ridden land, it was the custom to place a lid, saucer, or even a piece of bread over the top of a wine glass. An enterprising proprietor, it is suggested, conceived the idea of attracting custom by placing an appetizing morsel on each lid. Strictly speaking, *tapas* should be just that, a tiny nibble – perhaps a few toasted almonds, a stuffed olive, a piece of fried fish, a prawn or two, or a slice of *chorizo* or *jamón*. These days, though, more elaborate dishes, including largish portions of fried squid or

The Cult of the Pig

The 800-year occupation of Spain by the Moors had long-lasting effects on many aspects of daily life, not least diet. The Moors introduced a range of exotic spices – saffron, nutmeg, pepper – and fruits and nuts like bitter oranges, lemons, grapefruit, almonds: products and foods that remain essential flavours of the Spanish diet today. On the other hand, Islamic strictures forbid, of course, the consumption of pork.

Thus, during the centuries of struggle when Christians strove to regain control of the peninsula, the raising of pigs and the consumption of pork and its products, *jamón serrano* and other preserved sausages and *embutidos*, took on almost religious significance. Moreover, even after the completion of the *Reconquista*, the unfortunate subsequent expulsion of Moors and Jews from Spain, and their continued persecution throughout the horrors of the Inquisition, the consumption of pork came to represent something of a shibboleth of faith. For example, those *marranos* (converted Jews) who continued to refrain from eating it could be decreed heretics and have their property confiscated by the Church; they were then expelled from the country, tortured, or even burnt at the stake.

Andalucía, long at the leading edge of the struggle between Christian and Moor, came to specialize in the raising of pigs and production of pork products. Even today, two of Spain's greatest regional hams come from here: *jamón de Jabugo* from Jabugo in the Sierra Morena mountains of Huelva, produced from the native black-foot Iberian pig; and *jamón de Trévelez*, produced in the high Alpujarras near Granada.

fish, *cazuelitas* of seafood *guisos* (cooked dishes or stews), or portions of fresh shellfish *salpicón* may be offered as *raciónes* (large portions), generally considerably more expensive than the original bar-top snacks, and substantial enough to be almost a meal in itself.

Andalucía is known foremost as a zone where foods are fried. Certainly fish from both the Mediterranean and Atlantic coasts are enjoyed most frequently simply dredged in flour, then quickly fried in abundant boiling olive oil. Paper-wrapped packets are picked up from any of a number of fried fish stands or shops, *freidurías*, in Jerez, El Puerto de Santa María, Cádiz, or Málaga.

¡Que aproveche! Regional Specialities of Andalucía

Cazon en adobo Shark, first marinated in tasty spice mixture then deep-fried.

Almejas al marinera Small, sweet clams stewed in wine and garlic.

Puntillitas fritas The tiniest baby squid, usually deep-fried.

Huevas alinadas Marinated, seasoned fish roe.

Flamenquín Long, sausage-shaped croquette of *jamón serrano* rolled in veal, breaded and fried: typical drinking *tapa* in Córdoba and Montilla.

Pincho moruño Spicy mini-meat kebab usually grilled over charcoal and served as a *tapa*.

Ajo blanco Chilled, refreshing soup from Málaga made with olive oil, almonds and garlic pounded to a paste and mixed with iced water.

Gazpacho Classic vegetable soup from Andalucía, made with liquidized bread, olive oil, garlic, tomatoes, onion, cucumber, red pepper, sherry vinegar and iced water. Always served cold.

Salmorejo Very thick, garlicky, cold vegetable soup, garnished with *jamón serrano* and finely chopped egg. Speciality of Córdoba.

Boquerón Fresh baby anchovy. **Boquerones a la malagueña** Baby anchovies dredged in flour, then stuck together at the tails to form a fan before being deep-fried.

Chanquete Tiny, transparent fish similar to whitebait, usually dredged in flour, deep-fried, and eaten whole.

Chipirón Baby cuttlefish. **Chiperones en su tinta** Braised in a thick, black sauce made from their own ink.

Jamón serrano Famous mountain-cured, air-dried ham, eaten raw like *prosciutto crudo*. Andalucía is the source of two of Spain's best: *jamón de Jabugo* and *jamón de Trévelez*.

Dorada (pescado) a la sal
Whole bream (or other fish, such as *lubina, pargo,* or *mujol*) baked in a thick covering of sea salt, an exquisite and delicate method of preparation: the salt becomes a hard sealed container in which the fish steams gently; it emerges not salty at all, just extremely succulent and moist.

Urta a la rotena Exceptionally flavoured, firm-fleshed local fish usually served in a rich sauce made with tomatoes and *pimientos*.

Sherry Vinegar

Wine vinegar, of course, is a natural by-product of wine, that is to say, it is wine gone bad or sour through being attacked by the aceto-bacteria organism in contact with oxygen. Thus, through either carelessness or choice, vinegar can be and usually is produced in almost all wine regions.

Sherry vinegar is one of the world's most characterful and precious of all wine vinegars, highly prized not only in the zone itself but by gourmets everywhere. Indeed, so pungent and intensely flavoured is this marvellous essence that only a few drops are necessary to transform miraculously a dressing or sauce.

Occasionally a butt of wine turns into vinegar by chance. However, the commercial production of wine vinegar is something that cannot be left to chance, and nor can it be undertaken alongside the production of wine. For so pervasive is the aceto-bacteria that the production of vinegar must be kept entirely separate from any winemaking facilities, lest it invade and contaminate the entire stock.

Sherry vinegar is thus produced commercially only by a few specialists who take the same care in its unique production as do the winemakers themselves. *Vinos picados*, produced from the same authorized sherry grapes but low in alcohol and high in volatile acidity, are chosen to undergo a similar process of lengthy ageing by means of the *solera* system of dynamic fractional blending. It is this lengthy sojourn, in *soleras* sometimes 25 years or older, that gives sherry vinegar its great pungency, concentration and warm complex nutty flavours that are reminiscent of those found in the region's greatest wines.

ANDALUCÍA

Habas a la granadina Broad beans cooked with mountain herbs and *jamón serrano* from Trévelez.

Perdiz a la torera Partridge bullfighter's style, stuffed with bacon and anchovies, and stewed in white wine or sherry.

Pescaíto frito Any variety or varieties of small fish and shellfish, dredged in flour and quickly fried in boiling olive oil.

Tocino de cielo The dessert of the wine zones, traditionally made by nuns with egg yolks left after the whites were used for fining: a super-sweet, dense *crème caramel*-type dessert much loved in the zone.

Helado de pasas Raisin and wine ice cream, usually served with a glass of Pedro Ximénez wine poured over it.

WINES AND WINE ROADS OF ANDALUCÍA

Jerez and the Sherry Triangle

In Brief: Jerez de la Frontera, capital of the sherry wine trade, is located 84 km south of Seville. The excellent new motorway that connects Seville with Cádiz means that the journey takes less than an hour. Jerez certainly provides ample opportunities to visit world-famous and welcoming *bodegas* and it is a city of not inconsiderable charm. However, for more relaxing and intimate exploration of the sherry triangle, we suggest that either El Puerto de Santa María or Sanlúcar de Barrameda would make a better base. The Atlantic beaches, cleaner, less busy than their Mediterranean counterparts, allow wine travel to be combined with more traditional holiday pursuits.

SHERRY, THE WINE: PAST AND PRESENT

Sherry is not only one of Spain's greatest wines, but truly one of the great wines of the world. It is also one of those few select wines whose very success has resulted in its name being unlawfully stolen and abused by producers in any number of unlikely and far-flung places (Cyprus, South Africa, California, New York, Australia, even Britain, though in the latter case, the 'wine' so-called is not even produced from fresh grapes). Needless to say, none of the impostors bears any relation whatsoever to the real article. For sherry comes only from grapes grown and wines produced and aged in the

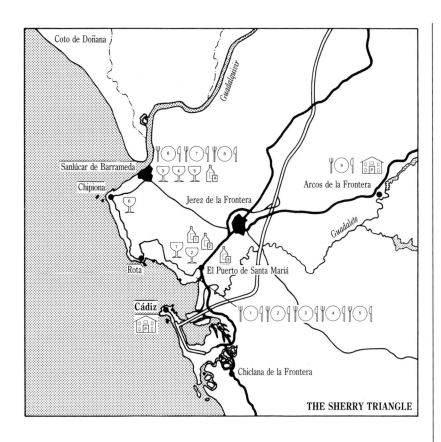

THE SHERRY TRIANGLE

delimited vineyard area primarily in the triangle formed by the principal sherry towns of Jerez de la Frontera, El Puerto de Santa María and Sanlúcar de Barrameda.

The vineyards are almost certainly among the earliest planted in western Europe, brought to Iberia by Phoenician merchants from Tyre who established the trading colony of Gádir (Gades under the Romans, now Cádiz) perhaps as early as 1100 B.C. The vineyards were certainly well in place by the time the Romans came to the peninsula, and under the conquerors they were greatly expanded, for the wines of the province of Baetica found great favour even in far-off Rome itself to where they were transported by sea in amphoras.

After the Romans came the Visigoths who were in turn overthrown by the Moors in 711 A.D. at the Battle of Guadalete. Yet, like the Romans who had preceded them, the Moors proved themselves to be not only brave and well-organized warriors, but, especially in the ninth century under the Caliphate of Córdoba, sophisticated and cultured rulers, so much so that Córdoba, capital of Al-Andalus, was to become for centuries one of western Europe's greatest cities, and a remarkable centre of enlightenment, learning and artistic achievement.

It should not be considered surprising that the teetotal Moors continued the cultivation of the grape. The vineyards of Jerez were even then considered among the most productive and important in the world and wine was of course a precious trading commodity; this essentially worldly and commercial empire was certainly not averse to making wines to sell to the Christians and Jews alike.

Yet if the wines of Al-Andalus in general, and Xeris (the Moorish name for Jerez) in particular, enjoyed some fame under the Moors, it was not until the sixteenth century that they began to earn lasting world renown. This was Spain's greatest epoch, her Golden Age, when the entire nation embarked on a great adventure of exploration and colonization of the New World. Seville and Cádiz were the ports from which the caravels and galleons sailed, and to which they returned, laden with unbelievable riches. With Spain the greatest maritime power of its day, and Andalucía the commercial and economic heart of the country, this tiny southern outpost became a great focus for all of Europe.

The void left after the expulsion of the Jews and the Moors was soon filled by foreign merchants and traders. The English settled in growing numbers in southern Spain, and one of the commodities that they began to trade in ever increasing quantity was the region's wine, known as 'sherris sack', from the Spanish verb *sacar*, to take out or export. Though the term came to be used primarily in association with sherry, there were at that time any number of different types of 'sack', most notably Málaga sack and Canary sack.

Of course, the sherry wine trade (though it could hardly know it at the time) was given a great boost on that historic night in 1587 when Sir Francis Drake led a famous night invasion into Cádiz harbour, routed the Spanish fleet that was being prepared to sail against the English, and, as part of the loot, got away with some 2900 pipes of sack which he brought back with him on his victorious homecoming. Thus was sealed the Englishman's long-standing and still ardent love affair with this great historic wine.

'If I had a thousand sons,' declares Falstaff in Shakespeare's *Henry IV*, 'the first humane principle I would teach them should be, to foreswear thin potations, and to addict themselves to sack.'

Generations of Englishmen ever since have been patriotically following Sir John's advice. In spite of the deterioration in Anglo-Hispanic relations following the defeat of the Armada, sherry continued to remain popular in England certainly throughout the seventeenth century. And in the eighteenth and nineteenth centuries, English, Irish and Scottish merchants continued to settle in the area to blend and ship wines, thus establishing some of the great sherry dynasties, such as Osborne, Duff Gordon, John Harvey & Sons, Garvey, Terry, Sandeman and Williams & Humbert. Even today, the ties are strong; though consumption has dropped in recent decades, Britain still remains far and away the most important and significant single export market for sherry.

Sherry developed historically as one of the great fortified wines of its age, wines which, like Málaga, port, Madeira and Marsala, were able to withstand shipping in cask by sea without spoiling. The demands of transport were indeed probably the most significant considerations as regards the evolution of the style of wine. The naturally robust and high-alcohol wines of Jerez were clearly well suited to such less than delicate treatment; indeed, the character of some wines positively improved through oxidation. Also to help them survive the rigours of the voyage, they would have been fortified with *holandas*, or distilled grape brandy, and to make them more palatable and appealing to the British sweet tooth, they would have been sweetened with *arrope*, a syrupy concentrate produced by boiling down unfermented grape must (a process perfected by the Moors). Whether they reached their eventual destination without further adulteration or alteration is less than likely, but the basic parameters for 'sherris sack' were thus roughly established at an early stage.

Today, sherry remains a wine fortified with grape brandy; *arrope* is still a constituent part of *vino de color* used to make the sweeter blends; and some old *soleras* still in production date back to the Peninsular Wars. (Cape Trafalgar lies just south of Cádiz; Nelson's body – the admiral died almost at the moment of victory over Napoleon's fleet, one of the greatest naval battles in history – was reputedly transported back to Britain preserved in a butt of sherry.)

That is not to say that sherry today bears a close resemblance to those historic wines of old. Methods of viticulture and winemaking have changed beyond all recognition even in the last few decades. The styles and types of wines made today are vastly impressive and superior, and certainly extend well beyond the medium-sweet and sweet cream and brown sherries upon which the success of the export market was historically based and which have for so long dominated the British market as the nation's favourite drawing-room wines. Indeed, true dry *amontillados* and *olorosos*, or elegant *finos* and *manzanillas* as drunk in the region itself, are as far from those commercial blends and brands as can be imagined.

The delimited sherry vineyard lies in a broad triangle formed by the Guadalquivir and Guadalete rivers, embracing its three principal towns, Jerez de la Frontera, El Puerto de Santa María and Sanlúcar de Barrameda. The finest vineyards lie mainly to the north and west of Jerez, planted on bare white *albariza pagos*. This dazzling white soil is composed of a deep layer of spongy chalk which maintains moisture even throughout the driest and hottest summer weather without cracking. The most prestigious *pagos* have names such as Macharnudo, Balbaina, Carrascal and Miraflores and they are the finest habitat for the Palomino grape, the most important variety for the production of sherry. *Barros* (heavy darker soil made up of clay, limestone and sand) and *arenas* (mainly sand) are more suitable for the cultivation of Pedro Ximénez and Moscatel grapes.

Within the region, there are more than 5000 winegrowers, ranging from the large *bodegas* themselves, who in many cases have substantial vineyard holdings in the finest zones, to small individual growers working only a few hectares part-time. The independent growers usually sell their grapes or pressed must to one of the large *bodegas de crianza* (many have long-standing agreements reaching back for generations) or they may choose

Sherry vinescape.

instead to sell the grapes to one of the region's seven co-operative wineries.

Sherry begins life in much the same way as any other modern white wine. The harvest normally starts in early September, though in exceptional years it may begin as early as late August. It usually lasts about a month. The grapes are harvested by hand by local labour as well as itinerant workers and gypsies who travel from region to region as and when the crops are ready. The damaging strike in 1991, which caused much of the harvest to be lost, demonstrates the delicate symbiosis that exists between land-owner and worker.

In the past, once harvested, the grapes were laid out to dry in the sun on *esparto* mats, perhaps for only a day or two before pressing. Today, however, the finest Palomino grapes are accorded the same treatment and urgency essential to modern white winemaking anywhere else in the world. They are, for example, harvested in small plastic tubs which can be stacked in trailers, minimizing premature crushing, bruising and oxidation; and once full, the trailers are taken as quickly as possible to each *bodega*'s press house.

The days when the *pisadores*, wearing their nail-studded *zapatos de pisar*, used to press the grapes in *lagares* amidst the vineyards are long gone (except during the annual *Fiesta de la Vendimia*). Today, the great sherry houses employ the most modern technologies, including both horizontal and continuous presses, to process the grapes as quickly as they can. Generally the grapes are de-stalked and crushed lightly between rubber rollers first, then placed in the presses where the free run must, or *primera yema*, is collected without the addition of any external pressure. This free-run grape juice is used almost exclusively for the production of delicate *fino* wines. The mass of crushed grapes then releases further must in response to light pressure, and this can be used for either *fino* or *oloroso* wines. Finally, the remaining juices left in the presses are extracted under hard pressure and sent away to be distilled.

The grape must then ferments, in modern temperature-controlled stain-less steel tanks, in horizontal resin-lined vats, in concrete deposits, in con-crete or earthenware *tinajas*, or else, in exceptional cases (as at the ultra-traditional A. R. Valdespino) in oak *botas*, previously the universal receptacle within the zone. During the first or tumultuous fermentation, the wines normally reach about 11.5–13° alcohol; after this, the slower, secondary fermentation converts harsher malic acid to smoother lactic acid. By December or January, the wines have usually stabilized and clarified naturally and are ready to be classified.

Up to this point the wines have been produced in a classic manner not dissimilar to the way in which white wines are made virtually anywhere else in the world. Now the wines enter a system of elaboration that is virtually unique and which gives sherry its tremendous personality and character.

The wines are classified by the *capataz*, or skilled cellarmaster, into two main families: *finos* and *olorosos*. *Finos* are wines that have a peculiar capacity to grow *flor* on their surface. Those vats of wine deemed to have this propensity are marked with a single *raya* (wines from this family will include *manzanilla*, *fino* and *amontillado*). Vats of those wines destined to be *olorosos* are marked with two slashes, *dos rayas* (wines from the *oloroso* family will include not only natural dry *olorosos* but also the medium, sweet and cream blends). Those wines whose future can still not yet be divined and which may prove to be either *finos* or *olorosos* are marked with a slash and a dot, *una raya y punto*. Poor, coarse or sour wines are eliminated with three slashes, or *tres rayas*.

The wines are then fortified, in the case of *finos* up to only 15.5° alcohol (the highest level at which *flor* can exist) and 18° for *olorosos*. Then they pass into their particular chosen *soleras* to begin a wholly unique process of dynamic ageing.

For, unlike most quality wines that undergo a static ageing process and are the product of one vintage year only, sherry is always a blended wine, which means that there can be continuity and consistency in style and quality, year after year. This is achieved in part by the fascinating method of fractional ageing and blending known as the *solera* system, an ongoing process that will be viewed in action by every visitor to the *bodegas de crianza* of Jerez. Basically the *solera* system works like this. Imagine, as an illustration, a four-scale *solera*. The oldest scale, called the *solera* itself, usually sits on the *suelo*, nearest the ground. On top of this tier there may be a row of butts containing wines of the first *criadera* (the word means 'nursery'), followed on top of this by the second *criadera*, and finally, above this, the third *criadera*. As a certain quantity of wine is drawn off from the *solera* itself (never more than 25% of the total), those barrels are replenished by topping up with wines from the next oldest, or first *criadera*; these barrels are in turn replenished with wines from the row above it, and so on. The process repeats itself throughout the chain, with the youngest wines blending with the next youngest and being blended in turn with new wines from that vintage (such new wines are known as *añadas*).

In practice, the butts of wine may not necessarily actually be located in neat tiers, one *criadera* above the next. They may not even be in the same

...as Domecq, Jerez de la Frontera.

parts of the *bodega*. Usually, *finos* are kept on the lower tiers to help maintain humidity, critical for the continued growth of *flor*, while *olorosos* may be on the higher tiers where they enjoy a slightly hotter temperature. Hoses and pumps facilitate the transfer of wines from one part of the *bodega* to another. Yet even so, the physical demands of 'running the scales', as the process of transferring wines from one *criadera* to the next is called, are immense: this is a complex and hugely labour-intensive process which will not be viewed on such a scale anywhere else in the world.

There is an advertising campaign that states quite simply, 'Real sherry comes from Spain', to distinguish this aristocratic wine from the many impostors which masquerade under its rightful name. Myriad factors – soil, climate, grape variety, methods of elaboration – contribute to the uniqueness of sherry. But perhaps one single factor, more than any other, cannot be duplicated anywhere else on earth: the magical and spontaneous appearance, even here on some wines only, of *flor*, a delicate layer of wrinkled yeast that forms on the surface of the wine, protects it from oxidation, feeds on the wines and contributes inimitable flavour, freshness and bouquet.

Flor is the miracle of *fino* sherry, allowing wines of remarkable freshness and scent to be produced from a hot-house vineyard where conditions would seem to preclude wines of delicacy and finesse. It is a fickle, temperamental living entity that must be nurtured and cared for lest it die out prematurely and so spoil the wine. In Jerez, the dirt floors of the *bodegas* are hosed down continuously in summer to reduce temperatures and promote humidity. Elsewhere, in El Puerto de Santa María, the proximity of the Guadalete allows in a thicker natural layer of *flor* and results in *finos* of exceptional elegance and grace. In Sanlúcar de Barrameda, the cool, well-ventilated *bodegas* facing the mouth of the Guadalquivir and the humid *marismas* of the Coto de Doñana, fanned by damp sea breezes, are able to promote a particularly thick and luxuriant growth of *flor* that lasts year round and results in the finest and most delicate sherry of all, *manzanilla*. In old *soleras* of *fino*, the *flor* eventually dies off, giving way to another family of wines known as *amontillados*, for this fine style of wine, too rarely seen in its authentic and natural state (many commercial wines utilize the term to indicate any type of medium-dry sherry), is nothing less than an aged *fino*, in which the glorious freshness of *fino* is replaced by more profound yet still fine and delicate nuances and a complex and pronounced nutty character.

The running of the scales is the key to the *solera* system, through the constant transference and blending of younger wines with old. For the rationale behind the *solera* system is that small quantities of young wines that are gradually mixed with larger quantities of old will eventually absorb their style and character; the new or younger wines, meanwhile, serve to refresh the old.

Once the wines have passed through their individual *soleras* they may or may not be ready to be bottled and drunk. Generally, they must undergo further treatments such as blending for homogeneity, assembly of constituent wines to produce the consistent house brands, and finally filtration and chilling for stabilization. *Finos* destined for export may be fortified further, from 15.5° up to a finished 17.5° (though there has been a recent welcome tendency by many *bodegas* to lower the alcohol of the export *finos* to about 16°). The *oloroso* wines rarely leave the *bodegas* in their natural unblended state, though this is indeed a pity, for a true dry *oloroso* is without doubt one of the great wines of sherry. Rather more often than not, *olorosos* serve as the base for the famous blended brands of medium, sweet and cream sherries that remain so popular in northern Europe and North America. To this end, they are usually blended with *vino dulce* produced from sun-dried Pedro Ximénez and Moscatel grapes, as well, possibly, with *vino de color* produced from *arrope* (boiled down concentrated grape must) to add colour.

The range of wines produced in the sherry region is thus quite remarkable, and the overall standard, even of the commercial brands available worldwide, is extremely high. None the less, to truly appreciate not only the quality of sherry, but the wine as it is meant to be drunk, it is essential to come to Jerez de la Frontera to experience it at the source.

THE SHERRY TRIANGLE

It might be suggested that sherry developed historically as a wine mainly suited to the particular tastes of the British. The same can certainly be said of other historic wines such as port or Marsala. Witness the fact that the most popular brands of medium and sweet sherry find virtually no market in their home country; port is not particularly a wine to drink in Portugal; and Marsala is wholly out of place with the almost African climate and cuisine of western Sicily. And yet sherry is undoubtedly also very much a wine of its own land, wholly fitting to be enjoyed within its zone of production, in a variety of styles and on every occasion, at all times of the day and night. The crucial fact to remember is that sherry, as drunk in Spain, is essentially a dry wine.

Don Bartolomé Vergara, the genial Public Relations Director of the *Asociación de Criadores Exportadores de Vinos de Jerez*, explained to us over a mid-morning *copita* and a nibble of salted almonds, 'Here in Jerez, we usually start the day with a dry *amontillado* or *oloroso* before moving on later to the *finos*.'

Indeed, these wines in their natural state, little encountered outside the region, are so outstandingly fragrant, nutty and pungent that they usually come as something of a revelation to those who have previously shunned the darker styles of sherry. Indeed, it is not going too far to suggest that wines such as (to name a few) Valdespino's Tio Diego or Duff Gordon's Club Dry (both natural dry *amontillados*), and Domecq's Rio Viejo, González Byass's Apostoles, or Osborne's Bailen (all dry *olorosos*) are among the best kept secrets of Spain, and rank alongside the great wines of the world.

Undoubtedly, though, it is the lighter dry, *bodega*-fresh *finos* and *manzanillas* that taste so utterly delicious in their home region, and which are so much a part of the unique southern way of life in the sherry triangle. In other parts of Spain, even in other parts of Andalucía, and certainly outside the country, these delicate and elegant wines are too often served at room temperature and from long-opened bottles that have lost all semblance of freshness and scent. But here in the sherry zone itself, a *copita* sampled in even the humblest bar always tastes as if it has just been drawn from the *bota*, wonderfully fresh, tasty and stingingly full of scent.

Jerez de la Frontera is of course the capital of the wine zone and undoubtedly one of the great wine towns of the world, totally dominated by the immense *bodegas* that have brought wealth and fame to the city. There are more than 50 such wine firms located in Jerez, and the largest and most famous, in their whitewashed, low-lying warehouses found throughout the

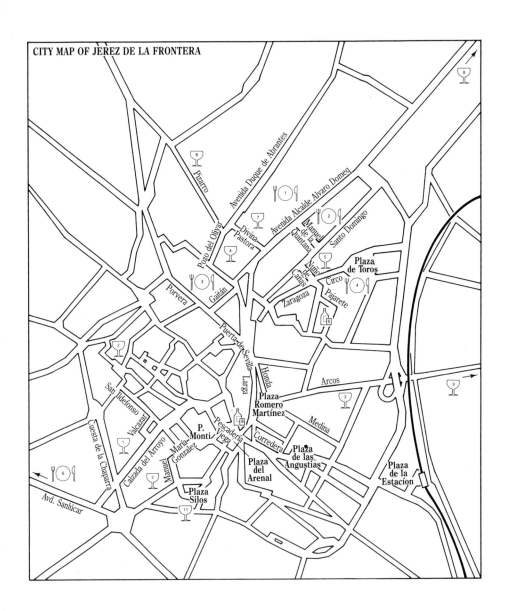

CITY MAP OF JEREZ DE LA FRONTERA

town, their names emblazoned in black on the outer walls, provide exceptional and hospitable opportunities for the serious wine lover or casual wine tourist alike.

Modern Jerez is a bustling Andalusian hub, a busy banking and commercial centre as well as an intimate wine town. Yet come here to find the *casco antiguo*, located behind the old Moorish Alcázar and the remnants of the medieval fortified walls. This is a quiet, crumbling and rather dilapidated *barrio*, wholly authentic and atmospheric. It is a place simply to wander through, following the irregular and narrow lanes and alleys, down orange-tree-lined streets of whitewashed houses with window-high grilles. As you meander, the sweet smell of orange blossom mixes with the heady scent of evaporating wine to make a particularly pleasant cocktail of aromas. This old part of town, dominated by its seventeenth-century Collegiate Church, the city's principal monument, seems always cooler, quieter, somehow apart from the bustle of the modern city.

The Collegiate Church, incidentally, is the focus of the famous *Fiesta de la Vendimia*, for it is here each year that the proclamation of the grape harvest takes place, the first grapes are pressed by foot, and the must is blessed. This is one of Spain's most important wine festivals, each year dedicated to a different foreign country, and there is always considerable Andalusian pageantry: flamenco dancing, bullfights, and of course, much eating and drinking. It should be pointed out, though, that this may not be the best time of year to visit *bodegas*, for many of them close lock, stock and barrel, in order that everyone may take part in the festivities.

Other notable monuments in Jerez include the Santo Domingo Convent; the numerous and prosperous civic manor houses and private palaces dating from the sixteenth, seventeenth and eighteenth centuries; the clock museum; and, located about four kilometres outside town, the Cartuja, with its splendid Gothic cloisters. The Cartuja, or Carthusian monastery, was once a breeding stable, and gave its name to the beautiful Carthusian horses of the region. These splendid white beasts, almost a symbol of the proud Andalusian spirit, can be seen in training each day at the Royal School of Equestrian Art.

After an exploration of Jerez, it is essential to strike out into the sherry country and explore the zone's other two principal wine towns, El Puerto de Santa María and Sanlúcar de Barrameda.

El Puerto lies 15 km south of Jerez on the Guadalete river. Once the major shipping port for sherry, in the sixteenth and seventeenth centuries its waterfront was extremely busy, with hundreds of ships moored along-side, and millions of butts of wine being rolled on board to be shipped to Britain and northern Europe, as well as to the Spanish colonies of the New World. Today, like most small towns whose principal *raison d'être* has long passed, El Puerto appears somewhat dilapidated, though atmospheric and lively none the less, its old working shipyards mirrored by the cranes of the historic port of Cádiz across the bay.

ANDALUCÍA

One of many *bodega*-lined streets in El Puerto de Santa María.

El Puerto is still dominated by the ageing warehouses of its principal *bodegas*, Osborne, Terry, Duff Gordon, Luis Caballero and others, *bodegas* that are possibly even more impressive than those of Jerez simply because they so totally dominate this otherwise small and unexceptional river town. The *bodegas*, whitewashed and with their names boldly painted in black, stretch the length of entire streets, and as you wander through the old back lanes to the Iglesia Mayor or the atmospheric Castillo de San Marcos (owned by Luis Caballero), the ever present aromas of evaporating sherry and brandy are intense and intoxicating. The proximity of the Guadalete to these riverside wine warehouses, incidentally, is more than beneficial for the wine: indeed, the higher humidity of El Puerto over Jerez results in a much more active and thicker growth of *flor*, making Puerto's *finos* some of the finest and most aromatic.

This undoubtedly remains a maritime town, historically and intrinsically linked with the sea. Christopher Columbus was a guest in the town between 1483 and 1486, and here he prepared for his famous voyage of discovery, his flagship named in its honour, the *Santa María*. The ship, in fact, was the property of a native son of El Puerto, Juan de la Cosa, who served as Columbus's pilot in 1492, and who on his return issued the first world chart incorporating the 'Indies'.

Trade with the New World brought prosperity to El Puerto, and during the sixteenth and seventeenth centuries many merchants built splendid palaces in the town, some of which still remain intact, notably the palaces of Vizarrón, Aranibar and the Marqués de Cañada. Today, El Puerto's port, if no longer a great shipping centre, is the home to a small fishing fleet, and the town's principal *paseo*, the Ribera del Marisco, or 'shellfish way', is one of the great gastronomic meccas of the zone. The maritime connection, moreover, continues at nearby Puerto Sherry, a vast purpose-built yacht centre, residential compound and marina.

Sanlúcar de Barrameda, the third major wine town in the sherry region, is equidistant from Jerez de la Frontera and El Puerto de Santa María, about 20 km away. The road from Jerez leads through the heart of the region's vineyards, while the route from El Puerto to Sanlúcar can mainly follow the coast by way of Rota and Chipiona, both minor wine towns. Rota is dominated by a large US military base, but the coast between it and Chipiona remains wild and relatively unspoiled. Chipiona is famous for its sweet Moscatel wines.

Sanlúcar de Barrameda, our favourite sherry town, exists on two levels. The old *barrio alto*, or high town, dominated by the Castillo de Santiago, is a maze of narrow alleys and whitewashed cottages, stark, blinding in the sun, free of tourists and almost African in feel. This is primarily still a residential zone, not a commercial area, though the great *manzanilla bodegas* have premises here as well as down below. The lower town, on the other hand, is altogether livelier, even a little crazy; it is down here, one senses, that the town lives today. Seek out the small central Plaza del Cabildo, lined with orange trees, crumbling mansions decorated with ceramic *azulejos*, and gay, bright higgledy-piggledy houses. Sit down at an outdoor table and enjoy an *helado de pasas* – raisin-and-Moscatel-wine ice cream – together with a short, sharp *café cortado* and watch the world go by.

Then make your way down to the waterfront *paseo* along the Bajo de Guía seafront. Though this has been extended and paved since our last visit some years ago, it still leads nowhere, except down to the beach where the traditional shipbuilders are still at work, building and repairing the great wooden fishing boats that ply the waters of the Guadalquivir and beyond. This seafront promenade, overlooking the wild, roadless expanses of the Coto de Doñana across the estuary, remains one of the great secret corners of Spain, and one of our favourite spots in the world.

Sanlúcar, of course, is the home of *manzanilla*. Wines so named can only

Barrio alto, Sanlúcar de Barrameda.

be elaborated here. If *fino* is the most delicate of sherries, then *manzanilla* is the finest and most elegant of *finos*. The secret of this great wine's exceptional delicacy, scent and finesse lies both in the selection of wines destined to be so elaborated, and in the moist, salty air of Sanlúcar, which promotes the thickest, most luxuriant growth of *flor* found anywhere in the region. This *flor* lasts throughout the year, not even dying back in the heat of midsummer, and the *bodegueros* utilize many more scales of wine in their *manzanilla soleras*. At Barbadillo, the town's leading producer, for example, its *manzanilla solera* may have as many as 33 different *criaderas*, the wine being constantly refreshed and invigorated in its running passage down the scales.

In Sanlúcar, such *bodega*-fresh wines may never even see the bottle: rather, in bars throughout the town, and especially in the waterfront restaurants and bars of the Bajo de Guía, *manzanilla* is drawn direct from casks and served in tall, straight-sided glasses known as *cañas* after the bamboo *venencias* that are used in the *bodegas* here. Served in this manner, and accompanied by a plate of freshly-boiled *langostinos de Sanlúcar*, it is unquestionably – at that moment and in that particular place – the finest wine in the world.

La Venencia

One of the highlights of a visit to a sherry *bodega* is to witness the remarkable skill and drama of the *venciador* as he fills a handful of waiting *copitas* with a careless, apparently effortless sweep and dash.

He achieves this through the use of the *venencia*, an instrument of great tradition and beauty, yet still of daily necessity to the *capataz* or cellarmaster. Traditionally in Jerez, the *venencia* has a long slender handle made of flexible whalebone; both the hook by which it is hung, as well as the cup that holds wine should be made of pure silver. The shape of the instrument, apparently, is based on a similar utensil which the ancient Greeks dipped into their narrow-necked amphoras. In Sanlúcar de Barrameda, the *bodegueros* use an altogether humbler tool known as a *caña*, similar in shape and function, but there made simply out of a length of bamboo cane. In either case, the *venencia* serves an essential function, for its skilful use allows samples of wines to be drawn out of the cask without unduly disturbing the fragile and delicate surface layer of *flor*.

Bodegas: Stop to Taste; Stop to Buy

Jerez de la Frontera

1

PEDRO DOMECQ SA
SAN ILDEFONSO 3
11404 JEREZ DE LA FRONTERA
CÁDIZ
TEL: (956) 33 18 00; FAX: (956) 34 99 66

WINES PRODUCED: La Ina *fino*; Amontillado 51-1a; Rio Viejo dry *oloroso*; Sibarita; Celebration Cream; Venerable (100% Pedro Ximénez).
BRANDIES PRODUCED: Fundador, Carlos III, Carlos I, Carlos I Imperial.
VISITS: Mon–Fri 10h30–12h30. Telephone Dept of Public Relations for appointment.

One of the oldest and largest of the great sherry firms, founded in 1730 by Patrick Murphy, an Irishman. In the early nineteenth century, under the direction of Frenchmen Pedro Domecq and his brother Juan Pedro Domecq, the firm expanded considerably, and established great inroads into the British market which are still of utmost importance today.

Domecq has some 80 *bodegas* located mainly in Jerez (the Miraflores *bodega* is in Sanlúcar for the production of *manzanilla*). The most notable that visitors will see

ANDALUCÍA

is the El Molino, which dates back to the company's foundation, and includes rare casks containing wines over 200 years old, dedicated to Napoleon, William Pitt, Admiral Nelson and other historic personages. The Mezquita *bodega*, so named because its columns are reminiscent of Córdoba's great Moorish monument, houses under a single roof some 42,000 *botas* of La Ina *fino*, one of the great wines of Jerez.

While La Ina is the company's best-known and -selling wine, its entire range is of a consistently high quality. Particular favourites include the long and nutty Amontillado 51-1a and the outstanding dry *oloroso* Rio Viejo. For the production of these fine wines, the company owns some 1500 hectares of its own vineyards.

The Domecq family was one of the first to begin the commercial production of sherry brandy, and today its brandies, such as Fundador, Carlos III, and the prestigious Carlos I brands, are enjoyed and appreciated nationally and internationally.

English, French, German spoken.

---

2 GONZÁLEZ BYASS
MANUEL MARÍA GONZÁLEZ 12
11403 JEREZ DE LA FRONTERA
CÁDIZ
TEL: (956) 34 00 00; FAX: (956) 32 20 13

WINES PRODUCED: Tío Pepe *fino*; El Rocio *manzanilla*; Amontillado del Duque; Apostoles *oloroso*; Matusalem.
BRANDIES PRODUCED: Soberano, Insuperable, Conde Duque, Lepanto.
VISITS: Mon–Fri 10h30–13h30. Telephone Dept of Public Relations for appointment.

González Byass, alongside Domecq, is one of the great firms of Jerez. Yet both of these world-famous giants have ably demonstrated that it is possible to produce quality wines in quantity. Tío Pepe is by far the largest selling *fino* in the world, yet it is also, unquestionably, one of the finest.

The company was founded in 1835 by Manuel María González, with the assistance of a maternal uncle, José Angel Moreno de la Peña (after whom the wine Tío Pepe was named). So successful was the firm that by 1855, exports to England alone numbered 3000 butts; by 1873 that number had risen to over 10,000.

The *bodegas* of González Byass are among the most impressive in Jerez. The original is La Sacristía. La Union *bodega* contains the rare 'Los Apostoles' *oloroso solera*, named after the 12 apostles; this consists of just 33 butts of rare old wines laid down in the 1860s and blended with a very small amount of old PX. The La Concha *bodega* is the most unusual, steel-constructed after a design by Gustave Eiffel. The more recent Las Copas *bodega* is the modern vinification plant and is noteworthy for the sheer scale of its winemaking installations.

English, French, German spoken.

3

JOHN HARVEY & SONS SA
CALLE COLÓN 1 (PRINCIPAL OFFICE)
CALLE ARCOS 53–57 (BODEGAS)
11401 JEREZ DE LA FRONTERA
CÁDIZ
TEL: (956) 15 10 30; FAX (956) 15 10 54

WINES PRODUCED: Tío Mateo Superior; Bristol *fino*; Bristol Medium Dry; Bristol Cream; '1796' *amontillado, palo cortado, oloroso*.
VISITS: Mon–Fri 9–13h.
Appointment preferable.

Harveys of Bristol has been shipping fine wines since 1796. Indeed, for much of that time, the company based its success on the traditional practice of purchasing wines in Jerez and shipping them to Bristol to be blended in its cellars there, and it was on this basis that the spectacular success of its Bristol Cream brand was achieved. The company owned neither *bodegas* nor vineyards in the sherry region.

However, in 1970 Harveys decided that, to ensure an adequate supply of grapes for world demand of its famous wines, as well as in anticipation of the trend for bottling sherry in its zone of production, it needed to establish a *bodega* in the Jerez. It achieved this through the purchase of various old sherry houses, including Mackenzie & Co, Terry, and Palomino & Vergara. The company thus now has impressive *bodegas* with lovely gardens, a wine museum, even pet alligators.

English spoken.

4

A. R. VALDESPINO SA
POZO DEL OLIVAR 16
11401 JEREZ DE LA FRONTERA
CÁDIZ
TEL: (956) 33 14 50; FAX: (956) 34 02 16

WINES PRODUCED: Inocente *fino*; Tío Diego *amontillado*; Solera 1842.
VISITS: Generally, visitors not received but wines can be purchased.

One of the few independent family-owned *bodegas* left in Jerez, and one of the most traditional. Valdespino is the Krug of sherry, for like that great *champenois* firm of tradition and prestige, here too at Valdespino wines are made as they have been in the past, on an artisan scale utilizing the old methods and craftsmanship which compromise quality not one iota. For example, the majority of wines still ferment in wood, simply because this results in a range of more individual wines with a variety of characteristics that would be lost if fermented in neutral stainless steel. The transfer of wine between the different *criaderas* is still done with the old museum-like hand instruments.

This is perhaps not surprising in a company that can trace its family history back to 1264 when one Don Alonso Fernández Valdespino fought alongside Alfonso X for the Reconquest of Jerez from the Moors and was rewarded with a grant of the reoccupied land. The family have been winegrowers ever since and the firm claims to have been founded in 1340. Inocente *fino*, its best-known wine, is produced almost entirely from the family's Inocente vineyard in the prestigious Macharnudo *pago*.
English spoken.

---

5 WILLIAMS & HUMBERT LTD
NUÑO DE CAÑAS 1
11400 JEREZ DE LA FRONTERA
CÁDIZ
TEL: (956) 33 13 00; FAX: (956) 34 51 91

WINES PRODUCED: Pando *fino*; La Cilla *manzanilla*; Dry Sack; Dos Cortados dry *oloroso*; Canasta Cream; Walnut Brown; Don Guido (white table wine from the Palomino grape).
VISITS: Mon–Fri at 12h and 13h30. Appointment necessary. Williams & Humbert, a historic firm founded in 1877, was a casualty of the Rumasa crash, though its future looks rosier since it was acquired in 1987 by the Sanlúcar firm of Barbadillo.

The wine that has been the basis of the company's success is Dry Sack, a classic medium *amontillado*, produced from a blend of true *amontillado*, with *oloroso* and select Pedro Ximénez wines. The less well-known wines in the range are equally superb, especially the fresh, fruity Pando *fino* and superbly pungent and concentrated Dos Cortados dry *oloroso*.

Williams & Humbert's *bodegas* in Jerez are concentrated in a single complex, famous for its beautiful gardens, stables and tasting room. They are located near the town's Plaza de Toros.
English, French, German spoken.

6

THE HOUSE OF SANDEMAN
SANDEMAN-JEREZ
PIZARRO 10
11400 JEREZ DE LA FRONTERA
CÁDIZ
TEL: (956) 30 11 00; FAX: (956) 30 00 07

WINES PRODUCED: Don Fino;
Medium Dry *amontillado*; Royal
Esmeralda *amontillado*; Royal
Ambrosante *palo cortado*; Character
oloroso; Royal Corregidor Cream.
BRANDIES PRODUCED: Capa
Negra, Capa Vieja.
VISITS: Mon–Fri 9–13h30.
Appointment necessary.
The House of Sandeman was
founded in 1790 by George
Sandeman, a Scotsman from Perth.
From its earliest days, it was
engaged in the purchase and
shipping of those two cornerstone
wines of the British market: sherry
and port.

The company acquired its own
bodegas and stocks of wine in the
sherry region in 1897 when it took
over Bodegas Pemartín, and it
remained in family hands until
1980 when it was purchased by the
international drinks conglomerate
Seagrams. There are two *bodega*
complexes, the main headquarters
in the centre of Jerez where visitors
are received, and the Cerro Viejo
complex in the middle of the
Macharnudo vineyard.
English, French, German spoken.

7

GARVEY SA
DIVINA PASTORA 3
11402 JEREZ DE LA FRONTERA
CÁDIZ
TEL: (956) 33 05 00

WINES PRODUCED: San Patricio
fino; La Lidia *manzanilla*; Tío
Guillermo *amontillado*; Ochavico
oloroso, Long Life *oloroso*; Flor de
Jerez *dulce*; Viña Monteguil (white
table wine from the Palomino
grape).
BRANDIES PRODUCED:
Espléndido, Gran Garvey,
Renacimiento Special Reserve.
VISITS: Mon–Fri 11h30–14h30.
Appointment necessary.
Garvey, founded by the Irishman
William Garvey in 1780, is one of
the great historic firms of sherry.
Though it too was purchased by
Ruiz-Mateo's ill-fated Rumasa
group, and subsequently taken over
by the Spanish government, it is
now back in private ownership, and
seems poised to re-establish its
position among the top companies of
the sherry hierarchy.

Garvey's most famous *bodega* is
the San Patricio, named after
Ireland's patron saint, and for long
the largest single *bodega* in Jerez. It
is used today, as since its inception,
for the production of the company's
flagship wine, San Patricio *fino*.
English, German, French spoken.

ANDALUCÍA

8 CROFT JEREZ SA
CRTRA MADRID–CÁDIZ, KM 636,300
11407 JEREZ DE LA FRONTERA
CÁDIZ
TEL: (956) 30 66 00; FAX: (956) 30 37 07

WINES PRODUCED: Croft Delicado *fino*; Croft Classic *amontillado*; Croft Original Pale Cream.
VISITS: By appointment only.
By sherry standards, Croft is a positive upstart, the company organized only in 1970, and its impressive colonial-style *bodega* complex located just outside Jerez built in 1979.

Croft represents a modern, non-traditional market-led expansion in the sherry zone. Its hugely successful Croft Original Pale Cream pioneered a wholly new type of wine, a sweet cream sherry that appeared, due to its pale appearance, to be dry. So successful was this new type that many sherry houses have followed suit with the production of their own Pale Creams. The company is owned by International Distillers & Vintners (IDV).
English, German, French spoken.

9 BODEGAS PAEZ MORILLA
CALLE DUERO 2
11400 JEREZ DE LA FRONTERA
CÁDIZ
TEL: (956) 34 39 32; FAX: (956) 34 12 65

VINEGAR AND TABLE WINES PRODUCED: Range of *solera* aged sherry vinegars; table wines from Arcos de la Frontera: Tierra Blanca (white, produced from Riesling/Palomino), Vina Lucia (produced from Tempranillo/Cabernet Sauvignon, aged in American oak

barricas).
VISITS FOR DIRECT SALES: Mon–Fri 7h30–15h.
The largest producer of sherry vinegars made by the *solera* system, also noted for superlative white and red table wines from grapes grown on the Vicaria estate at Arcos de la Frontera. This lovely estate winery, located off the road to San José del Valle, can be visited by appointment.

Almacenistas: Exceptional Storehouses of Precious Wines

Almacenistas are private stockholders of rare sherries. Neither vineyard owners nor commercial merchants, they are often private individuals who nurture and elaborate rare *soleras* of wines not as a full-time vocation, but seemingly simply for the sheer passion of it. They have always played a particularly important role in the production of fine sherry, for the large *bodegas de crianza* have traditionally looked to the *almacenistas* to supply them with quantities of wines of great individual character with which to improve their large-scale *soleras*. Rarely if ever were *almacenista* sherries bottled and sold on their own.

At Bodegas Maestro Sierra, for example, Doña Pilar Plá, Viuda de Antonio Borrego, continues to elaborate wines in an artisan fashion, employing the utmost hand-care in ways that would simply not be possible in the immense commercial *bodegas*. She purchases unfermented *mosto* from select vineyards in the prestigious Balbaina *albariza pago* that the family has worked with for generations, and the subsequent wines are nurtured and hand-cosseted at every stage of their considerable development. Greater numbers of scales can be worked into the *soleras*, even for *finos*, by maintaining, for example, extreme delicacy in the transfer from butt to butt to preserve the delicate layer of *flor*. This is achieved by working with the old hand instruments instead of electric pumps. Such tools as the *canoa* (boat-shaped funnel), *rociador* (curved stainless steel implement that extends below the surface of the wine so as not to disturb the *flor*), and the old-fashioned, fat-bellied *jarras* appear more like museum pieces than working tools, but they remain essential to achieve the finest quality. Some of the old *soleras* at this tiny *bodega* are of venerable age, dating back to its foundation in 1830. In short, the wines are made today as they have been since that early date, and as such, they demonstrate the greatest character and individuality.

In the past, the *almacenistas* almost always sold their wines to the great sherry firms, who valued them highly to be added to and blended with their own *soleras*. However, one firm, Emilio Lustau, specializes in the bottling and export of these rare unblended *almacenista* wines. A figure such as 1/25 on the label indicates that a single butt has been bottled out of a *solera* containing only 25 butts; clearly, the smaller the number, the rarer the wine. Such wines can never be produced in quantity – the very nature

ANDALUCÍA

of their production precludes this – but for the *aficionado*, they stand as benchmark sherries of the greatest individuality, quality and personality.

10

EMILIO LUSTAU SA
PLAZA DEL CUBO 4
11400 JEREZ DE LA FRONTERA
CÁDIZ
TEL: (956) 34 89 46

WINES PRODUCED: Dry Lustau; Fino Balbaína; Amontillado Macharnudo; Oloroso Carrascal; Old East India; plus rare *almacenista* wines from a range of sources.
VISITS: By appointment only.

11

BODEGAS 'MAESTRO SIERRA'
VIUDA DE ANTONIO BORREGO
PLAZA DE SILOS 5
11400 JEREZ DE LA FRONTERA
CÁDIZ
TEL: (956) 34 24 33

WINES PRODUCED: Fino, Oloroso, Cream from old *almacenista soleras*.
VISITS: Working hours, for direct sales. Appointment appreciated. Located near the Alcázar.

El Puerto de Santa María

1

OSBORNE Y CIA SA
DUFF GORDON & CO.
CALLE FERNÁN CABALLERO 3
11500 EL PUERTO DE SANTA MARÍA
CÁDIZ
TEL: (956) 85 52 11; FAX: (956) 85 34 02

WINES PRODUCED (OSBORNE): Quinta *fino*; Coquinero *amontillado*; Bailen *oloroso*; Osborne Cream.
BRANDIES PRODUCED (OSBORNE): Magno, Veterano, Carabela Santa María, Independencia, Conde de Osborne.
WINES PRODUCED (DUFF GORDON): Feria *fino*; Club Dry *amontillado*, El Cid medium

amontillado; Santa María Cream.
VISITS: Mon–Fri 9–14h. Appointment necessary.
Osborne and Duff Gordon are the two great sherry names that dominate El Puerto de Santa María. Duff Gordon was founded in 1734 by Sir James Duff, and when Sir Thomas Osborne, a native of Exeter, Devon, came to the region as a young man, he joined that firm, and later began shipping sherries under his own name. The two companies were finally joined together when the Osbornes bought out Duff Gordon in 1872; however,

even today, the companies, still family-owned by the Osbornes (together with substantial other interests), are run separately and continue to maintain their own long-established and separate lines of *soleras*.

Osborne's Quinta *fino* is one of the best examples of a Puerto *fino*, demonstrating how this style balances somewhere between the elegance and scent of a *manzanilla* and the somewhat fuller and more forceful character of a Jerez *fino*. Bailen is a fine, full-flavoured dry *oloroso*. Duff Gordon, which has traditionally supplied wines for the export market, produces a range of fuller sherries; its Club Dry is a true unsweetened *amontillado* of considerable character.

Osborne is the largest producer of sherry brandy, its striking black bull billboards a now classic feature of the Spanish countryside. The brandy *bodegas* lie just outside the town on the road to Jerez; the sherry *bodegas* for both Osborne and Duff Gordon are in the historic centre of the town.

English, French, German and Norwegian spoken.

---

2 FERNANDO A. DE TERRY
SANTÍSIMA TRINIDAD 2 Y 4
11500 EL PUERTO DE SANTA MARÍA
CÁDIZ
TEL: (956) 85 77 00

WINES PRODUCED: Maruja *fino*; Sherry de Terry (Camborio) *fino*, medium dry *amontillado*, *oloroso*; Amoroso Cream; Viña Alta (white table wine produced from Palomino grapes).
BRANDIES PRODUCED:
Centenario, Imperio, 1900, Primero.
VISITS: Mon–Fri 9–14h.
Appointment necessary.
Fernando A. de Terry was founded in 1883 by descendants of the Terry family who settled in the region from Ireland in the fifteenth century. Another historic *bodega* that fell prey to the Rumasa take-overs in the early 1980s, the company was subsequently nationalized before being purchased by John Harvey & Sons in 1985. Terry is noted above all for its fine Maruja *fino*, which demonstrates how fresh and distinctive the Puerto *finos* can be. However, today the company is probably better known for its sherry brandies, for its Centenario is one of the country's most popular and best-selling brands.

The de Terry family was once as famous for its horses as for its wines. Today, on the *bodega* complex located just outside El Puerto, there is still a stable of Carthusian horses as well as a fine collection of traditional Jerezano carriages. English spoken.

Sanlúcar de Barrameda

3 ANTONIO BARBADILLO
LUIS DE EQUILAZ 11
11540 SANLÚCAR DE BARRAMEDA
CÁDIZ
TEL: (956) 36 08 94; FAX: (956) 36 51 03

WINES PRODUCED: Manzanilla de Sanlúcar, Eva *manzanilla*, Solear *manzanilla pasada*; Fino de Balbaina, Cuco *fino*; Cuco *amontillado*, Principe dry *amontillado*; Cuco *oloroso*, San Rafael *oloroso*; Eva Cream, Pedro Ximénez; Castillo de San Diego (white table wine produced from Palomino grapes).

VISITS: Daily, by appointment. Barbadillo, located in the high old *barrio alto* of Sanlúcar de Barrameda next to the Castillo de Santiago, is the town's dominant sherry house, founded in 1821 and still in family hands. The company has 16 *bodegas* in Sanlúcar, and some 60,000 *botas* of wine, primarily *manzanilla*. For it is only in Sanlúcar that this remarkable and unique wine can develop, and Barbadillo is a specialist in its production. The *manzanilla soleras*, for example, have more than 30 scales and from this remarkable palette, a unique range of wines is produced, from the young, bone-dry and tangy Barbadillo *manzanilla fina* (usually about four years old) to the aged and exceptional Solear *manzanilla pasada*, a wine that is on average fifteen years old. It is the dampness, above all, that allows *manzanilla*, the lightest and most delicate of sherries, to be produced here, for the Poniente wind that blows across from the humid marshes of the Coto de Doñana encourages the thick growth of *flor* so characteristic of Sanlúcar. Yet not all *finos* produced in Sanlúcar are *manzanilla*: so delicate and fickle is this growth that of two adjacent *bodegas* at Barbadillo, for example, one may be utilized to produce *manzanilla* while the other, whose ventilation is blocked by the castle, produces instead *fino de Sanlúcar*, a slightly fuller and less delicate wine.

In addition to its fine sherries, Barbadillo produces an excellent fresh white table wine from early-harvested Palomino grapes. It is one of the most widely available and best table wines of the region. English spoken.

4 HIJOS DE RAINERA PÉREZ MARÍN SA
CALLE MISERICORDIA 1
11540 SANLÚCAR DE BARRAMEDA
CÁDIZ
TEL: (956) 18 13 86, 18 15 06;
FAX: (956) 18 28 00

WINE PRODUCED: 'La Guita' *manzanilla*.
VISITS: By appointment.
Old traditional Sanlúcar *bodega* founded in 1825 and located by the seafront specializing only in the production of 'La Guita' *manzanilla*, one of the finest examples of its type. This is still a relatively small, traditional *bodega* dedicated to quality. The name 'La Guita', incidentally, comes from the colloquial term for 'cash' for in the early part of the century when the wines were in great demand, they were only released on payment up front. The word also means 'string'; thus the wine has long been bottled in its distinctive presentation, with a piece of string extending from the capsule to the label.
English spoken.

---

5 HEREDEROS DE ARGÜESO SA
CALLE MAR 8
11540 SANLÚCAR DE BARRAMEDA
CÁDIZ
TEL: (956) 36 01 12, 36 08 17;
FAX: (956) 36 81 69
WINES PRODUCED: 'San Leon' *manzanilla*, 'Viruta' *manzanilla*, 'Argüeso' *manzanilla*; 'Argüeso' *amontillado*, Amontillado Viejo; 'Argüeso' *oloroso*; Moscatel Fruta; 'Argüeso' (white table wine).
VISITS: Mon–Fri mornings; appointment preferable.
Old family *bodega* founded in 1822 and located by the seafront producing traditional *manzanillas*.

Chipiona

6 BODEGAS JOSÉ MELLADO MARTÍN
CTRA DE ROTA, KM 3
11550 CHIPIONA
CÁDIZ
TEL: (956) 37 01 97

WINES PRODUCED: Moscateles de Chipiona.
VISITS: Daily, working hours for direct sales.
The richer, red clay-and-sand soil of Chipiona, a resort town south of Sanlúcar, is particularly well-suited to the cultivation of the Moscatel grape. Indeed, many of the large sherry *bodegas* have plantations here for the production of sweet Moscatel wines to be used for sweetening blends. This small private *bodega*, located outside town on the road to Rota, produces a range of exquisitely rich and extremely sweet dessert wines

ANDALUCÍA

produced from Moscatel grapes laid out to dry in the fierce autumn sun after the harvest. If you like sweet wines, it is worth stopping here to taste and buy.

The Rumasa Affair

Nearly a decade after the collapse of the Rumasa empire, the reverberations have not yet wholly ceased throughout the world of Spanish wine.

José María Ruiz-Mateos, a native Jerezano and member of the Zoilo Ruiz-Mateos sherry family, embarked in the early 1960s on an audacious course of acquisition and expansion in the sherry zone that resulted in his Rumasa 'empire' eventually owning a vast number of old and traditional sherry companies, including Williams & Humbert, Garvey, Palomino & Vergara, Misa, Pemartín, Varela, Bertola, Zoilo Ruiz-Mateos, Vergara & Gordon, Union de Exportadores de Jerez and others, a remarkable stable that accounted at its peak for some 35% of the region's production. Ruiz-Mateos did not stop there, either: wine interests in other Spanish regions included Bodegas Lan, Federico Paternina, Bodegas Franco Españolas and Bodegas Berberana in Rioja; Perez Barquero in Montilla; and René Barbier and Segura Viudas in Penedés. In other sectors, Ruiz-Mateos acquired banks, retail stores, hotels, shipping companies, insurance companies, travel agencies and much else. He was once described in a Madrid daily as 'the man who wanted to buy Spain'.

However, the sherry boom of the 1960s could not and did not last and the companies soon got into considerable difficulties with overproduction and sales. In early 1983 the company was expropriated by the State and nationalized. The government continued to run many of the companies in order to safeguard jobs, and gradually sold them back into private ownership. In the sherry zone, however, many of the great old names (still visible on their *bodega* walls) were lost, along with hundreds of jobs, still a tragedy for a region that suffers from the highest unemployment rate in the country.

Restaurantes, Hoteles y Paradores

Jerez de la Frontera

1

HOTEL JEREZ
AVDA ALVARO DOMECQ 35
11405 JEREZ DE LA FRONTERA
CÁDIZ
TEL: (956) 30 06 00; FAX: (956) 30 50 01

There are now more modern hotels in Jerez, but this somewhat dated but stylish hotel still remains the *bodegueros'* favourite.
Expensive

2

LA MESA REDONDA
MANUEL DE LA QUINTANA 3
11400 JEREZ DE LA FRONTERA
CÁDIZ
TEL: (956) 34 00 69

Considered by many the best restaurant in town, serving refined but classic dishes of the region: *gazpacho, bacalao dorado, pato al vino tinto, solomillo al oloroso.* Great selection of sherries and table wines.
Moderate to Expensive

3

RESTAURANTE GAITÁN
GAITÁN 3
11400 JEREZ DE LA FRONTERA
CÁDIZ
TEL: (956) 34 58 59

The proprietor has changed, but this old favourite, located just outside the old town walls of the *casco antiguo*, remains as popular as ever, serving classic Andalusian foods in a stylish and comfortable ambience.
Moderate

4

TENDIDO 6
CIRCO 10
11400 JEREZ DE LA FRONTERA
CÁDIZ
TEL: (956) 34 48 35

Located literally in the shadow of Jerez's bullring (hence the name), this popular restaurant serves *mariscos* and fish – *cazuela de pescado a la marinera, atun encebollado, almejas al jerez* – as well, naturally, as some notable beef specialities such as *rabo de toro.* Excellent selection of sherry, table wines of the zone and Riojas.
Moderate

ANDALUCÍA

5 VENTA LOS NARANJOS
CTRA JEREZ–SANLÚCAR, KM 4
11400 JEREZ DE LA FRONTERA
CÁDIZ
TEL: (956) 33 99 16

Located in the midst of the
vineyards on the road to Sanlúcar,
this popular roadside restaurant is
a genuine *venta*, serving a
superlative range of shellfish and
seafood to accompany sherries by
the half-bottle.
Moderate

El Puerto de Santa María

1 HOTEL MELIA EL CABALLO BLANCO
AVDA DE MADRID 1
11500 EL PUERTO DE SANTA MARÍA
CÁDIZ
TEL: (956) 86 37 45; FAX: (956) 86 27 12

Large modern hotel located just
outside the town on the NIV trunk
road to Cadíz, with restaurant
serving international and regional
foods, especially seafood.
Moderate to Expensive

2 HOTEL MONASTERIO SAN MIGUEL
CALLE LARGA 27
11500 EL PUERTO DE SANTA MARÍA
CÁDIZ
TEL: (956) 86 44 40; FAX: (956) 86 26 04

Located in the heart of old El
Puerto, this unique 4-star
hotel-restaurant has been recently
converted from the Monastery of
San Miguel Arcangel. Atmospheric
dining room in the vaulted *comedor*
of the convent.
Moderate to Expensive

3 CASA FLORES
RIBERA DEL MARISCO 9
11500 EL PUERTO DE SANTA MARÍA
CÁDIZ
TEL: (956) 86 35 12

Stylish, cool, tiled dining room
serving the usual range of
superlative shellfish and fish, as
well as an exceptionally rich and
tasty *arroz a la marinera*. Popular
tapas bar.
Moderate

4 RESTAURANTE LOS PORTALES
RIBERA DEL MARISCO 13
11500 EL PUERTO DE SANTA MARÍA
CÁDIZ
TEL: (956) 86 21 16

Traditional family-style restaurant serving *mariscos* and fried and grilled fish. Friendly *tapas* bar.
Inexpensive to Moderate

---

5 RESTAURANTE EL FOGON
AVENIDA DE LA PAZ 20-A
11500 EL PUERTO DE SANTA MARÍA
CÁDIZ
TEL: (956) 86 39 02

Closed 15 Jan–15 Feb; Tuesdays.

Small restaurant run by friendly couple, located up from Valdelagrana beach and serving creative foods using fresh local products. House wine from Arcos de la Frontera.
Moderate

Sanlúcar de Barrameda

6 HOTEL TARTANEROS
TARTANEROS 8
11540 SANLÚCAR DE BARRAMEDA
CÁDIZ
TEL: (956) 36 20 44; FAX: (956) 36 00 45

In the centre of the lower town near the seafront, this traditional *palacio*

has been renovated tastefully and traditionally. Formerly the offices of the sherry firm Bodegas Baron, arrangements can be made for visits to the *bodegas*. Exceptional suites overlook the town's main *paseo*.
Moderate

---

7 CASA BIGOTE
BAJO DE GUÍA
11540 SANLÚCAR DE BARRAMEDA
CÁDIZ
TEL: (956) 36 26 96

Closed Sun.
This famous fishermen's bar on the Sanlúcar seafront is as lively and popular as ever. Come to the bar to enjoy superlative stand-up *tapas* and *manzanilla* along with the fishermen; or repair across the

passage to the stylish dining room to sample brothers Paco and Fernando's superlative range of the freshest *mariscos, pescaditos fritos,* or, best of all, *guisos marineros* such as *atun encebollado, rape con mariscos, salpicón de mariscos, menudo de pulpo* and much else. Extensive list of *manzanillas* and table wines of the zone.
Moderate

ANDALUCÍA

8 MIRADOR DE DOÑANA
BAJO DE GUÍA
11540 SANLÚCAR DE BARRAMEDA
CÁDIZ
TEL: (956) 36 35 05

Also located along Sanlúcar's waterfront *paseo*; the seafood and shellfish served here is superb, and the view from the first-floor dining room across the Guadalquivir to the Coto de Doñana is unsurpassed. Superb selection of *tapas* and seafood *raciones* in the popular downstairs bar.
Moderate

Arcos de la Frontera

9 MESÓN DEL BRIGADIER
CURRO EL COJO
LAGO DE ARCOS
11630 ARCOS DE LA FRONTERA
CÁDIZ
TEL: (956) 70 10 03

Well-situated and authentic *mesón* located below this classic *pueblo blanco*, serving home-made foods of the zone on a vine-covered terrace overlooking the lake: home-cured local sausages and *jamones, ajo molinero, morcon de morcilla frita, conejo guisado, cordornices al vino*. The home-cured sausages and hams may be purchased to take away.
Moderate

Paradores

P PARADOR NACIONAL DE CÁDIZ
HOTEL ATLANTICO
DUQUE DE NÁJERA 9
11002 CÁDIZ
TEL: (956) 22 69 05; FAX: (956) 21 45 82

This modern hotel is not typical of the *parador* chain, but its superb position on the headland overlooking the bay makes a stay here memorable.
Moderate to Expensive

P PARADOR NACIONAL 'CASA DEL
CORREGIDOR'
PLAZA DEL CABILDO S/N
11630 ARCOS DE LA FRONTERA
CÁDIZ
TEL: (956) 70 05 00; FAX: (956) 70 11 16

Arcos de la Frontera, an atmospheric hill town, is located about 40 km from Jerez. The *parador* is sited dramatically above the Guadalete river in the town

square, and its restaurant serves excellent regional foods, including *berenjenas al estilo de Arcos, langostinos de Sanlúcar a la parrilla, riñones a la manera de Jerez, carne al estilo de Arcos*, and sweets from the local convent. Drink the local Tierra Blanca and Viña Lucia wines produced from vineyards near the lake.
Moderate to Expensive

Tomar Unas Copas: Stop for a Drink; Stop for a Bite

El Puerto's 'Shellfish Way'

On holiday weekends, or on every Saturday and Sunday from Easter to early September, El Puerto's Ribera del Marisco, or 'Shellfish Way' is the place to be. This main street opposite the town's lively park and *paseo* is quite simply a mecca for lovers of shellfish, one of the most congenial (if hectic) places in which to enjoy a range of *mariscos* and other seafood together with chilled half-bottles of Puerto *fino*. The Ribera del Marisco, as the name suggests, is literally lined with bars and restaurants, all serving exceptional arrays of *tapas* and *raciones*. But there is only one place to repair to: Romerijo's. Romerijo is no more than a bar/*cervecería* with pleasant pavement tables. But it has two exceptional adjoining outlets: a typical *freiduría* selling fried fish – *boquerones, puntillitas, salmonetes, calamares, chocos, gambas* – on one side, and a *cocedería* offering an unrivalled range of freshly-boiled *mariscos* on the other: *gambas, langostinos de Sanlúcar, quisquillas, langostas* and much else. A visit here is a must. The system is: you purchase your paper-wrapped packets of fried fish or boiled shellfish bundled into a Romerijo carrier bag, then take it round the corner to an outdoor table (preferably but not necessarily at Romerijo's bar), order a half-bottle of Puerto *fino* and attack this simple but unbeatable finger feast while the town's quotidian pageant rolls by: the aristocratic but down-at-heel lottery ticket seller; a guitar player (not bad) followed by a singer (terrible); then the balloon man and the vendor of home-fried potato crisps. And so it goes on: the half-bottle is finished . . . another demands to be ordered.

ANDALUCÍA

1

> ROMERIJO
> RIBERA DEL MARISCO
> 11500 EL PUERTO DE SANTA MARÍA
> CÁDIZ
> TEL: (956) 86 12 54

2

ECHATE PAYÁ
RIBERA DEL MARISCO
11500 EL PUERTO DE SANTA MARÍA
CÁDIZ

Tiny cubby-hole stand-up bar – name means 'move over' – serving full range of sherries, together with a remarkable selection of tasty hot *tapas*.

3

RINCÓN DEL JAMÓN
PASEO MARITIMO
VALDELAGRANA
11500 EL PUERTO DE SANTA MARÍA
CÁDIZ

Good selection of *jamones serranos* from Jabugo and Extremadura

together with other simple drinking snacks to accompany a good range of Puerto sherries as well as a selection of Riojas. Rincón del Jamón II is a sister establishment located in the town centre near the port.

4

BAR MARTÍNEZ
PLAZA CABILDO 25
11540 SANLÚCAR DE BARRAMEDA
CÁDIZ
TEL: (956) 36 25 13

In the main square of the lower town, serving an excellent range of *tapas* and *manzanillas*.

5

BAR BODOSKI
COMANDANTE PAZ VARELA 1
11400 JEREZ DE LA FRONTERA
CÁDIZ

Jerez is full of atmospheric bars serving good wines and *tapas*. This

one is singled out mainly because it is authentic, located near the main hotels opposite the fairground, and quite simply serves exceptional *pescaditos fritos* accompanied by *bodega*-fresh sherry.

6 BAR JUANITO
PESCADERÍA VIEJA 8–10
11400 JEREZ DE LA FRONTERA
CÁDIZ

Closed Mon.

Located in the old *judería* down a small passage off the Plaza del Arenal, this popular friendly bar is very typical and is noted for its good *tapas.*

Los Campings

CAMPING PLAYA LAS DUNAS
PASEO MARITIMO DE LA PUNTILLA
11500 EL PUERTO DE SANTA MARÍA
CÁDIZ
TEL: (956) 87 01 12

Open all year.

EL PINAR DE CHIPIONA
CTRA ROTA–CHIPIONA, KM 3,2
11550 CHIPIONA
CÁDIZ
TEL: (956) 37 23 21

Open all year.

Vinos y Comestibles: Stop to Taste; Stop to Buy

HIPERCOR
CTRA SEVILLA 34
11407 JEREZ DE LA FRONTERA
CÁDIZ

This great super-store is part of the Corte Ingles chain and has a superlative selection of wines and sherries (including a range of half-bottles) at competitive prices.

Compras Deliciosas: Stop to Taste; Stop to Buy

CONFITERÍA GUERRERO
CALLE ANCHA
11540 SANLÚCAR DE BARRAMEDA

Come here to taste and buy paper-wrapped packets of sugar-dusted biscuits of Sanlúcar known as *tortas de polvorón*, a great favourite with our young son.

Córdoba and the Montilla-Moriles Hinterland

In Brief: Córdoba, one of the great cities of Spain, lies just over the Sierra Morena mountains that separate Castilla-La Mancha from Andalucía. Situated about 140 km east of Seville and 180 km north of Málaga, it is a world away from the southern *costas*, a major tourist destination in its own right, and no visitor to Andalucía should miss the opportunity of stopping here.

Córdoba provides ample opportunities for sampling Montilla wines in any of its numerous and atmospheric bars and restaurants. The Montilla-Moriles wine country itself lies between Montilla, 45 km to the south of the city, and Lucena, and can most enjoyably be dipped into as a day trip from Córdoba, or else en route from Córdoba to Málaga.

Córdoba is a living palimpsest on which the history of Spain has been written, rewritten and overlaid. The town was probably first founded by the Carthaginians, became the capital of the Roman province of Baetica, and later greatly expanded as an independent caliphate, capital of Moorish Spain, and, during a golden age that lasted nearly 500 years, one of the largest and most prosperous cities of Europe with a population of over a million. Its most famous monument, the Mezquita, was built on the site of a Roman temple and a Visigothic church; after the expulsion of the Moors, this great shrine was further overlayered in the sixteenth century with the construction of a bizarre baroque cathedral within its interior. The town's Alcázar fortress ironically later served as the headquarters for the Holy Inquisition; the Judería, or Jewish quarter, still has one of Spain's only three remaining synagogues.

Today, Córdoba, located on the banks of the Guadalquivir river below the Sierra de Córdoba to the north, poised over the fertile wheatfields, olive groves and vineyards of its Campiña plains, is a bustling and reasonably prosperous provincial capital and, for the visitor, a town dense with atmosphere and history.

The Mezquita is rightly considered Córdoba's mecca. Indeed, after the Kaaba of Mecca itself and the el-Aksa mosque of Jerusalem, this magnificent mosque became the most sacred place of pilgrimage in the Islamic world: today it continues to attract visitors, if no longer pilgrims, from all over the world.

After the expulsion of both the Moors and the Jews, who contributed so

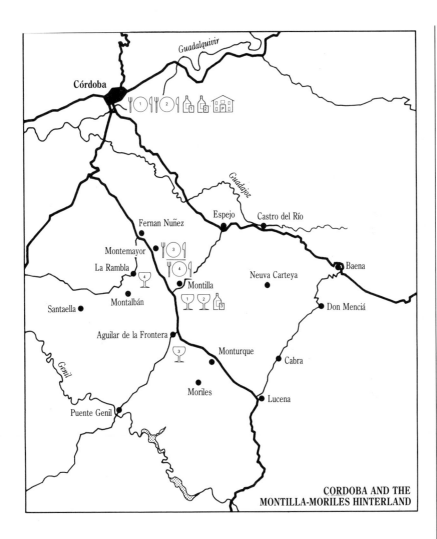

**CORDOBA AND THE
MONTILLA-MORILES HINTERLAND**

much intellectual life and fervour to this major European centre of learning, Córdoba fell into irreversible decline. The Jews, like the Moors, are long gone, but the Judería *barrio* where they lived remains an area of great charm and atmosphere, the narrow labyrinthine lanes lined by white-washed houses with metal grilles over their windows revealing now and then glimpses into the most beautiful patios, decorated with flowers, fountains and colourful *azulejo* tiles.

One such typical house in this old part of town is now a fine restaurant, El Churrasco, specializing above all in superlative charcoal-grilled meats

The *bodega* of Restaurante El Churrasco, Córdoba.

and fish, and other Córdoban specialities such as the delicious cold soup, *salmorejo*. A few doors down, the restaurant keeps its *bodega* in another house typical of the Jewish *barrio*, and this can be visited on request. Here, wooden barrels of the house wine, a yeasty and fresh Montilla *fino*, are kept on hand, as well as an exceptional collection of old Riojas. In typical fashion, the old house is built around its sunny, central patio, and this is a most pleasant place to enjoy a tall *copita* of the wine, drawn directly from the cask with the *venencia*. So served, the wine, flecked with yeasty *flor*, is at its freshest and most delicious. Though Montilla is a sherry-type *vino generoso*, the wine as drunk in the zone itself is unfortified and remarkably fragrant, fruity and delicious. A good Montilla may not have the austere rasping dryness of, say, a Puerto *fino*, nor the salty tang of a *manzanilla*: yet it is delicious in its own right, always somewhat fuller, fruitier and apparently less dry than sherry. Paradoxically, though heavier in the mouth, it is a lighter wine, one that is easier to drink in quantity. But it must be fresh, exceedingly fresh.

Córdoba used to be the home of a number of Montilla *bodegas*, and one or two still remain. One such is Bodegas Campo, most noteworthy for its collection of old barrels signed by local and national stars and dignitaries, especially famous bullfighters and flamenco dancers. However, though the wines continue to be stored here, and can be tasted and purchased, they must now by law be produced within the delimited Montilla-Moriles wine zone which lies outside the city.

The Montilla-Moriles vineyard is centred on the busy wine town of Montilla itself. To reach it, leave Córdoba on the road to Seville, then, about 8 km out, find the N331 turning left to Málaga. This leads through a dramatic sweep of the country, the high, rolling Campiña of Córdoba. In April or May this makes a magnificent vista of waving fields of still green and soft wheat, olive trees, and, further towards Montilla, endless rows of stumpy, close-cropped vines, with a profusion of wildflowers punctuating the view and adding a splash of colour. By June, the great colourful sunflowers stand to attention, and the grapes have already begun to form. But in July and August, after the harvests of wheat and sunflower, the landscape is baked, cracked and dry under parched, brown stubble and only the vine and the olive survive.

The delimited wine zone extends over most of the southern half of the Córdoba province, bordered by the Genil river to the south and the Guadajoz to the north, and encompassing the communities of Montilla, Moriles, Montalbán, Puente Genil, Monturque, Nueva Carteya, Don Mencía, and parts of Montemayor, Fernan Nuñez, La Rambla, Santaella, Aguilar de la Frontera, Lucena, Cabra, Baena, Castro del Río and Espejo.

Here the Pedro Ximénez vine sends down deep roots, searching far underground for moisture stored in the spongy layer of chalk subsoil, the prized white *albero* on which the finest vineyards lie, especially in the hills of the Sierra de Montilla and the Moriles Alto. Pedro Ximénez, or PX as it is also known, is utilized in both Jerez and Málaga for sweetening blends of those great wines. Here, in the hotter inland climate of Montilla, this remarkably versatile grape produces wines that can reach natural alcohol levels of 14–16°, fully fermented and so naturally bone dry. If anywhere else in the world you allowed white grapes to reach such huge degrees of ripeness, then fermented them out to reach their full potential alcohol, the result would be fat, flabby and coarse wines with no pretension to quality or finesse. Yet in Montilla, such grapes, fermented in clay *tinajas* and matured dynamically under a protective veil of *flor*, produce wines that are surprisingly fresh and fine, if undoubtedly fatter, less elegant than the finest *finos* from Jerez, Puerto or Sanlúcar.

Tinajas, the immense earthenware urns that are direct descendants of the fermentation *dolium* found throughout the ancient Roman world, are one of the most distinctive features of the Montilla-Moriles wine production. Today, while earthenware *tinajas* still do remain in use, many have been replaced with concrete versions, while in the most modern *bodegas* stainless steel fermentation vats may be preferred. None the less, it is a remarkable sight to view an enormous *bodega* filled with these unique vessels, like lines of so many giant, bulging Ali Baba jars. *Tinajas* have no aperture at the bottom, and so all the liquid has to enter and be removed from the narrow neck at the top of each jar by hoses, siphons and pumps. Moreover, to clean them, a man must enter each vessel down a ladder, an unpleasant and labour-intensive task to say the least. Yet *tinajas* are still used even by the most up-to-date *bodegas* as storage receptacles wherein the wines undergo their secondary or malolactic fermentation for the unique character that they impart to the wines of Montilla.

Once the wines have been fermented, as in Jerez they are classified into *fino* and *oloroso* families. *Finos* are generally produced from free-run juice and *mosto de yema* (juice from a light first pressing), from grapes grown on the superior zones of the Sierra de Montilla and Moriles Alto. As in Jerez, *finos* are wines that possess the rare propensity to grow *flor* on their surface in casks that are filled only to about two-thirds. *Oloroso* wines come from the second pressing, and from grapes grown on the lower-lying, sandy soils in the zones known as Ruedos. Casks of *oloroso* wines are filled to the bung and do not grow *flor*. Once classified, the wines are usually transferred to the maturation *bodegas* in Montilla, Moriles and a few other permitted municipalities. There they enter into different *soleras*, to undergo that unique process of dynamic fractional ageing.

It has to be said that the great strength of the wines of Montilla is exactly that: their great natural strength. The range of wines produced here is similar to that of Jerez, and runs the full gamut, from fresh, early-picked table wines (an innovation in both zones), through *fino*, *amontillado* (the term means 'in the style of Montilla'), *oloroso*, medium dry, medium sweet and cream blends. However, due to their higher initial natural alcohol levels, the *finos* of Montilla rarely need to be fortified, and even the *olorosos* require far less grape alcohol to bring them up to their finished state, an important factor that perhaps makes them easier to drink in quantity, as well as easier on the head the next morning. On the other hand, few would argue that Montilla can ever achieve the complexity, finesse and depth of flavour of the best sherries.

Montilla's similarity to Jerez has in recent years been something of a drawback as producers have struggled to establish for their wines an individual identity as something other than bargain or supermarket sherry look-alikes. To a certain extent they have failed, for the wines really are more similar to than different from sherry; as a result, combined with a general trend by the consumer away from *vinos generosos* in favour of lighter table wines (the sherry market has also suffered in recent years), many of the great Montilla *bodegas* have not survived.

Today, in the town of Montilla itself, two great *bodegas* remain, Alvear and Perez Barquero, while Carbonell y Cia is located in the nearby town of Aguilar de la Frontera. Furthermore, within the zone itself there are still literally scores of small to medium-sized *bodegas* that continue to purchase must or wine to mature in cask by the *solera* system, not to sell internationally or even nationally, but primarily to supply by the barrel, *garrafa*, or bottle to slake the seemingly unquenchable thirst engendered in the bars of Córdoba and its surrounding villages.

Alvear is the great name of Montilla. The company was begun in 1729 when Don Diego de Alvear y Escalera moved to Montilla and purchased land and buildings to start the now famous *bodegas*. Over the succeeding centuries, family members served in Spanish America, and a descendant even rose to become President of the Republic of Argentina. Alvear greatly expanded in the first half of this century when Don Francisco de Alvear y Gómez de la Cortina, Conde de la Cortina, took charge of the *bodegas* and acquired numerous vineyards and extensive premises. The Alvear family manor house in the centre of the town remains one of the principal monuments of Montilla.

The Alvear operation is immense and impressive. The company has considerable vineyard holdings of its own but these account for only a small percentage of its total needs. For the rest, Alvear relies on the purchase of grapes direct from small growers, many of whom have supplied the company for generations, as well as buying in pressed grape must or wine from growers or co-operatives. Alvear has two main *lagares* or press houses, located in the midst of the vineyards themselves. Here the grapes are brought in, de-stemmed and pressed without delay in modern pneumatic horizontal presses which work to apply gentle, even pressure.

In the recent past, all the grape must would have fermented in *tinajas*. Today Alvear uses stainless steel fermentation tanks which control the temperature of the fermenting must through internal refrigeration units. This is a matter of considerable importance, especially for the finer wines destined to be *finos*. After the first fermentation, the wines are transferred to *tinajas* where they undergo their secondary or malolactic fermentation before classification and passing into the maturation *bodegas* to enter into the *soleras*.

Pedro Ximénez is virtually the sole grape cultivated in the Montilla vineyard and it is a remarkable one. It is instructive to view the full gamut of wines produced at Alvear from this single variety alone, all entitled to the Montilla DO and ranging in colour from the palest yellow to near black.

The lightest wine, Marqués de la Sierra, is a table wine of only 10° alcohol, produced from grapes early-harvested in mid-August a full three or four weeks before the start of the main *vendimia*. Light, fruity and with a good bite of acid, it is a refreshing beverage. CB Fino is Alvear's best-selling wine, a pale lemon yellow wine with a good, fragrant yeasty character, extremely dry, fresh in the mouth, light and elegant. Fino Festival is an aged *fino* based on the CB *solera*. The wines are drawn off from this *solera* and pass into another three-scale *solera* for further ageing; the wine that eventually emerges is a slightly darker straw-yellow, fuller in the mouth, and with a delicious soft and nutty character. Carlos VII Amontillado Viejo also comes from the same base *solera* but is aged even further: light amber in colour, with a warm and intense flavour of hazelnuts. Since it is not fortified, it remains remarkably light in body for such a flavoursome wine.

The *oloroso* wines continue to increase in colour down the scale. Oloroso Pelayo is a rich amber wine, fuller and considerably heavier on the nose than the *fino* family of wines: it has a candied toffee and butter nose and is rich and long in flavour, yet totally bone dry. Oloroso Asunción is slightly darker still in colour, a medium dry *oloroso* with a characteristic raisiny nose that comes from the addition of PX sweetening wine. Finally, at the end of the scale, comes Pedro Ximénez 1927, an old *solera* of rare dessert Montilla: dark like black coffee, extremely full, concentrated and raisiny, luscious and very long.

Montilla itself is a typical inland Andalusian wine town. Known as Munda Betica to the ancient Romans, it was here that Julius Caesar defeated the army of Pompey. Today a bustling town of about 25,000 inhabitants, it serves as an economic centre for the zone and home of its most important *bodegas*. It is certainly the place to come to see how Montilla is made and to taste it at its source, and it is a pleasant town in which to spend a few hours. The Church of Santa Clara, with its *mudéjar* decorations, is its most notable monument.

Moriles, which shares the name of the official *denominación*, is only a tiny and fairly undistinguished village, as famous for the size and quality of its *flamenquines* as for its wines. Stop here to try this typical drinking snack, a tasty roll of veal and *jamón serrano*, breaded, deep-fried and cut into slices, together with a bottle of the local Moriles wine. Produced from grapes grown in the superior zone of Moriles Alto, it is traditionally sold in a slender 'hock'-style bottle, not the more usual sherry shape.

Other noteworthy Montilla wine towns include Aguilar de la Frontera, Lucena, Puente Genil (renowned locally for its *carne de membrillo* quince jelly), and La Rambla (also noteworthy for its ceramics). Espejo is a fine perched hill town surrounded by vineyards and olive trees and famous for its *embutidos* (cured pork products). Baena, another steep white hill town, and its environs, though located within the Montilla wine zone, is today almost totally given over to the cultivation of olives, for this zone produces one of Spain's finest extra-virgin olive oils.

Bodegas: Stop to Taste; Stop to Buy

1

ALVEAR SA
AVDA Mᴬ AUXILIADORA 1
14550 MONTILLA
CÓRDOBA
TEL: (957) 65 01 00; FAX: (957) 65 01 35

WINES PRODUCED: Marqués de la Sierra; CB *fino* (Pale Dry), Fino Festival; Carlos VII *amontillado viejo*, Alvear Medium; Oloroso Pelayo, Oloroso Asunción; Cream, Pale Cream; Pedro Ximénez 1927.
VISITS: Mon–Fri 10–12h30; 15–17h. Summer hours (15 May–31 Aug) 10–14h. Appointment preferable.
Montilla's leading producer has an impressive maturation *bodega* complex near the entrance to the town by the park, comprising *bodegas* La Sacristía, El Liceo, Las Mercedes (known also as 'La Monumental'), and Conde de la Cortina. It may be possible to arrange to visit the 'Las Puentes' *lagar* or press house, located in the nearby Sierra de Montilla, most remarkable for its huge capacity of *tinajas*.

Bodegas Conde de la Cortina belong to the same group and produce a similar range of wines that are marketed separately. English, German, Dutch spoken.

2

PEREZ BARQUERO SA
AVENIDA DE ANDALUCÍA 27
14550 MONTILLA
CÓRDOBA
TEL: (957) 65 05 00; FAX: (957) 65 02 08

WINES PRODUCED: Los Amigos *fino*, Gran Barquero *fino*; Gran Barquero *amontillado*; Gran Barquero *oloroso*; Gran Barquero Pedro Ximénez; Los Palcos Pale Cream; Viña Amalia (white table wine).
VISITS: May–October Mon–Fri 8–14h; October–April Mon–Fri 9–13h30; 16–18h. Appointment advisable.
Another leading Montilla producer, formerly part of the Rumasa stable of companies.
English, French spoken.

ANDALUCÍA

3 CARBONELL Y CIA DE CÓRDOBA SA
CTRA AGUILAR-PUENTE GENIL
14920 AGUILAR DE LA FRONTERA
CÓRDOBA
TEL: (957) 66 06 43

WINES PRODUCED: Solera Fina 1ª;
Moriles Superior; Flor de Montilla
amontillado.

VISITS: Mon–Fri 8–13h.
Appointment necessary.
Carbonell is one of Spain's most
important and best-known
producers of olive oil but it is also
the proprietor of this traditional and
beautifully-constructed Montilla
bodega.

---

4 BODEGAS LUIS LUCENA BLANCO
14540 LA RAMBLA
CÓRDOBA
TEL: (957) 68 44 37

WINES PRODUCED: Fino Rocío,
Fino Blanqueto.
VISITS FOR DIRECT SALES: Daily,
working hours.
This tiny but fascinating *bodega* is
typical of the zone. Luis Lucena
purchases fermented must from

growers in the Moriles Alto and
raises the wine in small *soleras* in
his traditional *bodega* in the *pueblo*
of La Rambla. The only wines made
are *finos* ('*¡No hay vinos gordos
aqui!*' I was sharply told), and they
are sold almost exclusively to bars
in Córdoba. Come here to see the
small end of the business, and to
taste and purchase *bodega*-fresh
bottles of excellent wine.

Restaurantes, Hoteles y Paradores

1 EL CABALLO ROJO
CARDENAL HERRERO 28
14003 CÓRDOBA
TEL: (957) 47 53 75

Famous and discreet classic
Andalusian restaurant serving both
traditional and historic *mozárabe*

foods: *alcachofas a la montillana,
salmorejo andaluz con jamón
serrano, rape mozárabe, pez espada
a la cordobesa.* Excellent selection
of desserts and superlative *bodega.*
Moderate to Expensive

---

2 EL CHURRASCO
ROMERO 16
14003 CÓRDOBA
TEL: (957) 29 08 19

Closed Thur; Aug.

An old favourite, located in the
heart of the Judería, serving
exceptional charcoal-grilled meats
and fish in the comfortable patio
dining room. Specialities include
salmorejo, churrasco, parrillada

mixta (mixed grill), *pez espada a la cordobesa, tejas con helado de pasas.* Ask to visit the *bodega* to view an authentic and well-preserved medieval house, to taste a *copita* of Montilla drawn from the cask, or to choose your bottle of Rioja from a selection of old vintages.
Moderate

---

3 HOTEL DON GONZALO
CTRA CÓRDOBA–MÁLAGA, KM 47
14550 MONTILLA
CÓRDOBA
TEL: (957) 65 06 58; FAX: (957) 65 06 66

Recently up-graded 3-star hotel-restaurant located outside Montilla on the road to Málaga. Restaurant serves local foods, including *gazpacho, salmorejo, alcachofas al Montilla.*
Inexpensive to Moderate

---

4 RESTAURANT LAS CAMACHAS
CTRA CÓRDOBA–MÁLAGA, KM 42
14550 MONTILLA
CÓRDOBA
TEL: (957) 65 00 04

Montilla's best restaurant, located on the main road at the entrance to the town, serving stylishly prepared regional foods: *salmorejo, revuelto de gambas, rabo de toro, riñones al Montilla*, accompanied of course by the wines of Montilla.
Moderate

Parador

P PARADOR NACIONAL DE LA
ARRUZAFA
AVDA. DE LA ARRUZAFA, S/N
14012 CÓRDOBA
TEL: (957) 27 59 00; FAX: (957) 28 04 09

Modern *parador* located a little outside the town in a quiet suburb, the actual site where the Moorish Calif Abderramán I had his recreational palace and planted the first palm trees in Europe. Lovely gardens and views over the city.
Moderate

Tomar Unas Copas: Stop for a Drink; Stop for a Bite

Córdoba has no shortage of bars serving excellent wines and *tapas*, though inevitably those around the Mezquita and the Judería can be overrun with tourists.

1 CASA RUBIO
PUERTA DE ALMODÓVAR
14000 CÓRDOBA

Located off the main *paseo* by one of the old gates to the walled city, this typical Córdoban *taberna* serves good house Montilla and *tapas*.

---

2 BODEGAS CAMPOS
CALLE LINEROS
14000 CÓRDOBA

Just east of the Plaza del Potro, this old *bodega* is worth visiting to see the collection of barrels signed by famous dignitaries and local bigwigs and its lovely sunny patios. Wines can be tasted and purchased, but there is usually no food on hand.

---

3 BARRIL DE ORO
AVDA DE ANDALUCÍA 22
14550 MONTILLA
CÓRDOBA

This pleasant typical bar is located virtually opposite the Alvear *bodega* but it is indicative of the zone that the Montilla wine served here is not from that great producer but purchased, as a matter of pride, from small individual growers, served *flor*-fresh from the barrel. Good hot *tapas* (especially *flamenquín*) and seafood *raciones*.

Los Campings

CAMPAMENTO MUNICIPAL
14000 CÓRDOBA
TEL: (957) 47 20 00

Open all year.

CAMPING LA CAMPIÑA
SANTAELLA
CÓRDOBA
TEL: (957) 31 33 48

Open all year.
Small, friendly, family run, located in wine country between Córdoba and Seville.

Compras Deliciosas: Stop to Taste; Stop to Buy

Baena Olive Oil

Spain is the world's largest producer of olive oil, and, we conjecture, also one of its largest consumers. Olive oil is used for everything: as a dressing for salads and vegetables, for cooking, and as the preferred medium for frying and even deep-frying. As is the case elsewhere, there is olive oil and there is olive oil. That produced in the zone of Baena, from olives grown in the communities of Baena, Don Mencía, Luque, Nueva Carteya and Zuheros, is considered among the finest in the country, entitled to its own Baena *denominación de origen*. Olive oils that have been produced to stringent standards and regulations receive a seal of authenticity from the Consejo Regulador, a guarantee of quality for the consumer.

Baena extra-virgin olive oil is of very high quality indeed, the best of which can even stand alongside single-estate olive oils from Tuscany. At their traditional Santa Lucía mill in Baena, for example, the Núñez de Prado family have been making olive oil for seven generations, and undertake exceptional hand care in every stage of production. The olives grown on the family estates are all harvested by hand, transported quickly to the mill, and ground to a paste by immense traditional granite stones. Then, a unique system invented by the Marqués de Acapulco y Quintillana at the turn of the century is employed: known as partial extraction, this consists simply of collecting the 'free run' oil through a system of fine filters without any additional pressure whatsoever. It takes eleven kilos of olives to yield just one litre of precious oil. But what oil! Extremely low in acid, concentrated in flavour, yet unfatty, fine and elegant, this unfiltered virgin oil is too good for cooking, but is best used to flavour a bowl of cold *gazpacho* or *salmorejo*, or simply to dribble on to a slice of good home-made bread to accompany a goblet of wine.

NÚÑEZ de PRADO CB
CERVANTES 15
14850 BAENA
CÓRDOBA
TEL: (957) 67 01 41; FAX: (957) 67 00 19

ANDALUCÍA

Málaga and its 'Mountain' Wine

> **In Brief:** Málaga, the gateway to the Costa del Sol, is not usually considered a tourist destination in its own right, but this major city with a population of half a million is not without its charms and deserves more than cursory exploration. Though its once famous wine industry is in considerable decline, there are two famous *bodegas* producing traditional wines that can be visited. Moreover, the wine country itself, located on the Antequera plateau en route to Córdoba as well as the Axarquía zone in the rocky hills east of Málaga and behind the resort of Nerja provide pleasant excursions away from the coast. In the latter zone, the tiny grape-growing *pueblo* of Competa has become something of an English expatriate community, and there is a signposted *'Ruta del Sol y del Vino'*.

Málaga is best known to British visitors today as the gateway to the Costa del Sol, but to the Victorians the name was associated primarily with wine. For Málaga, or 'Mountain' wine as it was also known, is one of the great historic wines of Spain, produced probably since the time of the Phoenicians who first brought the vine to these shores, enjoyed by Greeks, Romans and Moors alike, not to mention Catherine the Great and English ladies in Victorian parlours and sitting rooms. In the last century, sales of 'Mountain' in Britain exceeded even those of sherry.

Though the Koran forbade the consumption of alcohol, it was the Moors, surprisingly, who developed the wine into a form that would not be unrecognizable even today. They, after all, were in this area for some eight centuries, and, with their famous love of all things sweet, they developed a method of producing a dessert wine so luscious that it was known as *Xarabe al Malaqui*, or Málaga syrup, ostensibly taken for medicinal purposes only. This super-sweet wine was produced by a process they developed to make *arrope*, a constituent of Málaga wine made in the same manner and used in the wine even today. Grapes that have been laid out in the sun to shrivel and raisin for 8–11 days are pressed, then the super-thick, sugar-rich juice is cooked in copper double boilers until it is reduced to 30% of its original volume. This sweet, dark, concentrated juice is then added to the wines in varying degrees.

The phylloxera louse arrived in Málaga in 1878, earlier than anywhere else in Spain, and much of the historic vineyard was lost for ever. In truth, the steep, schistose, decomposed mica and slate vineyards of Axarquía were and still are so labour-intensive to cultivate that it was probably not con-

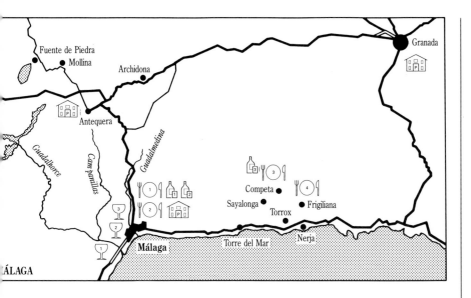

sidered worth the effort of replanting. Scores of grape-growing families emigrated to South America in search of a better life. Then traditional markets in Russia were lost after the Revolution. The isolation that followed Spain's own Civil War destroyed any remaining export markets, and in recent decades, increasing tourism has encroached ever further on those lands still under vines.

Today, the market for Málaga, formerly one of the great fortified wines of Europe, alongside sherry, port, Marsala and Madeira, is in considerable decline. Sweet fortified wines in general are out of favour with current drinking trends, and it is fair to say that Málaga has been out of favour so long that few wine drinkers have ever even encountered it. Today, apart from small grape-growers and producers, there remain only three major *bodegas* in Málaga still dedicated to the production of this once great wine, a pity given its lengthy historical pedigree. Although it is out of favour, Málaga is a wine that deserves to be better known and drunk by all those who seek to appreciate the grape in all its myriad and diverse manifestations. For Málaga is unique, it is authentic, and it can be very good, especially for those who like sweet raisiny pudding wines.

Those sweet dark 'stickies' on Victorian sideboards, you might think, were wines wholly at odds with their zone of production, developed not to quench the thirst of the locals themselves, but rather as export products mainly to satisfy the tastes of northern Europeans in colder climes. Yet the

ANDALUCÍA

Antigua Casa de Guardia, Málaga.

wine has an immense traditional following in Málaga today, and in the town's bars in the *casco antiguo* it continues to be drunk and enjoyed with considerable gusto.

Come to the Antigua Casa de Guardia, a famous and historic stand-up 'saloon' off Málaga's main avenue, the Alameda Principal, to gain an intimate and unforgettable acquaintance with the city's traditional wines. This is the place where the *malagueños* themselves pop in from nearby offices for a quick tot; they place a coin on the counter, down a straight glass of Añejo or Moscatel, collect the change, then just as quickly hustle out again. There are no seats, just the long, time-worn bar counter, and, behind it, a row of about 20 barrels, each containing a different Málaga wine.

Order a plate of *gambas* or *mejillones* from the shellfish vendor at the back and work your way through the wines. Try first a glass of Seco Añejo: amber, rather yeasty and a touch sour. Seco Trasañejo is better; the wine has been aged longer, and is correspondingly fuller and finer, slightly sweet in the mouth yet with a dry finish. The Moscatels should also be sampled; they are strikingly grapey, fragrant and lusciously sweet. Lágrima Añejo, produced traditionally from the free run must, is dark amber, a rich sweet wine with a bitter-coffee finish that is characteristic of Málaga. Pajarete 1908, the house speciality, comes foaming out of the barrel with a creamy froth almost like the foam on a glass of *espresso* coffee; it is darker than the Lágrima, drier, and with a beautiful long bitter-sweet finish of almonds and dried apricots.

The proprietor of the Antigua Casa de Guardia, José Garijo Ruiz, is also the owner of a small Málaga *bodega* of the same name, though almost all of his production is consumed in this popular *malagueño* spit-and-sawdust institution. Málaga's major producers, however, are both located somewhat out of the historic city centre in less than traditional surroundings on the industrial fringes of the town. Yet none the less, both Scholtz Hermanos and López Hermanos continue to produce traditional and historic Málagas based on old *soleras* containing rare and precious wines.

Scholtz Hermanos is the oldest firm, founded by a German, Christian Scholtz, in 1807. Scholtz's flagship wine, Solera 1885, is a classic Málaga, produced from both Pedro Ximénez and Moscatel together with the addition of concentrated old wines: deep amber, warm and figgy, it is probably the wine *par excellence* to drink with Christmas pudding, though *aficionados* would say that it is best enjoyed on its own.

López Hermanos, a family firm founded in 1885, continues to produce a full range of Málagas, from bone dry to very sweet. Trajinero, for example, is a dry Málaga produced from 100% Pedro Ximénez grapes and aged by the *solera* system. Cartojal Moscatel de Málaga is a new-style Moscatel produced with the most modern technologies; light, pale and intensely grapey, protected from oxidation in stainless steel tanks under a blanket of nitrogen, it is perhaps more in the style of fortified Muscat wines from southern France. The company's best-known wine, though, is wholly Spanish: Málaga Virgen, produced from 25% Moscatel and 75% Pedro Ximénez wines to which about 8% *arrope* is added. The resulting blend is fortified to 17° alcohol, then it is aged statically (not by *soleras*) for a minimum of two years in oak casks. Fresh, raisiny and not overly complex, the wine none the less maintains the characteristic and delicious bitter-sweet finish that is the classic hallmark of Málaga.

Like all airport destinations, Málaga is usually considered a town to escape from as soon as you have negotiated the rented car. In fact, the city itself can be very pleasant indeed, far more pleasant and certainly more authentically Spanish than many of the ghastly resorts both up and down the coast. The quarter around the strangely unfinished sixteenth-century cathedral is particularly bustling and hectic, while the palm-lined Paseo del Parque that leads to the Alcazaba is most pleasant. The Alcazaba and the hilltop Gibralfaro fortresses are of course reminders that this was one of the major strongholds of Al-Andalus. Málaga's seafront has been an important port for literally centuries, and so it remains today.

Our favourite Málaga destination is the beaches that line the city to the east, notably Pedregalejo and El Palo, just off the road to Almería. The city has ever encroached on these former fishermen's hamlets, but the *pescadores* still live here, in their tiny, toy-like houses, with their boats pulled up the beach, the womenfolk sitting out in front repairing the nets. Though today Pedregalejo is extremely popular as a hang-out for the city's youths, this waterfront is simply a fun place to relax and eavesdrop on how the Spaniards – both young and old – enjoy themselves in their free time. It is here, too, that you will find the finest *churrenguitos*, simple fishermen's bars that started out originally as shacks serving drinks and fried *pescaitos* (Málaga, together with Cádiz, can rightly claim to be the fried fish capital of the world) and *mariscos*. It is here, too, that you can enjoy that peculiar speciality of Málaga, the *espeto*. On the beach itself, sometimes in upturned old boats, fires of almond or olive wood are made, and sardines and other fish are threaded on to bamboo-and-cane skewers, stuck into the sand, and cooked in front of the fires.

Usually we believe that the wines of the land unquestionably go best with its local foods, and on the whole this holds true for Spain. What could be better than oak-aged Rioja and *lechazo asado? Gambas cocidas* and a *copita* of sea-fresh *manzanilla?* True, a glass of Trasañejo Seco and a plate of *mejillones* on the half-shell goes down very well in the Antigua Casa de Guardia. But Mountain wine with a *fritura malagueña* on the Pedregalejo seafront? Don't even consider it. Order a *caña* of draught beer instead, and relax and soak in the sun and the atmosphere . . .

As for further exploration of the wine country of Málaga, there are two zones worth seeking. The first is the plateau of Antequera, located up the mountain behind Málaga around the communities of Antequera itself, Mollina, Fuente de Piedra and Archidona. Here, the soil is a deep red on the surface, but underneath there is a rich bed of spongy white limestone. The vineyards are almost wholly given over to Pedro Ximénez, and in this hothouse environment the grapes ripen to exceptional degrees. Moreover, in some cases, after picking and before pressing, the bunches of grapes are laid out to be dried further to concentrate their sugars. Antequera is a white-walled fortified town in the heart of this fertile zone, with some pleasant and atmospheric old streets and churches, notably the Collegiate Church of Santa María la Mayor. There are also some interesting prehistoric caves and dolmens in the area, while the lagoon at nearby Fuente de Piedra is a sanctuary for migratory birds. One day in late April we saw thousands of pink flamingos in this small, shallow body of water. Archidona, another wine town, located above the ruins of a Moorish fort, is worth visiting for its splendid five-sided seventeenth-century central *plaza*.

The second principal Málaga wine zone is the rocky hills of Axarquía behind Nerja, east of Málaga. This, traditionally, is the foremost zone for

...iana

the cultivation of fragrant Moscatel grapes, used for Málaga wine or dried to be sold as Moscatel raisins, one of Málaga's great specialities. However, to witness how much this industry has declined, strike into the hills just past Torre del Mar to Sayalonga and Competa. It is tragic to view the steeply terraced, schistose slopes, once well-tended and cultivated with vineyards, now on the whole abandoned, the defined pattern of years and centuries of manual labour once more taken over by Nature. It is not difficult to understand why. These vineyards rank among the most labour-intensive in the world, and must be worked by man and donkey alone as no tractor could negotiate these steep and crumbling slopes. Yet, with the decline in the Málaga market, the prices fetched for the grapes are soul-destroyingly low. Here, and in neighbouring communities such as Torrox and Frigiliana, the fragrant Moscatel grapes are still cultivated by dedicated growers; on the hillsides beside their farmhouses there are *pasero* frames where the grapes are spread out each autumn to be dried into raisins. But it is a sign of the times, and perhaps not surprising, that many of these houses have long been abandoned or sold to foreigners.

Competa, high at the top of the valley, is a remote and charming hill town, once famous above all for its wines. Strangely, though, the town has been almost wholly taken over by a large and extended community of English families. Come here all the same to taste the Moscatel de Competa in any of the village's numerous bars, where ex-pats inevitably hang out, exchanging the day's news.

Another little town located on the signposted '*Ruta del Sol y del Vino*' is Frigiliana, situated in the steep balcony of hills high above Nerja. This is another wine *pueblo* for the curious and intrepid wine traveller to make

ANDALUCÍA

for, as it truly is a charming (and as yet still fairly unspoiled) typical Andalusian hill town. Climb up the cobbled alleyways to the top of the town for a panorama of the terraced hills leading down to the sea, and reward yourself with a *copa* of *vino de Frigiliana*.

Bodegas: Stop to Taste; Stop to Buy

1 SCHOLTZ HERMANOS SA
CTRA CÁDIZ, KM 238
29004 MÁLAGA
TEL: (952) 31 36 02, 23 08 04

WINES PRODUCED: Seco Añejo; Moscatel Pálido; Lágrima; Scholtz Solera 1885.
VISITS: Mon–Fri 9–15h.
Appointment necessary.
Málaga's oldest *bodega*, located near Málaga airport.

---

2 LÓPEZ HERMANOS SA
POLÍGONO INDUSTRIAL EL VISO
CALLE CANADA 10
29004 MÁLAGA
TEL: (952) 31 94 54; FAX: (952) 35 98 19

WINES PRODUCED: Trajinero; Málaga Virgen; Moscatel Cartojal.
VISITS: Mon–Fri 9–14h.
Appointment necessary.

Located in an undistinguished industrial park on the outskirts of town, it is still worth making an appointment to visit this long-established *bodega* in order to learn about and sample these traditional wines at the source. English, French spoken.

---

3 LARIOS SA
POLÍGONO INDUSTRIAL
   GUADALHORCE
CALLE CÉSAR VALLEJO 24
29004 MÁLAGA
TEL: (952) 24 11 00; FAX: (952) 24 03 82

WINES PRODUCED: Málaga Larios (Málaga *dulce color*); Benefique

(Málaga *seco oloroso*).
VISITS: Mon–Fri 8–15h.
Appointment necessary.
Spain's largest producer of Spanish gin also makes a range of Málaga wines.
English, French spoken.

Restaurantes, Hoteles y Paradores

1
BAR/RESTAURANT EL CALEÑO
PASEO MARÍTIMO
29016 PEDREGALEJO
MÁLAGA
TEL: (952) 29 91 48

There are so many good seafood bars and restaurants along Málaga's seafront that it is hard to single out one. However, El Caleño is a typical and authentic fishermen's *churrenguito* serving superb fish, shellfish, and fish cooked *al espeto*. The almond-and-olive-wood fire is made on the beach in front of the tables in the hull of an old fishing boat.
Inexpensive

2
CASA PEDRO
PASEO MARÍTIMO
29017 EL PALO
MÁLAGA
TEL: (952) 29 00 13

Closed Mon eve.
Famous and always busy old eating house on the fishermen's beach at El Palo (about 5 km east of Málaga on the road to Almería) serving the city's classics: *fritura malagueña*, *espetones de sardinas*, and a more than passable *paella*.
Moderate

3
BAR FRANQUELO 'EL BUEN GUSTO'
PLAZA D. PANTALEÓN ROMERO 2
29754 COMPETA
MÁLAGA
TEL: (952) 51 60 24

This little bar-restaurant just off the main square is nothing special but it has pleasant outdoor tables. Ask for the *plato del día* for some good hearty local fare: *cazuela de papa con calabaza*, *lomo al ajillo*, *bacalao*, *albondigas* and, of course, home-made *vinos de Competa*.
Inexpensive

4
RESTAURANTE EL BODEGUILLA
IGLESIA 1
FRIGILIANA
MÁLAGA
TEL: (952) 53 34 28

Open midday only out of season.

Good home cooking served at outdoor tables set in the cobbled passages near the church of this lovely whitewashed wine *pueblo*.
Inexpensive

ANDALUCÍA

Paradores

P

PARADOR NACIONAL DE GIBRALFARO
GIBRALFARO
29016 MÁLAGA
TEL: (952) 22 19 03; FAX: (952) 22 19 02

Located on the heights of the Gibralfaro beside the old Moorish fortress, with beautiful views over the city and sea. Good local foods, especially *fritura malagueña*.
Moderate

P

PARADOR NACIONAL DE ANTEQUERA
PASEO GARCÍA DEL OLMO, S/N
29200 ANTEQUERA
MÁLAGA
TEL: (952) 84 02 61; FAX: (952) 84 13 12

Newly constructed *parador* set among the ruins of the Moorish fortress above Antequera. Swimming pool.
Moderate

P

PARADOR NACIONAL 'SAN
      FRANCISCO'
REAL DE LA ALHAMBRA, S/N
18009 GRANADA
TEL: (958) 22 14 41; FAX: (958) 22 22 64

This former Arab palace which dates from 1302 was converted into a Franciscan convent founded by the Reyes Católicos immediately

after they seized the city. Located actually within the enclosure of the Alhambra, it is today one of the great hotels of Spain, and certainly its most popular. Reservations are required many months in advance, but it is worth while stopping here if only for a drink or a meal.
Very Expensive

Tomar Unas Copas: Stop for a Drink; Stop for a Bite

1

ANTIGUA CASA DE GUARDIA
ALAMEDA PRINCIPAL 18
29005 MÁLAGA
TEL: (952) 21 46 80

Traditional spit-and-sawdust *malagueño* bar open for over 150

years, serving an outstanding range of own-produced Málaga wines – dry Transañejo and outstanding Pajarete 1908 – direct from the barrel. Simple drinking snacks and *mariscos*.

2 BAR 'LA TASCA'
CALLE MARÍN GARCIA 12
29004 MÁLAGA
TEL: (952) 22 20 82

Popular city centre bar serving excellent selection of *tapas, jamón serrano*, wines of Jerez and Montilla, and simple *comidas caseras*.

---

3 BAR 'LA BUENA UVA'
AVDA CONSTITUCIÓN 2
29754 COMPETA
MÁLAGA
TEL: (952) 51 63 10

Good *semi-seco* and *dulce* wines of Competa – fragrant Moscatels from the steep slopes of Axarquía – served from the barrel by Paco in this lovely hill town taken over by the English.

Los Campings

CAMPING BALNEARIO DEL CARMEN
29004 MÁLAGA
TEL: (952) 29 00 21

Open all year.
Situated by Pedregalejo seafront.

CAMPING TRÉVELEZ
TRÉVELEZ
GRANADA
TEL: (958) 85 85 75

Open all year.
Atmospheric campsite in the high Alpujarras in *pueblo* famous for its superb *jamones*.

Compras Deliciosas: Stop to Taste; Stop to Buy

ULTRAMARINOS LA MALAGUEÑA
SAN JUAN 48
29004 MÁLAGA
TEL: (952) 21 27 46

Traditional grocery with good selection of Málaga wines, and other typical products such as *uvas pasas de Moscatel* – exquisite dried Moscatel raisins.

ANDALUCÍA

Las Alpujarras

The Alpujarras, a series of valleys and mountains bounded to the north by the great chain of the Sierra Nevada, remains one of the most remote parts of Spain, surprisingly so, given the region's proximity to Granada and the great coastal resort of Almería. First settled by Berber refugees from Seville, this mountainous zone was later populated with Moors fleeing Granada after its fall in 1492 until their final expulsion from Spain in 1568. They developed complex systems of irrigation that transformed the harsh land into a fertile paradise. After they left, new settlers from Galicia and Asturias came to settle in these still little visited hill communities.

Today, the zone is finally being developed for tourism and improvements in the road system have made villages like Trévelez now accessible. Trévelez claims to be the highest permanently inhabited community in Spain. It is a small *pueblo* famous for its hams since the days of the Catholic Kings. So fresh, so cool, so exceedingly dry is the mountain air up here that it results in hams that are noted for their exceptional sweetness, prized nationally as among the finest in the land. To produce them, the Trévelez hams are dry-salted for just a week, then they are hung up in airy, well-ventilated lofts to cure for 12–18 months. Gastronomes come from all parts of Spain to eat this great delicacy and to purchase whole hams at the source.

MESÓN JOAQUÍN
TRÉVELEZ
TEL: (958) 76 50 14

Come to this typical *mesón* at the entrance to the *pueblo* to dine under a ceiling of own-produced *jamones*, eating the simple, authentic foods of the Alpujarras: *sopa de ajo, habas con jamón, plato alpujareño* (mixed fry of *longaniza, morcilla, jamón serrano de Trévelez* and an egg), or *trucha con jamón*, accompanied by a *jarra* of delicious *rosado* wine from the Lower Alpujarras. Ask to view the family's traditional ham loft, 'Jamones Joaquín González', just across the road. The hams, *longaniza, chorizo* and *morcilla* are available for purchase.
Inexpensive

Condado de Huelva and its 'Discovery' Vineyards

> **In Brief:** The vineyards of Condado de Huelva lie between Seville and the Portuguese border, so the wine country can be dipped into when travelling from Spain to the Portuguese Algarve, or else by those who are in the province to explore the nature reserve of the Coto de Doñana. The Consejo Regulador runs a welcoming '*Casa del Vino*' tasting kiosk at the entrance to Bollullos Par del Condado, the zone's principal wine town. The Romería del Rocío celebration is a colourful annual pilgrimage to the shrine located near Almonte on the edge of the Coto de Doñana.

West of Seville towards Huelva and the Portuguese border, the land is cultivated with almond groves, olive trees, wheat fields, strawberries and vines. This is a rich, fertile *comarca*, its soil, particularly in the basin of the Tinto river, stained a deep and striking orange-red. The small whitewashed towns that stretch out towards the border – Niebla, Bollullos Par del Condado, Moguer, Palos de la Frontera and others – are classic Andalusian *pueblos*, sun-baked and sleepy.

Though few may yet have heard of it, this is the *denominación de origen* of Condado de Huelva, a notable wine region in terms of sheer quantity alone, if nothing else, with some 13,000 hectares of vines under cultivation. These vineyards have a lengthy pedigree, too, for the Greeks established much of the wine country, and wines from this corner of the peninsula were traded by the Romans. However, it was in the fifteenth century that they received their greatest boost, when they were taken on the first voyages of discovery to the New World. Christopher Columbus set out from the now silted river port of Palos de la Frontera with his three caravels on 3 August 1492, and it is more than probable that he and his men carried as cargo considerable amounts of the local wines. Certainly just ten years later there is clear documentary evidence that 25 *arrobas* of wine from Villalba del Alcor were purchased to be transported by ship on a voyage to the 'Indies'. This trade continued and expanded throughout the next two centuries, though by the eighteenth century it was already in decline as wines from elsewhere, notably nearby Jerez, gained in favour.

In fact, after the vineyard was replanted following the destruction of phylloxera at the turn of this century, most of the wines subsequently produced were sent in bulk to be blended with the wines of Jerez. Within the *comarca* itself, though, there was a steady and faithful market for Condado's old-style *vinos generosos*; heavy and oxidized, such wines were noted and appreciated foremost for the hefty alcoholic kick that they carried.

However, in recent years the local Consejo Regulador has recognized the need to modernize both the zone's winemaking installations and its types of wines. Thus, today, in addition to the classic *generosos*, a range of lighter *vinos jóvenes* are being produced which at best can be excellent local products of the *tierra* to accompany the seafood and shellfish of Huelva and its province.

Admittedly, few but the most fanatical wine tourists would come to this little-visited corner of the country just for the liquid refreshments on hand.

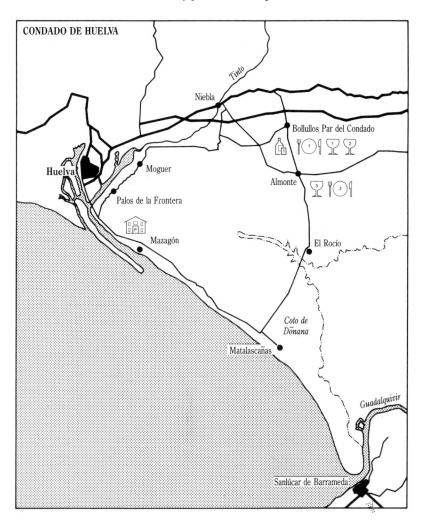

But for those coming into Spain from Portugal, or heading from Andalucía to the Algarve, it is certainly an area worth pausing in to quench your thirst.

Bollullos Par del Condado, the capital of the wine zone, located just off the main Seville–Huelva motorway, is a whitewashed one-street town that is awash with wine. '*In Vino Veritas*' a placard proudly proclaims at the town's entrance. Along the way there are literally scores of *bodegas*, all offering their wares, as well as simple *mesones*, *ventas* and *bodeguitas*, enticing you with offers: '*gambas, mariscos y vinos*'. The new-style *vinos blancos jóvenes* do go exceedingly well with such foods on the spot. Drunk cave cool in a *bodeguita*, accompanied by freshly boiled *gambas* or a plateful of *coquinas* from Matalascañas, they can be exceedingly quenching.

The *vinos generosos* may still be enjoyed locally, but for our money, if we choose to drink this style of wine, we would probably plump for a sherry or a Montilla any day of the week. None the less, Condado Pálido, the zone's *fino* equivalent, can be a pleasant enough accompaniment to a platter of *jamón de Jabugo*, the tasty dry-cured Iberian ham from Huelva's hilly hinterland. The *oloroso*-style wines are known as Condado Viejo and range from bone dry to very sweet.

The wine zone of Condado de Huelva is a rather sprawling one, but it is not without its charms. The Coto de Doñana can be reached by heading south from Bollullos Par del Condado through Almonte and El Rocío to Matalascañas. The Romería del Rocío is one of the great spring *fiestas* of Spain, a colourful annual pilgrimage at Pentecost when families, groups, fraternities, whole villages descend on this tiny and remote shrine by foot, ox cart, or horse to pay homage to the miracle of *Nuestra Señora del Rocío* (Our Lady of the Dew). Many of the pilgrims cross the Guadalquivir at Sanlúcar de Barrameda and make their way through the wild Coto de Doñana to reach El Rocío, a classic and joyous journey that takes some days.

The Parque Nacional de Doñana is one of Europe's great nature reserves, an immense protected roadless area located at the delta of the Guadalquivir and its inlying marshes that flood each winter, providing the conditions which attract millions of migratory birds from all over Europe (rare Imperial eagle, heron, pink flamingo, stork, spoonbill, griffon vulture, buzzard, black tern, purple gallinule, marsh harrier and many others), as well as numerous other rare species, including the elusive and endangered Iberian lynx, wild boar, mongoose, red deer, polecat, genet, badger and weasel. The Coto de Doñana extends over 300 square kilometres of marshlands; much of the area was (and still is) owned by aristocratic sherry families who treated it traditionally as their private hunting preserve. Today hunting is forbidden, and the park is so well monitored and controlled in order to preserve it that it can only be visited by special tours arranged through the visitors' centre. None the less, an excursion through this rare wild corner of Europe should be on the itinerary of every visitor to the region.

After spending some time in the Coto de Doñana, complete the circuit of Huelva by following the coast road from Matalscañas back towards Huelva itself. Palos de la Frontera today stands well above the silted estuary of the Tinto river, but it was from this tiny *pueblo* that not only Columbus, but scores of other discoverers and *conquistadores* sailed on their voyages to the New World. For this reason, it is known as the 'Cradle of the Discovery'.

Platero y yo, Moguer.

Today, though, Palos looks inland, not out to sea, and is best known for its luscious early-ripening strawberries.

Moguer is another lovely, quiet wine town, otherwise undistinguished save for the fact that it was immortalized in the Nobel Prize winning author Juan Ramón Jiménez's charming and poignant book, *Platero y Yo*. Juan Ramón was a native of Moguer, his father a wealthy landowner who had among other interests a wine *bodega*. Any children or adults who have delighted in those timeless tales of the author and his silver-grey donkey, Platero, and of life (and death) in rural Andalucía, will certainly wish to visit the Museum House of the poet.

Niebla today is just another small, depopulated *pueblo*, but it still has remains of its occupation by Romans and Moors. It was from here that the Condes de Niebla ruled in the twelfth–fifteenth centuries and gave the name Condado de Huelva to the *comarca*.

Visiting the Coto de Doñana

The Parque Nacional de Doñana, one of Europe's most important and best preserved nature reserves, can only be visited at present by organized guided tours in 4-wheel-drive Land Rovers or larger 4-wheel-drive buses. These tours last about 4 hours and take you well into the depths of this wild and still relatively untouched zone, and there are usually ample opportunities to view wildlife and birds at close hand. The jeep or bus rides are rugged to say the least, but the group tours may come as something of a disappointment for serious naturalists and ornithologists. None the less, since at present this is the only way to visit the park, they are still well worth joining. The tours run year round daily (twice daily in high season), and must be booked as far in advance as possible (however, if in the area, it is worth telephoning to see if there have been any cancellations). The administrative centre is located at El Acebuche, near Matalascañas, and there is an informative visitors' centre as well as bird-watching hides.

PARQUE NACIONAL DE DOÑANA
CENTRO ADMINISTRATIVO
EL ACEBUCHE
21760 MATALASCAÑAS
HUELVA
TEL: (955) 43 04 32

The Coto de Doñana, Huelva.

ANDALUCÍA

Bodegas: Stop to Taste; Stop to Buy

1 SOVICOSA
CALLE CASTILLA, S/N
21710 BOLLULLOS PAR DEL
  CONDADO
HUELVA
TEL: (955) 41 28 88, 41 20 87;
  FAX: (955) 41 10 34

WINES PRODUCED: Viña Odiel
blanco (dry), Viña Saltes *blanco*
(medium dry), Viña Saltes *rosado*.
VISITS: Daily, working hours for
direct sales.
This well-equipped *bodega* was
founded in 1984 by the Consejería
de Agricultura y Pesca of the
Government of Andalucía for the
production and promotion
especially of young new-style white
wines. Early picking and
fermentation in stainless steel vats
with temperature control ensure
that the wines are fresh and fruity.
Viña Odiel, produced from 100%
Zalema, is an excellent dry white
table wine, one of the best such
table wines produced in Andalucía.
It should always be drunk as young
as possible.
English, French, Italian spoken.

---

2 BODEGA COOPERATIVA VINÍCOLA
  DEL CONDADO
CALLE SAN JOSÉ 2
21710 BOLLULLOS PAR DEL
  CONDADO
HUELVA
TEL: (955) 41 02 61

WINES PRODUCED: Privilegio del
Condado *blanco*, Par del Condado
blanco; Mioro Condado Pálido;
Botaroble Condado Viejo.
VISITS: Daily, working hours.
Co-operative *bodega* producing
good fresh young table wines as well
as traditional *vinos generosos*.

---

3 COOPERATIVA SAN ISIDRO
  LABRADOR
CALLE MANUEL SIUROT 32
21730 ALMONTE
HUELVA
TEL: (955) 40 65 55

WINES PRODUCED: Los Tejares
blanco; Los Tejares *tinto*; Los
Tejares Condado Viejo *seco y dulce*.
VISITS: Mon–Fri 8–14h.
Fresh lemony Los Tejares *blanco*
and nutty Condado Viejo *seco*.

Restaurantes y Paradores

1 EL REÑIERO
CRUZ DE MONTEÑINA 6
21710 BOLLULLOS PAR DEL
   CONDADO
HUELVA
TEL: (955) 41 08 75

Closed Mon; Aug and Sept.
The best restaurant in town,
serving well-prepared foods of
Huelva: *mariscos, jamón de
Jabugo, rape a la marinera*. The
name signifies a cock-fighting ring,
reputedly still in use.
Inexpensive to Moderate

---

2 MESÓN EL TAMBORILERO
CALLE UNAMUNO 15
21730 ALMONTE
HUELVA
TEL: (955) 40 73 80

Closed Sun.
'*Esa es la carta*,' said the patron
taking us by the arm and drawing

us into the kitchen to see great
cauldrons of *menestra, pimientos
rellenos, lubino en salsa de
almendras, atun encebollado*, and
other seafood *guisos*. Located on a
small back street, but worth the
search.
Very Inexpensive

Parador

P PARADOR NACIONAL CRISTÓBAL
   COLÓN
CTRA MAZAGÓN–MOGUER
21130 MAZAGÓN
HUELVA
TEL: (955) 37 60 00; FAX: (955) 37 62 28

Isolated *parador* in front of the
great immense stretch of the sandy
Playa de Mazagón, this is
probably the best base from which
to explore the nearby Coto de
Doñana, 25 km further to the east.
Moderate

Tomar Unas Copas: Stop for a Drink; Stop for a Bite

Bollullos Par del Condado is literally lined with '*bodeguitas*' – small, vaulted
bodegas serving the town's tasty wines from the barrel to accompany a
range of seafood *tapas* and *mariscos*. The *Casa del Vino* is a friendly tasting
stand at the entrance to the town which serves to promote the wines of

ANDALUCÍA

Condado de Huelva. Wines can be sampled by the glass, and purchased at the same prices ex-*bodega*.

1 CASA DEL VINO
21710 BOLLULLOS PAR DEL
   CONDADO
HUELVA

Hours: Daily 11–15h; 18–20h.

Los Campings

CAMPING DOÑANA PLAYA
CTRA HUELVA–MATALASCAÑAS,
KM 28
21130 MAZAGÓN
HUELVA
TEL: (955) 37 62 81

Open all year.

———

CAMPING ROCÍO PLAYA
21760 MATALASCAÑAS
HUELVA
TEL: (955) 43 02 38

Open all year.

Compras Deliciosas: Stop to Taste; Stop to Buy

CHARCUTERÍA/CARNICERÍA DE LA
   COOPERATIVA SÁNCHEZ
   ROMERO-CARAVAJAL
CTRA DE SAN JUAN, S/N
21290 JABUGO
HUELVA
TEL: (955) 12 11 70

Jabugo, located in the Sierra Morena hills above Huelva, is widely regarded as the foremost zone for the production of air-cured *jamón serrano* from native Iberian pigs fed on a natural diet of acorns (*jamón de bellota*). Ham *aficionados* will certainly want to make the pilgrimage here to purchase these and other native Iberian pork products at the source.

¡Fiesta! Wine and Other Related Celebrations

Easter	Semana Santa	Seville, Arcos de la Frontera, Ronda, and many other towns.
April	Feria de Abril	Seville
last week of April	Cata de Vino	Córdoba
early May	Feria del Caballo	Jerez de la Frontera
mid-May	La Romería del Rocío	Almonte, near Huelva
last week of May	Feria de la Manzanilla	Sanlúcar de Barrameda
15 August	Noche del Vino	Competa, Málaga
end of Aug	Fiestas de la Recolección	Antequera, Málaga
early Sept	Fiestas de la Vendimia de Montilla-Moriles	Montilla
1st Sun in Sept	Feria de la Vendimia	Manilva, Málaga
2nd week of Sept	Gran Festival de Moscatel	Chipiona
2nd week of Sept	Feria de la Vendimia	Jerez de la Frontera
mid-Sept	Fiesta de la Vendimia	Bollullos Par del Condado
early Oct	Fuente del Vino	Cádiar, Granada
Sun before Christmas	Fiesta de las Migas y Vino del Terreno	Torrox, Málaga

ANDALUCÍA

Seville's *Feria de Abril*

Seville's *Feria de Abril* takes place each year in the last weeks of April, a gay and colourful spring pageant that sprawls over a vast fairground area beside the river known as the Prado de San Sebastián. For ten days and ten nights, all of Seville is caught up in the sheer exuberance and overflowing spontaneity and energy of this annual city-wide party. Canvas *casera* pavilions are constructed in the fairground area, and they are the scene of all-night drinking and, above all, frenetic all-night dancing, especially of the classic *sevillanas*. *Señoritas* dressed in their most colourful full-skirted polka dot flamenco dresses, with flowers in their hair, all become dark, sensuous beauties; and the men, riding on frisky white horses, or at the reins of polished horse-drawn carriages, epitomize the arrogance and pride of the Andalusian *caballero*. Naturally, it goes without saying that the *Feria de Abril* is a city-wide excuse to down endless quantities of *fino* sherry, accompanied by a range of tasty *tapas*.

Y para saber más Additional Information

Oficina de Informacion de Turismo
(Junta de Andalucía)
Avda de la Constitucion 21
41004 Seville
tel: (954) 22 14 04

The Sherry Institute of Spain
Institute for Foreign Trade
Spanish Embassy Commercial
Office
66 Chiltern Street
London W1M 1PR
tel: 071-486 0101; fax: 071-487 5586

Asociación de Criadores
Exportadores de Vinos de Jerez
(ACES)
Calle Eguiluz 2, 1°
11402 Jerez de la Frontera
Cádiz
tel: (956) 34 10 46;
fax: (956) 34 60 81

Consejo Regulador de Jerez
Avda Alvaro Domecq, s/n
Apdo Correos 324
11405 Jerez de la Frontera
Cádiz
tel: (956) 33 20 50;
fax: (956) 33 89 08

Consejo Regulador de Condado de
  Huelva
Calle Antonio Machado 8, 1⁰
21710 Bollullos Par del Condado
Huelva
tel: (955) 41 03 22

Consejo Regulador de
  Montilla-Moriles
Ronda de los Tejares 24
14001 Córdoba
tel: (957) 47 54 84;
fax: (957) 47 75 19

Consejo Regulador de Málaga
Edif. Advo Servicios Multiples
Avda de la Aurora 47, planta 6
29002 Málaga
tel: (952) 31 21 37

Consejo Regulador Brandy de Jerez
Calle Córdoba 3
11405 Jerez de la Frontera
Cádiz
tel: (956) 30 38 12;
fax: (956) 18 11 19

ANDALUCÍA

ARAGÓN

Alquézar, Somontano

Aragón, a landlocked region located strategically where the high Pyrenees descend to the broad, flat basin of the Ebro, has been historically a link between Catalunya to the east and Castile to the west and south. Today it is one of Spain's least populated regions, an area more usually passed through than stopped in.

This is a region of immense contrast. The dramatic Pyrenees in Alto Aragón reach upwards of 3500 metres, the highest points in that great mountain chain, snow-covered in summer as in winter. The broad valleys that carve down from the jagged peaks and form the Ordesa National Park provide some of the most beautiful and dramatic natural scenery in the Iberian peninsula. Yet below Huesca, by the time the Ebro valley is reached, the land, while fertile enough by the river itself, at times resembles nothing so much as a parched desert, tawny and barren, sun-scorched and hellish. Further south, in the province of Teruel, the mountains rise from the plains once again towards the rugged Sierra de Albarracín leading up to the high central *meseta* of Old Castile and the remote and still wild Maestrazgo, adjoining and extending into the region of Valencia.

Zaragoza, its name a corruption of that of the Roman city of Caesar Augusta, founded in 25 B.C., remains today as in the past the central focus of this otherwise depopulated rural region. A busy capital of just under a million inhabitants, it is the fifth largest city in Spain. Its position, linking the rich Basque and Catalan regions with Madrid, has brought prosperity: there is a sophistication to the city which comes as a contrast to the region's poor and abandoned rural areas. And if nationalist ambitions and resentment against the central powers in Madrid still run high in neighbouring Euskadi and Catalunya, one senses here a spirit of tolerance; as if Aragón, unfettered by animosity or centuries of injuries and resentments, untainted by the perceived arrogance of the *castellanos*, can stand as something of a bridge between the disparate nations which constitute modern Spain.

Indeed, it has probably always been so. The region was invaded by the Moors in 714, and Zaragoza was the seat of the short-lived Kingdom of Zaragoza under the Spanish-Muslim Beni-Casi dynasty. Even after its recapture by the Christians in 1118, Christian, Moor and Jew cohabited the city peacefully for many centuries. When the Kingdom of Aragón joined together with the maritime state of Catalunya, Zaragoza further prospered as a cosmopolitan capital while Catalan-Aragonese influence extended over Roussillon, the Balearic Islands, even over large parts of Italy. When Ferdinand II of Aragón married Isabel of Castile in 1469, and Isabel a decade later assumed the crown of Castile, these two great kingdoms were united, leading to the eventual unification of the Spanish nation.

Today it is difficult to imagine this remote and impoverished region playing such a central part in national and world affairs. Though Zaragoza is one of Spain's major cities, the rest of Aragón remains an introverted agricultural land, its role in national affairs today apparently peripheral. Certainly in its wine country, life on the whole appears timeless and little changed. The vine after all has been planted in Aragón for over two millennia and winegrowers continue to grow and harvest grapes as they have always done, not least because in many areas of this great arid region little else would grow.

In truth, the wines of Aragón have never enjoyed great fame or reputation and have long been noteworthy mainly in terms of sheer quantity, rather than quality. Within Spain, certainly, Aragón is viewed as the virtually unlimited source of cheap and heady *tintos del año* produced from the workhorse Garnacha grape, wines that are sold in supermarkets in litre or two-litre bottles, or, even more irreverently, from cardboard tetra-briks. Moreover, these stout, beefy red wines of Aragón, produced from grapes harvested late to increase their already high sugar levels, have long been valued for their immense power, alcohol, colour and tannin and have traditionally found ready markets as potent blending wines, sold *en granel* to producers in France, Germany and Switzerland as well as other parts of Spain.

This image has not yet been wholly dispelled today. The region is still undoubtedly dominated by its co-operative wineries. However, in recent years, even the giant co-ops themselves have begun to wake up to the fact that the future cannot lie in the continued supply of such unambitious wines. Changing attitudes have been apparent in improvements in the vineyards, modernized winemaking installations, and, most importantly, a commercial mentality which recognizes the need to produce wines that can be sold in bottle not bulk. But private initiative remains on the whole a preciously scarce commodity in zones such as Cariñena, Calatayud, or Campo de Borja.

Aragón's smallest delimited wine zone, Somontano, located in the cooler, higher foothills of the Pyrenees, is however emerging as something of an exception to the rest of the region. Indeed, huge investment, partly funded by the Government of Aragón, has already demonstrated the potential for this as yet little-known wine zone to produce superlative red and white wines which in the near future, we conjecture, will help to put the wines of Aragón on the quality map of Spain.

Orientation

Aragón, a land-locked region, is made up of three provinces: Zaragoza, Huesca and Teruel. Zaragoza, the region's capital, is Spain's fifth largest city, located in the Ebro valley on the historic crossroads linking Catalunya to the east with the Basque country to the west, and with Madrid to the south.

Zaragoza's airport is served by limited international flights, as well as by domestic flights. The region, however, is easily accessible by those arriving at international airports in Madrid, Barcelona, Bilbao, or Valencia. Zaragoza stands astride the main rail and road routes between the Basque country and Barcelona, while the main Barcelona–Madrid motorway skirts the capital. Aragón, together with Navarra, was a historic point of entry for the famous *Camino de Santiago* by way of the mountain pass of Puerto de Somport that descended from the Pyrenees down to Jaca. There are still numerous frontier crossing points between Aragón and France.

The wine country south of Zaragoza – especially Cariñena and Cala-tayud – can be combined with an exploration of the region's particularly rich *mudéjar* heritage. The small but up-and-coming wine zone of Somon-tano provides opportunity for exploration of the Aragonese Pyrenees. Campo de Borja is a virtual enclave tucked into the Navarra/Rioja borders.

Maps: Michelin No. 443 (Northern & Eastern & Balearics); Firestone Hispania C-3.

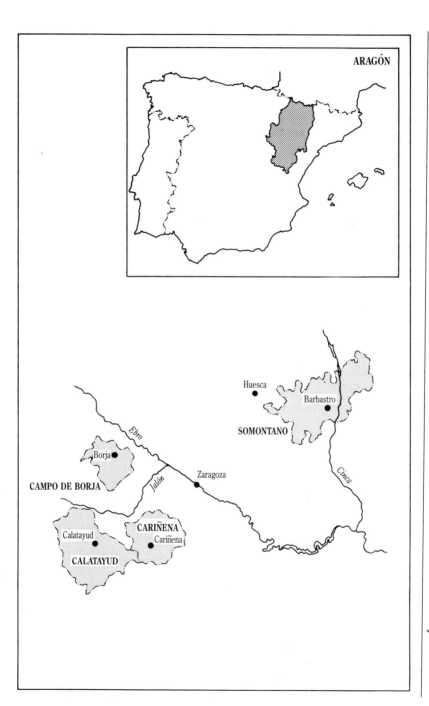

Mudéjar Architecture and Art

The term *mudéjar* is given to a style of architecture and art practised in Christian Spain by Moors who continued to live and work there after the Reconquest, utilizing Islamic-inspired forms and styles of decoration. Until the onset of the Inquisition, the Kingdom of Aragón enjoyed a reputation for its enlightened attitude to foreigners, and thus Moor and Jew were able to prosper alongside Christian and make significant contributions in the spheres of commerce, art and architecture. One of the greatest legacies of the Moors in Aragón is the particular and distinctive style of *mudéjar* architecture that they developed between the eleventh and sixteenth centuries. The style can be seen at its best in numerous churches with tall and graceful belltowers reminiscent of minarets, and with characteristic brickwork façades decorated with beautiful geometric patterns and whimsical strapwork. The contrast of such light and soaring edifices with the mainly heavy, down-to-earth stone Romanesque architecture in northern Aragón along the *Camino de Santiago* could not be greater. Examples of *mudéjar* architecture in Zaragoza include parts of the Seo Cathedral and the Castillo de la Aljafería, the Moorish fortress later taken over and expanded as a residence for the Kings of Aragón. The wine town of Calatayud is particularly rich in *mudéjar* work; especially noteworthy are the beautiful octagonal belltower of the Collegiate Church of Santa María and the Church of San Andrés.

LOS VINOS: THE WINES OF ARAGÓN

Calatayud DO   The most recently granted of Aragón's four DOs applies to some 17,800 hectares of vineyards spread over 29 municipalities in the westernmost part of the Zaragoza province, centred on the *mudéjar* town of Calatayud. This is a region that has long been noted for its powerful reds and *rosados* capable of reaching upwards of 16° alcohol, but recent trends, as elsewhere, are towards lighter, more approachable wines. White wines are produced mainly from Macabeo, Malvasia, Moscatel and Garnacha Blanca, and must reach a minimum alcohol level of 10.5°; *rosado* (minimum 11°) and *tinto* (minimum 12°) are produced from Garnacha, Tempranillo, Cariñena (Mazuelo) and Monastrell.

Campo de Borja DO   The demarcated wine region of Campo

de Borja is one of Spain's least known, extending over 10,000 hectares in the far west of Aragón in the Ebro valley bordering the vineyards of Rioja and Navarra. As elsewhere, the region is co-operative-led and has long been noted primarily as a producer of hefty blending wines to sell in bulk. However, some good value wines are today being produced in the zone: white from mainly Macabeo (minimum alcohol 10.5°), and *rosado* and red primarily from Garnacha (minimum 13°). Small amounts of fragrant Moscatel wines are made in Ainzón.

Cariñena DO   Aragón's best known *denominación* is long famed as the source of plentiful, inexpensive, but tasty *vinos corrientes*, produced primarily from Garnacha grapes grown on 21,000 hectares of vineyards located in 14 municipalities. Garnacha is still the predominant variety, but there are further plantations of Cariñena (Mazuelo), Tempranillo and Cabernet Sauvignon for the production of not only red wines (minimum alcohol 12°), but also good *rosados* (minimum 11°). White wines are produced mainly from Macabeo and must reach a minimum of 10.5°. There is also a local following for old-style *rancio*

(minimum 14°) and fortified *vino de licor* (minimum 17.5°). Cariñena, the grape which has taken its name from the municipality, is no longer widely planted here, though it is still an important variety in Catalunya, Rioja and parts of southern France (Carignan).

Somontano DO   Tiny but high-quality wine zone located in the province of Huesca comprising only 3300 hectares of vineyards, the majority of which are concentrated in nine municipalities. A great variety of grapes are cultivated, some on an experimental basis, for the production of white (minimum alcohol 10°), *rosado* (minimum 11°), and red (minimum 11.5°) wines. Grape varieties include white Alcañon, Macabeo, Chardonnay, Chenin Blanc, Riesling, Gewürztraminer; and black Moristel, Tempranillo, Garnacha, Cabernet Sauvignon, Pinot Noir, Merlot.

Cava DO   Classic sparkling wines produced by secondary fermentation in the bottle and entitled to the Cava *denominación* are made in Cariñena and Campo de Borja primarily from Macabeo, Parellada, Xarel-lo and some Chardonnay.

ARAGÓN

LA GASTRONOMÍA: FOODS OF ARAGÓN

Aragón is a hard land and its *cocina* reflects this. At once basic, simple and still in touch with its rural roots, it presents the products of its uplands and lowlands directly and with little fuss or pretension.

In the mountains of Huesca and Teruel, game is widely enjoyed, such as *jabalí* (wild boar), *liebre* (hare) and *venado* (venison), while the fast-flowing mountain rivers and streams provide ample fresh *truchas* (trout). Traditional *conservas caseras* – home-produced meat or game conserved in oil in earthenware crocks or glass jars – are still made in upland farms and serve as part of the regular diet throughout winter, even though modern refrigeration now makes such foods obsolete. And of course, the production of traditional pork *embutidos* remains an important local food industry – above all, fine *longaniza* from the province of Huesca and the exquisite and famous *jamón de Teruel.*

The arid central plains of Zaragoza provide scrubby grazing lands for herds of sheep and goat, and indeed, two classic dishes of Aragón are *ternasco asado* and *cabrito asado*, while *migas* is of course the classic breakfast of the *pastor*. The Ebro valley, which passes through the region, waters a fertile market garden and provides ample fresh produce of the highest quality: *pimientos* for the classic *chilindrón*, *borraja* (an edible thistle that is much loved in the region), luscious *melocotones* (peaches), *ciruelas* (plums) and *manzanas* (apples).

While no one would claim that Aragón is a region of great gastronomic delights, its foods, like its wines, are above all forthright, honest and robust.

¡Que aproveche! Regional Specialities of Aragón

Jamón de Teruel　One of Spain's outstanding air-cured *jamones serranos*, produced in the mountains of the province of Teruel and entitled to its own *denominación de origen*.

Borraja　Type of edible thistle with a refreshing bitter flavour, somewhat similar to the cardoon and cultivated and widely enjoyed throughout the region.

Judías blancas　White beans, a ubiquitous Aragonese accompaniment.

Magras con tomate　Cubes or slices of slightly fried pork or ham served with slices of fried bread in a tomato sauce.

Bacalao zaragozano　Dried salt cod, stewed with onion, potato, garlic and tomato.

Chilindrón Method of cooking meat such as chicken, lamb or pork, in a sauce made with dried red pepper, tomatoes, *jamón*, and fried onions. Most frequent manifestation in Aragón is *pollo a la chilindrón*.

Ternasco asado Young roast lamb, sometimes cooked on the spit. A *ternasco* usually indicates a baby lamb of only eight or nine kilograms.

Espárragos montañeses 'Mountain asparagus' – stewed sheep's tail – speciality from province of Huesca.

Melocotón en vino Peach stewed in wine.

Migas

No dish in the entire Spanish national repertoire is simpler or more loved than this humble shepherd's favourite. Devised as a means of using up hard chunks of stale bread – soaked in water, crumbled or cut into cubes, and fried in abundant oil or lard together with garlic, *chorizo* or *longaniza*, perhaps some chopped tomatoes and *pimentón* (the variations are countless) – it is one of those simple peasant dishes which has transcended social and regional boundaries and is today enjoyed wholeheartedly by all. In the wine zones of Cariñena, Calatayud and Campo de Borja, *migas* are usually served in autumn garnished with Garnacha grapes and sometimes even chocolate.

THE WINE ROADS OF ARAGÓN

In Brief: Aragón's four separate DO wine zones are located across a broad area of the region, and only the most dedicated wine traveller will wish to visit all of them.

Somontano is the smallest and arguably the most interesting: located in the foothills of the Pyrenees, it can be combined with excursions into the mountains, or else dipped into as a detour en route to the Catalan wine region of Costers del Segre.

Cariñena is located 46 km south of Zaragoza on the main road to Teruel and Valencia. Although not a particularly pleasant town in its own right, it is the centre of a large and important wine zone, and it may be worth while stopping here to stock up on its well-known and inexpensive *caldos*.

ARAGÓN

Calatayud, Aragón's most recent *denominación*, is centred on the eponymous town located 86 km south-west of Zaragoza on the main road to Madrid; it certainly is a destination in its own right, not simply for its wines but for its remarkable *mudéjar* architecture. The Parque Natural del Monasterio de Piedra is located nearby, a rare oasis of lush vegetation, fast-flowing streams and waterfalls in the midst of this otherwise parched and arid land.

Campo de Borja lies just across the border from Rioja and Navarra, and its wine country in a sense is another (very different) manifestation of the great Ebro valley vineyard. Borja and Ainzón, its two most important municipalities, are located just off the main Bilbao–Zaragoza highway.

Somontano

Somontano is a small but fertile *comarca* that lies at the base of the Pyrenean foothills, centred on the historic Roman town of Barbastro. It is Aragón's smallest delimited quality wine zone, but the one with possibly the greatest potential. Little visited in its own right, it is a region of great charm and a marked contrast to the arid, flatter wine zones of the region which lie to the south. Somontano, moreover, can serve as a jumping-off point for excursions into the dramatic mountain country.

Indeed, the name signifies 'under the mountain' and the proximity of the Pyrenees is always apparent. On a clear day, their jagged, snow-covered peaks seem remarkably close. The myriad rivers that tumble down from the high slopes have over millions of years scoured the gravel riverbeds and carved dramatic gorges and canyons such as those of the remote Sierra de Guara, a natural wonderland of carved sandstone cliffs, rock formations and cascades.

One such river that descends from the Guara is the Vero, which emerges from a grandiose gorge at the old Moorish citadel of Alquézar, today a picturesque and characteristic Somontano mountain *pueblo*, sited dizzily on the edge of the precipice, its splendid fortified Basilica de Santa María built on the remains of the Arab *alcázar* which gives the town its name. From Alquézar, the river waters a surprisingly lush and fertile valley as it descends to Barbastro, the focal community for this small mountain zone.

Barbastro today is a pleasant and bustling market town, with some fine old mansions, a tree-lined *paseo* with outdoor tables, and a notable Gothic cathedral. Centre of this small wine zone, it is also renowned for its antique shops which boast rustic stone fireplaces, old furniture, windows and doors,

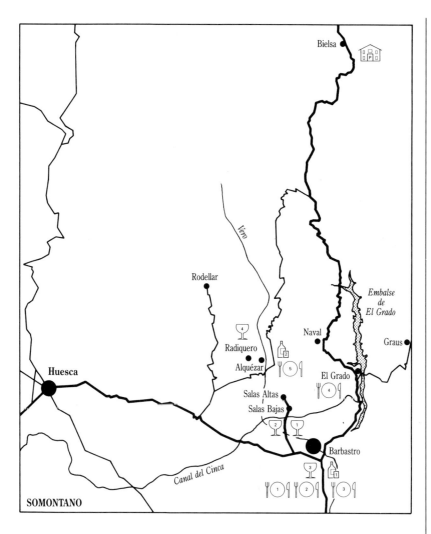

salvaged in many cases from the homes and *pueblos* which have been abandoned as younger generations continue the unending exodus from country
to city.

It was in this small historic town that the union of Aragón and Catalunya
was declared in 1137, sealed by the marriage of Princess Petronella, daughter of King Ramiro of Aragón, to Ramón Berenguer IV, Count of Barcelona.
It is probable that the marriage ceremonies were enlivened by liberal consumption of the local wines, for the vineyards of the *comarca* have been
planted since at least the time of the Reconquest. Since then, wine and

ARAGÓN

olives have been the main products of Somontano, commodities which, even up to the end of the last century, were traditionally used for barter.

However, like the other wines of Aragón, those of Somontano were generally not valued as precious in their own right but were produced and sold primarily *en granel* for blending, mainly across the border to France, a mere 60 km to the north. Indeed, the French connection is a logical and long-established one. In 1894, the Lalanne family, *viticulteurs* in Bordeaux, abandoned their native vineyards after the devastation of phylloxera and, after much searching, decided to settle near Barbastro and planted vineyards with Cabernet Sauvignon, Merlot and Moristel. The wines subsequently produced on the Finca San Marcos and sold under the Laura Lalanne label enjoyed considerable success and fame earlier this century and won medals in Bordeaux and Brussels as long ago as 1908. However, as happened throughout Spain, the isolation that set in after the Civil War put an end to the export market, and until even a decade or so ago, the wines of Somontano were mainly known and enjoyed only within their zone of production.

That, however, is set to change in future years. Significant investment and a rigorous campaign of experimental plantations of a wide variety of grapes have already borne fruit, and it is safe to predict that Somontano will soon be recognized internationally as one of Spain's most exciting quality wine zones.

In truth, it will probably never be a household name, simply because the vineyard zone is so tiny, at present a mere 3300 hectares of which only about 1700 are currently under vine, planted at between 300 and 600 metres above sea level primarily from the banks of the Cinca river below Barbastro up the slopes of the Sierra de Salinas. The greatest concentration of vineyards is between Barbastro and Salas Altas.

Most of the production remains at present in the hands of the Bodega Cooperativa Comarcal del Somontano de Sobrarbe, which has upwards of 250 grape-growing *socios* and controls over 800 hectares of vineyards. Located just outside Barbastro on the road to Naval, this, however, is no sleepy Aragonese co-operative such as some of those lumbering giants still dozing in the hot sun below Zaragoza. After Bodegas Lalanne, the Cooperativa del Somontano was the second company in the zone to begin to market its wines in bottle. It has recently modernized its installations and it continues to produce a range of well-made wines, primarily from the two local autochthonous grape varieties: Alcañon for whites and Moristel for reds.

Alcañon is no world beater; lacking aroma and potential alcohol, some say that it is a better grape for eating than for making wine. However, it can be zesty, refreshing and somewhat distinctive. The co-operative also produces white wines from Macabeo, one version of which is aged in wood to considerable effect. Its Montesierra *tinto* is typical of the reds of the zone, produced from a blend of Tempranillo and Moristel, with good, deep berryish fruit and an almost bitter, stalky finish. The top of the range wine, Señorío de Lazán, another Tempranillo/Moristel blend, is altogether more polished, having spent some time in new or nearly new American oak.

The Compañia Vitivinicola Aragonesa (CoViSa) is located near the co-operative, just opposite Bodegas Lalanne. CoViSa, more than any other *bodega*, has brought the wines of Somontano to the world's attention, not so much for what has yet been produced, but for the promise that has already been demonstrated. The autonomous Government of Aragón, anxious to give a higher profile to the wines of the region, identified Somontano as the zone with the greatest potential for quality and, working with other financial backers, put together a considerable investment package for the creation of this young and exciting company.

In 1986, CoViSa embarked on an ambitious programme of acquisition and the plantation of more than 600 hectares of new vineyards in the Somontano wine zone. Not content to produce wines only from the zone's traditional grape varieties, the company undertook massive experiments with both native and foreign grape varieties: white grapes planted by CoViSa include Macabeo, Chenin Blanc, Chardonnay, Gewürztraminer and Riesling; black grape varieties are Tempranillo, Cabernet Sauvignon, Pinot Noir and Moristel.

A small experimental *bodega* was established at Salas Bajas in the heart of the wine country, and scores of trials and mini-vinifications were carried out utilizing a variety of innovative techniques: skin contact at chilled temperatures to extract greater varietal character for the whites; experiments with barrel-fermentation; whole-grape fermentation (semi-carbonic maceration) for young reds; myriad trials with different types of wood for the *crianza* of both reds and whites. In the vineyard, different systems of trellising were tried; mechanical night harvesting was introduced; even sacred cows such as the ban on irrigation (technically illegal in Europe, though allowed by special dispensation for 'experimental' vineyards) were disregarded if necessary in the quest for quality.

Encouraged by the results, CoViSa has now begun the construction of an ultra-modern winery that is wholly 'new world' in outlook, and which, on

ARAGÓN

its completion in 1994, should be well equipped to take full advantage of
the astounding variety of high-quality grapes grown in this unique sub-
mountain zone. At present, there are already some 11 different wines in
production, ranging from the traditional Duque de Azara, a Tempranillo/
Moristel blend aged in American oak, to varietal wines made from Riesling,
Gewürztraminer, Chardonnay, Chenin Blanc, Cabernet Sauvignon and
Pinot Noir.

The vines are still very young and not all the wines are yet ready to take
on the rest of the world. But preliminary results are more than merely
encouraging. While the wines we sampled may still be somewhat green and
not yet complex, they already demonstrate a pedigree that is potentially
classic, with restrained, not overly obvious varietal character and a racy
balance of fruity acidity and aroma that comes from grapes grown in this
cooler, high altitude vineyard.

CoViSa is significant in a much broader sense too. For this young and
energetic company provides much needed evidence of a dynamism that is
certainly not usually considered in relation to Aragón and its wines. Indeed,
this is encouraging not simply for the future profile of Somontano and its
wines, but for the wines of Aragón and Spain as a whole.

CoViSa purchased much of the historic Finca San Marcos from the Lalanne family, who still remain just across the road in their historic farmhouse and *bodega*. This once pioneering company may no longer be the force
it once was historically, but it still retains about 20 hectares of vineyards
mainly around the *finca*, and continues to produce a range of highly
respected wines.

For the visitor to Somontano, excursions can be made from here up the
Vero valley to Alquézar, into the Sierra de Guara at Rodellar, or up the
river valley to Ainsa, from where trips can be made into the Ordesa
National Park.

One other winery should be singled out on our brief tour: Bodegas
Monclus, located at Radiquero near Alquézar. This is a tiny operation, in
complete contrast to CoViSa's ambitious size, run almost single-handedly
by the enthusiastic Mercedes Monclus, who in 1980 returned to her rural
home from Zaragoza to take over the family farm and begin the production
of quality wines from 12 hectares of vineyards.

Mercedes Monclus is as determined as she is charming and hospitable;
not content simply to dabble with the grapes already on the farm, she set
to her task with considerable zeal and replanted her entire vineyard in
order to be able to work part of it mechanically (the old vineyard had to

be worked by mules). She has also built a tiny but technically-advanced mini-*bodega* the size of a large garage on the road below Radiquero.

The wines of Bodegas Monclus are impressive. The white, produced from Macabeo with small quantities of grapes from her experimental plantations of Chardonnay, Chenin Blanc and Riesling, is aromatic with a finely balanced fruity acidity, while the *tinto del año*, produced by classic carbonic maceration in sealed tanks, is thick and bursting with fruit. Her finest wine, though, is a serious *vino de crianza* called Viña Vallarma, a wine which demonstrates the high quality and potential of the Somontano zone.

Cariñena

The road south from Zaragoza to Teruel and eventually to Valencia leads immediately from the regional capital into a harsh and remote landscape of bare ugly hills and scrubby chaparral, apparently suited for little other than the grazing of sheep and goats, or perhaps the occasional field of cereal. However, before too long, odd patches of vines begin to punctuate the deep red, iron-rich soil, becoming increasingly dominant by the time the wine town of Cariñena is reached some 46 km on. Indeed, here vines extend across the plains as far as the eye can see, and up and on to the flanks of the Sierra de Algairén beyond.

This is hot, arid Aragón, where the robust Garnacha grape reigns supreme over a harsh, hot-house terrain in which other more highly touted but temperamental and delicate grapes would simply wilt. In July and August the heat is hellish, compounded by the prevailing *cierzo* wind which takes almost all moisture out of the air. There is very little rainfall. Perhaps not surprisingly in this co-operative-led region, Cariñena is most noted for its massive, powerful wines that are still sold mainly in bulk either to be used as blending wines, or to be drunk anonymously in the bars of Barcelona, Bilbao or Madrid.

Cariñena itself is a miserable, crumbling town with apparently little to offer save vast quantities of wine. On a drizzly October morning when we were last there, the atmosphere was grim, even somewhat threatening. The previous night's rain had delayed the harvest, and the hundreds of itinerant workers, many of them *gitanos* from the south, were impatient to begin the day's work since they are paid by the amount harvested. If there is no work, then there is no money. The crowds of swarthy men milled around by the small central square, smoking, fooling around, fighting, as they waited for the tractors that would take them to the fields for another day's back-

breaking labour. It could almost have been a scene from the last century.

Tourism is virtually non-existent in Cariñena. Spaniards en route from Zaragoza or Bilbao to the Levante might choose to pause for lunch and to purchase wine in bulk, usually by the 16-litre *garrafa*, to be bottled at home. The main road leading into and out of town is literally lined with *bodegas*, great grey factories in functional, warehouse-like premises, their antiquated concrete fermentation vats or vast outdoor deposits more reminiscent of refineries or factories. This is winemaking and wine at its least romantic, wholly devoid of illusions of happy rural bliss and the bucolic pleasures of Bacchus.

Yet it is too easy simply to dismiss Cariñena and its wines. Admittedly, few of them are world beaters, or ready to take their place in Spain's vinous hall of fame. Yet, over the last few decades, Cariñena has quietly and unsensationally demonstrated its ability to produce well-made wines of every type, wines which – *peseta* for *peseta* – can represent quite exceptional value for money. These are wines that are sold in both litre and standard bottles in virtually every supermarket in Spain. When well-made, the wines are more than merely acceptable; and they are still ridiculously cheap. Internationally, too, Cariñena has provided the market with *crianza* wines aged in oak that can give surprisingly generous pleasure. As the best wines of Spain continue to escalate in price to match their higher international profiles, the time will come when more consumers outside Spain will perforce turn to such unflashy, low-profile, workhorse regions as Cariñena for their daily fix of ripe, juicy oak-aged wines.

Of course, Cariñena remains a region dominated by its immense co-operatives, and this has been cited as one reason why its profile remains so unexceptional and unexciting. For co-operatives on the whole, not just in Aragón but throughout Spain, have been singularly lacking in commercial vision, most remaining satisfied with producing wines only to sell *en granel*. Yet, one co-operative in Cariñena, the Cooperativa de San Valero, has defied this trend and indeed has led the way in demonstrating what can be done in the zone. Indeed, San Valero, founded in 1944 and with more than 1000 grape-growing *socios*, began to bottle and market its wines as early as the 1960s, one of the first co-operatives in Spain to do so. Today, almost all of the production is sold in bottle, not bulk. As such, it serves as something of a model for co-operatives not only in Aragón but throughout the country.

The sheer scale of winemaking at such a co-operative is simply staggering. In a normal harvest, San Valero handles some 18–20 million kg of grapes; on an average day of the *vendimia*, about 1.5–2 million kg of grapes are pressed. Of course, winemaking on this scale is not without considerable problems. First and foremost, the greatest challenge is to control the quality of such vast quantities of grapes. This is achieved in part by giving technical support to the *socios* throughout the growing season. In those parts of the vineyard identified as more suited to grapes such as Tempranillo and Cabernet Sauvignon, the co-operative has given incentives to plant these varieties.

At the time of the harvest, the co-operative's technicians make frequent checks on different parts of the vineyard to ascertain the optimum moment for harvesting in each zone or sub-zone. When they decide on the right moment, they rule that growers from each particular zone must harvest their grapes on a certain specified day or days. Should the growers bring in their grapes earlier or later, or should their grapes not be of the required quality, then they are penalized in the price paid for their crop.

Of course, San Valero has modern installations such as pneumatic presses and temperature controlled fermentation tanks, essential for the production of lighter and finer styles of wines. Admittedly, much of San Valero's production remains fairly unexciting, wines sold in litre bottles or tetra-briks mainly for the home market. Yet even its basic standard bottle range of white, *rosado* and red *vinos jóvenes*, marketed under the Don Mendo brand, demonstrates technical and marketing expertise, for these are well-made, easy-drinking beverage wines with some regional character.

The wines that the co-operative is most proud of in an international context, though, are its *vinos de crianza*, red wines produced primarily from Garnacha, with some Tempranillo, Cabernet Sauvignon and Cariñena, and aged in new or nearly new American oak *barricas* of 225 litres. Monte Ducay Crianza, in its distinctive black smoked glass bottle, spends only 6 months in wood but emerges with a very attractive light, soft, fruity vanilla character. Marqués de Tosos Reserva and Monte Ducay Gran Reserva are also both wines of considerable stature, even elegance.

While the Cooperativa de San Valero accounts for nearly a quarter of the production in the entire DO zone, there are literally scores of other *bodegas* in Cariñena itself as well as throughout the delimited wine zone. As such, they are also certainly worth seeking, if only because San Valero's wines are

ARAGÓN

widely available both nationally and internationally, while the individual private *bodegas* provide opportunities to taste wines made on a much smaller scale which may rarely be encountered outside the zone. Such wines, made by artisan methods with no concession to international taste – *rosados* aged for upwards of a decade in wood, and blockbuster, old-style,

Co-operatives

Aragón may be one of their great bastions, but wine co-operatives are found throughout Spain and remain at the heart of agricultural life today. Though they have been much derided, it is important to realize the key social and economic functions that co-operatives have played since their inception in the early 1940s.

In Aragón, as elsewhere, there is little tradition of estate winemaking on a small scale. Thus, earlier this century, the small grape-growers would usually seek to sell their grapes to wine merchants who would then ferment, age and market wines under their own brand names. However, under this system, the small growers were continually at the mercy of the merchants who could band together and collectively keep the price of grapes artificially low. The individual grower had little option but to accept whatever price was offered, and so existed at a level barely above subsistence.

The establishment of co-operative wine cellars undoubtedly improved the growers' lot, for co-operatives guaranteed to pay their grape-growing members a fair price for their crop based on the sale of the wines collectively made. There was a steady demand for the wines of Aragón, valued for their immense colour, alcohol and tannin by markets such as Rioja and France where they were used for blending. There was no need to produce quality wines; nor did the individual grower have any incentive to produce anything but the largest quantity of grapes at the highest, ripest potential alcohol levels.

Unfortunately, this is still the attitude in many co-operatives today. Yet the wine world has moved on, and Europe is now awash in its own wine lake. The best co-operatives, therefore, have realized that they must modernize their facilities and winemaking installations; they must encourage their growers to improve their grapes and pick at the optimum moment; and they must develop a more hard-headed commercial mentality. Change, though, comes slowly in such dinosaur institutions, many of which remain reluctant to break with the past.

inky reds – may not be our idea of what we wish to drink every day, but they are curiosities certainly well worth sampling on the spot.

Therefore, explore the town of Cariñena and its *bodegas*, then strike out into the thicket of wine country in virtually any direction: north-west to Almonacid de la Sierra, where the highly-regarded Bodegas Lopez Pelayo is located; west to Aguarón and the road that leads over the Sierra de Algairén to Calatayud; east to the wine *pueblo* of Tosos; or south along the main road to Teruel and Valencia, which crosses the mountains at the Puerto de Paniza: here the El Balcón shop and restaurant provides probably the best opportunity to purchase wines from a variety of small producers, together with the excellent products of Aragón such as *jamón de Teruel*, *longaniza*, local cheeses and conserved fruits.

Calatayud

Calatayud is an ancient town, located 86 km south-west of Zaragoza in the folds of the *sierras* leading up to the central *meseta* of Old Castile. There was a Celtic-Iberian settlement here in the fourth century B.C., and the Romans later established the town of Bilbilis Augusta on the imperial Zaragoza–Mérida road. The Latin poet Martial was born here in 40 A.D. Though the great master of the epigram spent much of his life in Rome under imperial and senatorial patronage, he never forgot his roots and eventually returned to Bilbilis where he ended his days, enjoying, no doubt, the native wines about which he wrote so lovingly.

When the Moors overran the Iberian peninsula in the eighth century, the site became an important strategic point, and a stout castle was built here that became known as the Qalat Ayub (castle of Ayub), from which is derived the name the town still enjoys today. The remains of Roman Bilbilis and the ruined Castillo de Ayub are located above present-day Calatayud, but it is below, within its medieval walls built under and into the cliff face itself that the town is at its most interesting and atmospheric. For Calatayud is one of the great *mudéjar* towns of Aragón.

The town, it has to be said, may have seen better days, yet it is still hugely impressive simply to wander through the narrow streets of the *casco antiguo*, admiring such notable monuments as the Colegiata de Santa María, with its lovely, geometrically-decorated octagonal belltower; the Church of San Pedro de los Francos, with its remarkable leaning tower; and the Church of San Andrés, the town's oldest, probably built over the remains of a Moorish mosque.

The Plaza de España is the centre of the old town, a rather charming if crumbling eighteeth-century square, surrounded by covered arcades, antiquated shops and shuttered houses with iron balconies and balustrades. Sit down on a bench here beside the old men in berets, and simply enjoy glimpses down the alleys and streets of Calatayud. The tall minaret-like belltowers of the many churches poke out over the rooftops; with their soaring lines and elegantly precise strapwork decoration, they come as something of a contrast to the simple adobe townhouses which line the narrow streets.

My three-year-old son and I had haircuts in a *peluquería* here in the town square, one of those old-fashioned male barber shops that have virtually disappeared from the rest of Europe since the advent of trendy stylists and unisex hair salons. As I sat on the old cracked leather chair, cape tightly wrapped and pinned around my neck, the old barber snipped away in that unhurried and leisurely fashion that seems altogether from another age, and we discussed the wines of Calatayud.

Calatayud, one of the great *mudéjar* towns of Aragón.

'In the past, we judged the quality of our wines by their alcoholic grade. Our *caldos*,' he added proudly, lowering his scissors to emphasize the point as he looked at me in the cracked mirror, 'our *caldos* could quite easily reach 16° alcohol, sometimes even higher. But since the advent of the *denominación*,' he continued with a disappointed shake of his head, 'the wines are much lighter and weaker, now no more than just 13 or 14°.' (I could only grunt in agreement at such a travesty, not wishing to spoil the male camaraderie that such places naturally engender.)

While locals such as my barber friend may still value the old-fashioned,

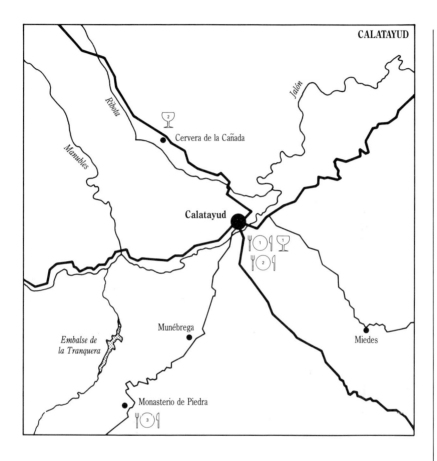

enormous, strapping wines of old, the world at large, it must be added, has long been less than enamoured with wines of this type. It is no wonder, then, that the wines of Calatayud in past decades were primarily sold in bulk as blending wines. Even in nearby Zaragoza, they remained wholly anonymous, rarely if ever seen in bottle. None the less, we understand that locally at least Munebrega was traditionally famous for its *tintos*, Cervera de la Cañada for its whites, and Miedes for its *rosados*.

Not just changing attitudes towards wine but also new technological advances, particularly the advent of temperature controlled fermentation in stainless steel, have persuaded *bodegas* in zones like Calatayud, and scores of others, to rethink their priorities and indeed to realize a potential previously never even dreamed of. The granting of the DO only as recently as 1990 is a recognition of the strides that have already been made. Make no mistake, Calatayud will probably never be a great wine region. But with

ARAGÓN

care in the vineyard and in the *bodega*, it does have the capacity to turn out well-made wines of interest and character. The vineyard, located at between 500 and 800 metres above sea level, is considerably higher than, say, Cariñena, and grapes such as Tempranillo, Mazuelo, even Cabernet Sauvignon stand a better chance here, alongside the ever-present workhorse Garnacha.

The Cooperativa del Campo San Gregorio has already demonstrated its ability to produce well-made and fresh new styles of wine and it is hoped that other co-operatives may follow its lead. Furthermore, Langa Hermanos, a private winery located just north of Calatayud on the Zaragoza road, has invested in modern winemaking installations and is turning out an impressive range of wines: young white, *rosado* and red *vinos jóvenes* under the Portalet brand; varietals from Cabernet Sauvignon, together with new plantations of Chardonnay and Chenin Blanc; traditional, thick *vinos de crianza*; even a classic sparkling Cava.

Notwithstanding the fact that we appreciate that Calatayud has made its wines more socially acceptable by lowering their alcohol content, the finest wine I tasted was Langa's Castillo de Ayud Reserva 1982. This is a dense, inky, thick *caldo* that weighs in at all of 14° (considered light here) and which is packed with dense Aragonese character – thick, liquoricy, raisiny, powerful. This is a massive wine that goes so well with the simple, strong and forthright foods of a bare and forthright land: *migas*, *chilindrón* and *ternasco asado*.

Campo de Borja

Campo de Borja, located in the far west of Aragón along the southern flank of the Ebro valley, is a wine region that few, in or out of Spain, have ever even heard of. Though the zone was granted its *denominación de origen* as long ago as 1978, Campo de Borja to a large extent remains today a *comarca* dominated by its co-operative wineries, still content to produce large quantities of anonymous wines mainly destined for the blending tanks.

Yet Campo de Borja certainly has potential as a wine region in its own right. One need only look at the map to notice that this relatively small zone of some 10,000 hectares extending over fifteen municipalities is a virtual peninsula abutting the regional frontiers with Rioja and Navarra (it is only 25 km to Alfaro in the Rioja Baja and 13 km to the prestigious Navarra wine town of Cintruénigo). The vineyards of Campo de Borja, mainly planted at between 300 and 600 metres above sea level,

Above: Arcos de la Frontera

Right: Sol y sombra: Plaza de Toros, Jerez de la Frontera

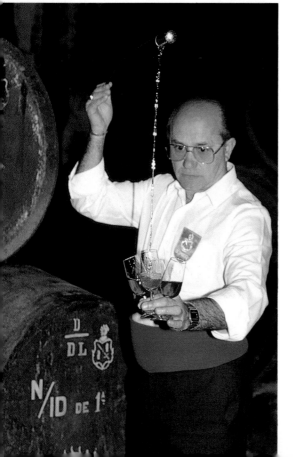

Above: Bodegas of Gonzàlez Byass, in the shadow of the cathedral in Jerez de la Frontera

Left: Venciador in Bodegas Domecq

Below: Tinajas

Right: Windmills, Campo de Criptana, La Mancha

Below: Landscape in the Montilla-Moriles vineyard

Left: Monasterio de Piedra, Aragón

Below: Valdepeñas vinescape

Above: Bombas of traditional *vino rancio*, ageing outdoors in Rueda

Right: Main square, Calatayud, Aragón

Left: Tordesillas, Castilla y León

Right: Lechazo asado, the great Castilian favourite, prepared in a wood-fired baker's oven

Below: Stainless steel and new American oak barrels in ultramodern winery of Raimat, near Lérida

Left: Courtyard of the De Muller winery, Tarragona, Catalunya

Below: Cavas Freixenet, San Sadurní de Noya, Catalunya

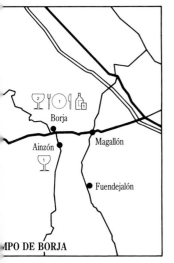

receive the humid influences from the river and the grapes ripen well: too well in most years, unless the harvest is monitored meticulously. The co-operatives control 95% of production; it is estimated that not even 10% of the zone's annual production is bottled.

In a sense, at least, Campo de Borja does not suffer from the problem of a negative image; it could be said that this little-heard-of zone has no image at all, to speak of. Perhaps this may be a positive factor in the future. For in truth, this is a minor Ebro valley wine zone of not inconsiderable charm; it is only just off a main highway; and some of its wines certainly deserve further attention.

While the zone is almost wholly dominated by its co-operatives, a long-standing private family firm is one of its leading flagbearers. Indeed, Bodegas Bordejé, founded in 1770, has demonstrated how, with private initiative, the wines of the zone can rise above the general level of co-operative mediocrity. Don Miguel Angel Bordejé, today a sprightly septuagenarian, is a man of energy and vision, and with a great passion for wine. As long ago as 1962 he decided to break with the long-standing family tradition of selling wines *en granel* and began to produce table wines in bottle. Trips to France, in particular to Beaujolais, led him to study and consider such techniques as carbonic maceration, still used today for all the company's red wines, even those destined for lengthy *crianza* in wood. Carbonic maceration, Bordejé discovered, not only resulted in fruitier wines, it also protected the delicate musts from oxidation (a great problem in hot wine zones), and contributed greater glycerine and thus roundness to his wines.

In 1970, Don Miguel Angel decided that he wanted to make an Aragonese sparkling wine, and so he turned his attentions towards the development of a high-quality Cava produced by the classic method of secondary fermentation in the bottle. Since 1974, Bodegas Bordejé has been making just such a wine, a fine sparkler made from Macabeo that is greatly appreciated locally, particularly in Zaragoza. Today the family owns some 100 hectares of its own vineyards, and uses only its own grapes for the production of its broad range of wines.

'Here in Campo de Borja, and in any other hot arid zone,' explained

Fernando Bordejé, Don Miguel Angel's son, who is now in charge of the day-to-day running of the *bodega*, 'the key to winemaking is to harvest at the optimum moment, that is, the precise moment when potential alcohol and acid are in balance. Many of the co-operatives still pay their *socios* to bring in grapes with the highest sugar levels, thus encouraging them to harvest late to produce wines for blending. Because we use only our own grapes, we can control these factors ourselves.'

The old Bordejé family cellars are located in Ainzón, a small wine town near Borja literally riddled with underground caves. The hand-dug cellars are hugely atmospheric, the installations workmanlike if not particularly up-to-date. But close family attention, hand care and control of every minute phase of the winemaking process more than make up for lack of the latest technologies.

For example, Bordejé insists that the grapes are harvested in small plastic tubs holding only 11 kg of grapes each in order that they arrive at the press house in optimum condition, and with the least possibility of bruising and premature oxidation. After fermentation in small stainless steel vats by carbonic maceration, the red wines pass to ancient, traditional Aragonese barrels holding some 3600 litres. Venerable though these receptacles undoubtedly are (they are over 100 years old and look like museum pieces), their large size protects the wine from oxidation, especially important when handling wines made from Garnacha, a grape notoriously prone to turning brown.

Remarkably, for a wine zone not known at all for its *vinos de crianza*, Bodegas Bordejé has an impressive underground store where over 100,000 bottles of Reserva and Gran Reserva wines lie in perfect storage conditions. These old aged wines are remarkably good, especially considering that the family seems to break all the established rules of oenology. For a start, Garnacha wines are not supposed to age well, while wines made by carbonic maceration are generally considered most apt for immediate consumption only. Ageing in large vats of old wood is said to result in tired wines lacking in fruit. Yet the proof is in the wines: we tasted, for example, Bordejé's 1979 Reserva that was still outstanding, with a well focused concentration of fruit and complex bottle nuances, slightly liquoricy on the palate, warm, not at all oxidized and beautifully long.

'The problem with these wines,' lamented Fernando, 'is selling them. We are so close to Rioja where there are so many fine and famous Reservas and Gran Reservas that few would ever look to Campo de Borja for wines of this type.' He shrugged, then grinned as he reached for the corkscrew. 'So we have to drink them ourselves!'

Campo de Borja will probably never be a zone known for its aged wines. However, its *vinos jóvenes* can be excellent, too. I was less impressed with Bordejé's white Macabeo, but his young *rosado* and *tinto* are both outstanding, vivid wines, intensely fruity and round and supple in the mouth.

Exceptionally good young wines are being produced, too, at the Bodega Cooperativa Agrícola de Borja, an indication, perhaps, that quality is not simply a matter of private versus collective initiative.

'There are undoubtedly good co-operatives and bad ones, just as there are good private producers and bad ones,' says Teodoro Pablo Pardo, the co-operative's down-to-earth and genial winemaker. 'We have 1000 *socios* in this co-operative, and likewise, we have good ones and less good ones. However, it is important to give them the incentive to produce better quality grapes. For example, it is essential that the grapes are harvested at just the right moment, and most of our *socios* will pick when we tell them to. At present, we award them a 10% bonus for bringing in their grapes at the right moment, that is when our technicians advise that this or that sub-zone is ready to be harvested. Likewise, we similarly penalize them if their grapes come in overripe or in poor condition. I would like to see these bonuses and penalties increased.'

Campo de Borja is traditionally a land of reds and *rosados*. The vineyard is planted overwhelmingly with Garnacha. Indeed, until the modification of the DO in 1989, white wines were excluded from the *denominación*. However, market demand for fresh, young white wines has led to further plantations of primarily Macabeo. Even in this hot, arid land, the Cooperativa de Borja demonstrates that it is possible to make fresh young white wines with character. For example, the Macabeo grapes are harvested early to retain their essential fruity acidity, and are pressed in modern pneumatic presses. But before drawing off the grape must, it is allowed to steep in contact with its skins for up to 8 hours at a low temperature to extract greater aroma and varietal character. The result is certainly successful: a fairly full-bodied white wine with a nice creamy almond fruit, and a zesty green apple freshness that is quite delicious.

The young *rosado* and *tinto* (all three young wines are marketed under the Borsao label) similarly demonstrate fine and fresh expressions of fruit.

'We have identified different zones for Garnacha,' explained Teodoro. 'For example, on vineyards at about 300 metres on mainly alluvial clay soil, we find that Garnacha gives wines that are very fruity and aromatic. We utilize those grapes for our *tintos jóvenes* vinified by carbonic maceration. On the other hand, on our higher vineyards, extending up to 500 metres, where the soil has more of a sandstone base, we find that the wines are less aromatic but have considerably more body and structure. We select those wines for *crianza* in wood and vinify them traditionally with de-stemming and crushing.'

The Cooperativa de Borja, incidentally, is not dedicated solely to wine. Many of its *socios* have not only vineyards but also fields of grain, olive and almond trees, and market gardens. The co-operative serves also to process their wheat harvest, and is furthermore a fine producer of excellent extra virgin olive oil.

While the wine country extends over 15 municipalities, Borja itself is definitely the economic, market and social centre for this small *comarca*. The ancestral home of the infamous Borgias, today it is a most pleasant wine town of about 4000 inhabitants; its historic centre has some fine mansions and public buildings and an excellent local restaurant. It is well worth

---

A Fat Problem

'*Hay una problema gordita*,' said Fernando Bordejé, shaking his head. A big fat problem.

It was late September. The white Macabeo grapes had all been harvested. In almost every vintage that Fernando could remember, once the white grapes were all in, the pickers were able to move straight on to the harvesting of the black grapes. But after the storms of the last fortnight, the sugar levels of the Garnacha had only reached about 10.5° potential alcohol, still some way from the minimum 12 to 12.5° that Fernando required.

The harvesters, a *cuadrilla* of itinerant gypsies hired for the *vendimia*, were impatient, unhappy. They wanted to work, for they were paid by the kilogram harvested. '*Las naranjas*,' they said, 'the oranges in Valencia are now ripe.' If Fernando couldn't keep them working, the threat implied, then they would just have to head south. Fernando knew that if they left, then it would be impossible to find another team, for by this time of year they had all been hired for the harvest not only here but also in Cariñena, Navarra, or nearby Rioja.

For a small, private winery like Bodegas Bordejé, whose quality wines are dependent on harvesting at the optimum moment, it was very worrying: '*una problema gordita*'.

making a detour off the main motorway to discover this unknown wine zone and to sample its tasty wines at the source. Other important wine towns in the *comarca* include Ainzón, Fuendejalón and Magallón.

Bodegas: Stop to Taste; Stop to Buy

Somontano

1

COMPAÑIA VITIVINICOLA
   ARAGONESA SA (CoViSa)
FINCA SAN MARCOS
CTRA BARBASTRO–NAVAL, KM 3700
22300 BARBASTRO
HUESCA
TEL: (974) 30 22 16; FAX: (974) 30 20 98
ADMINISTRATIVE OFFICE: AVDA
   INDEPENDENCIA 8, 9° C, 50004
   ZARAGOZA
TEL: (976) 23 52 47; FAX: (976) 21 06 42

WINES PRODUCED: Viña del Vero *blanco, rosado, tinto*; Chardonnay, Chardonnay Crianza (barrel fermented); Gewürztraminer; Riesling; Chenin Blanc; Cabernet Sauvignon *rosado*; Duque de Azara *tinto*; Val de Vos Cabernet Sauvignon.

VISITS: Mon–Fri 9–20h, by appointment through the administrative office. Working hours for tasting and direct sales. CoViSa was only founded in 1986, but the level of investment combined with the preliminary results from newly planted vineyards are encouraging enough to suggest that this will be a significant modern Spanish winery of the future. The experimental *bodega* is still in place and functioning at Salas Bajas, while the ultra-modern and technically highly advanced new *bodega* should be fully functional by 1994.

This is undoubtedly a new wave winery whose inspiration is more new world than old, with an emphasis on varietal wines produced from a host of local and international grapes. Results so far demonstrate a restrained and elegant style, with an emphasis on a good balance of fruit and acidity. English, French, Dutch spoken.

2

BODEGA COOPERATIVA COMARCAL
   DEL SOMONTANO DE SOBRARBE
CTRA BARBASTRO–NAVAL, KM 3800
22300 BARBASTRO
HUESCA
TEL AND FAX: (974) 31 12 89

WINES PRODUCED: Montesierra *blanco, rosado, tinto*; Camporocal *blanco, rosado, tinto*; Macabeo *blanco* Crianza; Monasterio *tinto* Crianza; Señorío de Lazan *tinto* Reserva.

ARAGÓN

VISITS: Working hours, by appointment. Kiosk open working hours for direct sales.

The well-run, well-equipped co-operative winery of Somontano still produces most of this small zone's wines.

French spoken.

---

3 BODEGAS LALANNE
CASTILLO SAN MARCOS
22300 BARBASTRO
HUESCA
TEL: (974) 31 06 89

WINES PRODUCED: Laura Lalanne *blanco, rosado, tinto*; Viña San Marcos *blanco, rosado, tinto*; Lalanne *tinto* Crianza, Reserva, Gran Reserva.
VISITS: Working hours for direct sales.

Bodegas Lalanne was founded in Bordeaux in 1842 and established in Somontano in 1894 after the outbreak in France of phylloxera. Bodegas Lalanne first brought fame to the wines of Somontano, for these wines were renowned internationally in the early years of this century. Today no longer the force that it once was, this is none the less a historic estate with about 20 hectares of its own vineyards, still producing a range of high-quality wines.

Old vintages are available for sale, as well as the full range of younger wines.

French spoken.

---

4 BODEGAS MONCLUS
CTRA ALQUÉZAR–RADIQUERO, S/N
22145 RADIQUERO
HUESCA
TEL: (974) 31 81 20

WINES PRODUCED: Monclus *blanco, rosado*; Monclus *tinto del año*; Monclus Viña Vallarma *tinto*; Monclus Viña Capana *tinto*.
VISITS: Daily, working hours. Appointment advisable to ensure someone is in.

Bodegas Monclus is a tiny operation, producing well-made wines from 12 hectares of its own vineyards planted mainly with Garnacha together with Moristel, Macabeo, Tempranillo, and small experimental amounts of Cabernet Sauvignon, Chardonnay, Chenin Blanc and Riesling. The aim in planting the 'foreign' grapes is not to make varietals but to use them to improve the wines in conjunction with the native varieties.

Mercedes Monclus is a great enthusiast for the wines and region and a dedicated winemaker. Her small artisan-*bodega* is located on the main road below the entrance to the *pueblo* of Radiquero.

Cariñena

1 BODEGA COOPERATIVA SAN VALERO
CTRA ZARAGOZA–VALENCIA, KM
   46,200
50400 CARIÑENA
ZARAGOZA
TEL: (976) 62 04 00; FAX: (976) 62 03 98

WINES PRODUCED: Perçebal *vino de aguja blanco, rosado*; Don Mendo *vino joven blanco, rosado, tinto*; Monte Ducay *blanco, rosado*; Monte Ducay *tinto* Crianza, Monte Ducay *tinto* Gran Reserva; Marqués de Tosos *tinto* Reserva; Gran Ducay Cava.
VISITS: Daily, working hours for tasting and direct sales.
Central Aragón is much derided as a dull wine zone of co-operatives incapable of producing quality wines. Yet San Valero demonstrates how a range of enjoyable and in some cases prestigious wines can be made on an immense scale. This is not a pretty *bodega*, but it is an extremely important one. There is a welcoming tasting salon just off the main road where the full range of wines can be sampled and purchased.

---

2 HEREDAD DE BALBINO LACOSTA
HERMANA MATILDE 33
50400 CARIÑENA
ZARAGOZA
TEL: (976) 62 03 89

WINES PRODUCED: *Vino joven rosado y tinto*; Viña Matilla *tinto* Crianza; Vega Lagunas *tinto* Reserva.
VISITS: By appointment.
Established in 1897 and a good source of the traditional, meaty wines of Cariñena.

---

3 HEREDEROS DE GENARO TEJERO
PRIMO DE RIVERA 1
50400 CARIÑENA
ZARAGOZA
TEL: (976) 62 01 83

WINES PRODUCED: Tres Hojas *blanco*; Seco Ambar *blanco* Crianza; Ojo de Perdiz *rosado*; Cepa Somera *tinto*; Tempranillo.
VISITS: Mon–Fri 11–18h.
Appointment preferred.
One of the region's oldest *bodegas*, located on the road to Calatayud. Traditional wines produced from grapes grown in own vineyards.

ARAGÓN

4 BODEGAS LOPEZ PELAYO
LA CRUZ 1
50108 ALMONACID DE LA SIERRA
ZARAGOZA
TEL: (976) 62 70 15

WINES PRODUCED: Cueva de
Algairén *blanco, rosado, tinto*;
Señorío de Arcano *tinto*; Cueva de

Algairén *tinto* Reserva; Siete
Rincones *tinto* Gran Reserva.
VISITS: Mon–Fri, working hours.
Appointment preferred.
Well-regarded range of wines made
entirely from own-grown grapes in
a historic and atmospheric *bodega*.

Calatayud

1 BODEGAS LANGA HERMANOS SL
CTRA NACIONAL II, KM 241,700
50300 CALATAYUD
ZARAGOZA
TEL AND FAX: (976) 88 18 18

WINES PRODUCED: Portalet
blanco, rosado, tinto; Castillo de
Ayud *rosado* Reserva; Castillo de
Ayud *tinto* Reserva; Cabernet
Sauvignon; Cava.
VISITS: Daily, by appointment.

Open working hours for direct sales.
The most advanced private winery
in the newly demarcated zone.
Modern installations and an
impressive range of fresh, lighter,
'new wave' Calatayud wines, as
well as traditional heavyweights
such as the aged Castillo de Ayud
rosado and Castillo de Ayud *tinto*
Reserva.

---

2 BODEGA SAN GREGORIO
COOPERATIVA DEL CAMPO SAN
    GREGORIO
CTRA DE VILLALENGUA, S/N
50312 CERVERA DE LA CAÑADA
ZARAGOZA
TEL: (976) 89 92 06; FAX: (976) 88 04 65

WINES PRODUCED: Monte
Armantes *blanco, rosado, tinto*;
Viejo Armantes *blanco* Gran
Reserva.
VISITS: Mon–Sat 9–13h; 14–20h.

No appointment necessary.
The San Gregorio co-operative has
demonstrated that with the use of
temperature controlled
fermentation, an attractive range of
young wines can be made. But the
most noteworthy and unusual wine
is the old-style traditional Gran
Reserva *blanco*, which reaches a
hefty 16° alcohol.
English spoken.

Campo de Borja

1

BODEGAS BORDEJÉ SAT
CTRA BORJA–RUEDA, KM 3
50570 AINZÓN
ZARAGOZA
TEL: (976) 86 20 61; FAX: 86 80 80

WINES PRODUCED: Bordejé
blanco, rosado, tinto; Bordejé *tinto*
Gran Reserva; Cava Bordejé Brut
Nature; Mari Dulcis Moscatel.
VISITS: Daily, working hours.
Appointment appreciated.
This historic family *bodega* was
founded in 1770 and maintains its
original and hugely atmospheric
hand-dug caves. This is very much a
serious working winery, producing
a range of well-made young wines,
some exceptional Gran Reserva
tintos, a good Aragonese Cava, and
a poignant and fragrant Moscatel,
made in honour of Fernando
Bordejé's late mother. The reds are
all produced entirely by carbonic
maceration.

Fernando is a young enthusiast
and, if time permits, will delight in
explaining his wines and the zone.

2

BODEGA COOPERATIVA AGRICOLA
    DE BORJA
CALLE CAPUCHINOS 10
50540 BORJA
ZARAGOZA
TEL: (976) 86 71 16; FAX: (976) 86 77 52

WINES PRODUCED: Borsao *blanco*,
rosado, tinto; Gran Campellas *tinto*
Crianza; Pedernal *tinto* Crianza;
Señor Atares *tinto* Reserva.
VISITS: Daily, by appointment.
Working hours for direct sales.
This little-known wine zone's best
co-operative produces a well-made
range of *vinos jóvenes* as well as
some good reds which undergo
crianza in *barricas*. The
co-operative was founded in 1956
and it has been producing wine in
bottle since 1975 prior to the
granting of the DO in 1978. Modern
technology is utilized to maintain
above all the fruit and aroma in the
finished wines.

Also good production of extra
virgin olive oil.

ARAGÓN

Restaurantes, Hoteles y Paradores

Somontano

1
HOTEL REY SANCHO RAMIREZ
NACIONAL 240 TARRAGONA–SAN
  SEBASTIAN, KM 162,700
22300 BARBASTRO
HUESCA
TEL: (974) 31 00 50, 31 00 54;
  FAX: (974) 31 00 58

Comfortable, recently renovated
3-star hotel with restaurant serving
local foods – *ternasco asado
Somontano, magras de jamón con
tomate* – together with the wines of
Somontano and Rioja.
Inexpensive to Moderate

2
BAR-RESTAURANTE L'ARRABAL
AVDA PIRINEOS 7
22300 BARBASTRO
HUESCA
TEL: (974) 31 16 73

Closed Sun.
Friendly restaurant on the edge of

town serving a well-prepared menu
of local and imaginative foods:
*escabeche de capon al vinagre de
Jerez, revueltos con setas y gambas,
conejo guisado*, and superb
home-made ice creams.
Moderate

3
RESTAURANTE FLOR
GOYA 3
22300 BARBASTRO
HUESCA
TEL: (974) 31 10 56; FAX: (974) 31 13 18

Local foods utilizing excellent
seasonal produce – *verduras del
tiempo, ternasco al horno, guisos
varios* – and the wines of Somontano
in this stylish popular restaurant.
Moderate

4
HOSTAL-RESTAURANTE TRES
  CAMINOS
22390 EL GRADO
HUESCA
TEL: (974) 30 40 52; FAX: (974) 30 41 22

Large roadside inn on the route to
the Pyrenees and France located
just south of the little hill *pueblo* of

El Grado. Restaurant is noted for its
authentic *cocina aragonesa*,
especially home-made *longaniza,
cabritillo, ternasco al horno* and
conservas caseras. Good selection of
wines of Somontano, as well as
longaniza for sale in the bar.
Inexpensive to Moderate

5 CASA GERVASIO
ALQUÉZAR
HUESCA

Alquézar is located about 27 km from Barbastro, sited dramatically on the remains of an Arab fortress above the steep Vero gorge. Wander the old streets, then find this simple but exceedingly atmospheric *fonda*. The sign above the door reads simply *'comidas'* and that is what you get: no menu, just whatever is on hand for the day: mountain-cured *jamón*, perhaps some pasta, *chuletillas de cordero*, rounded off by cheese, fruit, coffee and a lethal home-made *licor*. House wine is best mixed with lemonade.
Inexpensive

Parador

P PARADOR NACIONAL DE BIELSA
VALLE DE PINETA
22350 BIELSA
HUESCA
TEL AND FAX: (974) 50 10 11

Splendidly located in the Alto Cinca above Somontano, and a perfect retreat for relaxation in the Ordesa National Park.
Moderate

Cariñena

1 HOTEL-RESTAURANTE CARIÑENA
CTRA ZARAGOZA–VALENCIA, KM 47
50400 CARIÑENA
ZARAGOZA
TEL: (976) 62 02 50

On the main road virtually opposite the San Valero co-operative, this roadside traveller's inn serves a hearty *menú del día*. *judías verdes salteadas, lomo de cerdo plancha, ternasco asado, jamón de Teruel*. Good selection of local wines. Hotel has 30 rooms, most with private facilities.
Inexpensive

---

2 EL BALCÓN
CTRA ZARAGOZA–VALENCIA, KM 57
PUERTO PANIZA
ZARAGOZA
TEL: (976) 62 05 18

Primarily a motorist's stop in the hills south of Cariñena, this *tienda-restaurante* serves good tasty meals utilizing fine Aragonese products: *jamón de Teruel, longaniza, chorizo, quesos*.
Inexpensive

ARAGÓN

Calatayud

1 HOTEL-RESTAURANTE CALATAYUD
CTRA MADRID–BARCELONA, KM 237
50300 CALATAYUD
ZARAGOZA
TEL: (976) 88 13 23; FAX: (976) 88 54 38

Comfortable hotel on the main
Madrid road with restaurant serving
Aragonese specialities – *ternasco
asado, pollo a la chilindrón* –
together with wines of the zone.
Inexpensive

---

2 RESTAURANTE LISBOA
PASEO CALVO SOTELO 10
50300 CALATAYUD
ZARAGOZA
TEL: (976) 88 25 35, 88 14 59

On the main *paseo* just outside the
walls of the *casco antiguo*, this

traditional restaurant serves
well-prepared and authentic foods of
Calatayud: *judías con chorizo y
oreja, perdiz estofado, paletilla de
cordero*, and a good selection of
local wines.
Inexpensive to Moderate

Monasterio de Piedra

Given that the most striking feature of central Spain is its soul-scorching
aridity, the Monasterio de Piedra, with its lush surrounding natural park, is
a miraculous oasis which should not be missed.

Located only 25 km from Calatayud, the monastery was founded by
Cistercian monks from the Monasterio de Poblet in 1194 at the request of
King Alfonso II of Aragón. Royal patronage ensured ample endowments,
and over subsequent centuries it gained power and influence. For example,
a Papal Bull issued by Innocent III in 1201 granted rights to extensive
surrounding lands, including the vineyards of Calatayud, and it is to be
assumed that the sybaritic monks of Piedra enjoyed this legacy with lip-
smacking gusto. (Indeed, the old abbey kitchens, with their numerous
smoke-blackened fireplaces, and the vast underground *bodega*, give ample
evidence that life at Piedra was probably something less than austere.)

The site of the monastery is itself propitious, for it is located where the
arid Aragón plateau gives way to a remarkable waterland, at the point
where the Piedra river branches to lead down into a stepping-stone canyon
of beautiful cascades, waterfalls, pools and lush undergrowth. This natural
park is today open to the public. Notwithstanding its perennial popularity

(there are always coachloads of visitors), it remains a place of rare tranquillity and beauty. A signposted, self-guided walk takes about two hours to complete.

The monastery itself has been converted into an atmospheric luxury hotel: the old monks' cells have been turned into well-appointed bedrooms and there is an excellent restaurant that serves simple but well-prepared foods of Aragón to accompany, of course, the famous *caldos* of Calatayud.

3 MONASTERIO DE PIEDRA
50210 NUEVALOS
ZARAGOZA
TEL: (976) 84 90 11;
FAX: (976) 84 90 54

Moderate

The natural park of the Monasterio de Piedra, near Calatayud.

Campo de Borja

1 RESTAURANTE LA BOVEDA
PLAZA DEL MERCADO
50540 BORJA
ZARAGOZA
TEL: (976) 86 82 51, 86 88 44

Closed Mon.
What a surprise to find such a stylish restaurant in this charming but rather sleepy wine *pueblo*! It is located in a converted underground *bodega* decorated with beautiful paintings, and serves imaginative and well-prepared foods: *pasta fresca con salmón, anchoas y mejillones; migas con uva Garnacha; merluza al Cava de Ainzón; gallina de las Concepcionistas con ciruelas*. Wines from Bodegas Bordejé and the local co-operative, among others.
Moderate

ARAGÓN

Tomar Unas Copas: Stop for a Drink; Stop for a Bite

Somontano

1 BAR VICTORIA
PASEO DEL COSO 19
22300 BARBASTRO
HUESCA

Sit out under the trees of Barbastro's main *paseo* and watch the world go by. Reasonable wine and good hot *tapas*.

---

2 MESÓN EL VERIO
ALQUÉZAR
HUESCA

Stop for a glass of Somontano wine and linger at a pleasant outdoor table overlooking the Vero gorge, and across to Alquézar's beautiful basilica.

Campo de Borja

1 CAFÉ MONTESOL
PLAZA MAYOR
50540 BORJA
ZARAGOZA

In the main square of this quiet wine *pueblo*, stop for a glass of wine and a plate of *gambas*.

Los Campings

Somontano

The province of Huesca is a paradise for campers and there are scores of beautiful and well-equipped sites mainly in the mountains and the Ordesa National Park. The two best campsites for the Somontano wine region are:

LAGO DE BARASONA
CTRA N123 BARBASTRO–GRAUS, KM
     25
LA PUEBLA DE CASTRO
HUESCA
TEL: (974) 33 03 22

ALQUÉZAR RIO VERO
ALQUÉZAR
HUESCA
TEL: (974) 31 83 50

Calatayud

CAMPING CALATAYUD
CTRA MADRID–BARCELONA, KM 239
50300 CALATAYUD
ZARAGOZA
TEL: (976) 88 05 92

Zaragoza

CAMPING CASABLANCA
CTRA N-II, KM 316
50000 ZARAGOZA
TEL: (976) 33 03 22

Vinos y Comestibles: Stop to Taste; Stop to Buy

Zaragoza

BARBACIL
BODEGA LICORERÍA
CALLE JUAN PABLO BONET 4
50006 ZARAGOZA
TEL: (976) 27 10 64; FAX: (976) 27 29 23

Closed Sat afternoon, Sun.
Extensive wine and liquor store
(wholesale and retail) located in an
old winery in the centre of
Zaragoza.
French, a little English spoken.

LA FILOXERA
CADENA 2
50001 ZARAGOZA

Wine shop with *bodega* and
sampling cellar where wines,
sausage and cheese can be enjoyed.

Cariñena

EL BALCÓN
CTRA ZARAGOZA–VALENCIA, KM 57
PUERTO PANIZA
ZARAGOZA
TEL: (976) 62 05 18

Restaurant (see above) and shop on
main road in hills south of Cariñena.
Excellent selection of wines from
smaller growers, as well as good

ARAGÓN

Aragonese products: *jamón de Teruel, longaniza, quesos*, preserved fruits, home-made conserved meats. This is probably the best outlet for the wines of Cariñena, sold generally at very competitive prices.

¡Fiesta! Wine and Other Related Celebrations

about 15 Sept	Fiesta de la Vendimia	Cariñena
last week in Sept	Concurso Provincial de Vinos de Huesca	Barbastro
2nd fortnight in Oct	Fiesta del Vino del Somontano	Barbastro
12 October	Fiesta de la Virgen del Pilar	Zaragoza

Fiesta de la Virgen del Pilar

Zaragoza's famous *fiesta* is an event of much more than merely local or regional interest. The Virgen del Pilar, patron saint of Spain, is reputed to have descended from Heaven by way of the pillar now in the city's great Gothic basilica when she appeared to Saint James the Apostle in the year 40. Greatly venerated (witness the number of Spanish women named Pilar), her saint's day on 12 October is a major religious festival of great faith and devotion, as well as a national holiday. In Zaragoza itself, the 'El Pilar' festivities last for a week, and include the moving Rosario de Cristal procession, vibrant *jota* dancing, bullfights, and the *gigantes y cabezudos* procession of colourful cardboard giants and dwarfs.

For the winegrowers of Aragón (and indeed in many other regions of Spain too), it was traditional that the *vendimia* never started before 'El Pilar'. This, presumably, was to ensure that the grapes were harvested when they were as ripe as possible, the priority then being to make wines as powerful and as alcoholic as possible. Today, an indication of change even in this conservative bastion (now that modern taste and the market is for lighter, fresher, fruitier wines) is that the harvest begins earlier and earlier each year. Indeed, nowadays, in all the regions of Aragón, it is almost always in full swing well before the beginning of this important festivity.

Y *para saber más* Additional Information

Diputación General de Aragón
Departamento de Industria,
  Comercia y Turismo
Plaza de los Sitios 7
50000 Zaragoza
tel: (974) 22 14 00

Consejo Regulador de Cariñena
Calle Mayor 30
50400 Cariñena
Zaragoza
tel: (976) 62 06 94

Consejo Regulador de Calatayud
Polígono Industrial de la Chaluca,
  parcela 31
50300 Calatayud
Zaragoza
tel: (976) 88 59 12

Consejo Regulador de Somontano
Avda Navarra 1, 1 dcha
22300 Barbastro
Huesca
tel: (974) 31 30 31

Consejo Regulador de Campo de
  Borja
Barrio Curto 2
50570 Ainzón
Zaragoza
tel: (976) 86 88 06

ARAGÓN

CASTILLA-LA MANCHA

Windmills on the vast plains of central
La Mancha.

Castilla-La Mancha, known historically as New
Castile, occupies a vast central portion of the
country extending over the southern half of
Spain's great interior *meseta*. High, flat and
broad, constituting a bridge between Castilla y
León to the north and Andalucía to the south,
this is one of the most strikingly singular regions
of Spain, not easily or perhaps immediately
appealing to the visitor, but an essential element
of the enduring core which defines Spain and the
Castilian Spaniards.

No city in Spain could be more archetypically Spanish than Toledo, the
region's capital. Dramatically sited on a rugged granite promontory almost
surrounded by the Tagus river, it was the capital of Spain under the Visigoths in the sixth century, conquered by the Moors in 711, and reconquered
by King Alfonso VI in 1085 with the aid of El Cid. A cultural melting-pot
for Christian, Moor and Jew alike, Toledo then became the capital of Spain
after the Reconquest until Philip II decided to move his court to Madrid in
1561. After that, Toledo declined in importance, yet even today it seems to
hold and safeguard something of the very spiritual essence of the country
within its narrow medieval alleys, its great monumental churches, and in
the paintings of El Greco, sombre, intense and otherworldly.

Outside Toledo, beyond its dark and claustrophobic streets, it is the vast,
open and endless space of Castilla-La Mancha that is most striking. From
horizon to horizon, this is one immense flat landscape of vines, olive groves
and great tracts of wheat. Vines, above all, dominate, sweeping right across

the land in virtually all directions. This, after all, is the *denominación de origen* of La Mancha, the largest delimited quality vineyard in Europe, and the source of a massive 35–40% of total Spanish wine production. So prevalent is the vine that the Airén, La Mancha's predominant grape variety planted almost exclusively here and nowhere else, is claimed to be the most widely cultivated variety in the world, surpassing by far even such internationally ubiquitous superstars as Cabernet Sauvignon or Chardonnay.

La Mancha's great vineyards sprout from a land that is arid and climatically extreme. Yet there is a grandeur here, simply in its seemingly boundless space. La Mancha is a land without confines, diametrically opposite in feel to the claustrophobia of Spain's cities, where people live packed together in what must rank as some of the ugliest urban developments in the world. Here in the Manchegan countryside, unpolluted by industry, in a high rarefied atmosphere where the air is clean and fresh and where there are few distractions from the lights of large cities, the sky that is revealed at night is immense and immensely beautiful – larger even than the sky at sea.

It is a sky, above all, for dreamers and lunatics, like La Mancha's old knight errant whose eccentric and individual spirit even still today seems not wholly out of place or vanished in the *pueblos* and wine towns of the region.

Orientation

Castilla-La Mancha comprises 5 provinces: Toledo, Ciudad Real, Albacete, Cuenca and Guadalajara. The region's capital, Toledo, is one of the great historic cities of Spain, and should be on every visitor's itinerary.

Located south and east of Madrid, the region is best served by air via Madrid's international airport, although the eastern provinces of Cuenca and Albacete are accessible from Valencia. All major rail and road routes to the south and east pass through the region.

While the entire region of La Mancha makes up Europe's single largest delimited vineyard, the most notable wine country is found around the separate *denominación* of Valdepeñas. This zone is best dipped into en route to Andalucía.

Maps: Michelin No. 444 (Central); Firestone Hispania C-5, T31.

CASTILLA-LA MANCHA

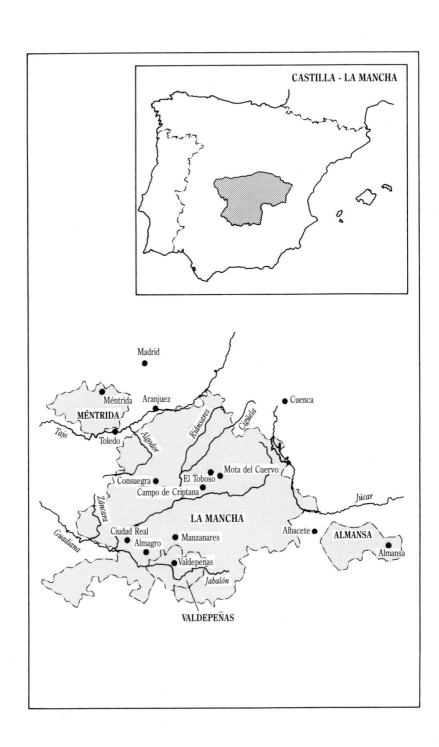

La Ruta de Don Quijote

Apart from Toledo, Castilla-La Mancha does not rate as an obvious tourist destination. However, the region serves as an important corridor to the south and south-east and millions of tourists and visitors pass through it each year. In an effort to encourage travellers to stop awhile, the tourist authorities have somewhat hopefully devised *'La Ruta de Don Quijote'*, a suggested itinerary that leads through some of the characteristic towns and sights mentioned in Cervantes' great work.

Some of the principal *'lugares de La Mancha'* within the La Mancha wine country include: El Toboso, the *pueblo* where Don Quixote found his Dulcinea (there is a well-restored *'Casa de Dulcinea'* here as well as the *Centro Cervantino*); Puerto Lápice, where in the local *venta*, Don Quixote was knighted by the innkeeper (Cervantes himself is said to have stayed in the same inn, still open and serving travellers today); Consuegra, famous for its windmills and its exquisite crop of saffron; Mota del Cuervo, an important wine town also dominated by its windmills; and Campo de Criptana, yet another wine town with an impressive collection of well-preserved windmills.

It has to be said that these Manchegan villages and towns are on the whole unremarkable: whitewashed, little-visited *pueblos* baking under the glare of a ferocious midday sun in the middle of Spain's great, lonely central *meseta*. Yet even the casual visitor will not want to miss dipping into one or two of them to experience something of the Cervantine qualities of this vast and wholly singular region. The ironic genius of Cervantes' masterpiece, after all, was to envisage the fantastic and the heroic within the realms of the everyday and wholly ordinary.

LOS VINOS: THE WINES OF CASTILLA-LA MANCHA

Almansa DO   Delimited wine region in the south-east of Castilla-La Mancha bordering the Levante and centred on the town of Almansa, famous for its well-preserved medieval castle. Wine production is principally *rosado* and red wines produced from Monastrell and Garnacha Tintorera. Minimum alcohol 12°.

La Mancha DO   Europe's largest delimited vineyard extends over a vast superficial area of 174,000 hectares in some 180 municipalities extending over the provinces of Toledo, Albacete, Ciudad Real and Cuenca. The most widely planted variety is overwhelmingly the white Airén, while there are much smaller plantations of the white Macabeo, Pardilla and Verdoncho, as well as black Cencibel (Tempranillo) and Garnacha. White wines still account for some 90% of production and must have 11–14° alcohol; *rosados* must reach the same levels, while red wines must attain 11.5–15° alcohol.

Méntrida DO Delimited region located south-west of Madrid and north of Toledo producing mainly heavyweight, old-style red and *rosado* wines from Garnacha, Tinto Madrid and Cencibel grapes. Much of the production goes for blending or distillation. Paradoxically, one of Spain's leading private estates, Marqués de Griñon, is located within the zone, but its classy red Cabernet Sauvignon wine is wholly untypical and in any case not entitled to the *denominación*. Méntrida wines must reach a minimum 13° alcohol but may soar up to natural levels of 16° or higher.

Valdepeñas DO *Denominación* for the best wines of La Mancha, produced from delimited vineyards in the south of the region in the province of Ciudad Real centred on the important wine town of Valdepeñas. Though renowned primarily for its red and light red *clarete* wines, the vineyard is still paradoxically planted with up to 90% white grapes, mainly the ubiquitous Airén. Valdepeñas *claretes*, the most famous wines of the zone, have traditionally been produced with up to 80% white grapes, coloured with blending from the black varieties. However, in recent years there has been a significant increase in the plantation of the aristocratic Cencibel (Tempranillo) for the production of outstanding oak-aged Reserva and Gran Reserva wines of high quality, and it is these wines that have received the most attention internationally. Alcohol levels are for white 11–13.5°, *rosado* 11.5–14.5°, and red 12.5–15°.

LA GASTRONOMÍA: FOODS OF CASTILLA-LA MANCHA

Central Castilla-La Mancha appears something of an austere and arid interior region, a complete and utter contrast to the colourful and lush coastal *huertas* of the Levante or Andalucía. Landlocked and about as far

Vinos Jóvenes

Central Spain, and Castilla-La Mancha in particular, has long enjoyed a dubious reputation as the purveyor of traditional, heavy and often oxidized bulk wines, supplied in quantity both to its own home market and to international markets. This is not surprising, given the region's arid and semi-arid climate, the nature of its unrelieved flat terrain, and the hellish temperatures which in summer average upwards of 40°C.

However, in recent years, a quiet revolution in winemaking has been taking place here not just in some of the region's few outstanding private wineries, but also in some of its dinosaur-like co-operatives. In the past, growers were encouraged to pick as late as possible as this resulted in higher levels of potential alcohol. Now, by encouraging their members to pick their grapes earlier – sometimes as much as a month or more before the traditional harvest – and through the use of refrigeration to control the temperatures during fermentation, some co-operatives are producing a new breed of light, fruity *vinos jóvenes*. Such wines – mainly white, but with some *rosado* and red – may never be world beaters, but they are clean, well-made and, most important of all, still extremely inexpensive.

As Europe's largest single delimited vineyard and the vast potential source of such sound, good value wines, and with the opening of the single European market in 1993, La Mancha may well finally come of age.

from the sea as you can get in Spain, its cuisine is a reflection of the harsh and bare nature of its terrain and of a climate which, if hellishly hot in summer, is bitterly freezing in winter. None the less, it is a cuisine that is simple, rarely less than satisfying, and, like everything else in the region, wholly and uncompromisingly authentic.

This is a region of great winter stews such as *gazpacho manchego*, a filling winter bean, vegetable and meat hot-pot, *caldereta de cordero*, made with best end of lamb stewed with tomatoes and peppers, or the everpresent *cocido castellano*, a one-pot dish to which any variety of vegetables, beans and meats is added, usually including *chorizo*, potatoes, cabbage and chickpeas. In bars or roadside *ventas* and *mesónes*, such simple but full-flavoured *tapas* as morsels of fried *chorizo* and *morcilla*, *tortilla española* (the famous and ubiquitous cake-like Spanish potato omelette), and cubes of *queso manchego* soaked in olive oil are offered, to accompany copious amounts of honest if anonymous Manchegan wine.

CASTILLA-LA MANCHA

The scrubby, dusty grazing lands of the central *meseta* provide sustenance for little save flocks of sheep and goats; as in the neighbouring region of Castilla y León, they find their way into the roasting ovens, the great wood-fired *hornos de asar* that are so characteristic of central Spain. Such classic roast meats are superb accompaniments to the great oak-aged wines of Valdepeñas. And of course, La Mancha's great flocks of sheep provide the raw material for the region's greatest contribution to Spanish gastronomy, *queso manchego*, one of the great cheeses of the world.

Other dishes which reflect the harsh and self-sufficient nature of the diet include *tojunto*, a robust rabbit stew characteristic of Ciudad Real (the name is a contraction of '*todo junto*', meaning everything put together). *Perdiz estofado* is similarly typical and recalls the region's prevalent fondness for small game, the perennial privilege of the countryman who has traditionally had a pot shot at virtually anything that moves.

Don't come to Castilla-La Mancha for sophisticated or fussy *haute cuisine*: do come to enjoy the strong, forthright and always filling foods of a vast and great central region.

¡Que aproveche! Regional Specialities of Castilla-La Mancha

Sopa de ajo   Supremely simple soup of garlic, bread, olive oil and paprika: served throughout central Spain.

Berenjenas de Almagro   Small baby aubergines, cooked first then pickled in vinegar and spices.

Asadillo   Mixture of roasted vegetables – tomatoes, peppers, onions and garlic – served hot or cold.

Duelos y quebrantos   *Cazuelita* of *chorizo*, *tocino*, fried brains, scrambled eggs and bread, baked in an oven.

Callos a la madrileña   Classic and favourite tripe dish, cooked with tomatoes, onions, *morcilla*, *chorizo* and ham.

Cocido castellano   Typical Spanish stew, consisting always of meat, chickpeas, potatoes, cabbage, turnips, beef, *chorizo* and *morcilla*. May be served in several courses, the liquid first as a soup, then the vegetables and beans, and finally the sliced meat.

Pisto manchego   Vegetable stew from La Mancha made with red and green peppers, tomatoes, squash, onions cooked slowly in olive oil or lard. Sometimes garnished with scrambled eggs.

Perdiz estofado Partridge stewed in white wine, onions, garlic and herbs.

Tojunto Substantial rabbit stew containing garlic, onion, green beans, rabbit and anything else the cook cares to throw in.

Mazapán de Toledo The Arabs probably passed on the method of making delicious sweetmeats from pounded almonds and sugar: Toledo specializes in its production, made in any number of whimsical shapes and colours.

Cheese: *Manchego DO* Spain's most famous cheese is produced from pasteurized or raw ewe's milk cured for a minimum of 60 days. It is generally available in two versions: *curado* (hard, well-aged and strong in flavour) and *semi-curado* (fresher, softer and mild). The wine zones of Valdepeñas and La Mancha are the principal regions of production.

Saffron

Saffron, the most colourful and expensive spice in the world, comes from this otherwise parched and monochromatic land. Introduced to Spain by the Arabs (its Spanish name, *azafrán*, comes from the Arab word for 'yellow'), it is cultivated especially around Consuegra, an otherwise unexceptional Manchegan town most famous for its splendid windmills that stand high on a ridge overlooking the plain. Saffron comes from the stigma of the pale purple crocus plant (*Crocus sativus*) which blooms for a brief and glorious fortnight only, usually sometime towards the end of October. At this time the red and rather ugly, endless landscape of La Mancha is transformed into a glorious purple wonderland.

The precious stigmas must be harvested by hand as soon as the flowers bloom, yielding a miserly three threads per plant. These are then dried, packaged and sold in minuscule amounts at great expense (it takes some 300,000 stigmas to make up a pound weight of saffron, and this would sell for upwards of £1000). In spite of its exorbitant cost and rarity, this unique ingredient is considered an essential flavouring for many classics of the Spanish table, including that orange-tinted national favourite, *paella a la valenciana*. Not only does saffron lend a vivid colour to the dishes it enhances, it imparts subtle but unmistakable flavours and scents which are truly the inimitable taste of Spain.

CASTILLA-LA MANCHA

THE WINE ROADS OF CASTILLA-LA MANCHA

In Brief: The delimited wine region of La Mancha DO is so vast and sprawling that it would be impossible and probably undesirable to attempt to cover it comprehensively. Towns are few and far between and there is little developed tourist industry. Most wine production continues to lie in the hands of immense co-operative wineries. None the less, visitors heading either south to Andalucía or south-east to the Levante will pass through the region and it deserves some exploration.

Valdepeñas is the finest wine zone, entitled to its own separate *denominación de origen*: indeed, the town itself, located about 200 km south of Madrid, is riddled with old *bodegas*, and with its unique *tinaja*-lined Avenida del Vino, must be considered one of the great wine towns of Spain.

The town of Almansa, which gives its name to another separate *denominación*, is dominated by its fine medieval castle and can be visited en route to Alicante.

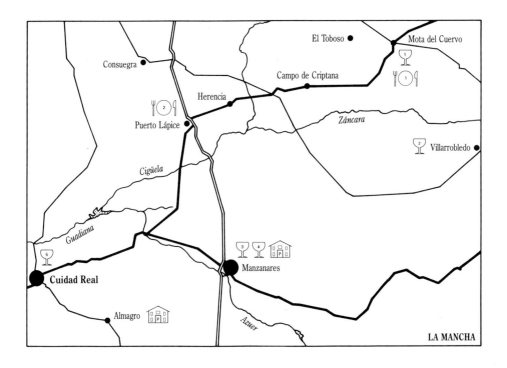

LA MANCHA

La Mancha

In many ways, La Mancha seems at odds with the image of modern Spain that has emerged over the last two decades. Its outlying *pueblos* remain timeless, baked dry and cracked under the glaring midday sun; the arid land is cultivated in much the same way as it has been for centuries, in many cases still worked by donkey or mule. There is certainly an impression of somnolence, a torpor that comes from a heat that is inescapable, in contrast to the demanding sense of urgency that is part of modern Spain's frenetic *movida*, as the country races to establish its place beside other European nations.

Come to La Mancha, and the rest of Europe seems a world away. Not even the Moors found much reason to populate this vast, seemingly isolated central plateau. Yet, if its people are poor, living off the land as they have done for centuries, the youth having long ago chosen to migrate to the cities, they are proud and remarkably friendly.

I met a Communist Republican on the train one day, an intellectual involved in local politics. He was going to Madrid for a left-wing rally, gave me some of his pamphlets. He strongly believed that Spain's future lies in the land.

'So, you are here in La Mancha researching our *caldos*,' he said warmly when he learned what I was doing. It turned out that he himself is a small grape-grower, selling his crop to the local co-operative to be processed.

'The co-operatives have been the great salvation of the *campesino*. Of course they make the best wines, too. How could any of we small growers ever hope to have the equipment, technology or knowledge that our modern co-operatives possess today? However, our principal problem,' continued my fascinating companion, 'is that our local Airén grape ripens in some years to produce wines with only as little as thirteen or fourteen degrees potential alcohol.'

Believe me, he was not joking and leaned over conspiratorially so that I could smell the strong menthol sweets that he was sucking. 'I'll tell you my secret,' he said, wagging a yellow nicotine-stained finger. 'Whenever I bottle wines for my own consumption, I always first add about a finger of *coñac*, then top the rest up with wine. I leave it to marry together for a year or so and the resulting wine is magnificent. Sixteen to eighteen degrees alcohol!'

My friend on the train may not be wholly representative of Spanish winedrinkers today, yet it is clear that the time when many Spaniards judged the quality of a wine solely by its alcoholic content has not yet wholly passed. Indeed, the demand for such traditional *caldos*, perhaps oxidized, certainly hardly fine or elegant, but always rich and heady in alcohol, remains considerable.

And vast oceans of such wines continue to be made, primarily in La Mancha's immense and numerous co-operative wineries. For the region's wine industry still remains predominantly in the hands of these collective village industries. While I would like to share my friend's blanket enthusiasm for such large-scale and originally well-intentioned enterprises, I have to say that many co-operatives that we have visited do not and cannot live up to the lofty ideals that he envisages. Many co-operatives throughout the country and in particular in La Mancha can only be described as antiquated at best. Crumbling through age and lack of investment, poorly equipped, and run by conservative and ageing committees who lack any trace of marketing initiative, their primary role today seems in many cases simply to process vast quantities of their member *socios'* grapes to make wines with no greater ambition than to be distilled into grape alcohol.

However, although La Mancha has long been considered a region of bulk wines only, destined to be distilled, sold *en granel*, or packaged in cardboard tetra-briks or returnable litre bottles to be sold at the lowest prices possible, changes and improvements in recent years demonstrate that the region is by no means without considerable potential. A market-led evolution in consumers' demand for fresher, lighter styles of wine (both in Spain itself and certainly internationally), allied with improvements in winemaking technologies, has enabled such changes to be brought about, though not without certain resistance locally.

Mota del Cuervo is a typical Manchegan town located in the heart of Don Quixote country on the road to Alicante. On the ridge of hills above the town there is a line of old white windmills, and the local hostelry beside the town's co-operative is called, what else, the Mesón de Don Quijote. For all that, it is a good typical roadside inn, with a friendly bar serving tasty hot *tapas* of *chorizo* and *morcilla* to accompany stout *chatos* of local wine.

The village co-operative, the Sociedad Cooperativa del Campo Nuestra Señora de Manjavacas, appears little different from the vast, whitewashed co-operative wineries found in virtually every *pueblo* in the region. It is neither modern nor picturesque. However, since 1981, it has been at the forefront of a quiet vinous revolution of considerable significance, for it has demonstrated that fresh, fruity modern wines can be produced from native grapes grown on the arid plains of central Spain.

The Manjavacas co-operative has about 2500 grape-growing members, all located within the municipality of Mota del Cuervo. A full 95% of the grapes grown are the white Airén, while the small amount of black grown is mainly Cencibel with a little Garnacha. There are experimental plant-ations of Viura, Verdejo and Parellada for the production of white wines, and Cabernet Sauvignon, Merlot and Pinot Noir for reds and *rosados.* The large industrial winemaking facility is capable of processing 25 million kg of grapes in just a single month. Of this vast amount, 65% is immediately discarded to be distilled; but most of the remaining amount (and that still represents a considerable ocean of wine) will bear the La Mancha *denominación.*

With so many winegrowing members, the quality of the fruit brought in must be controlled rigorously; thus, as the grapes come into the *bodega,* they are examined for their overall state of condition, potential alcohol and total acidity. No longer are *socios* encouraged to pick late simply to achieve super-high sugar levels. Indeed, for the new-style *vinos jóvenes,* they are rewarded for producing grapes considerably lower in potential alcohol, but in good condition and with reasonably high acidity.

This co-operative claims that it was the first in the region to invest in a large-scale refrigeration plant, necessary equipment for the production of modern-style white wines, and crucial for winemaking in a region where temperatures can still reach 40°C at the time of the *vendimia.* However, the co-operative has not yet had the necessary funds to replace all of its 500-odd concrete fermentation *tinajas* with more modern stainless steel. These old-style vessels date back to the 1940s when they in turn replaced the traditional earthenware *tinajas* that are still in use in parts of La Mancha and Valdepeñas and which themselves are direct descendants of the Roman fermentation *dolium. Tinajas* are one of the most primitive types of fermentation vessels available; they are extremely labour-intensive and must be emptied and cleaned by hand. Yet the co-operative of Manaja-vacas manages to produce its impressive range of modern *vinos jóvenes* in them by means of an ingenious traditional method of vinification.

To achieve this, the cleaned and selected grape musts are first chilled to just above 0°, then each *tinaja* is only filled to about one-tenth of its total capacity. As the must begins to ferment and the temperature naturally rises, additional chilled must is added in stages to maintain the temperature between 16° and 18°; this continues until the *tinaja* is full and the wine is totally fermented. This labour-intensive and unique form of manual tem-perature control results in a slow, very regular fermentation that conserves the primary aromas and flavours of the grape; the finished wines are low

CASTILLA-LA MANCHA

in alcohol (normally between 10.5° and 11.5°) and maintain their refreshing bite of acidity.

In spite of the success of such wines, the local taste remains undoubtedly in favour of the traditionally vinified wines, fermented without any form of temperature control at upwards of 30°. Both styles are marketed under the co-operative's 'Zagarron' label and it is interesting to taste them side by side. The Zagarron *blanco joven* is very pale in colour; it has a fresh vinous nose (not greatly aromatic); and it is a clean, refreshing beverage, if neither long nor complex. The Zagarron *blanco tradicional* has a straw yellow colour, rather flat oxidized nose and is full-bodied with plenty of gutsy flavour and extract. To my way of thinking, the *joven*, however paradoxically, has less character: it is more neutral and inoffensive and would probably be deemed more acceptable internationally. The *tradicional*, on the other hand, might find little acceptance in the international market, yet within the region itself, it is probably the better wine to accompany its forthright and full-flavoured local foods.

The co-operative of Manjavacas also makes a good, fruity Zagarron *rosado joven* from Cencibel, Garnacha and Airén, as well as both *joven* and *tradicional* reds. The *tinto joven* is particularly supple and easy to drink.

Mota del Cuervo makes a good base to explore some of the so-called *lugares de La Mancha*, towns and sites that are mentioned in Spain's greatest picaresque novel, *The Adventures of Don Quixote*. Nearby El Toboso, for example, boasts the so-called '*Casa de Dulcinea*', a rather grand *casa solariega* which actually dates from a later period than Cervantes. It is worth visiting all the same to view a well-preserved example of a 17th-century manor house, complete with a home *bodega*, olive mill and enormous wine press still *in situ*. El Toboso also houses the *Centro Cervantino*, founded in 1926, with a rare collection of editions of *Don Quixote* in some 33 languages, many signed by world heads of state. From El Toboso, head next to Campo de Criptana, above which is a collection of well-preserved Manchegan windmills, some of them open to the public. Herencia is another typical *lugar de La Mancha* and also has a Manchegan dairy worth visiting for probably the best hand-made Manchego cheese you will ever eat (see below), while Puerto Lápice, back on the main Madrid–Seville road, claims the inn where Don Quixote had himself knighted by the innkeeper.

Perhaps rather surprisingly, given the fact that over 90% of the zone is planted with white grapes, La Mancha is today fast gaining something of a reputation for its red wines. Historically, the reason growers have preferred the white Airén grape over virtually all others has been its ability to give reasonable yields from a poor, dry terrain, up to three times as much per plant as from other varieties. However, now that improved winemaking techniques have led the way in opening new markets, the cultivation of lower-yielding but superior grapes is on the increase, particularly black grapes such as Cencibel.

Cencibel is another name for Spain's greatest native grape, known as Tempranillo in Rioja, Tinto Fino or Tinto del País in Ribera del Duero, Tinto del Toro in Zamora, and Ull de Llebre in Catalunya. In the far south of La Mancha, in the separate *denominación* of Valdepeñas, it excels marvellously, so it is perhaps natural that it is now being increasingly used throughout the La Mancha zone for soft, fruity *tintos jóvenes* as well as full-bodied *vinos de crianza* aged in oak casks.

One firm making excellent red wines is Fermin Ayuso Roig in Albacete, whose Estola Reserva and Gran Reserva wines, given lengthy ageing in both *barrica* and bottle, demonstrate considerable class and stature. Two other Manchegan *bodegas* producing good wines, both located in the wine town of Manzanares just on the border with the Valdepeñas vineyard, are Vinícola de Castilla, an impressive and super-modern installation formerly under the Rumasa umbrella producing Castillo de Alhambra wines, and the town's co-operative, Cooperativa del Campo Nuestro Padre Jesus del Perdón, whose tasty and inexpensive Yuntero white and red wines ably demonstrate what excellent value the wines of La Mancha can be. The long-established firm of Rodriguez y Berger, located in the small wine *pueblo* of Cinco Casas, has long supplied international markets with good value Manchegan wines, produced since 1983 by cold fermentation. While it still supplies European supermarkets and wine chains with products blended to suit their exact market requirements, its more characterful wines, Viña Santa Elena white and red, demonstrate La Mancha's future and its potential.

Valdepeñas

The Valdepeñas vineyard is a natural extension of the La Mancha *denominación*, located in the far south of the central Castilian *meseta* virtually on the slopes of the Sierra Morena leading up to the regional frontier with Andalucía. There is little apparent difference in the terrain save that it is slightly more undulating, the soil perhaps even poorer and stonier.

Yet for centuries Valdepeñas has enjoyed a special separate status, its wines singled out as pre-eminent and appreciated far and wide since even

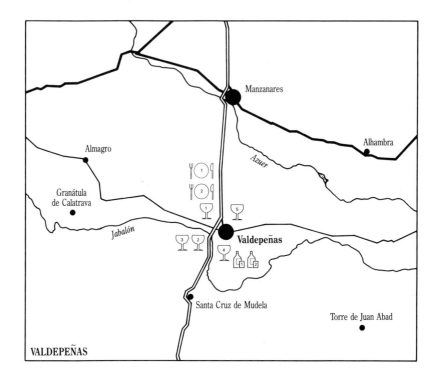

VALDEPEÑAS

the days of the Romans. It is a town that has always lived by and for its wine, and from as early as the sixteenth to nineteenth centuries it enjoyed something of a golden age, selling primarily red wines to the country's new capital in Madrid, 200 km to the north, to Andalucía, and to Spanish American countries such as Mexico, Venezuela, Puerto Rico and Argentina. When the new railway between Madrid and Seville was built in 1861, passing through Valdepeñas, it enabled the town's winegrowers to benefit further, and by 1895 a 'wine train' loaded with hundreds of goatskins of the local *clarete* was departing daily for the capital. Even today, many of the best bars in Madrid take it as something of a matter of pride that their house wine is a good Valdepeñas *clarete*.

Valdepeñas itself appears much less inviting from its industrial outskirts the rest of La Mancha, the Valdepeñas vineyard is predominantly planted with white Airén grapes. This may seem immediately paradoxical, but in fact the classic Valdepeñas *clarete*, though in appearance a light red wine, historically has been and continues to be made from up to 80% white grapes blended with the macerated juice from black grapes to gain its colour, traditionally stored if not fermented in earthenware *tinajas*, and usually drunk some time during the second year after its production.

Although there is still a considerable local taste for the 'stony' character that earthenware *tinajas* give to the wine of Valdepeñas, these remarkable receptacles are no longer quite so central to its production as they were in the past. *Tinajas* certainly remain in place in almost all of the town's numerous *bodegas* and co-operatives, but generally it is claimed that they are retained only for storage purposes. Certainly in the immense installations located on the outskirts of the town, gleaming stainless steel fermentation vats and gigantic steel outdoor deposits have all but replaced these charming though now antiquated vessels.

Valdepeñas wine today is produced in principally three distinct styles. As in the rest of La Mancha, there is a considerable vogue for the production of light, fruity new-style *vinos jóvenes*, made from grapes picked as early as a month before the main harvest. The white *vinos jóvenes* which make up the majority of such wines are usually cold fermented in stainless steel, and may be released as early as the December after the vintage. They should always be drunk as young as possible in order to enjoy their fleeting charms of freshness, fruity acidity and the delicate green apple aromas which the Airén at best can display. Red *vinos jóvenes*, unlike the traditional *claretes* or *tintos del año*, may be produced from 100% Cencibel grapes with no addition of Airén, macerated on the skins for a relatively short period of 48–50 hours, then fermented at controlled temperatures. Though these soft, fruity and supple wines are also best drunk when young and fresh, they certainly come to no harm if kept for upwards of a year.

Valdepeñas' standard *claretes* or *tintos del año* still form the backbone of the zone's production in terms of volume and such wines continue to slake an enormous national thirst. Indeed, mention Valdepeñas to a Spaniard and it is this type of wine that most readily comes to mind. For indeed, Valdepeñas *clarete* remains the archetypal Spanish wine with which to indulge in the nation's favourite custom, the *chateo*: pausing in one or a number of bars or *tascas* to meet friends, down a short *chato* (tumbler) or two of wine, and nibble on a tasty *tapa*. *Clarete* is an easy-to-drink red wine which is above all soft, fruity and quenching, not harsh or high in tannin, and so it is the preferred drink for this activity, a sort of Spanish equivalent of English 'session' bitters.

In recent years, however, Valdepeñas has attracted most attention internationally for its superb oak-aged Crianza, Reserva and Gran Reserva wines produced from 100% Cencibel grapes. These wines are not only fantastically rich in flavour and character, they are also very good value, certainly among the best wine buys that Spain has to offer today.

Cencibel, of course, is the local version of Tempranillo, the aristocratic grape of Rioja. However, it has been grown in Valdepeñas probably for centuries, and, on this high arid central *meseta* where the average altitude is 750 metres above sea level, it has taken on its own distinctly individual style. Though the stony terrain of Valdepeñas has an underlying bedrock of chalky clay, like the best parts of Rioja, the grapes naturally reach higher degrees of maturity here and give significantly lower yields in terms of quantity. Though the grapes are harvested earlier today than in the not so distant past, the wines of Valdepeñas are still generally richer in body, concentration and alcohol than their Rioja counterparts.

The practice of ageing in wood casks, one might consider, must be something of a novelty in this land of the *tinaja*. In fact we have been told that wines have been wood-aged in Valdepeñas since as long ago as the seventeenth and eighteenth centuries in the traditional *bocoy castellano* of 300–400 litres. Casks were probably also used to transport *clarete* to Madrid by the turn of the century, alongside the traditional goatskins. Be that as it may, Valdepeñas has only in the last two decades come on to the modern Spanish wine scene as the purveyor of such fine old wood-aged wines. However, the levels of investment in the town's major private wineries such as Bodegas Los Llanos and Bodegas Félix Solís clearly demonstrate the commitment to this important and already highly successful style of wine.

Los Llanos, for example, inaugurated an immense new *bodega* in 1981, excavated some 12 metres underground and with a capacity for 8000 American oak *barricas* of 225 litres (the company holds total stocks of 10,500 *barricas*, probably the largest quantity in any Spanish *bodega* outside Rioja). Indeed, today Reservas and Gran Reservas make up as much as 70% of the company's production. The Señorío de Los Llanos Gran Reserva 1983 is a superb example: voluptuous, full and warming, and particularly excellent with the lamb dishes of Castilla-La Mancha, or, perhaps best of all, simply with a wedge of grainy, aged Manchego cheese.

Bodegas Félix Solís is the region's leading exporter and the largest private *bodega* in Castilla-La Mancha. The company's principal winemaking installation, located along the main Madrid carriageway, is mind-boggling in its sheer scale, for it appears more like some sort of refinery than what we would consider a traditional producer of quality wines. The company's immense outdoor vats can hold 2½ million litres each, and its total capacity is some 40 million litres. This is winemaking on a colossal scale. Naturally,

gas Félix Solís, Valdepeñas.

the great majority of its wines are destined to be drunk without great fuss or pretension, from litre bottles or tetra-briks purchased at local supermarkets throughout Spain.

Yet notwithstanding its vast industrial size, Félix Solís, still a family company, maintains its old traditional *bodegas* in the heart of Valdepeñas, such as the beautiful Viña Albali *bodega* where wines are still stored in earthenware *tinajas* under charming hat-like covers made from straw. In addition to *tinajas*, this *bodega* also holds some 3500 *barricas* of the company's Viña Albali Reserva and Gran Reserva wines, which are among the most successful examples of the classic Valdepeñas wood-aged style. Viña Albali Reserva 1986 is a compact, concentrated wine, full of black fruit flavours, with a smooth, polished balance between sweet new oak and fresh primary fruit. Viña Albali Gran Reserva 1981 is deeper and more complex, with rich, figgy bottle nuances, and a long, smooth, concentrated finish that combines power and finesse.

Valdepeñas itself appears much less inviting from its industrial outskirts than it actually is. However, even if you are just passing through en route to the south, stop here all the same. The very entrance to the town is remarkable, the Avenida del Vino, lined with hundreds of earthenware *tinajas*, which leads to the heart of the old town itself. At the end of the Avenida there is an immense Manchegan windmill and a fascinating *Museo de los Molinos* which is open to the public. The centre of Valdepeñas is literally riddled with old *bodegas*, many of them still in use, providing local 'stony' *tinaja* wines for immediate consumption in the town's many welcoming bars. Even the town's civic museum has an old *bodega* in the basement.

The Plaza de España, as in all Spanish towns, is the central focus of life.

CASTILLA-LA MANCHA

Pleasantly arcaded, dominated by its surprisingly large cathedral notable for its octagonal belltower and open roof rafters, this is where the whole town turns out after the lengthy afternoon *siesta*. Even the fountain in the square is a winepress, worked haphazardly and in fits and starts by chubby infant cherubs. Stop here awhile and enjoy a glass of the good local wine at the Bar Penalty together with tasty hot *tapas*, or around the corner at the atmospheric Casa El Cojo.

The Valdepeñas *denominación* applies to grapes grown not only in the municipality of Valdepeñas, but also in a further nine communities located within the province of Ciudad Real, including Alhambra to the north-east, Granátula de Calatrava to the west, Santa Cruz de Mudela to the south, and La Torre de Juan Abad to the south-east. Though almost all the principal *bodegas* are located in Valdepeñas itself, it may be of interest to explore the wine country none the less, perhaps stopping just outside the zone in the lovely town of Almagro, the old university centre of La Mancha, which has a charming town square, one of the oldest working theatres in Europe (Corral de Comedías), and a most welcoming *parador* located in a sixteenth-century convent.

Other Manchegan Wine Zones

Castilla-La Mancha covers an immense superficial area and there are *bodegas* and *cooperativas* located throughout. However, as a wine region, it must be said that those companies currently producing wines of interest to the international consumer or wine traveller are still definitely few and far between.

Almansa is another of Castilla-La Mancha's *denominaciónes de origen*. The region may be of interest to wine travellers heading to Alicante or Murcia. Indeed, it is actually nearer in both proximity and in style of wine produced to the Levantine wine regions of Yecla and Jumilla than to La Mancha. The predominant grape grown is the black Monastrell in addition to Cencibel and Garnacha Tintorera. As in Yecla and Jumilla, much wine is produced with little more ambition than to supply anonymous blending wines to be sold in bulk. However, one private firm, Bodegas Piqueras, produces an excellent range of wines under the Castillo de Almansa label that are certainly worth sampling, while the town of Almansa itself is worth pausing in to visit its fine well-preserved medieval castle.

The *denominación* of Méntrida lies west of Madrid in the province of

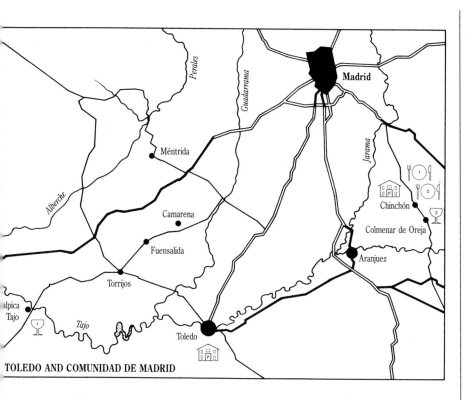

TOLEDO AND COMUNIDAD DE MADRID

Toledo. It too produces wines which on the whole never find their way into the bottle but are destined only for either bulk sales or distillation. However, Toledo's hinterland is the home of one of Spain's leading wine producers, Carlos Falcó, Marqués de Griñon, who has a family estate at Malpica de Tajo where he produces superlative Cabernet Sauvignon wines entitled only to the humble *vino de mesa* designation as well as top-quality white wines from Rueda.

The vast sprawl of hinterland that surrounds the nation's capital and makes up the Comunidad de Madrid falls outside the bounds of the autonomous region of Castilla-La Mancha, but large quantities of wine are made here which should at least be noted. This area has been granted the provisional *denominación de origen* Vinos de Madrid, an all-encompassing label for vineyards stretching all the way from the slopes below the Escorial south of the capital to Aranjuez. One notable town certainly worth visiting is Chinchón, famous not for its wines but for its anisette liqueur; the neighbouring *pueblo*, Colmenar de Oreja, produces some local wines of note.

CASTILLA-LA MANCHA

Bodegas: Stop to Taste; Stop to Buy

La Mancha

1

COOPERATIVA NUESTRA SEÑORA DE
   MANJAVACAS
CAMINO REAL 7
16630 MOTA DEL CUERVO
CUENCA
TEL: (967) 18 00 25; FAX: (967) 18 11 20

WINES PRODUCED: Zagarron
blanco, rosado y tinto jóvenes;
Sandogal *tinto;* Parra Verde *blanco,
rosado y tinto;* Hoja Blanca (*blanco
ecológico*).
VISITS: Mornings, by appointment.

Direct sales working hours.
This well-run co-operative has a
mixture of modern and old
installations, including more than
500 concrete *tinajas* still used for
fermentation, and is well worth
visiting to view the vast
winemaking facilities, and to
sample and purchase the new style
Zagarron *vinos jóvenes,* excellent
examples of their type.

2

FERMIN AYUSO ROIG
CALLE MIGUEL CARO 4
02600 VILLARROBLEDO
ALBACETE
TEL: (967) 14 04 58; FAX: (967) 14 49 25

WINES PRODUCED: Estola *blanco,*
Armiño *blanco;* Viña Q *blanco,
rosado y tinto;* Estola *tinto* Crianza,
Reserva, Gran Reserva.
VISITS: By appointment.

Villarrobledo was once the centre
of production for earthenware
tinajas and the town is still noted
for its ceramic ware, as well as for
its wines. Fermin Ayuso Roig is its
leading private producer and its
Estola Reserva and Gran Reserva
wines are particularly worth
sampling.
English spoken.

3

VINÍCOLA DE CASTILLA SA
POLÍGONO INDUSTRIAL, S/N
13200 MANZANARES
CIUDAD REAL
TEL: (926) 61 04 50; FAX: (926) 61 04 66

WINES PRODUCED: Castillo de
Alhambra *blanco, rosada y tinto;*
Señorío de Guadianeja *tinto*
Reserva, Gran Reserva.

VISITS: Mon–Fri, appointment
appreciated but not essential:
(winter) 8–14h; 15h30–18h;
(summer) 7h30–14h30.
Modern, large-scale winery
formerly part of the Rumasa group
producing a range of well-made
wines utilizing up-to-date
technologies. The Castillo de

Alhambra range of varietal wines (Garnacha, Cencibel and Airén) are good examples of the sound, value-for-money wines that La Mancha can provide, while the Señorío de Guadianeja Reserva and Gran Reserva wines, produced from both Cencibel and Cabernet Sauvignon, demonstrate remarkable quality and value. Manzanares is located 25 km north of Valdepeñas on the principal route to Madrid. English spoken.

---

4 COOPERATIVA DEL CAMPO NUESTRO PADRE JESUS DEL PERDÓN
POLÍGONO INDUSTRIAL
CTRA DE ALCÁZAR, S/N
13200 MANZANARES
CIUDAD REAL
TEL: (926) 61 03 09; FAX: (926) 61 05 16

WINES PRODUCED: Lazarillo *blanco y tinto*; Yuntero *blanco*, *rosado, tinto*; Yuntero *tinto* Crianza; Casa La Teja *tinto* Crianza.
VISITS: Weekdays, working hours.
Another of La Mancha's well-regarded co-operatives. Yuntero wines, especially the soft, fruity red produced from 100% Cencibel, have been well received in international markets.

---

5 RODRIGUEZ Y BERGER
PRINCIPAL 2
13720 CINCO CASAS
CIUDAD REAL
TEL: (926) 52 60 41; FAX: (926) 52 60 34

WINES PRODUCED: Gota de Oro *blanco*; Senescal *blanco, rosado, tinto*; Viña Santa Elena *blanco, rosado, tinto*.
VISITS: Mon–Fri, working hours.
This long-established company, founded in 1922, has supplied international markets for decades with millions of bottles of sound, good value Manchegan wine sold under a host of labels. Its Viña Santa Elena wines are modern examples from La Mancha, more than capable of standing on their own two feet. English spoken.

CASTILLA-LA MANCHA

Valdepeñas

Tinajas

Tinajas.

Tinajas are immense earthenware vessels usually some three metres in height, bulbous towards the top but tapering down to a narrow, pointed foot. They are propped up in the *bodega* most often by some form of wooden scaffolding which allows access to their top apertures, themselves covered with lazy-looking straw '*sombreros*'. A double row of these antiquated cool clay vessels is a remarkable sight, for it is one hardly changed since the days of the ancient Romans. Once utilized throughout central Spain, *tinajas* remain in use today in Valdepeñas, La Mancha, Montilla-Moriles, Extremadura and a few other isolated parts of the country only.

Of course, before the introduction of stainless steel or resin-lined concrete, wine was most usually fermented in vessels made of wood. But Spain's central *meseta* is noteworthy for its lack of afforestation, although there has always been a plentiful supply of clay. Villarrobledo was long the principal area for the production of *tinajas*. Not only was its own local clay ideal for their manufacture: the local potters had the generations-old skills to make such immense, one-piece vessels, as well as kilns large enough to hold them for firing.

Tinajas are no longer being manufactured today, but it is our belief, in spite of the fact that the best *bodegas* are doing away with them (witness the number lining Valdepeñas' Avenida del Vino), that they will remain in use for some years to come, not least because the people of Valdepeñas still love the unique 'stony' character that they impart to wines stored in them.

1 BODEGAS FÉLIX SOLÍS SA
CTRA N-IV MADRID–CÁDIZ, KM 199
13300 VALDEPEÑAS
CIUDAD REAL
TEL: (926) 32 24 00; FAX: (926) 32 24 17

WINES PRODUCED: 'Los Molinos'
blanco, rosado, tinto; Viña Albali
tinto Crianza, Reserva and Gran
Reserva.
VISITS: Mon–Fri 8–14h; 16–19h.
Sat 8–13h. Appointment not
essential.
Located just south of the town on the main Madrid–Cádiz route,
Bodegas Félix Solís is the leading
bottler in this important zone.
Though the main wine installation
is ultra-modern, visitors may be
able to visit the Viña Albali *bodega*
where traditional *tinajas* are still in
use, as well as thousands of
barricas for the production of the
superlative range of Viña Albali
Reserva and Gran Reserva wines.
English, French spoken.

---

2 BODEGAS LOS LLANOS
COSECHEROS ABASTECEDORES SA
CTRA N-IV MADRID–CÁDIZ, KM 200,5
13300 VALDEPEÑAS
CIUDAD REAL
TEL: (926) 32 03 00, 32 27 38;
    FAX: (926) 32 27 34

WINES PRODUCED: Armonioso
blanco joven; Torneo *tinto* Reserva;
Señorío de Los Llanos *tinto*
Reserva, Gran Reserva; Pata Negra
tinto Gran Reserva.
VISITS: By appointment. Direct
sales daily at the *bodega*.
One of the oldest *bodegas* in Valdepeñas, founded in 1875 by the
Caravantes family, whose wines
were exported to America more than
a hundred years ago. Today the
company has concentrated on the
production above all of fine
wood-aged wines intended for export
markets. Though the immense
outdoor vats that dominate the
bodega give an industrial look to
this vast winery, below ground there
are more than 10,000 *barricas* of
Reserva and Gran Reserva wines
patiently ageing.
English spoken.

---

3 LUIS MEGIA SA
SALIDA DEL PERAL 1
13300 VALDEPEÑAS
CIUDAD REAL
TEL: (926) 32 06 00; FAX: (926) 32 53 56

WINES PRODUCED: Islero *blanco*,
rosado, tinto jóvenes; Marqués de Gastañaga *blanco*; Luis Megía
tinto; Duque de Estrada *tinto*
Reserva, Gran Reserva.
VISITS: Mon–Fri 9–13h30;
15h30–19h. Appointment
necessary.
The third great company of

CASTILLA-LA MANCHA

Valdepeñas, today part Japanese owned, produces zesty *vinos jóvenes* as well as highly regarded *vinos de* *crianza* under the Duque de Estrada label.

English, French spoken.

---

4 BODEGA COOPERATIVA 'LA INVENCIBLE'
TORRECILLA 102
13300 VALDEPEÑAS
CIUDAD REAL
TEL: (926) 32 27 77

WINES PRODUCED: La Invencible *blanco, rosado, tinto*; Valdeazor *tinto*.
VISITS: Daily, working hours.
It may be worth seeking out Valdepeñas' best co-operative winery simply to view its immense lines of *tinajas* still in use.

---

5 BODEGA VEGA FRÍA
CRISTO 35
13300 VALDEPEÑAS
CIUDAD REAL
TEL: (926) 32 18 05; FAX: (926) 32 47 31

WINES PRODUCED: Vega Fría *tinto* Reserva.
VISITS: Mon–Fri, working hours.

One of the most interesting Valdepeñas wines we tasted comes from this small idiosyncratic private *bodega*, aged for lengthy periods not in wood but in *tinaja*, followed by lengthy time in bottle: immense, rustic and powerful.

Almansa

BODEGAS PIQUERAS SA
JUAN RAMÓN JIMÉNEZ 1 Y 3
02640 ALMANSA
ALBACETE
TEL: (967) 34 14 82; FAX: (967) 34 54 80

WINES PRODUCED: Castillo de Almansa *tinto* Reserva, Gran Reserva; Marius *tinto* Reserva.
VISITS: Mon–Fri 8–13h; 16–19h.
Almansa's leading private *bodega* is located within the city and is

renowned for its full-bodied Reserva and Gran Reserva wines. Almansa is a picturesque town with a fine medieval castle; visitors heading south from Madrid to Alicante or Murcia should stop here, if just to visit the castle, and taste and purchase good-value wood-aged reds to drink on the coast.
English, French spoken.

Toledo

Marqués de Griñon

Toledo's hinterland, like the rest of Castilla-La Mancha, is covered with vines, but it has long been considered a zone of bulk wines only. The Méntrida DO, for example, is a co-operative-led zone producing wines mainly destined for blending or distillation.

Carlos Falcó, Marqués de Griñon, studied agricultural economics at the University of California at Davis in the 1960s and on returning to his family estate at Malpica de Tajo, he eventually planted a vineyard with Cabernet Sauvignon. The results proved to be exceptional, and the wine was for some years produced for Falcó by Antonio Sanz in Rueda (Sanz also makes the Marqués de Griñon Rueda DO white wine). However, since 1989, a new well-equipped and computer-controlled *bodega* has been installed on the *finca* and all the red wines are now estate-bottled.

The Marqués de Griñon red wines are not entitled to a *denominación de origen*, so they are bottled as humble *vino de mesa tinto de Toledo*. This clearly has not harmed their considerable commercial success. Like Italy's super-Tuscan *vini da tavola*, wines made outside the limitations imposed by bureaucratic dictates, the Marqués de Griñon Cabernet Sauvignon manages to stand alongside the greatest wines of the country based purely and simply on its own excellence and on the high profile it has gained through the marketing acumen of its producer. This proves, as always, that the name and reputation of a producer is far more important to the consumer than a broad and general *denominación* on its own.

1

VIÑEDOS Y BODEGAS DE MALPICA
FINCA CASA DE VACAS
45692 MALPICA DE TAJO
TOLEDO
TEL: (925) 87 71 70
ADMINISTRATIVE ADDRESS: SERRANO 213, 28016 MADRID
TEL: (91) 458 17 08; FAX: (91) 457 75 93

WINES PRODUCED: Marqués de Griñon *blanco* Rueda DO; Marqués de Griñon Rueda Selección Especial (fermented and aged in new *barrica*); Marqués de Griñon *tinto* Cabernet Sauvignon.
VISITS: Afternoons, by appointment.
The Finca Casa de Vacas is located 50 km from Toledo and 110 km from Madrid.
English, French, Italian spoken.

Vinos de Madrid

2 BODEGAS JESUS DIAZ E HIJOS SA
CALLE CONVENTO 38
28380 COLMENAR DE OREJA
MADRID
TEL: (91) 894 32 43

WINES PRODUCED: Jesus Diaz e
Hijos *blanco, rosado y tinto*.
VISITS: Daily, working hours.
Tasty award-winning wines
produced in a quiet, typical wine
pueblo near Chinchón.

Chinchón Anisette

Chinchón is a charming little town located about 50 km south-east of Madrid. It is worth coming here simply to view its Plaza Mayor, one of the prettiest in Spain, surrounded by arcades and houses with wooden and iron-railed balconies. Each year, in July, August and October the Plaza is closed off and a series of highly regarded bullfights takes place as a benefit for a local hospice for the aged.

Throughout Spain, Chinchón is known for one thing: its famous anisette liqueur. Indeed, there may be as many as seven distilleries still producing this popular and potent anis-flavoured spirit, though the one located in the basement of the town's castle unfortunately is no longer functioning. Come here to linger over a memorable tumbler or two, turned milky by a cube of ice, at a balcony table on Chinchón's Plaza de España.

Restaurantes, Hoteles y Paradores

La Mancha

1 MESÓN DE DON QUIJOTE
CTRA MADRID–ALICANTE, KM 139
16630 MOTA DEL CUERVO
CUENCA
TEL: (967) 18 02 00

Atmospheric Manchegan roadside inn with a fine, open bar serving good hot *tapas* and local wines, as well as a decent restaurant noted for its authentic *cocina manchega*: *pisto manchego, judías con perdíz, sopa de ajo con huevo, perdices escabechadas*, washed down with the heady wines of Mota.
Inexpensive to Moderate

2 VENTA DEL QUIJOTE
EL MOLINO 4
CTRA DE ANDALUCÍA, KM 136
13650 PUERTO LÁPICE
CIUDAD REAL
TEL: (926) 57 61 10

Cervantes apparently actually stayed in this famous old *venta* and immortalized it for ever, for it was here that he had his great comic hero Don Quixote de la Mancha knighted by the innkeeper. This typical Manchegan roadside *venta*

is thus a true '*lugar de La Mancha*', atmospheric and still today as in the past serving the needs of travellers en route across the broad expanses of Castilla-La Mancha. Restaurant serves classic foods of central Spain: *migas de pastor, caldereta de cordero, pisto manchego, duelos y quebrantos, asadillo* and wines of La Mancha and Valdepeñas.
Inexpensive to Moderate

Valdepeñas

1 HOTEL MELIÁ EL HIDALGO
CTRA MADRID–CÁDIZ, KM 194
13300 VALDEPEÑAS
CIUDAD REAL
TEL: (926) 32 32 50; FAX: (926) 32 33 04

Well-equipped and conveniently-located motel with swimming pool just north of the wine town, set amidst the vineyards. The restaurant specializes in game in season.
Moderate

———

2 RESTAURANT 'LA AGUZADERA'
CTRA MADRID–CÁDIZ, KM 197
13300 VALDEPEÑAS
CIUDAD REAL
TEL: (926) 32 32 08

Located at the entrance to the town adjacent to the campsite, not far from the great *bodegas*, this simple

grill-restaurant is a winegrowers' favourite and serves the typical foods of La Mancha – *berenjenas de Almagro, asadillo, perdíz estofada, cordero asado* – together with a good selection of old Valdepeñas Reserva and Gran Reserva wines.
Inexpensive to Moderate

Paradores

P

PARADOR NACIONAL DE ALMAGRO
RONDA DE SAN FRANCISCO, S/N
13270 ALMAGRO
CIUDAD REAL
TEL: (926) 86 01 00; FAX: (926) 86 01 50

Located in the 16th-century
Antiguo Convento de San
Francisco, in the heart of this

atmospheric and fascinating
Manchegan town. Restaurant
serves good local foods –
*berenjenas de Almagro, pisto
manchego, magras con pisto* – and
local wines.
Moderate

P

PARADOR NACIONAL DE
    MANZANARES
CTRA MADRID–CÁDIZ, KM 175
13200 MANZANARES
CIUDAD REAL
TEL: (926) 61 04 00; FAX: (926) 61 09 35

Located about 25 km north of
Valdepeñas along the main road

from Madrid to Andalucía, this
parador is less atmospheric than
Almagro's, being housed in a
modern installation, but it is a
comfortable and convenient stop
none the less.
Moderate

Almansa

MESÓN PINCELÍN
LAS NORIAS 10
02640 ALMANSA
ALBACETE
TEL: (967) 34 00 07

Closed Mon.
Typical and well regarded

restaurant serving *comidas caseras*
and *platos típicos*, including
gazpacho manchego and *paletilla de
cabrito*, accompanied by the
full-bodied and forthright wines of
Almansa.
Inexpensive

Toledo

P

Parador

PARADOR NACIONAL CONDE DE
  ORGAZ
PASEO DE LOS CIGARRALES, S/N
45000 TOLEDO
TEL: (925) 22 18 50; FAX: (925) 22 51 66

Located outside the city, but offering sensational views over the Tajo gorge to Toledo reminiscent of the paintings of El Greco. Swimming pool and good restaurant serving specialities of Toledo: *perdices, pepitoria de gallina, mazapán.*
Expensive

Chinchón

1

MESÓN DE LA VIRREINA
PLAZA MAYOR 21
28370 CHINCHÓN
MADRID
TEL: (91) 894 00 15; 894 13 02

Sit on a wooden balcony overlooking Chinchón's lovely square while sipping an *anís de Chinchón*, then enjoy simple but well prepared Castilian foods: *chorizo asado, duelos y quebrantos, judías con chorizo, cochinillo, lechazo asado* and local wines.
Moderate

2

MESÓN CUEVAS DEL VINO
BENITO HORTELANO 13
28370 CHINCHÓN
MADRID
TEL: (91) 894 02 06

Installed in a vast, ancient *bodega* with beam press and *tinajas* still in place, this is today an atmospheric *mesón* with wood-fired ovens specializing in the roast meats of Castile: *cochinillo, cordero lechal asado, chorizo del mesón a la brasa.*
Moderate

CASTILLA-LA MANCHA

Parador

P

PARADOR NACIONAL DE CHINCHÓN
AVDA GENERALÍSIMO 1
28370 CHINCHÓN
MADRID
TEL: (91) 894 08 36; FAX: (91) 894 09 08

Lovely atmospheric *parador* located just off the Plaza Mayor, installed in the Augustinian convent of Chinchón, founded in the fifteenth century. Cool central patio and gardens, friendly bar with good *tapas* and *raciones*, and restaurant serving typical foods of the zone: *pincho de morcilla, lentejas guisadas con chorizo, chuletitas de cordero a la brasa* and the luscious *yemas de Chinchón*.
Moderate

Tomar Unas Copas: Stop for a Drink; Stop for a Bite

Valdepeñas

1

CAFE-BAR EL PENALTY
PLAZA DE ESPAÑA 2
13300 VALDEPEÑAS
CIUDAD REAL
TEL: (926) 32 15 15

On the main square, serving good *tapas calientes – morcillejas, chorizo, callos, setas, calamares* – together with quaffable Valdepeñas *clarete*.

2

CASA EL COJO
BALBUENA 2
13300 VALDEPEÑAS
CIUDAD REAL

Located just around the corner from the main square, this is a highly atmospheric old tavern serving excellent *tapas* and local wines.

Los Campings

La Mancha

CAMPING LA CELADILLA
CTRA DE LA MESAS, KM 4
EL PEDERNOSO
CUENCA
TEL: (967) 16 43 13

Open all year.
Near Mota del Cuervo.

Valdepeñas

CAMPING 'LA AGUZADERA'
CTRA MADRID–CÁDIZ, KM 197
13300 VALDEPEÑAS
CIUDAD REAL
TEL: (926) 32 32 08

Toledo

CAMPING EL GRECO   Open all year.
CTRA PUEBLA DE MONTALBÁN   Swimming pool.
45000 TOLEDO
TEL: (925) 22 00 90

Aranjuez

CAMPING SOTO DEL CASTILLO   Open all year.
CTRA DE ANDALUCÍA   Bourbon palace and convenient for
28300 ARANJUEZ   excursions to Chinchón.
MADRID
TEL: (91) 891 13 95

Compras Deliciosas: Stop to Taste; Stop to Buy

DULCINEA DE LA MOTA
CALLE CAMINO REAL 14
16630 MOTA DEL CUERVO
CUENCA
TEL: (967) 18 26 73

Good place to stop for provisions for
a classic Manchegan picnic to take
up to the windmills of Campo de
Criptana: bread cooked in a
wood-fired oven, *queso manchego*,
chewy air-cured *jamón serrano* and
wines from the local co-operative as
well as a good selection of old
Reservas from Fermin Ayuso Roig.

Queso Manchego

The semi-arid pastures of La Mancha are the habitat for a scraggy, tough
breed of sheep, the *manchega*, from whose rich, fatty milk since time
immemorial the shepherds have made one of the great cheeses of Spain,
if not the world, Manchego. Protected, like the country's finest wines, by a
denominación de origen granted in 1985, Manchego cheese is produced
only in the region of Castilla-La Mancha, from either pasteurized or raw

CASTILLA-LA MANCHA

ewe's milk from the *manchega* breed, according to strict guidelines and methods.

While there are immense large-scale dairies producing the cheese, we visited a small artisan *quesería* where Juan Moreno Manzanaro produces Manchego entirely from the unpasteurized milk of his own herd of 600 sheep. Each day of the year, seven days a week, he produces 18 to 20 hand-made cheeses weighing about 2½–3 kilograms each. The hard-pressed cheeses, recognizable by the characteristic zig-zag pattern left on the rind by *esparto*-mat binders, must age for a minimum of sixty days before they become *semi-curado* Manchego. The fully-cured *quesos viejos* of a year or older become hard and very full-flavoured, definitely piquant, with a long, savoury salty flavour. Manchego cheese accompanied by a glass of oak-aged Valdepeñas wine is undoubtedly one of the great food/wine combinations of Spain.

Juan Moreno Manzanaro, artisan-producer of Manchego cheese at his dairy in Herencia.

Hunt out this small dairy to see how authentic Manchego cheese is made, and to taste and to buy it at the source. Remember, though, that if you want to observe the cheesemaking process, work begins early in the morning and is usually finished by midday.

QUESERÍA DE JUAN MORENO
MANZANARO CORRALES
SANTIAGO 12
13640 HERENCIA
CIUDAD REAL
TEL: (926) 57 12 18; 57 11 99

Open daily, mornings.

¡Fiesta! Wine and Other Related Celebrations

end of Aug	Fiesta de la Vendimia	Tomelloso
1st week Sept	Fiesta del Vino	Valdepeñas
1st week Sept	Fiesta de la Vendimia	Socuéllamos, Toledo
last Sun in Oct	Día de la Rosa de Azafrán	Consuegra

Y para saber más Additional Information

Departamento de Turismo
Comunidad de Castilla-La
  Mancha
Palacio de Fuensalida
Plaza del Conde 2
45000 Toledo
tel: (925) 22 45 00

Consejo Regulador de Valdepeñas
Constitución 19
13300 Valdepeñas
Ciudad Real
tel: (926) 32 27 86;
fax: (926) 32 10 54

Consejo Regulador de La Mancha
Calle Canalejas 37
13600 Alcázar de San Juan
Ciudad Real
tel: (926) 54 15 23;
fax: (926) 54 65 39

Consejo Regulador de Almansa
Calle Méndez Nuñez 5
02640 Almansa
Albacete
tel: (967) 34 02 58

Consejo Regulador de Méntrida
Calle Ramón y Cajal 6
45510 Fuensalida
Toledo
tel: (925) 78 51 85

Consejo Regulador de Vinos de
  Madrid
Calle Bravo Murillo 101, 3°
28020 Madrid
tel: (91) 534 85 11

CASTILLA-LA MANCHA

CASTILLA Y LEÓN

Isabel la Católica, Medina del Campo.

Old Castile, the historic name for the modern autonomous region of Castilla y León, is the great Catholic heartland of Spain. As the Reconquest edged ever further south from Asturias, the capital of Christian Spain was established in León as early as 914, while a hundred years later the capital of the newly founded Kingdom of Castile was established at Burgos. Over the succeeding centuries, Castile and León spearheaded the expansion ever south, gradually and finally, through conquest and marriage, expelling the Moors and uniting for the first time the various kingdoms, principalities and provinces of the peninsula under a single banner.

A statue of Isabel la Católica stands in the vast, empty central Plaza de España of Medina del Campo, today a quiet town on the fringe of the Rueda vineyard, but in the fourteenth century one of the great trading centres of Europe, its fairs attracting foreign merchants in search of high-quality merino wool. It may have been here that Spain's greatest monarch passed from this world, but her spirit lives throughout the region even today. For Isabel of Castile together with her husband Ferdinand of Aragón oversaw a Golden Age when Spain not only consolidated her position in Europe (after centuries of domination by the Moors), but also dispatched those audacious sea voyages which were to culminate in the discovery and colonization of the New World.

Castilla y León, set on the high, lonely central *meseta* of the Iberian peninsula, embraces a full fifth of the Spanish mainland, and encloses within its bounds the great cities of the Spanish interior: Salamanca, León, Burgos, Valladolid, Segovia, Avila, Zamora. In a sense, the region embodies the very essence of Spain. This is the land of El Cid, Spain's greatest legendary hero. It is the region, too, where General Franco established his headquarters during the bitter years of the Civil War. The Spanish language itself is known in Spain as Castellano, the language of Castile, to distinguish it from Catalá, Gallego or Euskera, separate languages which were all officially banned under the dictatorship.

It is an uncompromising, staunchly conservative and severe region, its great cities separated by vast tracts of empty country. Villages are hard and crumbling, streets of limewashed adobe houses set under an unrelenting sun. Yet many of the region's unprepossessing, sun-scorched *pueblos* and towns played mighty parts in Spanish history. Tordesillas, for example, was where Portugal and Spain signed a treaty in 1494 dividing the New World – even those parts of it not yet discovered – between themselves on the basis of an arbitrary line drawn some 370 leagues west of the Cape

Orientation

Castilla y León is located north of Madrid and encompasses some of the country's most important and historic cities. There are nine provinces: Avila, Burgos, León, Palencia, Salamanca, Segovia, Soria, Valladolid and Zamora. Hemmed in by the mountains of the Sierra de Guadarrama and Sierra de Gredos to the south and the Cordillera Cantábrica to the north, the region is situated on Spain's vast central *meseta*. The landscape is thus harsh and austere, dominated by fortresses and castles that recall the Reconquest, and sparsely populated between its major provincial capitals. The principal wine zones are along or near the Duero river valley, Spain's most extensive and fertile basin which extends across the region into Portugal.

The region is best served by Madrid airport. All the provincial capitals can be reached from Madrid by rail and road. The principal NI motorway extends north to Burgos and beyond, while there are principal roads to Salamanca, Valladolid and León. For those arriving in Spain at the ferry port of Santander, the region can be easily dipped into en route to Madrid and the south. For exploration of the wine country, the use of a car is essential.

Maps: Michelin No. 442 (Northern & Central); Firestone Hispania C-2.

CASTILLA Y LEÓN

CASTILLA Y LEÓN

● Villafranca del Bierzo

León ●

EL BIERZO

Burgos ●

Pesquera de Duero

Aranda de Duero

Valladolid ●

Tordesillas

Duero

Portugal

Duero

Zamora ●

Toro ●

Rueda ●

Peñafiel ●

RIBERA DEL DUERO

TORO

● Medina del Campo

Nava del Rey

RUEDA

Salamanca ●

● Segovia

● Avila

Verde islands. At nearby Toro, the same two countries had previously fought a decisive battle over the succession to the Castilian throne, the Portuguese backing Juana la Beltraneja against the ultimately victorious Isabel and Ferdinand.

As a wine region, Castilla y León today ranks among Spain's greatest, the purveyor – this austere Catholic, nationalist heartland – of mighty wines that are similarly uncompromising. This is the home not only of Vega Sicilia, arguably Spain's greatest and certainly its most expensive wine, but also excellent white wines from Rueda as well as highly touted red wines from Ribera del Duero and from Toro. The best of these red wines are massively concentrated, packed with extract, colour and tannin; they are wines, one imagines, that the Cid himself would have enjoyed drinking, before setting out to storm an enemy fortress or to vanquish 10,000 Moors. They are wines that could only come from the harsh, austere and uncompromising landscape of the Spanish interior, the region of Castilla y León.

LOS VINOS: THE WINES OF CASTILLA Y LEÓN

Ribera del Duero DO Castilla y León's most famous wine region has risen from virtual obscurity in the last decade to the point where it is now considered one of the great wine regions of Spain. The delimited vineyard is large, extending for some 110 km from San Esteban de Gormaz in the east almost to Valladolid in the west, and encompassing vineyards in 6 municipalities in the province of Soria, 59 in Burgos, 5 in Segovia and 19 in Valladolid. The *denominación* applies only to red and *rosado* wines produced primarily from Tinto Fino (also known locally as Tinto del País), a sub-variety of Tempranillo; there are also smaller plantations of Garnacha, Cabernet Sauvignon, Malbec and Merlot (the last three grapes planted a century ago at Spain's most famous *bodega*, Vega Sicilia). The red wines of Ribera del Duero are noted foremost for their great capacity to improve with age, but there are attractive young wines being made in the region, too. Red wines must reach a minimum 11.2° alcohol; *rosado* wines 10.5°.

Rueda DO *Denominación* for light, pale white wines of excellent quality, as well as traditional sherry-like wines produced from delimited vineyards primarily in the south of the province of

Castles of Castile

More than anywhere else in Europe, Spain is a land of castles. The centuries-long struggles of conquest and reconquest meant that frontiers were constantly aligned and realigned, and scores of medieval castles were built to retreat into in times of need. Indeed, it is estimated that there were once some 10,000 castles throughout the nation, and of those that remain, many are located in Old Castile, the region whose name reflects the fact that historically it was a kingdom of fortifications.

The castles of Castile on the whole even *look* like every schoolboy's image of a medieval military fortification. Segovia's Alcázar, though somewhat overzealously reconstructed and restored in the nineteenth century, is a magnificent, soaring evocation of chivalry and romance. At Medina del Campo, once one of the most important market towns in Europe, the immense, moated brick castle where Isabel la Católica lived for some years before her death is a fine example of the *mudéjar* style. Our favourite castle in Castilla y León, however, is that of Peñafiel, located in the heart of the Ribera del Duero wine region. The great ship-like structure, strikingly built out of the region's soft white tufa stone, with its turrets and crenellated walls, dominates a narrow ridge overlooking the great Duero river valley.

Peñafiel.

Many towns and *pueblos* of Old Castile are not merely dominated by their castles, but are actually located within extensive fortified enclosures and old town walls that served, in times of attack, to protect their inhabitants. Avila is as famous for its old town ramparts as it is for Saint Teresa. Zamora, town of beautiful Romanesque churches, still has the remains of its stout castle and town walls intact. Other notable castles along the Duero valley wine country include those at Berlanga de Duero, Gormaz, El Burgo de Osma and Peñaranda de Duero.

Valladolid, as well as in tiny areas of Segovia and Avila. Grape varieties are Verdejo and Viura for young, fruity light table wines and Palomino for traditional *vinos generosos*. Four types of wine are elaborated: Rueda (produced with a minimum of 25% Verdejo) and Rueda Superior (minimum 60% Verdejo), minimum alcohol for both 11.5–14°; Rueda Pálido (pale dry sherry-type wine produced under a veil of *flor*, minimum alcohol 15°); and Rueda Dorado (dark, oxidized dry or sweet *vino generoso*, minimum alcohol 15°).

Attractive and well-made sparkling wines (*vinos espumosos*) produced by the classic method of secondary fermentation in the bottle are being produced in the zone from the characterful Verdejo grape, and it is anticipated by the Consejo Regulador that such wines may soon be included under the *denominación*. There are also experimental plantations of Sauvignon Blanc that have

produced excellent results and which also may soon be authorized.

Toro DO   Demarcated region located primarily in the province of Zamora around the medieval town of Toro for the production of red wines of immense power and strength (12.5–15° alcohol) from the Tinto de Toro grape, a sub-variety of Tempranillo which has been planted in the zone for centuries, as well as lesser amounts of white wines (primarily from Malvasia; 11–13°) and *rosados* (from Tinto del Toro and Garnacha; 11–14°).

El Bierzo DO   Somewhat remote and little-known demarcated vineyard located in the far west of the province of León, adjacent to the regional frontier with Galicia, for the production of white, *rosado* and red wines. Principal grapes include Doña Blanca, Godello, Malvasia and Palomino for white wines and Mencía and Garnacha Tintorera for red wines and *rosados.* White wines must reach 10–13° alcohol; *rosados* and reds, 11–14°.

Cigales DO Small zone located north of Valladolid noted primarily for its excellent *rosados*, light red *claretes* and robust red wines produced primarily from Tinto Fino with some Garnacha. Traditionally the *rosados* of Cigales spend some time maturing in wood, though today's taste is for lighter, fruitier wines.

Cebreros Vineyard zone adjacent to La Mancha in the far south of the region below Avila: principal grape varieties are Garnacha for the *tintos* and Albillo for the *blancos.* The zone is noted foremost for its heady reds which reach alcohol levels of 14–17°.

Benavente Traditional wine zone located in the north of the province of Zamora, most famous for its scores of peasant *bodegas* producing light, slightly fizzy *vinos de aguja*, primarily *claretes* from a variety of mixed black and white grapes, including Mencía, Garnacha, Palomino and Malvasia.

LA GASTRONOMÍA: FOODS OF CASTILLA Y LEÓN

Castilla León is so hard, so massive, so blunt. Its towns are nothing if not solid, timeless, enduring. The gastronomy of the region presents, not surprisingly, a similar uncompromising character. The favourite start to a meal is *sopa de ajo*, little more than hot water poured over stale, dried bread, fried (even slightly burnt) garlic, *pimentón* and a few cubes of chewy *jamón serrano.* If times are good, an egg might be broken into the mixture. *Bacalao al ajoarriero* is another typical and strongly flavoured dish, the old muleteers' favourite of salt cod stewed with dried peppers and garlic. The most popular and prevalent meal of the Duero valley is simply *lechazo, lechuga y vino* – lamb cooked in a wood-fired oven, salad and a clay *jarra* of wine. What more do you need, *hombre*? Perhaps a few thick slices of *jamón serrano*, carved off with a knife, black, tough and chewy. Or a wedge of well-cured ewe's milk cheese, hard, almost, as a rock, but full of grainy, strong flavour.

And the bread: indeed, nowhere else in Spain makes such fine breads. This, after all, is Spain's greatest area of wheat cultivation, and the region is known as '*tierra de pan*'. The round loaf, *torta de pan*, is particularly excellent: with a golden-yellow, smooth, hard crust, and an inside that is dense, soft and delicious. *Torta de azeite*, with its shiny, oil-washed crust, is another favourite.

If its foods are simple, robust, direct, they are ably partnered by a range of wines which is on the whole equally forthright and probably unrivalled anywhere in Spain for diversity of styles and types: soft, creamy whites and superb sparkling wines from Rueda; exquisite *rosados* from Cigales and Ribera del Duero; dense inky *tintos jóvenes* and elegant, wood-aged Reservas and Gran Reservas from Ribera del Duero; rustic *tintos* from Valladolid and Rueda; immense, powerful *caldos* from Toro; even dry and sweet fortified *vinos generosos* from Rueda and La Nava.

¡Que aproveche! Regional Specialities of Castilla y León

Sopa de ajo; sopa castellana
Typical soup made with hot water, garlic, *pimentón*, bread and sometimes a poached egg.

Bacalao al ajoarriero   Dried salt cod prepared with garlic and dried red peppers, in the style of the old muledrivers of León. This dish has become popular throughout the country.

Cabrito asado   Roast kid.

Chanfaina salmantina
Salamancan fricassée made with rice, chicken giblets, lamb sweetbreads and *chorizo*.

Cochinillo asado   Roast sucking pig, cooked until extremely tender and melting (it should be so tender that it can be cut into portions with the edge of a plate). Speciality of Segovia, but found throughout the region. Also known as *tostón*.

Lechazo; cordero lechal   Young milk-fed baby lamb. **Lechazo asado**   Baby lamb cooked in a wood-fired bread oven.

Olla podrida   Classic one-pot meal containing a combination of ham, bacon, beef or chicken, together with chickpeas, cabbage, tomatoes, garlic and onions.

Ropa vieja   Traditional Castilian dish made with left-over meat and vegetables, cooked in a *sofrito*.

Yemas   Sugar and egg yolk sweets, traditionally made by nuns. The most famous come from Avila, city of Saint Teresa.

Cheeses: *Queso de Burgos* Creamy, cured ewe's milk cheese from Burgos. *Queso de Zamora* Notable local cheese made either from pure ewe's milk, or from a mixture of ewe's and cow's milk.

CASTILLA Y LEÓN

Hornos de Asar: The Great Roasting Ovens of Castilla y León

Nothing is more typical of Castilla y León than its great *hornos de asar* – wood-fired brick bakers' ovens found in roadside inns or town- or city-centre taverns for the succulent preparation of roast *cochinillo* (sucking pig), *lechazo* (milk-fed baby lamb), or *cabrito* (kid). These establishments range from the flamboyant and famous, such as Segovia's Mesón de Cándido, an actual declared National Monument, to simple, basic eating houses, like Casa Corrales in Aranda de Duero, where you pass the baker's oven on your way upstairs to eat an unchanging menu of *lechazo*, salad, bread and wine at simple, scrubbed, wooden trestles.

Mesón de Cándido, Segovia.

The provinces of Segovia and Avila are the home foremost for *cochinillo* or *tostón*, a new-born sucking pig that weighs no more than 3 or 4 kilograms. So succulent and tender does the meat emerge from the oven that it is traditionally sliced with the edge of a dinner plate. The provinces of Valladolid, Soria and Burgos, and especially the town of Aranda de Duero, on the other hand, are considered the premier zone for one of Spain's greatest national dishes, *lechazo asado*. The baby lamb, cooked simply in an earthenware *cazuela*, flavoured only with thyme, garlic, wine and salt, is simplicity itself; yet served with a bottle of one of the great wines of Ribera del Duero this is one of the classic food/wine combinations of Spain.

No visitor driving south to Madrid should miss the opportunity to stop for lunch in any number of these great Spanish institutions.

THE WINE ROADS OF THE DUERO VALLEY

In Brief: The Duero river valley is central Spain's natural river basin, and, together with the Ebro, its most important single valley vineyard.

This is not one but at least three major wine regions (and a few minor ones as well), which have all emerged from obscurity only in the last decades and are now considered among the foremost in Spain.

Ribera del Duero currently produces some of Spain's most sought-after and expensive red wines. The best centre for exploring this important 110 km-long region is Aranda de Duero, though the wine country can also easily be dipped into from Valladolid to the west.

Rueda, located south-west of Valladolid, is today considered the source of some of Spain's best dry white table wines. In truth, the wine country is dreary, but it can be explored from the charming and historic town of Tordesillas, or else dipped into en route south to Salamanca.

Toro is a fine historic town in its own right, and the source of powerful red wines that have received favourable attention in recent years. The vineyard can be explored en route to Zamora, one of Castilla y León's most charming provincial capitals.

Ribera del Duero

Castilla y León's premier wine region, Ribera del Duero, has shot into the world's limelight from virtually nowhere in only the last ten years or so. Admittedly, this is the home of Vega Sicilia, the most famous of all Spanish wine estates, whose Unico wines are considered by many to be the nation's finest and certainly its most expensive and prestigious. Yet for well over a century this famous and idiosyncratic estate has stood in splendid isolation, alone on the high Castilian *meseta* by the banks of the Duero river, with hardly any neighbours, let alone rivals.

Today Vega Sicilia still has few rivals, not here nor anywhere else in Spain for that matter. Its Unico wines are produced from a blend of French and native grapes: Cabernet Sauvignon, Merlot, Malbec and Tinto Fino. Low yields, high altitude, extremes in temperature, high fixed acid levels and a ruthless selection both in the vineyard and in the *bodega* results, in the best years, in rare, concentrated wines of immense power and breed which cannot be compared to any others in the world simply because nowhere else that we know of submits its wines to such an unusual and

CASTILLA Y LEÓN

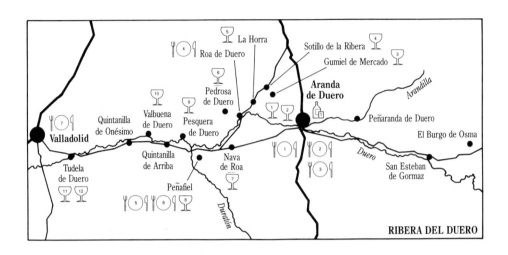

lengthy ageing discipline, first in large wooden vats, followed by upwards of decades in new and old 225-litre oak *barricas*. The result is wines of almost unbelievable concentration and intensity, comparable in weight to nothing so much as fine vintage port (produced, after all, further down the same river valley), and with hosts of rich and complex flavours, aromas and associations. Unico can be made only in those years when it is deemed that the wines will be able to support such lengthy wood ageing. Otherwise, compact, concentrated wines under the Valbuena label are produced; they are superlative in their own right, not lesser or second-label Vega Sicilia in any sense. But they are not Unico.

As recently as a decade ago, the only other wine producer of note in the region was the co-operative *bodega* of Peñafiel, which, in cellars underneath that town's splendid Moorish castle, has since the 1920s been producing and bottling wines that have gained both awards and international attention, most notably the immense blockbuster known as Protos.

Elsewhere, small winegrowers continued to grow grapes and produce large quantities of wine, as evidenced by the *zarceras de bodegas* – chimney-like ventilation stacks poking out of the brown earth above virtually every village in the wine zone. The wines were either made in such primitive home *bodegas* as they had been for centuries, or more often, after the creation of the village co-operatives in the decades following the 1940s, the grapes were sold to those great industrial grape processors which, with the notable exception of Peñafiel, usually sold the resulting wines in bulk for blending.

Yet in recent years especially, particularly since the granting of the *deno-*

minación de origen in 1982, the expansion and levels of investment in the zone have been rapid in the extreme. New generations of local winegrowers have recognized their region's potential to make great wines. Dissatisfied with the mentality of the co-operatives, they have set their sights much higher, and have invested in new *bodegas* and modern winemaking installations. Already a finely-tuned marketing expertise has emerged, as the region's best wines now rank alongside the finest in the country, and command prices to match. Success breeds success and new proprietors from outside the region have entered the fray, purchased properties and land, and invested in modern winemaking installations, while even the region's co-operatives are finally catching up too, modernizing their facilities and producing wines to sell in bottle, not bulk. There are now more than 30 producers marketing their wines under the Ribera del Duero DO and it is probable that this number will greatly increase over the next years and decades.

To understand how rapid the rise has been from virtual obscurity, it is only necessary to visit the *bodegas* of Alejandro Fernández, whose wine, Pesquera, is considered one of the region's – indeed the country's – finest and which has gained a considerable international profile.

Alejandro Fernández and his family are natives of the unassuming and undistinguished *pueblo* of Pesquera de Duero. He only began to make wine in 1972, originally both for his own consumption and to sell to some of his *amigos*. Indeed, he produced those early vintages in a village peasant *bodega* adjacent to the modern one that has since been built. The wines were fermented in the timeless traditional manner, on the stalks and skins in a primitive open-topped stone *lagar*. After the wine had macerated for a sufficient period, the *orujo* – grape skins and stalks – was pressed utilizing an ancient wooden beam press, an antique piece of equipment that was still in use by Fernández as recently as 1982.

Fernández, apparently, always knew what style of wine he wished to produce – immensely structured, rich in tannin and suitable for lengthy conservation – and the wines were immediately successful locally. He liked them himself, anyway, though naturally those early vintages had something of a rustic character; fermented on the stalks, they were undoubtedly bitter and tannic, yet they already clearly demonstrated the remarkable potential of the fruit, and were robust, manly wines in the style that Pesquera still maintains. In 1982 Fernández modernized his installations. Little by little, and with no marketing or any publicity whatsoever, the wine has gained an immense following, simply by word of mouth.

Today, a mere decade later, Alejandro Fernández's Pesquera wines have achieved international fame if not stardom, and the newly constructed *bodega* holds stainless steel fermentation vats and row after row of new American oak *barricas*. About 250,000–300,000 bottles are produced each year, and such is the remarkable clamour for the wine that most of this is pre-sold even before it is bottled. The original 65-hectare vineyard at Pesquera de Duero, planted exclusively with Tinto Fino, has been supplemented with a further 100 hectares at Roa, though whether this will be used to expand production of Pesquera, or to produce a new and separate wine, has not yet been decided.

I talked to Señora Fernández about their rapid success (her husband was unavailable, having jetted to the States to present the new vintage), and she seemed remarkably unsurprised by all that had happened.

'The wines of Pesquera de Duero,' she explained, 'have always had much fame. In the past, before the days of truck transport, the *arrieros* of León would come here to buy wine in *pellejos de cabra* – whole goatskins – both to sell to local *posadas* and *ventas* and to transport by mule train to the north of Spain. Our wines of Pesquera de Duero were always considered excellent and in great demand, but because they were made in a primitive manner, they never lasted much more than a year. Today we are taking the same excellent fruit and utilizing modern methods to produce a great wine.'

Pesquera is a great wine. What stands out foremost in a tasting of recent vintages is its sheer concentration of fruit and extract. An unlabelled 1986 bottle destined to be a Reserva or possibly a Gran Reserva tasted at the *bodega* displayed a deep purple youthful robe and an intense, silky, voluptuous bouquet of new oak and ripe blackberry fruit. In the mouth it was undoubtedly rich in tannin and extract, yet the tannins were not overly aggressive: it was the lingering, almost sweet concentration of fruit that was most memorable. This is clearly a great wine, and one that will benefit from further bottle ageing for upwards of a decade.

Pesquera is produced entirely from Tinto Fino, the great grape of the Duero valley, also known locally as Tinto del País; it is a sub-variety of the Tempranillo of Rioja which has adapted itself to these very different microclimatic conditions over the decades and centuries. The *Estación y Bodega Experimental de Pedrosa* is currently undertaking experiments to verify whether this is indeed the case by planting Tempranillo alongside Tinto Fino to see if the former acquires the local characteristics of the latter. Be that as it may, what is certain is that this noble variety, when grown on the high Castilian *meseta*, produces grapes that are unique to the Ribera del Duero vineyard.

Altitude certainly plays a great part in this. Though the vast central *meseta* appears flat and in part featureless, the wine country lies at a dizzyingly high altitude, upwards of 800 metres above sea level. Thus, on a baking hot end of May day in Aranda de Duero, for example, you may look across to the nearby Sierra de Niela mountains which are still covered in snow. And in midsummer, though it may be hellishly hot by day – 35°C or more – by night the temperatures may plunge to a chilly 6–8°C. These immense fluctuations contribute greatly to the aromatic qualities and fruity acidity of grapes grown in this rarefied atmosphere.

Moreover, though the soil here is similar to parts of the Rioja, consisting primarily of light, chalky clay, yields per hectare are generally considerably lower. Much of the delimited vineyard is still planted with large amounts of extremely old vines yielding tiny quantities of concentrated and high-quality fruit. Another notable feature of the Tinto Fino as grown in Ribera del Duero is its considerably high level of acidity, a factor that makes the wines of the zone ideal for lengthy *crianza* in wood. Tempranillo in Rioja, on the other hand, generally lacks acidity, one reason why it must be blended with Mazuelo and other grapes.

Though Pesquera was always famous for its *tintos* produced entirely from black grapes, further east, particularly around Aranda and its surrounding *pueblos*, both black Tinto Fino and smaller amounts of the steely white Albillo grape were traditionally cultivated and harvested together to produce a robust dark-pink *clarete*. Such wines are still much favoured locally, and it is usually the *claretes* which are most enjoyed here together with a midday lunch of *lechazo asado* in any of the zone's superlative *hornos de asar*.

Aranda de Duero is certainly the place to come to try this sensational Castilian speciality. There are literally scores of such typical restaurants all serving excellent food (we recommend three but there are many more, all, we imagine, excellent). The town is noteworthy, too, as the centre for the wine zone, and some of its best *bodegas* lie nearby in outlying *pueblos*. As it is virtually on the main north–south route about 75 km south of Burgos, we strongly advise that no wine lover or wine traveller should miss stopping here.

Aranda may prove to be something of a holiday destination in its own right. Isabel la Católica, after all, used to come here as a summer retreat, so the townsfolk claim proudly, as if it happened only yesterday, not 500 years ago. Certainly it is a pleasant enough place, a typical Castilian town,

CASTILLA Y LEÓN

Aranda de Duero.

and the best base for exploration of the wine zone. The town has a couple of notable churches, a fine park on its outskirts – particularly lively on Sundays – and an interesting old quarter riddled with underground *bodegas*. Come here simply to wander for an hour or two, stop for a glass of wine and *tapas* or for a lamb lunch, then strike out into the wine country.

East of Aranda, the delimited Ribera del Duero wine zone extends as far as El Burgo de Osma, notable for its surprisingly large and ornate baroque cathedral, and includes such other typical Castilian towns as Peñaranda de Duero, with its characteristic Plaza Mayor, and wine *pueblos* like San Esteban de Gormaz, which has a fine castle and some notable Romanesque architecture. The heart of the wine country, though, extends west, from around Aranda de Duero to as far as Tudela de Duero, almost on the outskirts of Valladolid.

Aranda de Duero itself is the home of the prestigious Bodegas Peñalba Lopez, whose Finca Torremilanos, located just outside the town, was one of the earliest estates to begin the production of fine oak-aged wines. The estate was actually founded as long ago as 1903, but the new modern winery was built in the mid-1980s. Today the Torremilanos range of wines includes the typical *clarete* much loved in the zone; fresh and vivid *tinto del año*; and Crianza, Reserva and Reserva Especial wines that demonstrate the concentration and maturity of the region's best aged red wines.

The historic centre of Aranda is riddled with deep underground *bodegas*, but most of these were abandoned when the town's co-operative, the Bodega Cooperativa Virgen de Las Viñas, was founded. Today many of these atmospheric old caves have been restored by the town's *peñas*, and serve as gathering places for like-minded *amigos* to get together to drink, eat snacks, sing and drink even more. These days, however, the wine stored in the *bodegas* is usually purchased from the co-operative in either barrels or *garrafas* (16-litre demi-johns). The Tierra de Aranda wines of Aranda's co-operative, while not overly exciting or exceptional, are well made and sound.

From Aranda, strike out into the wine country. Leave the town on the C619 road to Palencia, then, after about 18 km, find the small road right to Gumiel de Mercado. As you approach this wholly unassuming Castilian *pueblo*, you will probably pass through more fields of wheat than vines, yet this is a notable wine community none the less. Gumiel is little more than a clutch of stone and adobe houses dominated by its church. But above the town, leading up to the top of the hill that it is built around, there are literally scores of characteristic ventilation stacks, indicating a substantial warren of small private underground *bodegas* that have for centuries served as the store for the wines of the community.

Today the wine industry has been revitalized through the establishment of an important private winery, Bodegas Valduero. In this quiet and unremarkable *pueblo*, this young, go-ahead company has brought in outside engineering expertise to enlarge its underground storage facilities, linking up old hand-dug peasant *bodegas* and, with mining technology from Asturias, excavating new galleries 16 metres underground to serve as the store for up to 3000 *barricas* for the ageing of Crianza, Reserva and Gran Reserva wines.

Bodegas Valduero has about 70 hectares of its own vineyards, planted primarily in Gumiel de Mercado and its environs, and it supplements its requirements through the purchase of grapes mainly from small local farmers with mixed holdings. The bulk of the vineyard is planted with Tinto Fino, but there are also significant plantations of Albillo, the traditional white grape of the zone.

The Ribera del Duero *denominación* does not at present allow for the production of white wines, only *rosados* and reds. None the less, Bodegas Valduero produces an excellent white wine from Albillo that is extremely fresh, crisp, even tart, a sort of Spanish Gros Plant which would, we imagine, be excellent with coastal shellfish. Albillo also finds its way into

Valduero's *rosado*, for this is produced in the classic traditional *clarete* manner, that is, by harvesting Tinto Fino and Albillo grapes together (in proportions of about 70:30), pressing the grapes together, and leaving them in contact with the skin for a period of about 6–8 hours. Only the free run must is utilized, and the result is a very fresh *rosado*, high in acid yet full-bodied and well-structured.

The range of Valduero reds demonstrates the various styles of red wine produced in Ribera del Duero. I particularly like the zone's *tinto joven* wines for they are generally rich in fruit and colour, yet have a sufficient bite of acidity that makes them slightly astringent and refreshing in the mouth, while a relatively high glycerine content rounds off any sharp edges: as such they are excellent accompaniments to slightly fatty foods such as the classic roast lamb. While even the young wines have plenty of fruity acidity, those with markedly higher levels are ideal for lengthy *crianza* in both wood and bottle. The resulting Crianza, Reserva and Gran Reserva wines are capable of lengthy conservation, and indeed may positively need considerable time to soften and develop; on the other hand, if sampled before fully mature, they may reveal a character that is far leaner than, for example, the fleshier, more immediately appealing wines of a zone like the Rioja Alavesa. Indeed, it may not be wholly fanciful to suggest, in this great bastion of the monarchy, that the wines of Ribera del Duero, with their concentration of colour, acid and tannin, may be more suited to austere nationalist tastes than the essentially republican wines of Rioja which are so easily and unstintingly appreciated by all and sundry.

From Gumiel, continue a tour through the wine country, passing through such quiet but characteristic wine *pueblos* as Sotillo de la Ribera (Bodegas Ismael Arroyo), La Horra (Bodegas Balbas), Roa de Duero (Cooperativa Virgen de la Vega), and Pedrosa de Duero. Pedrosa is where the Consejo Regulador has its experimental vineyards and *bodega* and undertakes much critical research for the development of vines and wines. This small *pueblo* of only about 200 inhabitants is also the home of Bodegas Hermanos Pérez Pascuas, run by the brothers Benjamin, Manuel and Adolfo. The Pérez Pascuas family has always cultivated vines and indeed the brothers' grandfather was a leading figure in the local wine scene and was instrumental in the founding of the co-operative at Roa. While previous generations may have been content to sell their grapes to the co-operatives that they themselves had helped establish, when the brothers took over running the family business they immediately set their sights considerably higher.

'The problem with co-operatives,' explained Manuel, 'is quite simply that they have not been able to commercialize the wines of the zone as they deserve to be. They have not been able to fully realize the potential of our fruit to make great wine.'

The original family *bodegas* by their house in Pedrosa remain, but the Pérez Pascuas brothers are now putting the finishing touches to a brand new winemaking installation on the edge of the village. Looking at the rows of stainless steel fermentation tanks and the striking *bodega de crianza*, constructed with Moorish-inspired arches and filled with new American oak *barricas*, it is awesome to contemplate how quickly and surely the zone has picked itself up from virtual obscurity and catapulted itself into the world's limelight. The jump from selling fruit to co-operatives to producing wines recognized as potentially world class has been achieved in little more than a decade and should inspire winegrowers throughout Spain.

From Pedrosa, return to Roa, then find the small back lanes that lead eventually down to Peñafiel. Peñafiel is the most striking and atmospheric of all the wine towns of the Ribera del Duero, and should not be missed. Its castle is one of the great medieval fortresses of central Spain and is definitely worth a visit, even though its interior is mainly dilapidated and abandoned. The wine lover will also wish to visit the great *bodegas* of the Cooperativa Ribera del Duero which are hollowed out of the very heart of the hill upon which the castle rests, and which are a depository for one of the region's legendary wines, Protos. Produced only in the best years, always from a selection of its members' oldest vines, this is a massive, dense, powerful wine, aged usually for at least three years in wood and three years in bottle before release. The co-operative also produces excellent Peñafiel Reserva and Ribera Duero Crianza wines, but one of my favourites is its basic and excellent value Ribera Duero *tinto joven*. This vivid and well-focused wine is produced, like the others, entirely from Tinto Fino, and again demonstrates the prime quality and concentration of the region's fruit.

Peñafiel itself is a charming if somewhat crumbling old town, brooding beneath its castle, seemingly half-abandoned, yet still strongly Castilian in character. Search out the shabby old Plaza del Coso and explore the atmospheric *barrio de la judería* which leads up towards the castle, then settle into one of the town's excellent restaurants for a meal of, what else, lamb, bread and tasty local wine. Or else follow your nose to any of a number of traditional *panaderías* making good round Castilian breads, purchase some chewy *jamón* and local cheese, and a bottle of wine from the co-operative, and settle in at the pleasant picnic area on the road up to the castle.

From Peñafiel, cross the river to visit Pesquera de Duero and the *bodegas* of Alejandro Fernández, then return to the south bank and continue towards Valladolid on the main N122 road. The great Vega Sicilia is located along this road opposite Valbuena de Duero, though unfortunately it is not open for visits. The wines are not even available for sale at the estate: so great is the world demand for this unique wine that it is rationed out in miserly quantities – not even the King of Spain, it is said, may necessarily receive his full quota. The Ribera del Duero wine region continues on towards Valladolid through typical wine towns such as Quintanilla de Arriba and Quintanilla de Onésimo (Bodegas Mauro), ending finally at Tudela de Duero.

Rueda

Rueda, the delimited vineyard located south of Valladolid and famous for its creamy, fresh white table wines, is, I am sorry to say, quite the least obviously charming wine zone we have ever visited. The wine country, set high on the wide Castilian *meseta*, is flat and totally uninteresting; the climate is hellishly hot in summer and freezing in winter; the villages on the whole are dull and uninviting (with the exception of Tordesillas), with little to offer the visitor but their undeniable and unmistakable *casticismo* – their hard but wholly authentic Castilian character. It is difficult even to find many vines, for the land is dominated above all by endless, soul-numbing stretches of wheat.

Rueda itself is a one-street town on the main Madrid–La Coruña road, and probably used to be a minor rest halt for the numerous lorries that ply this route, a place to stop and quench the thirst which driving on these long, dusty roads inevitably works up. But now a dual carriageway by-pass has been built, depriving the town of even such passing trade. The town itself seems virtually moribund, and its great baroque church is an apparent anachronism – how could this dull and crumbling *pueblo* ever have supported such a bombastic edifice?

The answer, here and in the surrounding villages and communities of this remarkable wine zone, lies deep underground. In spite of its interminable flatness and its crumbling dilapidation, Rueda sits on a secret warren of underground *bodegas*, carved deep out of the limestone bedrock, and dating back in some cases to the fourteenth century or earlier. Many of these underground *bodegas* have long been abandoned, but scores of others, in Rueda itself and in neighbouring wine communities such as La Seca and

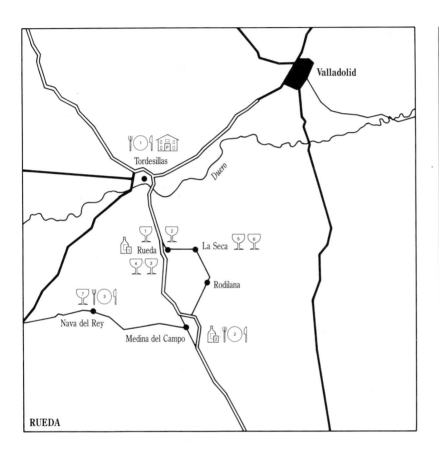

RUEDA

Nava del Rey, are in the process of being rehabilitated and restored.

The region's extensive underground cellars, plus the presence of mansions and immense churches in even the smallest *pueblos*, are evidence of a former prosperity based on wine. The wines of this zone enjoyed easy access to the Castilian court in the years of Spain's Golden Age, while as early as the sixteenth century they were exported throughout Europe. The Tsars of Russia were particular *aficionados* of the wines of Nava del Rey. And throughout the north of Spain, in Asturias, Cantabria and Galicia, the wines, transported by *arrieros* – mule drivers – from León, had a great following, so much so that even today in those regions, you may come across a sign over a bar door proudly proclaiming 'Vinos de La Nava'.

Historically, the wines of Rueda and its surrounding communities were *vinos generosos*, sherry-type wines produced from the characterful Verdejo grape which were naturally high in alcohol, produced in both *pálido* (pale,

CASTILLA Y LEÓN

matured under a veil of *flor*) and *dorado* (oxidized *oloroso* type) styles. Given
the difficulties of transporting wine in those far-off days, no small part of
their national and international success must have been based on the fact
that such wines were virtually indestructible. The *arrieros* transported
them in *pellejos de cabra*, whole goatskins, traditional and uniquely Spanish
containers that were still in use in the zone as recently as twenty years ago.

'Make no mistake,' Señor Jesús González Yllera of Bodegas SAT Los
Curros told me, '*pellejos* were excellent containers for conserving wine well,
provided they were cleaned scrupulously. Here in Castile, our traditional
vinos generosos were sold from house to house, *pueblo* to *pueblo*, in either
pellejos or *garrafas*. A *garrafa* holds one *cántaro*, sixteen litres. A *pellejo*
would contain usually four to five *cántaros*. It was easy enough for a strong
man to carry a full *pellejo* over his shoulders.' The amiable owner of one of
the zone's best and most forward-looking *bodegas* demonstrated to me how
it was done, hunched over, gripping the imagined fore and rear legs of the
animal skin over his shoulders.

If the wines of Rueda and its surrounding communities enjoyed considerable renown in past times, sometime earlier this century they lost their
way. As throughout the country, phylloxera devastated the vineyards, and
many were never replanted after that terrible blight. Later, after the Civil
War, Spain was isolated from the rest of the world and needed to develop a
self-sufficient economy. Much of Castilla y León was singled out to supply
the nation with wheat and other cereals, and thus many low-yielding and
uneconomic vineyards (in comparison to higher-yielding parts of the
country such as La Mancha) were abandoned. For this reason, even today
Rueda is a wine zone with apparently few vines. They are there, but tucked
amidst the dominating fields of wheat that are still the most characteristic
feature of the Castilian plain.

Many of those vineyards that remained were replanted at the time with
the higher-yielding Palomino and Viura vines, at the expense of the much
finer but parsimonious Verdejo. Moreover, while the best traditional wines
of the zone had always been matured in oak casks, often utilizing the *solera*
system of dynamic ageing, an alternative method of accelerating the process
of oxidation gained favour which was considerably cheaper and quicker.
This was achieved by filling bulbous 16-litre *bombas* about three-quarters
full, loosely stoppering them, then placing the bottles outside in the open
air to suffer the intense heat and sun of the summers, followed by the
numbing cold of the winters, a method still employed today by a handful of
the zone's *bodegas*. Though this accelerated method is not conducive to

making fine wines (they lack the complexity and nutty nuances of wines aged traditionally by the *solera* system), there is still a strong local and regional following for them, and they are also, apparently, widely used and excellent for cooking.

None the less, by the early 1970s the market and taste for such wines had contracted severely, and more and more farmers had turned to growing wheat, sugar beet or potatoes in preference to vines. It was a bold and imaginative move, therefore, when the pioneering Rioja firm, Marqués de Riscal, abandoned white winemaking in its traditional homeland, and, after searching the country for a suitable alternative venue, came to Rueda with the intention of making new-style, light white table wines from the Verdejo grape.

'Everyone thought we were *loco*,' recalled Pedro Aznar Escudero, Technical Director at Bodegas Vinos Blancos de Castilla, as Riscal's new company was named when it was founded in 1972. 'This zone was virtually dead as a wine area when we arrived because no one else had considered making *vinos jóvenes* here. Yet the Verdejo had everything we sought in a white grape: it is aromatic, has plenty of *cuerpo* [body], good acidity, and a most pleasing characteristic bitter finish. It makes wine with personality and is certainly far more interesting and exciting than Rioja's dull Viura.'

Marqués de Riscal, impressed above all with the quality and potential of the zone's fruit, set to putting in place all the necessary installations for the production of modern white wine, as well as impressing on the local growers the need not only to tend the vines well but to harvest at the optimum moment, as much as a month earlier than they were accustomed to. By paying a considerable premium for top-quality Verdejo grapes, they achieved this, and furthermore encouraged increased plantations of Verdejo at the expense of Viura and Palomino.

At the time, the Spanish taste was overwhelmingly for wood-aged white wines, so Riscal's early Rueda vintages spent about 6–8 months in wood. Over the following years, both Spanish and international tastes evolved towards lighter, fruitier wines, and the modern unoaked style of Rueda eventually emerged. The Marqués de Riscal Rueda Superior is still considered one of the best examples: produced from 85% Verdejo and 15% Viura, this is a full-bodied dry white table wine that is intensely fruity and concentrated in the mouth, with a ripe, almost creamy fruit, yet with the characteristic bitter finish that is the hallmark of Verdejo. It is a wine, above all, to enjoy young. Riscal also produces a Rueda Reserva Limousin from 100% Verdejo aged in *barricas* made with oak from the French

Limousin forests. The charming, creamy fruit of the Verdejo is finely balanced with the new oak, and the wine is long, rich, exciting.

Experiments with a range of other white grapes followed; although Albariño, Treixadura, Riesling, Chardonnay and Sauvignon Blanc were all planted, only the last fared well on this high Castilian vineyard. Riscal's first Sauvignon Blanc wine was released in 1985 and the results were superlative, so much so that other *bodegas*, aware of this leading producer's keen winemaking and marketing intuitions, have also begun planting the variety, and the Consejo Regulador, we understand, is on the point of authorizing it for inclusion under the Rueda DO.

Just as more than a hundred years earlier Marqués de Riscal had pioneered French winemaking techniques in the Rioja to result in a new style of wine that achieved international success not just for itself but for the entire region, so here in Rueda has its pioneering work and the superlative results and success that followed led to a great revival for the entire zone.

Rueda's *denominación de origen* was granted in 1980. Today, there are about 20 *bodegas* in Rueda marketing modern, light table wines in bottle, though this number will almost surely greatly increase in years to come. Almost all of them have modern installations essential to the production of quality white wines, especially stainless steel fermentation tanks with temperature control and up-to-date bottling equipment.

Another significant development in Rueda is the production of superlative sparkling wines produced by the classic method of secondary fermentation in the bottle, utilizing the Verdejo grape. In rehabilitated and restored *bodegas* deep underground, traditional slanting *pupitres* are in place for the hand *remuage* of thousands and tens of thousands of bottles, and the early results are certainly more than encouraging. Such wines may have difficulty in establishing a market identity within Spain since they are unlikely to be granted the Cava *denominación*; none the less, wines such as Los Curros' Cantosán Brut Natural – fine persistent mousse, fresh creamy nose, full and elegant in the mouth – demonstrate how superb such Castilian sparklers can be.

Rueda today is clearly one of the great success stories of the Spanish wine scene. Indeed, it is not going too far to say that it is, without doubt, one of the most exciting and vital wine zones in the country, even if, in this harsh but dull Castilian environment, you may have to search deep underground to discover this.

The best base for exploration of the Rueda wine zone is Tordesillas, a historic town along the Duero river just outside the delimited wine zone north of Rueda. There is a pleasant modern *parador* on the town's outskirts, a friendly well-run campsite, and some good local restaurants. The main north–south trunk road now by-passes the town, leaving it somewhat somnolent, especially during midsummer afternoons when everything and everyone shuts up shop to escape the tremendous heat. Yet this now quiet and pleasant town was, in its heyday, at the centre of events of world importance, most notably when the shamelessly libertine and corrupt Borgia Pope Alexander VI, father of Lucrezia and Cesare, devised the Treaty of Tordesillas in 1494 which divided the New World between Spain and Portugal, and defined their respective spheres of world influence. It was in Tordesillas' Monasterio de Santa Clara, too, that the unfortunate Juana la Loca (Joanna the Mad), daughter of Ferdinand and Isabel, spent 40 years locked up in a windowless cell, following the death of her husband, Philip of Habsburg, son of the Emperor Maximilian. This royal monastery can be visited and is particularly noteworthy for its beautiful *mudéjar* patio.

Rueda itself lies just 10 km south of Tordesillas. Apart from wine, it has little to offer, but there is plenty of that to satisfy the thirstiest wine traveller. Indeed, this is by far the most important town in the eponymous wine zone, and the home not only of the region's most important producers, but also of the Consejo Regulador and the *Estación Enologica de Castilla y León*. Rueda's *bodegas*, moreover, still document the evolution of the zone's types and styles of wines. For example, head off the town's main road on the dirt lane behind the baroque church to the Calle de las Bodegas, a street lined with crumbling old houses and mainly abandoned wine *bodegas* where the growers used to produce their traditional *vinos generosos*. One such firm still making old-style wines from its own harvest – *cosecha propria* – is Bodegas Pimental. This ramshackle but still functioning wine installation, with its old wooden casks and deep, cobwebbed cellars, could not provide a greater contrast to the super-modern installations of Riscal's Bodegas Vinos Blancos de Castilla or the welcoming new *bodegas* and public tasting room of SAT Los Curros.

Los Curros, noted for its fine white Ruedas and excellent sparkling wines, is also well known for its Yllera red wines, produced from grapes grown at Boada del Roa in the Ribera del Duero zone but bottled in Rueda, and so not at present entitled to that prestigious *denominación*. No matter: the wine has already made a great name for itself in Spain certainly as well as abroad, and though the new *bodega* has since been constructed at Boada, its success is already assured. It is certainly one of my favourite red wines of the Duero.

CASTILLA Y LEÓN

Another important *bodega* in Rueda which can be visited is Antonio Sanz's Bodegas de Crianza Castilla la Vieja. Sanz is one of Rueda's foremost winemakers; since the early 1980s, he has been making a prestigious white Rueda for Carlos Falcó, Marqués de Griñon, from 100% Verdejo grapes, and he is now producing for that Toledan aristocrat a Rueda Selección Especial fermented and aged in oak *barrica*. Castilla la Vieja also produces a full and diverse range of wines under its own label, from the creamy Palacio de Bornos Rueda and tasty oak-aged Almirante de Castilla red to superlative sparkling wines, as well as the region's old-style *vinos rancios*, aged outdoors in bulbous glass *bombas*.

While the town of Rueda is without doubt the centre of its wine industry, the greatest concentration of vineyards lies around the *pueblo* of La Seca, and particularly extends from La Seca towards Medina del Campo. La Seca itself is a quiet Castilian village whose inhabitants continue to work the land as they have for generations. This is not a wholly specialized wine zone, and the farmers have traditionally cultivated a range of crops in addition to grapes, including wheat, sunflowers, sugar beet, alfalfa and potatoes. As a result, rather than making wine themselves, most remain content to sell their grapes either to the private wine companies or to co-operatives such as the immense Agrícola Castellana, which lies on the outskirts of the village on the road to Rodilana. This outwardly antiquated co-operative remains the zone's largest producer. In recent years, it too has followed developments and changes and has invested in modern installations, including stainless steel fermentation tanks, gentler horizontal presses, and modern bottling lines. As important as modernizing its facilities, though, Agrícola Castellana has also attempted to change its members' way of thinking, in particular by stressing the need to harvest their grapes far earlier. Even so, Agrícola Castellana is one of the few remaining large-scale producers of the traditional old-style wines of the zone, Rueda Pálido and Rueda Dorado.

As in Rueda, the adobe houses of La Seca sit on a great underground warren of *bodegas*, some of which are in the process of being rehabilitated. Antonio Sanz, for example, is in the process of restoring extensive antique caves dug out by hand centuries ago for a newly formed venture, Bodegas Con Class. This up-market wine company intends to produce Rueda Superior from 100% Verdejo as well as a Verdejo sparkling wine by the classic method of secondary fermentation in the bottle.

Medina del Campo, south of La Seca, has for centuries been an important market centre for the surrounding countryside. Indeed, in the Middle Ages, this town, located on the strategic route from Galicia to central and southern Spain, was considered one of the most important market towns in Europe, a centre of commerce especially for wool traders from northern countries in search of high-quality merino wool from Castile, as well as goods from the Moorish-held south and the Levante. Medina's lovely brick castle recalls the town's Moorish past, while its grandiose Plaza de España is fittingly self-important since Isabel la Católica lived here for some years and died in the palace next to the Ayuntamiento.

One final wine town should be visited, Nava del Rey, located about 18 km west of Medina del Campo. Today, driving out to this lonely Castilian town well off the beaten track, there is little to suggest that before Spain's Civil War it was one of the country's largest wine communities in terms of volume. As recently as 30 years ago, there were 4000 hectares of vineyards planted here, but today, as elsewhere in the zone, most of the land is given over to wheat and other such crops. Yet historically, Nava del Rey was always famous for its wines, far more famous than its neighbour Rueda.

Wine may no longer be its inhabitants' principal occupation, but an important company has established itself in the town and is reviving its wine industry. Alvarez y Díez has now purchased eight extensive historic underground *bodegas* located throughout Nava's old centre, and has also built an extremely modern and well-equipped *bodega* on the outskirts of the town near the railway line. The company owns 75 hectares of its own vineyards and purchases almost all of the town's remaining production. All its wines – from young, light modern-style Rueda to wood-aged traditional Rueda Pálido and Dorado – are produced entirely according to ecological or organic precepts both in the vineyard and in the *bodega*. Indeed, Alvarez y Díez claim that they are the first commercial *bodega* in Spain (and possibly the world) to produce wines without using any sulphur dioxide during the winemaking process, a considerable and remarkable achievement.

While its Mantel Nuevo is a zesty, young organic white wine that has received considerable attention, the company continues to hold great stocks of its traditional *pálido* and *dorado* wines. Unlike *dorado* wines produced by accelerated methods through sunning in *bombas*, Alvarez y Díez continue to produce such wines by classic traditional methods, that is, through lengthy ageing in wooden casks using the *solera* system. These ancient and precious wine butts lie deep underground in the secret *bodegas* of Nava del Rey, filled with the traditional old-style wines of Rueda. In truth, such wines can be very good indeed, but no one (save a loyal local following) seems to want to drink them any more.

Why continue to make them? I asked Etelvino Sánchez Pastor, the enthusiastic Technical Director who has masterminded the company's organic, sulphur-free wine production. '*Hombre*,' he replied, not a little disapprovingly, 'if we were to lose *bodegas* and wines like these, it would be to lose something of our personality, our very roots.'

Toro

A wine journey heading west down the Duero valley passes first through the vineyards of Ribera del Duero and Rueda before entering the province of Zamora and the vineyards of Toro. Though Toro was only granted its *denominación de origen* in 1987, like those other prestigious zones it is a wine region with a lengthy historic pedigree. In the thirteenth century, the Cathedral of Santiago de Compostela was granted 20 *aranzadas* of vineyards in Toro by King Alfonso IX. Throughout the Middle Ages, the wines of Toro were traditionally the favourite tipple of the dons of Salamanca, that great Castilian university to the south, and they were also enjoyed by the Kings of León to the north. Indeed, so renowned was this region for its wines that the lands south of Toro itself were and still are traditionally known as the *comarca* Tierra del Vino, even though today most of the vineyards have long been abandoned in favour of the cultivation of cereals.

Historically, Toro was always an immense blockbuster of a wine produced from the Tinto del Toro grape, yet another manifestation of the Tempranillo or Tinto Fino found further east in Ribera del Duero and, of course, in Rioja. This sub-variety has probably been planted here for many centuries, and it is very well adapted to its extreme Castilian microclimate. The province of Zamora is the second driest in Spain (after the Manchegan province of Almansa), and the temperature here is even hotter than in the other Castilian wine zones to the east. The characteristic soil in the best Toro vineyards is sandy clay covered with a dense blanket of enormous stones, some as large as a man's shoe. These stones, like their similar counterparts in the French vineyard of Châteauneuf-du-Pape, serve as most effective night storage heaters, warming the vines on summer nights when temperatures can plummet dramatically. The Tinto del Toro vines in this extreme vineyard yield only tiny amounts of fruit, but of great concentration and character.

'Traditionally in the past,' explained Manuel Fariña Lopez, head of the zone's most advanced and forward winery, Bodegas Fariña, 'the grapes were harvested as late as possible and our Toro wines could reach 15.5° alcohol

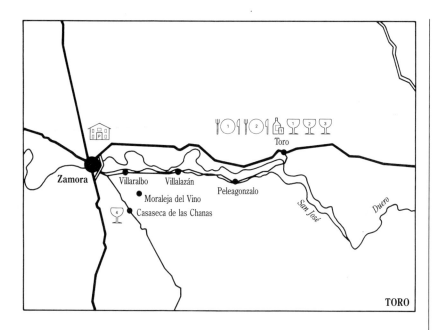

and still retain noticeable residual sweetness. Here in the zone, a wine's quality was always measured by its alcoholic content, not by its taste or aroma. The wines were elaborated in the primitive peasant manner utilizing a process known as *"embabujar"* whereby we fermented them on the skins and stems, stirring in the mass to further extract more colour and tannin. They were aggressive and powerful wines and were drunk only in Castilla y León and the north of Spain.'

The isolation that occurred after Spain's Civil War and the subsequent abandonment of low-yielding vineyards in favour of the cultivation of wheat almost resulted in the total loss of the Toro vineyard. Tastes began to change even within this traditional heartland in favour of the lighter, easier to drink wines of La Mancha, and by the early 1970s the market had almost been completely lost. Only a handful of *bodegas* continue to believe in the zone's history and potential. Led by Bodegas Fariña, they have since successfully revived the zone and are now producing superb oak-aged wines which, in terms of their quality-to-price ratio, must rank among the best in Spain.

'Our first task,' continued Señor Fariña, 'was to learn to pick our fruit considerably earlier to reduce potential alcohol levels. Those old-style wines with 15° alcohol or more were coarse, toasted and jammy and lost all the

CASTILLA Y LEÓN

primary aromas of the fruit. Today we are seeking lighter wines with about 13.5–14° alcohol only. Though this may still seem rather high, we have found that if we reduce alcohol levels any more then the wines lose their particular Toro character.'

Make no mistake, even modern, 'light' Toro is not a wine for the faint-hearted. Yet scrupulous care in every phase of the winemaking process, particularly during maceration in the initial stages of fermentation, can result in powerful wines that at best combine deep fruit with a characteristic round softness. Because the wines of Toro have a far greater glycerine content than their Ribera del Duero counterparts, they are initially much more forthcoming and approachable. They will probably never have the great longevity of the best Ribera wines, but on the other hand, in spite of their great strength, they come around far earlier and indeed can be delicious to drink young.

We tasted Fariña's wines from the vat and they illustrated the point. The Tinto del Toro grapes harvested in 1990 had been vinified separately to produce both wines to be drunk young as *tinto joven* as well as wines destined for ageing in wood. The *joven*, for example, had received only 2 days' maceration on the skin and was fermented at a temperature of 23–24°: the resulting wine had picked up a nice bright purple colour and was intensely fruity, round and easy to drink already. The same grapes selected and vinified for ageing in wood were macerated on the skin for about 6 days with frequent *remontaje*, then fermented at a temperature of about 26°: this wine had a much deeper, dense, purple-black colour, a profound blackberry-and-spice nose, and in the mouth was rich and filling, packed with soft but grippy sweet tannins. Fariña's best wine, Gran Colegiata Reserva, spends 12 months in wood (about 20–25% new American oak each year), followed by at least a year in bottle prior to release. It is by any

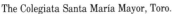
The Colegiata Santa María Mayor, Toro.

standard a classy, concentrated wine of great ripeness and finesse.

Señor Fariña is in the process of constructing a new and well-equipped *bodega* on the outskirts of Toro. When we visited, the proposed barrel store was still just a great hole excavated in the ground.

'We wanted to use some of the existing old *bodegas* in Toro itself, some of which are deep, very large and provide optimum conditions for wine storage and maturation. Most of these have long been abandoned, so it would have been a way of preserving our heritage. But the Ayuntamiento did not allow us, for it was anxious to keep any industry outside the historic *casco viejo* of the town. A pity.'

Toro remains one of the great wholly unspoiled medieval towns of the Duero, rising above its long Roman bridge out of the carved and twisted sandstone cliffs where the river makes a mighty bend from north to west. Dominated by the fortress-like Romanesque Colegiata Santa María Mayor church, the historic centre is extremely atmospheric, with its narrow lanes, old houses, colonnaded square and baroque Torre del Reloj. The main square is lined with small bars serving the town's famous wines together with simple drinking snacks. It was in Toro, incidentally, that a famous battle took place in 1476 when Ferdinand and Isabel defeated the forces of Juana la Beltraneja to usurp the Castilian throne from its probable rightful heir. How different Spanish history might have been had the outcome been different.

From Toro, the wine traveller may wish to dip into the so-called Tierra del Vino en route to Zamora. Descend out of town and cross the river, then find the old Roman bridge and pause here for a dramatic view back to the town, looking beyond the river to the sandstone cliff topped by the grand Colegiata, one of central Spain's finest Romanesque monuments. Then find your way to the provincial capital by way of small typical *pueblos* like Peleagonzalo, Villalazán and Villaralbo, or dip further south to Moraleja del Vino and Casaseca de las Chanas. Though much of the wine country has been long abandoned, before the arrival of phylloxera almost the entire region was devoted to wine production; and most towns and villages are still riddled with underground *bodegas*, as the chimney-like *zarceras de respiración* emerging from the ground still indicate. The Tierra del Vino *comarca* has traditionally been noted for its lighter *claretes* produced from red and white grapes harvested and vinified together. Bodegas Fariña, in addition to its new premises outside Toro, has its old family *bodega* in the wine town of Casaseca de las Chanas and produces probably the best wines of the *comarca*.

CASTILLA Y LEÓN

Zamora is far less visited than the other great cities of Old Castile, but it is one of our favourites. Its medieval quarter, packed with at least a dozen Romanesque churches, is quite simply one of the most charming that we know, and the *parador* located in its heart, in a fifteenth-century mansion of the Counts of Alba and Aliste, is one of Spain's most atmospheric.

Other Wine Zones in Castilla y León

Castilla y León is a vast region and wine is produced extensively throughout it. Even its best-known demarcated wine zones are remarkably recent creations, so it is probable that in due course some of its other long-standing traditional wine zones will pick themselves up from obscurity and begin producing wines of quality and prestige.

Cigales, for example, is a historic wine region located north of Valladolid, more or less in line with the other great wine regions of the Duero basin, forming a triangle with Ribera del Duero and Rueda. If the former is famous for its red wines and the latter for its whites, Cigales has traditionally supplied Valladolid and central Spain with *rosados* and *claretes*, some of which can be very good indeed. Such is the potential of the local fruit, especially Tinto Fino, that we conjecture that the zone could soon emerge as a serious red wine region, too.

Another notable wine zone in the province of Zamora is Benavente, an extensive *comarca* extending from the town of Benavente to the frontier with Galicia, most notable for its ant-like clusters of peasant *bodegas* located above almost every *pueblo*. These ancient cellars have since time immemorial served as press houses and wine stores for the small farmers who have traditionally cultivated grapes alongside other crops, to make wines primarily for their own consumption. Indeed, it is a remarkable sight to come to any number of these tiny towns and follow the dirt lanes to the tops of the hills where lines of stone portals mark the entrance to scores of such private *bodegas*. A small town like Colinas de Transmonte, on the road to Galicia, may have as many as a hundred or more such subterranean structures.

Traditionally the wine produced in these primitive *bodegas* was a *clarete* made from a mixture of black and white grapes fermented on the skins together. The wines, stored in *garrafas* or wooden *bocoys* in the cool, damp caves, were noted foremost as *vinos de aguja*, for they usually retained a refreshing and sharp characteristic carbonic prickle. One firm in Benavente, Bodegas Otero, continues to produce wines in this traditional style.

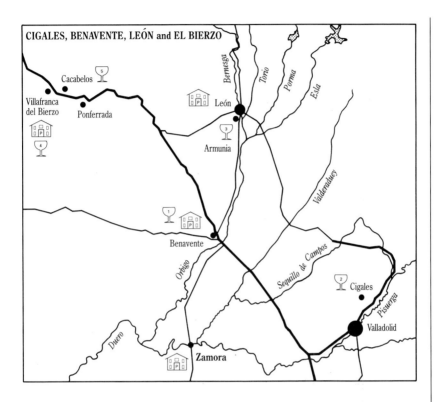

Further north, in the province of León, a large firm with the unfortunate acronym of VILE (Vinos de León) is blending as well as producing some sound white, *rosado* and red wines. In the same province, meanwhile, on the foothills of the Cordillera Cantábrica leading into Galicia, the delimited wine zone of El Bierzo, centred on the town of Villafranca del Bierzo on the old *Camino de Santiago*, is the source of some tasty wood-aged reds, especially from the characterful local Mencía grape. The best wines are produced by Bodegas Palacio de Arganza. This minor wine zone can be visited by any heading west to Galicia.

CASTILLA Y LEÓN

Bodegas: Stop to Taste; Stop to Buy

Ribera del Duero

1

BODEGAS PEÑALBA LOPEZ
FINCA TORREMILANOS
09400 ARANDA DE DUERO
BURGOS
ADMINISTRATIVE ADDRESS:
 PLAZA PRIMO RIVERA 4–5°A,
 09400 ARANDA DE DUERO
TEL: (947) 50 13 81; FAX: (947) 50 80 44

WINES PRODUCED: Torremilanos *rosado*; Torremilanos *tinto joven*; Torremilanos *tinto* Crianza, Reserva, Gran Reserva.
VISITS: By appointment, after 16h.

Pablo Peñalba Lopez's Finca Torremilanos, located on the outskirts of Aranda, is considered one of the zone's leading estates and produces an excellent range of wines under the Torremilanos label. The new winery is extremely well equipped and up-to-date, while the old underground *bodega* continues to serve as a barrel store for the ageing of Reserva and Gran Reserva wines.

2

BODEGA COOPERATIVA VIRGEN DE
 LAS VIÑAS
CTRA BURGOS, S/N
09400 ARANDA DE DUERO
BURGOS
TEL: (947) 50 13 11

WINES PRODUCED: Tierra de Aranda *rosado, tinto*.
VISITS: Daily, working hours for direct sales.
Aranda's co-operative winery, producing sound, if not overly exciting wines under the Tierra de Aranda label.

3

BODEGAS VALDUERO
09440 GUMIEL DEL MERCADO
BURGOS
TEL: (947) 54 54 59
ADMINISTRATIVE ADDRESS: DR
 ESQUERDO 165, 28007 MADRID
TEL: (91) 409 54 40; FAX: (91) 409 51 70

WINES PRODUCED: Viadero *blanco*; Viña Valduero *rosado*; Viña Valduero *tinto joven*; Viña Valduero *tinto* Crianza, Reserva,

Gran Reserva.
VISITS: Weekdays, by appointment.
It is worth visiting this young, well-run company to view its remarkable underground caves, excavated with mining equipment from Asturias. The old two-storey stone *bodega* has been converted into a pleasant tasting room and still has the ancient beam wine

press in place. Valduero's superlative range of wines includes the unusual white Viadero, produced from the local Albillo grape, as well as lean but powerful Reserva and Gran Reserva wines.

---

4 BODEGAS ISMAEL ARROYO
CALLE LOS LAGARES 71
09441 SOTILLO DE LA RIBERA
BURGOS
TEL AND FAX: (947) 54 51 09

WINES PRODUCED: Mesoneros de Castilla *rosado*; Mesoneros de Castilla *tinto joven*; Val Sotillo *tinto* Reserva, Gran Reserva.
VISITS: Weekdays, 10–14h; 16–20h. Appointment appreciated.

Highly regarded family-run wine estate with both modern installations and extensive underground caves producing tasty Mesoneros de Castilla *tinto joven*, as well as fine Val Sotillo Reserva wines. The family live above the *bodega* so there is usually someone on hand to show visitors around, though a telephone call first is always appreciated.

---

5 BODEGAS BALBAS
LA MAJADA, S/N
09442 LA HORRA
BURGOS
TEL: (947) 54 03 81

WINES PRODUCED: Balbas *rosado*; Balbas *tinto joven*; Balbas *tinto* Crianza, Reserva.
VISITS: By appointment.
The Balbas family has been making wine in its private

underground *bodega* in La Horra since 1777, but today's generation has set its sights somewhat higher: Juan José Balbas now presides over a new winemaking installation on the outskirts of Roa and is producing an impressive range of wines utilizing Tinto Fino with some Cabernet Sauvignon, aged in both American and French Limousin *barricas*.

---

6 BODEGA HERMANOS PÉREZ PASCUAS
CALLE LAS ERAS, S/N
CARRETERA DE ROA
09314 PEDROSA DE DUERO
BURGOS
TEL: (947) 54 04 99; FAX: (947) 54 11 00

WINES PRODUCED: Viña Pedrosa *rosado*; Viña Pedrosa *tinto joven*; Viña Pedrosa *tinto* Crianza, Reserva, Gran Reserva.
VISITS: Mon–Fri 9–14h; 16–20h. Appointment not necessary.
The Pérez Pascuas family have always been key figures in the local

CASTILLA Y LEÓN

winemaking scene, the grandfather having helped in the foundation of the co-operative winery at Roa. However, brothers Manuel, Benjamin and Adolfo have embarked on a quality-led path that will allow them, they feel, to make wines that will fully realize the potential of the remarkable fruit from their Ribera del Duero vineyards. While the old winery by the family house in Pedrosa remains, they are currently constructing an entirely new winemaking installation on the outskirts of the town. When functioning, this *bodega* should have visiting facilities, and possibly even a picnic area.

The Consejo Regulador, incidentally, has its experimental *bodega* in Pedrosa. English, French spoken.

---

7 BODEGAS SEÑORÍO DE NAVA SA
CTRA VALLADOLID–SORIA
09318 NAVA DE ROA
BURGOS
TEL: (947) 20 97 90; FAX: (947) 20 98 00

WINES PRODUCED: Señorío de Nava *rosado*; Señorío de Nava *tinto joven*; Vega Cubillas *tinto*; Señorío de Nava *tinto* Crianza, Reserva.
VISITS: Weekdays 9–13h; 16–19h. Appointment advisable.
Bodegas Vinos de León (VILE – see below) purchased the old co-operative winery at Nava de Roa and in its place has established a new company, Señorío de Nava. Considerable investment has transformed the old, antiquated co-operative, and the new winery is equipped with both the most modern winemaking installations and an extensive store of new oak *barricas*. The company owns 140 ha. of vineyards, planted primarily with Tinto Fino together with some Cabernet Sauvignon and Merlot, trained on wires. The considerable levels of investment indicate that this will be a *bodega* to watch.

---

8 BODEGA RIBERA DUERO
COOPERATIVA DE PEÑAFIEL
GENERAL SANJURGO 64
47300 PEÑAFIEL
VALLADOLID
TEL: (983) 88 00 16, 88 18 24

WINES PRODUCED: Ribera Duero *rosado*; Ribera Duero *tinto joven*; Ribera Duero *tinto* Crianza; Peñafiel *tinto* Reserva; Protos *tinto* Gran Reserva.
VISITS: Mon and Fri only, 13h30–14h; 18h30–19h. Call for an appointment.
Direct sales working hours at '*La Primera Bodega*' on the road to

Aranda just outside the town. One of Spain's oldest co-operative wineries, founded in 1926 by 12 members, today has 250 grape-growing *socios* in Peñafiel and its surrounds. Unusually, Bodega Ribera Duero began to bottle its wines at its foundation, and the famous Protos won its first gold medal at a wine fair in Barcelona in 1928. The extensive *bodega*, burrowing into the hill below Peñafiel's castle, was constructed in 1972 and today holds nearly 4000 *barricas* of Crianza, Reserva and Gran Reserva wines. While the fame of the co-operative was firmly established by its oak-aged wines, we consider its punchy *tinto joven* one of the best-value young reds of central Spain.

9

BODEGAS ALEJANDRO FERNÁNDEZ
LOS LAGARES, S/N
47315 PESQUERA DE DUERO
VALLADOLID
TEL: (983) 88 10 27

WINES PRODUCED: Pesquera *tinto* Crianza, Reserva; Janus *tinto* Gran Reserva.
VISITS: By appointment. Wines available for direct sales 'if there are any'.
Alejandro Fernández's Pesquera wine has become, after Vega Sicilia, the best-known and most sought-after of all the wines of the Ribera del Duero zone. While the wine is consequently in great demand and mostly pre-sold, it is none the less worth coming here, if only to view the primitive *bodega* where Fernández made his first wines, simply to gain an insight into how quickly the region has emerged on to the world wine scene. Today the newly constructed *bodega* is well-equipped and has a stock of 3000 mainly new *barricas*.

Vega Sicilia

Vega Sicilia is legendary. For more than a century, this imposing French-style château has stood above the banks of the Duero in splendid isolation, quietly and methodically producing wines that have long been considered Spain's finest and certainly her most expensive, virtually its only wine of international renown, worthy of investment, speculation, and lengthy conservation.

The estate was established in 1864, and the Cabernet Sauvignon, Merlot,

CASTILLA Y LEÓN

Malbec and Tinto Fino vines have been planted here ever since then, continually regenerated with clonal selection through the estate's own propagating nursery. The entire estate runs to over 1000 hectares, but only about 120 are given over to vineyards, extending over the tongues of sheltered, well-drained east-facing valleys sited at over 750 metres above sea level. Some of the vines are more than 80 years old, dating from the vineyard's replanting after phylloxera. Yields are very low, and the vineyards are always harvested in several passes, collecting each time only those grapes that have reached optimum ripeness and maturity.

The selected grapes are vinified parcel by parcel, before being transferred to American oak *tinas* where they undergo the malolactic fermentation and age for upwards of a further two years. Throughout this period, Don Mariano Garcia, Vega Sicilia's Technical Director, is constantly monitoring and tasting the wines, earmarking this vat, rejecting that one, choosing those destined to be Vega Sicilia Unico. Once assembled, the wines then undergo a further lengthy ageing discipline in *barrica*, starting in new oak then ageing progressively in older and older wood, for upwards of a decade, sometimes much longer. The wine is bottled but never released until deemed ready, usually after a further five years minimum. Thus, Vega Sicilia Unico is often fifteen years old or more before it is released.

'But we have no fixed rules here,' explained Mariano. 'Each year is

Vega Sicilia, Spain's most famous wine estate.

different, so it is rather like playing jazz. We improvise a lot, but always within the long-established Vega Sicilia framework. It is only possible to make Unico in those years when the wine is very concentrated and extremely high in fixed acid, necessary to support this extended barrel ageing. The wine stays in the barrel each year precisely as long as it needs to. In those years when we cannot make Unico, it does not signify that it is necessarily a poor vintage. We give the same care and attention to the production of Valbuena.'

We tasted the great Unico 1973 in the Vega Sicilia château, together with a *tapa* of own-produced *chorizo* and nuggets of good, dense Castilian bread. The wine was astounding, most notable for its concentrated fruitiness, power and intensity. In spite of its lengthy sojourn in wood, it was still remarkably vivid, overlayered above all with a complex cornucopia of dried fruits, cedar and leather. Its finish was sweet, velvety and astonishingly long.

10

BODEGAS VEGA SICILIA
CTRA VALLADOLID–SORIA, KM 40.2
47359 VALBUENA DE DUERO
VALLADOLID
TEL: (983) 68 01 47

WINES PRODUCED: Valbuena; Vega Sicilia Unico, Vega Sicilia Unico Reserva Especial.
VISITS: By appointment for wine professionals only, as long in advance as possible.

11

HIJOS DE ANTONIO BARCELO
CTRA VALLADOLID–SORIA, KM 14
47320 TUDELA DE DUERO
VALLADOLID
TEL: (983) 52 10 11; FAX: (983) 52 05 13
ADMINISTRATIVE ADDRESS: AVDA
   DE CÓRDOBA 21, 2°–3, 28026
   MADRID
TEL: (91) 475 80 12; FAX: (91) 476 15 25

WINES PRODUCED: Peñascal *blanco, rosado, tinto*; Santorcal Rueda; Viña Mayor Ribera del Duero Crianza.

VISITS: By appointment.
This long-established and large wine company has based its success on a fortifying tonic wine, Sanson, as well as on its distinctively bottled Peñascal range of wines, especially the excellent dry and medium-dry *rosados*. The company also produces good red Ribera del Duero Viña Mayor as well as Santorcal Rueda Superior.
English spoken.

CASTILLA Y LEÓN

12 BODEGAS MAURO SA
CALLE CERVANTES 12
47320 TUDELA DE DUERO
VALLADOLID
ADMINISTRATIVE ADDRESS AND
BODEGA FOR DIRECT SALES: CTRA
N-112, KM 328, 47350
QUINTANILLA DE ONÉSIMO,
VALLADOLID
TEL AND FAX: (983) 68 02 65

WINES PRODUCED: Mauro *tinto* Crianza, Reserva.
VISITS: Daily, by appointment. Direct sales at Quintanilla de Onésimo.
It is right that the Mauro wines should now be entitled to the Ribera del Duero *denominación* for, though previously located just outside the delimited zone, this has long been one of the region's finest examples of how stylish and classy the wines of this region can be. While there are tasting and direct sales opportunities at Quintanilla, the principal *bodega* is located in the charming, typically Castilian town of Tudela de Duero, in a lovely seventeenth-century town house with vaulted cellars. This is a small estate, producing only limited amounts of wine entirely from its own 6-ha. vineyard, aged primarily in French oak *barricas*.

Rueda

1 VINOS BLANCOS DE CASTILLA SA
CTRA N-VI, KM 172,600
47490 RUEDA
VALLADOLID
TEL: (983) 86 80 83, 86 80 29;
FAX: (983) 86 85 63

WINES PRODUCED: Marqués de Riscal *blanco*; Marqués de Riscal *blanco* Reserva Limousin; Marqués de Riscal *blanco* Sauvignon.
VISITS: Mon–Fri 9–13h; 15–19h. Appointment necessary.
It is not possible to overestimate the pioneering role that this famous Rioja house has played in the development and creation of the modern white wines of Rueda. Scores of other *bodegas* have since followed their lead, but the Marqués de Riscal Rueda wines remain the benchmark against which all others are measured. The winery is extremely well-equipped, but, being purpose built in 1972, not particularly picturesque or atmospheric.
English, French spoken.

2 BODEGAS SAT LOS CURROS
ENCERRADILLA, S/N
47490 RUEDA
VALLADOLID
TEL: (983) 86 80 97

WINES PRODUCED: Tierra Buena *blanco* (50% Verdejo/50% Viura); Young Life *blanco joven* (100% Verdejo); Viña Cantosan *blanco* (100% Verdejo); Viña del Val *rosado, tinto*; Yllera *tinto* Crianza, Reserva; Viña Cantosán Brut *vino espumoso*, Viña Cantosán Brut Nature *vino espumoso*.

VISITS AND DIRECT SALES: Daily 9–21h including weekends and holidays.

The Yllera family have been winegrowers in the Rueda zone for five generations (the original *bodegas*, still in use, are located at Fuente el Sol), but until 1975, all their wines were old-style *vinos generosos* sold in bulk, originally in *pellejos de cabra* and 16-litre *garrafas*. Today, the new *bodega* built near the entrance to the town is extremely up-to-date and well-equipped, and the Los Curros wines – Viña Cantosán white and Yllera red – are well-known throughout Spain, particularly in some of the country's finest restaurants. In Rueda itself, Señor Yllera is in the process of restoring a remarkable and atmospheric ancient underground *mudéjar* cellar dating from the fourteenth century, to be utilized primarily as a store for the company's exceptional traditionally-made sparkling wines.

———

3 BODEGAS DE CRIANZA DE CASTILLA
LA VIEJA SA
CTRA MADRID–CORUÑA, KM 170,6
47490 RUEDA
VALLADOLID
TEL: (983) 86 81 16, 86 83 36;
FAX: (983) 86 84 32

WINES PRODUCED: Palacio de Bornos *blanco*; Marqués de Griñon *blanco* (100% Verdejo), Marqués de Griñon Selección Especial (100% Verdejo fermented in *barrica*); Huerta del Rey *rosado*; Almirante de Castilla *tinto* Reserva; Palacio de Bornos Brut Nature *vino espumoso*; Dorado '62' *vino rancio*.

VISITS: Mon–Fri 10–13h; 16–19h. Appointment advisable, though not necessary for direct sales.

Antonio Sanz has probably received most attention for his production of the Marqués de Griñon Rueda, for this is one of the zone's best and certainly highest profile wines. However, Sanz is a skilled winemaker and he demonstrates this further in his remarkable range of wines produced and sold under the Castilla la Vieja labels. In addition to good young white wines, the oak-aged reds and traditional sparkling wines deserve to be

CASTILLA Y LEÓN

sampled. Come here, too, to see the rows of old-style *bombas* sunning in the courtyard.
English, French, Italian spoken.

---

4 BODEGA J. PIMENTEL Y CIA
CUATRO CALLES, S/N
47490 RUEDA
VALLADOLID
TEL: (983) 86 80 68

WINE PRODUCED: Montico Rueda Dorado.

VISITS: Mon–Fri 9–13h30.
Seek out this old ramshackle *bodega* in the dirt lanes behind the church to visit one of the few remaining producers of traditional wood-aged Montico Rueda Dorado.

---

5 AGRÍCOLA CASTELLANA, S. COOP
LTD
CTRA RODILANA, S/N
47491 LA SECA
VALLADOLID
TEL: (983) 81 63 20; FAX: (983) 81 65 62

WINES PRODUCED: Cuatro Rayas *blanco*; Pampano *blanco semi-seco*; Campo Grande Rueda Pálido; '61' Rueda Dorado.
VISITS: Mon–Fri 9–13h; 15h30–19h.
Still the zone's largest producer by far, controlling through its member winegrowers some 2000 ha. of vineyards (the entire DO zone comprises less than 5000 ha. in total). Recent investment has brought modern improvements, particularly the installation of stainless steel fermentation tanks for the production of fresh *vinos jóvenes* such as Cuatro Rayas. The co-operative is still a large producer of traditional Rueda *pálido* and *dorado* wines.

---

6 BODEGAS CON CLASS
47491 LA SECA
VALLADOLID
TEL: (983) 86 83 36; FAX: (983) 86 84 32

WINES PRODUCED: Con Class Rueda Superior *blanco* (100% Verdejo); Con Class *vino espumoso*.
VISITS: By appointment.

Old subterranean *bodegas* in the heart of this small wine town, stylishly reconstructed and remodelled in 1988 for the production of high-quality young white wines and sparkling wines, entirely from the Verdejo grape.

Vinos Ecológicos: Organic Wines

Just as there has been enormously increased consumer interest in the production of organically grown vegetables and organically reared meat in recent years, so has there been much greater world awareness of the production of organic wines.

Castilla y León, with its harsh semi-arid climate, is a vineyard that is capable of producing high-quality fruit with minimal or no chemical interference in the vineyard. The great challenge for Etelvino Sánchez of Alvarez y Diéz, however, was to transform such healthy, organically grown fruit into wine without the use of any chemicals whatsoever, even eschewing the use of sulphur dioxide, universally considered by oenologists an essential adjunct to the winemaking process.

The methods by which Sánchez achieved his aim are complex, based primarily on the isolation and multiplication of the strongest natural yeasts present on the Verdejo grapes. The addition of large quantities of such selected natural yeasts, it was discovered, actually strengthened a wine's natural defence against its greatest enemy, acetobacteria.

Sánchez's basic winemaking principals are of further relevance even to non-organic winemakers, for they are based on an almost manic preoccupation with speed and cleanliness from the moment the grape is harvested through each stage and phase of the winemaking process.

'We are not saying that our Mantel Nuevo *vino ecológico* is better than other wines, nor are we saying that other wines are not natural. However, we can say that we have successfully produced our wines with the elimination of all unnatural steps in the winemaking process, and above all through the total elimination of the use of sulphur dioxide.'

For those of us who have suffered from headaches and hangovers from poorly made or over-sulphured wines, this is a not inconsiderable achievement, and one to be applauded, especially given the fact the resulting wines are also excellent.

CASTILLA Y LEÓN

7 ALVAREZ Y DÍEZ SA
CALLE JUAN ANTONIO CARMONA 16
47500 NAVA DEL REY
VALLADOLID
TEL: (983) 85 01 36
ADMINISTRATIVE ADDRESS:
SIMANCAS 21, PORTAL F 1° A, 28029
MADRID
TEL: (91) 323 48 15

WINES PRODUCED: Mantel
Blanco; Mantel Nuevo Ecológico;
Lanzos *tinto*; Mantel Pálido;
Mantel Dorado.
VISITS: Mon–Fri 9–14h. Arrange

appointment with Administrative
Office.
Spain's first commercial producer of
vino ecológico, utilizing no sulphur
dioxide whatsoever in the
winemaking process. The Verdejo
grapes grown in Nava del Rey are
used to produce various styles of
wines from fresh, fruity wines,
through wood-aged *vino de crianza*,
to the traditional *vinos generosos*,
probably the finest examples of their
type in the wine zone.

Toro

1 BODEGAS FARIÑA SL
CTRA DE TORDESILLAS, S/N
49800 TORO
ZAMORA
TEL: (988) 69 18 82
ADMINISTRATIVE ADDRESS: CALLE
FRAY TORIBIO DE MOTOLINÍA 10,
49004 ZAMORA
TEL: (988) 51 45 62; FAX: (988) 51 15 88

WINES PRODUCED: Valderreyes
blanco joven; Valderreyes *rosado*;
Colegiata *tinto* Crianza; Gran
Colegiata *tinto* Reserva.
VISITS: Mon–Fri, by appointment.

Bodegas Fariña still maintains its
principal *bodegas* at Casaseca de las
Chanas, located about 9 km south
of Zamora (see below). However,
these newly constructed premises
are the source of one of central
Spain's great undervalued wines,
Gran Colegiata, and visitors may
wish to make an appointment to
visit, taste and purchase at the
source.
English, French spoken.

2 BODEGAS LUIS MATEOS SA
ERAS DE STA CATALINA, S/N
49800 TORO
ZAMORA
TEL: (988) 69 08 98

WINES PRODUCED: Valdeví
blanco, rosado, tinto; Tinto Toro;
Vega de Toro *tinto* Crianza; Tío
Babú *tinto* Reserva.
VISITS: Daily, by appointment.
Another good source for the
powerful, four-square wines of Toro.

3 VINOS DE TORO, S. COOP.
CTRA TORDESILLAS 13
49800 TORO
ZAMORA
TEL: (988) 69 03 47

WINES PRODUCED: Cermeño *blanco, rosado, tinto*; Bardales *blanco, tinto clarete*; Cañus Verus *tinto* Crianza; Marqués de Toro *tinto* Reserva.

VISITS: Mon–Fri, working hours. No appointment necessary. Co-operative winery with 300 *socios* working over 1000 ha. of vineyards. Cañus Verus is a typical and robust example of the *denominación*.

La Tierra del Vino

4 BODEGAS FARIÑA SL
CTRA DE MORALEJA, S/N
49151 CASASECA DE LAS CHANAS
ZAMORA
TEL: (988) 57 76 73; FAX: (988) 57 77 20

WINES PRODUCED: Comarca del Vino *tinto*; Fariña *tinto* Crianza.
VISITS: Daily, working hours.
The Tierra del Vino *comarca* has historically produced wines

considerably lighter than its more famous neighbour, Toro. Bodegas Fariña is a leading producer in both zones. Its Fariña *tinto* Crianza produced at Casaseca de las Chanas is a wine that deserves attention, produced from a mix of 50% Tinto del Toro and 50% Cabernet Sauvignon.
English, French spoken.

Benavente

1 BODEGAS OTERO
AVDA GENERAL PRIMO DE RIVERA 22
49600 BENAVENTE
ZAMORA
TEL: (988) 63 16 00

WINES PRODUCED: El Cubeto *rosado*; Peña Trevinca *tinto* Crianza; Señor de Donado *tinto* Crianza.
VISITS: Weekdays, 16–19h.
Benavente is not a well-known wine zone, but there is a strong local following for its home-made

rosados which usually retain a refreshing slight carbonic prickle. In a zone still dominated by its scores of primitive peasant *bodegas*, Bodegas Otero is the largest commercial producer. Red wines are produced from a mix of local grapes, including Mencía, Preto Picudo, Garnacha and Alicante.

CASTILLA Y LEÓN

Cigales

2 BODEGAS VICENTE CONDE
CAMAZON
LOS GATOS, S/N
47270 CIGALES
VALLADOLID
TEL: (983) 30 55 59

WINES PRODUCED: Vicente Conde
rosado; Tercer Año *rosado*; Reserva
del 70 *rosado*.

VISITS: Daily, working hours.
Cigales has been noted historically
for its *claretes* produced from a
mixture of red (Tinto Fino,
Garnacha) and white (Albillo,
Verdejo, Viura) grapes, often aged
for considerable periods in wooden
barrels. This is the source of
well-made traditional examples.

León

3 BODEGAS VINOS DE LEÓN – VILE SA
CALLE LA VEGA, S/N
ARMUNIA
24080 LEÓN
TEL: (987) 20 97 12; FAX: (987) 20 98 00

WINES PRODUCED: Palacio de
León *blanco, rosado, tinto*; Palacio
de los Guzmanes *tinto* Crianza; Don
Suero *tinto* Gran Reserva.
VISITS: Weekdays 9–13h; 16–19h.

Appointment necessary.
This large-scale winery produces a
range of sound, well-made wines
and has recently invested massively
in a top-end-of-the-market
operation at Bodegas Señorío de
Nava in the Ribera del Duero zone
(see above).
English spoken.

El Bierzo

4 BODEGAS PALACIO DE ARGANZA
AVDA DÍAZ OBELAR 17
24500 VILLAFRANCA DEL BIERZO
LEÓN
TEL: (987) 54 00 23

WINES PRODUCED: Palacio de
Arganza *blanco, rosado, tinto*;
Señorío de Arganza *tinto* Crianza,
Reserva, Gran Reserva.
VISITS: Daily, by appointment.
El Bierzo is a little-known wine
region located in the mountains

west of León on the ancient
pilgrims' route to Santiago de
Compostela. This *bodega*
undoubtedly produces its best wines,
notably oak-aged Reserva and
Gran Reserva wines from the
characterful Mencía grape, said by
some to be a lookalike of Cabernet
Franc. Certainly, at best, it can
share a berryish, herbaceous
character that is most distinctive
and pleasant.

5 BODEGA COMARCAL COOPERATIVA
'VINOS DEL BIERZO'
AVDA DE LA CONSTITUCIÓN 106
24540 CACABELOS
LEÓN
TEL: (987) 54 61 50; FAX: (987) 54 92 36

WINES PRODUCED: Fontousal *blanco*; Viña Oro *rosado*; Guerra *tinto* Gran Reserva; Señorío del Bierzo *tinto* Gran Reserva.
VISITS: Mon–Fri 9–13h; 15–19h.
No appointment necessary.
This large co-operative has about 2000 grape-growing *socios*. The oak-aged Señorío del Bierzo wines are the best.

Restaurantes, Hoteles y Paradores

Segovia

MESÓN DE CÁNDIDO
PLAZA DEL AZOGUEJO 5
40001 SEGOVIA
TEL: (911) 42 59 11; FAX: (911) 42 81 03

Literally in the shadows of the great Roman aqueduct, this famous old *horno de asar* has been roasting *tostones* (sucking pigs) so long that it has actually been declared a National Monument. Cándido himself has retired, but his son and grandson continue the tradition of slicing the tender meat theatrically with the edge of a plate; after touring the city, a meal here is a virtual must for all visitors to central Spain.
Expensive

Ribera del Duero

1 MESÓN DE LA VILLA
PLAZA MAYOR 3
09400 ARANDA DE DUERO
BURGOS
TEL: (947) 50 10 25

Closed Mon.
Aranda is lamb country and the town is literally packed with fine *hornos de asar*, all vying for custom. This restaurant, though, is considered the finest, located on the main square a stone's throw from the Duero in a renovated underground wine cellar. Typical specialities include *chorizo a la braza*, *morcilla de matanza*, *cordero asado*, *leche frita*, accompanied by an excellent selection of local wines.
Moderate

CASTILLA Y LEÓN

2 ASADOR EL CIPRÉS
PLAZA PRIMO DE RIVERA 1
09400 ARANDA DE DUERO
BURGOS
TEL: (947) 50 74 14

Another faultless and typical Castilian *horno de asar*, serving excellent *morcilla casera*, followed by, what else, *cordero asado* and home-baked bread.
Moderate

3 CASA RAFAEL CORRALES
OBISPO VELASCO 2
09400 ARANDA DE DUERO
BURGOS
TEL: (947) 50 02 77

Closed Thur eve.

This basic *casa* is the archetypal Castilian *horno de asar*: pass the wood-fired baker's oven on the way to your upstairs trestle table and enjoy the classic feast of the zone: *lechazo asado, lechuga, pan y vino.*
Inexpensive

4 RESTAURANTE LA CHULETA
PAZ ESPAÑOLA 5
09300 ROA DE DUERO
BURGOS
TEL: (947) 54 03 12
—
Roa is a rather out-of-the-way and run-down wine *pueblo*, so this restaurant comes as something of a welcome surprise. Open kitchen and

cool, comfortable dining room serving good grilled fish as well as meats: *potaje de garbanzo, revuelto de setas, trucha a la plancha, cordero,* and of course the superlative wines of the surrounding communities.
Moderate

5 MESON 'EL CORRALILLO'
GENERAL YAGÜE 2
47300 PEÑAFIEL
VALLADOLID
TEL: (983) 88 07 33

Closed Mon.
Remarkable ancient underground wine *bodega* converted into a

restaurant in the hillside beneath Peñafiel's famous castle. Menu serves little more than the basics of the region, but this is a welcome stop, especially in midsummer, since it is always refreshingly and naturally cave-cool.
Inexpensive

6 ASADOR MAURO
CALLE ATARAZANAS, S/N
47300 PEÑAFIEL
VALLADOLID
TEL: (983) 88 08 16

Closed Sun eve.

Located just below the castle in the old part of town, this is another famous *horno de asar* serving both *lechazo* and *tostón*, together with the great wines of Peñafiel.
Moderate

7 LA FRAGUA
PASEO DE ZORRILLA 10
47006 VALLADOLID
TEL: (983) 33 87 85

Closed Sun eve.
Valladolid is not our favourite city, but if you come here to visit the National Museum of Religious Sculpture, it may be worth seeking out this classic Castilian eating house, one of the most famous

restaurants of central Spain. Noted primarily for its meats roasted in the *horno de asar*, other specialities include *bacalao con patatas y puerro, rape castellano, mollejas con setas, crema de arroz con leche*. Great wine list, especially strong on Ribera del Duero, Rueda and old vintages of Vega Sicilia.
Very Expensive

Rueda

1 MESÓN VALDERREY
CTRA MADRID–CORUÑA 1
47100 TORDESILLAS
VALLADOLID
TEL: (983) 77 11 72

Typical Castilian restaurant located by Tordesilla's medieval bridge serving good roasted and grilled meats alongside excellent white wines of Rueda and reds of Ribera del Duero and Toro.
Moderate

2 RESTAURANTE CONTINENTAL
PLAZA DE ESPAÑA 15
47400 MEDINA DEL CAMPO
VALLADOLID
TEL: (983) 80 10 14

Join the locals at this basic,

old-fashioned restaurant on the main square for an uninspired but substantial *menú del día – sopa castellano, merluza a la cazuela, leche frita*.
Inexpensive

CASTILLA Y LEÓN

3 FONDA MARTÍN
GONZALEZ PISADOR 1
47500 NAVA DEL REY
VALLADOLID
TEL: (983) 85 00 10

Basic but authentic *fonda* serving good *comidas caseras – setas a la plancha, chuletillas, merluza a la cazuela* – together with the full range of wines of Nava del Rey. **Inexpensive**

Parador

P PARADOR NACIONAL DE
TORDESILLAS
CTRA N-620, KM 152
47100 TORDESILLAS
VALLADOLID
TEL: (983) 77 00 51; FAX: (983) 77 10 13

This modern *parador* with swimming pool, located just outside town on the road to Salamanca, makes the most comfortable base for exploration of the Rueda wine country. Restaurant serves typical Castilian *cocina: sopa de ajo, perdiz estofada a la casera, lomo y longaniza de la olla* accompanied by a good selection of local wines from Rueda, Ribera del Duero, Toro and Cigales.
Moderate

Toro

1 HOTEL JUAN II
PASEO DEL ESPOLÓN 1
49800 TORO
ZAMORA
TEL: (988) 69 03 00

Comfortable and friendly 3-star hotel opposite Toro's famous Colegiata, with rooms overlooking the Duero river far below.
Moderate

---

2 BAR-RESTAURANTE 'ALEGRÍA'
PLAZA ESPAÑA 10
49800 TORO
ZAMORA
TEL: (988) 69 00 85

Under the *soportales* in the old part of town, a simple basic bar-restaurant serving good *tapas* and a popular *menú del día*. Packed with locals.
Inexpensive

Paradores

P

PARADOR NACIONAL CONDES DE
  ALBA Y ALISTE
PLAZA DE VIRIATO 5
49001 ZAMORA
TEL: (988) 51 44 97; FAX: (988) 53 00 63

Historic and atmospheric *parador* installed in a splendid fifteenth-century palace in the heart of Zamora's *casco viejo*. Swimming pool.
Moderate to Expensive

P

PARADOR NACIONAL REY
  FERNANDO II DE LEÓN
PASEO RAMÓN Y CAJAL, S/N
49600 BENAVENTE
ZAMORA
TEL: (988) 63 03 00; FAX: (988) 63 03 03

Installed in the twelfth-century castle that formed part of Benavente's medieval defences.
Moderate

P

HOTEL SAN MARCOS
PLAZA DE SAN MARCOS 7
24001 LEÓN
TEL: (987) 23 73 00; FAX: (987) 23 34 58

This magnificent sixteenth-century plateresque edifice in the heart of León was formerly the headquarters for the *Orden de los Caballeros de Santiago*, and served as a hostel for pilgrims on the *Camino de Santiago*. Today it is a deluxe hotel, part of the *parador* chain, but it maintains its timeless atmosphere and grandeur. Highly reputed restaurant with dining room overlooking the Bernesga river.
Expensive

P

PARADOR NACIONAL VILLAFRANCA
  DEL BIERZO
AVDA DE CALVO SOTELO, S/N
24500 VILLAFRANCA DEL BIERZO
LEÓN
TEL: (987) 54 01 75; FAX: (987) 54 00 10

Located in the mountains of León on the road to Santiago de Compostela, El Bierzo is a little visited *comarca* of great natural beauty as well as a wine zone of minor importance. This modern *parador* is located in the high part of town and enjoys splendid views of the surrounding countryside.
Moderate

CASTILLA Y LEÓN

Tomar Unas Copas: Stop for a Drink; Stop for a Bite

Ribera del Duero

1 BAR EL CIPRÉS
PLAZA PRIMO DE RIVERA 1
09400 ARANDA DE DUERO
BURGOS
TEL: (947) 50 74 14

Aranda is packed with bars serving good house wines and *tapas*, but El Ciprés stands a notch above: a stylish and popular wine bar serving a selection of *rosados* and *tintos* from Ribera del Duero by the glass, together with a good range of tasty hot *tapas*. Adjoining restaurant serves excellent roast lamb (see above).

Rueda

1 BAR LEONES
CTRA MADRID–CORUÑA
47490 RUEDA
VALLADOLID

This bar is nothing special but it is a good place to sample the fresh, new-style Verdejo wines of Rueda by the glass together with a *bocadillo*. Small selection of wines for sale.

----

2 BAR MONACO
PLAZA DE ESPAÑA 26
47400 MEDINA DEL CAMPO
VALLADOLID
TEL: (983) 80 10 20

Pavement tables under the broad *soportales* of Medina's famous square, and an excellent selection of *tapas* and wines by the glass – whites from Rueda, reds from Ribera del Duero and *rosados* from Cigales. Stylish upstairs restaurant.

Toro

1 BAR LA ESQUINA
PLAZA DE ESPAÑA 27
49800 TORO
ZAMORA

Corner bar on the main square serving freshly made *tapas* and *bocadillos* to accompany the wines of Toro.

Zamora, the provincial capital, is filled with atmospheric bars. The best area is the zone near the Cathedral known as '*Los Herreros*'.

Los Campings

Ribera del Duero

CAMPING COSTAJAN
CTRA N-I, KM 162
09400 ARANDA DE DUERO
BURGOS
TEL: (947) 50 20 70

On the main road south to Madrid. Swimming pool.

Rueda

CAMPING EL ASTRAL
CTRA N-620, KM 155
47100 TORDESILLAS
VALLADOLID
TEL: (983) 77 00 53

Friendly, family run. Swimming pool.

Vinos y Comestibles: Stop to Taste; Stop to Buy

AREA TUDANCA
CTRA N-I, KM 152,8
09470 FUENTESPINA
BURGOS
TEL: (947) 50 60 11; FAX: (947) 50 60 15

Open 7 days a week until midnight. This superior highway rest area located 8 km south of Aranda de Duero on the main road to or from Madrid has a restaurant serving Castilian specialities (*morcilla de Burgos, chorizo, chuletillas a la brasa, cordero asado*), as well as a shopping centre offering regional specialities and an outstanding selection of wines, especially from Ribera del Duero and Rioja. Conveniently situated for a break for those heading south from the Santander ferry, and a good place to stock up on wines for those on their way back home. English spoken.

TIENDA DE PINCHA PECES
GENERAL FRANCO 9
47300 PEÑAFIEL
VALLADOLID

General shop run by local wine enthusiasts: good selection of old vintages of Protos, Peñafiel, and Vega Sicilia Unico and Valbuena.

CASTILLA Y LEÓN

Compras Deliciosas: Stop to Taste; Stop to Buy

JAMONES Y EMBUTIDOS CASEROS
PLAZA CTE REQUEJO 10
09400 ARANDA DE DUERO
BURGOS
TEL: (947) 50 01 33

Good selection of home-cured sausages and *jamones*, as well as local cheeses and wines.

PANADERÍA 'LA ROSARIO'
PLAZA GENERAL BERUGO
09400 ARANDA DE DUERO
BURGOS

Excellent Castilian breads cooked in a wood-fired oven, especially the typical *torta de azeite* and *canillas* – long, floury breadsticks.

REAL MONASTERIO DE STA CLARA
47100 TORDESILLAS
VALLADOLID

Delicious almond sweets made and sold from behind a revolving

turntable by unseen Clarissa nuns who still live and work in Tordesilla's famous Real Monasterio – try the sensational, crunchy *pasta de almendras*.

¡Fiesta! Wine and Other Related Celebrations

Carnaval (Feb)   Fuente del Vino   Cebreros
    (During Carnival festivities, the town's fountain flows with wine)

end of Aug   Fiesta de la Vendimia   Cacabelos
    (Festival of the wines of El Bierzo)

last Sat in Sept   Fiesta de la Vendimia   Cigales

last Sun in Sept   Fiesta de la Vendimia de la   Rueda, La Seca
    DO Rueda

1st Sun in Oct   Fiesta de la Vendimia de la
    Ribera del Duero
(Wine festival takes place in a different town within the DO zone every year)

Tauromania: An Obsession with Bulls

The Spanish passion for the bullfight is well known, if somewhat inexplicable to most foreigners. Clearly, there is a primordial obsession with bulls that is uniquely part of the Spanish temperament, and which goes back to the days when neolithic Iberians painted pictures on the cave walls at Altamira. In Castilla y León, bizarre, cruel annual festivals still take place which are little short of barbaric, again demonstrating the nation's mania for bulls.

At Tordesillas, each year on the Tuesday after 8 September, the locals enact the *Toro de la Vega* in which a full-size *toro bravo* (fighting bull) is let loose in the Plaza Mayor and chased through the narrow streets to the edge of the town. Once over the medieval bridge, it is attacked by youths and men on foot and horseback, some of them brandishing Roman-style pikes. This festival dates back to 1355 when it was inaugurated by the aptly-named Pedro I El Cruel.

At Benavente in the province of Zamora, another bizarre ritual is enacted each year, the so-called *Toro Enmaromado* in which a *toro bravo* is tied to a 200-metre-long rope and led and teased through the streets of the town; finally the rope is twisted tighter and tighter around a pole until the bull is killed.

Since Spain joined the European Community, there has been increased outside pressure to curb such ritual animal abuse. At the very least, such traditions are evidence, if any is needed, that the country still remains very different from the rest of Europe.

Y para saber más Additional Information

Junta de Castilla y León
Dirección General de Turismo
Paseo de Zorrilla 48, 1°
47000 Valladolid
tel: (983) 33 00 99

Consejo Regulador de Ribera del
　Duero
Plaza Primo de Rivera 3
09400 Aranda de Duero
Burgos
tel: (947) 50 56 06

Consejo Regulador de Rueda
Santísimo Cristo 26
47290 Rueda
Valladolid
tel: (983) 86 82 46

Consejo Regulador de Toro
Plaza de España 7
49800 Toro
Zamora
tel: (988) 69 03 35

Consejo Regulador de El Bierzo
Los Morales 1
24540 Cacabelos
León
tel: (987) 54 61 50;
fax: (987) 54 92 36

Consejo Regulador de Cigales
Onésimo Redondo, s/n
47270 Cigales
Valladolid
tel: (983) 33 55 83

CATALUNYA

ués.

More so than all the other autonomous regions of Spain, Catalunya is a virtual state within a state. At once the wealthiest, most sophisticated, most *avant garde* of all regions, it is viewed as something of a promised land by its native and adopted sons alike, a nation with a fiercely independent culture and language, a unique sense of its own worth, and a deep-seated resentment of power and control emanating from central Madrid, a city which the Catalans dismiss as little more than a backwater in contrast to their own vital, throbbing, crazy Barcelona. Catalunya is as different from stereotypical Spain as can be imagined. Little wonder, then, that its inhabitants despise bullfights and flamenco.

Independent Catalunya was established as early as the ninth century after the expulsion of the Moors and more than 500 years before the Catholic Monarchs' formation of the Spanish state. The Generalitat, Catalunya's autonomous parliament, celebrated in 1988 the thousandth anniversary of its foundation. Union with Aragón in 1137 brought a further expansion of power, and during the fourteenth century the kingdom was an important commercial and maritime force, its influence extending not only over the eastern Iberian seaboard and the Balearic islands, but over parts of southern France, Sardinia, Corsica, Italy, even parts of modern-day Greece. However, after Ferdinand of Aragón and Isabel la Católica married, uniting the Kingdoms of Castile and Aragón, Catalunya's fortunes declined as power was transferred to central Spain.

In modern times, under the decades of Franco's dictatorship, Catalan culture was severely repressed, an act which created a widespread resentful undercurrent that undoubtedly still simmers today and which leaves the visitor to the region in little doubt that he or she is in an entirely separate world from Castilian Spain.

For a start there is Catalá, the Catalan language, not a dialect of Spanish but a Romance language in its own right, related to the ancient *langue d'Oc* of Occitaine, today spoken not only throughout the region, but also in most of Valencia, parts of Aragón, the Balearic islands, and in isolated pockets of French Roussillon. Though Franco tried to wipe it out, banning its use in schools and broadcasts and ordering all books published in Catalá to be destroyed, it remains overwhelmingly the first language of the people of Catalunya, spoken widely by all.

In many senses, Catalunya is the California of Spain. Certainly both are states of immense wealth, influence and incredible natural beauty. The rocky coastline of the Ampurdán and Costa Brava is reminiscent of the Pacific shores of northern California, while the interior wine lands of both lead up from a Mediterranean littoral through rolling hills towards dramatic mountain ranges. Catalunya, furthermore, like California, is a region where prosperity is based on both traditional and new 'high-tech' industries (biotechnology, telecommunications, microelectronics) as well as a strong agricultural base. There is something of a forward-looking New World attitude evident in Catalunya, too, that contrasts with traditional, conservative, Catholic attitudes found in other parts of Spain. One senses here a boundless confidence, an inherent self-belief, perhaps even a hubristic arrogance.

Certainly, from a wine point of view, Catalunya has emerged in recent decades as the most open-minded of all Spain's great wine regions in terms of technical innovation, experimentation with both native and foreign grape varieties, and in the creation of a remarkably broad and eclectic range of wines. Today the region is the source of superlative sparkling Cava wines produced by the classic method of secondary fermentation in the bottle; fine white and world-class red wines produced in the Penedés, Catalunya's premier wine zone; excellent sparkling and table wines from Alella, north of Barcelona, and the Ampurdán-Costa Brava extending up to the French frontier; traditional old-style *vinos rancios* and luscious Moscatel altar wines from Tarragona; immense, almost black wines from the slate slopes of the Priorato; and exceptionally clean sparkling Cava, fine white, and oaky, smooth red wines from the Costers del Segre, especially from the Raimat estate, created literally out of desert through the imagination, efforts and belief of the Raventós family.

Catalunya is an exciting region to visit. Though parts of its coast have been blighted by thoughtless mass development, there are still many areas of outstanding beauty both by the Mediterranean seaboard, as well as in its hinterland, especially leading up to the mountains of Montserrat and the Catalan Pyrenees. Barcelona is one of the great cities of Europe; Tarragona, one of the most important cities in the ancient Roman empire, still has considerable and impressive remains from that classic age. For the wine lover, this is one of Spain's most welcoming regions with numerous opportunities for in-depth wine visits and tours. The range of wines produced, moreover, is an always excellent accompaniment to the varied and delicious cuisine of Catalunya.

Orientation

The large and prosperous autonomous region of Catalunya comprises four provinces: Barcelona, Tarragona, Lérida and Gerona.

Barcelona's international airport is located at El Prat de Llobregat, 14 km to the south of the city. There are smaller airports served by international charter flights at Gerona for the Costa Brava, and Reus for Tarragona and the Costa Dorada. The region's location adjacent to the French frontier makes it one of the principal overland routes into or out of the country, and road and rail connections are excellent. There are major road and rail routes that extend north–south along the coast to Valencia, as well as north-west via Zaragoza to Bilbao and the Basque country. The direct motorway link between Barcelona and Madrid is in the process of completion.

Catalunya's extensive wine country is found throughout the region, and holidaymakers can most easily and enjoyably take excursions away from the beaches into the wine hills of Penedés, Alella, the Costa Brava and Tarragona. There are ample opportunities for visiting wine producers. For exploring the wine country, the use of a car is essential, though there may be opportunities for organized group visits.

Maps: Michelin No. 443 (Northern & Eastern & Balearics); Firestone Hispania C-3, T-25.

CATALUNYA

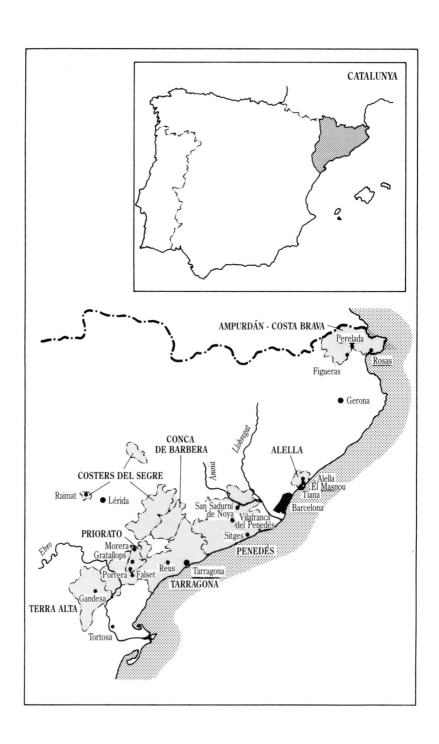

Modernisme

Catalunya is the home of *Modernisme*, a branch of *art nouveau* which flourished at the turn of the century, especially in the city of Barcelona. *Modernisme* is best known for fantastic and bizarre architecture, with curving lines, rounded edges, mosaic façades, elaborate collages of pottery, glass and porcelain, twisted wrought iron door and window fittings, sinuous archways and gateways, and polychromatic stone roofs. Its greatest exponent was Antonio Gaudí i Cornet, and its greatest monument is the unfinished Sagrada Familia cathedral, Barcelona's most striking landmark.

Art nouveau became wildly popular all over Europe for a brief period, and it embraced all the applied arts, not just architecture. At its heart was the essential belief that objects – churches, factories, apartment blocks, even park benches or domestic kettles – could be decorative as well as functional.

Don Manuel Raventós, son of José Raventós, the innovative and energetic Catalan who created the first sparkling Cava wines in 1872, was a great follower of the movement. The Codorníu cellars in San Sadurní, a declared National Historical Artistic Monument, were designed and constructed by Gaudí's contemporary and colleague, José María Puig y Cadafalch. This remarkable cathedral to wine mirrors the outline of the Montserrat mountain in the background, and, with its splendid stained glass windows and sweeping, elliptical brick arches, is one of the most striking *bodegas* in the world.

The basic functionalism of *Modernisme* is evident also in the Raventós' Raimat winery, constructed in 1918 on the estate above Lérida. Designed for Raventós by Rubió Bellver, it was the first reinforced concrete construction built in Spain. This, too, is a cathedral-like temple of wine; yet the striking, step-shaped exterior served a practical purpose as well. During fermentation periods, the interior of the building was kept cool by cascades of water descending the outside steps of the building.

LOS VINOS: THE WINES OF CATALUNYA

Alella DO Tiny but historic demarcated region north of Barcelona centred on Tiana, Alella and Santa María de Martorelles, producing primarily pleasant, light white table wines, as well as some *rosado* and red wines. Principal grape varieties include white Pansá

Blanca (Xarel-lo) and Garnacha Blanca and black Pansá Rosada, Tempranillo and Garnacha. White, *rosado* and red wines must attain 11.5–13.5°. This zone is also the source of excellent Cava.

Ampurdán-Costa Brava DO
Most northerly wine region in Catalunya, extending along and into the Costa Brava hinterland up to the frontier with France. Source of both white (from Macabeo and Xarel-lo; minimum alcohol 11–13.5°) and *rosado* and red wines (from Garnacha and Cariñena; minimum alcohol 11.5–14°) as well as fine sparkling wines (both Cava and Granvás) and traditional fortified *vinos rancios* from the Garnacha grape similar in character to the *vin doux naturel* (VDN) wines from nearby French Roussillon.

Vinos Espumosos: Spanish Sparkling Wines

Cava DO *Denominación* applying to Spain's finest sparkling wines, produced by a process of elaboration and ageing whereby secondary fermentation and elimination of the bottle sediment takes place in the same bottle. Minimum *crianza* of 9 months is required prior to release. Cava is the only *denominación* for Spanish wines that does not apply to a geographical area: it is granted to wines produced by the specified classic process of elaboration, utilizing authorized grapes, and taking place in a variety of regions extending over mainly 9 provinces: Barcelona, Gerona, Lérida and Tarragona (all in Catalunya), as well as Zaragoza, Navarra, La Rioja, Alava, Valencia and in a few isolated individual *bodegas* granted the *denominación* by special dispensation. In practice, however, some 90% of Cava is produced in the Penedés zone, with the industry centred on the sparkling wine capital of San Sadurní de Noya. The principal grape varieties are Macabeo (Viura in Rioja), Xarel-lo and Parellada, while Chardonnay is also authorized and is increasingly being planted and used. The levels of sweetness are defined as follows:

Brut Natural or *Brut Nature*
Totally bone dry, released without the addition of *licor de expedición*.
Extra Brut Less than 6 grams of sugar per litre.
Brut 0–15 grams of sugar per litre.

Extra seco   12–20 grams of sugar per litre.

Seco   17–35 grams of sugar per litre.

Semi-seco   33–50 grams of sugar per litre.

Dulce   More than 50 grams of sugar per litre.

Método Tradicional   Fine sparkling wines produced by the same classic method as employed for Cava, but outside those zones delimited by the Cava *denominación*. Such wines, particularly those produced in the Castilla y León wine zone of Rueda from the Verdejo grape, can be excellent and in no way inferior.

Método Fermentación en Botella   Transfer method, whereby secondary fermentation takes place in the bottle, then the wine, once rendered sparkling, is filtered and transferred to a clean bottle in order to eliminate the lees. Wines must age for minimum of 2 months on the lees. Label may say *Vino Espumoso Natural* or *Fermentación en Botella*.

Método Granvás   Charmat or *cuve close* method whereby the secondary fermentation takes place in large hermetically sealed stainless steel vats, after which the wine is filtered and bottled under pressure.

Vino Gasificado   The lowest quality sparkling wine, produced by injecting carbon dioxide into the base wine.

Conca de Barberá DO   Recently demarcated region west of Penedés, most noteworthy for the Torres flagship Milmanda estate which is located here. Those great Chardonnay wines, however, are atypical of the zone and have not, as yet, utilized the *denominación*. Much of the resources of Conca de Barberá goes to the production of Cava. In addition to the white Macabeo, Xarel-lo and Parellada, principal black grapes include Garnacha and Ull de Llebre (Tempranillo) and these are utilized for the production of *rosado* and red wines mainly in co-operative wineries. White and *rosado* wines must reach 10–12° alcohol; red wines must attain 10.5–13° alcohol.

Costers del Segre DO   While the *denominación* Costers del Segre applies to vineyards extending over some 29 municipalities in the province of Lérida and one in the province of Tarragona, in practice there is only one commercial producer of note at present, Raimat. The *denominación* applies to white, *rosado*, red and sparkling wines

CATALUNYA

produced from a variety of authorized grapes: white varieties include Macabeo, Parellada, Xarel-lo, Chardonnay and Garnacha Blanca; black varieties are Ull de Llebre (Tempranillo), Cabernet Sauvignon, Merlot, Pinot Noir, Monastrell, Trepat and Mazuelo (Cariñena). White, *rosado* and red wines must reach 9.5–13.5° alcohol.

Penedés DO Catalunya's premier table wine zone extends into the hinterland above coastal Sitges and Vilanova i la Geltrú and is centred on the wine town of Vilafranca del Penedés. The *denominación* applies to white, *rosado* and red wines produced from both native and international grapes: white varieties include Macabeo, Xarel-lo, Parellada, Moscatel, Malvasia, Chardonnay, Chenin Blanc, Gewürztraminer, Riesling; authorized black grapes are Garnacha, Cariñena, Ull de Llebre (Tempranillo), Samsó, Monastrell, Cabernet Sauvignon, Merlot and Pinot Noir. Much of the zone's production goes to the Cava industry. White wines must reach 9–13° alcohol; *rosado*, 10–13°; red, 10–14°.

Priorato DO Tiny but historic wine enclave located in the west of the Tarragona province over 11 municipalities, producing primarily traditional red wines of great personality and immense power, as well as smaller amounts of white and *rosado* wines and traditional *vinos rancios*. Permitted grape varieties include white Garnacha Blanca, Macabeo, Chenin Blanc and Pedro Ximénez, and black Garnacha, Garnacha Peluda and Cariñena. White, *rosado* and red wines must all reach a minimum of 13° alcohol but can traditionally reach upwards of 18° naturally. *Vino rancio* must have 14–20° alcohol.

Tarragona DO The Tarragona *denominación*, Catalunya's largest, applies to a zone noted primarily for its sturdy, high-alcohol white, *rosado* and red wines mainly today sold and exported in bulk. However, historically this was one of Spain's great wine regions, famous above all for its Tarragona Gold *vinos rancios* much loved in Victorian England. Such traditional wines, today known as Tarragona Clásico, continue to be made, albeit on a much reduced scale. The Tarragona vineyard extends over 75 municipalities, and is further divided into two sub-zones: Tarragona Campo to the east of the capital and Falset to the south-west. The principal grape varieties are white Macabeo, Xarel-lo, Parellada and Garnacha Blanca and black Garnacha, Mazuelo (Cariñena) and Ull de

Brandy de Penedés

Catalunya is one of Spain's traditional centres for the distillation of wine into grape brandy, a practice carried out here since the thirteenth century when Arnau de Vilanova, a Catalan alchemist, learned the secret art of distilling from Arabs and made the first Catalan brandies at the court of Pere II, Count of Barcelona. The resulting unaged grape brandy, or *aguardiente*, not only had antiseptic and medicinal uses, it was furthermore discovered that when added to the rather thin, low in alcohol wines of the region, it allowed them to be conserved for lengthy periods and shipped without undue deterioration. The production of *aguardiente* became an important part of the Catalan wine industry and by the eighteenth century more than 7000 pipes (casks of about 485 litres each) were being shipped annually from Vilanova i la Geltrú, principally to Russia, America, London and Amsterdam, in addition to much greater quantities of fortified wines such as Tarragona.

Today, the region remains an important distilling centre; indeed Penedés is the only Spanish zone other than Jerez entitled to a geographical designation for brandy under EC regulations, Brandy de Penedés. The best examples are produced in Charentais pot stills by a process of double distillation as employed in Cognac and are subsequently aged statically before blending and assembly (rather than dynamically in *soleras* as in Jerez). Brandy de Penedés is generally somewhat leaner and drier in style than sherry brandy, at its best an extremely fine, fragrant and smooth expression of the distilled essence of the grape.

Llebre (Tempranillo). White, *rosado* and red wines from Tarragona Campo must attain 11–13° alcohol; Falset is noted for its robust red wines which must reach a minimum of 13° alcohol. Tarragona Clásico, produced in both red and white as well as in sweet and dry versions, must contain at least 15° alcohol.

Terra Alta DO   Relatively small delimited wine region in the south-west of the province of Tarragona extending across 12 municipalities, producing robust white, *rosado* and red wines, much of which are sold in bulk for blending. Authorized grapes include the white Macabeo and Garnacha Blanca and black Cariñena, Garnacha and Garnacha Peluda. The wines must attain 12–15° alcohol.

CATALUNYA

LA GASTRONOMÍA: FOODS OF CATALUNYA

Just as Catalunya has possessed and safeguarded its historic, cultural and linguistic identity down the centuries, so has Spain's most idiosyncratic and individual autonomous region developed and maintained a regional cuisine that is uniquely its own. The powerful Catalan state, whose influence in the Middle Ages extended as far as the eastern Mediterranean, naturally received and assimilated a vast variety of foreign influences; moreover, unusual ingredients from afar, especially spices, flowed through its ports as one of its principal maritime trading commodities. Thus, over the centuries, a Catalan cuisine developed which, while utilizing its abundant natural produce and products of both sea and land and remaining essentially in touch with its country roots, at the same time developed a character more European, sophisticated, even slightly whimsical compared to the heavier, serious *cocina* of Castilian Spain.

Take *zarzuela*, one of the region's great classic dishes. *Zarzuela* is a distinctively Spanish genre of operetta, and indeed this dish is a colourful and slightly unpredictable symphony of the sea, incorporating any type of fish and shellfish available, cooked together in a rich, saffron-scented sauce of onions, garlic and tomatoes.

Spanish cuisine, unlike French, is generally not noted for its sauces, but Catalunya claims an impressive range, including *ali-oli*, that pungent garlic mayonnaise that has become a favourite across the Mediterranean (mayonnaise itself, it is claimed, was invented on the Catalan island of Menorca and was named after its capital city, Mahon); also *romesco, samfaina* and *picada*. Though these sauces are not in themselves difficult to prepare or particularly sophisticated or refined, they add considerable variety to the daily Catalan diet, and certainly provide a colourful contrast to the more predictable and unimaginative foods of the central Spanish interior.

That said, only a Catalan would claim that this is Spain's premier gastronomic region. As one might expect from a wealthy and forward-looking region that thinks more than highly of itself, there is no shortage in Barcelona and in outlying country areas and coastal resorts of restaurants serving what may be considered modern, fashionable foods, even so-called *nueva cocina*, Spain's answer to *nouvelle cuisine*. If that is your scene, by all means go for it. However, for our money, we far prefer to seek out the traditional Catalan country inns, *masías* and *hostales* serving the basically

Porrón-manship

The *porrón* is a drinking vessel unique to Catalunya, the region's answer to the leather wineskin *bota* used elsewhere in the Iberian interior. Made of glass, with a bulbous body and a long, pointed spout pierced only by the tiniest aperture, the *porrón* used to grace the tables of virtually every Catalan house at mealtimes, a communal drinking vessel to be picked up and drunk from at arm's length, the wine squirting into the mouth in a fluid parabolic arc.

An octogenarian Ampurdán farmer whom we met explained, 'In our house, we always had two *porrones*: one filled with wine, the other filled with water mixed with a little wine for the young ones. Even as very young children, we drank from the *porrón*. Today, since everyone has refrigerators, the *porrón* is hardly used any more. And it is frowned upon now to give children wine, even wine mixed with water.' He banged his cane angrily and added, 'I say better wine with water than Coca Cola.'

While the *porrón* may no longer be in daily use in most homes, in these heady days of Catalan culturalism it has taken on the significance of something of a modern shibboleth. Restaurants purporting to be typically Catalan may serve their house wines in the *porrón*. Or chauvinistic or macho Catalans may order wine by the bottle, then transfer it to the *porrón*. Like knowing how to dance the *sardana*, the ability to drink from this uniquely Catalan vessel without making a fool of yourself – dribbling red wine down your white shirt, squirting it into your eye or over your partner's silk blouse – is one sure way of establishing Catalan street credibility.

Porrones.

simple but distinctive foods of the land: *pan con tomate, esqueixada, escalivada, fideua, pollo con samfaina* and well-prepared fish and simple grilled meats.

Catalunya likes to consider itself different from the rest of Spain, even superior to it, but in one respect at least this region is far the poorer in that it lacks the great tradition of *tapas* bars. However, Catalan cuisine has no shortage of good little dishes, and many restaurants will provide a selection of nibbles and appetizers if you ask for a 'pica-pica' at the start of your meal.

¡Que aproveche! Regional Specialities of Catalunya

Pan con tomate (pa amb tomàquet) A Catalan *crostino* of toasted bread, rubbed first with a clove of garlic and a ripe mashed tomato, then dribbled with extra-virgin olive oil.

Esqueixada de bacalao Raw, de-salted *bacalao* (salt cod), flaked and mixed with onions, tomatoes, and red pepper, dressed with oil and vinegar and served as a first course or *tapa*. Very refreshing in summer.

Escalivada Roasted and peeled red peppers and aubergines, mixed with chopped tomatoes and onions, served as a salad dressed with olive oil and vinegar, or eaten on toasted bread as a *tapa*.

Xató Fish salad, made with *bacalao*, tuna, anchovies, lettuce, olives, onions and a special dressing: speciality of Sitges.

Ensalada catalana Substantial salad made with lettuce, boiled potatoes, green peppers, beans, tomatoes, tuna and hard-boiled eggs in a creamy dressing.

Habas a la catalana Broad beans cooked with herbs, spices and *butifarra*.

Ali-oli Supremely simple sauce made from finely mashed garlic and olive oil, mixed together to form a creamy mayonnaise-like emulsion: served with meat, fish and vegetables. **Rape con ali-oli** Monkfish first poached, then spread thickly with *ali-oli* and baked in a hot oven.

Samfaina Half-cooked Catalan sauce made with tomato, red pepper and aubergine, often served with chicken (*pollo con samfaina*) or rabbit (*conejo con samfaina*).

Romesco Spicy delicious sauce from Tarragona served with fish and shellfish and made with dried red peppers and chillies, vinegar, bread, garlic and toasted almonds.

Romescada Salad with dried

beans, raw *bacalao* and *romesco* sauce.

Picada   Catalan sauce containing garlic, parsley, toasted almonds, toasted hazelnuts and chopped pine nuts.

Fideua   One of the great dishes of Catalunya: tiny vermicelli noodles cooked in a *paella* pan together with plenty of fried garlic and concentrated fish stock, and served with pungent *ali-oli* on the side.

Mar i muntanya   Extravagant Ampurdán 'surf 'n turf' consisting usually of a combination of chicken, rabbit or snails with prawns, lobster, crayfish, monkfish or whatever else is at hand.

Butifarra   Large fat white Catalan pork sausage flavoured with spices like cumin and cinnamon as well as almonds and pine nuts; usually served grilled.
Butifarra con mongetes
Butifarra sausage cooked with *mongetes*, a type of white bean.

Escudella i carn d'olla   Catalan variation of the national *cocido*, containing chickpeas, *butifarra*, *pilota*, and any variety of meats and vegetables such as chicken, bacon, beef, pig's trotters, potatoes, carrots, cauliflower, usually eaten in two courses, first as a soup together with rice or noodles, then the meats and vegetables.

Caracoles en cacerola   Snails stewed with garlic, tomatoes and *pimientos*: speciality of Lérida.

Fideos a la cazuela   Ample Catalan stew made with sausages, *butifarra*, spare ribs, bacon and vermicelli noodles, cooked in a thick tomato and onion *sofrito*.

Conejo al ajo   Country stew of rabbit cooked in an earthenware *cazuela* together with wine, seasonings and ample quantities of garlic.

Pilota   Meatball made with ground meat, parsley, breadcrumbs and egg.

Suquet   Fisherman's pot containing different rock fish cooked in a thick *sofrito*.

Zarzuela de pescado
Substantial and spectacular fish stew made with a variety of fish and shellfish, cooked with tomatoes, garlic, olive oil, saffron and wine.

Crema quemada a la catalana
Catalan *crème brûlée*, made usually with a creamy egg custard topped with hard caramelized sugar, sometimes flamed in Chartreuse.

Cheese: *Mató i mel muntanyes de Montserrat*   Curd cheese from Montserrat served with mountain honey.

CATALUNYA

THE WINE ROADS OF CATALUNYA

In Brief: Most of Catalunya is wine country, so visitors to the region are fortunate in being able to dip into it from virtually wherever they are based.

For those entering the country from the north, the wine zone of Ampurdán-Costa Brava begins almost as soon as the French frontier is crossed. Apart from its wine interest, this rocky, far northern coast is one of the region's most beautiful and there are ample opportunities for traditional seaside holiday pursuits as well as forays into the vineyards.

South of the Costa Brava and just north of Barcelona itself, Catalunya's tiniest wine region, Alella, can be dipped into by heading inland from the coast at El Masnou. This is still quite beautiful wine country, but the suburbs of the nearby capital are encroaching upon it ever further each year.

The Penedés is without doubt Catalunya's most important wine region as well as its most welcoming. Located south-west of Barcelona, its centre is Vilafranca del Penedés, though the best and most enjoyable base for forays into the wine country is probably the seaside resort of Sitges, a fairly crazy yet still charming resort, popular both locally and internationally. San Sadurní de Noya is located within the Penedés wine zone and is the centre for the important Cava wine industry.

The beach resorts south of Tarragona are another popular holiday destination. Tarragona itself is a fascinating old town, with extensive Roman ruins and an atmospheric medieval *casco viejo* still located within its massive and ancient town walls. While much of the Tarragona hinterland is given over to vines, the most remarkable wine zone to visit is the Priorato, with its fascinating ruined Scala Dei monastery, and its bizarre slate terrain and isolated villages.

Inland Lérida is probably the least visited of Catalunya's provincial capitals and this arid hinterland would attract little interest for its wines were it not for the Raimat estate located north of the city just off the road to Huesca. This is without doubt one of Spain's most important and forward-looking wineries, and it is well worth making an appointment to visit and to taste the wines at the source. From Lérida, the wine traveller can head north into Aragón, and the up and coming wine zone of Somontano.

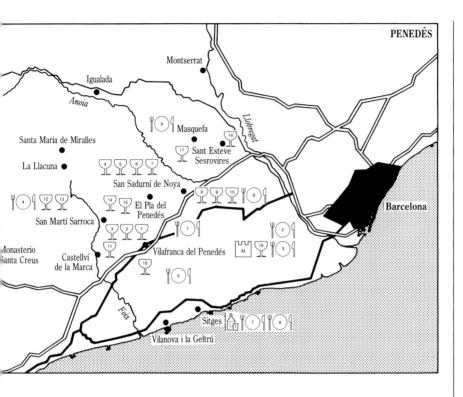

Penedés and San Sadurní de Noya: Exceptional Table Wines and Sparkling Wines

In recent decades, the Penedés has emerged as one of Spain's premier wine regions, the source of fine everyday and oak-aged white wines, exceptional red wines, sparkling Cava, even sweet dessert wines, traditional *vinos rancios* and fine brandies. It is one of the most dynamic and fastest-developing wine regions in Spain, and the scene of considerable experimentation with both native and foreign grape varieties, methods of training, winemaking, and the creation of a range of different styles of wine aimed at both the home and international markets.

Much of the credit for the high profile that the Penedés enjoys today must be given to the Torres family who have led the modernization of the local wine industry, pioneered a hugely impressive range of wines, and successfully marketed them throughout Spain as well as internationally. When, after studying oenology and viticulture in Dijon, Miguel A. Torres returned to the Penedés and his family wine firm in 1962, he was convinced that

CATALUNYA

there were precise limits to the quality of the wine that could be made from the native grapes of the region. He therefore embarked on an ambitious planting programme with noble grape varieties from abroad, not excluding the zone's native varieties, but alongside them. Thus, on the Torres estates, white grapes such as Riesling, Gewürztraminer, Muscat and Chenin Blanc are now grown alongside native Parellada, and black grapes such as Cabernet Sauvignon, Cabernet Franc, Merlot and Pinot Noir complement native Tempranillo, Garnacha and Cariñena. Torres' aim was, and still is, not to set out to make single varietal wines only, but rather to experiment with the blending and ageing of a variety of grapes to see what could be achieved.

In those days, it should be remembered, Spanish wine suffered from a poor reputation not only internationally but even within Spain itself. With the exception of aged red wines from Rioja, the isolated and unique Vega Sicilia, and fortified wines from Jerez, there were few quality Spanish wines of note.

It was a great moment for Spanish wine as a whole, therefore, when in 1979 at the so-called 'Wine Olympiad' in Paris, organized by the French gourmet publishers Gault-Millau, Torres' Gran Coronas Reserva 'Black Label' 1970, produced primarily from Cabernet Sauvignon grapes grown on the family estate of Mas La Plana, took top honours, beating even the great *premier grand cru classé* Château Latour. This event astonished the wine world both in Spain and abroad, and awoke producers and consumers alike to the fact that Spain has the potential to make truly great wines of world class, second to none.

Torres has since gone from strength to strength and today produces a masterly range of wines blended from a varied palette of both native and foreign grapes: Gran Viña Sol from Chardonnay and Parellada; Gran Viña Sol 'Castell de Fransola' from Parellada with Sauvignon Blanc fermented in French oak; Viña Esmeralda from Gewürztraminer and Muscat; Milmanda from Chardonnay fermented and aged *sur lie* in French oak; Sangre de Toro and Gran Sangre de Toro from Garnacha and Cariñena; Viña Magdala from Pinot Noir and Tempranillo; Coronas and Gran Coronas from Cabernet Sauvignon and Tempranillo; Las Torres from Merlot; and the now legendary Gran Coronas Reserva 'Black Label' from 100% Cabernet Sauvignon.

It is remarkable that such a diverse range of grape varieties can be cultivated successfully within a single wine zone. However, this is made possible by the particular climates and microclimates of the Penedés, which extends across three separate sub-zones ranging from sea level to altitudes of upwards of 800 metres. Lower Penedés (Bajo Penedés), the area extending into the coastal littoral above Sitges and Vilanova i la Geltrú, is the hottest sub-zone and is best suited to the cultivation of particularly fragrant grape varieties such as Moscatel and Malvasia, from which are made traditional fortified dessert wines such as the famous Moscatel de Sitges. These coastal hills, extending up to 200 metres above sea level, are also planted with native black grape varieties such as Garnacha, Cariñena, Ull de Llebre (Tempranillo) and Monastrell.

A higher range of coastal hills separates Vilafranca del Penedés from the lower zone, and the flattish depression formed between this range and the range of mountains leading up to the Montserrat makes up the Central Penedés, located at between 250 and 500 metres above sea level. This cooler but well-sheltered zone yields the grapes for some 60% of the zone's table wine production and has also traditionally been the source of prodigious quantities of the white grapes Xarel-lo, Macabeo and Parellada, grown to meet the seemingly insatiable requirements of the giant international firms producing sparkling Cava. Central Penedés has further proved itself a propitious habitat for international superstar grapes such as Cabernet Sauvignon, Pinot Noir, Chardonnay and Chenin Blanc.

Penedés Superior extends into the lower slopes of the Montserrat *sierra* to the north, as far as 80 kilometres inland from the coast and ranging in altitude from 500 to 800 metres above sea level. The microclimate here is considerably cooler, and this zone has been the traditional source of Parellada, the most delicate and aromatic of the three native grapes utilized to produce Cava. However, other grapes that are even more aromatic and characterful than Parellada can also fare well on these cool mountain slopes, notably Gewürztraminer, Riesling, Chenin Blanc and Chardonnay.

Given the undoubted potential of the Penedés, as well as the proximity of its coastal ports for shipping, it is perhaps surprising that the region historically never really enjoyed an outstanding reputation for its table wines. The fault, in part, may have lain with the antiquated Catalan system of farming known as the *Rabassa Morta*, a form of rigid sharecropping that was still in place until the late nineteenth century. By this system, not only did the peasant workers, known as *rabassaires*, have to share their crops with the landowners, they were only entitled to work the land for the duration of the life of the first planted vines. Thus, as under any form of sharecropping, the priority was always to grow as large a quantity of grapes as possible, rather than to strive for quality. When the vineyards of Catalunya were decimated, first by oidium in the mid-nineteenth century and later by phylloxera, the replanted vines, grafted on to American rootstock, had a much shorter life and this led to considerable discontent, legal arguments and the ultimate abandonment of the system.

The most significant event in the Penedés occurred in 1872 when Don José Raventós returned from his travels in France and on the family Codorníu estate in San Sadurní de Noya produced the first bottles of Penedés sparkling wine by the classic method of secondary fermentation in the bottle that he had witnessed and learned about in Champagne. The sparkling wine (called in those days 'champaña') was an immediate success and within ten years, it had taken the Penedés by storm. Such was the demand in subsequent decades – such is the continued demand today – that the majority of the vineyards of the Penedés were soon given over to the cultivation of Xarel-lo, Macabeo and Parellada, the established trio of grapes from which the base wine later rendered sparkling by secondary fermentation was produced.

The success of Cava, as the sparkling wine has come to be known, has undoubtedly brought considerable prosperity and success to the Penedés zone, where the overwhelming majority of such sparkling wines are produced. Immense profits have been ploughed back into the industry and have led to improvements in the vineyard, and to the creation of advanced winemaking installations utilizing the latest technologies, most notably the widescale introduction of cold fermentation equipment. Since many firms produce both Cava and table wines, these advances are leading to the production not only of improved sparkling wines, but also of better still table wines, above all crisp, clean and fruity cold-fermented white wines as well as outstanding fruity, supple red wines. The latter in particular can be quite different from the traditional Spanish reds from wine regions like Rioja, for in Penedés there is generally less emphasis on extended wood-ageing, for example, and more concentration on bringing out the seductive ripe flavours of the fruit.

One firm that has been producing excellent table wines for decades is Jean León SA. When Jean León, a successful Los Angeles restaurateur of Catalan descent, came to the Penedés in the early 1960s, purchased a 60-hectare property in the heart of the Cava country near San Sadurní de Noya, and promptly grubbed up the local white vines and replaced them with cuttings of Cabernet Sauvignon from Château Lafite and Chardonnay from Corton-Charlemagne, the locals thought he was absolutely crazy: they called him 'el americano loco'. After all, from their point of view, he was throwing away a guaranteed profit and return and replacing it with untried foreign vines that they had never even heard of.

The risk and indeed the investment was great, for at the time no one else, not even Torres, had yet planted these untried grape varieties in the Penedés, nor, for that matter, virtually anywhere else in Spain. Today, two wines only are produced, Jean León Cabernet Sauvignon and Jean León Chardonnay. They are undoubtedly among the finest wines not only from the Penedés but from all of Spain, produced entirely from grapes grown on the estate.

The white Chardonnay is fermented and aged in American oak *barricas* (50% new each year) and to my taste it is one of the most successful of such wines, very rich in colour with a full, buttery Chardonnay nose, and a balance in the mouth between the fatness of the fruit, the soft toasty vanilla of the oak, and the refreshing grapefruity zing of fresh fruity acid.

The red wines are fermented in stainless steel, and the period of maceration has in recent years been reduced from as much as 14 days to only 3–5 in order to produce more supple wines that can be enjoyed younger, yet which still have sufficient extract and tannin to age well. We tasted a variety of vintages from both the bottle and the vat and were impressed with the consistent quality of the wines, their intense colour, deep, concentrated berryish fruit, and elegant and firm tannins.

Superlative table wines are also being produced at Masía Bach, an outrageously flamboyant neo-classical mansion in the heart of the Penedés Superior near the little wine town of Sant Esteve Sesrovires. The estate was constructed by the Hermanos Bach, two brothers who had amassed a fortune selling uniforms to the British and French armies during World War I. The brothers were Francophiles and particularly loved the sweet wines of Sauternes. More as a hobby than anything else, they began to produce a sweet white wine on the estate, and named it Extrísimo Dulce, after the finest *extrísimo* cotton which they imported from India to make the uniforms. The wine achieved considerable fame as one of Spain's greatest sweet dessert wines and is still produced today. The Bach brothers had no children, and they therefore sold the estate in 1932 to the Mata family, who in turn sold it to Codorníu in 1975.

Currently Masía Bach is producing a range of fascinating wines that deserve attention. Magnificat, for example, is a white wine produced at present in only minuscule quantities from Chardonnay, Pinot Noir vinified off the skins *en blanco*, Xarel-lo and Chenin Blanc. Masía Bach Extrísimo *tinto* and Extrísimo *tinto* Reserva are both successful blends produced from Cabernet Sauvignon, Garnacha and Tempranillo, the latter given longer ageing in new wood, while Masía Bach Cabernet Sauvignon is a flavoursome, well-made varietal.

CATALUNYA

There are scores of other wine companies, large and small, producing good to excellent table wines in the Penedés. René Barbier, located in a beautiful twelfth-century estate outside San Sadurní de Noya, was purchased by the Freixenet group after the collapse of the Rumasa empire and today produces particularly noteworthy red wines from Tempranillo and Cabernet Sauvignon. Marqués de Monistrol is another beautiful estate located in the heart of the wine country in the tiny hamlet of Monistrol de Noya, noted not only for its sparkling wines, but also for its white Blanc de Blancs and Blanc en Noirs table wines. Cavas Hill, located at Moja just south of Vilafranca del Penedés, also produces excellent still wines as well as sparkling. Duarte de Siò produces both artisan Cava and still table wines, most notably a fine oak-aged red from Cabernet Sauvignon and Tempranillo, while Mont Marçal, another small but excellent Cava house, utilizes Chardonnay and Cabernet Sauvignon in its table wines.

One of the most interesting family enterprises is Ramón Balada's Celler Hisenda Miret, located in the charming wine *pueblo* of San Martí Sarroca. Balada produces single varietal Viña Toña wines from each of the three Cava grapes grown on his own vineyards only. These wines are all excellent in their own right and furthermore provide a fascinating opportunity to examine the qualities which each contributes to the Cava blends: Macabeo, most noteworthy for its fresh, zingy acidity, Xarel-lo for its peary opulence and full body, and Parellada for its finely scented green apple fruit.

The Penedés wine country is vast and there are literally hundreds of winegrowers and producers of excellent wines, both still and sparkling, located throughout. However, apart from some well-known and a few famous names, this still remains relatively uncharted wine country. As small growers decide in future years to produce their own wines and consequently up-grade their winemaking installations, it is probable that there will be many more new names emerging on to the regional, national and even international wine scene. Therefore it is an exciting wine region to visit, with more than ample scope for wine exploration.

Visitors will certainly wish to spend time in the capital of the Penedés, Vilafranca del Penedés, and should not miss visiting the Torres winery as well as the excellent *museo del vino* in the old part of town. From Vilafranca, strike into the heart of the wine country by heading first to San Martí Sarroca, passing the Torres winery at Pacs del Penedés along the way. San Martí has a beautiful Romanesque church and castle complex from which there are superb views of the Penedés vineyard leading up to the higher zones. There is also a small exhibition and sale of wines and Cava from the *pueblo* in the castle. From San Martí, continue into the high Penedés Superior as far as La Llacuna and Santa Maria de Miralles, then circle around by way of Igualada back to Vilafranca or San Sadurní. Or else, from Vilafranca, head through the vineyards to San Sadurní de Noya, capital of Cava, and then strike out to fascinating wine hamlets like El Pla del Penedés, Monistrol de Noya, or, further towards the dramatic Montserrat, Masquefa and Sant Esteve Sesrovires.

Museo del Vino

MUSEU DEL VI
PLAÇA DE JAUME I
08720 VILAFRANCA DEL PENEDÉS
BARCELONA

HOURS: 10–14h; 16h30–19h30. Closed Sun afternoon, Mon. Superlative and extensive wine museum tracing the history of wine in the Penedés from ancient to present times. Good diorama models, collection of Catalan barrels and *porrones*, and

explanation of the geology of the zone. This is possibly the best and most welcoming wine museum in Spain. The visit ends in a tavern with a complimentary glass of wine, a flûte of Cava, or for groups or families, a communal *porrón* to pass around. Wines are changed each fortnight, and the wines on display from participating *bodegas* are available for purchase.

San Sadurní de Noya

San Sadurní de Noya, located 45 km south-west of Barcelona, is one of the great sparkling wine capitals of the world. Though signs and noticeboards leave you in little doubt as to the principal activity of this otherwise rather unprepossessing town, it is still hardly possible to imagine the scale of this vast industry. Some 140 million bottles of sparkling Cava, produced by the classic method of secondary fermentation and expulsion of the lees within the same bottle, are made each year. While Cava can legally be produced in other parts of Catalunya (good examples come from Alella and Ampurdán-Costa Brava), as well as in parts of Rioja, Aragón and Navarra, some 90% of the total output comes from the Penedés. Amazingly, of that vast amount a full 80% is produced by the two giants of the industry and their

CATALUNYA

subsidiaries, Codorníu and Freixenet, both located in San Sadurní de Noya along with literally dozens of other medium-large to tiny producers alike.

Though Cava has been produced for over a century, the last decades have seen a virtual revolution in winemaking technology that has transformed the industry and allowed even finer and better sparkling wines to be made in Catalunya. Cava sometimes used to suffer from a rather coarse earthiness, but the best wines today demonstrate a character that is exceedingly fresh, even citrusy, overlayered with attractive creamy fruit.

Because of the high temperatures during the *vendimia*, which begins in early September, it is essential that the grapes are picked at the optimum moment of ripeness, and that they remain whole and intact during transport as quickly as possible to the press house. The grapes are then de-stemmed and pressed extremely lightly, generally in horizontal pneumatic presses or in ultra-modern continuous presses. Harsh or excessive pressing would give poor or coarse grape must. The musts of each grape variety are then classified into different qualities, the best of which will be made into Cava; the rest will end up at the distillery. The musts are next clarified, in the best houses by means of sophisticated vacuum filters. Fermentation takes place in stainless steel deposits at low temperatures and may last upwards of two or three weeks to result in base wines that are meticulously clean, fresh and attractively round and fruity.

Once the base wines have been fermented, the wines made from each of the separate different grape varieties, Xarel-lo, Macabeo, Parellada and, increasingly, Chardonnay, are classified then blended together. Each house naturally has its own style and combines the different wines in varying proportions. Generally, Macabeo is deemed to contribute finesse and acidity, Xarel-lo gives the wine its power and body, and Parellada is the most fine and aromatic of the native varieties. If Chardonnay is brought in, it contributes fine fruity acidity as well as the rich and distinctive buttery flavours and aroma of that great grape, giving a style that is recognized by consumers as more international.

After blending, a measured amount of cane sugar and yeast is added to the wine to precipitate the secondary fermentation, and the wines are bottled and sealed with temporary crown corks. They are then laid to rest in horizontal positions, traditionally arranged manually in blocks known as *rimas*, these days more often in crates or cube-shaped racks that can be moved mechanically. The secondary fermentation occurs slowly, and the action of the yeasts feeding on the sugar mixture produces a small amount of additional alcohol and an abundance of carbon dioxide, which slowly

Cadaqués, a charming fishing village in the Ampurdán, Catalunya

The dramatic Montserrat *sierra* is the backdrop to the vast vineyards of the Penedés, Catalunya

Above: Horreos – small stone barns raised above the ground on pillars – are a familiar sight in Galicia

Left: The Virgin of Guadalupe, Extremadura

Below: Medellín, Extremadura, birthplace of Hernán Cortés, conqueror of Mexico

Right: Paella, though Spain's national dish, is authentically a speciality of Valencia

Below right: Sowing rice on the flooded paddies of the Albufera, Valencia

Above: Vineyards of Getaria, overlooking the Basque fishing village

Left: Murcia street scene

Right: The 15th-century castle of Olite, former residence of the Kings of Navarra

Above: The Remelluri farmhouse, a prestigious family-run single vineyard estate in the Rioja Alavesa

Left: Stone carving in 12th-century cloisters of the Collegiate Church, Santillana del Mar

Opposite page, top: Bodegas R. López de Heredia is one of the oldest and most traditional Rioja producers

Opposite page, bottom: Bottles of Viña Tondonia Gran Reserva ageing in the cellars of R. López de Heredia

Left: Racking, a labour-intensive and daily task in the *bodegas* of the Rioja

Below: Grape harvest on the Contino estate, Laserna, near Logroño

becomes dissolved, giving the wine its sparkle. The slower and more careful this secondary fermentation, the finer, lighter and more persistent are the resulting bubbles. The time that each house leaves the wines to undergo the secondary fermentation varies, but all non-vintage Cava must so age for a minimum of nine months and vintage Cava for a minimum of three years.

Once the secondary fermentation is considered complete, the final process is to clarify the wine by removal of the bottle sediment, a process known as *remoción* or *remuage*. To achieve this, the fine yeasty sludge that has collected in the bottles as a by-product of the yeasts feeding on the sugars during the secondary fermentation must be induced to collect in the necks of the bottles, from where it can be expelled. Traditionally this process is achieved manually, by placing the bottles in wooden racks known as *pupitres* where skilled workers gradually twist and nudge each bottle from a near horizontal position to an almost up-side down vertical one, a process that takes upwards of 30 days. At the end of it, the bottles, lying *en punta*, have the yeasty sludge resting against the bottle's stopper.

age, the process of hand riddling to clear sparkling wines of their sediment after the secondary ...ntation in the bottle.

This manual process, however, is extremely slow and expensive. The Spanish Cava industry has led the way in the development of a remarkable automatic or semi-automatic system that has revolutionized sparkling wine production: by this process some 500 bottles at a time can be placed in metal cubic racks known either as *girasoles* or *girapaletas* which are then mechanically turned or rocked to achieve the same result of gradually settling the sediment in the necks of the bottles. This process, though by no means as picturesque as the manual one, is far less labour intensive: while a single manual *remueur* could perhaps turn and riddle 40–60,000 bottles a day, under this system three men can turn one and a half million bottles a day. The development of special yeasts that are slippery rather than sticky means that the resulting clarity of the wine is in no way impaired.

When the sediment has collected in the neck of the bottle, the next stage is its expulsion. Traditionally, this too was undertaken manually, but today the process has been mechanized. The bottles are placed neck down on an automatic line which passes them through a freezing brine solution. This freezes the collected sediment into a block of ice in the neck of the bottle next to the crown cork. Once frozen, the crown cork is taken off, the bottle is given a sharp tap, and the pressure inside the bottle expels the block of frozen wine, and with it the collected sediment, thus rendering the remaining wine crystal clear.

The process of expelling the sediment results naturally in an ullage within each bottle that must be refilled. At this stage, the sparkling wine in the bottle is bone dry; to produce the range of styles of wines – Brut, Seco, Semi-Seco, or Dulce – a *licor de expedición* is added to top the bottle up to its full level. The *licor de expedición* consists of older reserve base wines mixed with pure cane sugar in varying degrees of sweetness. While both the export and the Catalan taste is almost overwhelmingly for dry Brut or Brut Nature wines with little or no sugar added, in the rest of Spain there is still a preference for semi-sweet and sweet Cava, probably because much of the wine is drunk at weekends with pastries. Once topped up, the bottles are given their final corks, wired muzzles, labels and capsules.

Visitors to San Sadurní will be able to witness this remarkable and lengthy process in its entirety. Both the giants of the industry, Freixenet and Codorníu, are extremely welcoming to visitors, even those who turn up without previous appointments. They trundle through the vast and endless galleries in the comfort of little trains and afterwards there is always a generous tasting of the wines.

Though Freixenet, with its excellent creamy Cordon Negro Cava in the distinctive black satin bottle and its classy, bone dry Brut Nature Vintage, and Codorníu, with its Première Cuvée and its light and elegant Anna de Codorníu, both produce first-class wines that represent the benchmarks of the Cava industry, San Sadurní de Noya and the surrounding countryside is literally riddled with scores of medium to tiny wine firms, many of whose wines will never be seen outside Catalunya.

Within the region itself, certainly, a distinction is made between Cavas produced by the giant firms and Cavas from small *artesanal* companies. While in no way disparaging the wines made by the giants, which are of a remarkably high standard and overall quality and consistency, one senses a consensus among the local Catalan consumers that smaller is better. As, for example, in Córdoba, where every bar prides itself on its own local source of Montilla, *flor*-fresh and drawn direct from the barrel, so in Barcelona or Sitges would most bars and restaurants, as something of a matter of pride, seek to offer their own exclusive Cava from a small artisan house. For it should be remembered that in Catalunya, it is as natural to enjoy a flûte of Cava in a bar as it is a '*chiquito*' of red wine in northern Spain or a *copita* of *fino* in Andalucía. There are literally scores of establishments producing such wines to meet the seemingly unquenchable local demand.

Moreover, if Cava initially owed its spectacular success to its excellent price/quality ratio (even today Cava is remarkably inexpensive, given the massive investments in technology and the overall high quality of the wine), a new tier of premium Cavas is now emerging on the scene. When Josep María Raventós i Blanc, namesake and great-grandson of the founder of Codorníu, split his ties with the family business in 1982, he not only kept the family house, located within the grounds of Codorníu, but also some of the company's best vineyards surrounding the estate. Following his untimely death, his son, Manuel Raventós i Negra, constructed a strikingly modern, state-of-the-art winery directly across the road from Codorníu, not with the intention of competing directly with it, but instead of filling a niche at the top end of the Cava market. Raventós i Blanc Brut, in its distinctive and classy livery, is certainly one of the best premium Cavas I have tasted, fresh yet rich, with fine persistent bubbles and a good, yeasty depth of flavour and fruit.

Other good top end Cavas that we have enjoyed from medium to smaller companies include Reserva de la Familia from Juve y Camps, Gran Tradición from Marqués de Monistrol, Brut Imperial from Rovellats, Brut Brutísimo from Cavas Hill, Gran Reserva from Josep Masachs, Brut Nature from Cavas Montsarra, and Extra Brut from Duart de Sió. Outside Penedés, other excellent Catalan Cavas include the superlative and fragrant Raimat Chardonnay from Costers del Segre, Parxet Brut and Parxet Chardonnay from Alella, and the deluxe Gran Claustro from the Castillo de Perelada winery in the Ampurdán-Costa Brava.

The Catalans themselves are immense lovers of Cava and down the stuff in prodigious quantity, as an *aperitif* (rarely will you see anyone drinking sherry in Catalunya), throughout meals, after lunch or dinner with *postres*, even for *desayuno*, I imagine. When we are in this lovely region, I must confess, we tend to follow local custom, too.

CATALUNYA

Bodegas y Cavas: Stop to Taste; Stop to Buy

1

MIGUEL TORRES SA
COMERÇIO 22
08720 VILAFRANCA DEL PENEDÉS
BARCELONA
TEL: (93) 890 01 00; FAX: (93) 817 02 07,
817 07 03

WINES PRODUCED: *Vinos blancos*:
Viña Sol; San Valentin; Gran Viña
Sol; Viña Esmeralda; Gran Viña
Sol 'Castell de Fransola'; Waltraud;
Milmanda. *Vino rosado*: De Casta.
Vinos tintos: Sangre de Toro; Gran
Sangre de Toro; Coronas; Gran
Coronas; Gran Coronas Reserva
Black Label 'Mas La Plana'; Mas
Borrás; Viña Magdala; Gran
Magdala; Viña Las Torres.
Fortified wines: Vino de Licor;
Moscatel de Oro; Sangre Brava.
BRANDIES PRODUCED: Solera
Selecta; Gran Reserva; Fontenac;
Miguel Torres; Miguel I; Honorable.
VISITS: Mon–Fri without
appointment (except for groups).
Tours every hour on the hour 9–
12h; 15–17h. While the visiting
facilities are at present located in
the *bodega* at Vilafranca, Torres are
currently in the process of
constructing a new visitors' centre
in Pacs del Penedés. Opening hours
and days have not yet been fixed, but
should be in place by summer 1993.
Telephone the above number and
ask for the Public Relations
Department for further information.
The Torres family have been
making wine in the Penedés since
the seventeenth century, but the
present company was founded in
1870, and is still located in its
original *bodegas* opposite the
railway line at Vilafranca del
Penedés, which enabled the wines to
be easily shipped to Barcelona.
Though noted today primarily for its
innovative range of modern wines
produced from both native and
international grapes, the company
still produces a fascinating range of
traditional wines, including *vinos
rancios* aged in *bombas* outside in
the sun. The Torres brandies are
also distilled on the site, the best in
impressive copper Charentais pot stills.
   The vinification plant at Pacs del
Penedés is one of the most modern
in Europe. Torres owns some 800
hectares of its own vineyards,
accounting for almost 50% of its
needs; the remaining grapes are
purchased from local winegrowers
in the different zones who receive
considerable support from the
company's technicians. There are 7
separate Torres estates: Masía
Torres and Mas La Plana (Pacs del
Penedés); Mas Rabell de Fontenac
(San Martí Sarroca); Mas Jané
(Pontons); Fransola (Santa María
de Miralles); Milmanda Castle
(Poblet); Agulladolç (San Joan de
Mediona).
English, French, German spoken.

2 CELLER COOPERATIU DE
VILAFRANCA DEL PENEDÉS SCCL
CALLE BISBE MORGADES 18
08720 VILAFRANCA DEL PENEDÉS
BARCELONA
TEL: (93) 890 10 49; FAX: (93) 890 04 18

WINES PRODUCED: Els Castellers
Xarel-lo *blanco*, Els Castellers
Macabeo *blanco*; Els Castellers
rosado; Els Castellers *tinto*.
CAVAS PRODUCED: Els Castellers
Extra Brut, Brut, Rosat, Extra Seco,
Extra Semiseco.

VISITS: Daily, working hours.
Appointment not essential but
appreciated.
Vilafranca's largest co-operative
winery has some 400 member *socios*
who collectively work over 1000 ha.
of vineyards and produce a range of
wines and Cavas named after the
acrobatic human castle teams for
which Vilafranca is famous.
A little English spoken.

3 CELLER GRIMAU-GOL SA
CALLE NORD 8
08720 VILAFRANCA DEL PENEDÉS
BARCELONA
TEL: (93) 892 03 72

CAVAS PRODUCED: Duart de Siò
Brut; Duart de Siò Brut Nature;
Duart de Siò Cuvée de les Flors.
WINES PRODUCED: Vi Novell

Penedés; El Blanc Brisasol *blanco*;
El Rosat Cabernet *rosado*; El Negre
Grana *tinto* Reserva.
VISITS: Daily, working hours.
Traditional family winery
producing good Cavas, still white
table wines, and a notable oak-aged
red from Tempranillo and Cabernet
Sauvignon.
English, French spoken.

4 RENÉ BARBIER SA
CTRA SANT QUINTÍN, KM 5
08770 SAN SADURNÍ DE NOYA
BARCELONA
TEL: (93) 899 51 11; FAX: (93) 899 60 06

WINES PRODUCED: René Barbier
blanco, rosado, tinto; René Barbier
Kratliner *blanco*; René Barbier
Cabernet Sauvignon; René Barbier
tinto Reserva.
VISITS: Mon–Fri 9–11h30; 15–
17h. Appointment necessary.

The René Barbier winery was
established in 1880 by a Frenchman
who left his own country after it
was devastated by phylloxera.
Today it shares the beautiful estate
outside San Sadurní with its sister
company Segura Viudas. Both
properties were purchased from the
Spanish government by the
Freixenet Group following the
collapse of Rumasa. This well run
and modern winery is the second

CATALUNYA

largest producer of Penedés table wines, noted for its sound range of dry white, *rosado* and red table wines.

English spoken.

---

5 FREIXENET SA
CALLE JOAN SALA 2
08770 SAN SADURNÍ DE NOYA
BARCELONA
TEL: (93) 891 07 00; FAX: (93) 891 12 54

CAVAS PRODUCED: Freixenet Carta Nevada; Freixenet Cordon Negro; Freixenet Brut Rosé; Freixenet Brut Nature; Freixenet Brut Barroco; Freixenet Reserva Real.
VISITS: 9–11h30; 15–17h. Advisable to arrange an appointment in advance with the Public Relations Department. Freixenet, one of the great giants of the Cava industry, remains a family-owned concern, its Freixeneda estate in the hands of the Ferrer family since the thirteenth century. Today the Freixenet Group comprises an important conglomerate of companies located not only in the Penedés, but also in California, Mexico, even Champagne itself: the Group as a whole is, so it claims, the world's largest producer of sparkling wines by the traditional method of secondary fermentation and expulsion of the lees within the same bottle. Its Spanish Cavas alone – Freixenet itself, along with Segura Viudas, Castellblanch and Conde de Caralt export more than 40 million bottles annually – account for some 70% of all Cava exported.

The winery is vast, consisting of no less than ten storeys of galleries, seven of which are underground, and it is awesome to witness the scale of its operations. Yet Freixenet undoubtedly proves that quality can be achieved and rigorously maintained even on such an immense volume. The production of fine sparkling wines by the classic method is an operation that requires considerable investment as well as the latest technological advances, and Freixenet has always been at the forefront of such developments. Freixenet, for example, pioneered the use of *girapaletas*, the cubic rocking racks that hold some 500 bottles and which have revolutionized the process of clearing the wines of their sediment.

Freixenet's Carta Nevada range of Cava is the market leader in Spain, while Cordon Negro, in its distinctive black matt bottle, is the leading export Cava. Our favourite wine is the distinctive and very fine Brut Nature.
English, German, French spoken.

6

CODORNÍU SA
CASERIO, S/N
08770 SAN SADURNÍ DE NOYA
BARCELONA
ADMINISTRATIVE ADDRESS: AVDA
  GRAN VÍA 644, 08007 BARCELONA
TEL: (93) 891 01 25, 301 46 00;
  FAX: (93) 317 96 78

CAVAS PRODUCED: Codorníu Blanc de Blancs; Codorníu Chardonnay; Codorníu Brut Clásico; Codorníu Première Cuvée; Anna de Codorníu Brut; Codorníu Non Plus Ultra.

VISITS: Mon–Fri 8–11h30; 13–15h30. Closed Fri afternoon, weekends and holidays.

Codorníu is the home of Cava, and the Codorníu buildings, designed at the end of the nineteenth century by the *art nouveau* architect José María Puig i Cadafalch, are a declared National Monument: no wine lover, therefore, should miss a visit to this remarkable and historic winery. Today the old buildings of the press house serve as a wine museum, a contrast to the equally impressive new winemaking installations, with their ultra-modern continuous presses, immense and sophisticated vacuum filters, and banks of stainless steel tanks for the temperature controlled fermentation of the base wines. Beneath the beautiful gardens of the estate, there are over 25 kilometres of underground galleries containing some 100 million bottles of wine! Fortunately for the many thousands of visitors who make their way here each year, tours are conducted from the comfort of small trains.

As is the case at its great rival Freixenet, what is most remarkable about the Codorníu operation is that in spite of its immensity, the overall standard of production remains so very high. Codorníu takes the utmost care at every stage of production. For example, to ensure that the grape must is of the highest quality, Codorníu has installed local presshouses amidst far-off vineyards to ensure that grapes are pressed as quickly as possible and do not oxidize in the hot autumn sun. Such is the demand for grapes, that the Raimat estate in Lérida was originally planted with native Cava grapes to supplement Codorníu's own local supply; today Raimat supplies its sister company not only with Xarel-lo, Macabeo and Parellada but increasingly with larger amounts of Chardonnay as the company seeks to refine further its wines and give them a more international style and profile. English, French, German spoken.

CATALUNYA

7 CASTELLBLANCH SA
AVDA CASETAS MIR, S/N
08770 SAN SADURNÍ DE NOYA
BARCELONA
TEL: (93) 891 00 00; FAX: (93) 891 01 26

CAVAS PRODUCED: Gran Castell Brut; Il Lustros Brut; Brut Zero; Clásico Seco, Semi-Seco; Extra Brut, Seco, Semi-Seco; Cristal Brut, Seco, Semi-Seco; Grand Cremant Seco, Semi-Seco.
VISITS: Mon–Fri 10–12h; 15–17h (except Fri afternoon); Sat & Sun & holidays 10–13h. There is a small charge for the visit, which includes an audiovisual, tour and tasting and lasts about 2 hours.

San Sadurní today has scores of small to tiny family businesses producing Cava. Notwithstanding the fact that Castellblanch today stands at the opposite end of the spectrum as one of the zone's largest producers, with an ageing capacity of 20 million bottles, the company's origins were exactly thus, founded in 1908 as a family business with only three employees, producing and maturing wines in hillside caves.

Castellblanch is now part of the Freixenet Group.
English, French, German spoken.

8 JUVÉ Y CAMPS SA
SANT VENAT 1
08770 SAN SADURNÍ DE NOYA
BARCELONA
TEL: (93) 891 10 00; FAX: (93) 891 21 00

CAVAS PRODUCED: Cava Gran Reserva 'Gran Juvé'; Cava Gran Reserva 'Reserva de la Familia'.

WINES PRODUCED: Vino Blanco Reserva 'Ermita d'Espiells'.
VISITS: Only for wine professionals, by appointment.
Highly regarded, medium-sized family producer of excellent Cava as well as a fine white table wine, Ermita d'Espiells.
English, French spoken.

9 SEGURA VIUDAS
CTRA SANT QUINTÍN, KM 5
08770 SAN SADURNÍ DE NOYA
BARCELONA
TEL: (93) 899 51 11; FAX: (93) 899 60 06

CAVAS PRODUCED: Segura Viudas Brut Reserva; Segura Viudas Brut Vintage; Segura Viudas Heredad Reserva.

VISITS: Weekdays, 9–11h30; 15–17h. Appointment necessary.
The Heredad Segura Viudas estate, on which is also located the table wine firm of René Barbier, is an extensive *finca* of 180 ha., located around a charming and well-restored 12th-century *masía*.
A former Rumasa property, now

part of the Freixenet Group, it is highly regarded both within Spain and internationally for its quality Cavas. English spoken.

---

10 RAVENTÓS I BLANC SA
PLAÇA DEL ROURE, S/N
08770 SAN SADURNÍ DE NOYA
BARCELONA
TEL: (93) 891 06 02; FAX: (93) 891 25 00

CAVA PRODUCED: Raventós i Blanc Brut.
WINES PRODUCED: Raventós i Blanc 'Vi de Tiratge' *blanco*; Raventós i Blanc Chardonnay.
VISITS: By appointment.
Super-modern 'boutique' winery just opposite Codorníu owned and run by a branch of the Raventós family, producing top-quality Cava as well as table wine. Just as, at the turn of the century, Codorníu built what was for its time a remarkable modern and *avant-garde* winery, so has Raventós i Blanc constructed a strikingly modern and futuristic winery, equipped with the latest technologies, as a fitting home for its 'new wave' prestige wines. English spoken.

---

11 MONT-MARÇAL
MANUEL SANCHO E HIJAS SA
FINCA MANLLEU, S/N
08732 CASTELLVÍ DE LA MARCA
BARCELONA
TEL: (93) 891 82 81; FAX: (93) 215 35 46

WINES PRODUCED: Mont-Marçal Vi Novell del Penedés *blanco*; Mont-Marçal *blanco*; Mont-Marçal *rosado* Rubí; Mont-Marçal *tinto joven*; Mont-Marçal *tinto* Crianza; Mont-Marçal *tinto* Cabernet Sauvignon.
CAVAS PRODUCED: Mont-Marçal Cava Demi-Sec, Sec, Brut, Extra Brut, Rosado Brut.
VISITS: Mon–Fri 9–13h; 14–19h. Appointment necessary.
Mont-Marçal is a château-style winery, located within its own 60-ha. estate in Castellví de la Marca in the heart of the Penedés, south-west of Vilafranca. The lovely old *masía* where the Sancho family lives is over 200 years old. English, French, German, Dutch spoken.

---

12 CAVA ROVELLATS
FINCA ROVELLATS
LA BLEDA
08731 SAN MARTÍ SARROCA
BARCELONA
ADMINISTRATIVE ADDRESS: CALLE
PAU CLARÍS 136, ENTLO. 2A, 08009
BARCELONA
TEL: (93) 488 05 75; FAX: (93) 488 08 19

CAVAS PRODUCED: Rovellats
Cava Grand Cru Masía s. XV;
Rovellats Cava Brut Nature;
Rovellats Cava Brut Imperial;
Rovellats Cava Brut Especial;
Rovellats Cava Rosé; Rovellats

Cava Super Extra.
VISITS: Daily 8–13h; 15–19h.
Telephone for appointment.
Family firm located in the country
outside San Martí Sarroca
specializing in artisan-produced
Cava produced by traditional
methods (*pupitres* for riddling) but
utilizing modern winemaking
technology. The *masía* dates from
the fifteenth century and its
star-shaped underground cave is
noteworthy.
English, French, Italian spoken.

---

13 R. BALADA SL
CELLER HISENDA MIRET
AVDA ANSELMO CLAVÉ 7
08731 SAN MARTÍ SARROCA
BARCELONA
TEL: (93) 899 13 56; FAX: (93) 899 15 02

WINES PRODUCED: Blanc Joliu;
Viña Toña Macabeo *blanco*; Viña
Toña Xarel-lo *blanco*; Viña Toña
Parellada *blanco*.

VISITS: Mon–Fri 8–13h; 16–18h.
Weekends 10–13h.
Small but well-equipped family
winery with 12 ha. of own
vineyards. Blanc Joliu is produced
from a blend of the zone's three
native white grapes, while the
single varietal wines are fascinating
and individual.
English, French spoken.

---

14 JEAN LEÓN SA
CHATEAU LEÓN
08733 EL PLA DEL PENEDÉS
BARCELONA
TEL: (93) 899 50 33
COMMERCIAL OFFICE: CALLE PAU
CLARÍS 106, ENTLO. 2A, 08009
BARCELONA
TEL: (93) 412 24 42; FAX: (93) 301 54 99

WINES PRODUCED: Jean León
Chardonnay; Jean León Cabernet
Sauvignon, Jean León Cabernet

Sauvignon Reserva.
VISITS: By appointment for
professionals only.
One of the Penedés leading estates,
producing impeccable Chardonnay
and Cabernet Sauvignon varietal
wines entirely from grapes grown on
its own 158 ha. of vineyards.
   Though the wines of Jean León
are well known and have a high
international profile, by Spanish

standards the operation remains a small-scale one; the commercial offices are located in Barcelona, and unfortunately there are limited opportunities for visits from the general public. English spoken.

15

ALSINA SARDÀ SA
LES TARUMBES, S/N
08733 EL PLA DEL PENEDÉS
BARCELONA
TEL: (93) 898 81 32; FAX: (93) 898 86 71
ADMINISTRATIVE ADDRESS: CALLE
    HERMENEGILDO CLASCAR 25,
    08720 VILAFRANCA DEL PENEDÉS,
    BARCELONA
TEL: (93) 890 01 77

CAVA PRODUCED: Alsina & Sardà Brut Reserva.
WINE PRODUCED: Alsina & Sardà *vino joven blanco.*
VISITS: Mon–Fri 10–13h; 15–19h. Small family firm in the heart of the vineyards making good artisan Cava and white wine from grapes grown on own 30-ha. estate. English, French, Italian spoken.

16

MASÍA BACH
CTRA CAPELLADES, KM 20,5
08781 SAN ESTEVE SESROVIRES
BARCELONA
TEL: (93) 771 40 52
ADMINISTRATIVE ADDRESS:
    CODORNÍU, AVDA GRAN VÍA 644,
    08007 BARCELONA
TEL: (93) 891 01 25, 301 46 00;
    FAX: (93) 317 96 78

WINES PRODUCED: Extrísimo *blanco seco y dulce*; Magnificat *blanco*; Extrísimo *tinto*, Extrísimo *tinto* Reserva; Cabernet Sauvignon.
VISITS: By appointment. Arrange by telephoning the Public Relations Department in the administrative office.

The Masía Bach estate, located in the Penedés Superior, is a unique château-style winery created in the 1920s by the Bach brothers, and purchased in 1975 by Codorníu. The fame of the estate was based on its oak-aged sweet white wine, one of the rare examples of this style of wine produced in Spain. However, today the modern winery is producing not only that sweet dessert classic, but also dry white and oak-aged red wines of the highest quality.

CATALUNYA

Agro 2001

At the time that Codorníu purchased Masía Bach, it also formed, in conjunction with the Government of Navarra, a separate company on the same estate, Agro 2001. Its goal was to undertake in-depth experiments in clonal selection as well as the development of virus-free clones of both native and foreign grape varieties. Virus-free clones, it is claimed, can improve yields by as much as 50–100% as well as giving up to a degree more in potential alcohol and improved colour and acidity, significant achievements in an arid country where yields are often tiny and unprofitable. Agro 2001 is furthermore undertaking considerable experiments with new trellising systems, modern methods of pruning, and the use of fungicides and fertilizers. Much of the work has been based on studies undertaken in conjunction with the University of California at Davis, one of the world's leading wine research institutes, and there are constant exchanges of information and ideas.

17

MARQUÉS DE MONISTROL
PLAZA IGLESIA, S/N
08770 MONISTROL DE NOYA
BARCELONA
TEL: (93) 891 02 76
ADMINISTRATIVE ADDRESS: APDO.
  CORREOS 14, 08100 MOLLET DEL
  VALLÉS, BARCELONA
TEL: (93) 593 24 00; FAX: (93) 593 98 55

CAVAS PRODUCED: Marqués de Monistrol Brut; Marqués de Monistrol Gran Coupage Semi-seco; Marqués de Monistrol Brut Selección; Marqués de Monistrol Gran Tradición Brut Nature.
WINES PRODUCED: Marqués de Monistrol *blanco, rosado*; Marqués de Monistrol Blanc de Blancs; Marqués de Monistrol Blanc en Noirs; Marqués de Monistrol *tinto* Gran Reserva.
VISITS: Daily, by appointment. While it is documented that vineyards have existed in Monistrol de Noya since 986 A.D., the aristocratic Marqués de Monistrol began producing wines and sparkling wines in 1882. Nearly a century later, in 1980, the company was purchased by the international drinks company Martini & Rossi. The winery is still housed in beautiful old buildings and both the table wines and Cavas are highly regarded.
English, French spoken.

18

CAVAS HILL SA
BONAVISTA 2
08734 MOJA
BARCELONA
TEL: (93) 890 05 88; 890 08 78;
    FAX: (93) 817 02 46

CAVAS PRODUCED: Brut de Brut
Gran Reserva; Rosado; Brut
Brutísimo.
WINES PRODUCED: Oro Penedés
blanco; Blanc Cru *blanco*; Blanc
Brut *blanco*; Castell Roc *rosado*;
Gran Civet *tinto*; Gran Toc *tinto*
Reserva.
AGUARDIENTE: Marc de Cavas
Hill.
VISITS: Daily, by appointment.

Although Cavas Hill was founded
in 1660 by an eponymous English
emigrant, the winery did not
expand until the beginning of the
twentieth century when cellars
were built for the production of
sparkling Cava. Today, Cavas Hill
is noted not only for its fine
sparkling wines but increasingly
for its excellent white and red
Penedés table wines. Small,
modern and very well-equipped
winery and cellars amidst the
vineyards about 3 kilometres
outside Vilafranca del Penedés.
English, French spoken.

Restaurantes y Hoteles

1

HOTEL RESTAURANT SOL I VI
CTRA SAN SADURNÍ A VILAFRANCA,
    KM 4
CAN BAS
08739 LAVERN
BARCELONA
TEL: (93) 899 32 04, 899 33 26

The best hotel in the wine country,
located in a Catalan farmhouse
among the vineyards on the road
between Vilafranca and San
Sadurní, with an adequate
restaurant serving *cocina típica
catalana* accompanied by the wines
and Cavas of the region.
Moderate

2

HOTEL DOMO
FRANCESC MACIÀ 2 I 4
08720 VILAFRANCA DEL PENEDÉS
BARCELONA
TEL: (93) 817 24 26; FAX: (93) 817 08 53

Vilafranca's best hotel is brand new
and aimed more at the business user
than the tourist but it is
comfortable and well-equipped none
the less. Cafeteria and restaurant.
Moderate to Expensive

CATALUNYA

3 CASA JOAN
PLAZA DE L'ESTACIÓN 8
08720 VILAFRANCA DEL PENEDÉS
BARCELONA
TEL: (93) 890 31 71

This comfortable and stylish winegrower's favourite is located just opposite the railway station, across the pedestrian bridge from Bodegas Torres, and serves exceptional Catalan foods: *fideos con sepia, farcellets de marisc gratinados, magret de pato, estofado de ternera, melocotón al vino tinto* together with a fine selection of both Catalan and Rioja wines.
Moderate

---

4 RESTAURANTE CA L'ANNA
LA ROCA 4
08731 SAN MARTÍ SARROCA
BARCELONA
TEL: (93) 899 14 08

Closed Sun eve, Mon.
Highly regarded local restaurant recommended by the winegrowers in this quiet but important wine town in the heart of the Penedés Central. Located just below San Martí's church and castle complex, with a lovely terrace dining room serving imaginative and well-prepared Catalan cuisine, accompanied by an extensive selection of local wines and Cavas.
Moderate

---

5 CELLER DEL PENEDÉS
ANSELM CLAVÉ 13
08734 SAN MIGUEL D'OLERDOLA
BARCELONA
TEL: (93) 890 20 01; FAX: (93) 890 46 50

Famous old eating house off the main road between Vilafranca and Sitges, serving typical foods of the Penedés: *escalivada, conejo al ajo, parillada de carne a la brasa, crema catalana*, and good selection of local wines. Refresh yourself, if you dare, with a slug from the giant *porrón* chained outside the restaurant before entering.
Moderate

---

6 RESTAURANT MIRADOR DE LES
    CAVES
CTRA ORDAL–SAN SADURNÍ,
    KM 3,800
08770 ELS CASOTS
BARCELONA
TEL: (93) 899 31 78, 899 33 39

Closed Sun eve, Mon eve; 2 weeks in August.
Classy restaurant located outside San Sadurní on the road to Ordal enjoying outstanding views across the vineyards to the mountains of Montserrat. Freshly prepared

seasonal foods utilizing market produce, as well as foods prepared in Cava and *vinagre de Cava*.
Expensive

---

7 RESTAURANTE LA MASÍA
PASEO VILANOVA 164–166
08870 SITGES
BARCELONA
TEL: (93) 894 10 76

Old *masía* on the road out of town, with a lovely outdoor shaded terrace serving simple but authentically prepared foods of Catalunya –

locally-cured *embutidos, escalivada, esqueixada, rape con ali-oli, cazuela de pollo al ajillo* – accompanied by a good selection of local wines. Meal ends with a *porrón* of sweet Moscatel de Sitges, served together with *musico*, a mixture of dried fruits and nuts.
Moderate

---

8 MARE NOSTRUM
PASEO RIBERA 60
08870 SITGES
BARCELONA
TEL: (93) 894 33 93

Closed Wed.
This long-established restaurant on Sitges' crazy waterfront

promenade remains a faithful favourite, serving classic, unflashy foods: *cogollos de Tudela, fideuada al brou de peix, pollo con samfaina, rape con langostinos al ali-oli, crema catalana* and a good selection of wines and Cava.
Moderate to Expensive

---

9 HOSTAL RESTAURANT CAN
   PARELLADA
URB. CAN PARELLADA
MASQUEFA
BARCELONA
TEL: (93) 772 51 25

Closed Wed.
Old rustic country *masía* under the

Monserrat in the heart of the wine country, serving simple but authentic foods of the region: *pan con tomate, esqueixada, escalivada,* homemade *butifarra* and grilled meats.
Inexpensive

Tomar Unas Copas: Stop for a Drink; Stop for a Bite

1 BODEGAS CANDELARIA
CALLE MAYOR 41
08870 SITGES
BARCELONA

The popular seaside resort of Sitges has been renowned since the Middle Ages for its sweet Moscatel and Malvasia wines. The latter has all but disappeared, but sweet, treacly Moscatel wines, drawn from the barrel, can be sampled by the glass in this old drinking den-cum-wine shop near the train station.

Los Campings

CAMPING SITGES
CTRA C246, KM 38
08870 SITGES
BARCELONA
TEL: (93) 894 10 80

Friendly, family run. Swimming pool.

Vinos y Comestibles: Stop to Taste; Stop to Buy

GRAN COLMADO
CALLE CONSELL DE CENT 318
08007 BARCELONA
TEL: (93) 318 51 84

Closed Sun.
International grocery with bar and restaurant located in the heart of Barcelona. Cellar is stocked with extensive selection of Catalan, Spanish, and international wines. Bar has good selection of open wines and Cavas to enjoy together with a range of *tapas* while the restaurant offers full meals.
English, French, Italian spoken.

———

RAÏM
CAVAS VINOS I LICORS CATALANS
PLAÇA DE JAUME I 3
08720 VILAFRANCA DEL PENEDÉS
BARCELONA

Small but well stocked specialist wine shop next to Vilafranca's famous wine museum.

———

LA LLAR DEL VI I DEL CAVA
    PENEDÉS
AVDA TARRAGONA 3
08720 VILAFRANCA DEL PENEDÉS
BARCELONA
TEL: (93) 890 45 94; FAX: (93) 892 08 12

Extensive wine shop with a full selection of both table wines and Cavas, not only from well-known producers but also from smaller growers. There are usually open wines for tasting.

MON DEL CAVA
PAU CASALS 1
08770 SAN SADURNÍ DE NOYA
BARCELONA
TEL: (93) 891 04 03; FAX: (93) 891 12 06

Remarkable shop selling all the equipment necessary to produce Cava or wine on a small to medium scale, as well as a good selection of wine-related articles for the consumer.

Costers del Segre: Raimat and the Varietal Revolution

Lérida is probably Catalunya's least visited provincial capital, located far inland near the regional frontier with Aragón, on the high road to Zaragoza, below the mighty Pyrenees and at the start of the flat, seemingly endless *meseta* of central Spain. This is certainly another world from Barcelona, some 200 km to the east, and from the holiday resorts of the Costa Brava and Costa Dorada. Set in a fertile basin crossed by the Segre river, the city has a history dating back at least to Roman times, and was later the capital of a small Arab kingdom. Today, though parts are prosperous, even stylish, much of it appears rather crumbling and half-forgotten, like the Seu Vella basilica within the ruined castle walls, deconsecrated, used as a fortress during the War of Spanish Succession, now virtually abandoned. Northwest of Lérida, the road leads towards high Aragón: Barbastro, Huesca and the Pyrenees.

When Don Manuel Raventós, whose family had already achieved spectacular success with its Codorníu sparkling wines, first came to the zone in 1914, the extensive lands above the capital were no more than a desert, the surface badly eroded and what topsoil there was contaminated by salt to such a degree that it could support no vegetation. It was thus widely considered an act of madness when he purchased a 3200-hectare estate, said to contain within that vast space just one solitary tree and a ruined castle

CATALUNYA

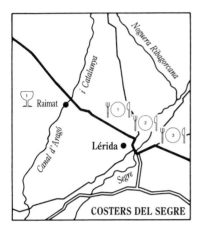

COSTERS DEL SEGRE

of Arab origin. Carved into the gate of the castle was the date 1627, a bunch of grapes (*raïm* in Català) and a hand (*mà*), an indication to Raventós, it is now said, that vines had once been grown on the estate. Accordingly (and perhaps hopefully), he named the estate Raimat, and within four years, long before any still imaginary vines could have borne fruit, he commissioned the construction of a remarkable Modernist winery, a vast, airy cathedral of a *bodega*, designed by Rubió Bellver, a pupil of Gaudí.

Perhaps Don Manuel was a visionary; others say he may have been the beneficiary of inside knowledge: within just a few years of his purchasing the property, the Aragón–Catalunya canal was approved and subsequently constructed, bringing with it an ample and constant supply of fresh, clean water from the Pyrenees and passing directly through the heart of the estate. Over the next thirty years, this source of water enabled Raventós to transform his Raimat estate completely and utterly, though not without massive investment both financially and in human effort. Hundreds of local workers were employed, hills were levelled to provide a sufficient depth of topsoil, thousands of trees were planted to leach the salt from the earth, and kilometres of irrigation canals were dug to water the estate. The ecological changes to the landscape were so immense that the zone's natural equilibrium took time to stabilize. At one point there was a terrible plague of rabbits. Raventós' solution was to introduce snakes to control the teeming population.

So successful has been the transformation that today desert truly has been turned into oasis. There are 17 lakes on the estate, filled with water from the canals; parts have been designated a nature reserve and are now the habitat of rare and protected species. There is even a small private zoo on the estate. More than 500 different species of trees have been planted. Within the estate itself, Raventós constructed a model village for its employees, with a railway station, school, sports centre, church, cemetery, bar and restaurant for the 130 families who live and work there, many of whose forebears have been on the estate since its foundation.

And there are vines; and more vines, almost as far as the eye can see. Originally, the estate was planted only with Spanish native varieties such as Macabeo, Parellada and Xarel-lo, primarily grown for the production of

Codorníu sparkling wines. However, the Raventós family has long maintained close connections with the Californian universities of Davis and Fresno, world leaders of research into viticultural and oenological innovations and technologies. When viticultural experts from UC Davis visited the estate in the early 1970s, they believed the potential was there to grow not only native but a variety of non-Spanish grapes, both white and black, and they assisted in an ambitious and still continuing programme of replanting.

Today, about 1200 hectares, or over a third of the estate, is planted mainly with a range of virus-free varietal clones trained on wires. Grapes planted on the estate include Cabernet Sauvignon (400 hectares), Chardonnay (300 hectares), Pinot Noir (128 hectares), Tempranillo (75 hectares), Merlot (55 hectares), and the original trio of Catalan white grapes (250 hectares). There are furthermore experimental plantations of other grape varieties, including Albariño, Sauvignon Blanc and Syrah. Important trials of different vine training systems are undertaken, using methods from as far afield as Coonawarra, Australia; Geneva, New York; and Ruakura, New Zealand. The estate is undertaking its own clonal selection, and is furthermore researching such crucial aspects of viticulture as rootstock selection, the minimal use of fertilizers and pesticides, methods of irrigation, and mechanical harvesting. A futuristic winery, inspired by Egyptian temple architecture and constructed in the shape of a truncated pyramid, has been built into a hill and connects underground with the old Modernist winery, to which an ultra-modern state-of-the-art Cava cellar was added and inaugurated in 1991.

Designated an official 'model agricultural estate', Raimat is today undoubtedly at the forefront of Spanish wine technology and one of Spain's leading and most forward-looking wineries. Yet notwithstanding the vision, the great land-moving exercises, the total ecological and environmental transformation, the seemingly bottomless investment, the years and decades of experimentation, trial and error, and all the recent favourable publicity, the question has to be asked: Is it possible, even with all of this, to manufacture great wines from what, at its outset, was clearly an inhospitable, even hostile territory for the vine?

Study of all the great wine regions of Europe has led us to believe that, whatever operations and innovations are undertaken in the vineyard and the winery, Nature not Man has the final say. Why else, in Burgundy, for example, have adjoining and seemingly identical plots of land produced for generations and centuries wines that are wholly different in character, not to mention quality and value, the one merely ordinary, the other an undisputed *Grand Cru*? Terrain – the chance presence or absence of prehistoric fossils in the Kimmeridgian clay of the vineyards of the Yonne – and minute, hardly measurable differences in microclimate – the delicate and particular combination of hours of sunlight, temperature, precipitation, risk of frost and hail, and myriad other such factors – have always been deemed the ultimate determinants of quality.

But Spain as a whole, and the Raimat estate in particular, works on another and wholly different scale: indeed, Raimat seems to have turned such basic Old World assumptions on their head. Perhaps Manuel Raventós simply refused to believe them. The land at Raimat was too salty to support vines? No problem. He desalinated it and transported and distributed thousands of tons of topsoil to boot. Underneath, the profounder layers of subsoil were of excellent quality for the vine, consisting of a layer of clay followed by spongy, friable sedimentary sandstone that is capable of retaining moisture and can be pierced by deep, moisture-seeking roots.

The climate of the zone may also seem at odds with the ideal for viticulture, for in summer it is hellishly hot by day, too hot, one might think, for the production of quality wines. However, by night the temperature plummets dramatically, and this contrast, it has been proved, is excellent for maintaining good acid levels and fruity aromas. The arid desert-like conditions of inland Lérida, like those of most of central Spain, would seem too dry and inhospitable to support the vine and give reasonable and profitable yields. The solution at Raimat is blindingly obvious: the use of selective irrigation. Though irrigation is anathema to European viticulture, and technically illegal within the rules of the EC, the 'experimental' nature of much of Raimat's plantation has allowed such rules to be circumvented when necessary.

Without any doubt whatsoever, the results speak for themselves, for the wines of Raimat – white, red and sparkling – certainly rank among the country's most exciting. That is not to say that Raimat can yet claim individual wines of undisputed world class, comparable to Torres' Gran Coronas 'Black Label', Vega Sicilia Unico, or wholly individual and incomparable Reservas and Gran Reservas from the Rioja. But the range of wines that Raimat is now producing – and it should be remembered that Raimat wines have only been bottled since 1978 – are innovative and of the highest quality; moreover, they are being produced in relative quantity, and thus fill a niche in the quality middle market, immediately accessible and available to all.

Raimat Chardonnay, is one of Spain's most successful examples of this internationally popular varietal, ripe, full yet with a fresh biting acidity. A Chardonnay 'Selección Especial', fermented and matured in new oak *barrica*, is now also being produced in limited quantity, richer, oaky, full in the mouth and packed with ripe fruit.

While the estate was originally planted entirely with white grapes, it is now probably Raimat's red wines that are making the biggest impact internationally. An extensive range is produced, including Raimat Clos Abadía, from 60% Cabernet Sauvignon, 30% Tempranillo and 10% Merlot; Raimat Cabernet Sauvignon, from 85% Cabernet Sauvignon and 15% Merlot; Raimat Tempranillo; Raimat Merlot; and Raimat Pinot Noir. Clos Abadía has beautifully ripe fruit and is a well balanced, medium-weight wine that has benefited from about 12 months' ageing in wood. The Cabernet Sauvignon is a bigger, more serious wine, with an intense blackcurrant palate and lots of tannin and grip. Pinot Noir is a notoriously difficult grape, far less easy to transplant than Cabernet Sauvignon, but the Raimat example is particularly successful, demonstrating a deep and distinctive vegetal nose and a restrained, lean character that is more Burgundian than New World.

Finally, the Raimat Chardonnay Cava deserves special mention. On the whole, I believe that one of Cava's greatest assets is its unique character that comes from the native grape varieties of the Penedés. The Raimat Cava, however, is produced from 100% Chardonnay, and it is certainly more international in style, yet it is undoubtedly an excellent and well-made wine with a zesty, pineappley fruit that is simply delicious.

Raimat, clearly, has revolutionized wines and winemaking in deepest inland Lérida. Almost singlehandedly as a result of its efforts, a new *denominación* was granted in 1988, Costers del Segre DO, which embraces not only the vineyards of Raimat as a sub-zone in its own right, but also three other sub-zones, Artesa to the north-east of Lérida and Las Garrigas and Vall de Riu Corb to the south-east, extending into the Tarragona province and located on the depression of the Ebro. The regulations for the DO were clearly based on the success of the varieties of grapes grown and styles and types of wines produced at Raimat. However, no significant producers within the region have as yet benefited from Raimat's expertise and experience. The majority of wines from the zone that are not produced by Raimat come from co-operative wineries.

None the less, Raimat represents to me the incredible, almost boundless potential of Spain. The estate, an oasis amidst desert, demonstrates what can be done on even the most apparently inhospitable and unpromising terrain. This does not mean that Raimat is necessarily the future for Spain, nor that similar estates will soon be appearing in La Mancha, Jumilla or León. Raimat has proved that with water, with immense financial resources, with viticultural and oenological expertise and the newest technologies, much can be achieved. But there are other qualities, too, that are more elusive and rare: above all, Raimat is the result of vision, patience, faith and remarkable imagination.

Bodega: Stop to Taste; Stop to Buy

1 RAIMAT
AFUERAS S/N
25111 RAIMAT
LÉRIDA
TEL: (973) 72 40 00; FAX: (973) 72 40 61

WINES PRODUCED: Chardonnay, Chardonnay 'Selección Especial'; Raimat Clos Abadía; Raimat Cabernet Sauvignon; Raimat

Tempranillo; Raimat Merlot; Raimat Pinot Noir.
VISITS: Wines can be purchased during working hours; visits to the estate should be arranged in advance by contacting the Office of Public Relations.
English, French, Italian, German spoken.

Restaurantes y Hotel

1 FONDA DEL NASTASI
CTRA HUESCA, KM 2,500
25000 LÉRIDA
TEL: (973) 24 92 22

Closed Sun eve, Mon.
On the outskirts of Lérida on the road to Huesca, this famous old eating house is considered the best in town, serving authentic and well prepared foods of Catalunya as well as some innovative and modern dishes: *tosta de escalivada y anchoas, bacalao al forn, salmón con cangrejos.* Extensive and highly regarded cellar of Catalan and Spanish wines.
Expensive

2 LA DOLCETA
CAMÍ MONTCADA 48
25000 LÉRIDA
TEL: (973) 23 13 64

Closed Sun eve, Mon.
Popular, homely restaurant serving good home-cooked foods of Lérida, especially *caracoles.*
Inexpensive

3 SANSI PARK HOTEL
AVDA ALCALDE PORQUERAS 4
25000 LÉRIDA
TEL: (973) 24 40 00; FAX: (973) 24 31 38

Modern, well-equipped and
centrally located hotel.
Moderate

Los Campings

CAMPING LES BASSES
CTRA HUESCA, KM 5
25000 LÉRIDA
TEL: (973) 23 59 54

Located on the road to Huesca, not
far from the Raimat estate.
Excellent swimming pool complex.

CAMPING CEL DE RUBIO
CTRA C-1313 LÉRIDA-PUIGCERDÁ,
  KM 48
ARTESA DE SEGRE
LÉRIDA
TEL: (973) 39 02 05

Open all year.

The Costa Brava

The coast north-east of Barcelona, stretching from Blanes up to the frontier
with France, is one of Spain's most popular holiday destinations, the so-
called Costa Brava, the Wild or Rugged Coast. Although some of its most
(in)famous resorts are probably best avoided, representing the worst of
low-budget, concrete jungle overdevelopment, the northernmost stretches
of the coast, particularly from the Gulf of Roses and Cadaqués to the border,
though by no means free of development, are still relatively unspoiled, the
rocky coastline beyond Cabo de Creus dramatically beautiful.

This is historic wine country, and though tourism is no doubt the
mainstay of the economy, significant and important wines produced in
two separate DO zones are enjoyed in prodigious quantity by the area's
holidaymakers and deserve to be better known.

ALELLA
Alella is one of Spain's smallest but most historic wine-producing areas,
located just north of Barcelona, off the coast road that leads to the Costa
Brava and traversed by the A7 motorway that connects the region with
France to the north, Zaragoza and Castilian Spain to the west, and Valencia
to the south. It is this motorway, begun in 1967, that has probably done the

CATALUNYA

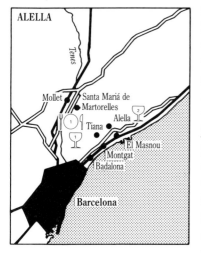

most harm to this charming hill region, for it brought the area within commuting distance of the great Catalan capital, and much of its former vineyards have subsequently been developed into countless *urbanizaciones*. So great has been the move from city to suburb that the total area under vine has shrunk since 1967 from 1400 hectares to just 550. Today the Alella DO applies to vineyards that extend across 17 municipalities in the north of the province of Barcelona, particularly centred on El Masnou, Tiana, Alella itself, and Santa María de Martorelles. The zone is subdivided into two separate *comarcas*, the Maresme, comprising the coastal littoral above El Masnou, and the higher inland Valles.

In the earlier part of this century, the wines of Alella enjoyed considerable renown. The Alella Vinícola Sociedad Cooperativa was founded in 1906, and produced *vinos de Alella* that were particularly well-liked in Barcelona, and which came to be associated with the great political and cultural upheavals of the Catalan capital. Most of them were white, produced from the distinctive Pansá Blanca, a sub-variety of Xarel-lo, wines which retained a pleasant, off-dry touch of sweetness. Over the subsequent decades, the co-operative was powerless to stop the decline in viticulture, as more and more grape-growers, especially those in the higher, terraced wine country of the Valles, chose to sell their land to the property developers. However, in recent years, the Alella Vinícola has modernized its installations, and as well as the traditional medium-sweet wines of Alella, now produces a range of other white, *rosado* and red wines under its well-known 'Marfil' label.

The zone's best producer, and virtually its only other one, is the firm of Parxet SA, which has a *bodega* for the production and maturation of its excellent Parxet Cava at Tiana, as well as a beautiful estate winery located on an old restored *masía* in the Valles sub-zone at Santa María de Martorelles. In the early 1980s, as local concern grew over the decline of the historic wine country, a company was set up to safeguard this heritage. The company was named Alta Alella, and in the Marqués de Alella it found a patron and believer in the wines who agreed to lend his name to the wines so produced. Today Alta Alella is wholly owned by Parxet SA and its Marqués de Alella wines are certainly the best of the zone.

Marqués de Alella Clásico is to my way of thinking the most interesting; produced from 100% Pansá Blanca, vinified to retain a touch of residual sweetness, it is the true traditional medium-dry wine of Alella, quite creamy, round, even opulent in the mouth. There is also a Marqués de Alella Seco, produced from Pansá Blanca with Macabeo and Chenin Blanc; though lemony fresh and undoubtedly a good partner to seafood and shellfish, it is not as characterful as the Clásico. Parxet owns or controls some 200 hectares of vineyards within the Alella DO and has significant plantations of Chardonnay. This great international grape is utilized to produce Marqués de Alella Chardonnay, a full well-structured wine that is not wood aged and which thus allows the fruity ripeness of the Chardonnay to stand out as well as the recently released Marqués de Alella Allier, aged in new French oak from the Allier, the ripe, creamy fruit overlaid with a toasty vanilla character.

All the Marqués de Alella table wines are produced at Parxet's winery at Santa María de Martorelles. This is an impressive and super-modern estate winery set amidst its vineyards in the heart of the wine country, and seems almost more Californian than Spanish. The eighteenth-century Catalan farmhouse that it has been constructed around still has its old fermentation *tinas* and wine press in place, but it is furnished incongruously with a mixture of the traditional and modern. Parxet will probably eventually move its offices and administration to this site from Tiana.

The *bodegas* in Tiana, however, will always be kept on for the maturation of Cava for they are an integral part of the history of the company. Tiana is a historic wine town: vines have been planted in this community since the Roman era, when the town was the important municipality of Titiana. Cava has been produced here since 1920. Today, Parxet is one of the largest of the medium-sized Cava firms, tiny compared to the giants of San Sadurní de Noya, but none the less a significant player on both the national and international scene, noted above all for its fine and individual premium Cavas. Parxet's Brut Nature is one of my favourite Cavas, a very rich, full-bodied wine that demonstrates the power and character of the Pansá Blanca. Parxet Brut Nature Chardonnay, produced from 80% Chardonnay, 10% Macabeo and 10% Parellada, is another excellent and richly flavoured wine.

In order to expand production, Parxet is trying to buy more land to increase the extent of its own vineyards. Though the company can only achieve this by paying the market price for residential development, it is determined in its efforts to put a stop to the gradual erosion of this historic

CATALUNYA

wine country, and to safeguard the table and sparkling wines of Alella. We toast their efforts with a delicious cup of *vino de Alella* and wish them well.

AMPURDÁN-COSTA BRAVA

Like Alella, the wine region of Ampurdán-Costa Brava, extending across the province of Gerona up to the French frontier, is one of Spain's oldest, its vineyards planted not by the Romans, not even by the Greeks, but earlier still, by the Phoenicians, on one of their earliest forays to the Iberian peninsula. That this corner of Spain remained important to the ancients is well evidenced by the extensive and impressive Greco-Roman ruins of Ampuria, just north of La Escala. Even the old Greek jetty is still *in situ* off the beach there, today incongruously scrambled over by laughing northern European children and topless *fräuleins*.

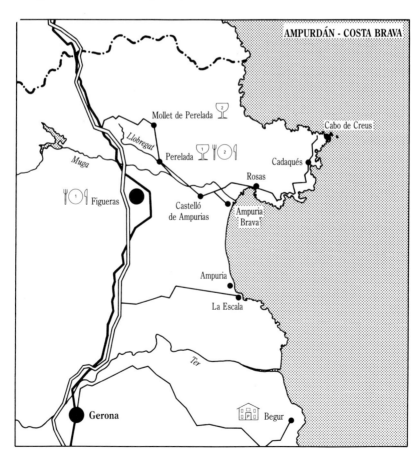

Though the wine region of Ampurdán-Costa Brava is still considerably larger than that of tiny Alella, this too is a historic zone that has contracted considerably. The back-breaking effort required to tend mainly terraced hill vineyards scorched by sun and swept by a hellish and unceasing wind, combined with the easier lures of tourism, have led the younger generation to abandon the land and seek their fortunes elsewhere, in the stylish and fashionable resorts of La Escala, Ampuria Brava and Rosas.

Today, the Ampurdán-Costa Brava DO is considered neither one of Catalunya's particularly significant wine regions nor one which is in the process of picking itself up and looking to the future. The farmers are usually not full-time grape-growers, but also tend sheep and pigs, as well as cultivating other crops. As a consequence the great majority of the wines continue to be produced in village co-operative wineries, few of which are yet particularly well-equipped.

This is a harsh, rugged land. Drive from medieval Castelló de Ampurias over the rugged promontory that juts out at the northern end of the Bay of Roses, climb over the hills and descend to the now fashionable fishing village of Cadaqués. All along the way, the hills bear witness to literally centuries of toil: the steep dry-stone slate terraces, once covered with vines and olives, are now crumbling and almost wholly abandoned. How quickly Nature reasserts herself as the scrub and earth recovers literally centuries of toil.

These vineyards, like their counterparts across the national frontier in French Roussillon, were historically the source of fortified liqueur wines. It was a Catalan, after all, one Arnau de Vilanova, who in the thirteenth century not only perfected the art of distillation, but also found that the addition of grape brandy to the previously unstable and mainly light wines of Catalunya improved them immeasurably and also enabled them to be conserved for lengthy periods. Such old-fashioned traditional *vinos rancios*, particularly those produced from the Garnacha (Garnatxa) grape, are still enjoyed locally in the Ampurdán, produced for home consumption in private cellars, as well as by some of the region's better co-operative wineries.

The Ampurdán-Costa Brava has also long been noted for its robust and full-bodied *rosado* wines, produced from Garnacha, Cariñena, Alicante and Cinsault. In the past they would probably have spent some time ageing in old, tired wooden casks, emerging years later with the orange tints that betray oxidation and flavours of old wood. Such wines may still be produced and enjoyed locally. Today, though, the nearly unquenchable thirst of the region's holidaymakers down on the coasts has led the producers to seek fresher, more supple styles of wine.

As in Alella, there is one private firm that is head and shoulders above the rest, and which is noted not only for its excellent and modern range of table wines, but equally for its Cava as well as other sparkling wines. This is Bodegas y Cavas Castillo de Perelada, a group made up of Cavas del Castillo de Perelada (with ageing cellars in the Carmen monastery of Perelada and modern vinification installations in the Penedés), Cavas del Ampurdán, which in Perelada produces still wines as well as sparkling wines by the tank method, and Covinosa, a joint venture for the production of still wines and fortified traditional *vinos rancios* with the Cooperativa de Mollet de Perelada.

The tiny *pueblo* of Perelada, located in the hills between Castelló de Ampurias and Figueras, is thus today the most important in the zone from a wine point of view. Bodegas y Cavas Castillo de Perelada has the nucleus of its wine operations located here; moreover, the fourteenth-century Castillo de Perelada itself can be visited, and there is a fascinating wine museum located in the old cellars of the Carmelite monks. This museum houses Greco-Roman artefacts, a fine collection of glass and ceramics, and some fascinating old Catalan barrels and other winemaking equipment. These cellars are also the repository for the company's most prestigious Cava, Gran Claustro, the distinctive bottles resting *en rimas* or else in *pupitres* undergoing the manual process of *remuage*.

Castillo de Perelada's Blanc de Blancs and Blanc Pescador are among the most popular wines on the Costa Brava and are excellent accompaniments to the feasts of shellfish served up and down the coast. We were impressed, too, by the company's deliciously fruity and supple young red wines. Indeed, the Ampurdán-Costa Brava has earned something of a reputation for its zesty, Beaujolais-like 'new wines' – *vi novell* or *vi de l'any* – vinified by carbonic maceration and meant to be imbibed within just weeks or months of the harvest.

Figueras stands in the heart of the Ampurdán-Costa Brava wine zone; no visitor to the Costa Brava will wish to miss visiting this otherwise unremarkable market town, for the Dali Museum is, well, quite unique (its exterior is decorated with 'loaves of bread' in the shape of matador hats – no more need be said).

Bodegas: Stop to Taste; Stop to Buy

Alella

1

PARXET SA
CALLE TORRENTE 38
08391 TIANA
BARCELONA
TEL: (93) 395 08 11; FAX: (93) 395 55 00

WINES PRODUCED: Marqués de
Alella Clásico *blanco*; Marqués de
Alella Seco *blanco*; Marqués de
Alella Chardonnay *blanco*, Marqués
de Alella Allier *blanco*.

CAVAS PRODUCED: Parxet Brut;
Parxet Brut Nature; Parxet Brut
Nature Chardonnay.
VISITS: Daily, by appointment.
Production of well-made white
wines as well as impeccable
premium Cava from grapes grown
in the suburbs of Barcelona.
English, French spoken.

2

ALELLA VINÍCOLA SOCIEDAD
   COOPERATIVA
ANGEL GUIMERÁ 70
08328 ALELLA
BARCELONA
TEL: (93) 555 08 42

WINES PRODUCED: Marfil *blanco
seco y semi-seco, rosado y tinto.*
VISITS: Mon–Fri working hours
for direct sales.
Historic co-operative winery.

Ampurdán-Costa Brava

1

BODEGAS Y CAVAS CASTILLO DE
   PERELADA
PLAZA DEL CARMEN 1
17491 PERELADA
GERONA
TEL: (972) 53 80 11; FAX: (972) 53 82 77

VISITS: Daily except Sun afternoon
and Mon. Guided visits from 10h.
The timetable of visits depends on
the season. After the guided visit,
the wines can usually be tasted and
purchased.

Castillo de Perelada is not only the
wine zone's most important
producer, it is also its most
welcoming. Tours of the castle and
Carmen cellars are open to all
without appointment. In the
medieval castle there is the glass
and wine museum together with a
large library of more than 60,000
volumes.
French spoken. English-speaking
guide can be provided for groups, if
arranged in advance.

CATALUNYA

2

COVINOSA (COMERCIAL VINÍCOLA
DEL NORDESTE SA)
CALLE ESPOLLA 9
17752 MOLLET DE PERELADA
GERONA
TEL: (972) 56 31 50

WINES PRODUCED: Conde Bravo
blanco, rosado, tinto; Garrigal tinto;
Garnatxa de l'Empordà *vino rancio;*
Moscatell; *vi de l'any* (new wine).
VISITS: 9–12h; 15–18h.
Mollet is a historic wine town
located towards the French border
whose wines were mentioned in
documents in 844.
French spoken.

Restaurantes, Hoteles y Paradores

Alella

1

RESTAURANT MAS CORTS
CTRA BADALONA–MOLLET, KM 7,650
SANT FOST DE CAMPCENTELLES
BARCELONA
TEL: (93) 593 55 55

Closed Mon.
Climb into the Alta Alella, the
heart of the wine country, and make
your way to this isolated old
country *masía* serving a good
selection of foods from both sea and
upland hill: *esqueixada de bacalla,
fideuas, butifarra a la brasa, conejo,
rape a la piña,* and the wines of the
tiny Alella zone.
Inexpensive to Moderate

Ampurdán-Costa Brava

1

HOTEL RESTAURANTE AMPURDÁN
ANTIGUA CARRETERA A FRANCIA
17600 FIGUERAS
GERONA
TEL: (972) 50 05 62; FAX: (972) 50 93 58

Famous and highly regarded
hotel-restaurant on the outskirts of
Figueras noted for its innovative
cuisine based on the typical produce
and foods of the Alt Ampurdán
prepared in lighter and imaginative
ways: *ensalada de escalivada con
sardinas, terrina de conejo a la
menta, pescados de la costa al
horno,* accompanied by an excellent
selection of wines not only from the
zone but also the rest of Catalunya
and Spain.
Expensive

2 RESTAURANT MAS MOLI
CTRA ANTIGUA DE VILABERTRÁN A
    PERELADA, KM 44,800
17491 PERELADA
GERONA
TEL: (972) 53 81 25

Closed Sun eve, Mon.
Cool old restored mill house just a few kilometres outside Perelada serving fresh, well-prepared local foods: *ensalada de berenjenas, exqueixada de bacalao Mas Moli, pato con nabos de Vilabertrán, paletilla de cordero lechal al horno,* plus the full range of Perelada wines.
Moderate

Parador

P PARADOR NACIONAL DE
    AIGUABLAVA
PLAYA DE AIGUABLAVA
17255 BEGUR
GERONA
TEL: (972) 62 21 62; FAX: (972) 62 21 66

Modern *parador* located dramatically on a secluded wooded peninsula just north of the Cabo de Sant Sebastià. Restaurant serves well-prepared Catalan foods: *zarzuela de pescado, suquet de pescado, crema catalana.*
Expensive

Los Campings

Alella

CAMPING MASNOU
CTRA N-II, KM 633
MASNOU
BARCELONA
TEL: (93) 555 15 03

Open all year.
On the main highway just north of Barcelona not far from Tiana, with an underpass directly to the beach.

Ampurdán-Costa Brava

The Costa Brava is without doubt one of Spain's most popular holiday destinations and the coast is therefore lined almost non-stop with campsites.

CAMPING MAS NOUS
CTRA FIGUERAS–ROSAS, KM 38
CASTELLÓ DE AMPURIAS
GERONA
TEL: (972) 25 05 75

Conveniently located for excursions to Perelada and the Ampurdán wine country.

CATALUNYA

Vinos y Comestibles: Stop to Taste; Stop to Buy

CAN BERRETINA
MERCADERS 28
17004 GERONA
TEL: (972) 20 30 77

Large selection of wines, wine
skins, casks and other accessories.

Tarragona and the Priorato

TARRAGONA

As in other parts of Catalunya, Tarragona and its province is one of the
great historic vineyards of Spain. The Phoenicians probably first brought
the vine to these shores, but it was the Romans who extensively encouraged
the systematic planting and development of efficient agricultural estates
that were the forerunners of the Catalan *masías*. Tarraco, after all, was the
capital of the Roman province of Tarraconensis which extended all the way
across the north of Spain to the Atlantic, and also the Imperial capital of
the entire Iberian peninsula. The wines produced in the Campo de Tarragona were not only enjoyed by thirsty Roman legions; so excellent were
they deemed, that they were exported in considerable quantity even back
to Rome itself. This transport was undertaken both overland on the Via

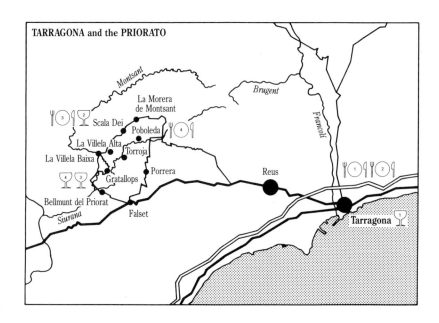

Augusta (the ancient Roman road that hugged the Mediterranean coastline around present-day Spain, France and Italy), and by sea in specially designed boats capable of carrying as many as 10,000 amphoras of wine. Viticulture in Tarragona subsequently declined during the Dark Ages and the occupation by first the Visigoths, then the Arabs; the province was not reconquered until 1099.

Viticulture was only revived in the region by the foundation of important monasteries such as Scala Dei in the Priorato, and Poblet and Santa Creus. Wine, of course, is essential for the celebration of Mass; and all three of these monasteries were noted wine producers, not to say consumers.

From early times, the traditional wines of Tarragona were the classic fortified *vinos rancios*, wines which by the eighteenth and nineteenth centuries were known as Tarragona Gold and Tarragona Sweet, and they were exported all over the world. Such wines were not only popular and inexpensive (they were known in England as 'poor man's port'), they were also virtually indestructible: indeed, when maritime freight was still cheap, Tarragona wines were traditionally shipped in hogsheads to the Philippines and back, a passage that took them over the Equator twice, simply to maderize and age them.

Tarragona today is a significant wine region in terms of quantity only,

Roman remains in Tarragona, former capital of the extensive ancient province of Tarraconensis.

not quality. Indeed, for decades if not centuries, the province has been the source of mainly bulk wines, noted foremost for their powerful alcohol levels, shipped *en granel* to be blended. The majority of the wines of Tarragona are made in co-operative wineries, few of which even bother to bottle and market their products, selling them instead in bulk to the large-scale wine merchants.

There are three principal DO zones in the province, Tarragona DO (which is divided into three sub-zones: Campo de Tarragona, Falset and Ribera de Ebro); Terra Alta DO, the southernmost, adjoining the provinces of Teruel and Zaragoza; and Priorato DO, the tiniest but most prestigious.

Tarragona itself is a fascinating old city, with considerable Roman remains including an amphitheatre, forum, aqueduct and triumphal arch. The medieval town stands within the ancient Roman walls, themselves constructed on immense monolithic blocks built by indigenous Iberians even centuries earlier. It is undoubtedly one of the most atmospheric old quarters in Spain, a maze of stone-paved alleys and streets, beautiful Gothic and Romanesque churches and other buildings, ruined walls and crumbling town houses with wrought iron balconies overflowing with flowers and cacti.

The old town is located in the heights above the sea port, but to gain a further acquaintance in particular with the wines of Tarragona, it is necessary to make your way down to the waterfront. This district, the Serrallo, is a fascinating part of the town in any case: the seafront *paseo* is lined with superb fish restaurants serving the daily catch straight off the boats, and a lively fish auction takes place each afternoon between 3 and 5 P.M.

The De Muller winery is located just up from the waterfront, and it is the only traditional firm still located in the city itself. The company, founded in 1851 by a Frenchman, Augusto de Muller y Ruinart de Brimont, continues to produce wines entitled to the various *denominaciones* of Tarragona: Tarragona DO, Terra Alta DO and Priorato DO, as well as its unique house speciality, altar wines (*vinos de misa*). Indeed, De Muller has been purveyor to the Vatican since 1888, in the reign of Leo XIII, and today supplies some 49 countries all over the world with pure, organically produced sacramental wines made according to special regulations laid down under Pope Benedict XV.

The De Muller winery is a fascinating and rambling old place, a real working winery, not a museum showcase. Large quantities of wines are still sold in bulk, notably to Britain where they are supplied to the professional restaurant trade as high-quality speciality cooking wines. In addition to its famous traditional wines, De Muller has introduced a range of white, *rosado* and red 'Solimar' wines, tasty, well-made, and excellent accompaniments to the local foods. The company also maintains a historic *bodega* in the Priorato for the production not only of the immense, almost black Priorato Legítimo, a table wine that weighs in at a hefty 15° alcohol, but also for the production of the extremely rare *soleras* of Priorato *rancios*. Dom Juan For, for example, dates back to a *solera* laid down in 1865, a

Sacramental Wines and the Church

The Church has always been closely linked to wine production because of its constant need of wine to celebrate the Holy Sacrament. When Spanish missionaries went to the New World, they took the vine with them, and as Catholicism spread to all the corners of the globe, large quantities of wines were needed even in those countries or continents with no indigenous or imported tradition of grape-growing, especially Africa and Asia.

Today the production of sacramental or altar wines is carried out under strict regulations as laid down by Pope Benedict XV (1914–22). The wines must be very pure and unadulterated; only minimal sulphur may be used; stabilization takes place usually by physical means, not chemical; and if fortified, then grape alcohol must be added and only up to certain prescribed levels. All of De Muller's wines are approved and carry a certificate from the Archbishop of Tarragona.

Altar wines are usually sweet, the priestly tooth being that way inclined (the company does make a dry *vino de misa* for diabetic priests). The most popular wine is Vino de Misa Dulce Superior, which is produced from Macabeo and Garnacha Blanca grapes grown in the Terra Alta. More interesting and a worthy drink in its own right is the company's fragrant varietal Vino de Misa Moscatel.

Because the requirements for purchasing altar wines are quite particular, the wines, though they are available in standard bottles, are more usually shipped in demi-johns, plastic drums or metal drums containing anything from 5 to 230 litres. An archdiocese in western Africa, for example, might purchase a couple of hundred 20-litre plastic drums of Vino de Misa Dulce Superior and then pass out, say, two drums to each parish church to last it throughout the whole year. Not surprisingly, wines expected to stand up to such treatment need to be virtually indestructible: the classic fortified wines of Tarragona suit such needs almost perfectly.

CATALUNYA

tawny wine with penetrating flavours of nuts, butterscotch and marzipan, extremely long, fine and powerful, still vividly full of fire and life.

THE PRIORATO

The Priorato is a tiny, historic wine enclave actually located within the much larger Tarragona zone. Only a few decades after the Moors left the region, a handful of Carthusian monks from Grenoble came to the zone, and crossed the Montsant mountain west of Tarragona. There they met a shepherd who told them that he had seen a host of angels who ascended into the heavenly clouds above Montsant as if by means of a stairway; the monks took this to be a divine message, and as the site had a source of abundant water as well as wild medicinal herbs, they founded the Cartoixa and named it Scala Dei, 'stairway of God'.

The priory rose to become extremely important and wealthy. Its immediate jurisdiction embraced seven surrounding *pueblos* which collectively made up the *comarca* known as Priorato: Scala Dei itself, Gratallops, Porrera, La Villela Alta, Torroja, La Morera de Montsant and Bellmunt del Priorat. Since the Cartoixa of Scala Dei had established and planted much of the zone's vines, by tradition it was entitled to 10% of the wine from each *pueblo*. The peasants of course tried to deliver to the Cartoixa early picked or green grapes, so it was decreed that the harvest could not begin until the day of San Bruno, patron saint of Scala Dei, which occurred in the first week of October. Because the wines of Priorato were always made from such late harvested grapes, they could reach 17–19° alcohol naturally and gained fame even in the Middle Ages for their exceptional power.

The Priorato is not only a historical entity, but also a tiny, compact geographical whole made up of land quite unlike that which surrounds it. The steep hills that lead up from Falset to the higher Montsant *sierra* consist mainly of loose schistous slate (*pizarro* – large, flat slabs of slate; or *grava* – looser, pebbly slate) that is extremely acid and difficult to cultivate. The zone receives very little rain in summer and not much grows here but the vine, the olive and the hazelnut tree. Not surprisingly in this hostile environment, it is a poor region made up of mainly small subsistence farmers working tiny, isolated patches of terrain.

Traditionally, black Garnacha and Cariñena grapes have been cultivated here, though the former is considered best for the production of the authentic Priorato. The vines yield minuscule amounts – perhaps as little as half a kilo per plant – and the resulting grapes have huge concentrations of black colour, flavour and potential alcohol. Yet due to the particular

Scala Dei, 'stairway of God'.

nature of the terrain, its wines, especially those produced entirely from Garnacha, have a characteristic and extremely high glycerine content that gives them a roundness and soft fruitiness that is quite delicious and intriguing. This is fascinating because, almost everywhere else in Spain, Garnacha is generally disparaged as a grape of little worth for the production of quality wines.

Earlier in the century, the wines of the Priorato were almost exclusively sold to be blended with lighter wines from the north. But growers would always keep back their best grapes to produce the deep, almost black Priorato wines, if only for their own consumption. Some of those were tucked away in wooden barrels in deep cellars and left to age for decades and more, to become the old-fashioned Priorato *rancios*.

Today, in this isolated and harsh zone, there are only a handful of producers still making Priorato wine. The prices that the wines fetch are still far too low considering the considerable efforts required to make viticulture a feasible proposition. Not surprisingly, most of the region's youth have long departed to the cities in search of work, and who can blame them? None the less, Priorato remains one of the great, authentic wines of Spain and it would be a tragedy if it were to be lost altogether.

Fortunately, its future seems secure since the Cellers de Scala Dei established itself in the *pueblo* of Scala Dei in 1973. The winery belongs to a group of families who have set themselves the task of safeguarding not only the wines of Priorato, but something of the *comarca*'s history as well. Just as the monks recovered the land when they came to the zone after the Moors, the proprietors of Scala Dei are attempting to revitalize the lands and vineyards of the Cartoixa, as well as to oversee the eventual restoration

CATALUNYA

The small wine village of Scala Dei, tucked around the ruined Carthusian monastery in the remote and harsh Priorato.

of the ruined and long-abandoned monastery itself. Much of the credit for the attention that Scala Dei and its wines have received must be given to Asunción Peyra for her tireless and energetic efforts on behalf of both.

Cellers de Scala Dei has both planted new and restored long-abandoned vineyards (the company owns or controls some 80 hectares of vineyards around Scala Dei), and its winery is extremely modern and well-equipped. While traditional wines continue to be made, particularly the company's flagship Cartoixa de Scala Dei Reserva, it has reinterpreted the wines of Priorato and is now producing them for modern tastes. This may mean that the Cartoixa Priorato has 'only' 14.5° alcohol, but for most of us, that is quite enough! More innovative yet is the planting of foreign grapes such as Cabernet Sauvignon and even, surprisingly, the white Chenin Blanc which is combined with Garnacha Blanca for the production of a white Priorato.

At first, I confess I was surprised at the decision to plant foreign grapes. Priorato, after all, is unique, while Cabernet Sauvignon is everywhere. Why bring it here, of all places? Yet this great international grape, when grown on the slate *pizarro* soil of Priorato creates a quite individual wine that is a magnificent expression of the land. Cellers de Scala Dei do not use it to produce a varietal, but blend it with Garnacha to make a fascinating and intense wine called Negre Scala Dei.

De Muller of Tarragona maintains a small *bodega* in the tiny hamlet of Scala Dei, the repository for its rare old *soleras* of Priorato *rancios*. Many locals say that these are the real traditional wines of the Priorato, and indeed, they can be outstanding. When Asunción Peyra first came to the *pueblo* in the early 1950s, she produced her own traditional *vinos rancios* in a simple peasant *bodega*. Some of these old wines are still in small oak barrels in her private '*bodega de los angelitos*', a remarkable bitter-sweet collection and recollection of her early years in the Priorato.

Scala Dei is without doubt the most interesting and important *pueblo* in the Priorato, but once you have made it this far, it is fascinating to wander through some of the zone's other villages. From Scala Dei, wind your way around to La Villela Alta (the co-operative produces excellent olive oil as well as wine), La Villela Baixa and Gratallops (home of the zone's most important co-operative winery), then descend to Falset and from there find the road to Bellmunt del Priorat.

Just before Bellmunt, the winery of Hermanos Barril should be visited. Rafael Barril is a lawyer from Madrid, but he has dedicated much of his life to restoring his family farmhouse and 8-hectare vineyard in the Priorato. He makes a fascinating range of artisan-produced wines, including the traditional Masía Barril Clásico Priorato (16.5° alcohol) and the lighter Masía Barril Extra (13.5–14°); Masía Barril Añejo, a *vino rancio* aged in wood for upwards of 10 years; Masía Barril *vino aromatizado*, produced by macerating Priorato wine with extracts from herbs grown on the estate; and Masía Barril Especial, a fortified, semi-sweet port-like wine. There is also a *vinagrería* for the production of high quality herb-infused wine vinegars. The Masía Barril is Rafael Barril's passion; he is currently expanding his botanical herb garden, and hopes to have a *centro turístico* open to the general public before too long. The wines can always be sampled and purchased, though it is generally best to telephone in advance to ensure that someone is on hand to receive you.

Bodegas: Stop to Taste; Stop to Buy

Tarragona

1
DE MULLER SA
CALLE REAL 38
43004 TARRAGONA
TEL: (977) 21 02 20; FAX: (977) 21 04 00

WINES PRODUCED: Viña Solimar *blanco, rosado, tinto*; Vino de Misa Dulce Superior; Vino de Misa Moscatel; Vino Rancio Seco; Priorato Legítimo; Aureo Dulce;

Aureo Seco; Solera 1926; Solera 1865 Dom Juan For.
VISITS: Mon–Fri, by appointment. Historic working winery by Tarragona's waterfront, and the source of excellent table wines, rare *vinos rancios*, and altar wines. English spoken.

CATALUNYA

Priorato

2 CELLERS DE SCALA DEI SA
RAMBLA DE LA CARTOIXA, S/N
43379 SCALA DEI
TARRAGONA
TEL: (977) 82 70 27; FAX: (977) 82 70 44

WINES PRODUCED: Blanc Scala Dei; Novell Scala Dei; Rosat Scala Dei; Negre Scala Dei; Cartoixa de Scala Dei Reserva.
VISITS: Daily, by appointment.

Open 'always' for tastings and direct sales.
This tiny wine zone's leading producer is extremely welcoming. Ask Asunción Peyra if it is possible to visit the ruined Cartoixa (at present, she is the only one who holds a key).
French spoken.

---

3 COOPERATIVA COMARCAL DEL
PRIORATO
PIRÓ 33
43737 GRATALLOPS
TARRAGONA
TEL: (977) 83 91 67

WINES PRODUCED: Priorato; Priorato Rancio.

VISITS: Daily, working hours for direct sales.
The Gratallops co-operative is the umbrella organization of the zone's nine co-operatives, and handles the bottling and marketing of their wines.

---

4 HERMANOS BARRIL
MASÍA BARRIL
43738 BELLMUNT DEL PRIORAT
TARRAGONA
TEL: (977) 83 01 92
ADMINISTRATIVE OFFICE: AVDA DE
AMÉRICA 54, 28028 MADRID
TEL: (91) 356 27 53; FAX: (91) 355 64 10

WINES PRODUCED: Masía Barril *blanco*; Masía Barril Extra; Masía Barril Clásico; Masía Barril Aromatizado; Masía Barril Añejo; Masía Barril Especial.
VISITS: Open daily, working hours. Advisable to telephone before coming. Rafael Barril hopes that the *Centro Turistico* will be open by 1993.

Restaurantes y Hoteles

Tarragona

1
RESTAURANTE BAR LA PUDA
MUELLE PESCADORES 25
43000 TARRAGONA
TEL: (977) 21 10 70, 21 15 11

Located in the Serallo harbour district opposite Tarragona's important fish market, this popular restaurant opens at 4 A.M. for the fishermen to breakfast before going to sea. Needless to say, the fish and shellfish served are impeccable: good seafood *tapas* served at the bar, *entremeses del mar, fideua, gambas grillé, sepieta a la plancha, crocanti quemada con Chartreuse.* After lunch, wander across to watch the fish auction which takes place each day between 3 and 5 P.M.
Moderate

2
HOTEL IMPERIAL TARRACO
RAMBLA VELLA 2
43000 TARRAGONA
TEL: (977) 23 30 40

Modern well-equipped hotel near the entrance to town.
Moderate to Expensive

Priorato

3
HOSTAL ELS TRONCS
RAMBLA 26
43379 SCALA DEI
TARRAGONA
TEL: (977) 82 71 58

This simple bar-restaurant is next to the Celler de Scala Dei and serves basic but good food. The house wine, served in the *porrón*, is pretty thick and heavy: so first pick up a bottle of Novell Scala Dei to enjoy with your *ensalada* and *cordero a la brasa.*
Very Inexpensive

4
HOSTAL ANTIC PRIORAT
43379 POBOLEDA
TARRAGONA
TEL: (977) 82 70 06; FAX: (977) 82 72 25

A peaceful retreat in the heart of the Priorato not far from Scala Dei in this friendly and atmospheric *hostal* with swimming pool. Restaurant serves authentic foods

CATALUNYA

of the Priorato: *romescada, conill amb samfaina, carnes a la brasa,* game in season together with local Priorato as well as the wines of Scala Dei.

Moderate

Los Campings

The coastline above and below Tarragona has numerous campsites which allow easy access to Tarragona as well as excursions into the Priorato.

Vinos y Comestibles: Stop to Taste; Stop to Buy

Tarragona

SUMPTA
PRAT DE LA RIBA 34
43001 TARRAGONA
TEL: (977) 22 61 58

The city's best wine shop has a friendly but hectic adjoining bar serving good *bocadillos* together with a range of quality open wines, and light meals at a handful of tables.

Priorato

MOLI D'OLI COMARCAL
SOCIEDAD COOPERATIVA VITICOLA
 DEL PRIORAT
LA VILLELA ALTA
TARRAGONA

One of Spain's best extra-virgin olive oils, produced from the tiny but fine Arbaquina olive of the Priorato, is made here and is offered for sale along with the wines of the village co-operative.

¡Fiesta! Wine and Other Related Celebrations

end of August	Fiesta Mayor	Vilafranca del Penedés
mid-Sept	Fiesta de la Vendimia	Alella
mid-Sept	Festa de la Verema	Sitges

(One of the region's most important and best wine festivals, with such events as grape-crushing contests, and a fountain that spouts wine)

Els Castells

Both Tarragona and Vilafranca del Penedés are famous for their *els castells* — human towers of men and boys. This may sound like little more than an amusing diversion, but believe me, it is much more than this. Teams are extremely dedicated: they train and practice regularly, and there is fierce rivalry between teams and towns to make the most difficult formations. A 3 × 8, for example, has three men on its base and lower levels and reaches up to eight levels of men and boys high. To make the human castle, dozens of men, usually dressed in colourful local costume, surround the base men, who are the strongest and stockiest of the team and who stand with arms linked to create a platform for the others to climb up. As another three men climb on to their shoulders, the surrounding dozens link together to spread the weight and help pin the first two tiers. The subsequent levels climb into place, and the final tier is usually made by an extremely light, agile and fearless boy. Such castles can stand upwards of 10 metres or more! At festivals such as Tarragona's Santa Tecla or Vilafranca's Fiesta Mayor the successful completion of such difficult constructions is a moment of supreme emotion and pride.

Als Castellers, Vilafranca del Penedés.

CATALUNYA

mid-Sept	Fiesta de la Vendimia	Espluga de Franguli, Tarragona
mid-Sept	Fiesta de la Vendimia	Capmany, Gerona
23 Sept	Fiesta de Santa Tecla	Tarragona

(famous for its *els castells*, human tower demonstrations)

last Sun in Sept	Festa de la Verema	Barcelona
first Sun in Oct	Festa de la Verema del Penedés	Vilafranca del Penedés
after the harvest	Bal del Most	Pla del Penedés
10 Oct	Nit Jove del Cava	San Sadurní de Noya

Y para saber más Additional Information

Regional Government Tourist
  Dept
Generalidad de Catalunya
Diagonal 341
08000 Barcelona
tel: (93) 209 28 89

Instituto Catalán de la Vid y el
  Vino (INCAVI)
Consejo de Ciento 333
08007 Barcelona
tel: (93) 317 81 36

Consejo Regulador de Alella
Párroco Desplá 22
08328 Alella
Barcelona
tel: (93) 555 08 42

Consejo Regulador de
  Ampurdán-Costa Brava
Calle Blanch 10, 1°
17600 Figueras
Gerona
tel: (972) 50 75 13

Consejo Regulador de Conca de
  Barbera
Apartado Correos 12
Calle Arnac de Pons 16
43400 Montblanc
Tarragona
tel: (977) 88 70 07

Consejo Regulador de Costers del
  Segre
Campo de Marte 35
25004 Lérida
tel: (973) 24 66 50

Consejo Regulador de Penedés
Amalia Soler 27
Apartado Correos 226
08720 Vilafranca del Penedés
Barcelona
tel: (93) 890 48 11

Consejo Regulador de Priorato
Po Sunyer, s/n
43202 Reus
Tarragona
tel: (977) 31 20 32

Consejo Regulador de Tarragona
Avda Catalunya 50
43002 Tarragona
tel: (977) 21 79 31

Consejo Regulador de Terra Alta
Avda Catalunya 5
43780 Gandesa
Tarragona
tel: (977) 42 01 46

Consejo Regulador de Vinos
  Espumosos
Avda Tarragona 24
08720 Vilafranca del Penedés
Barcelona
tel: (93) 890 31 04;
fax: (93) 890 15 67

CATALUNYA

EXTREMADURA

Trujillo, cradle of *conquistadores*.

Extremadura, cut off from the heart of the country by the Sierra de Gredos, Sierra de Bejar and Sierra de Guadalupe, crushed against the bleak frontier with inland Portugal, has long stood apart from the rest of Spain, a poor, isolated, half-forgotten corner of the country that is rarely visited, even by the Spaniards themselves.

Yet cross over the mountains from Castilla y León in early spring and descend the boulder-strewn valley to Plasencia, and it is like entering another world. Already the wild flowers are in bloom beside the road and the meadowlands are a lush deep green. In Plasencia, palm trees grow beneath the half-ruined eighth-century aqueduct, the delicate mimosa is in flower, and the fresh new leaves of the weeping willows droop down to the banks of the Río Jerte, where barefoot washerwomen wade in the still icy waters, skirts drawn up around their waists, scrubbing and pounding the laundry against the rocks as they have done for centuries.

Extremadura may be forgotten by the twentieth century but it was not always so. This was the capital of the Roman province of Lusitania, as the splendid ruins of Mérida attest (the city, known to the Romans as Emeritus Augustus, oversaw territory that included much of present-day Portugal). Extremadura was the home, too, of the *conquistadores* who set out from this bleak land to discover and conquer a New World. Her past glories may have long faded. So be it. Today the region is a splendid, unspoiled corner of Europe that remains in its isolation wholly authentic, untouched, even wild, almost threatening. In the Parque Natural de Monfragüe, rare species such as the black vulture and the imperial eagle soar above the quartzite

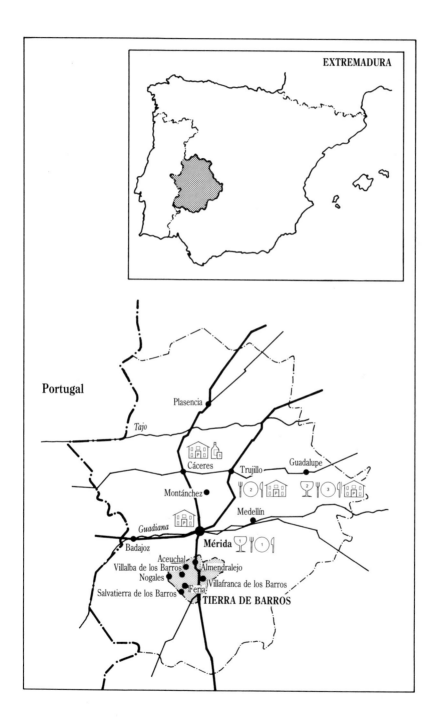

cliffs that tower over the Tajo gorge, while in the dense woodlands, the rare and elusive Iberian lynx makes his home.

As a wine zone, admittedly, Extremadura is strictly in Spain's minor league. The region as yet possesses no zones entitled to *denominación de origen* status. But as elsewhere throughout the Iberian peninsula, the vine is grown and wine is produced, if mainly for home and local consumption. The rough, throat-burning *pitarra* served in the bars of Cáceres and Plasencia is definitely an acquired taste, for locals or the foolhardy only. In the slopes below the remote shrine of Guadalupe, grapes are grown and produce robust red and curious sherry-type wines of local repute, drunk in prodigious quantity by the scores of pilgrims who have marched or made their way to this important shrine from throughout the Hispanic world. In Montánchez, a town located between Trujillo and Mérida most famous for its superlative *jamones serranos*, red and white wines are produced, noteworthy because

---

Orientation

Extremadura comprises two provinces: Badajoz in the south and Cáceres in the north.

Madrid's international airport is the best starting-point for those exploring northern Extremadura, while Seville's international airport is better for those heading to the south of the region. A north–south rail line passes through the region, with connections to Portugal. Roads are generally poor, though there are major highways that lead eventually from Madrid to Lisbon in the west, and to Seville in the south. For those heading for Andalucía, a journey through Extremadura provides a fascinating alternative route to the rather dreary haul through the parched central plain of La Mancha.

Mérida, located on the historic and important crossroads known as the Vía de la Plata, makes the best base for visitors, for it is also convenient for dipping into the region's most notable wine zone, Tierra de Barros, centred on the wine town of Almendralejo. Other notable towns include Cáceres and Trujillo, both hugely atmospheric, with their crumbling old palaces and churches topped with storks' nests. They certainly deserve to be visited, as does the remote, isolated *pueblo* of Guadalupe, built around the famous monastery. Guadalupe is about 1½ hours' drive south of Navalmoral de la Mata, off the NV Madrid–Mérida highway. Montánchez, the famous ham town, is located between Cáceres and Mérida.

Maps: Michelin No. 444 (Central Spain); Firestone Hispania C-5.

they both have the rare propensity for growing *flor*. They are certainly worth sampling if passing through the region, together with a plate of the thinly sliced, chewy ham.

The zone which has mainly put the wines of Extremadura on the vinous map of Spain is the *comarca* south of Mérida known as Tierra de Barros, a region in the past noted only for its cheap bulk wines destined on the whole for distillation, but which in recent years, through the considerable efforts of a single producer, has proved its ability to produce red wines of power and elegance that have rightly gained an international reputation.

Extremadura may well be off the beaten track. But to us, that is all the more reason to come here.

Los Conquistadores

How strange that remote, land-locked Extremadura gave birth to scores of native sons who left their home and crossed an unknown ocean to conquer and colonize the New World. Of the many adventurers who set sail in the wake of Columbus' discoveries, some 600 came from Extremadura. Many had never even seen the sea before. Francisco Pizarro, conqueror of Peru, came from Trujillo as did Francisco de Orellana, the first navigator of the Amazon. They and their descendants later returned home and built wondrous palaces with the gold that they had plundered. Hernán Cortés, the conqueror of Mexico, came from the little and wholly undistinguished village of Medellín, while Vasco de Nuñez de Balboa, who discovered the Pacific Ocean, and Fernando de Soto, who explored the North American Mississippi valley both came from the southern Extremaduran town of Jerez de los Caballeros.

In a sense, the *conquistadores* were the first winemakers of the New World. It is documented that they took the wines of Extremadura with them on their great sea voyages. Cortés, for example, offered the *clarete* of Guadalcanal to the Aztec Moctezuma as one of his greatest gifts. In later voyages, vine stocks from Extremadura were taken to the New World and grafted on to native roots, for the missionaries who followed the *conquistadores* needed wine to celebrate Mass as well as to drink. It is even conjectured by some that California's trendy mystery grape, the Zinfandel, could originally have come from Extremadura.

LOS VINOS: THE WINES OF EXTREMADURA

Tierra de Barros   The Tierra de Barros is a vast wine zone centred on the town of Almendralejo and includes 22 other municipalities with a total of 60,000 hectares of vines. Since 1979, the zone has benefited from provisional *denominación de origen* status for the production of white, *rosado* and red wines, though significant improvements have not been forthcoming to date to warrant the granting of the full DO. The predominant grape varieties are the indigenous high-yielding and insipid whites Cayetana and Pardina. However, Macabeo is increasingly replacing these white varieties, while there are also significant plantings of Tempranillo, as well as lesser amounts of Garnacha, Graciano and some Cabernet Sauvignon, Chardonnay and Sauvignon Blanc. The wines of Tierra de Barros have traditionally either been sold in bulk for blending, or else distilled in the town, then sent elsewhere for the production of liquors and brandies. However, restructuring in the zone, and the considerable efforts of one private company, Bodegas Inviosa, may result in more wines being bottled within the zone in the future.

Montánchez   Municipality located in the hills between Cáceres and Mérida more famous for its hams than wines, but a source none the less of curious *flor*-growing red and white wines produced from a variety of local indigenous grapes. Rarely encountered outside the region, such unusual wines are worth seeking out and trying when in the area.

Cañamero   Small wine zone planted at 600–800 metres above sea level mainly centred on the town of Cañamero, located in the Sierra de Guadalupe. The most widely planted grapes are the indigenous whites Alarije and Malvar, which in some cases produce unique wines that grow a veil of *flor*. There are lesser plantations of Tempranillo and Garnacha for the production of *rosado* and hefty red wines which can reach upwards of 15° alcohol.

Pitarra y Pinchos

Extremadurans, especially in Cáceres and Plasencia, love nothing so much as going into the local bars to enjoy *pitarra*. This is a unique, rustic wine, served usually in stout tumblers accompanied by a selection of hot bar-top *pinchos* such as *pruebas de chorizo* or stewed *setas en caldereta*. The spicy, tasty foods may mask any defects in the home-made wine, and anyway, after three or four *chatos* of this always heady beverage, who cares? Every bar throughout the province prides itself on the source and authenticity of its *pitarra*.

The word '*pitarra*' signifies a terracotta clay receptacle somewhat like a *tinaja* though usually considerably smaller. The rustic method of wine-making especially throughout the province of Cáceres is simply to add all the grapes – white and black, uncrushed and still on their stems – into the *pitarra* and then simply leave them to ferment untouched and of their own accord. This is primitive winemaking at its most basic, the way that wine has been made here for centuries if not millennia.

Needless to say, the folksy, old-style wines so produced, genuine though they undoubtedly are, may be something of an acquired taste.

LA GASTRONOMÍA: FOODS OF EXTREMADURA

As Spain's poor, forgotten and neglected corner, it is not surprising that the Extremaduran diet is a frugal one. Yet like many great regional kitchens, it is one which has taken basically humble ingredients and treated them with considerable skill and ingenuity, so emerging as one of the richest and tastiest, if least well known, of all Spanish regional cuisines.

The bleak land, in truth, yields little. The scrubby Extremaduran terrain is suited to little other than the raising of goat and sheep, and indeed, the great national dish of the region is *caldereta extremeña*, based on the shepherd's ever-present and well-blackened pot placed over the open hearth, and stocked with whatever is at hand: scraggy but tasty scraps of goat or lamb flavoured and stretched out with wine, meat broth, chillies, abundant garlic and *pimentón*.

Elsewhere, in the remote upland hill country of the region, the rare indigenous black-footed Iberian pig still roams. The sweet and tasty meat from this sub-species of the wild boar is acknowledged as pre-eminent for

EXTREMADURA

Bundles of *trigueros* (wild asparagus) sold by the roadside.

the production of the finest *jamón serrano*, *lomo*, *chorizo* and other such *embutidos*, cured meats based on artisan mountain traditions which are considered one of the pinnacles of the Spanish national table, sought-after, wildly expensive, but in the region itself virtually taken for granted as a daily staple and served in all manner of ways.

Another example of the basic frugality and ingenuity of the Extremaduran diet is its dependence on wild foodstuffs – *trigueros* (wild asparagus), *criadillas de la tierra* (earth truffles), and *setas* (wild mushrooms) – natural products which must be foraged for, discovered only by those poor but crafty peasants who possess little more than an innate and intimate knowledge of their own *tierra*.

These foods and many others are served unselfconsciously and in great abundance in the restaurants of the region, many of which have never had to survive by catering to outsiders or tourists with different, more refined tastes. Hardly delicate, and with no concession whatsoever to international requirements, the *cocina extremeña* is wholly authentic and delicious and one of the great pleasures of travelling in the region.

¡Que aproveche! Regional Specialities of Extremadura

Jamón de Montánchez   Claimed by many to be Spain's greatest *jamón serrano*: produced from the indigenous black-footed Iberian pig cured traditionally in the hill zone of Montánchez, north of Mérida.

Pruebas de chorizo; pruebas de morcilla   Tasty mixtures of seasoned *chorizo* or *morcilla*, served hot as a *tapa* in earthenware *cazuelitas*.

Revueltos de trigueros y criadillas de tierra   Scrambled eggs served with wild asparagus tips and *criadillas de tierra*, the wild, unaromatic earth truffle.

Migas de la Tierra de Barros   Stale bread soaked first in water, then cubed and fried in olive oil with garlic, dried red peppers and smoked bacon, sometimes topped with a fried egg.

Setas en caldereta   Wild mushrooms stewed in wine, oil and garlic, the sauce sometimes thickened with a little liver paste.

Caldereta extremeña   Hearty lamb or kid stew, seasoned piquantly with red peppers, chillies, wine and plenty of garlic.

El frite extremeño   Cubed lamb fried with plenty of *pimentón* and garlic.

Tenca frita   Fried freshwater tench.

Arrope   Boiled-down grape must thickened with squash to make a honey-like jelly. Usually served with fresh cheese.

Cheeses: *Torta de la Serena* or *Torta del Casar*   Highly valued, creamy semi-soft cheeses made from ewe's milk curdled with vegetable rennet, available only in winter and spring. *La Majada* Creamy paprika-coated goat's cheese from Cáceres.

THE WINE ROADS OF EXTREMADURA

In Brief: Even the most intrepid oenophile will not come to Extremadura simply in search of wine: there are far better and more fruitful zones and regions to explore elsewhere throughout the country. Yet wherever one is in this remote region, there will be interesting or curious local wines to sample, if not always wholeheartedly to enjoy. Mérida is the best base for exploring Roman ruins and the wines of the Tierra de Barros. Visitors to

EXTREMADURA

Cáceres and Plasencia should at least sample its unique *vinos de pitarra*. Travellers en route between Cáceres and Mérida should make a brief detour to Montánchez to enjoy *jamón* and wine in that atmospheric hill town. And wine pilgrims to Guadalupe, one of the most atmospheric shrines in the country, can most enjoyably slake their thirst with the wines of Cañamero.

The Tierra de Barros

Mérida, the Roman town of Emeritus Augustus, was founded in 25 B.C. on the crossroads of two important thoroughfares, the roads that connected Cádiz to the south with Gijón to the far north, and Lisbon to the west with Tarragona to the east. Its strategic position by the sluggish Guadiana river helped it to prosper and eventually become the capital of the extensive Roman province of Lusitania which included much of present-day Portugal.

The Roman theatre in Mérida, built by Agrippa in 24 B.C.

Today, viewing the Roman ruins, which are among the most extensive and best preserved outside Italy, one can only wonder at the achievements of that remarkable civilization: the theatre built by the Emperor Agrippa, the amphitheatre, hippodrome, triumphal arch, bridge and aqueduct are all still in a fine state of preservation. When the Romans came to far-off outposts like this, built such awe-inspiring monuments, and gave the people their bread and circuses, surely one understands why even the most stubborn barbarians laid down their arms willingly and chose to become citizens of that unique ancient civilization.

Emeritus Augustus was settled by people from every corner of the Roman Empire who migrated there for commercial, administrative, and military reasons. Every class of civil servant, merchant, manual worker, craftsman, artist, doctor and soldier existed in the city, which enjoyed good contact and communications with Rome itself. Veteran soldiers from the legions V Alaudae and X Gemina were granted extensive tracts of land to cultivate and exploit on their retirement.

And of course, as elsewhere throughout the Roman world, vineyards were planted and vast quantities of wines were produced. Roman amphoras have been excavated in the immediate surroundings of Mérida, and beautiful mosaics in excavated villas depict bucolic scenes celebrating the grape harvest.

Today, the wine country begins almost immediately south of Mérida: low, head-trained bushes of vines sprout out of the deep red, stony soil as far as the eye can see. This is the start of a vast wine zone, the delimited *comarca* of Tierra de Barros, extending over 60,000 hectares and encompassing 23 municipalities.

The busy town of Almendralejo, located 24 km south of the Roman town on the main N630 road to Seville, is the undoubted centre of the wine trade. Almendralejo, at first glance, appears a rather sprawling transit town, a place to pass through not to stop in. Yet it is one of Spain's most unlikely great wine towns, in sheer volume if nothing else. In the past there were some 300 *bodegas* in Almendralejo; today there are still well over 100, as well as the enormous co-operatives, while the town is also an important centre for the distillation of wine into grape alcohol. Indeed, so important is wine in the local scheme of life that even the town's bullring has a cellar underneath it, still holding the old cement fermentation *conos*.

The vast majority of the wines of the Tierra de Barros have little claim to fame, save for the dubious distinction of traditionally being the cheapest in the country, selling for even less than the bulk wines of La Mancha. Produced mainly from obscure but high-yielding indigenous grapes such as Cayetana and Pardina, they are ideally suited for distillation; and indeed this is an important local industry in Almendralejo itself and in nearby Villafranca de los Barros. As beverages to drink in their own right, though, the bulk of the wines are strictly for local consumption only, produced by rudimentary techniques without recourse to technology, and prone to quick oxidation.

However one producer, Bodegas Inviosa, has demonstrated the potential of the zone, and in so doing has placed the wines of Tierra de Barros on Spain's vinous map. For the red wines Lar de Barros Reserva and Lar de Lares Gran Reserva are outstanding – at once fine, powerful, and elegant – and must rank alongside the great red wines of Spain.

EXTREMADURA

When Marcelino Díaz returned to Almendralejo and his family wine business in the early 1970s, he had spent many years outside the region, learning about both winemaking and wine marketing. Indeed, for a time he was involved in exporting Spanish wines to London, and thus acquired not only an excellent command of the English language, but also an insight into the sophisticated demands of the international export market.

His family is a large one; between them the Díaz family control some 400 hectares of vineyards in Tierra de Barros. When Marcelino returned from the north, happy to be back in his native land and charged with the enthusiasm and broader outlook which travel engenders, he decided that the family business needed to be restructured. His professional training as an agricultural engineer enabled him to recognize that the underlying soil of the *comarca*, sited on a long extinct inland sea and with profound deposits of white chalk beneath its topsoil of red clay, was not wholly dissimilar to the chalky terrain of parts of the Rioja Alavesa. In 1974 he decided to grub up the unexciting indigenous vineyards and replant them with the classic grape varieties of Spain: Macabeo for white wines and Tempranillo, Garnacha and Graciano for reds. The vines have adapted to their remote new homeland admirably.

Lar de Barros *blanco*, admittedly, is not the most exciting white wine in Spain, but even in Rioja, where it goes by the name of Viura, Macabeo has never been noted for its complexity or racy flavours. However, the grape variety is highly resistant to oxidation, an important concern in this hot southern vineyard, and is capable of producing a fresh lemony wine that is well made and tasty, a particular contrast to the flat, oxidized wines for which the region is perhaps more notorious. More interestingly, Macabeo also serves as the base for a noteworthy sparkling wine made by the classic method of secondary fermentation in the bottle, the only such wine entitled to the prestigious Cava *denominación* in Extremadura.

Lar de Barros *tinto* Reserva is the finest wine produced by Bodegas Inviosa, made from a blend of about 70% Tempranillo, 25% Garnacha and 5% Graciano, a recipe not dissimilar to that used in the Rioja. The wines, fermented in modern stainless steel vats with temperature control, are assembled and aged for at least a year in large deposits, then given a further 12 months in new American oak *barricas* followed by at least 6 months in bottle prior to release. Lar de Barros is a fine red wine; the ripe fruit of the 1986 is vividly focused, and the wine displays a rich velvety elegance and firmness which marks it as a distinct product of this far-flung vinous outpost. Remarkably, for a wine of this quality, it is marked only as a *vino de la tierra*, Spain's equivalent to the humble French *vin de pays*. Yet this is not entirely without its advantages.

Says Marcelino Díaz, 'I am afraid of the *consejos* and the politicians in Madrid who tell you how to make wine, as would be the case if we were granted the full DO. Take this 1986 Reserva, for example. Two years in *barrica* would have been too much for it; far better to take it out of wood when it is ready, and then give it further ageing in bottle. I prefer to make these sort of decisions myself, according to the needs of each vintage and to my own, not somebody else's, standards.'

Díaz has also planted Cabernet Sauvignon, Chardonnay and Sauvignon Blanc in his Tierra de Barros vineyards, and it will be interesting to follow the results in future years. More significantly for the zone as a whole, the success of Bodegas Inviosa has inspired other *bodegas* to begin to restructure both in the vineyard and in the cellar. Within the entire *comarca* now, for example, Díaz estimates that the Tierra de Barros vineyard is planted with as much as 15–20% Macabeo and perhaps 5–10% Tempranillo, in place of the duller local varieties. Other *bodegas*, too, are following his lead in such essential (but hitherto ignored) viticultural practices as reducing yields and harvesting earlier, while there has also been some limited investment in modern technology and equipment. Even the co-operative wineries are beginning to restructure as they recognize the need as well as the potential rewards.

There is still, undoubtedly, a long way to go before Tierra de Barros will be recognized as a quality wine zone in its own right. But Marcelino Díaz has demonstrated the remarkable and hitherto unrealized potential of Extremadura to make quality wines that can compete on a world basis and he should be applauded for his efforts.

For those who care to explore the Tierra de Barros beyond Almendralejo itself, it is worth striking out into the country. The *comarca*, located in the centre of the province of Badajoz between the plains of the Guadiana and the mountains of the Sierra Morena to the south, comes as quite a contrast to the bleak and mainly uncultivable Extremaduran lands to the north. For this is fertile agricultural land, planted extensively not only with vines but with vast tracts of cereal.

Aceuchal, to the west of Almendralejo, is a typical agricultural *pueblo*, as famous for its cultivated garlic and melons as for its wines. Bodegas Inviosa has one of its *bodegas* here. The town is also noteworthy for its bullfighting museum, the *Museo Taurino de Mahiz-Flor*. Villalba de los Barros, just across the Guadiana river, is characteristic of the region in that it boasts the remains of a notable castle constructed over an Arab fortress, a reminder that this border country was hotly disputed during the Reconquest. Other noteworthy but isolated and little-visited *pueblos* of the *comarca* include Feria, with its typical whitewashed houses, and Salvatierra de los Barros, most famous for its pottery. There are a number of workshops where such wares may be purchased. Nogales has the remains of another noteworthy castle.

Guadalupe: Shrine and Wines

Guadalupe is one of the great hidden secrets of Spain, a small unspoiled medieval *pueblo* located in the dense and remote Sierra de Guadalupe, dominated by its famous, fortress-like Monasterio de Nuestra Señora de Guadalupe.

In the thirteenth century an illiterate shepherd stumbled upon a miraculous wooden statue of the Virgin, purportedly carved by Saint Luke himself. The relic took on new importance and significance in 1340 during the struggles to expel the Moors when King Alfonso XI vowed at the battle of Salado that, if victorious, he would build a monastery on the site in honour of the Virgin. Needless to say, this was one of the great victories of the Reconquest, and the subsequent monastery prospered and rose in importance as a major site of pilgrimage, second in Spain only to Santiago de Compostela. Christopher Columbus met Queen Isabel la Católica here to sign the documents authorizing his first voyage of discovery; on his return, the first native Americans were baptized in the town fountain. The island of Guadalupe was named after the shrine, and indeed the Virgin, who later appeared to a Mexican peasant in another miraculous vision, was subsequently adopted as the patron saint of many of Spain's New World colonies, a role she still fulfils today throughout the Americas.

Throughout the medieval age, the monastery was rebuilt, expanded and enlarged. The Hieronymite monks kept a *ganadería* of some 30,000 head of cattle, not only to feed the thousands of pilgrims who came to the Virgin's shrine, but also as a source of high-quality hide for the parchment for their illuminated choir books and manuscripts; indeed the monastery possessed what was, at its time, one of the finest libraries in the world. Wealthy beyond belief, it held control over extensive lands cultivated with both crops and vines. In Guadalupe there were hospitals, a medical school and inns for travellers; indeed, the town's *parador* is located in old fifteenth-century Hospital de San Juan Bautista.

And yet, for the visitor today, Guadalupe stands in splendid and remote isolation. To arrive here even by car is still something of an adventure. The town can be reached from either Madrid, Cáceres, or Mérida, though not without considerable effort: the final leg of the journey is on winding mountain roads that pass through the densely wooded mountains of the Sierra de Guadalupe. Finally, at the Ermita del Humilladero, the road opens to reveal Guadalupe far below, the massive Gothic monastery brooding down in the valley. Imagine how pilgrims who had walked here must have felt on reaching this point!

Though a destination for pilgrims for literally centuries, Guadalupe remains relatively unspoiled, simply because of its inaccessibility. The medieval town itself is charming, with its old stone houses with overhanging balconies and heavy wooden porches, its shaded arcades, winding narrow stone-paved streets and numerous bars and inns on or just off the main square.

Gothic cloisters of the monastery of Guadalupe.

The place to make for is the Hospedería del Real Monasterio, installed in the sixteenth-century Gothic cloisters of the monastery itself. This is an authentic pilgrims' hospice, since 1971 run as a 2-star hotel open to the public. The bedrooms are located in the dormitories of the upper cloisters, while the *comedor* is actually in the old refectory of the monastery. The hospice connects directly with the monastery by way of the mozarabic cloisters where about a dozen Franciscan monks still live. To stay in this remarkable inn is to experience something of the history of this holy and peaceful place.

Many of today's pilgrims come to Guadalupe for the day only. The Franciscans give them a guided tour of the monastery, first showing the illuminated choir books made by the Hieronymites; the beautiful and detailed embroidered robes; the sacristy with its series of paintings by Zurbarán; the treasury with its overwhelming collections of riches, crowns and relics; and finally, last of all, the baroque Camarín, a tiny but overblown room in a tower that backs on to the main altar of the Church. The visit culminates in a dramatic and emotional moment when the hooded Franciscan monk throws back a curtain to reveal the decorated gold throne which faces into the church; the throne is revolved and the tiny but much venerated black statue of the Virgin of Guadalupe is revealed, almost swamped by the splendour of her crown and flowing robes. For those who have made their way here from every corner of the Hispanic world, this is a moment of extreme faith and deep emotion. Even for non-believers it is a moving experience, simply to be within touching distance of so many centuries of unquestioning faith.

Yet, on leaving the monastery there is an overwhelming sense of relief: such belief undoubtedly weighs heavy. Once outside in the brightness of the Extremaduran day, a rather giddy atmosphere of exhilaration is about, and most pilgrims, it seems, want little more than to repair straight away to a restaurant to nourish the body, after having replenished the needs of the soul. There are naturally a number of restaurants in Guadalupe which cater for the influx of visitors. Indeed, it has probably always been so. Most serve the basic but authentic foods of Extremadura, accompanied by wines from nearby Cañamero.

Cañamero is conveniently located about 20 km south-west of Guadalupe, and so has long been able to benefit from a ready market for its wines. In truth, they are of little more than local interest. Cañamero is best-known for its white sherry-type wines which have the propensity to grow *flor*, and they may be sampled in the bars of the pilgrim town. The most frequently encountered wines, though, are the Cepa de Cañamero *claretes* from Bodegas Ruiz Torres, made from a mixture of red and white grapes, robust if slightly oxidized, but thirst-quenching in the heat.

Bodegas: Stop to Taste; Stop to Buy

1

BODEGAS INVIOSA
AVDA DE LA PAZ 19
06200 ALMENDRALEJO
BADAJOZ
TEL: (924) 66 09 77; FAX: (924) 66 59 32

WINES PRODUCED: Lar de Barros *blanco, rosado, tinto*; Lar de Barros *tinto* Reserva; Lar de Lares *tinto* Gran Reserva; Cava Bonaval.
VISITS: Working hours, by appointment.
The wines of Extremadura remain

relatively undiscovered, but Bodegas Inviosa is putting them on the vinous map of Spain, especially with its outstanding Lar de Barros *tinto* Reserva and Lar de Lares *tinto* Gran Reserva. Marcelino Díaz has modernized his winemaking installations and restructured his vineyard: most importantly, however, he has a modern and sophisticated outlook and mentality, and is closely in touch with market demands and international tastes.

Cava Bonaval is produced by artisan methods in small quantity and is well worth trying when in the zone.

Marcelino Díaz has plans to develop a tourist centre for visitors, possibly with a wine shop and restaurant, but this project has not yet been finalized. English, French spoken.

---

2 BODEGAS RUIZ TORRES
CAÑADAHONDA 61
10136 CAÑAMERO
CÁCERES
TEL: (927) 36 90 27; FAX: (927) 36 93 02

WINES PRODUCED: Cepa de Cañamero *blanco*, *clarete*; Trampal *blanco* Reserva; Trampal *tinto* Reserva; Feliz Ruiz *tinto* Reserva.
VISITS: Daily 8–14h; 15h30–18h30.
About the only reliable source for the traditional wines of Cañamero, widely available in Guadalupe.

Restaurantes, Hoteles y Paradores

1 BAR-RESTAURANTE 'El PARAISO'
CTRA GIJÓN–SEVILLA, KM 312
06200 ALMENDRALEJO
BADAJOZ
TEL: (924) 66 10 01

Located on the main road to Seville just south of the town, this is a convenient and most pleasant stop for any heading south or north on this main thoroughfare. Owner Juan Campomanes Puerto has won many prizes for his *cocina extremeña*. Specialities include *pruebas de chorizo, revuelto de triguero y criadillas de tierra, setas en caldereta, cabrito asado, arrope de Almendralejo*, served together with a good selection of local wines, including Lar de Barros Reserva. **Inexpensive to Moderate**

EXTREMADURA

2 MESON LA TROYA
PLAZA MAYOR 10
10200 TRUJILLO
CÁCERES
TEL: (927) 32 13 64

Typical and famous Extremaduran eating house, located in the main square of the town that is known as the 'Cradle of the *Conquistadores*'. Set menu only serving gargantuan portions: *tortilla, migas, caldereta extremeña*, salad, fruit, wine and mineral water.
Very Inexpensive

---

3 HOSPEDERÍA DEL REAL
MONASTERIO
PLAZA JUAN CARLOS I, S/N
10140 GUADALUPE
CÁCERES
TEL: (927) 36 70 00

One of the most genuinely atmospheric hotels we have ever encountered. Rooms are simply furnished but spacious with private facilities, and the *comedor* is noted above all for its faithful *cocina extremeña – criadillas de tierra, migas, habas con jamón, caldereta extremeña* – served with good local Cañamero wines.
Inexpensive to Moderate

Paradores

P PARADOR NACIONAL VÍA DE LA PLATA
PLAZA DE LA CONSTITUCIÓN 3
06800 MÉRIDA
BADAJOZ
TEL: (924) 31 38 00; FAX: (924) 31 92 08

Located on the site of a Roman temple and Visigothic basilica, this stylish *parador* has been a convent, hospital, church and prison: today it probably makes the best base for visiting this fascinating Roman city and the wine country of Tierra de Barros to the south.
Expensive

P PARADOR NACIONAL DE TRUJILLO
PLAZA DE SANTA CLARA
10200 TRUJILLO
CÁCERES
TEL: (927) 32 13 50; FAX: (927) 32 13 66

Installed in the ancient convent of Santa Clara in the atmospheric town of the *conquistadores*. The Clarissa nuns used to sell their sweets and pastries from behind the wooden *torno* by the front entrance: today they are installed

P

in modern premises across the road, but the sweets are still just as

good (see below).

Moderate

PARADOR NACIONAL DE CÁCERES
CALLE ANCHA 6
10003 CÁCERES
TEL: (927) 21 17 59; FAX: (927) 21 17 29

Located within the walled medieval town in the fourteenth-century Palacio del Comendador. Restaurant serves good local foods, including *cabrito asado*.

Moderate

P

PARADOR NACIONAL DE ZURBARÁN
MARQUÉS DE LA ROMANA 10
10140 GUADALUPE
CÁCERES
TEL: (927) 36 70 75; FAX: (927) 36 70 76

The *parador* is not as friendly nor as authentically atmospheric as the

Hospedería del Real Monasterio, but if that is full, this is the next best alternative. Installed in the fifteenth-century Hospital de San Juan Bautista, just across the road from the monastery itself.

Moderate

Tomar Unas Copas: Stop for a Drink; Stop for a Bite

Extremadura is a great region for bars and *tapas*. The custom, especially in the Cáceres province, is to go out for *pitarra y pinchos*, and bars pride themselves equally on the quality of their home-made wines as well as their bar-top snacks. In the historic centre of Cáceres there is no shortage of such places, though El Palacio del Vino is a popular favourite serving a good selection of bottled wines. In Mérida, try any of the bars along both the Plaza de España and the Plaza de Santa Clara. In the latter, Bar Lusi is always popular.

1

EL PALACIO DEL VINO
CALLE ANCHA 4
10003 CÁCERES
TEL: (927) 21 08 59

Bar/wine *bodega*/restaurant located in a sixteenth-century

palace in the historic centre of town. Good selection of wines from Extremadura, Rioja, Ribera del Duero and Catalunya served with tasty drinking snacks – *morcilla*, *chorizo*, *chanfaina*, *magro* and local cheeses. Restaurant specializes in Brazilian-style grilled meats.

Located next to the Parador Nacional de Cáceres.

Los Campings

CAMPING MÉRIDA
MÉRIDA
BADAJOZ
TEL: (924) 30 34 53

Open all year.

Vinos y Comestibles: Stop to Taste; Stop to Buy

ULTRAMARINOS ZANCADA
SANTA EULALIA 38
06800 MÉRIDA
BADAJOZ

Stylish tile-fronted old-fashioned grocery along the pedestrian precinct, with a good selection of *productos extremeños – jamones, embutidos, quesos, dulces, vinos y licores.*

———

FELICIANO BECERRA
CALLE JOSÉ R. MELIDA 56
06800 MÉRIDA
BADAJOZ
TEL: (924) 31 45 52

Another good shop for cured pork products and local wines, conveniently located just opposite the Roman museum and amphitheatre complex.

Compras Deliciosas: Stop to Taste; Stop to Buy

CONCEPCIONISTAS FRANCISCANS
CONVENTO STA CLARA
(OPPOSITE THE PARADOR
   NACIONAL)
10200 TRUJILLO
CÁCERES
TEL: (927) 32 06 38

Exquisite *pastas de Sta Clara, pastas de almendra*, meringues and other sweets and pastries, sold by unseen nuns out of the revolving *torno.*

Along the road watch out for women selling bundles of *trigueros* – wild asparagus – and *criadillas de tierra* – earth truffles. Cook them with scrambled eggs for a real taste of Extremadura.

¡Fiesta! Wine and Other Related Celebrations

mid-August   Fiestas de la Vendimia   Almendralejo

Y para saber más Additional Information

Junta de Extremadura
Consejerías de Turismo,
  Transportes y Comunicaciones
Cárdenas 11
06800 Mérida
Badajoz
tel: (924) 31 30 11;
fax: (924) 31 19 25

EXTREMADURA

GALICIA

Galicia has preserved much of its tradition and culture through its physical and rural isolation.

Green, rainy Galicia, located way up in the northernmost, westernmost corner of Spain: it would be hard to find a greater contrast between its lush damp countryside, rolling hills and deep estuaries and the brown, arid and endless plains of Castile. This is indeed another world from the rest of Spain. Literally hours or days from anywhere else due to the nature of the terrain and the poor network of roads, its physical isolation has allowed the region over the centuries to maintain its unique cultural, historic and linguistic roots. The Moors, who overran virtually every other corner of the Iberian peninsula, never managed to conquer the region. Or perhaps they deemed it hardly worth their while.

Indeed, rural Galicia remains a region that time has passed by. This is a raw and still primitive land, settled by Celtic tribes a thousand years before Christ. Today, teams of oxen harnessed with carved wooden yokes still pull wooden-wheeled carts. The peasants work tiny smallholdings divided and sub-divided time and again into a confused patchwork, too small to be mechanized or economical. I have seen farmers preparing their fields with primitive stick ploughs, a method of cultivation unimproved since the Stone Age. Women dressed in black still carry baskets or bundles balanced on their heads as they walk from *pueblo* to *pueblo*. At times one can hardly believe that this is Europe.

Here the farmers grow a little bit of everything – potatoes, cabbage, turnips, and always a row or two at least of vines, trained high up wooden or granite posts to free the land below for other valuable crops. Memories of poverty and famine run generations deep, and even city-dwellers do not feel comfortable unless they are assured of their own supply of potatoes, above all, and wine. In many cases, the domestic pig is still kept by rural families, slaughtered in the ritual *matanza* each autumn by itinerant butchers and salted down to provide the staple storehouse of preserved meats and sausages.

Virtually unknown as a wine region simply because its wines are rarely exported outside Galicia itself, this is none the less a propitious habitat for the vine. From the high, terraced mountain pass at Valdeorras, down to the Sila and Miño river valleys and the vineyards of Ribeiro at Ribadavia, across to the coast and the rolling, gentle hills of the Rías Baixas, the vine flourishes, sometimes to the exclusion of virtually all else. Admittedly, the vast majority of wines produced are indifferent at best, made by primitive methods and sold in unlabelled bottles. Such rustic wines serve for little more than to quench a near insatiable local thirst, for the Gallegans are the country's greatest topers, consuming per capita almost twice the country's average.

Yet they are not wholly indiscriminate. *Aficionados* have long extolled the virtues of a rare wine produced from a shy, delicate and low-yielding grape variety known as Albariño. Today this fickle variety has been revived, and Galicia's Albariño wines from the Rías Baixas are now considered among the greatest and certainly most expensive white wines of Spain.

The traveller to Galicia is not likely to go thirsty. He never has. For more than a millennium, pilgrims have made their way to this remote corner from throughout Christendom to the shrine of Santiago de Compostela. Across the Pyrenees, from France, Germany, Italy, Britain and other parts of northern Europe, they descended, then marched westward until there was virtually nowhere further to go. The thousands and millions who had struggled for weeks or months to reach Santiago were in need of considerable sustenance, and the winegrowers of Galicia have for centuries found the region's capital a virtually unquenchable market for their wines.

In truth, as a destination, Galicia has much more to offer than its wines. Its beaches, especially along the Rías Baixas, are clean and beautiful, washed by the tremendous breaking rollers of the Atlantic. There are scores of charming fishing villages still virtually untouched by tourism, while the inland countryside remains even more uncharted. History abounds in the Romanesque churches, bridges and buildings along the *Camino de Santiago*. Galicia, furthermore, boasts a magnificent regional gastronomy based on a feast of the nation's finest fish and shellfish, wonderful accompaniments to its overlooked but by no means minor wines.

GALICIA

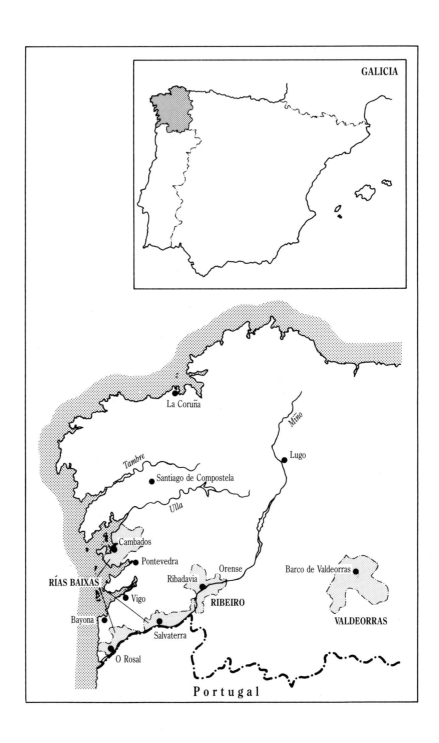

Orientation

Galicia, an autonomous region with its own language, traditions, history and climate, comprises four provinces: La Coruña, Lugo, Orense and Pontevedra. Place names are often written on road signs in Gallego.

The region can be reached direct by international flights to Labacolla, near Santiago de Compostela. La Coruña has an airport served by domestic flights. The region's position as an important and historic pilgrimage destination means that many roads lead here, though there is as yet no complete main dual carriageway or motorway. Galicia thus remains well off the beaten track, and is not reached without considerable effort or time. Visitors from Britain can most enjoyably visit Galicia from the ferry port of Santander by way of the lovely Cantabrian and Asturian coasts, or inland by way of León.

Almost all the region's significant wine country is located in the provinces of Orense and Pontevedra. The most beautiful and important wine region is the Rías Baixas, a tourist destination in its own right, so there is considerable scope in Galicia for combining wine touring with more traditional holiday pursuits.

Maps: Michelin No. 441 (North-West Spain); Firestone Hispania C-1, T-20.

The Cult of *Santiago Matamoros*

It is claimed (though not without considerable dispute) that Saint James the Apostle, son of Zebedee, brother of Saint John, came to the Iberian peninsula after the Crucifixion to preach the Gospel. In the year 40 the Virgin Mary reputedly descended from Heaven by way of a pillar to appear in an apparition before the Apostle in Zaragoza. However, on his return to Jerusalem four years later, James suffered martyrdom at the hands of Herod Agrippa. His remains, say the chroniclers, were taken by boat to Spain, landed at the little Galician town of Padrón, and buried and forgotten. Several centuries later, in 813, a pious hermit, led by a star to a field ('*campus stellae*') fortuitously discovered the Apostle's bones just at a

Ecclesiastical window shopper, Santiago de Compostela.

moment of great importance for the Catholic Church in Spain. For the Moors had by then overrun the peninsula, only failing to subdue remote Galicia and neighbouring Asturias. Saint James, or Santiago, became the rallying cry for the Christians, ever more so after the Battle of Clavijo in 844 when the Apostle, mounted on a furious white charger, sword in hand, intervened to ensure a famous victory for the righteous, so earning for himself the title of *Santiago Matamoros*, Saint James the Moor Slayer. In this frightful guise, as seen in images in churches throughout the country, he inspired Christian soldiers to complete the Reconquest and so rid the peninsula of the Infidel.

The town of Santiago de Compostela was built on the site where the Apostle's remains were reputedly found, and the great Romanesque cathedral with its beautiful baroque façade became the focus for a pan-European shrine of pilgrimage second in importance only to Rome and Jerusalem. Even today it remains a holy and venerated pilgrim destination for the faithful.

LOS VINOS: THE WINES OF GALICIA

Rías Baixas DO   Granted the DO only in 1988, Rías Baixas has already established itself as a zone capable of producing white wines of the highest quality, primarily from the prestigious Albariño grape. Other permitted local white grapes include Caiño Blanco, Loureira, Torrontés and Treixadura. The delimited wine zone applies to vineyards located across 18 municipalities mainly in the west and south of the province of Pontevedra, extending down to the national frontier with Portugal. The wine zone is further subdivided into three sub-zones: Val do Salnés, located mainly around Cambados between the *rías* of Arosa and Pontevedra; O Rosal, a tiny area located south of Bayona, near the natural border with Portugal formed by the mouth of the Miño; and Condado do Tea, an inland wine zone that follows the banks of the Tea river and the north bank of the Miño, mainly from Salvaterra do Miño to Crecente.

The minimum alcohol content for white wines of Rías Baixas is 10°, but this rises to a minimum of 11.3° for varietal wines made from Albariño. Tiny amounts of red wines are produced, primarily from local grapes such as Brancellao, Caíño Tinto, Espadeiro, Loureira Tinta, Mencía and Sousón; red wines must reach a minimum of 9.5°.

Ribeiro DO   The Ribeiro DO extends over 13 municipalities mainly located along the Miño valley west of Orense to Ribadavia, as well as along the slopes of tributaries that drain into this great waterway.

The greater part of the vineyard is planted with Palomino, the high-yielding grape which, outside Jerez, makes white wines of very little character or distinction. Alicante, as the Garnacha grape is known locally, is the principal red variety, and produces similar wines of little marked character. However, in recent years, there has been a move towards the recovery and replanting of the zone's traditional and characterful native grape varieties, such as Treixadura, Torrontés, Godello and Loureira for white wines, and Sousón, Brancellao, Caíño Tinto and Mencía for reds. White wines must attain 9–13° alcohol; reds must reach 9–12°.

Valdeorras DO   The Valdeorras wine zone is located in the north-eastern section of the Orense province near the border with the province of León where the mountain pass descends to the Sila river valley. The delimited vineyard extends over 8 municipalities. While the area under vine was once reasonably extensive, today the Valdeorras vineyard is in a process of continual decline, for this harsh mountainous terrain is extremely difficult to work and the prices its obscure wines fetch make the cultivation of grapes hardly worth the effort. The best red wine is produced from the Mencía grape, though it is exceeded by plantations of the blander Alicante; most distinctive white wine is made from Godello. White, *rosado*, and red wines must all reach a minimum of 9° alcohol.

Orujo

Orujo is the residue of skins and pips left over after the pressing of grapes during the winemaking process. In almost all winemaking countries, including Spain, this dense mass is distilled into a fiery and usually fairly raw and powerful spirit. Like French *marc* and Italian *grappa*, *orujo* or *aguardiente de orujo* may be considered something of an acquired taste to the uninitiated.

Though produced wherever wine is made, the best *orujo* is generally deemed to come from Galicia, and the best *gallego* versions, according to those who actually drink the stuff, are home-produced in tiny pot stills by traditional artisan methods. These rustic spirits are usually not available commercially, though enterprising locals may be persuaded to part with an unlabelled bottle or two. (If it proves to be undrinkable, it can always be used to start the barbecue.) Some of the best versions are those in which herbs and aromatic plants have been macerated. The Cooperativa Vitivinicola del Ribeiro produces a fine and well-regarded *orujo* which will not make you blind (they do suggest, however, that before drinking it you pin to your jacket a card bearing your name and address).

Queimada This potent brew is made from a pot of *orujo* to which coffee beans, sugar and fruit are added; the mixture is set alight, the flames are allowed to die down, then it is poured into white china bowls. Seemingly innocuous, it is to be consumed at your own peril.

LA GASTRONOMÍA: FOODS OF GALICIA

Galicia is one of the great gastronomic corners of Spain, and indeed its regional *cocina* is one of the major attractions for visitors. No other region of Spain – not even the Basque country – can surpass Galicia in the excellence of its shellfish and fish. From the Rías Altas to the Rías Baixas, in Santiago de Compostela, Pontevedra, or Vigo, the range of *mariscos* and seafood *tapas* on offer in even the simplest bars and restaurants is quite overwhelming. The deep, broad *rías* – wide estuaries that extend into the country – are a source of exceptional orange-tinted *mejillones* (mussels) and *ostras* (oysters); *pulpo* (octopus) is served everywhere; and the array of simply prepared shellfish is unsurpassed: *vieiras* (scallops, symbol of Saint James), *percebes* (a highly prized edible barnacle), *navajas* (razor shell clams), *cigalitas* (tiny crayfish), *choquitos* (tiny cuttlefish), *almejas* (clams), *berberechos* (cockles), *langostinos* (Dublin Bay prawns), *centollo, buey* and *nécora* (all types of crab), *gambas* and *camarones* (shrimps and prawns), and of course, *bogavante* (lobster) and *langosta* (spiny lobster or crawfish).

It is hard to go wrong with such fresh-from-the-sea foods. The Galician methods of preparation are generally simple and unfussy. The classic *merluza a la gallega* is a case in point: little more than poached hake and potatoes, served in a simple sauce of oil, garlic and *pimentón*. Yet how delicious it is! Other typical hearty foods include the simple potato and cabbage soup known as *caldo gallego, lacón con grelos* (knuckle of ham cooked with turnip greens), and *callos a la gallega* (tripe and chickpeas). These are rustic, filling foods, nothing refined about them, and they continue to satisfy farmers and fisherfolk alike.

Generations of men from Galicia have traditionally emigrated to South America; once they have made their proverbial fortunes, most long to return to their homeland, bringing back with them the taste of their adopted countries in the form of *churrasquerías*. These simple grill houses, sometimes set up in private houses or outdoor gardens, serve great feasts of meats (usually pork), simply grilled over charcoal and served with a mouth-searing South American-inspired *moja picante* sauce.

Galician fish and shellfish is perfectly accompanied by the region's white wines, both its basic, tart 'green' wines and the aristocratic and expensive Albariños. Heartier meats, stews and soups are usually accompanied by bottles or clay jugs of red wine, remarkably light in alcohol, yet stainingly dark in colour, and with a most peculiar yet not wholly unpleasant mouth-puckering bite of acidity. These red wines are unlike any others found in Spain, yet, with the local foods, they can be excellent.

¡Que aproveche! Regional Specialities of Galicia

Pimientos de Padrón Tiny green peppers, fried in oil, then seasoned with sea salt; usually eaten with the fingers as a *tapa*, they are deliciously sweet, except for the odd rogue pepper which is as hot a chilli as you would care to eat!

Xouvàs Tiny sardines, usually grilled and eaten traditionally with *pan de maiz* (corn bread), especially at *fiestas*.

Salpicón de mejillones Mussels cooked and served cold with finely chopped onion, egg, pickles, red pepper, and dressed with vinegar and oil.

GALICIA

Caldo gallego   Hearty Galician soup of cabbage, potatoes, beans and bacon or sausage.

Caldeirada   Fish stew made with the catch of the day, together with potatoes, garlic, oil and *pimentón*. Sometimes the broth is served first, followed by the fish.

Empanada de xouvàs   Pie or tart filled with fried onions and tiny sardines. **Empanada de berberechos**   Similar flat pie filled with cockles.

Lacón con grelos   Boiled shoulder or knuckle of ham served with tender turnip tops, *chorizo* and potatoes.

Filloas   Classic Galician dessert of home-made pancakes filled with either cream or jam.

Cheeses: *Queso Tetilla*   Creamy, breast-shaped cheese. Not to be missed. *San Simón*   Strong Galician smoked cheese, similarly breast-shaped, smoked over a birch-wood fire.

Pulpo a feira

The favourite and most characteristic food of Galicia is *pulpo*, octopus: there are even whole restaurants known as *pulperías* devoted to serving it. Every bar in the region worth its salt, moreover, offers *pulpo a feira* as a *tapa* or *ración*.

It is at country festivals, though, that *pulpo* is really enjoyed. Great metal drums are transported outdoors, and a fire is set ablaze beneath them; into these bubbling primitive cauldrons whole octopus are pitched, boiled for considerable lengths of time until tender, fished out unceremoniously, then quickly chopped up into small pieces, seasoned with oil and *pimentón*, and served always on small wooden platters. The rather fatty octopus may be something of an acquired taste, but it is a particularly good accompaniment to the region's tart, sometimes sour local wines, served in white ceramic *tazitas* like handleless teacups.

THE WINE ROADS OF GALICIA

In Brief: After Santiago de Compostela, the region's capital and greatest attraction, the most popular destination in Galicia is probably the Rías Baixas country that extends south to the frontier with Portugal. This is fortunate for the wine tourist, for it is also the region's premier wine zone. For exploration of the Val do Salnés Albariño wine country, Cambados, with its atmospheric Parador Nacional del Albariño, makes an excellent base, while El Grove at the tip of the peninsula is a fine resort with nice beaches and plenty of restaurants and seafood bars. Further south below Vigo, one of Galicia's large cities, Bayona is another pleasant resort from which the O Rosal wine country can be dipped into en route to La Guardia, located at the mouth of the Miño overlooking Portugal. Inland from Vigo, exploration of the Rías Baixas sub-zone of Condado do Tea makes a pleasant excursion en route to Ribadavia.

Ribadavia is a fine inland market town located on the Miño river and the centre for the important and extensive Ribeiro wine zone. The Valdeorras wine zone is passed through en route to León and the Cantabrian coast, though it is not a wine region that warrants extensive exploration.

The Rías Baixas

The Rías Baixas country extends south from Santiago de Compostela, below Padrón, the little inland port where Saint James's body was reputedly landed – in the Church of Santiago there is the *padrón* (mooring post) to which the blessed boat was allegedly tied. Here a series of deep and wide river estuaries known as *rías* carve their way far inland, creating broad peninsulas flanked by pine- and eucalyptus-covered hills extending down to the edge of the rocky shores. In the *rías* themselves, there are extensive networks of rafts, *mejilloneiras* for the cultivation of mussels, while the seaside communities base their economy on fishing, the gathering of shellfish, and, ever increasingly, tourism.

Yet, popular though its resorts undoubtedly are, Galicia will never be a mass tourist destination: it is too far away and inaccessible, its climate too unpredictable to compete with Spain's famous holiday destinations on the Mediterranean seaboard. Those of us who love the region are anxious to keep it that way.

Inland, the country is characterized by its small mixed farms, peasant

GALICIA

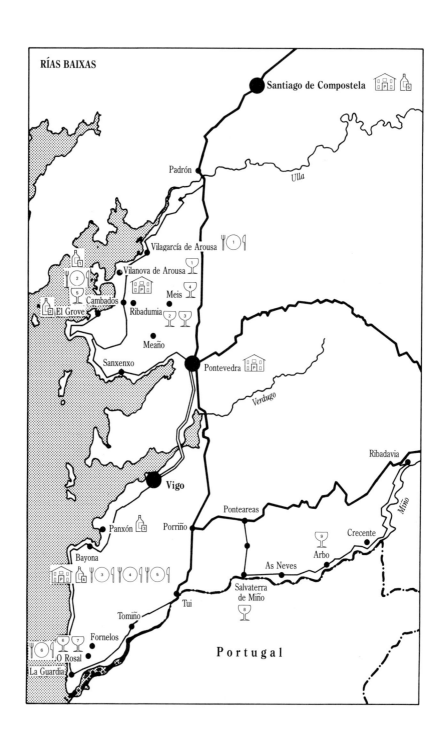

allotments and smallholdings where the cultivation of potatoes, grain, cabbage and turnips is carried on alongside a few rows of vines, trained high on granite or wooden posts. Most farms boast their own *horreos*, freestanding stone granaries raised from the ground on granite supports, decorated often with a cross or with religious carvings, and looking like so many mini-chapels amidst the fields and vineyards.

While most of the farmers grow vines and make their own wine, the Rías Baixas was not traditionally known as one of Galicia's great wine regions. Indeed, it was long considered a marginal wine zone at best due to its high annual precipitation, the risk of hail and strong storms, and the damp mists that often cause the grapes to rot. It is no wonder that in bad years, the wines can be notoriously thin and sour.

Such simple wines of the country, home-made by traditional country methods, are generally light in alcohol (only 8–10°) and may have a quite sharp taste of malic acid rather reminiscent of some farm ciders. Usually they slip down well enough *in situ*, and are adequate accompaniments to the simple but always tasty foods of Galicia.

These local, mainly home-made wines may be nothing much to write home or books about. However, *aficionados* have long come to the Rías Baixas in search of a rare vinous marvel, a legendary but elusive wine made from the aristocratic and unique Albariño grape. It is not fully established whether Albariño is a true autochthonous grape variety of Galicia, or whether it is perhaps a clone of Riesling, brought to the region by Cistercian monks on pilgrimage to Santiago as long ago as the twelfth or thirteenth centuries. By now it doesn't really matter, for the grape has been here so long that it has developed its own characteristics which make it unlike any other in the world.

Manuel Otero Candeira, a local businessman whose primary family concern is the important 'Guau' fish and shellfish conserving plants, explains: 'For those of us who love Albariño, it was always a constant search to find the real thing. And it was always a lottery. You would hear that this farmer had made a good wine, so you would rush to his house to taste and buy it! It might be sensational this year, but when you go back the next it is undrinkable, adulterated and no longer genuine. Unlabelled bottles would be passed over in bars or restaurants, changing hands for the price of a Gran Reserva from Rioja! Some were not pure Albariño, many were horrible and badly made, but the occasional bottle was genuine and unsurpassable, and made the whole search worthwhile. For when Albariño is good and genuine, there is no other wine in the world like it. The quest for Albariño became, for me and for other *aficionados* who come from all classes of Galician society, an obsession.'

In the early 1970s, people from outside agricultural sectors or from other parts of Spain who recognized the great potential of the Albariño grape, set to work to provide the impetus to change the structure of the wine zone, which at that time was still wholly haphazard, and poorly equipped and organized. Land was purchased and replanted exclusively with Albariño; forests were cleared for planting vines; small growers were encouraged to replant with Albariño and to sell their grapes at premium prices never heard of before (the Albariño grape today is by far the most expensive grape per kilogram in Spain, second in the world, claim the growers, only to the grapes of Champagne); and scores of new and generally well-equipped *bodegas* sprang up in the zone. Such considerable efforts were rewarded with the granting of the Rías Baixas DO in 1988.

For Manuel Otero Candeira, the quest thus turned from searching for genuine Albariño, to an obsessive dream of creating a château-style winery. In the early 1980s he embarked on this project with characteristic zeal; on high land the family had always owned outside Cambados, he cleared some 12 hectares of mainly forest and planted it entirely with Albariño in the traditional manner trained up granite posts in *parra* or pergola. The *bodega*, newly constructed but in the traditional style of a Galician *pazo* (palace) from old reclaimed stones, is a small but super-modern estate winery equipped with the latest technology and state-of-the-art winemaking installations.

In his Granbazán wines, Otero seeks to make an Albariño of considerable structure and weight, not a fruity wine to drink within its year of production, and to achieve this he combines traditional methods with modern technology. The rustic, artisan-made Albariños that Otero had always enjoyed and admired were usually produced by the traditional method of macerating the crushed grapes on the skins to extract body and flavour. However, this method can yield wines that are coarse and prone to oxidation. In order to gain sufficient body and extract while maintaining the delicacy and scent of the Albariño, Otero first de-stems and crushes the grapes, then chills them to about 5° before placing them in special stainless steel vats where they are allowed to macerate at low temperature on the skins for 8–10 hours.

Afterwards, the *lágrima*, that is the free run juice that descends from the vats simply by its own gravity, is drawn off separately and this only is used for the production of his amber-bottled Granbazán wine. The remaining mass of grapes is lightly pressed in pneumatic Vaslin presses, and some of this gently-pressed juice is mixed with the *lágrima* (60%) for the production of his green-bottled wine. Both undergo extremely slow and long fermentation in small fermentation tanks at the low temperature of 12–13°, then are bottled not before the August following the harvest.

The wines so produced are outstanding. Granbazán amber, for example, is an Albariño of considerable body and weight, high in glycerine, with a soft, creamy ripeness and a lovely voluptuous fruitiness of ripe peaches and pears. In character, the wine is something of a paradox: full and well-structured, yet delicate and seductive in the mouth, it provides almost more of a sensation than a flavour. When tasting a wine like this, you understand how it could be seriously addictive!

Otero has also experimented with a *barrica*-fermented Albariño, the first *bodega* in the zone to attempt this. I tasted the wine only days after it had been drawn from the new Limousin barrel, so admittedly it was not yet fully knit together. Yet, though the wine was packed with complex oak and fruit flavours, to me it had lost something of the particular charm of the Albariño, its extremely subtle and delicately creamy fruit. However, it is still early days, and I would not be surprised if fine *crianza* wines could be produced in the zone, for the Albariño has the structure, extract and weight to warrant ageing in wood.

The Val do Salnés sub-zone, mainly centred on Cambados and the hills and villages that surround it and extend down the peninsula towards El Grove, remains today the heart of the Rías Baixas DO zone, and certainly the sub-zone that has seen the most investment and plantation of Albariño. As such, it also has the greatest concentration of the region's *bodegas* and accounts at present for some 75% of its production.

The Conde de Creixell, owner of the prestigious Marqués de Murrieta estate in Rioja, has established a *bodega* at his family home, the Pazo de Barrantes near Cambados, and will soon be producing a pure Albariño wine to be marketed alongside those famous and prestigious Riojas. Though at the time of writing the wine had not yet been commercially released, we tasted a *bodega* sample over lunch at the Castillo de Ygay in Logroño, and it promises to be a wine of considerable elegance and class, with enough weight and structure to stand alongside even the famous oak-aged El Dorado de Murrieta.

Another significant development in the region is the coming together of small groups of *cosecheros*, individual grape growers who jointly have significant plantations of Albariño and have subsequently pooled resources to invest in well-equipped communal winemaking facilities. The Agrupación de Cosecheiros Albariño do Salnés, situated in Ribadumia, was one of the first such groupings founded in 1975, and its Dom Bardo Albariño remains one of the classic wines of the zone. Another such grouping, in this case of 140 winegrowers, is the Bodegas de Vilariño-Cambados, whose Martin Códax Albariño, vinified to be drunk while young and extremely fruity, is one of the most widely available wines, though no less excellent for that. It should be stressed that these small co-operatives of *cosecheros* function much the same as private *bodegas* in relation to their winemaking goals and marketing initiatives, and as such, bear little relation to the immense and usually torpid co-operative wineries found in many other Spanish wine zones.

Cambados could well be called the capital of the Albariño; indeed, in August, the town even boasts a *Fiesta del Albariño* which provides one of the best opportunities to taste a range of this otherwise rare and elusive wine. It is a charming town, located on the Ría de Arousa, with its impressive stone-paved Plaza de Fefiñanes dominated by the old and austere Pazo de Fefiñanes, a seventeenth-century church with Celtic carvings, and a small bridge spanning the road. Park in the square, knock on the door of the *bodega* of the Pazo to purchase a bottle or two of its distinctive wood-fermented traditional wine, or enjoy a glass of Albariño under the *soportales* of Bar Laya. Then wander down to the waterfront, through narrow stone-paved streets which still retain the feel of the medieval town. Many of the houses are grand old mansions, with impressive *escudos* (coats-of-arms) on their walls, and granite *horreos* standing proudly in front of them.

Other important wine towns and villages in the Val do Salnés sub-zone include Meaño, Sanxenxo, Ribadumia, Meis, Vilanova de Arousa and Portas. Some of these are little more than hamlets, but in each, in addition to the larger *bodegas*, there are opportunities to purchase *vino de cosechero* direct from the growers themselves. El Grove, though not actually located within the delimited wine zone, is another town that ought to be visited. This popular and busy resort located almost at the tip of the peninsula boasts some fine, protected and shallow beaches; and on the waterfront of the town itself, there are literally scores of welcoming bars and restaurants.

Pontevedra, located at the base of the same peninsula, is the bustling market centre for the surrounding country, an old atmospheric town that is extremely lively and authentic. Its *casco antiguo* is almost wholly intact, and it is a delight simply to wander through the old stone-paved streets, down the bar-lined Calle Figueroa to the charming Plaza de la Leña, then along to the waterfront where the Lerez river joins the Ría de Pontevedra. The covered market is located down here, and displays a quite exceptional and mouthwatering array of fish and shellfish.

Though the vine is grown throughout the Rías Baixas country, the official delimited zone for wines entitled to the *denominación de origen* does not begin again until the far south of the region in the two further sub-zones of O Rosal and Condado do Tea.

O Rosal is located in the lowest basin of the Miño river in the zone known as Baixo Miño. This is a rare, undiscovered land, south of the popular resort of Bayona, inland from a rocky and strikingly beautiful coast. La Guardia is located virtually at the southernmost tip of Galicia, overlooking Portugal on the other side of the mouth of the Miño, a little visited but charming fishing town most famous for its fine shellfish, especially crawfish or spiny lobster (*langosta*) and lobster (*bogavante*). The wine country is located just inland in the hills above the Miño in tiny communities such as O Rosal itself, Tomiño and Pesegueiro, near Tui, the region's principal frontier post, overlooking Valença do Minho in Portugal.

This sub-zone of O Rosal is nowhere near as developed or as intensive as the wine country of the Val do Salnés. However, two famous Rioja companies have demonstrated their faith in the region through the establishment of noteworthy *bodegas*. La Rioja Alta SA of Haro worked with the Lagar de Fornelos, located at Fornelos near O Rosal, for many years before purchasing it outright. Today this forward-looking company has 25 hectares of Albariño, planted in traditional *parra* (up stone posts in pergola fashion) as well as trained in a new and innovative *espaldera alta*, that is, on a high-wired trellis. This method maintains the advantages of the old *parra*: the vines are protected from rot or mildew in this, the wettest part of Spain, while at the same time preserving the grape's fresh, fruity acidity; on the other hand, the new method is much more viable economically because much of the vineyard work can be done mechanically.

Lagar de Fornelos is a small but very up-to-date *bodega*, well-equipped for the production of a sleek, modern 100% Albariño wine. Angel Suarez Vicente, the oenologist at the *bodega*, is modest about his efforts. 'The miracle,' he says, 'is this quite exceptional grape, the Albariño. When you have such a rich and characterful grape as this, it is not difficult to make a great wine, provided you follow the precepts of modern white winemaking. We harvest in small plastic boxes, crush the grapes without de-stemming, and press them lightly in pneumatic presses. Then we chill the must and

GALICIA

allow it to clarify naturally for 24 hours before fermenting in small stainless steel deposits at 16° for about two months. This long, slow fermentation is essential to maintain fruit and aroma.'

The Lagar de Cervera is a delicate and quite delicious Albariño wine, with a slight but refreshing carbonic prickle and delicate flavours of green apples and pears. Yet, for all its delicacy, it is a rich wine with a lovely roundness that comes from a high glycerine content, and which gives the wine a delightful touch of apparent sweetness.

Suarez is himself a native of the zone and knows the land, its people and wines, intimately. 'While pure varietal Albariño wines are the fashion today,' he adds, 'here in O Rosal we have always believed that making good wine is like making a good *caldo gallego*. For a *caldo gallego*, you take a bit of everything: some good broth, vegetables, perhaps a chicken or piece of beef, each adding its flavour. Similarly, to make a good wine, say the᛫ locals, you need a bit of Albariño, together with some Loureira, perhaps some Treixadura and Caiño Blanco, all added to the vat and mixed' together.'

Something of this essential peasant philosophy is followed at Bodegasᵢ Santiago Ruiz, the sub-zone's leading and most longstanding producer, today owned by the Rioja Bodegas Lan. To qualify as a designated 'O Rosal' wine (as distinct from a mono-varietal Albariño), wines must be produced from a minimum of 70% Albariño and Loureira, the rest being made up of authorized autochthonous varieties such as Treixadura, Caiño Blanco and Torrontés. Santiago Ruiz makes just such a wine; while lacking the intensity and richness of a pure Albariño, it too is superlative, full of scent and flavour, yet with a fine, perhaps less unctuous and intense character.

Inland from O Rosal, mainly along the north bank of the Miño mirroring the hills across the river in Portugal, lies the third sub-zone of the Rías Baixas, Condado do Tea. This is a lush, unspoiled, little-visited corner of Galicia, a rural land quite unlike anywhere else in Spain. Here every farm and smallholding grows vines, but there is as yet little specialization. Rather, the vines, trained high on pergolas, are planted here and there, sometimes around the edges of the fields, freeing the land for other crops.

Yet the wines of the area have always enjoyed considerable renown, and bars and houses everywhere offer '*vinos de Condado*'. However, as elsewhere throughout the Rías Baixas, there has been an increase in specialized plantations in recent years as the landowners have recognized the potential of the zone to produce on a commercial scale wines of great character. As at

O Rosal, pure varietal Albariño wines are made as well as wines entitled to the sub-designation 'Condado do Tea'. For the latter, such wines must be produced from a minimum of 70% Albariño and Treixadura, the remainder made up with preferred authorized varieties.

To reach Condado do Tea, either follow the Miño upriver from O Rosal to Salvaterra do Miño, or else, from Pontevedra or Vigo, follow the main road towards Portugal, then at Porriño find the road east to Orense before turning south at Ponteareas to Salvaterra do Miño. Principal wine *pueblos* include Salvaterra do Miño, As Neves, Arbo and Crecente; noteworthy *bodegas* include Granja Fillaboa and Bodegas Condasat in Salvaterra, and Bodegas Marqués de Vizhoja near Arbo. Arbo is known as the '*meca do lamprea*'; lampreys are still caught in ancient wicker traps on the river here and much enjoyed locally. From Crecente, it is a brief but lovely drive upriver to Ribadavia.

Ribeiro

If Rías Baixas has emerged as the aristocratic wine zone of Galicia, Ribeiro remains the source of much of the region's sound everyday drinking. Ribeiro is Galicia's best-known wine region, located in the western flank of the province of Orense, centred on the lovely stone-built river town of Ribadavia. It has long been the unstinting fount of inexpensive and mainly light wines – both white and red – enjoyed up and down the Galician coast, and in urban centres such as Santiago de Compostela, Vigo, La Coruña and Orense itself.

It was not always so. In the fourteenth century, John of Gaunt's English longbowmen paused in Ribadavia en route to Portugal and found the local wines so strong and to their liking that they were literally taken legless and had to rest for a further two days to recover before moving on. The wines of Ribadavia thus gained a certain international fame and were widely shipped by the English, especially after the loss of their vineyards in Aquitaine following the Hundred Years War with France. Indeed, we might still be drinking them today but for the cooling of Anglo-Hispanic relations after Drake's raid on Cádiz and the later rout of the 'Invincible' Armada.

However, it is more than likely that the wines of Ribeiro were never destined for greatness or lasting fame. After phylloxera, in order to satisfy the Gallegos' own monumental and historic thirst, the winegrowers of Ribeiro chose to abandon their traditional grape varieties. In their place they

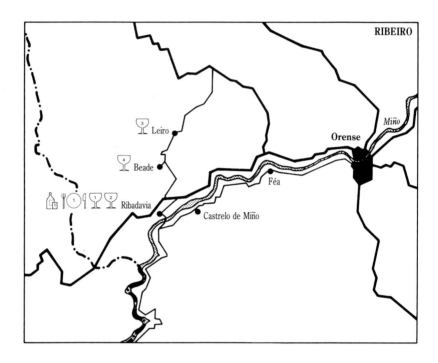

planted with the high-yielding but mainly insipid Jerez and Alicante (as Palomino and Garnacha are respectively called locally), and these two varieties are still dominant today, accounting for well over half the area under vines. As elsewhere in Galicia, in recent years there has been the belated realization that the wine zone's future lies not in the continued production of indifferent bulk wines (which can never compete in price or alcoholic grade with those from the hot zones of central Spain), but in the reclamation of its local indigenous varieties, characterful grapes like the whites Treixadura, Torrontés and Godello and blacks Sousón, Brancelao, Caiño Tinto and Mencía. These grapes are unique and distinctive, grown virtually nowhere in Spain outside Galicia: they deserve to be safeguarded.

The wine country which follows the Miño between Orense and Ribadavia is possibly Spain's most beautiful. The steep and verdant valley has been carved into ancient drystone terraces known as *socalcos* and the vines are trained high up poles or in lovely shaded pergolas. If you enter the region from, say, Castilla y León, it is impossible to imagine a greater contrast: after the parched brown plains of the central *meseta*, punctuated only by black, stumpy head-trained vines, comes the almost unbelievably lush and verdant green of Ribeiro, its steep slopes, planted with tall and upstanding vines, reminiscent almost of Germany's Mosel valley.

By far the largest and most important producer in Ribeiro, and the one which has done most to improve the wines of the zone, is the Cooperativa Vitivinicola del Ribeiro. Indeed, with over a thousand grape-growing *socios* it is in a position to encourage quality, and it achieves this with a range of wines, the best of which reward those growers who have maintained or replanted with autochthonous varieties. In white wines, for example, the Pazo label, one of the most widely available of all Galician wines, is produced mainly from Palomino, with only a minimal addition of local grapes. The superior Viña Costeira, however, is produced almost entirely from local varieties, especially Torrontés, Treixadura and Godello; only marginally more expensive, it demonstrates far greater depth of character and is well worth seeking. The co-operative's top white wine is Amadeus (which replaces the previous Brandomín label), produced entirely from a rigorous selection of the best local grapes, and only made in small quantities in the best years. Difficult to find, it is numbered among the finest wines of Galicia.

One tends to think of Galicia as primarily a white wine region, perhaps because of its lush and damp green colour, or the excellence of the region's seafood. Be that as it may, Ribeiro is also noted for its red wines, and they too should be tried when in the region. Even those produced primarily from Alicante bear little relation to Garnacha wines from, say, hot zones such as central Aragón. Those produced from local grapes are even better: generally surprisingly deep in colour, relatively low in alcohol, and with a rasping acidity that comes as something of a shock. Served in white ceramic *tazitas* which show off the colour beautifully, they are certainly something of an acquired local taste, best sampled in traditional *tabernas* and drinking dens in Ribadavia or Santiago.

For those passing through Ribadavia en route to the Galician coast, it may well be worth stopping at the co-operative to stock up on Costeira wines for everyday drinking, for they are certainly more accessible than the always expensive Albariños of the Rías Baixas. Further exploration of the Ribeiro wine zone can be undertaken by venturing into the thickets of wine villages that lie in side valleys off the main Orense–Ribadavia road. Strike out into the country north and south of the Miño and pass through typical wine hamlets such as Leiro, Gomariz, Castrelo do Miño, Féa and scores of others. This is still a zone of small private winegrowers, and there is plenty of scope for the intrepid wine traveller to hunt out new wines.

VALDEORRAS

Valdeorras

For visitors entering Galicia from the inland route by way of Castilla y León, the main road from León flanks the massive and formidable barrier of the Cordillera Cantábrica to the north and crosses the rugged Montes de León. In the small Castilian wine *comarca* of El Bierzo, the road forks, either northwards towards Lugo and eventually Santiago de Compostela (this was the principal route of the Pilgrim's Way), or southwest, following first the Sil then the Miño river valleys to Orense, Ribadavia and the Rías Baixas.

The remote and minor Galician wine zone of Valdeorras lies just over the mountains, not far from the regional frontier, and is noteworthy for little else save the fact that the wine traveller heading to the Rías Baixas will pass through the heart of it. But this is striking wine country, brown, parched and mountainous, the steep and bald hills especially around the gorge of Puebla de Trives carved into an amazing network of drystone terraces. It is heartbreaking to consider that most of the vineyards have been long abandoned, the years, indeed centuries of labour allowed to fall back into ruin as Nature once more reasserts herself. And yet, how could grape-growing ever, in this day and age, be economic or worthwhile in such a labour-intensive, remote and unheard-of land?

Around Larouco, La Rúa and Vilamartín de Valdeorras, however, the valley floor opens up and vines still thrive on the flatter, easier to cultivate sedimentary plains. As elsewhere in Galicia, though perhaps more understandably here, local varieties have long been abandoned in favour of the high-yielding duo of Jerez and Alicante. However, it is generally agreed that the best wines of Valdeorras are produced from the local white grape Godello and the black Mencía. Rare, difficult to find wines made from these characterful local grapes should be sought and tried if passing through the Valdeorras.

Bodegas: Stop to Taste; Stop to Buy

Rías Baixas (*Val do Salnés sub-zone*)

1

AGRO DE BAZÁN SA
TREMOEDO
36628 VILANOVA DE AROUSA
PONTEVEDRA
TEL: (986) 55 55 62; FAX: (986) 54 32 27

WINES PRODUCED: Granbazán
Albariño (amber bottle), Granbazán
Albariño (green bottle); Granbazán
Albariño Crianza.
VISITS: Working hours for direct
sales.
Manuel Otero Candeira has
realized a dream in the creation of
this remarkable estate winery. The
bodega is located in the
reconstructed *pazo*, a wholly new
country palace built in the style
typical of the Val do Salnés. The
upstairs offices are furnished with
antiques and paintings, while the
winemaking installations below are
state-of-the-art modern. The
well-equipped tasting salon provides
the opportunity to taste these
prestigious and impeccable wines,
and serious wine lovers are always
welcome.

2

PAZO DE BARRANTES
BARRANTES
36636 RIBADUMIA
PONTEVEDRA
ADMINISTRATIVE OFFICE:
  MARQUÉS DE MURRIETA SA,
  CASTILLO DE YGAY, CTRA DE
  ZARAGOZA, KM 5, 26080 LOGROÑO,
  LA RIOJA
TEL: (941) 25 81 00; FAX: (941) 25 16 06

WINE PRODUCED: Pazo de
Barrantes Albariño.
VISITS: By appointment through
the administrative office in Logroño.
The Pazo de Barrantes is the
ancestral home of the Condes de
Creixell. The present Count, Don
Vicente Cebrián Sagarriga, is the
owner of the prestigious Bodegas
Marqués de Murrieta in Logroño, so
it is perhaps not surprising that he
has now decided to turn his
considerable efforts to the creation
of a top-class Albariño to offer
alongside his stable of classic and
famous Riojas. At the time of
writing, the wine is still not
available commercially, though a
sample we tasted at Murrieta
demonstrates its quality and the
classic winemaking expertise
which is the hallmark of Murrieta.
English, French spoken.

GALICIA

The Creixell Foundation

The Creixell Foundation is a humanistic and cultural foundation based in the Pazo de Barrantes and inspired by the Conde de Creixell's friendship with the British author Graham Greene. A principal objective of the Foundation is to encourage and promote an exchange of cultural ideas and values particularly between young people of different countries. Each year it organizes an Anglo-Hispanic Literature Seminar that lasts for three weeks during the summer and is based at the Pazo de Barrantes. Students and academics from universities in Great Britain and Spain can apply to take part. For further information, write to Marqués de Murrieta SA (address above).

3 AGRUPACIÓN DE COSECHEIROS ALBARIÑO DO SALNÉS
SISÁN
36638 RIBADUMIA
PONTEVEDRA
TEL AND FAX: (986) 71 00 52

WINE PRODUCED: Dom Bardo Albariño.

VISITS: By appointment.
The relatively small co-operative of *cosecheros* was founded in 1975 and was one of the first to produce and market commercially a modern Albariño. Its Dom Bardo Albariño remains an archetype.
French spoken.

4 BODEGAS DE VILARIÑO-CAMBADOS SA
BURGÁNS 91
VILARIÑO
36633 CAMBADOS
PONTEVEDRA
TEL: (986) 52 10 01;
FAX: (986) 52 08 75

WINE PRODUCED: Martin Códax Albariño.
VISITS: Daily, working hours. Appointment necessary.
Another highly regarded co-operative of *cosecheros* producing the popular and widely available Martin Códax Albariño.
English spoken.

5 BODEGAS DEL PALACIO DE
  FEFIÑANES SA
  PLAZA DE FEFIÑANES, S/N
  36630 CAMBADOS
  PONTEVEDRA
  TEL: (986) 54 22 04

WINE PRODUCED: Albariño de
Fefiñanes.
VISITS: By appointment.
Classic old-style Albariño,
fermented and aged in wood.

as Baixas (*O Rosal sub-zone*)

6 LAGAR DE FORNELOS SA
  BARRIO DE CRUCES
  FORNELOS 34
  36770 O ROSAL
  PONTEVEDRA
  TEL: (986) 62 58 75; FAX: (986) 62 50 11

WINE PRODUCED: Lagar de
Cervera Albariño.

VISITS: Daily, without
appointment 9–13h30; 15–18h.
Owned by La Rioja Alta SA in
Haro, this small but modern wine
estate makes a notable Albariño
wine near La Guardia. It is at
present one of the few such wines
widely available in Britain.

7 BODEGAS SANTIAGO RUIZ VINOS DE
  EL ROSAL
  SAN MIGUEL DE TABAGÓN
  36770 O ROSAL
  PONTEVEDRA
  TEL: (986) 61 05 68

WINE PRODUCED: Santiago Ruiz.
VISITS: By appointment.
Another Rioja-owned *bodega*
(Bodegas Lan), producing the classic
wine of O Rosal from a mix of local
grapes, including Albariño,
Loureira, Treixadura and others.

Rías Baixas (*Condado do Tea sub-zone*)

8 GRANJA FILLABOA
  36450 SALVATERRA DO MIÑO
  PONTEVEDRA
  COMMERCIAL OFFICE: PLAZA DE
  COMPOSTELA 6, 36201 VIGO,
  PONTEVEDRA
  TEL: (986) 43 70 00; FAX: (986) 43 24 64

WINE PRODUCED: Fillaboa
Albariño.
VISITS: By appointment,
preferably at weekends.
Highly regarded estate producing
Fillaboa Albariño from own grapes
grown on 21 ha. of vineyards.
English, some French spoken.

GALICIA

9 BODEGAS MARQUÉS DE VIZHOJA SA
FINCA LA MOREIRA
CEQUELIÑOS
ARBO
PONTEVEDRA
COMMERCIAL OFFICE: AVDA
ATLÁNTIDA 37, 36208 VIGO,
PONTEVEDRA
TEL: (986) 23 69 64

WINES PRODUCED: Marqués de
Vizhoja; Torre La Moreira Albariño.
VISITS: Mon–Fri by appointment.
Eighteenth-century estate located
in the rolling hills above the Miño
overlooking the Minho vineyards of
Portugal, across the river.

Ribeiro

1 COOPERATIVA VITIVINICOLA DEL
RIBEIRO
VALDEPEREIRA, S/N
32417 RIBADAVIA
ORENSE
TEL: (988) 47 01 75

WINES PRODUCED: Pazo *blanco*,
tinto; Viña Costeira *blanco*;
Amadeus *blanco*.

AGUARDIENTE: Pazo Orujo.
VISITS: Mon–Fri 8h30–13h;
14h30–18h.
This large co-operative is the
reliable source for some of Galicia's
most widely drunk and enjoyed
wines. The potent *orujo* is
legendary.

---

2 COSECHEROS DEL VINO DEL
RIBEIRO
SAMPAIO, S/N
32414 RIBADAVIA
ORENSE
TEL: (988) 47 07 87; FAX: (988) 47 03 63

WINE PRODUCED: Campo
Hermoso *blanco*.
VISITS: Daily, working hours.
Co-operative of *cosecheros*
producing tasty white wine from
Treixadura, Lado, Torrontés and
Palomino.

---

3 RICARDO VAZQUEZ ALEMPARTE
GOMARIZ
32429 LEIRO
ORENSE
TEL: (988) 48 82 95

WINES PRODUCED: Alemparte
blanco, Alemparte Treixadura;

Alemparte *tinto*.
VISITS: By appointment.
Located in a side valley off the Miño
above Ribadavia, this small family
bodega makes sound Ribeiro wines
of which the Alemparte Treixadura
is most noteworthy.

---

4 BODEGAS CAMPEON
32431 BEADE
ORENSE
TEL: (988) 47 09 24

WINES PRODUCED: Campeon *blanco, tinto*; Val do Pereiro *blanco*.
VISITS: Daily, working hours.

Family *bodega* located on the road from Ribadavia to Leiro in the midst of vineyards. There is a bar attached to the *bodega* where the wines can be sampled. Val do Pereiro is mainly Treixadura and Torrontés.

Valdeorras

1 BODEGA COOPERATIVA JESUS
NAZARENO
AVDA 18 DE JULIO 62
32300 O BARCO DE VALDEORRAS
ORENSE
TEL: (988) 32 02 62; FAX: (988) 32 02 42

WINES PRODUCED: Albar *blanco, rosado, tinto*; Gran Vino Godello; Menciño *tinto*; Valdouro *tinto* Crianza.

AGUARDIENTE: Conxuro.
VISITS: Weekdays, working hours. The zone's largest producer offers a rare opportunity to taste and purchase Godello (Gran Vino Godello) and Mencía (Menciño) wines.

---

2 BODEGA JOAQUIN REBOLLEDO
SAN ROQUE, S/N
32350 LA RUA DE VALDEORRAS
ORENSE
TEL: (988) 24 17 14

WINES PRODUCED: Blanco Godello; Tinto Mencía.
VISITS: Open daily for direct sales. Located on the main road.

Restaurantes, Hoteles y Paradores

Rías Baixas

1 CHOCOLATE
CTRA VILAGARCÍA–LA TOJA, KM 2
VILLAJUÁN
36600 VILAGARCÍA DE AROUSA
PONTEVEDRA
TEL: (986) 50 11 99

Located on the main road between Cambados and Vilagarcía de

Arousa, this is reputed to be the best restaurant in Galicia. Manolo Cores is a great personality, and the restaurant is decorated with accolades from his famous friends. Specialities include exceptional seafood and shellfish from the *rías*, while the restaurant is also famous

GALICIA

for its enormous charcoal grilled steaks and meats. Good selection of wines, particularly Albariños from the Rías Baixas.
Expensive

2

RESTAURANTE O' ARCO
CALLE REAL 14
36630 CAMBADOS
PONTEVEDRA
TEL: (986) 54 23 12

Lovely comfortable restaurant down from the main square serving faithfully prepared traditional foods: good selection of shellfish, home-made *empanada de berberecho, rape al Salnés, lomo de merluza al Albariño, filloas.* Good wine list with extensive selection of Albariños, as well as old Reservas from Rioja and Vega Sicilia.
Moderate

3

RESTAURANTE NAVEIRA
ALFÉREZ BARREIRO 8
36300 BAYONA
PONTEVEDRA
TEL: (986) 35 50 35

Located directly opposite the *lonja* (fish market), this simple but highly regarded restaurant is noted for serving the freshest catch of the day.
Moderate

4

EL MOSQUITO
VENTURA MISA 32
36300 BAYONA
PONTEVEDRA
TEL: (986) 35 50 36

Old traditional bar/restaurant serving good *mariscos* and Galician home cooking: *caldo gallego, merluza a la gallega,* and reasonable house wine.
Inexpensive

5

CHURRASQUERÍA FRANKY
VISO DE CALVOS
SABARIS
36300 BAYONA
PONTEVEDRA
TEL: (986) 35 11 59

Located in the hills between Bayona and Ramallosa, this typical family-run *churrasquería* serves simply grilled meats, salad and home-made wines.
Inexpensive

6

EL GRAN SOL
MALTESES 32
36780 LA GUARDIA
PONTEVEDRA
TEL: (986) 61 05 52

Closed Sun and holiday evenings. Quite simply one of our favourite restaurants in Spain: a simple rustic tavern in the old town overlooking the fishing port, serving some of the best fish and shellfish that you will ever eat: *percebes, centolla, langosta, bogavante* accompanied by light, home-made O Rosal wine.
Inexpensive (Moderate to Expensive for *langosta*)

Paradores

P

PARADOR NACIONAL DEL ALBARIÑO
PASEO DE CERVANTES, S/N
36630 CAMBADOS
PONTEVEDRA
TEL: (986) 54 22 50; FAX: (986) 54 20 68

Located down by the waterfront in the reconstructed Pazo de Bazán, this is a quiet and comfortable *parador* with a good restaurant serving local shellfish and seafood.
Moderate

P

PARADOR NACIONAL CASA DEL
    BARÓN
CALLE MACEDA, S/N
36002 PONTEVEDRA
TEL: (986) 85 58 00; FAX: (986) 85 21 95

Well restored typical Gallegan palace.
Moderate

P

PARADOR NACIONAL CONDE DE
    GONDOMAR
CTRA DE BAYONA, KM 1,600
36300 BAYONA
PONTEVEDRA
TEL: (986) 35 50 00; FAX: (986) 35 50 76

Installed in the Monte Real fortification on the peninsula guarding the entrance to the Bayona bay, this remarkable *parador* is actually located within the old castle fortifications. Ask for a room with views over the Atlantic for a memorable stay.
Expensive

GALICIA

P

HOSTAL DE LOS REYES CATÓLICOS PLAZA DEL OBRADOIRO 1 15705 SANTIAGO DE COMPOSTELA LA CORUÑA TEL: (981) 58 22 00; FAX: (981) 56 30 94	Quite simply one of the great historic hotels of Europe, founded by Ferdinand and Isabel in 1499 as a hospice for pilgrims to the great shrine of Santiago. To stay here is to experience a part of Spanish history. **Very Expensive**

Ribeiro

1

RESTAURANTE PLAZA PLAZA MAYOR 2 32400 RIBADAVIA PONTEVEDRA TEL: (986) 47 05 76	Closed Mon eve. Simple but friendly bar-restaurant serving *pulpo, bacalao a la gallega, anguilas a la Ribadavia* and a good selection of local wines. **Inexpensive**

Tomar Unas Copas: Stop for a Drink; Stop for a Bite

Galicia is one of Spain's finest regions for bars and *tapas*. On the coasts, certainly, almost every village boasts a host of bars, all serving quite exceptional arrays of shellfish and other hot *tapas*, accompanied, of course, by the local wines. The following suggestions are simply a few that we have found particularly congenial, but there are so many in the region that it is hard to go wrong.

1

BAR LAYA PLAZA DE FEFIÑANES 36630 CAMBADOS PONTEVEDRA	On the main square, with outdoor tables: come to the capital of the Albariño to sample this delightful wine under the shaded *soportales*.

2

PARAÍSO DEL MARISCO AVDA ORILLAMAR 36980 EL GROVE PONTEVEDRA TEL: (986) 78 20 71	Competition is intense in the bars of El Grove to offer the best and freshest array of shellfish and *tapas*. For the record, this friendly and popular bar serves a

sensational range of *tapas* and *raciones* but I would guess that so do most other bars along the Orillamar waterfront.

---

3 CAFE-BAR BEIRAMER
CALLE MUJINES 11
PANXÓN
PONTEVEDRA
TEL: (986) 36 59 38

Panxón is located on the opposite side of the bay from Bayona, and so is considerably quieter and less visited. The waterfront is lined with bars all serving good *tapas* but this one, run by a young friendly couple, is recommended for its hospitality and good food.

---

4 BAR EL PATIO
CALLE CONDE 19
36300 BAYONA
PONTEVEDRA
TEL: (986) 35 69 75

This street behind the main thoroughfare is literally lined with bars, but El Patio is particularly friendly and serves a good array of hot *tapas*: *navajas, pulpo a feira, pimientos de Padrón, mejillones,* together with good house wine from Ribeiro.

---

5 BAR ABRIGADOIRO
CARRERA DEL CONDE, 5 BAJO
15700 SANTIAGO DE COMPOSTELA
LA CORUÑA
TEL: (981) 56 31 63

This outstanding wine tavern is located just outside the *casco antiguo*, but it is well worth seeking out to enjoy house Ribeiro cooled in a trough fed by a waterwheel, and accompanied by a good range of simple but authentic *tapas*.

Tabernas

If you really want to experience Galician wines at the source, it is essential to hunt out an authentic drinking *taberna*. Like the great *Heurige* of Austria and the Italian Südtirol, true *tabernas* are located in the *bodegas* where the wines are actually made. A simple trestle table and a few stools may stand among the wooden barrels; perhaps there is a fire in winter; or in

GALICIA

Taberna do Papuxa, Ribadavia.

summer (if there is any wine left), there may be tables and chairs in the shade of the garden amidst the vines.

At the Taberna do Papuxa in the old *barrio xudio* of Ribadavia, for example, friends drop in and help themselves to a china *tazita* of white Ribeiro wine drawn direct from the wood. There are hams and sausages hanging from the rafters, and a loaf of bread with a knife stuck in it for any who are feeling peckish.

When I commented to Pepe Papuxa that his wine was excellent – light, creamy, and so easy to drink – the septuagenarian merely shrugged his ample shoulders. '*Moja,*' he replied. '*Moja la boca.*' It wets the mouth, lubricates conversation, and encourages singing and dancing. He then began to croon a deep, low sad lament in the clicking, slurring language of the Gallegos, and we all poured ourselves another cup of wine . . .

1 TABERNA DO PAPUXA
BARRIO XUDIO 5
32414 RIBADAVIA
PONTEVEDRA

Los Campings

Rías Baixas

BAYONA PLAYA
BAYONA
PONTEVEDRA
TEL: (986) 35 00 35

CAMPING PLAYA AMERICA
NIGRAN
PONTEVEDRA
TEL: (986) 36 54 04

ESTANQUE DORADO
TOMIÑO
PONTEVEDRA
TEL: (986) 62 25 26

Open all year. Near the Portuguese frontier.

CAMPING MOREIRAS
EL GROVE
PONTEVEDRA
TEL: (986) 73 16 91

Open all year.

CAMPING RÍAS BAIXAS
PORTONOVO-SANGENJO
PONTEVEDRA
TEL: (986) 69 00 15

EL TERRON
VILANUEUA DE AROUSA
PONTEVEDRA
TEL: (986) 55 43 94

Ribeiro

CAMPING LEIRO
LEIRO
ORENSE
TEL: (988) 48 80 36

Open all year.

Vinos y Comestibles: Stop to Taste; Stop to Buy

ADEGA GALLEGA
SANTA MARTA DE ARRIBA 56
15700 SANTIAGO DE COMPOSTELA
LA CORUÑA

Wine, sausage and other Galician products. Wares can be sampled, even after store hours.

GALICIA

VINOTECA
MARÍA BERDIALES 41
36203 VIGO
PONTEVEDRA
TEL AND FAX: (986) 43 43 89

Closed Sat afternoon, Sun.
Exceptional Spanish wine shop

owned and run by enthusiast
Enrique Lorenzo Feijóo. Extensive
range of wines for sale by bottle or
case from virtually every corner of
the country.
A little English spoken.

Compras Deliciosas: Stop to Taste; Stop to Buy

PANADERÍA BENIGNO ABELLEIRA
SARMIENTO 23
36002 PONTEVEDRA
TEL: (986) 85 14 52

Galician bread is more varied than
anywhere else in Spain. Come to
this old bakery in the *casco antiguo*
which has been supplying locals
with a range of breads and
empanadas for over 100 years.

LA CASA DE LOS QUESOS
RUA DE BAUTIZADOS 10
15700 SANTIAGO DE COMPOSTELA
LA CORUÑA

Small artisan shop in the old part
of town specializing in the famous
breast-shaped *queso de tetilla* and
queso de San Simón, as well as a
selection of home-made wines and
orujos.

Los Curros

On the bleak and remote hills below Vigo, every summer great country
spectacles take place: *curros*, the rounding up and branding of wild horses.
Each Sunday throughout the month of June, these hardly organized events
take place in the hills above villages like Mougás, Morgadanes, Bayona,
Torroña and Pinzas.

At Morgadanes, for example, great crowds have gathered on the hills
by early morning. Here in the high hills, amidst the eucalyptus and pine
woods, the wine flows freely from dawn to dusk: dense, inky *tinto* that
tastes as if it is made from foxy hybrid American grapes, and cloudy, turbid

The *curro* of Morgadanes, near Bayona.

home-made white, both served in handleless china cups. Cauldrons of octopus boil all day long, and chops, ribs and sausages are roasted over blazing fires.

The beasts, short-legged, with unkempt manes and distended bellies, are rounded up by *caballeros* on horseback and are brought in gradually and unwillingly. They are confused and angry at being captured, their eyes blazing in terror and rage. A baby foal, born this morning, is delivered in arms, placed in a smaller corral apart from its mother. It can barely even stand.

By afternoon, the corrals are full; groups here and there light fires, take out long home-made pikes, ropes and branding instruments. A horse is haltered, led out, and, while two or three men tug at the rope around its neck and another couple pull it by the tail, the red hot brand is thrust against the beast's exposed and taut flank. The smell of singed hair and burning flesh is overpowering. Then they produce a large pair of shears and ceremoniously cut off the tangled mane. Once done, the beast is released and wildly gallops away to disappear into the misty, green hills once more.

This is a raw and cruel country spectacle and an intoxicating and dangerous atmosphere prevails, no doubt lubricated by the copious amounts of wine consumed. We are stunned by the barbarity of this primordial event which has taken place since before the dawn of time: the capture, control and subsequent freeing again of beautiful wild beasts. Here in this harsh environment – so harsh that the menfolk have traditionally and for centuries had to go abroad to seek their living – it appears as a vainglorious demonstration that in spite of all, man can be the maker of his own destiny, can control and dominate even Nature itself.

¡Fiesta! Wine and Other Related Celebrations

end of April	Feria del Ribeiro	Ribadavia

(One of Galicia's most important regional festivals celebrating in particular the wines of the Ribeiro zone.)

early June	Fiesta de Langosta	La Guardia
1st Sun in June	Festa do Viño Tinto del Salnés	Ribadumia
1st weekend in Aug	Fiesta del Albariño	Cambados
1st Sun in Aug	Festa do Viño do Condado	Salvaterra do Miño
early Nov	Festa do Magosto	Orense

(New wine and chestnuts)

Y para saber más Additional Information

Regional Government Tourist
   Office
Junta de Galicia
Palacio de Rajoy
15700 Santiago de Compostela
La Coruña
tel: (981) 58 00 33

Consejo Regulador de Rías Baixas
Calle Michelena 1
36002 Pontevedra
tel: (986) 85 48 50

Consejo Regulador de Ribeiro
Calle Bajada de Oliveira, s/n
32400 Ribadavia
Orense
tel: (988) 47 10 15

Consejo Regulador de Valdeorras
Dr Perez Lista 12
32300 O Barco de Valdeorras
Orense
tel: (988) 32 03 18

THE LEVANTE

Dame de Elche, Elche.

The Levante is Spain's great eastern seaboard, extending from the Ebro delta south of Catalunya to the frontier with southern Andalucía. The area so called, while not actually an official entity, embraces two separate autonomous but contiguous regions, Valencia and Murcia. The name, moreover, connects this eastern section of the country with its eastern Mediterranean counterpart and recalls the centuries-long occupation of these lands by the Moors. Valencia, with its multicoloured *azulejo* domes and minaret-like belltowers, may even now appear, in the coruscating glare of the Mediterranean midday, something of an oriental apparition. The lush *huerta* of citrus groves and market gardens that closely encircles Spain's third largest city is a paradise of fecundity, a constant reminder of the Moors' legacy of an extensive, life-giving system of irrigation.

This is a land of great contrast: the intensive and often fly-by-night development of coastal resorts along the Costa Blanca and the timeless, unchanging *pueblos* of the interior; the lush, alluvial littoral of the *huerta* and the harsh and inhospitable mountain terrain leading up to Spain's central *meseta*; cosmopolitan city and rural agricultural country; the essentially Catalan culture of Valencia and the Castilian culture of Murcia.

From Castellón de la Plana south through Benidorm, Alicante and La Manga to Cartagena and beyond, this is one of Spain's great holiday destinations, a mecca not only for foreign tourists but for Spaniards too. It is, after all, the closest and most immediately accessible seaboard for Madrid and central Spain. Indeed, so popular is this eastern coastal strip that it is hardly possible to believe that just 30 years ago a resort like Benidorm was no more, apparently, than a small and charming fishermen's village. Today, with its ghastly, unending lines of concrete multi-storey apartments, its pubs, piano bars, discos and nightclubs, and its establishments serving English breakfast until mid-afternoon, it has, not without justification, come to be associated with the very worst elements of 'package holiday' Spain.

Yet it is too easy to dismiss the coastal resorts of the Levante wholesale; obviously for the many millions who continue to come here year after year, they must be satisfactorily providing the basic requirements for a holiday in the sun, whatever those particular requirements may be. And for those millions who do make their way here, English pubs notwithstanding, the region often provides the first real taste of Spain, and may serve as a jumping-off point for further exploration of the country.

Make no mistake, while most of the region's tourists may rarely leave their villa complexes, apartments or hotels, there is much on offer here for the curious and adventurous visitor. Valencia itself is one of our favourite large Spanish cities, its old baroque part of town delightfully intimate and easy to explore on foot. Alicante, most often used as an airport destination only, is still very much a real, living Spanish town. The palm groves of Elche are magnificent and really do have to be seen to be believed, while inland towns such as Murcia and Alcoy remain at once atmospheric, self-contained and authentic.

The Levante is one of Spain's great zones of specialized agriculture, yielding an overflowing cornucopia of fruits and vegetables that is despatched efficiently throughout the country, Europe and the world. It is not surprising to find, then, that the cultivation of the grape is of considerable importance here in addition to the region's other traditional crops, grown for the table as well as for winemaking. Indeed, the Levante is a vast and important wine region in its own right, the abundant source of rivers of mainly anonymous, branded Spanish white, *rosado* and red wines enjoyed throughout the world, even though such wines' provenance may never be known or realized. No one claims that this is one of Spain's great wine regions save in terms of volume, nor, admittedly, does the region have all that much to offer the curious wine traveller, with the exception of a few isolated gems. All the same, those who do come to the Levante will find the local wines both well made and more than satisfactory: they certainly need never go thirsty.

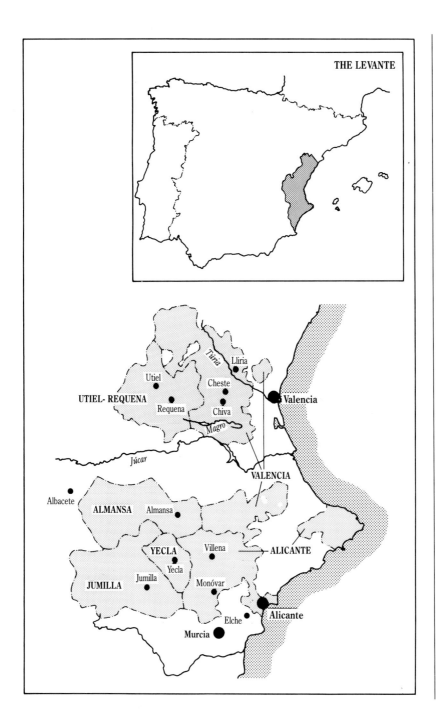

THE LEVANTE

Orientation

The broad eastern section of Spain known as the Levante comprises two separate regions, Valencia (which is made up of three provinces, Valencia, Alicante and Castellón) and Murcia. This seaboard region remains one of Spain's most popular and frequented, for both Spaniards and foreign tourists alike. It is inevitably extremely overcrowded in season, but the wine country, extending inland from Valencia and around Utiel-Requena, up from Alicante, and around the Murcian towns of Yecla and Jumilla in particular, remains virtually untouched.

Both Valencia and Alicante have international airports. The region is well served by rail connections with Madrid, as well as with Barcelona and France. The A7 motorway extends along the eastern seaboard from the French border through Valencia, Alicante and Murcia.

Maps: Michelin No. 445 (Central & Eastern); Firestone Hispania C-8, T28.

The *Huerta:* Legacy of the Moors

'La huerta empieza en las últimas calles de la ciudad,' say the Valencianos. Indeed, even today, it remains true that the lush market gardens and citrus orchards of Spain's third largest city begin on its very outskirts, with little or no transition between city and country.

Valencia and the Levante, like the rest of Mediterranean Spain, enjoys an extreme climate, with parchingly dry summers and rainfall in autumn and winter that is sometimes so fierce and violent that the water has no chance to even soak into the ground, but rather washes away in dry courses known as *ramblas*. Yet, due to an intricate system of irrigation first developed by the Moors, based on a patchwork of canals originally fed by mechanical waterwheels, this rich alluvial littoral has been transformed into a veritable sub-tropical paradise, considered one of the most fertile strips in Europe, a dense swatch of mainly orange and citrus groves, capable of giving three or even four crops each year.

In a land where water has traditionally held the key to prosperity, even to life itself, it is no wonder that rights over this precious substance have been so jealously safeguarded. In Valencia, for example, under the great Gothic Puerto de los Apostoles of its cathedral, in the shadow of the beautiful octagonal Miguelete belltower, an unusual yet still wholly func-

The Water Tribunal meets weekly before the Door of the Apostles of Valencia's Cathedral to settle disputes relating to water and irrigation in the *huerta*.

tional ritual is enacted on the stroke of noon every Thursday. This is the *Tribunal de las Aguas* – the Water Tribunal – which, since the Middle Ages, has met weekly to settle any water disputes. Representatives of each of Valencia's eight canals (*acequias*), accompanied by an *alguazil* (bailiff), sit outdoors solemnly. The proceedings are entirely oral and are conducted in Valenciano, a Catalan dialect still spoken daily throughout most of the region. Complaints and denunciations are presented and judgement is passed: the sentence, which may include the ultimate sanction of deprivation of water, is immediate and binding.

LOS VINOS: THE WINES OF THE LEVANTE

Alicante DO   The delimited Alicante vineyard lies inland from the coastal city, particularly centred on the two wine towns of Villena and Monóvar. The *denominación* applies to dry, medium dry and sweet wines produced from Merseguera, Moscatel and Verdil grapes (minimum alcohol 11°); dry, medium dry and sweet *rosado* wines (minimum alcohol 12°) and red wines from Monastrell (primarily) together with some Garnacha and Bobal (minimum alcohol 12°); *vino de doble pasta* (minimum alcohol 12°); *vino de licor rosado, vino de licor tinto* and *vino de licor Moscatel Alicante* (minimum alcohol 15°); and the zone's unique speciality, Fondillón (minimum alcohol 16°, eight years' minimum ageing period in wood).

Jumilla DO Delimited wine region north of Murcia producing heavyweight red wines normally with a very high alcohol content, primarily from the Monastrell grape. Though the system of *doble pasta* continues to be utilized for the production of wines primarily for blending, lighter, finer table wines are now also being produced here that demonstrate potential for the future. White, *rosado* and red Jumilla must attain 11–15° alcohol; Jumilla Monastrell, whether *rosada, clarete* or *tinto*, 14–17°; and Jumilla Monastrell *tinto doble pasta* 14–16.5°.

Vino de Doble Pasta

Vino de doble pasta or *vino de doble capa* is a unique speciality of the Levante, a wine produced not normally for drinking in its own right, but primarily for blending. The production of this dense, inky and concentrated wine is most distinctive and fascinating. Black grapes – usually here Monastrell – are first de-stemmed and crushed, then pumped into fermentation tanks to macerate. After a period of hours, the free run juice (*mosto de lágrima*) is drawn off separately simply by gravity, without the use of additional pressure. This grape must is usually stained a lovely coral to deep pink colour and is vinified separately into *rosado* wine. Meanwhile, the remaining mass of wine-drenched pulp and skins is left in the vat, and this is topped up with more freshly crushed grapes. There is consequently a double amount of grapes and grape skins in the fermentation tank. As the wine ferments, it thus gains an immense extract of concentrated colour and tannin, qualities which generally make it unpalatable on its own but excellent for blending with lighter and more insipid wines from less sunny regions.

Utiel-Requena DO
Utiel-Requena is probably Valencia's finest delimited winegrowing region, located west of Valencia on the edge of the Castilian *meseta* particularly around the wine towns of Utiel and Requena. While white, *rosado* and red wines are produced under the *denominación* from Macabeo, Merseguera and Planta Nova white grapes and Bobal, Tempranillo and Garnacha black grapes, the zone is best known for its *rosado* and red wines. Light, attractively fruity, these are the wines that are sent down to the great blending vats of Valencia to emerge ultimately on the world wine scene with little or no indication of their provenance. Minimum alcohol for all wines is 10°.

Valencia DO The vast delimited Valencia vineyard is divided into three sub-zones and is noted above all for the production of sound everyday white wines, lesser amounts of *rosado* and reds, and for specialities such as Moscatel de Valencia (minimum alcohol 14°). Principal grape varieties include white Merseguera, Planta Fina, Pedro Ximénez, Malvasía and black Monastrell, Garnacha, Garnacha Tintorera. The three sub-zones are:
Valentino The biggest sub-zone, accounting for over 60% of the production of the DO, and extending over some 29 municipalities in the centre and north of the province. A range of wines is produced, including dry, medium dry and sweet white wines (minimum alcohol 11°); *rosado* and red wines (minimum alcohol 11°); and *vino de licor* (minimum alcohol 15°).
Clariano The next largest sub-zone is located in the south of the province and accounts for about 30% of the Valencia DO's total, producing dry white, *rosado* and red wines (minimum alcohol 11°).
Alto Turia The smallest sub-zone, extending over only six communities in the north-east of the province, but producing the lightest, most delicate white wines (minimum alcohol 10°).

The names of Valencia's sub-zones, however, are rarely of importance to the consumer, since grape must or wines are usually purchased from the different zones, then blended together by the large firms that dominate the industry.

Yecla DO Murcian enclave bordering the Manchegan province of Albacete and the Valencian province of Alicante, noted primarily for its powerful red, *clarete*, *rosado* and white wines produced from grapes grown in the vineyards surrounding the eponymous wine town. Principal grape variety is Monastrell and the

THE LEVANTE

best sub-zone is Campo Arriba, entitled to its own sub-*denominación*, Yecla Campo Arriba. White wine, produced from Merseguera and Verdil, must reach 11.5–13°; *rosado*, 11.5–14°; *clarete*, 12–14.5°; red, 12–14°; *tinto doble pasta*, 14–16°; Yecla Campo Arriba *clarete*, 14.5–16° and Yecla Campo Arriba *tinto*, 14–16°.

Other drinks

Horchata   Light, refreshing beverage from Valencia made from the ground *chufa* root known as the 'earth almond'. Best *horchata* is said to come from Alboraya, a town in Valencia's *huerta* just north of the city.

Horchatería in Valencia.

Sangría

Sangría is as much a cliché of Spain as *paella*. It is perhaps no coincidence that while both are now known and enjoyed nationally and internationally, they are most at home and authentic in the Levante. No doubt through the popularity of this region as a holiday destination, both have come to be associated throughout the world with food and drink Spanish style. Light Valencia red wines, fruity and low in tannin, make the ideal base for this refreshing beverage, mixed together simply with slices of orange and lemon, a cup of Spanish brandy, plenty of ice, and topped up with lemonade to taste. While *sangría* may be a drink that wine *aficionados* normally sneer at, an ice-cold *jarra*, freshly made and served on an outdoor terrace in view of the Mediterranean, can be one of the most enjoyable drinks in the world.

LA GASTRONOMÍA: FOODS OF THE LEVANTE

No other country in Europe can surpass Spain when it comes to the sheer quality and variety of her fruit and vegetables, as a visit to Valencia's modernist *Mercado Central* clearly demonstrates. This is one of the largest markets in Europe, a vast, airy building which is a proud and almost permanent display of the abundant richness of the region. Not only is the glistening array of produce from Valencia's *huerta* beautifully and colourfully laid out, there are furthermore great halls devoted to fish, shellfish and salted fish; cured sausages, hams and fresh meats; cheese; breads and pastries; even snails.

ng *pimientos* in front of a bar on the Calle
n Femades, Valencia.

After viewing this remarkable emporium, appetite whetted by all that great display, head out to the little Calle Mosén Femades, a pedestrian alley lined with typical bars offering an outstanding range of *tapas*, especially delicious vegetable dishes made from the freshest produce of the *huerta*: *ajos tiernos* (young green garlic tops, stewed in olive oil), *pimientos asados* (peppers roasted over charcoal, peeled, and bathed in garlic and oil), cauliflower in *salsa picante*, *habas con jamón* (green beans with *jamón serrano*), *berenjenas al horno* (baked aubergine slices) and much else, most enjoyably accompanied by small *chatos* of rosado from Utiel-Requena, or glasses of simple, anonymous, chilled white Valencia wine.

Of course, rice is the most characteristic food of the Levante, and it appears in any number of guises, not simply in that form known to most foreigners as *paella a la valenciana*. In fact, here in the zone, the Valencian version does not include fish or shellfish; to be authentic, it is made with chicken and rabbit, and must contain the particular type of fresh bean known as *garrafon*, as well, always, as snails. Not only is *paella* in all its various manifestations enjoyed in restaurants up and down the coast (and at its best in the Albufera rice region), the locals like nothing better than to prepare this great festive dish themselves, in the enormous and characteristic flat pans cooked over an open fire out of doors.

While on the coast, a colourful Mediterranean array of fish and shellfish is enjoyed, the inland foods still reflect the harshness of the upland terrain, and the impoverished diet of the past. Dried fish in many different variations remains extremely popular, especially the dark, chewy, and strongly-flavoured *mojama*. Rabbit and game are shot not simply for sport but to put into the cooking pot, and snails are still gathered as a nourishing and delicious wild food that is free.

As in much of Spain, there remains an enormous contrast between the authentic *fondas, mesones* and *ventas* of the interior, and the more internationally-oriented restaurants of the coastal resorts.

¡Que aproveche! Regional Specialities of the Levante

Pericana Classic *picadita* of the Levante, a mix of dried peppers, dried salt cod, abundant garlic and olive oil.

Mojama Salted air-dried tuna, pressed in olive oil. Very strong and chewy.

Almadraba Mixture of dried fish and dried cod's roe: strong but authentic taste of the land.

All-i-pebre *Salsa picante* made with garlic, olive oil, *pimentón*, toasted almonds and chilli peppers, used to flavour fish dishes of Valencia, particularly roasted eels (*anguilas al all-i-pebre*).

Caldero al estilo del Mar Menor Fish stew from Murcia containing typical Mediterranean rock fish; the broth is eaten first with rice, then the fish is served with *ali-oli.*

Arroz abanda One of many of the region's famous rice dishes: made with any variety of local fish and shellfish, and flavoured with saffron. Like *caldero*, the rice is served first, with the fish and shellfish following as the second course.

Paella Famous saffron-flavoured rice concoction, cooked in a large open flat pan (*paellara*), together with broth and any combination of meats, vegetables, snails, seafood and/or shellfish. Though *paella* has become a national and even international dish, the Levante is its homeland and the region where it is prepared best and in the most variety. **Paella a la valenciana** In Valencia, the classic version is prepared with rice, saffron, chicken, rabbit, snails and *garrafon* green beans, but no shellfish or seafood. **Paella marinera** *Paella* made with a mixture of fish and shellfish, as well, usually, as vegetables and some meat. **Paella con conejo y caracoles** Inland

La Albufera

The Albufera lagoon lies just to the south of Valencia, a large body of fresh water separated from the sea by a narrow strip of sand dunes. Though within a half-hour drive of the city, it is still a rare and unspoiled corner of wild Spain, sanctuary for tens of thousands of migratory birds, and, in spite of increased pollution, a source of freshwater fish and especially eels.

The fringes of the lagoon are where Spain's rice is grown, on great tracts of paddies flooded by a complex patchwork of sluices and canals. In the past, the farmers of the Albufera lived amidst their rice fields, in distinctive steeply pitched and thatched whitewashed cottages, sowing the rice by hand in late spring, harvesting it by the end of September, and in the meantime fishing for eel, collecting snails, shooting duck, and tending market gardens on the rich patches of alluvial soil that lie on the higher ground. The paddies are still cultivated, but few farmers now lead this lonely life of self-sufficiency.

Valencian rice is a short grain variety, unlike either long grain rice or medium grain Italian *arborio*. Its great quality is that it can be cooked uncovered in a flat *paella* pan, absorbing the cooking stock and flavourings without leaving a hard or chalky centre, yet still retaining its characteristic *al dente* bite and separate grains.

Come out to the tiny *pueblo* of El Palmar, located in the midst of the rice country and once a town of rice growers and fishermen. Today, many of the characteristic cottages have been turned into restaurants, for this is where the Valencianos themselves head to at weekends, to enjoy great raucous feasts of *paella*, made in great variety with any number of local ingredients, cooked properly over a wood fire, and served in the pan, to be eaten communally with wooden forks.

Alicantine classic of rice, rabbit and snails, cooked in the *paellara* preferably over an open fire.

Arros amb fesols i naps
Another classic country rice dish, served in the *pueblos* of the Albufera lagoon where the special Valencian rice grows, made with the excellent vegetables of the region's lush *huerta*, especially *fesols* (Valencian for green beans) and *naps* (turnips).

Pato a la naranja   Duck, preferably wild from the Albufera lagoon, cooked with oranges, in a piquant orange sauce: speciality of Valencia.

Conejo de monte a la alicantina   Inland country stew made with wild rabbit slow-cooked with dried beans, bitter orange and spices.

Turrón   Almond, honey and sugar nougat. **Jijona; turrón de Jijona** Jijona-style nougat utilizes the same basic ingredients, but the almonds are first roasted more deeply, then ground to a thick paste. *Turrón de jijona* and a glass of Fondillón is one of the most exquisite of all Spanish food/wine combinations.

Pan de Elche   Typical Moorish-inspired sweetmeat made from dried figs.

THE WINES AND WINE ROADS OF THE LEVANTE

In Brief: Though the wine regions of Valencia and Murcia are immensely important in terms of sheer quantity, this in truth is not one of Spain's great zones for the wine traveller. The industry is dominated above all by immense co-operative wineries and huge export-orientated private firms, many of whom continue to sell wines primarily in bulk not bottle. None the less, such companies form an essential part of the Spanish wine scene.

Visitors driving to Valencia from Madrid pass first through the wine zone of Utiel-Requena and may wish to stop in either of those two wine towns, if only for lunch, before descending from the central *meseta* to the region's capital. Valencia itself is dominated almost exclusively by five huge firms, two of them Swiss-owned, with semi-industrial premises on the outskirts of the city. While a visit to any of these immense wineries would be fascinating simply to gain an understanding of how wine is produced on such a large scale, the thirsty traveller may find it a more enjoyable task simply to sample (and re-sample) the range of local wines by the glass or bottle in Valencia's welcoming and superb *tapas* bars.

Visitors to Alicante, on the other hand, should strike out into the hinterland to the little wine town of Monóvar to visit Bodegas Salvador Poveda which produces excellent everyday white, *rosado* and red wines, as well as one of the great historic wines of Spain, the legendary Fondillón.

Jumilla and Yecla, located in the autonomous region of Murcia, are rather grim inland towns with little to offer the visitor save vast quantities of wine, much of it vinified by the *doble pasta* method for blending with lighter, insipid wines from northern regions or countries. While opportunities to visit *bodegas* are limited, the wine museum of Ascencio Carcelén in Jumilla is certainly worth a stop. From Jumilla, on the return to the coast, stop in Murcia itself, and visit the nearby *Museo de la Huerta* in Alcantarilla. Elche lies between Murcia and Alicante, and no visitor should miss its amazing Huerto del Cura palm groves.

Valencia

The wine region of Valencia, extending to the west of Spain's third largest city mainly on the higher hills above its fertile *huerta*, is a vast vineyard, spread over three separate sub-zones, Alto Turia, Valentino and Clariano. Remarkably, the Valencia DO is second only to Castilla-La Mancha in terms of volume of wine produced, a vast amount accounting for some 8% of the national total. Yet to the wine consumer, even in Spain itself, it has been and to a certain extent remains today an anonymous zone whose wines have yet to establish a concrete identity.

The reason for this is not hard to find. In this region of specialized agriculture, the growing of grapes has traditionally been viewed much like the cultivation of any other cash crop. Indeed, far more table grapes are grown than wine grapes, and like the rest of the region's superb fruit and vegetables, they are exported throughout Europe and the world.

In the same way, the wine grape has traditionally been seen as a crop to grow for cash. The overwhelming majority of the region's 40,000 *cosecheros de vino*, for example, sell their grapes to the hundred-odd co-operative wineries found throughout the region. There is little tradition of small-scale estate winemaking. Even the co-operatives themselves have not usually made wine to be marketed direct; rather, they have prospered by selling either unvinified grape must or newly-made wine direct to the large Valencia wine firms who skilfully blend them into finished wines, primarily to

THE LEVANTE

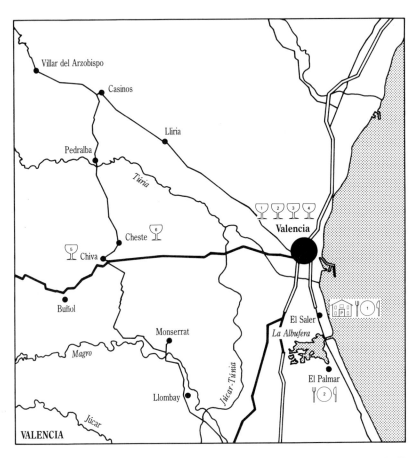

suit the tastes of export markets. Such blended wines, mainly sold in bulk and given brand names by the wholesalers, rarely disclose the fact that their origins are Valencian. For this reason, as much as any, the wines of Valencia have yet to establish their own market identity or following.

Be that as it may, the local wine industry is a remarkable one. Valencia has long been Spain's principal port, and its traders have a lengthy history of looking abroad for their markets. As long ago as the first century AD, there is archaeological evidence that wine was exported from these shores to Rome. The Moors, during their occupation of the Levante, continued the cultivation of the vine for winemaking as well as for the production of highly prized *uvas pasas*. Even after their expulsion from the region, this dual trade in wine and raisins was the basis of the principal export activity of the Valencianos alongside the silk trade. The Arabs also brought the art of distillation to the region, and as the demand for grape brandies increased in the eighteenth century, Valencia became an important port for the shipping of distilled *aguardiente* to France, Great Britain and Holland. Thus, while in other Spanish wine regions, producers were scarcely looking further than the distance they could transport their wines (carried in bulging, pitch-lined goatskins) by mule train, the wine merchants of the Levante had their sights set much further away.

This essentially cosmopolitan outlook remains the cornerstone of the Valencia wine industry even today. In a city where merchants from abroad have long been established, it is perhaps not wholly surprising that today two of Valencia's large wine companies are wholly Swiss-owned: Bodegas Schenk and Bodegas C Augusto Egli. These two, together with Vinival, the largest exporting wine company in Spain, Bodegas Vincente Gandía Pla, and Bodegas Cherubino Valsangiacomo, account for as much as a quarter of the country's total wine exports.

Massive investment in modern technology by these firms – immense outdoor fermentation and storage tanks, large-scale refrigeration plants, vacuum filters and high-speed bottling lines – means that they are able to produce clean, fresh, mainly light white, *rosado* and red table wines to be drunk young, usually within their first year of production. They are sound and well-made if uncomplicated wines which can represent outstanding value, especially to the large chain and supermarket buyers who make their way to the El Grao port area of the city where most of the principal *bodegas* are located. Moreover, the great strength of the Valencia wine industry, based on its traditionally pragmatic merchant mentality, has been its willingness to adapt its products to market requirements; buyers literally specify the exact type and style of wine that they require and the large firms can blend it for them precisely.

This export-led marketing approach, though it has resulted in immense bulk sales for Valencia wines over the past decades, has also contributed its own problems. During the last decade about 85% of the region's exports were accounted for in bulk sales *en granel*, not in bottle. Just as attracting masses of package holidaymakers to the region's resorts has ultimately devalued the image of its tourist industry, so the sale of bulk wines at very low prices has contributed directly to the poor or non-existent image of Valencia wine. Moreover, just as tourism in the region has suffered in recent years as holidaymakers have turned away from Spain's traditional resorts, during the same period the market for inexpensive bulk wines has contracted sharply.

THE LEVANTE

The almost total collapse of the Eastern European market, which accounted for nearly a fifth of total Valencia exports, was a particularly painful blow for many firms and co-operatives. Furthermore, bulk exports to other traditional markets such as Equatorial Africa, Switzerland, Scandinavia and Austria have also contracted in recent years. By contrast, the British and German markets have demonstrated signs of growth and vigour, primarily because these areas are interested not in bulk wines at the cheapest prices, but in quality Valencia wines bearing the *denominación de origen* and bottled in the region of origin.

Valencia's large export firms, as well as its most forward-looking co-operative wineries, have thus realized that the future must lie in the production of wines that can establish a marketable identity for themselves as unique products of the vineyards of Valencia. In recent years there has been a noticeable and crucial shift of emphasis to shipping in bottle, not bulk, and the percentage of wines exported *en granel* has continued to fall. The raw materials – the grapes – are already of sound enough quality, though naturally further improvements in the vineyard, in particular restriction of yields as well as planting more interesting grape varieties, will lead to better wines. The technology to produce sound, fresh everyday wines is also mainly in place, certainly in the large private firms, as well as, increasingly, in the co-operative wineries. It is only a matter of time, we conjecture, before Valencia emerges as a major player on the international wine scene in its own right.

Indeed, wines such as Vicente Gandía Pla's sound, best-selling Castillo de Liria range, Vinival's Viña Calderon white and red, Schenk's Castillo Murviedro red, and Egli's Rey Don Jaime Blanco, produced from Merseguera grapes grown in the Alto Turia, already demonstrate how good – and what good value – such Valencian wines can be. We have little doubt that in future years, we will be seeing and drinking more wines from Valencia. And we will be aware that this is where they have come from.

While we suggest that the best way to gain a further acquaintance with the wines of Valencia is simply to drink them (this not being a region overly attractive for wine touring), serious students of the grape may wish to make an appointment to visit one of the city's five large *bodegas*. For those interested in actually getting into the wine country, the main Madrid road that leads to Utiel-Requena passes, above Chiva, through the thick of the Valentino sub-zone. This is the most extensive of the Valencia DO's three sub-zones, and is widely planted with white grapes such as Merseguera, Planta Fina, Pedro Ximénez, Malvasia and the black grapes Garnacha and

Garnacha Tintorera. Important wine towns include Chiva, Cheste and Buñol in the centre, and Lliria and Casinos extending north into the Campo de Turia. The sub-zone is known primarily for its fruity white wines. The southeasternmost part of the Valentino zone, however, is an overlapping sub-zone in its own right, the source of particularly fragrant Moscatel grapes from which superb sweet, fortified Moscatel de Valencia wines are made.

The sub-zone of Clariano is Valencia's southernmost, a semi-arid area adjacent to the vineyards of Alicante, and the source of full-bodied white, *rosado* and red wines produced mainly from the white Merseguera grape and the black grapes Monastrell and Garnacha. This area is also the source of delectably sweet table grapes.

Valencia's finest sub-zone lies in the north of the Comunidad Valenciana, the Alto Turia, located at over 600 metres above sea level, and the source of particularly fine, crisp white wines from the Merseguera grape.

Most of the wines produced in the Valencia vineyard come from co-operative wineries, but there may be opportunities, when touring inland country zones, to visit winemakers and purchase wines locally. Look out for signs proclaiming '*vinos de cosechero*'.

Utiel-Requena

The Utiel-Requena vineyard lies west of Valencia on the high plateau leading up to the central Castilian *meseta*, planted at altitudes over 700 metres above sea level. This is probably Valencia's finest winegrowing district and the source of excellent *rosado* and red wines produced mainly from the tough-skinned Bobal grape, with increased plantations of Tempranillo and Garnacha.

The delimited vineyard is made up of 18 small wine *pueblos* in addition to the larger towns of Utiel and Requena. Each town or *pueblo* has its own co-operative winery, but to date only a handful of them bottle and market their wines themselves, the rest preferring to maintain longstanding custom and sell pressed, unfermented grape must or newly-finished wines to the large Valencia wine firms. There is hardly any tradition of estate winemaking, and the growers often work a number of tiny parcels of vines spread in different locations throughout the zone, the legacy of split inheritances down the ages, as well as a means of spreading the risk of crop failure through hail or frost.

Carlos Cárcel Pérez, for example, has a small *bodega* at Rebollar, a tiny

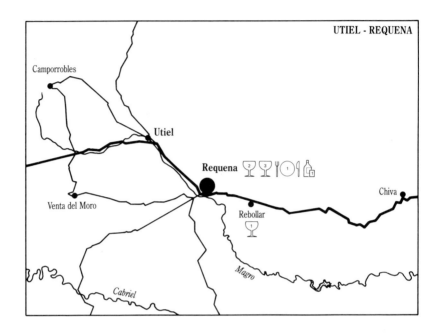

wine *pueblo* of only 250 inhabitants just off the main Valencia–Madrid road en route to Requena. His 20 hectares of Bobal grapes are divided between 20 separate parcels of vines ranging in size from under half a hectare to one-and-a-half. In addition, he has 10 hectares of Garnacha and has recently planted 5 hectares of Tempranillo.

Though there is a co-operative in Rebollar, Señor Cárcel is one of the very few small growers in the zone to make, bottle and market his wines himself, mainly to private customers as well as to bars and restaurants locally and in Valencia. His Rebollar *rosado* is typical of the tasty, full-bodied *rosados* of Utiel-Requena: attractive dark pink, luscious strawberry nose, fresh and full-bodied in the mouth. This wine, like most of the *rosados* of the zone, is a *vino de lágrima*, produced by macerating the crushed black grapes on their skins for a few hours, then drawing off the coloured grape must from the vat with no additional pressure, a process which makes particularly well-structured wines. The remaining wine-drenched grapes are subsequently left in the vat, which is filled again with more crushed black grapes to make *vino de doble pasta*.

Since most of the zone's co-operatives sell their pressed grape must or wine to the large Valencia wine firms who blend it, very little wine is marketed under the Utiel-Requena DO. This is a shame, as the wine zone has considerable potential in its own right to produce not only fine *rosados* but also noteworthy red wines of real quality. While Bobal, the zone's native grape, does well on the semi-arid plateau of Utiel-Requena, the most promising results are coming from Tempranillo, Spain's aristocratic black grape, which has adapted well and produces deep, full wines that maintain an attractive soft, ripe fruit.

Of the large firms, Vinival has a lovely estate, the Casa de Calderón, surrounded by an impressive 160-hectare vineyard that supplies much of the fruit for its flagship Viña Calderón wines. In addition to Bobal, Garnacha and Tempranillo, this vineyard is planted with some Cabernet Sauvignon and Merlot. Bodegas C. Augustus Egli also owns an estate in Utiel-Requena, the Casa Lo Alto *finca*, planted with a similar mix of grapes in addition to white varieties such as Merseguera, Macabeo and Airén.

Requena itself is a pleasant wine town with a broad, tree-lined *paseo* at the far end of which stands a rather grandiose *Monumento a la Vendimia*. During the town's wine festival, the fountain at its foot flows with wine. Requena is a good place to sample the wines of the zone, together with a hot *bocadillo* or a full lunch in the excellent Mesón del Vino in the town centre. Utiel is another busy if unremarkable wine town with a pleasant historic *casco viejo*. From Utiel, the road leads soon into the central plains of Castilla-La Mancha.

Alicante, Yecla and Jumilla

Alicante, the hinterland inland from the maritime provincial city, and Yecla and Jumilla, located in the separate autonomous region of Murcia, are parched, seemingly inhospitable Mediterranean wine regions, as great a contrast to the lush *huerta* of the Levante as you could imagine. This extensive and virtually contiguous hinterland is planted primarily with Monastrell, a small, tough grape able to survive the exceptionally dry climate, and which yields small quantities of grapes especially high in colour, tannin and potential alcohol. Such grapes have traditionally been vinified by the *doble pasta* system, producing both excellent *rosados* as a by-product, and immensely concentrated and tannic wines to be shipped in bulk for blending. Even today, there is a great demand for such wines, though by no means all those who purchase them, many of whom are located in far more prestigious Spanish and French wine zones than these unfashionable Levantine outposts, would like this fact to be widely known.

Alicante is a wine region with a great history. As part of the autonomous

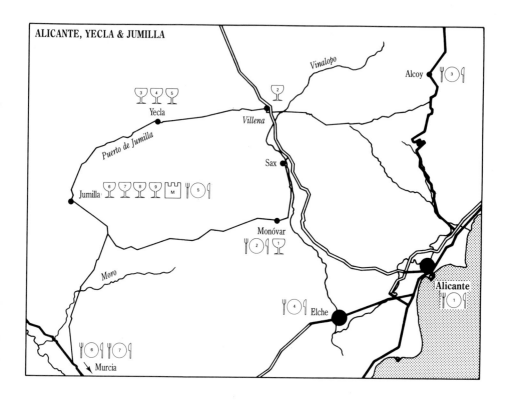

region of Valencia, it stands well apart from Yecla and Jumilla, proud of its separate *valenciano* heritage, and a stout Catalan-speaking region. The port of Alicante itself has long been the point of embarkation for the wines of the zone, which have a lengthy and prestigious pedigree. For example, Louis XIV, the great Sun King of France, reputedly enjoyed as his last worldly morsel a biscuit dipped in a crystal glass of Fondillón, Alicante's great *vino rancio*.

Fondillón apart, the wines of Alicante nowadays make little claim to greatness. Bodegas Salvador Póveda, located in Monóvar, a typical inland *pueblo* of Alicante, produces a full and characteristic range of Alicante wines in its atmospheric and rather ramshackle family *bodega* at the top of the town.

'*Mi vino es sencillo y auténtico*,' states Rafael Póveda, the serious young marketing director of the family firm. Indeed, Póveda's Viña Vermeta wines, and the table wines of Alicante in general, are proudly and unashamedly just that: simple but genuine country wines, to be drunk without fuss or pretension, in quantity and on virtually any occasion.

Póveda's white Alicante, produced from the Merseguera grape, is clean, fresh, well made, a good everyday beverage wine, but without much real character. The *rosado* is better, extremely pale, produced from grape must run off after only the briefest contact on the skins, but very fresh, fruity and full in the mouth. The standard red Viña Vermeta is a tasty, supple and fruity wine that is released without wood ageing to be drunk within a year or two of its production, but the best vats of red wine are selected for ageing in large oak deposits as well as in new oak *barricas*. These Reserva wines can be very successful, though they do have a tendency to oxidize rather quickly.

One of the most interesting wines is Póveda's *vino de doble capa*. This is the traditional blending wine of the region, produced after the pale, pink-tinged grape must has been drawn off for the production of *rosado*. The resulting wine, vinified in contact with a double amount of skins, is correspondingly intensely deep in colour and tannin, and can also reach levels in excess of 15 or 16° alcohol.

Though supposedly produced only for blending, within the zone itself there is actually a following for '*doble capa*' drunk as a table wine. Tasted from the vat, this immense, almost black wine was surprisingly round, with a touch of apparent sweetness, the result, explained Póveda, of its high natural glycerine content. While locals come to the *bodega* direct to purchase it by the 16-litre *garrafa* for home consumption, the wine, remarkably, is bottled and labelled and can even be found in the wine section of Valencia's prestigious El Corte Inglés department store. It may not be for everyone, but like *mojama*, the strong, chewy dried tuna so loved here, Póveda's '*doble capa*' is an authentic taste of the land.

If today the everyday wines of Alicante make no claim to greatness, the zone is still the source of one of the great historic wines of Spain. Fondillón may be little known and rarely encountered these days: only a handful of *bodegas* still produce this marvellous rarity. Yet during Spain's great Golden Age, it was considered the wine of kings. Even the ascetic Philip II, in isolation high up in his Escorial palace, reputedly enjoyed this special aged wine. During the seventeenth century the British navy was the principal purchaser and consumer of Fondillón, which was in its time more famous than sherry, port, Madeira or Málaga. Today, it may be only an obscure curiosity, but we consider it still one of the great wines of Spain.

It is unclear what the name signifies, though there is a theory that Fondillón was first produced by farmers who saved their choicest Monastrell grapes for themselves, storing them in wooden casks at the bottom (*fondo*) of their cellar. What is known is that the wine was first produced sometime after the Monastrell grape was introduced to these lands, probably during the fifteenth century when it was brought back to the zone by Catalan soldiers returning from the Middle East. The Monastrell adapted well to the harsh Alicante terrain and was able to produce wine of both intense colour and sufficient alcohol. Yet it was noted that the variety also had the tendency to oxidize rather quickly, a quality which made it ideal for the production of *vino rancio*.

Today, Fondillón is produced as in the past. At Bodegas Salvador Póveda, for example, selected Monastrell grapes are harvested as much as a month later than grapes destined to make table wines. These intensely concentrated, sugar-rich grapes (in the past they were further lightly sunned outside to concentrate them even more) are then pressed and vinified to make a wine that can reach 16° alcohol naturally and with no need of fortification, while retaining a slight natural residual sweetness. The wine is then left to age either statically in old and immense oak barrels for a legal minimum of eight years and usually much longer, or else it passes into a series of ancient *soleras* containing wines that have been resting since the Spanish Civil War. This is the Póveda family's 'Sacristía', the rare depository for a collection of exceptional *vinos rancios* quite unlike wines produced anywhere else in the world. To enter this hallowed cellar and taste these old wines from the cask – brick red to amber in colour, with a host of subtle and complex aromas, flavours and associations – is a rare experience indeed.

From Monóvar, the Alicante vineyard extends through other wine communities such as Sax and Villena. Other well-regarded producers in Villena include Garcia Póveda, Alfonso Abellan and Bodegas Eval. From Villena, it is a short drive across an invisible regional frontier into Murcia and the virtually contiguous vineyards of first Yecla then Jumilla.

In truth, as wine country goes, this is arid and most unpromising terrain. The towns themselves have little to offer the visitor. The vineyards appear bleak and harsh, planted mainly with Monastrell vines, head-trained low to the ground on a miserable chalky, stony terrain at altitudes of up to 650 metres above sea level, producing among the lowest yields in the country. The vast majority of the wines are made in immense and sometimes antiquated factory-like *bodegas* and co-operative wineries. On the whole, they can be sound enough if powerful beverages; they are still remarkably inexpensive, those wines, that is, which are bottled and sold as such, rather than destined for the blending tanks or wine lakes of Europe.

Yecla itself is probably better known in Spain today as a furniture centre than a centre for wines, but the immense Cooperativa 'La Purisima' still dominates the town and does produce some sound wines in bottle. Better offerings are probably available from private companies such as Bodegas Castaño and Bodegas Enrique Ochoa Palao, both of whom produce well-regarded wines, especially Yecla's characteristic rich and beefy reds.

From Yecla, drive over the Puerto de Jumilla, a hill pass that reaches 800 metres above sea level, then continue on to Jumilla itself. We rather like this inland Murcian town, overlooked by its ancient castle and totally focused on wine. The town's Bodega Cooperativa 'San Isidro' is the largest in Spain, and reputedly the third largest in Europe with immense installations built in 1976, while the town's largest private producer, Bodegas J. Garcia Carrion, exports vast quantities of Jumilla wines throughout Spain and the world, albeit a great proportion packaged in cardboard tetra-brik cartons, hardly the best way to improve the low image of the zone. Bodega Señorío del Condestable is another immense wine firm, belonging to the Bodegas y Bebidas group.

While such immense firms still dominate the Jumilla wine scene, and considering that much of the zone's wines are still produced primarily for blending, it is perhaps something of a surprise that a Frenchman, Jacques Germain, proprietor of Les Vins René Germain et Successeurs which has significant holdings in Bordeaux, has invested in a substantial wine estate of 300 hectares outside Jumilla and the construction of a small but well-equipped *bodega* amidst the vineyards.

Jean-François Gadeau, oenologist and Technical Director of the new enterprise, Vitivino SA, explained, 'It is the potential quality of the fruit that attracted us. The Monastrell is the same grape as the French Mourvèdre, utilized in the southern Rhône valley and in the Provençal vineyard of Bandol. It has the potential, if vinified carefully and skilfully, to make great wine.'

But to achieve this, Gadeau further explained, the zone's traditional methods of production had to be avoided, that is, the practices of harvesting late to gain increased sugar levels, and fermenting without temperature control at upwards of 30°, which inevitably results in cooked wines totally lacking in fruit or charm.

It was an innovation to construct the new *bodega* actually in the heart of the company's vineyards, not in the town of Jumilla itself like almost all the other wine companies.

'We considered this crucial to our operation,' continued Gadeau. 'Monastrell does have a tendency to oxidize easily, and at the time of the harvest the temperatures can still be over 35°. By siting the *bodega* actually in the vineyard, we can ensure that the fruit is harvested, de-stemmed and quickly crushed within a half hour at most.'

The wines then ferment in resin-lined concrete vats at carefully controlled temperatures. The fermentation vats are not wholly filled, and Gadeau believes that it is crucial to keep the *sombrero* – the dense mass of skins – well wetted throughout the fermentation period, with *remontaje* – pumping up grape must and spraying it over the cap – at least once a day. This not only ensures greater extract and colour, but also results in the extraction of rounder, softer tannins, as opposed to the mouth-numbing, stewed tannins of the traditionally-produced wines of the zone.

Vitivino's Altos de Pio normal unaged red wine, which spends no time in oak, is certainly a successful wine. It has a lovely, youthful ruby hue and is medium-weight in the mouth, with dense ripe fruit and a good grippy backbone of tannin. This is a modern, well-made wine, as far from those heavyweight, head-banging traditional Jumillas as can be.

But Jean-François Gadeau was saving the best for last. Since he was opposed to the traditional, old-style production of the zone's wines, it might be natural to assume that the *doble pasta* process would have no place in Vitivino's operations. Yet, remarkably, the *bodega*'s most interesting wine was an immensely concentrated experimental sample produced from the 1990 harvest by the much reviled *doble pasta* method and aged in new French oak *barricas*. To produce this wine, the vat had actually been filled up with crushed grapes three separate times, so the *sombrero* was unusually thick, and Gadeau had had to ensure that it was sprayed over regularly to keep it wet. After vinification and malolactic fermentation, this amazing wine was then placed in a series of experimental *barricas* from the French forests of the Allier, Vosges and Nevers. We tried some samples direct from the cask. This is a wine, certainly, that will need lengthy ageing in new wood to tame it, but the incredible colour, intensely gamey, meaty nose, and sheer structure and concentration suggests that it could be a new *grand cru* of the zone.

While this young and enthusiastic Frenchman had little doubt about the quality of his own wines, he was less optimistic about the future of the Jumilla wine zone.

'It will be very hard to change the image of Jumilla from that of a zone of cheap bulk wines, and thus it will always be difficult to sell quality wines

from here at the price that they would deserve or warrant. Because of this, we may have to choose to market our wines outside the DO scheme as simple *vinos de mesa*. We have not yet decided.'

From Jumilla, we suggest that the wine traveller heads down to Murcia, visits the *Museo del Huerta* in Alcantarilla, and completes the circuit back to Alicante, by way of the famous palm gardens of Elche.

The palm grove in Elche is the most extensive in Europe.

Museo de la Huerta

MUSEO DE LA HUERTA
AVDA DEL PRÍNCIPE, S/N
30820 ALCANTARILLA
MURCIA

Open 10–18h. Closed Mon. This important ethnographic museum has extensive exhibitions of life in rural Murcia, with collections of tools, utensils, domestic and farm implements, and costume. Set amidst the lush orange groves of

Murcia, there are furthermore full-scale reconstructions of typical thatched cottages, a *taberna tipica huertana*, and, most impressive of all, an enormous still-working waterwheel which demonstrates how arid semi-desert lands were traditionally irrigated and so turned into lush veritable gardens of Eden.

THE LEVANTE

Bodegas: Stop to Taste; Stop to Buy

Valencia

1 BODEGAS VINIVAL
EXPORTADORA VINÍCOLA
    VALENCIANA SA
AVDA NOV. BLASCO IBAÑEZ 2
46120 ALBORAYA
VALENCIA
TEL: (96) 371 01 11; FAX: (96) 371 01 54

WINES PRODUCED: Malvarrosa *blanco, rosado vino de aguja;* Torres de Quart *blanco, rosado, tinto;* Viña Calderon *rosado, tinto;* Moscatel Vival d'Or; Mellow Peach y Apple.

VISITS: Mon–Fri, by appointment. Spain's largest exporting wine firm, founded in 1969 through the amalgamation of five smaller private companies. *Bodega* is located near El Grao port, with distinctive brick-built domes for massive storage of wines. Vinival is also the proprietor of the lovely and important *finca* Casa de Calderón in Utiel-Requena.
English, German, French spoken.

---

2 BODEGAS C. AUGUSTUS EGLI
CALLE MADERAS 21
46022 VALENCIA
TEL: (96) 323 09 50; FAX: (96) 323 41 58

WINES PRODUCED: Perla Valenciana *blanco, rosado;* Rey Don Jaime *blanco, rosado, tinto;* Casa Lo Alto *blanco,* Casa Lo Alto *tinto* Crianza.

VISITS: By appointment. Swiss-owned firm founded in 1903 by a Zurich wine merchant with extremely modern and vast winemaking installations and flagship estate, Casa Lo Alto, in Utiel-Requena.
English, German, French spoken.

---

3 BODEGAS SCHENK
CAMINO HONDO DEL GRAO 78
46023 VALENCIA
TEL: (96) 323 09 81;
FAX: (96) 323 41 46

WINES PRODUCED: Cavas Murviedro *blanco, rosado, tinto;* Los Monteros *tinto;* San Terra *tinto* Crianza; Real Copero Moscatel.
VISITS: By appointment.

Another large Swiss firm, founded in 1927, with the Swiss consulate actually located within the *bodega.* Bodegas Schenk is the shipper of immense quantities of wines not only from the Levante but also from La Mancha, but the best wines are vinified in the plant at El Grao.
English, German, French spoken.

---

4 CHERUBINO VALSANGIACOMO
VICENTE BRULL 26
46011 VALENCIA
TEL: (96) 323 00 28

WINES PRODUCED: Vall de Sant
Jaume *blanco, rosado, tinto*;
Marqués de Caro *tinto*; Brut
Nature.

VISITS: By appointment.
The smallest of Valencia's five
large exporting firms, Spanish
owned but also with Swiss
connections.
English, German, French spoken.

---

5 VICENTE GANDÍA PLA SA
CTRA GODELLETA–CHESTE, S/N
46370 CHIVA
VALENCIA
TEL: (96) 367 02 58
ADMINISTRATIVE ADDRESS: CALLE
MADERAS 13, 46022 VALENCIA
TEL: (96) 323 06 09; FAX: (96) 367 93 26

WINES PRODUCED: Castillo de
Liria *blanco, rosado, tinto*; Sangría;
Moscatel.
VISITS: Not open for public visits.

Founded in 1885 by Vicente Gandía
and still owned and run by the
family, Gandía Pla has one of the
country's most modern and
up-to-date wine facilities and
installations at the recently
constructed *bodega* at Chiva. The
company's best-selling Castillo de
Liria range is extremely popular
both nationally and internationally.
English, French, German spoken.

---

6 SOCIEDAD COOPERATIVA CHESTE
VINÍCOLA Y CAJA RURAL
LA ESTACIÓN 5
46380 CHESTE
VALENCIA
TEL: (96) 251 06 40

WINES PRODUCED: Castillo de
Cheste *blanco, rosado, tinto*; Conde
de Cheste *blanco, rosado, tinto*;
Sechara *blanco, rosado, tinto*;
Moscatel.
VISITS: Daily, working hours for
direct sales.

Utiel-Requena

1 HIJOS DE ERNESTO CÁRCEL SL
CALLE BODEGAS 5
46391 REBOLLAR-REQUENA
VALENCIA
TEL: (96) 230 09 75

WINES PRODUCED: Rosado
'Rebollar', Tinto 'Rebollar'.
VISITS: Daily, by appointment.
One of the few small grower–
estates in this region dominated by

THE LEVANTE

immense concerns. Carlos Cárcel Pérez produces his Utiel-Requena wines entirely from his own vineyards.

2 COMPAÑIA VINÍCOLA DEL CAMPO DE
REQUENA SL
CASA DE DON ANGEL – FINCA LA
CABEZUELA
CALLE DE SAN AGUSTÍN 5
46340 REQUENA
VALENCIA
TEL: (96) 391 55 25, 230 12 10;
    FAX: (96) 391 49 04

WINES PRODUCED: CVCRE
Blanco Flor; Viña Carmina *rosado*;
Viña Mariola *tinto* Crianza

(Tempranillo); Vera de Estenas *tinto*
Reserva (Cabernet Sauvignon);
Juan de Argés Cava.
VISITS: Daily, by appointment.
One of Utiel-Requena's leading
wineries, established in 1919, and
producing good *rosado* and aged red
wines from its own 40 hectares of
vineyards, as well as an excellent
Utiel Cava.
French spoken.

3 COOPERATIVA VINÍCOLA
REQUENENSE
AVDA GENERAL PEREIRA 5
46340 REQUENA
VALENCIA
TEL: (96) 230 03 50

WINES PRODUCED: Fortaleza
rosado; Palacio del Cid *tinto*
Reserva; Tempranillo *tinto*;
Monumento Moscatel.
VISITS: Daily, working hours for
direct sales.
Modernized, well regarded
co-operative winery.

Alicante, Yecla and Jumilla

1 BODEGAS SALVADOR PÓVEDA
BENJAMÍN PALENCIA 19
03640 MONÓVAR
ALICANTE
TEL: (96) 547 01 80; 547 11 39;
    FAX: (96) 547 33 89

WINES PRODUCED: Viña Vermeta
blanco, rosado, tinto; Viña Vermeta
tinto Crianza, Reserva; Tinto 'Doble
Capa'; Fondillón.
VISITS: Daily, by appointment.

Direct sales working hours.
Excellent everyday table wines and
of course the legendary Salvador
Póveda Fondillón from this highly
regarded family *bodega* run by
youthful enthusiast Rafael Póveda.
Though the old *bodega* is located in
the high part of town, the company
is currently constructing new,
modern premises on the outskirts
of Monóvar.

2 BODEGAS EVAL SA
CTRA VILLENA–YECLA, KM 58
03400 VILLENA
ALICANTE
TEL: (96) 580 84 83
ADMINISTRATIVE OFFICE: CALLE
 PRINCIPE DE VERGARA 13-2°A,
 28001 MADRID
TEL: (91) 435 85 34; FAX: (91) 577 44 11

WINES PRODUCED: Lopez de la Torre *blanco, rosado, tinto*; Lopez de la Torre *blanco* (Chenin Blanc/Riesling); Lopez de la Torre *tinto* Cabernet Sauvignon; Lopez de la Torre *tinto* Crianza, Reserva; Lopez de la Torre 'Vino Heráldico' *tinto* Gran Reserva; Lopez de la Torre Moscatel; Lopez de la Torre *vino espumoso método tradicional*.
VISITS: Mon–Fri 9–14h; 16–19h. Large range of wines produced in a well-equipped modern *bodega* located 10 km outside Villena. French spoken.

3 COOPERATIVA AGRICOLA 'LA
 PURISIMA'
CTRA DE PINOSO, S/N
30510 YECLA
MURCIA
TEL: (968) 79 02 82; FAX: (968) 79 51 16

WINES PRODUCED: Estio *blanco, rosado*; Calp *rosado, tinto*; Alfeizar *tinto*; Calp *tinto* Reserva, Gran Reserva.
VISITS: Mon–Fri 10–13h; 16–19h. Immense co-operative winery producing some sound Calp Reservas.

4 BODEGAS CASTAÑO SA
CTRA FUENTEÁLAMO 3
APARTADO 120
30510 YECLA
MURCIA
TEL: (968) 79 11 15, 79 16 04;
 FAX: (968) 79 19 00

WINES PRODUCED: Viña Las Gruesas *blanco, rosado, tinto*; Castaño *tinto* (*maceración carbónica*); Pozuelo *tinto* Crianza.
VISITS: Mon–Fri 8h30–13h30; 15h30–19h30. Appointment appreciated.
English, French spoken.

5 BODEGA ENRIQUE OCHOA PALAO
PARAJE DE LOS PINILLOS, S/N
30510 YECLA
MURCIA
TEL: (968) 79 20 64

WINES PRODUCED: Altiplano *blanco, rosado, tinto*; Barahonda *blanco, rosado, tinto*; Señorío de los Angeles *tinto* Crianza; Ochoa *tinto* Reserva.
VISITS: Weekdays, by appointment.

THE LEVANTE

6 BODEGAS COOPERATIVA 'SAN
  ISIDRO'
CTRA A MURCIA, S/N
30520 JUMILLA
MURCIA
TEL: (968) 78 07 00; FAX: (968) 78 23 51

WINES PRODUCED: Sabatacha
blanco, rosado, tinto; Viña Celia
blanco, rosado, tinto; Sabatacha

Real *tinto* Reserva; San Isidro *tinto*
maceración carbónica; Solera; 50
Aniversario; Lacrima Viña Cristina
(*dulce natural*).
VISITS: Mon–Fri 8h30–13h; 15–
19h.
Spain's largest co-operative winery
with 1500 *socios*.
English spoken.

---

7 VITIVINO SA
CAÑADA DE ALBATANA, S/N
30520 JUMILLA
MURCIA
TEL: (968) 78 28 54, 78 14 28;
  FAX: (968) 78 26 03

WINES PRODUCED: Altos de Pio
blanco, rosado, tinto; Taja *tinto*.
VISITS: By appointment.
Immaculate French-owned and
-run *bodega* producing quality wines
entirely from grapes grown on own
300-ha. estate.
French spoken.

---

8 BODEGAS J. GARCIA CARRION
AVDA MURCIA, S/N
30520 JUMILLA
MURCIA
TEL: (968) 78 06 12; FAX: (968) 78 31 15
ADMINISTRATIVE OFFICE: JORGE
  JUAN 73–6°, 28009 MADRID
TEL: (91) 435 55 56; FAX: (91) 576 66 07

WINES PRODUCED: Covanegra
blanco, rosado, tinto; Montelago

blanco, rosado, tinto; Castillo San
Simon *tinto*; Don Simon *sangría*.
VISITS: Mon–Fri 9–19h by
appointment.
Immense private wine firm with
the capacity to process a million
litres of wine per day in both bottle
and tetra-brik.
English, French spoken.

---

9 BODEGA SEÑORÍO DEL
  CONDESTABLE
AVDA REYES CATÓLICOS, S/N
30520 JUMILLA
MURCIA
TEL: (968) 78 10 11; FAX: (968) 78 11 00

WINES PRODUCED: Condestable

blanco, rosado, tinto; Señorío de
Robles *rosado, tinto*.
VISITS: By appointment.
Another immense private winery,
part of the important Bodegas y
Bebidas group.

Museo del Vino

M

BODEGAS ASENSIO CARCELÉN
BARÓN DEL SOLAR, 1–3
30520 JUMILLA
MURCIA
TEL: (968) 78 04 18; 78 01 45

WINES PRODUCED: Acorde *blanco*, *rosado*, *tinto*; Bullanguero *blanco*, *rosado*, *tinto*; Con Sello *tinto* Gran Reserva; Pura Sangre *tinto* Gran Reserva; Sol y Luna *vino de licor*.

HOURS: Open working hours by appointment.
The traditional Bodegas Asensio Carcelén, one of Jumilla's best private producers, has a fine wine museum which traces the history of the vine and winemaking in the zone from Roman times to the present.

Restaurantes, Hoteles y Paradores

Valencia

1

CASA CARMINA
CALLE EMBARCADERO 4
46012 EL SALER
VALENCIA
TEL: (96) 183 02 54

El Saler, located on the way to the Albufera lagoon, is a popular beachside resort for Valencianos. It is also one of the places where locals come to eat rice and other regional specialities such as *anguilas al all-i-pebre*. This is a good, authentic and friendly eating house just off the town's main street.
Inexpensive

2

RESTAURANTE CAÑAS I BARRO
CAUDETE 7
46010 EL PALMAR
VALENCIA
TEL: (96) 161 10 97

Located outside Valencia in the middle of the Albufera rice-growing zone, El Palmar is the place to come to experience the authentic *paellas* of Valencia. There are scores of restaurants to choose from, but this is the fishermen's favourite. Dining room overlooking the rice paddies, and *paellas* cooked authentically over a wood fire: *paella conejo y pollo, paella a la valenciana, amb fesols i naps, arroz abanda, paella de mariscos* accompanied by fresh local white and *rosado* wines.
Inexpensive

THE LEVANTE

Parador

P

PARADOR NACIONAL LUIS VIVES
CTRA EL SALER, KM 16
46012 EL SALER
VALENCIA
TEL: (96) 161 11 86; FAX: (96) 162 70 16

This newly constructed *parador* with an 18-hole golf course is

located outside Valencia, on the isthmus separating the Albufera lagoon from the sea. Good base for exploration of the lagoon, beaches and excursions into Valencia.
Expensive

Utiel-Requena

1

MESÓN DEL VINO
AVDA GENERAL VARELA 13
46340 REQUENA
VALENCIA
TEL: (96) 230 00 01

Closed Tue.

Extremely lively bar and restaurant on Requena's main *paseo* by the market, serving typical foods of the Valencian hinterland: *habas con jamón, ajoarriero, gazpacho manchego, fideua, perdiz escabechada* together with an extensive selection of local wines.
Inexpensive

Alicante, Yecla and Jumilla

1

RESTAURANTE DELFÍN
EXPLANADA DE ESPAÑADA 12
03001 ALICANTE
TEL: (96) 521 49 11

It is worth stopping in Alicante at least long enough to enjoy a meal in this classic landmark restaurant along the town esplanade, serving

both traditional and innovative dishes: *arroz con atún y gambas rojas, almejas marinera, arroz abanda,* exceptionally fresh fish and shellfish, and meat dishes from the Alicante hinterland.
Moderate to Expensive

2

BAR-RESTAURANTE TRIBALDO
AMARGUÍN 29
03640 MONÓVAR
ALICANTE
TEL: (96) 547 00 24

In the country just outside the wine *pueblo* of Monóvar, this simple typical restaurant serves the authentic foods of inland Alicante:

almadraba, mojama, arroz con conejo y caracoles, chuletas a la brasa.

Inexpensive

Ventas: The Authentic Old Inns of Spain

Ventas are Spain's old wayside inns, found the length and breadth of the country, usually located on the outskirts of towns or along the old country routes and mule tracks of the interior. Traditionally, they were the stopping-off place for the country's travellers, merchants and mule train drivers, places where wayfarers put up for the night, watered their animals, ate and drank before moving on to the next town or market. They are as old as time and as Spanish as Don Quixote, who, after all, was 'knighted' by the innkeeper in the Venta del Quijote in Puerto Lápice.

Even today, *ventas* are renowned foremost for serving the typical and authentic foods of the land. They may be no more than simple and humble roadside inns serving *comidas caseras*, platters of home-cured *jamón*, *embutidos* and locally made cheeses, accompanied by clay *jarras* of local wines, or jugs of partially-fermented *mosto*; or they can be altogether more refined and sophisticated.

One of the great *ventas* of the Levante is the famous Venta del Pilar. This stylish and popular eighteenth-century coaching inn on the outskirts of Alcoy, a town best known for its April *Moros y Cristianos* festival, may these days attract well-off businessmen for extended expense-account lunches but it continues to serve the true foods of the Alicante hinterland. For example, though the menu includes such sophisticated dishes as *bulla-besa* and *solomillo trufas negras y setas*, one of the restaurant's most popular appetizers is *pericana*, a simple dish which to me typifies the true fare of an authentic *venta*. This simple *picadita* is made from the sort of ingredients that every upland farm would always have on hand – dried peppers, dried salt cod and garlic, fried together in abundant olive oil. Yet it is delicious! Other typical hearty foods include *atún en escabeche*, *croquetas de bacalao* and, of course, that favourite of the Alicante hinterland, *mojama.*

3

VENTA DEL PILAR
CTRA VALENCIA, KM 2,300
COCENTAINA
03800 ALCOY
TEL: (96) 559 23 25

Closed Sun.
Expensive

4 HUERTO DEL CURA
PORTA DE LA MORERA 14
03203 ELCHE
ALICANTE
TEL: (96) 545 80 40; FAX: (96) 542 19 10

Hotel-restaurant actually located within Elche's magnificent palm grove. The restaurant, Els Capellans, serves good fresh fish and rice dishes.
Moderate to Expensive

---

5 MESÓN EL CASTILLO
PLAZA REY D. PEDRO 1
30520 JUMILLA
MURCIA
TEL: (968) 78 21 14

Closed Mon eve.
Simple but friendly restaurant

serving *comidas caseras – sopa de cocido, lentejas con chorizo, atún a la plancha, cabrito frito con ajos –* accompanied by a good selection of local wines.
Inexpensive

---

6 RINCÓN DE PEPE
CALLE APÓSTOLES 34
30001 MURCIA
TEL: (968) 21 22 39; FAX: (968) 22 17 44

Restaurant closed Sun eve.
Famous hotel-restaurant located in the historic centre of Murcia near the cathedral. Restaurant serves local and international foods in a

classic setting: *arroz en caldero, caldereta de pescadores, lomito de lobarro del Mar Menor con ajos confitados, cordero lechal asado al estilo de Murcia*, together with an extensive list of Spanish wines. *Tapas* as well as meals served at the friendly and popular bar.
Expensive

---

7 RESTAURANTE MESÓN DE LA
  HUERTA
AVDA DEL PRÍNCIPE, S/N
30820 ALCANTARILLA
MURCIA
TEL: (968) 80 23 90

Closed Sun eve, Mon.
Excellent and atmospheric restaurant adjacent to the *Museo de*

la Huerta (see above) serving authentic and well-prepared foods of Murcia: *pisto murciano, migas, cordero, ajos tiernos, cabrito mesonero* together with a good selection of local wines. There is also a large, friendly *tapas* bar.
Inexpensive to Moderate

Tomar Unas Copas: Stop for a Drink; Stop for a Bite

Valencia

Valencia is renowned for its bars serving an enormous variety of *tapas* made from produce and products of both the inland *huerta* and the sea. While there are literally hundreds of bars to explore in Spain's third largest city, a compact but superlative offering can be found along the Calle Mosén Femades, a small pedestrian walkway in the centre of town. We particularly like the Cervecería Pema (C/ Mosén Femades 3) for its vegetable *tapas*, and the Palacio de la Bellota (C/Mosén Femades 7) for its exceptional selection of *jamones*.

Utiel-Requena

1 MESÓN DEL VINO
REQUENA
(SEE ADDRESS ABOVE)

This bar-restaurant on Requena's main *paseo* is the best place to sample the excellent *rosado* and red wines of Utiel-Requena, together with fine hot *tapas* such as *longanizas fritas, habas con jamón, embutido de orza* and superb *bocadillos*.

Los Campings

As one of Spain's premier holiday destinations, the Levante coast is literally jam-packed with campsites. Inland sites, however, are few and far between.

Valencia

CAMPAMENTO TURIS. VALENCIA
CTRA DE RIU 558
46012 EL SALER
VALENCIA
TEL: (96) 183 02 12

Open all year.

DEVESA GARDENS
CTRA EL SALER, KM 15
46012 EL SALER
VALENCIA
TEL: (96) 161 11 36

Open all year. Good restaurant.

Alicante

EL PALMERAL
CTRA VALENCIA–MURCIA, KM 62
03203 ELCHE
ALICANTE
TEL: (96) 545 27 62

Open all year.
Located virtually within Elche's famous palm groves. Swimming pool.

Vinos y Comestibles: Stop to Taste; Stop to Buy

Valencia

LAS AÑADAS DE ESPAÑA
JÁTIVA 3
46002 VALENCIA
TEL: (96) 352 24 73; FAX: (96) 394 00 42

Closed Sun.
Centrally located gourmet food and wine shop with an extensive selection of wines from throughout Spain, as well as gourmet foodstuffs – *embutidos ibéricos, quesos, ahumados.* There is always a selection of wines available for tasting.
English, French, German spoken.

EL CORTE INGLÉS
PINTOR SOROLLA 26
46000 VALENCIA
TEL: (96) 351 24 44

Spain's premier department store has an excellent food hall with an extensive selection of Valencia and other Spanish wines.

Compras Deliciosas: Stop to Taste; Stop to Buy

Alicante

> ## *Museo de El Turron*
>
> MUSEO DE EL TURRON
> TURRONES EL LOBO
> CALLE ALCOY 62
> 03100 JIJONA
> ALICANTE
> TEL: (96) 561 02 25; FAX: (96) 561 21 03
>
> Fascinating museum dedicated to the production of Spain's favourite Christmas sweet, *jijona* nougat, produced simply and purely from almonds, honey, sugar and egg white. The factory is usually in production between September to December so this is the best time to visit. Free samples at the end of the tour plus an enormous variety of sweets available for purchase.

EL HUERTO DEL CURA
PORTA DE LA MORERA 49
03203 ELCHE
ALICANTE
TEL: (96) 545 17 82

Elche's famous palm grove has about a thousand palm trees from throughout the world, as well as beautiful Mediterranean and tropical gardens. After touring this delightful garden, purchase loose packets of fresh, dried and candied dates – *datiles frescos, datiles naturales* and *datiles confitados* – from the grove's own palms, as well as other typical sweetmeats such as *pan de Elche*.

Jumilla

QUESERÍA DE JUMILLA SL
LA ALQUERÍA, S/N
30520 JUMILLA
MURCIA
TEL: (968) 78 10 92

Queso de Jumilla made from pure goat's milk together with a tumbler of Jumilla *tinto* is one of the great cheese and wine combinations of Spain – the pungency of the goat marrying well with the rather animal-like earthiness of the Monastrell wine.

THE LEVANTE

¡*Fiesta!* Wine and Other Related Celebrations

early Feb	Font del Vi	Burriana

(Town's fountain flows with wine during patronal *fiesta* of San Blas)

12–19 March	Las Fallas	Valencia
2nd fortnight of Aug	Fiesta de la Vendimia	Jumilla
last week of Aug/ early Sept	Fiesta de la Vendimia	Requena

(Wine festival of declared national touristic interest)

2nd week of Sept	Fiesta de la Vendimia	Titaguas
mid-Oct	Fiesta de la Vendimia	Cheste
8 December	Fiesta de la Inmaculada	Yecla

(presentation of new wines)

Las Fallas de Valencia

Valencia's *Fallas* is one of the country's wildest and most spectacular festivals, highlighted by a procession of giant satiric effigies that float through the streets of the city every year in mid-March on Saint Joseph's day. Joseph is patron saint of carpenters and it was no doubt the town's craftsmen who began this particular and peculiar custom, probably some time in the sixteenth century. Today the construction of the giant *fallas* has literally reached new heights: some of them are several storeys high and can be elaborately crafted models. Major *fallas* take nearly a full year of planning and construction and are extremely expensive to build. Local rivalries between competing groups are intense.

The *Fallas* festival is one of the highlights of the year for Valencianos, as well as for the thousands of Spanish and foreign tourists whom it attracts each year. The climax is on the final night when all but the best *fallas* are set on fire to light up the night sky as the hopes and dreams of another year's labour literally go up in smoke.

Y para saber más Additional Information

Dirección General de Turismo
Isabel la Católica 8, 2°
46004 Valencia
tel: (96) 352 61 77

Oficina Regional de Información y
  Turismo
Calle Alejandro Séiquer 4
30001 Murcia
tel: (968) 21 37 16

Consejo Regulador de Valencia
Micer Masco 7, 1°, pta 2a
46010 Valencia
tel: (96) 360 20 13

Consejo Regulador de Utiel
  Requena
Sevilla 12
Apdo Correos 61
46300 Utiel
Valencia
tel: (96) 217 10 62

Consejo Regulador de Alicante
Consellería de Agricultura, Pesca
  y Alimentación
Calle Profesor Manuel Sala 2
03003 Alicante
tel: (96) 511 54 11

Consejo Regulador de Jumilla
Calle San Roque 15
30520 Jumilla
Murcia
tel: (968) 78 17 61;
fax: (968) 78 19 00

Consejo Regulador de Yecla
Calle Corredera 14
30510 Yecla
Murcia
tel: (968) 79 23 52

NAVARRA AND THE
BASQUE COUNTRY

Pilgrim marker at Puente la Reina,
confluence of the two major routes along the
Camino de Santiago.

Spain has always been cut off from the rest of Europe by the Pyrenees which extend as a formidable barrier across the country's relatively narrow northern neck. The western end of the range, however, has served for millennia as a point of entry to and departure from the Iberian peninsula. It was at the Roncesvalles Pass, on the high road between Pamplona and St Jean Pied de Port, that in 778 fierce Basque warriors ambushed and wiped out Charlemagne's rear guard, an event immortalized in the *Chanson de Roland* (although that great French romantic epic, for dramatic convenience, changed the foe to a vast horde of Saracens). Some centuries later, millions of pilgrims braved the same dramatic mountain pass to begin their arduous march along the so-called *Camino de Santiago* to the shrine of Saint James in Galicia.

Notwithstanding the fact that this corner of Spain has thus been an historic thoroughfare for centuries, it remains today something of a separate and extremely individual area, made up of two autonomous but linked regions, Navarra and the Basque Country (País Vasco). Indeed, it has long been so. The Kingdom of Navarra, which at its height in the eleventh century not only extended across both the present region and the País Vasco, but also included the Basque provinces of France, much of La Rioja and parts of Old Castile, long enjoyed particular and independent rights. Under King Sancho El Mayor, a system of *fueros* was initiated which guaranteed a certain measure of autonomy and privileges to the towns and cities of the kingdom; in the thirteenth century, a *Fuero General* was written that applied to the Kingdom of Navarra as a whole and which for centuries defined its separate and independent relation to the rest of Spain.

The Basque provinces, though annexed by Pedro El Cruel of Castile in the fourteenth century, were also entitled to maintain their own laws, customs and economic privileges which the Spanish kings swore to maintain and preserve, traditionally under the sacred oak tree at Gernika, long a symbol of Basque national and cultural identity. And so it continued until the early nineteenth century when both the Basques and the Navarrans backed the Carlists in a dispute over the succession to the throne; the Carlists lost, and as a result, both regions were eventually deprived by Madrid of their ancient *fueros*.

Resentment in the Basque Country at lost liberties and freedom has thus long smouldered. During the Civil War, Navarra backed the Nationalists but the Basques threw in their lot with the Republicans. Franco never let them forget this; during the war, he allowed the Nazi airborne Condor League to obliterate the sacred town of Geruika on 26 April 1937 and in subsequent decades he systematically brutalized the region in an attempt to eradicate its identity, culture and language. It is perhaps not surprising, under the circumstances, that anger and disaffection led to the rise of violent resistance under the banner of ETA, an armed nationalist struggle that continues less explicably even in today's democratic Spain.

Be that as it may, this still remains one of Spain's most beautiful areas to visit, with clean sandy beaches washed by huge rollers from the Bay of Biscay, and charming, unspoiled fishing villages. As a wine region, the Basque Country encompasses the prestigious Rioja Alavesa sub-zone, the plentiful source here above all not of oak-aged Reservas and Gran Reservas but primarily of fruity young *vinos de cosecheros* to be imbibed in prodigious quantity in the bars of Bilbao and San Sebastián. And of course, there is Txakolì. Just as the safeguarding of the Euskera tongue, sports such as *pelota*, or the native cuisine are seen as a means of maintaining Basque national and cultural identity, this unique and traditional wine of the land, minor though it undoubtedly is in national terms, is another manifestation of longstanding country tradition and Basque identity.

In contrast to the lush Basque Country, Navarra marks the watershed between two different Spains – the wet, lush lands of the northern coast, and, looking down from the mountain slopes above the region's capital Pamplona, the endless, arid Spain of the central interior. Navarra is an enormously varied province and reflects this contrast, ranging from the snow-covered peaks of the high Pyrenees to the near-desert stretches of the Ribera Baja above the Ebro basin.

Though from a wine point of view long in the shadow of its neighbour

Rioja, Navarra has emerged in the last decade as one of Spain's most forward-looking and up-and-coming wine regions in its own right, the source of not only fine *rosados* but also increasingly of superlative oak-aged red wines of real class and quality.

Orientation

Navarra is a small northerly region at the western end of the Pyrenees, stretching from the mountains to the Ebro river basin. It consists of a single province administered from its capital city Pamplona. The Basque Country, also known as Euskadi, is an autonomous region with its own indigenous and mysterious language, Euskera. It comprises three provinces: Alava, Guipúzcoa and Vizcaya.

Long a point of entry to the Iberian peninsula, the Basque Country remains so today, via the Irun–Hendaye frontier crossing. Navarra can be reached by road from France via the famous Roncesvalles Pass. Both regions are easily accessible by sea via the Plymouth–Santander ferry.

There is an international airport at Bilbao, while Navarra can also be approached from Barcelona. Navarra is located north of La Rioja and can be dipped into by wine tourists visiting that important region.

Maps: Michelin No. 442 (Northern & Central); Firestone Hispania C-2, T-22.

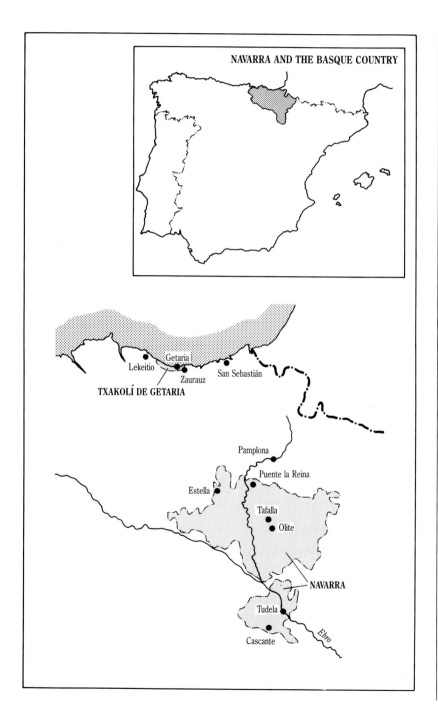

El Camino de Santiago in Navarra

The *Camino de Santiago* enters Spain by way of two principal routes: the Roncesvalles Pass in Navarra and the Puerto de Somport that descends to Jaca in neighbouring Aragón. The two routes come together in Navarra at the pilgrims' town of Puente la Reina, continuing as a single route (with minor variations) all the way to Santiago de Compostela.

As early as the year 1000, King Sancho El Mayor realized the importance of this great trans-European thoroughfare, and supported the creation of churches, hospitals and monasteries in the Navarran towns along the way. The *Camino de Santiago* thus became an important cultural, artistic and commercial thoroughfare, bringing with it, not least, exchanges of information regarding viticulture and winemaking.

Many of Navarra's towns along the *Camino de Santiago* retain not only superbly preserved monuments from that great epoch, but also something of a medieval flavour in their atmospheric stone-paved, and today mainly quiet, streets. The route from Jaca leads through Leyre, with its fortified Monasterio de San Salvador de Leyre, and Sangüesa, a charming, well-preserved town which boasts numerous lovely churches, notably the Iglesia de Santa María with its magnificently carved portal. Puente la Reina, where the two routes join, is a quiet but lovely medieval village, the river still spanned by the twelfth-century stone bridge that gave the town its name. Further south lies Estella, one of the most important and best preserved towns along the *Camino de Santiago*. Estella was singled out in the medieval *Codex Calixtus*, an early guide for pilgrims, for its '*buen pan, excelente vino, mucha carne y pescado, y toda clase de felicidad*'.

The *Camino de Santiago*, far from being a moribund relic, is still travelled by devout pilgrims even today. The ancient pilgrims' way sometimes follows modern roads, at other times traverses stone-paved tracks across the countryside. Just outside Estella the old pilgrims' route leads to Irache, once the site of an extremely important Cistercian monastery and medieval medical school. Beside the old monastery buildings, a new and extremely modern *bodega* has recently been constructed, Bodegas Irache; the company takes its position along this historic thoroughfare seriously, and has initiated plans to construct a fountain that will give each passing pilgrim either a measured drink of wine or a drink of water.

LOS VINOS: THE WINES OF NAVARRA AND THE BASQUE COUNTRY

Txakolí   Txakolì or Chacolí is the generic name for light, slightly sour 'green' wine from the Basque Country, produced in all three provinces from a range of local grapes. Txakolì can be either red or white (it is often made from a mix of grapes) and is often sold in unlabelled bottles. The quality of such wines can be extremely variable.

Txakolì de Getaria DO; Chacolí de Guetaria DO   The only Txakolì entitled to *denominación de origen* comes from a tiny area of wine country in the steep slopes above the fishing villages of Guetaria and Zarautz. The wine, produced from Hondarribi Zuri (white) and Hondarribi Beltza (black) grapes, usually harvested and vinified together, must reach a minimum of 9.5° alcohol, and is best consumed young while it still maintains a refreshing prickle of carbonic gas. It is an extremely quenching beverage to accompany grilled fish.

Navarra DO   The delimited Navarra wine zone extends throughout the province across five separate sub-zones and applies to the elaboration of white, *rosado* and red wines from white grapes Viura, Garnacha Blanca and Chardonnay and black grapes Garnacha,

Tempranillo, Mazuelo, Graciano, Cabernet Sauvignon and Merlot. White wines must reach 10–12.5° alcohol; *rosados*, 10–13.5°; reds, 10–14°. The sub-zones are Baja Montaña, located across 14 municipalities in the north-east of the region and representing 15% of the total vineyard; Valdizarbe, 24 municipalities in the north of the region: 10% of the vineyard; Tierra de Estella, 26 municipalities in the south-east of the region: 15% of the total vineyard; Ribera Alta, 24 municipalities in the centre of the region: 30% of the total vineyard; and Ribera Baja, 13 municipalities located in the south of the region and 30% of the vineyard.

While the Navarra DO is awarded to white, *rosado* and young red wines that pass organoleptic analysis, aged red wines come in three levels which will be indicated on the back label: Crianza (minimum of two years' ageing, one of which must be in oak barrels no larger than 500 litres); Reserva (three years' minimum total ageing with at least one year in oak barrel); and Gran Reserva (at least two years' ageing in oak barrel followed by a minimum of 3 years in bottle prior to release).

Rioja DO   Though the Rioja Alavesa is located entirely within the Basque province of Alava and there are furthermore 7 municipalities in Navarra entitled to the Rioja *denominación*, we have covered wines from those sub-zones in our chapter on Rioja.

It should be emphasized, however, that while from an export point of view, we may be mainly familiar with and interested in the great red oak-aged Reservas and Gran Reservas of Rioja, many winegrowers particularly in the Rioja Alavesa produce a particular style of wine primarily for sale and consumption in the Basque Country. Such wine, produced by a traditional system of whole grape or semi-carbonic maceration, is intensely fruity and gulpable and is particularly savoured in the bars and gastronomic societies of the region. It is known as *tinto joven de Rioja Alavesa*, or often simply as *vino de cosechero*.

Other Drinks

Pacharán Pacharán, a sort of Navarran sloe gin, has in recent years become something of a cult drink in bars not only in Pamplona but even as far off as the capital Madrid. Home-made versions are often preferred and available in specialist wine shops. Pacharán usually comes in both dry and sweet versions; we prefer the dry.

LA GASTRONOMÍA: FOODS OF NAVARRA AND THE BASQUE COUNTRY

Of all Spain's many regional cuisines, that of the Basque Country is universally considered paramount. The interior of the country is a fertile and verdant land of mainly self-sufficient smallholdings (*caseríos*), and a superb range of produce and products finds its way on to the table. All along the Basque coast, great fishing fleets return with a superlative catch of Atlantic fish and shellfish that is greatly loved and prepared most imaginatively. Ultimately, though, it is not simply a question of the excellence of the ingredients from both land and sea that determines the character of the Basque cuisine; rather there seems to be something innately part of the Basque national psyche – both male and female – that delights in the preparation and production of foods of the highest quality, both in the home and in restaurants and gastronomic societies alike.

This is a land that not only enjoys an immense repertoire of great traditional dishes – *bacalao al pil-pil, kokotxas en salsa verde, marmitako* and scores of others – it also enjoys a reputation for the creation of imaginative new dishes that are none the less essentially Basque-inspired: such dishes form the basis of the so-called *nueva cocina vasca* as developed and devised in some of Spain's greatest restaurants not only in the Basque Country itself but in Madrid and elsewhere.

Though the preparation of foods in Navarra may be influenced by its Basque neighbours, the region on the whole is considerably less innovative, innately more conservative in all things. The dishes that most come to mind in Navarra are simple, well-prepared and make good use of the region's excellent produce and products: *esparragos de Tudela, pimientos rellenos,* or fresh trout from a fast-running mountain stream, fried quickly over a hot griddle.

¡Que aproveche! Regional Specialities of Navarra and the Basque Country

Pimientos asados Navarra is the principal source of one of Spain's favourite vegetables, the red pepper: here *pimientos* are roasted over a fire until black, skinned, then stewed in olive oil with garlic. The best peppers are the pointed, slightly piquant *pimientos de piquillo* from the Llodosa area.

Pimientos rellenos Red peppers, roasted and skinned, then stuffed with a meat or fish mixture and baked.

Espárragos de Navarra Probably the best white asparagus in Spain, protected by a *denominación especifica,* served fresh in spring and early summer, and available tinned all year round.

Cogollo de Tudela Tiny 'little gem' lettuce from market gardens of Tudela.

Ajoarriero Dried salt cod prepared with garlic and dried red peppers, in the style of the old mule-drivers. This dish, a favourite of Navarra, has become popular throughout the country.

Paticas de cerdo Pig's trotters slowly cooked in wine and garlic: a favourite country food of Navarra.

Angulas Tiny elvers (they look like a bowl of thick noodles), usually fried in olive oil, garlic and red pepper, served in a wooden bowl and eaten with a wooden fork.

Bacalao al pil-pil Reconstituted salt cod boiled first, then fried gently in pungent garlic and chilli pepper oil; as the fish fries, it releases gelatine which flavours and thickens the sauce.

Chiperones en su tinta Squid stewed in its ink – unappetizing visually but delicious and not overly strong.

Cogote de merluza Favourite at the Basque *asadores* – head, neck and stripped out body of hake, grilled over hot charcoal.

Kokotxas en salsa verde Basque preparation of hake barbel (flesh stripped from the throat), simmered in *salsa verde* made from fish stock, olive oil, garlic and chopped parsley.

Txistorras Spicy, thin Basque sausage, usually grilled.

Txangurro a la vasca Spider crab, another favourite of the Basque coast, stewed in a rich tomato and garlic sauce.

Besugo a la brasa *Besugo*, a type of sea bream, is one of the most delicious and favourite fish of the north coast, best simply grilled over charcoal at an *asador*.

Marmitako Hearty traditional stew made with bonito tuna, tomatoes, peppers and potato.

Perdiz con chocolate Unusual Navarran speciality: partridge in a rich chocolate sauce.

Cordero al chilindrón *Chilindrones* – meats or poultry stewed with red peppers, tomato, *jamón* and onions – are as popular in Navarra as they are in Aragón,

The Gastronomic Societies of the Basque Country

One of the great traditions of the Basque Country is its profusion of male-only gastronomic societies. These are private clubs where friends and colleagues gather, free of the distractions of their womenfolk, to prepare foods communally, eat together, talk, play cards and drink good wine. Though this may sound like an anachronistic activity, fit only for old men in berets or cloth caps, even young men that we have met belong to such societies. The Basques pride themselves on their egalitarianism, and social barriers have little importance in such private clubs as farmers and fishermen share the serious task of preparing foods alongside lawyers, doctors and other professionals.

Women have always been barred from membership. I wonder, in today's evolving society, is this changing? A friend explained to me that these days, depending on the club, women might be allowed to visit or even to eat with the men on a weekday lunchtime. However, one thing that remains strictly forbidden is for them ever to enter the kitchen and prepare food!

though here it is lamb that is the most favoured meat.

Trucha a la navarra Trout soaked in wine, stuffed with a slice of air-cured *jamón*, dredged in flour, and pan-fried.

Cuajada Type of Basque junket made with curdled ewe's milk, authentically served in a wooden bowl.

Cheeses: *Idiazábal DO* Strongly flavoured sometimes smoked cheese hand-made in the Basque Country with pure milk from the indigenous, long-fleeced latxa sheep. *Roncal DO* One of the great cheeses of Spain, from the Pyrenees mountains of Navarra: long-cured, well-aged ewe's milk cheese.

THE WINE ROADS OF NAVARRA

In Brief: The most enjoyable and obvious place to gain an acquaintance with the wines of Navarra is in the region's capital, Pamplona. This is a pleasant, stylish city, and probably the region's principal tourist attraction, even outside the crazy San Fermín festival week (6–12 July). For the wine lover, there are two principal routes that lead south from Pamplona. The N121 passes through important wine towns such as Las Campanas, Olite and Tudela and is best for those en route to Aragón and Catalunya. Those wishing to gain a more in-depth insight into the work of EVENA, Spain's premier wine research institute, should certainly visit Olite and preferably stay overnight in the magnificent Parador Nacional situated in a castle that was once the residence of the Kings of Navarra. Those wishing to combine wine tasting with sightseeing along the *Camino de Santiago* should follow the N111, the old pilgrims' route south by way of Puente la Reina and Estella. This leads to Logroño, capital of the Rioja.

Navarra, notwithstanding that it has long lived in the shadow of its prestigious neighbour Rioja, has emerged in recent years as one of Spain's most exciting and fast-developing quality wine regions.

This is a long-established and historic wine region in its own right, with vineyards that date back to Roman times at least and an extensive and highly developed wine industry developed during the Middle Ages to slake the thirst of millions of passing pilgrims on the weary road to Santiago. The carved decorations of wine scenes and vine leaves on many of the

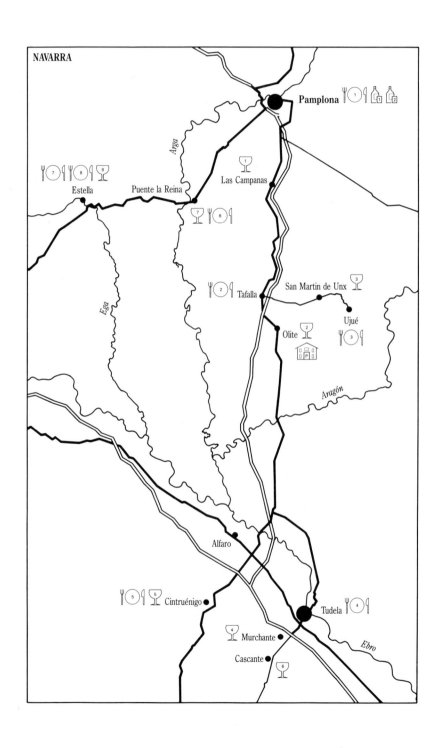

region's Romanesque churches attest to the importance of viticulture in the medieval period.

Of course, during this period much of Rioja came under the jurisdiction of the Kingdom of Navarra and, in a sense, the two regions' wine industries developed in parallel. In the past century, for example, Navarra like Rioja found its wines in great demand after phylloxera devastated the vineyards of France. This great scourge, though, was not long in crossing the Pyrenees, and while the extensive wine country was subsequently replanted as elsewhere on louse-resistant American rootstock, it never completely recovered its former extent.

After phylloxera, Rioja went its separate way as it developed its own unique style of oak-aged wines based on French winemaking techniques. Navarra, meanwhile, took the apparently collective decision to replant its vineyards primarily with higher-yielding Garnacha at the expense of the once traditional but more fickle Tempranillo. Land reforms which fragmented ownership into small or tiny smallholdings led to the inevitable rise and domination of co-operative wineries. As elsewhere, the co-operatives lacked private initiative, and for decades were more than content mainly to process their *socios'* grapes into bulk wines destined to be sold in bulk for blending, either south to Rioja up to the 1950s, or else to longstanding markets in France and Switzerland.

Such wines were produced primarily by the *doble pasta* method of winemaking used in the Levante which resulted in wines with a great concentration of colour, tannin and alcohol, qualities ideal for blending but not for drinking. However, as a by-product of this method, excellent *rosados* were produced that have long been enjoyed locally.

The introduction in the 1970s of modern stainless steel winemaking equipment with the facility for temperature control during fermentation revolutionized the production of Navarra's traditional *rosado* wines and enabled them to be made on a commercial scale that proved successful not only nationally but internationally. Indeed, so successful were such wines that a saying grew up in Spain that you look to Rioja for red wines, Catalunya for whites and Navarra for *rosados*: and there is still some validity in this generalization even today.

In spite of the success of such wines produced by the region's finest pioneering wineries (Julián Chivite, Vinícola de Navarra, Bodegas Irache, Señorío de Sarría), by the early 1980s the wine industry in Navarra was still in something of a state of crisis. With the exception of the products of a handful of excellent private companies, most of the region's wines were still being produced in poorly-equipped co-operative wineries and the actual area under vines was declining rapidly as farmers chose to cultivate more lucrative cereal crops. Therefore, at the initiative of the Government of Navarra, a decision was taken to try to rectify the situation and re-establish this historic wine region through the funding and establishment in 1981 of a viticultural and oenological research institute that came to be known as EVENA (*Estación de Viticultura y Enología del Gobierno de Navarra*). Its brief, quite simply, was to examine every aspect of grape-growing and wine-making in the region in order to improve quality.

An extensive programme of experimentation with different grape varieties, both native and foreign, was undertaken and already the results have led to a profound change in emphasis in both the vineyard and the *bodega*. For example, it was realized that while Garnacha is excellent for the production of both fresh and robust *rosados* and fruity young reds, it is not well suited to the production of red wines destined for oak ageing since it is particularly prone to early oxidation. As a result, it was decided to decrease the dependence on this single predominant variety; previously Garnacha was planted on over 90% of the region's total vineyard; today it accounts for only about 75% and is still further declining. In the meantime, there have been considerable increased plantations of Tempranillo, Graciano and Mazuelo (the great grapes of Rioja), as well as Cabernet Sauvignon and Merlot. Viura and Chardonnay have been identified as the white grapes with most potential, while on the higher, damper zones of the Baja Montaña, there have even been successful results from aromatic grapes such as Riesling.

There have furthermore been considerable experiments with different types of winemaking, with blending different grape varieties, and above all with ageing in different types of wooden barrels, as well as in the bottle. What has already been conclusively demonstrated is that Navarra has great potential as a region for the production of high-quality red wines capable of ageing. Today, the balance of production in Navarra is roughly 40% *rosado*, 40% red wines and 10% white.

What is most significant is that the region is gradually but surely gaining its own identity and not merely as the source of look-alike Riojas. The particular conditions and micro-climates of the Navarran sub-zones are quite distinct from the Rioja regions to the south; moreover, the enlightened attitudes developed at EVENA are allowing wholly individual types and styles of wine to emerge. For example, the use of Cabernet Sauvignon and Merlot (not officially authorized in Rioja) alongside traditional native grapes can result in wines with completely different, perhaps more international characters. Moreover, there is a minor but none the less significant trend towards the bottling of varietal wines produced from 100% Cabernet Sauvignon or 100% Tempranillo, and indeed some of these wines have already attracted considerable attention internationally.

The work at EVENA has only been going on for little more than a decade and it continues at a furious pace. Furthermore, recent investment in some of the region's private companies has been immense, and even the co-operative wineries are finally beginning to modernize their installations. The new wines of Navarra that have already emerged, from *bodegas* like Ochoa, Irache, Navarra, Cenalsa, Chivite, Señorío de Sarría, or the Romero co-operative, have conclusively demonstrated Navarra's potential. In the very near future, it is certain that we will see even better wines – *rosados*, oak-aged reds, even whites – emerging as Navarra establishes itself as one of Spain's premier wine regions.

Café Iruña, Pamplona.

Pamplona is the capital of the region in every sense, and no visitor will wish to miss spending some time in this lovely old town. The city comes as something of a surprise, for it is charming, surprisingly sober and northern in feel, in contrast to the way in which Ernest Hemingway described it during *fiesta* time in his great novel *The Sun Also Rises*. Modern Pamplona sprawls out into the folds of the Basque hills to the north and is prosperous and hard-working. But the old town, still roughly enclosed by its fortified walls, remains hugely atmospheric, particularly the small maze of streets between the Gothic cathedral, the Plaza de Castillo and the Plaza de Toros. Ask in the tourist office for a map of the old town, and trace on foot the path of the *encierro*, that insane daily event during the Fiesta de San Fermín when six murderous *toros bravos* are let loose to run through the streets along with hundreds of local youths and crazy or blind-drunk foreigners. Afterwards, make your way to any number of excellent and friendly bars to enjoy a glass or two of fresh Navarra *rosado* along with a tasty selection of *tapas*.

From Pamplona, the wine traveller has the choice of two principal routes. The N121 extends due south from the city (parallel to the A15 motorway) and passes through the important wine sub-zones of Valdizarbe, Ribera Alta and Ribera Baja; it is the best route for those heading towards Aragón and Catalunya. The first wine town of note that is reached is Las Campanas, home of Bodegas Vinícola de Navarra, one of Navarra's oldest, founded by a Frenchman escaping phylloxera in 1864 and the first *bodega* in Navarra to commercialize its wines in bottle, as well as the first to bottle Navarra *rosado* (in 1950). Today it is part of Spain's largest drinks group, Bodegas y Bebidas. The winemaking installations have been completely renovated in recent years, but this is still a historic and atmospheric *bodega* to visit. On the site of the *bodega* there is a basilica-hospital founded by the Brotherhood of San Nicolás de Bari to serve pilgrims en route to or from Galicia, now converted to an inn used by guests of the winery.

The road south leads through Tafalla to Olite. Olite today is little more than a small *pueblo*, yet its magnificent, perhaps rather overzealously restored castle attests to its importance in Navarra's Golden Age. The castle was once the residence of the Kings of Navarra, and today parts of it have been converted into a most comfortable and atmospheric *parador*. For the wine lover, of course, Olite is most significant today as the home of EVENA. It may be possible for serious wine lovers to tour this remarkable institute, located just north of the town in the old Alcoholera San Isidro, by prior appointment.

The Institute's dynamic director, Javier Ochoa, himself a trained oenologist, lives in Olite above his own private and highly regarded winery, Bodegas Ochoa. This is an impressive estate operation. Ochoa owns 13 hectares of his own vineyards, and controls a further 45 through family, friends and long-standing contracts. Perhaps not surprisingly, the wines of Bodegas Ochoa are at the leading edge of the 'new wave' wines of Navarra; the varietal Cabernet Sauvignon and Tempranillo wines are particularly vivid and well-focused.

From Olite, if time allows, a most enjoyable diversion should be made to little Ujué, a hill town 20 km east of Olite with a remarkable fortified sanctuary. On a clear day there are stunning views from here across to the Pyrenees. The Mesón Las Torres, located by the sanctuary, is a simple but outstanding restaurant of great charm.

Winemaking detail on the fortified sanctuary at Ujué.

The wine road continues south, passing through an arid landscape of mainly parched fields of vines or cereal on its descent towards the Ebro basin. By the time the river is reached, ridges of rounded earth replace other crops, for, around Tudela in particular, this is one of the country's premier zones for the cultivation of precious white asparagus. Indeed, if you are in the region in May or June, this local delicacy should on no account be missed.

This southernmost wine region is the Ribera Baja. Just as the Rioja Baja is considered a poor relation to the more temperate Alta and Alavesa sub-zones, Ribera Baja is often dismissed as an overly hot and dry sub-zone primarily producing little more than blending wines from Garnacha. True, vast amounts of such wines do continue to be made, especially in many of the area's vast co-operative wineries. But Ribera Baja is also the home of one of the region's largest and most respected private wineries, Bodegas Julián Chivite, located at Cintruénigo. The success of this remarkable, still wholly family-run firm has been based above all on its Gran Feudo *rosado*, one of the best examples of its kind. Yet wines such as Chivite Reserva, produced from Tempranillo and Garnacha and aged for at least two years in oak and one in bottle, and the superlative 125 Aniversario Gran Reserva, produced entirely from Tempranillo grapes grown on the family's own estates in the Ribera Baja and Ribera Alta, demonstrate that superlative oak-aged red wines can also be produced in this hotter sub-zone.

From Cintruénigo, the wine traveller can head either south-east into Aragón and Catalunya, or north-west into the adjoining Rioja.

An alternative option is to leave Pamplona on the N111, the road which follows the old pilgrims' route and leads eventually to Logroño. Small pilgrim towns such as Puente la Reina and Estella are still wholly medieval in character and certainly deserve to be visited. Today Puente la Reina is so quiet and peaceful that it is almost impossible to imagine what it must have been like in its medieval heyday when the traffic, the constant movement of people on foot or horseback going to and from Santiago, must have been immense.

Just above Puente la Reina lies one of Navarra's most remarkable wine estates, Señorío de Sarría, located in the Valdizarbe sub-zone at about 650–700 metres above sea level. Señorío de Sarría is the creation of the late Señor Felix Huarte, a local building magnate, who purchased some 1500 hectares of abandoned land in the early 1950s, and, with a workforce of gypsies and unemployed workers from Andalucía, cleared the land using only donkeys and created a self-sufficient model agricultural village, complete with its own school, church, playground and bar. The lands were cultivated with corn, beans, fruit orchards and vineyards and today some 25 families still live and work on the estate.

Señorío de Sarria, Puente la Reina.

However, in 1981, the vineyards (about 150 hectares) and *bodega* were sold to the Caja de Ahorros de Navarra, a bank owned by the Government of Navarra. Since then there has been a massive injection of capital to renovate both the vineyards and the winery. In particular, the vineyard has been replanted with more Tempranillo, Graciano, Mazuelo and Cabernet Sauvignon to improve its red wines, and with Chardonnay to improve its whites. The newly renovated *bodega* currently has about 7000 American oak *barricas* for the ageing of red wines and this number will double in the next few years, demonstrating the company's commitment to quality oak-aged reds. Señorío de Sarría's Reservas are particularly well-structured wines of some class, and should improve even more in future years as the new plantations come into fuller production.

Another important Navarra *bodega* that demonstrates the changes and improvements that have taken place within the last decade is Bodegas Irache, located next to the historic monastery of the same name south of Estella. Though parts of the old *bodega* date back to when it served as a gun store for the Carlists, a new and beautiful super-modern *bodega* is in the process of being constructed. Bodegas Irache, a historic winery founded in 1891, is located in the small but prestigious sub-zone of Tierra de Estella which claims to have the best balance between the hot arid lands of the Ribera vineyards and the colder, wetter climates of Valdizarbe and Baja Montaña. This, explained the oenologist José Javier Soto Lizarraga, has always been a zone noted foremost for its red wines. Although the company's vineyards are planted with an impressive array of grapes – Tempranillo, Cabernet Sauvignon, Merlot, Graciano, Mazuelo, Pinot Noir in addition to the workhorse Garnacha for red wines, and Viura, Chardonnay and Malvasia for whites – Soto is not one who necessarily believes that the Garnacha should be abandoned wholesale.

'There is no such thing as a super-grape that would be the salvation to all our problems,' he says. 'Besides, I don't believe that Garnacha is as bad as it is reputed to be. On the contrary, it is capable of producing excellent *rosado* as well as fantastic *tinto joven* red wines. Cabernet Sauvignon could never make such fruity and supple wines. True, generally Garnacha does not age well. But we do not want to drink Crianza or Reserva wines every day in any case.'

A future dream project that Bodegas Irache envisages is the creation, across the road from its existing premises, of a true château-style estate winery surrounded by its own vineyards. The vines have been planted and the future wine has already been given a registered name, Cható Irache.

Nearby, the Chivite family have also purchased an estate, Señorío de Arínzano, and have already planted 130 hectares with Cabernet Sauvignon, Merlot and Tempranillo. They too plan to produce château wines entirely from their own grapes, a relatively new concept in Navarra (rare, for that matter, even in nearby Rioja). These developments at the top end of the market demonstrate the forward direction that Navarra is moving in and are a further positive pointer to the future.

Bodegas: Stop to Taste; Stop to Buy

1 BODEGAS VINÍCOLA DE NAVARRA
CTRA PAMPLONA–ZARAGOZA, KM 14
31397 LAS CAMPANAS
NAVARRA
TEL: (948) 36 01 31; FAX: (948) 36 02 75

WINES PRODUCED: Las Campanas *blanco, rosado y tinto*; Bandeo *blanco, rosado y tinto*; Castillo de Javier *rosado*; Castillo de Tiebas *tinto* Reserva, Gran Reserva.
LICOR: Pacharán Alaiz.
VISITS: Mon–Fri working hours, by appointment.
Bodegas Vinícola de Navarra is located on the *Camino de Santiago* where monks from the brotherhood of San Nicolás de Bari built a hospital for pilgrims.

This is one of Navarra's oldest wineries, founded in 1864 by Julio Salvador Mihura, a Frenchman in search of a suitable place to restart winegrowing after the vineyards in his native land were destroyed by phylloxera.

Throughout its history, it has been one of the region's pioneering *bodegas*. It was, for example, the first in Navarra to bottle *rosado*; the wine, under the Las Campanas brand, was much appreciated by, among others, Ernest Hemingway on his visits to Pamplona for the San Fermín festival, and he was a frequent visitor to the *bodega*.

Today Bodegas Vinícola de Navarra is part of the large Bodegas y Bebidas group.
English spoken.

EVENA – *La Estación de Viticultura y Enología del Gobierno de Navarra*

EVENA, the most advanced wine research institute in Spain, is of considerable interest to the serious wine lover or wine professional. Once having decided in the early 1980s to embark on a quality-driven path, EVENA has undertaken with the most minute and meticulous care to investigate every aspect of grape-growing and winemaking in Navarra.

Experimental vineyards have been planted in all 5 of Navarra's subzones with some 36 different grape varieties and studies have been undertaken on individual rootstocks, virus-free clones, methods of training and pruning, the effects and efficacy of various forms of pest control, and ideal density of vines per hectare. The super-modern laboratory, computer analysers, and experimental *bodega*, converted from the former Alcoholera San Isidro just outside Olite, provide the facilities for wide-ranging studies and investigations. There are banks of tiny stainless steel fermentation tanks for 'mini-vinifications' to allow for experiments with fermentation at various temperatures, different lengths of maceration, whole or semi-whole grape fermentation; a variety of blends from a range of different grapes can subsequently be assembled; experiments take place on ageing in French, American and Spanish oak; if French, then from various forests, including the Limousin, Allier and Never; and experiments are carried out using different systems of clarification and stabilization.

What is significant about EVENA's research to date is above all the open-minded attitude with which it approaches its task. As regards wine, much of Spain remains steadfastly, even stubbornly, conservative. Yet here, anything and everything is being tested, given a chance to shine in Navarra, and from this EVENA is picking out the best, and using its results in conjunction with the region's Consejo Regulador to advise and steer the region's winegrowers and winemakers along the path to better quality.

ESTACIÓN DE VITICULTURAY
ENOLOGÍA DEL GOBIERNO DE
NAVARRA (EVENA)
VALLE DE ORBA
31390 OLITE
NAVARRA
TEL: (948) 74 00 54, 74 02 91;
FAX: (948) 71 20 92

WINES PRODUCED: Experimental wine station producing up to 50 different wines from a variety of native and experimental vines. Wines are not for sale.
VISITS: By appointment.

NAVARRA AND THE BASQUE COUNTRY

2 BODEGAS OCHOA SA
CTRA ZARAGOZA 21
31390 OLITE
NAVARRA
TEL: (948) 74 00 06; FAX: (948) 74 00 48

WINES PRODUCED: Ochoa *blanco, rosado, tinto joven*; Ochoa Tempranillo; Ochoa Cabernet Sauvignon; Ochoa *tinto* Crianza, Reserva.
VISITS: By appointment. Working hours for direct sales.

Javier Ochoa has acquired a reputation as one of Navarra's most exciting and innovative winemakers. Through his work at EVENA where he is the director, as well as in his own family *bodega*, he has pioneered a range of 'new wave' Navarra wines of the highest quality. The *bodega* is still located in the basement below the family home.
English spoken.

---

3 BODEGA BERAMENDI
CTRA TAFALLA–SAN MARTÍN
31495 SAN MARTÍN D'UNX
NAVARRA

WINES PRODUCED: Beramendi *rosado*, Beramendi *tinto joven*.

VISITS: Mon–Sat 10–14h; 16–20h. Sun 10–15h.
Brand new small private *bodega* 1 km outside San Martín on road to Ujué producing tasty, young *rosado* and red wines. The wines are for sale in bottle or in 16-litre *garrafas*.

---

4 BODEGAS CENALSA
CARRETERA TUDELA, S/N
31521 MURCHANTE
NAVARRA
TEL: (948) 83 83 85
ADMINISTRATIVE OFFICE:
   CIUDADELA 5, 31001 PAMPLONA
TEL: (948) 22 72 83; FAX: (948) 22 99 99

WINES PRODUCED: Agramont *blanco, rosado y tinto*; Campo Nuevo *tinto*; Príncipe de Viana Cabernet Sauvignon; Príncipe de Viana Tempranillo.
VISITS: Mon–Fri 9–14h; 15–18h. Appointment necessary for in-depth visit.

Cenalsa, part-owned by the Government of Navarra, is an important marketing company that advises some of the region's best co-operative wineries on both grape-growing and winemaking, then in its own *bodegas* in Murchante skilfully utilizes the resulting wines to create and bottle blends under its successful Agramont, Campo Nuevo and top-of-the-range Príncipe de Viana brands.
English, French spoken.

---

5 BODEGAS JULIÁN CHIVITE
CALLE RIBERA, S/N
31592 CINTRUÉNIGO
NAVARRA
TEL: (948) 81 10 00; FAX: (948) 81 14 07

WINES PRODUCED: Gran Feudo
blanco, rosado y tinto; Viña Marcos
tinto joven; Gran Feudo *tinto*
Crianza; Chivite *tinto* Reserva;
Parador *tinto* Reserva; 125
Aniversario *tinto* Gran Reserva.
VISITS: By appointment, Mon–Fri
11–13h30; 15–17h.
The Chivite family has been
making wine in Cintruénigo for
three and a half centuries, and
today the company is run by the
tenth generation to carry on this
tradition. It is one of Navarra's
leading private wineries, and
indeed a proud wine company of
national and international repute.
Cintruénigo is located on the
south side of the Ebro river virtually
adjacent to the delimited vineyards
of the Rioja Baja. The Chivite wines
are produced from grapes grown
primarily in the Ribera Baja and
Ribera Alta sub-zones. Though the
modern success of the company is
based on its phenomenally popular
Gran Feudo *rosado*, one of the best
of its type, Chivite also produces a
range of excellent oak-aged red
wines of the highest quality.
In addition to the large working
winery in Cintruénigo, the family is
currently embarking on an
ambitious project, the creation of a
château-style winery near Estella
called Señorío de Arínzano. There is
an ancient castle on the estate in
the process of being restored, while
the *bodega* has been designed by
one of Spain's leading modern
architects, Rafael Moneo. This is an
exciting project and the wines, to be
produced from Cabernet
Sauvignon, Merlot and Tempranillo,
are eagerly awaited.
English, French spoken.

---

6 BODEGA NUESTRA SEÑORA DEL
ROMERO
S. COOP. LTDA.
CRTRA TARAZONA 33
31520 CASCANTE
NAVARRA
TEL: (948) 85 14 11; FAX: (948) 85 14 36

WINES PRODUCED: Malon de
Echaide *blanco y rosado*; Torrecilla
blanco y rosado; Plandenas *rosado*;
Plandenas *tinto* Reserva; Señor de
Cascante *tinto* Gran Reserva.
VISITS: Daily, working hours, by
appointment. Open for direct sales
working hours.
Navarra has long been a land
dominated by its co-operative
wineries, and while in the last
decade their general standards have
improved immensely (more than
half now have temperature
controlled fermentation

equipment, and encourage their members to pick their grapes at the optimum moment), others remain antiquated in equipment and mentality and sell wines only in bulk not bottle. Cascante's Señora del Romero co-operative is reputedly the region's best and most forward co-operative winery and produces an excellent range of well-made wines at competitive prices. English spoken.

7

BODEGA DE SARRÍA SA
VINOS DEL SEÑORÍO DE SARRÍA
SEÑORÍO DE SARRÍA
31100 PUENTE LA REINA
NAVARRA
TEL: (948) 34 01 40
ADMINISTRATIVE OFFICE: PÍO XII
  31, 31008 PAMPLONA
TEL: (948) 26 75 62; FAX: (948) 17 21 64

WINES PRODUCED: Señorío de Sarría *blanco y rosado*; Señorío de Sarría *tinto* Crianza, Reserva, Gran Reserva; Señorío de Sarría Cabernet Sauvignon.
VISITS: By appointment only, as far in advance as possible.
When Don Felix Huarte, a local construction magnate, purchased the Señorío de Sarría estate in 1953, it was a completely abandoned, uncultivated tract of 1500 hectares located in the hills above Puente la Reina in Navarra's Valdizarbe sub-zone. There were no roads and the terrain was rough and overgrown, yet the land was cleared with the aid of 60 donkeys and itinerant gypsy workers from Andalucía. Huarte's aim was to create a model agricultural estate, and to this end he gave employment to Andalucíans who planted cereal, olive trees, fruit orchards and about 150 ha. of vineyards. He built housing for 50 families who came to live at Sarría, as well as a school, church, bar, cinema and playground, all self-contained on the grounds of the estate, and he constructed a grand château-style mansion for himself and his family.

In 1981, the estate was divided when the Caja de Ahorros, a savings bank owned by the Government of Navarra, took over the vineyards and *bodega*, which lies some 7 km from the model village isolated in the depths of the Altos de Sarría. The rest of the estate still belongs to the Huarte family, and there are still about 25 families living and working in the model village.

The Señorío de Sarría was always famed above all for its red wines destined for oak ageing, even when the rest of Navarra was producing mainly *rosados*. Since 1981, the *bodega* has been expanded and modernized, and there is even more emphasis on the production of fine oak-aged red wines (there are currently 7000 *barricas* but this number will more than double to 15,000 in the next few years), produced from the traditional grapes of the zone, Tempranillo, Mazuelo, Graciano and Garnacha.

There are also small but significant plantations of Cabernet Sauvignon and Chardonnay.
English spoken.

---

8 BODEGAS IRACHE SL
31200 AYEGUI-ESTELLA
NAVARRA
TEL: (948) 55 19 32; FAX: (948) 55 49 54

WINES PRODUCED: Castillo Irache *rosado, tinto*; Castillo Irache *tinto* Reserva; Gran Irache *tinto* Crianza; Real Irache *tinto* Gran Reserva.
VISITS: Mon–Fri, working hours. Appointment appreciated but not essential. There is a small wine museum in the historic cellars, and there are furthermore plans for a visitors' centre in the new *bodega*. There are plans to build a drinking fountain on the wall of the *bodega* that looks over the old pilgrims'

track which will give the thirsty passer-by either a drink of water or a measured drink of wine. There are shaded picnic tables in front of the monastery.

Bodegas Irache, located next to the famous monastery south of Estella, is a leading private winery producing a range of excellent oak-aged red wines. The old cellars, used as a gun store during the Carlist struggles, are a remarkable contrast to the newly constructed and impressive winery, with its beautiful arched nave which will serve as a depository eventually for 15,000 *barricas*.

Restaurantes, Hoteles y Paradores

1 JOSETXO
PLAZA PRÍNCIPE DE VIANA 1
31000 PAMPLONA
NAVARRA
TEL: (948) 22 20 97

Closed Sun; August.
Pamplona's finest and best-known restaurant is luxurious and sophisticated yet still serves typical

Navarra foods as well as international specialities: *foie gras, pimientos del piquillo rellenos de tartar de langostinos, ajoarriero a la Navarra, corderito en chilindrón*. Has reputedly one of the best wine lists in Spain.
Expensive to Very Expensive

2

HOSTAL TAFALLA
CTRA ZARAGOZA, KM 38
31300 TAFALLA
NAVARRA
TEL: (948) 70 03 00; FAX: (948) 70 30 52

This popular and well-known wayside inn with rooms is located on the main road between Tafalla and Olite. It is noted above all for its fine restaurant serving sophisticated *nueva cocina navaresa – foie gras hecha en casa, carpacio de pato y jamón iberico, magret de pato*. There is also an informal self-service cafeteria serving good tasty local dishes such as *sopa de garbanzos* and *cordero en chilindrón*, accompanied by the young wines of Olite.

Restaurant **Expensive**

Cafeteria **Inexpensive**

Parador

P

PARADOR NACIONAL PRÍNCIPE DE
 VIANA
PLAZA DE LOS TEOBALDOS 2
31390 OLITE
NAVARRA
TEL: (948) 74 00 00; FAX: (948) 74 02 01

One of Spain's great castle *paradors*, located in the old palace of the Kings of Navarra, this makes an excellent base for exploration of the Navarra wine country.
Restaurant serves good local foods: *espárragos de Olite, cogote de merluza, cordero en chilindrón*.

Moderate

3

MESÓN LAS TORRES
31496 UJUÉ
NAVARRA
TEL: (948) 73 81 05

Open midday daily. Evenings by reservation.
Located next to Ujué's fortified sanctuary, this is a typical and wholly authentic *mesón* that should not be missed. There is a huge open fire in the corner of the dining room where *chuletas* are cooked over vine shoots, and *migas de pastor* are prepared in a long-handled *sartén*. Other specialities include *cordero en chilindrón, chorizo casero* and game in season. Come here, too, to purchase excellent honey as well as the famous candied *almendras garapiñadas de Ujué*.

Inexpensive

4
CASA IGNACIO
CORTADORES 9
31500 TUDELA
NAVARRA
TEL: (948) 82 10 21

Closed Tue.
Only exceptional quality local produce is utilized in this typical, locally famous Navarran eating house: *cogollos de Tudela, espárragos, menestra de verduras, tortilla de ajos tiernos*, and good grilled meats. Excellent *tapas* bar.
Moderate

5
HOSTAL RESTAURANTE MAHER
RIBERA 19
31592 CINTRUÉNIGO
NAVARRA
TEL: (948) 81 11 50; 81 11 51

There is not a great deal to Cintruénigo save the impressive Bodegas Julián Chivite, but this restaurant is also worth a detour. Young chef Enrique Martínez has transformed his family's bar-restaurant located nearly opposite the Chivite *bodega* into a stylish establishment serving traditional and innovative foods utilizing the superlative seasonal produce of the zone: *espárragos de Tudela, jamón de Jabugo, bonito a la brasa, conejo de monte guisado con setas y caracoles*, with a good selection of the wines of Cintruénigo and the Rioja.
Moderate

6
FONDA LORCA
CALLE MAYOR 54
31100 PUENTE LA REINA
NAVARRA
TEL: (948) 34 01 27

Typical and wholly authentic Navarran *fonda* on the main square of this atmospheric and historic pilgrims' town serving simple but outstanding home-cooked local foods: *sopa de garbanzos, borraja, paticas de cerdo, calamares en su tinta, leche frita* together with a good selection of local wines.
Inexpensive

7
RESTAURANTE LA CEPA
PLAZA DE LOS FUEROS 18
31200 ESTELLA
NAVARRA
TEL: (948) 55 00 32

Closed Wed.

Stylish little restaurant on Estella's main square serving traditional foods – especially excellent roast meats – as well as more innovative dishes.
Moderate

NAVARRA AND THE BASQUE COUNTRY

8 BAR RESTAURANTE CASANOVA
NUEVA 8
31200 ESTELLA
NAVARRA
TEL: (948) 55 28 09

Simple friendly first floor dining room above a lively bar serving typical foods of Navarra: *menestra de verduras, alubias rojas, trucha a la navarra, cordero al chilindrón* and wines of the Tierra de Estella. **Inexpensive**

Tomar Unas Copas: Stop for a Drink; Stop for a Bite

1 BAR ERBURU
SAN LORENZO 19–21
31000 PAMPLONA
NAVARRA
TEL: (948) 22 51 69

Pamplona is literally jam-packed with excellent bars serving good wines and *tapas*, especially in the old part of town. This is one of our favourites, friendly and with an excellent selection of *pinchos* and *tapas – bacalao ajoarriero, pimientos rellenos, callos, jamón de Jabugo –* and good Navarra wines by the glass or bottle. Also a pleasant little restaurant.

---

2 CAFÉ IRUŇA
PLAZA DEL CASTILLO 44
31000 PAMPLONA
NAVARRA

This stylish old-world café on Pamplona's main square is the place to hang out, nursing a chilled *cerveza* or a glass of *rosado* at the outdoor tables while watching the world go by. Incongruously, the interior houses a bingo hall.

Los Campings

CAMPING EZCABA
CTRA PAMPLONA–IRÚN, KM 7
ORICAIN-PAMPLONA
NAVARRA
TEL: (948) 33 03 15

Nearest campsite to Pamplona, pleasant with swimming pool.

CAMPING LIZARRA
CTRA N-111, A 1 KM DE ESTELLA
31200 ESTELLA
NAVARRA
TEL: (948) 55 17 33

Open all year.
In the country, 1 km from the lovely
Romanesque pilgrim town.
Swimming pool.

Vinos y Comestibles: Stop to Taste; Stop to Buy

LA VINOTECA
AVDA CARLOS III 71
AND
CALLE ESQUIROZ 22
31000 PAMPLONA
NAVARRA
TEL: (948) 24 89 31; 27 80 06

Excellent selection of wines,
home-made Pacharán, wine books
and accessories. Luís Fernández
Olaverri, the proprietor, is an
enthusiastic amateur of wines and
the first president of the Cofradía del
Vino de Navarra.

MUSEO DEL VINO
AVDA SANCHO EL FUERTE, 77 BAJO
31008 PAMPLONA
NAVARRA
TEL: (948) 27 98 77

Closed Sun.

Specialist wine shop located about
10 minutes outside the *casco
antiguo*. List includes old vintages
dating back to 1925. Also conserved
vegetables and Pacharán.
A little French spoken.

LA BODEGA
AVDA DE ZARAGOZA, 54 BAJOS
31500 TUDELA
NAVARRA
TEL: (948) 82 68 64

Closed Sun.

Specialist wine shop with an
extensive list especially strong on
Rioja and Navarra wines. Also
conserved *pimientos del piquillo*,
espárragos and Pacharán, as well
as some wine accessories, wine
skins, etc.

La Botería: The Age-old Craft of Handmade Wine Skins

Navarra was once a great centre for the production of *pellejos de cabra* and *botas*. *Pellejos* are whole goatskin receptacles, skilfully sewn together in a shape which preserves the form of the beast, legs and all, and lined with pitch to make them watertight. With a capacity of about 120 litres each, in the past they served primarily as containers for the transport of wine by mule train throughout central Spain.

The *bota*, on the other hand, is an altogether more intimate article and one which is still widely in use today. Indeed, it is traditionally the working man's constant companion and friend, a crescent- or tear-shaped leather wine bag containing usually about a litre, to be carried to the fields or workplace to quench the thirst that a man's work brings. The *bota* is held high above the head and squeezed with both hands, the *vino blanco* or *tinto* squirting into the back of the throat with a loud, forceful and eminently satisfying hiss.

Botería La Estellica, Estella.

Marceliano Diaz de Cerio's business in Estella is the oldest *botería* in Navarra, founded in 1860. His father and grandfather were also *boteros*, and before the Civil War the business kept five men employed full-time, producing 40–50 *pellejos* a month. Then the trucks came to replace the mule trains, and the *arrieros* as well as the *boteros* found themselves out of work.

Señor Diaz still makes his *botas* by hand according to traditional artisan methods. The best *botas* are made from goatskins turned inside out, the trimmed fur interior lined with boiling pitch resin. The hairy, pitchy surface in contact with the wine gives it an altogether unique and peculiarly Spanish flavour.

However, such traditional *botas* must be used regularly or else they will crack, dry out and leak. Therefore today Señor Diaz also makes *botas* with inert latex linings, especially recommended for those of us who do not take our *botas* to the office every day.

BOTERÍA LA ESTELLICA
PASEO DE LA INMACULADA 44
31200 ESTELLA
NAVARRA
TEL: (948) 55 04 42

The Basque Country

In Brief: The Basque Country, known as Euskadi, is a special, separate corner of Spain. From the French border along the north coast to west of Bilbao, and into the green and rugged foothills of the Pyrenees and the Cantabrian massif, the region remains wholly self-contained, in feel virtually a separate country within a country. The Basque coastal beach resorts are extremely popular with both Spanish and foreign tourists, but the interior remains little visited, its isolated villages and clusters of whitewashed *caseríos* untouched by time.

This is a strictly minor wine region (with the exception of the prestigious Rioja Alavesa, covered in our Rioja chapter). However, a unique country wine, Txakoli, is produced throughout the region and should be sampled on the spot with shellfish or fish. Txakoli de Getaria has recently been granted a *denominación de origen* and is without a doubt the best and most reliable of such wines, which is fortunate because Getaria itself is a lovely fishing village with a selection of exceptional *asador* restaurants serving charcoal-grilled fish.

Ernesto Chueca had been working in the vineyards when we met at the Caserío Gurutze in the steep ladder of hills that rise above the colourful fishing village of Getaria. It was a hot day and he was sweating hard. We shook hands, then immediately repaired down to the cellar beneath the house where he lives with his family. He opened an unlabelled bottle of Txakoli 'Txomin Etxaniz' and poured out the wine into large, wide, thin-glass tumblers. We clicked glasses, then he downed his in a single, thirsty draught, refilled his glass and drank deeply again.

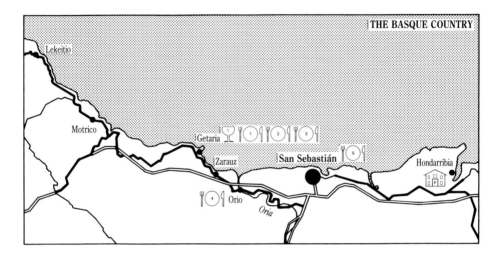

The wine was indeed deliciously quenching: extremely pale, with a delicate crab-apple perfume, and prickly bubbles that quickly rose in the glass but did not persist; it was light, refreshing and you felt that you could drink it in quantity all day and night.

Txakolì is a type of wine that is made throughout the Basque Country, traditionally in *caseríos* by rustic, primitive methods. The wine, which can be white, red or somewhere in between, is usually light in alcohol, slightly tart with malic acid and often turbid. Since it is usually home-made, the unlabelled bottles served in bars and restaurants can be of a standard that is more than variable, to say the least. Txakolì de Getaria is the only wine currently entitled to *denominación de origen* and as such, it is probably both the best example as well as the most reliable.

Ernesto Chueca explained to me that the wines of Getaria have been famous for centuries, protected from competition in the past by traditional and ancient *fueros*. When these were abolished in 1830, however, the vineyards declined as the market became flooded with stronger, cheaper wines from Navarra and Rioja. Yet, in small pockets here and there, winegrowing continued simply because Getaria was and remains a particularly favoured habitat for the vine and for the production of a unique wine that remains even today very much a part of the Basque cultural identity.

The balcony of hills between Getaria and Zarautz (there are only 47 hectares for the entire DO) is an extremely well-exposed corner of the Basque Country: though the annual rainfall is high, the vineyards face south-east and so receive maximum hours of sunlight, and they are well ventilated by the fresh breezes that come in from the sea. As a result, the Hondarribi Zuri (white) and Hondarribi Beltza (black) grapes ripen here to a reasonable degree – elsewhere Txakolìs may struggle to reach even as much as 8° or 9° alcohol; while Txakolì de Getaria must by law reach a minimum of 9.5°, the wines in this area almost always exceed 10.5° and often 11°.

Txakolì de Getaria is produced from a mixture of white and black grapes, planted together haphazardly in the steep terraced vineyards that look out to the sea. They are harvested together, quickly pressed, then the grapes are immediately separated from the skins and fermented *en blanco*. However, even this brief contact with black-skinned grapes (they usually account for about 15% of the harvest) always results in the leaching of some colour into the must so that, depending on the care of the winemaker, the resulting wine is either pale with the slightest blush of pink, or altogether somewhat deeper in colour.

Traditionally Txakolì is fermented in large oak vats known as *kupelaks*. Once fermented, the wines continue to age on their barrel sediment, a process that gives rounder, fuller flavour and helps to maintain the wine's refreshing *pétillant* prickle of carbonation.

Ernesto remembers that his father's customers would always come to the *caserío* in early spring to taste the wines direct from the wooden vat. This was known as the *probateko*, and it was an important annual event. Private customers, restaurateurs, men from Basque gastronomic societies would come to taste wines from the individual *kupelaks*, for there was always a certain degree of variation between each. A chef might choose to buy this entire *kupelak*, a buyer from a gastronomic society in San Sebastián might choose to buy those two in the corner. Deal struck, hands would be shaken and customer and winemaker would sit down together to a fish supper prepared by Ernesto's mother.

Many producers of Txakolì still make the wines in the old fashion, that is, fermented in wooden casks. The Chuecas, however, have modernized their winemaking installations and now enjoy the luxury of stainless steel fermentation vats which enable temperature-controlled fermentation. The wines are undoubtedly better for it, says Ernesto. True, the custom of the *probateko* no longer has quite the same meaning or purpose; none the less, long-standing family customers still come to the *caserío* each spring to taste wines from the stainless steel vat simply for the tradition of it. And indeed, such local customers still request that the wines are bottled unfiltered, as in the days of old.

Getaria, wine town and important Basque fishing port.

Chueca's Txakolì 'Txomin Etxaniz', produced from the family's 12 hectares of vineyards, is probably the best and best-known wine from Spain's
tiniest recognized quality wine region. There is a handful of other small
producers in Getaria and Zarautz producing and bottling wines, and they
too should be sought and tried by visitors to the area. These wines are best
enjoyed in quantity with great seafood feasts in any of the region's *asadores*
in fishing villages like Orio, Zarautz, Getaria, Motrico or Lekeitio. In these
basically simple eating houses, there is usually a simple iron grill set up
on four legs on the pavement in front of the restaurant, and this is used to
cook fish such as tuna steaks, sardines, *cogote de merluza* or that particularly Basque favourite, *besugo*.

Bodegas: Stop to Taste; Stop to Buy

1 TXAKOLÌ TXOMIN ETXANIZ
CASERÍO GURUTZE
20808 GETARIA
GUIPÚZCOA
TEL: (943) 83 27 02

WINE PRODUCED: Txakolì
'Txomin Etxaniz'
VISITS: Daily, working hours.
Telephone before coming.

Restaurantes, Hoteles y Paradores

1

TXOKO
KAIA GAINEAN
20808 GETARIA
GUIPÚZCOA
TEL: (943) 83 56 39

There are fancier and better-known restaurants in this popular fishing village, but the seafood here is impeccably fresh, it is well prepared, the outdoor tables overlook the harbour, and there are two or three Txakolìs on offer as well as a good selection of Riojas.
Moderate

2

TAILE-PE
SAN ANTÓN
20808 GETARIA
GUIPÚZCOA
TEL: (943) 83 16 13

Located at the far end of the fishing harbour at the base of 'El Raton', this fishermen's favourite specializes above all in shellfish: *txangurro, langosta, bogavante,* as well as good seafood *guisos* and grilled fish.
Moderate to Expensive

3

BAR AGUSTO
HERRERIETA 29
20808 GETARIA
GUIPÚZCOA
TEL: (943) 83 19 14

Just off the main road, this simple bar is handy for a hearty home-cooked Basque meal: *menu del día* may include *potaje, merluza frita, cuajada* and quaffable home-made Txakolì.
Inexpensive

4

BODEGÓN JOXE MARI
HERRICO ENPARANTZA
20810 ORIO
GUIPÚZCOA
TEL: (943) 83 00 32

Closed Mon.
Classic Basque *asador* with a pavement charcoal grill for the preparation of fish from the fleet in the harbour opposite. Orio is an unspoiled fishing village with a sheltered beach. It should be pointed out, incidentally, that fish throughout the region, especially the speciality *besugo,* is always expensive and sold according to weight at the prevailing market price, so always ask for the price beforehand to avoid unnecessary heart failure. Atmospheric rustic

beamed dining room and good
Txakolì de Getaria.
Moderate to Expensive

---

5 AKELARRE
BARRIO DE IGUELDO
20008 SAN SEBASTIÁN
GUIPÚZCOA
TEL: (943) 21 20 52

Closed Sun eve, Mon.
Pedro Subijana is one of the great
chefs of Spain: this wonderful
restaurant, located about 7 km
outside San Sebastián beyond

Monte Igueldo overlooking the sea,
has pioneered a sophisticated *nueva
cocina vasca* based on essential
Basque traditions and utilizing
superb Basque produce in a menu
of creativity and innovation that is
constantly evolving and adapting
to the seasons.
Very Expensive

Parador

P PARADOR NACIONAL EL EMPERADOR
PLAZA DE ARMAS DEL CASTILLO
20280 HONDARRIBIA
GUIPÚZCOA
TEL: (943) 64 21 40; FAX: (943) 64 21 53

Restored tenth-century castle of
Carlos V in the heart of this historic
medieval port town near the
French border.
Moderate

Tomar Unas Copas: Stop for a Drink; Stop for a Bite

Though the Basques like to distance themselves from all things 'Spanish',
in one sense at least they surpass all others in that most quintessential
Iberian activity: stopping at bars to '*tapear*'. No other region in Spain – not
Galicia, not even Andalucía – can surpass the Basque Country in either the
numbers or the excellence of its *tapas* bars. This is a land, after all, where
the custom of popping out for a '*chiquito*' – a small measure of red wine
usually served in a thin-glass tumbler – together with a nibble of this or
that is virtually an institution, and bars in cities and towns alike compete
fiercely for trade, attracting custom by the quality of their house wine as
well as by the variety of their usually exceptional bar-top snacks. Nowhere

is this activity better pursued than in the Parte Vieja of San Sebastián, the old quarter behind the fishing harbour, under the hilltop statue of Christ, and extending in from the far end of the famous Concha beach. This is a hive of narrow streets literally lined with bars, each serving a quite amazing and delicious array of bar-top *banderillas* unrivalled anywhere else in Spain – *pinchos*, *tapas*, *bocadillitos*, fried fish morsels, *tortillas*, *mariscos* and much else – accompanied by superb house wines usually from the Rioja Alavesa. There are too many such bars to single out: simply make your way here and enjoy.

Los Campings

GRAN CAMPING ZARAUZ
CTRA SAN SEBASTIÁN–BILBAO,
  KM 18,6
20800 ZARAUZ
GUIPÚZCOA
TEL: (943) 83 12 38

Open all year.

PLAYA DE ORIO
CTRA N-634, KM 19,5
20810 ORIO
GUIPÚZCOA
TEL: (943) 83 48 01

Open all year.
Situated by the beach; swimming pool.

CAMPING IGUELDO
CTRA SAN SEBASTIÁN–MONTE
  IGUELDO
20008 SAN SEBASTIÁN
GUIPÚZCOA
TEL: (943) 21 45 02

Open all year.
Situated outside San Sebastián, conveniently near the great Akelarre restaurant.

Vinos y Comestibles: Stop to Taste; Stop to Buy

VINOTECA OTAEGUI
CALLE SAN MARCIAL 5
20005 SAN SEBASTIÁN
TEL: (943) 42 18 92; FAX: (943) 42 97 19

Closed Sun, Mon morning, holidays.
One of the best speciality shops in Spain, located in the centre of San Sebastián. Vinoteca has a selection of over 900 wines from every region

of Spain, as well as the classic wine regions of the world. Good selection of Txakolì, as well as other products of the Basque Country. There is always a selection of wines to taste, changed every month. French spoken.

¡Fiesta! Wine and Other Related Celebrations

6–14 July	Fiesta de San Fermín	Pamplona
every Sun in Aug	Día del Txakolì	Getaria

Las Sanfermínes

Spain's craziest and most famous festival shows no sign of running out of steam as literally thousands of Spanish and foreign tourists descend on this otherwise sober capital for one week of the year to witness or join in Pamplona's famous *encierro* or 'running of the bulls'. Immortalized by Hemingway in his novel *The Sun Also Rises*, this remarkable event continues to be carried out today even though every year there are injuries, gorings, even deaths. Every morning for a week, precisely at 7 a.m., a skyrocket is launched marking the release of six fighting bulls from their corral in the old part of town near the Plaza Santo Domingo. As the bulls tear through the fenced-off cobbled streets, youths dressed all in white wearing red belts and bandanas, men, women, anyone crazy enough to attempt it, try to run in front of or alongside the bulls on their rampant journey to the Plaza de Toros. This terrifying and foolhardy event lasts just a few minutes and apparently the rest of the day (and night) is spent imbibing sufficient alcohol to summon up enough courage to attempt it again the next day. Meanwhile, the bullfights themselves are famous and attract the country's best *toreros*. Hotel rooms are virtually impossible to come by (and prices double at least).

Y para saber más Additional Information

Delegacion de Turismo
Arrieta 11-5°
31000 Pamplona
Navarra
tel: (948) 23 06 22

Viceconsejería de Turismo
Gobierno Vasco
Calle Duque de Wellington 2
01000 Gasteiz-Vitoria
Alava
tel: (945) 24 60 00

Consejo Regulador de Navarra
Conde Oliveto 2
31002 Pamplona
Navarra
tel: (948) 22 78 52

Consejo Regulador de Txakolì de
 Getaria
Caserío Gurutze
20808 Getaria
Guipúzcoa
tel: (943) 83 27 02

Consejo Regulador de Pacharán
Calle Serafin Olave 31, 1°
31007 Pamplona
Navarra
tel: (948) 26 59 60;
fax: (948) 27 84 31

LA RIOJA

La Granja Nuestra Señora de Remelluri.

Rioja may be Spain's most famous table wine, but La Rioja, the region, is far from well known. Like most of inland Spain away from the tourist-infested *costas*, it remains little visited and certainly not an obvious destination. It has not always been so: La Rioja, like Navarra to the north, lies along the *Camino de Santiago*, and for centuries at least, towns such as Logroño (the region's capital), Nájera and Santo Domingo de la Calzada were essential halts along one of Europe's main religious and cultural arteries. Medieval pilgrims no doubt sampled the fine wines of the region en route, for Rioja wine has been popular and applauded for centuries.

Today, La Rioja is a small inland autonomous region, located along the sheltered, verdant valley of the Ebro below the rugged Sierra de Cantabria. As in the past, it remains a crossroads, linking the northern Atlantic Basque and Cantabrian coasts with Catalunya; Navarra and the north with historic Old Castile. Basques, Romans, Arabs, Navarrese, Castilians, Jews, Aragonese: all have passed through and left their mark here.

As long ago as the 12th century, the *Codex Calixtus* (a medieval manuscript part of which includes a descriptive and practical account of the *Camino de Santiago* – possibly the first ever European tourist guide) commented on the hospitality of the people of the Rioja. Certainly centuries of catering to foreigners passing through has left the locals free of suspicion of outsiders (the same cannot be said for many parts of inland Spain), and La Rioja remains one of the friendliest and most welcoming of all the country's varied wine regions.

Of course, from our biased point of view, it is above all for wine that the region is renowned and the principal reason for visiting it. For La Rioja is quite simply Spain's greatest table wine region, producing a range primarily of warm, silky, oak-aged reds, as well as both modern and traditional white wines, that is unrivalled in prestige and quality anywhere else. There are literally scores of famous companies who welcome visitors and provide remarkable opportunities to witness cellar techniques in cobwebbed *bodegas* virtually unchanged since the turn of the century, alongside modern installations that are as up-to-date as anywhere in the world. This essential contrast between the arch-conservative and the ultra-modern is one of the most fascinating aspects of the region.

In addition to its famous wines, the Rioja also offers the wine lover a delicious regional cuisine based on the excellent fresh vegetables and market produce, as well as on roast lamb and chops cooked over vine shoots, basically simple foods that go so well with the red wines of the region.

La Rioja extends much beyond its fabled and famous wine country and the region has much to offer in addition to its great wines and foods. As in Navarra, the pilgrims' way to Santiago de Compostela has left a rich legacy of monumental sites, with notable Romanesque monasteries, convents, churches, hospitals and pilgrims' hospices all along the way, in Logroño itself, Navarrete, Nájera, San Millán de la Cogolla and its monasteries of Yuso and Suso, and Santo Domingo de la Calzada. Outside the wine country, the steep *sierras* which are never far from view provide spectacular mountain country, and *pueblos* such as Ezcaray are popular for walking excursions to Monte San Lorenzo, as well as with hunters. Valdezcaray, by contrast, is a winter resort with good facilities for skiing.

If in the past, pilgrims pushed through the region on their way to Saint James's shrine on the Galician coast, the wine lover today, even if en route to the sunny resorts of the south, will certainly want to stop here long enough to explore Spain's greatest wine area, and to sample the great wines of Rioja at source.

LOS VINOS: THE WINES OF RIOJA

Rioja DOCa Rioja is Spain's first recipient of select *denominación de origen calificada* status; this applies to red, *rosado* and white table wines produced to stringent guidelines and minimum ageing requirements from approved grapes grown within the demarcated vineyard extending approximately from Haro east along the Ebro

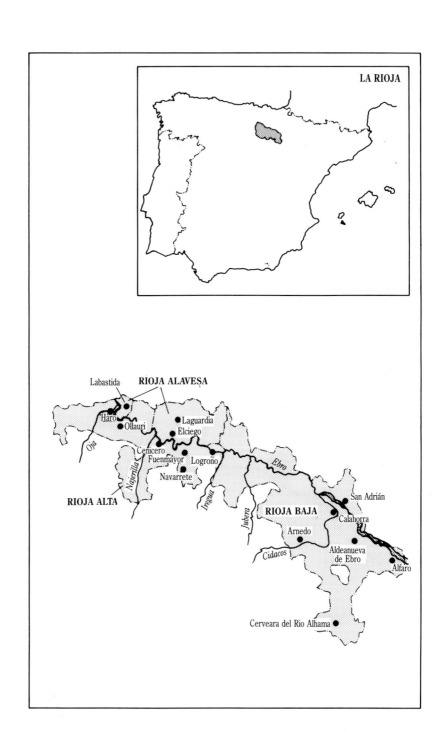

LA RIOJA

Labastida   **RIOJA ALAVESA**

Haro   • Laguardia
Ollauri   • Elciego
Oja
Cenicero
Fuenmayor   Logroño
Navarrete
Najerilla
Ebro
RIOJA ALTA
San Adrián
Iregua
Calahorra
Jubera   **RIOJA BAJA**
Arnedo
Cidacos   Aldeanueva
de Ebro   Alfaro

Cerveara del Rio Alhama   •

Orientation

La Rioja is the smallest autonomous region on the Spanish mainland, sandwiched between Navarra and the Basque Country to the north, Aragon to the east, and Castilla y León to the south and west. The delimited Rioja wine zone actually extends beyond the boundaries of the Rioja political region, and encompasses parts of the Basque Alava province and a tiny part of Navarra.

The most convenient international airport is Bilbao, which is about 2 hours by car from Logroño. There are also domestic flights to Vitoria. The region, located on the principal rail and road routes linking Bilbao with Zaragoza and Barcelona, is accessible and well served by communications. There are frequent direct train and coach services from Logroño to Madrid, 336 km away.

La Rioja can be most easily dipped into by those travelling north or south to or from France, or to or from Santander (by way of the ferry link with Plymouth).

Maps: Michelin No. 442 (Northern & Central); Firestone Hispania C-3.

valley to Alfaro about 100 km away. Red and *rosado* wines may be produced from Tempranillo, Garnacha, Mazuelo and Graciano. White wines are produced from Viura, Malvasia and Garnacha Blanca. The new '*calificada*' status imposes further strictures, including mandatory bottling in the zone of origin, further controls on viticulture and vinification, and the probable future creation of smaller designated quality sub-zones.

The Rioja demarcated vineyard measures about 44,000 hectares and is divided into three sub-regions: Rioja Alta, the westernmost area, producing sturdy, long-lived wines of medium strength (minimum alcohol 10° for reds, whites and *rosados*); Rioja Alavesa, so named because it lies within the Basque province of Alava, noted foremost for its wines of great delicacy and charm (minimum alcohol 11.5° for reds and 11° for whites and *rosados*); and Rioja Baja, the easternmost and hottest zone, producing sturdy red wines that are high in alcohol and ideal for blending (minimum alcohol 12.5° for reds and 12° for whites and *rosados*).

The *Consejo Regulador de Rioja* is one of the most rigorous and strict in the country, undertaking a variety of measures to ensure the

LA RIOJA

authenticity of wines entitled to the DOCa. It furthermore lays down minimum requirements relating to the ageing of wines, and to this end awards back labels to wines that have met the following qualifications (it should be borne in mind that the year of the harvest counts as the first year; thus a wine becomes second year – 2° *año* – in the January following its harvest):

Vino del año   Young wine usually from the latest harvest, although the vintage year does not need to be indicated.

Vino sin crianza   Rioja wine in its first or second year which has undergone less than one year's ageing in oak cask (in many cases such wines may spend no time at all in wood).

Vino de Crianza   Red Rioja wine that has undergone a minimum of 12 months in oak cask and a further 6 months in bottle. Such wine may not be released before its third year. White and *rosado* Crianza wines must undergo a mandatory 6 months' ageing in wood.

Reserva   Selected red Rioja wine that has undergone a minimum ageing of 12 months in cask, and in total 36 months between cask and bottle. Such wine may not be released until its fourth year after the vintage. White and *rosado* Reserva wines must undergo a minimum of 6 months' wood ageing and a total minimum ageing of at least 2 years.

Gran Reserva   Rare selected red Rioja produced in the best years only; minimum ageing requirements are 24 months in cask and 36 months in bottle (or vice versa). Red Gran Reserva wines may not be released until the sixth year after the harvest. White and *rosado* Gran Reserva wines must spend a minimum of 6 months in cask and not be released before a total of 4 years.

Other drinks

Zurracapote   Type of Riojan *sangría*, usually consumed in liberal quantity in local wine and other festivals: made from *rosado* or young *tinto* wine mixed with fruit, sugar, juice and brandy.

LA GASTRONOMÍA: FOODS OF LA RIOJA

The verdant Ebro valley is the abundant source not only of the great wines of the Rioja, but also of a huge variety of fine produce and food products which are employed in a basically simple but robust and authentic *cocina* that is among the most attractive of regional tables in all Spain.

Vegetables in abundance are the mainstay of the Rioja diet, prepared in

Eating in *Bodegas:* A Tradition of Hospitality

The great *bodegas* of the Rioja are among the most hospitable and welcoming that we have encountered anywhere in the world. There is a long-standing tradition here of '*reuniones en la bodega*' – cellar get-togethers among groups of friends to drink, talk, eat and drink some more.

At the Castillo Ygay of Marqués de Murrieta, the *bodega comedor*, a beautiful wood-panelled dining room, its enormous stately table laid with china, silverware and crystal goblets, has a large window that looks directly into the cellar below; as privileged guests, customers and friends enjoy the succession of dishes cooked by the Conde de Creixell's first-class private chef and accompanied by the great wines of Murrieta, it is rather bizarre to observe the blue-overalled cellar workers below, busily at work with the racking or finishing of the wines.

In other cases, the dining may be somewhat less formal, yet no less welcoming. At La Granja Remelluri, for example, we enjoyed the hospitality of a true family meal, seated at the long trestle table in the restored farmhouse in front of a crackling fire made from vine shoots. As we dined and discussed wine with the Rodriguez family, we gained an impression of how decisions are made by consensus around the kitchen table at this unique single-vineyard family estate.

Usually, the foods cooked in such settings are the simple but classic *platos riojanos* which go so well with the wines. The great French chef Paul Bocuse, for example, was brought over to cook in the private kitchens of CVNE for the celebration of its 100th anniversary in 1979, but when he tasted the *bodega* cook's *patatas riojanas*, he reputedly asked why he was needed. We have enjoyed such simple dishes as *pimientos asados* roasted on a fork by the *bodeguero* himself, the blackened skin peeled, the red peppers sliced then stewed in olive oil and garlic, while there is no finer meal than the supremely simple *chuletas al sarmiento*, tiny milk-fed lamb chops cooked over a fire of vine shoots in the *bodega* dining room.

Some *bodegas* have taken to opening their private dining rooms to the public by previous arrangement. For small groups of individuals or wine lovers, I can think of no finer way to experience something of the food, wine and hospitality of the region. *Bodegas* which offer this excellent service include La Rioja Alta SA, Bodegas Berberana and Bodegas Campo Viejo.

LA RIOJA

any number of imaginative ways. The most famous is the classic *menestra de verduras*, a sort of stewed vegetable medley found throughout northern Spain, though nowhere else is it prepared so carefully and meticulously: the individual vegetables are each cooked separately (sometimes dipped in egg and flour and fried), then assembled in a saffron-scented sauce of wine, garlic, onions and *jamón*. Other great vegetable dishes of Rioja include *pimientos asados, patatas a la riojana, pochas con chorizo*: all are supremely simple yet delicious and hearty foods of the land.

The Rioja region is inland and land-locked, yet because Haro was once an important market for the distribution of fresh and dried fish throughout central Spain, there is a great tradition of fish dishes that are still enjoyed. Thanks to its geographical and historical proximity, many are variations of Basque classics – *merluza en salsa verde, bacalao al pil-pil, besugo a la brasa* – while the favourite local dish is *bacalao a la riojana* – dried salt cod stewed with olive oil, garlic and *pimientos*.

However, above all, this is a land of meat-eaters. The *chorizo* sausage of the region is famed for its excellence; strongly flavoured, slightly hot, yet soft-textured and not overly chewy, it is a delicious nibble with a *chiquito* of young *vino de cosechero*. This is a region that enjoys game of every sort, while the popular *bodeguero*'s favourite is simply *chuletas al sarmiento* – tender baby lamb chops cooked over a fire of vine shoots. And of course, the great speciality of Rioja, as in Old Castile, is the preparation of meats – especially tender milk-fed lamb (*lechazo*) – classically roasted in a wood-fired *horno de asar*. As in Bordeaux, where a similar essentially simple cuisine has evolved to partner that region's great wines, in Rioja such foods perfectly complement the region's great oak-aged Reservas and Gran Reservas.

¡*Que aproveche!* Regional Specialities of La Rioja

Alubias con chorizo Tiny white beans, cooked with *chorizo* to make an orange-tinged soupy stew. In season, fresh undried beans known as *pochas* are favoured and are superlative.

Menestra de verduras Classic vegetable stew made with fresh produce such as peas, beans, artichokes, potatoes, onions, tomatoes, garlic, and whatever else may be in season. The vegetables are usually all cooked separately (sometimes fried first), then assembled and stewed with *jamón*, wine, saffron and oil.

Patatas riojanas Supremely simple but delicious first course of potatoes, stewed with *chorizo*, garlic and red pepper.

Pimientos asados Red peppers roasted over an open flame until the skin is blackened, then peeled, and dressed in olive oil and garlic.

Bacalao a la riojana Salt cod stewed with olive oil, garlic and red peppers.

Lechazo asado (cordero lechal asado) Very young milk-fed lamb, usually rubbed simply with garlic, and roasted in an extremely hot wood-fired baker's oven until meltingly tender: the classic food of Rioja.

Chuletas al sarmiento Tiny baby lamb chops grilled over a fire of vine shoots.

Cuajada Junket made from ewe's milk, usually served in a wooden bowl with honey or sugar.

THE WINES AND WINE ROADS OF RIOJA

In Brief: For such a famous and important wine region, the Rioja is relatively compact and easy to explore. The entire distance from Haro to Alfaro is only 100 km, and it is only 43 km between Logroño and Haro. The principal wine country, and the greatest concentration of *bodegas*, is found between those two important wine towns, and some days or weeks could be dedicated to exploring this area. The Rioja Baja, south-east of Logroño and centred on Calahorra, is for the less single-minded wine tourist. Both Logroño and Haro have excellent hotels and a range of superlative inexpensive to moderate restaurants serving local foods; each has a campsite.

The Wines of Rioja: Past and Present

In spite of challenges from up-and-coming wine regions such as Ribera del Duero, Penedés and Navarra, Rioja remains Spain's premier table wine region, a position it has held for well over a hundred years. Indeed, in a country where the concept of wine as a fine or precious commodity is still in its relative infancy, Rioja has for long been almost the only regional ambassador of premium Spanish table wines abroad. Even within Spain, Rioja has long stood as virtually the only table wine that could be found

LA RIOJA

reliably on almost every restaurant wine list the width and breadth of the country.

The vine certainly has deep and long-established roots in the fertile Ebro valley that extends from the lower slopes of the Sierra de Cantabria and the fringes of the Basque Country, way down to the wide, hotter plains of the Ebro basin south of Calahorra. Not only was this a propitious habitat from time immemorial, it was also a natural thoroughfare and corridor, a crossroads of cultures and civilizations. While the Romans almost certainly planted the first systematic vineyards in the region in the first and second centuries before Christ, it was the medieval age, after the Reconquest of the region from the Moors, that saw the wide-scale expansion and recovery of the wine territory of the Rioja.

Rioja, after all, was located along the *Camino de Santiago*, one of the most intensively used roads in medieval Christendom, traversed by literally millions of thirsty pilgrims for hundreds of years. Encouraged by the Kings of Navarra, whose jurisdiction much of the region came under, monasteries such as San Millán de la Cogolla, Santa María de la Real de Nájera, San Martín de Abelda and Santo Domingo de la Calzada planted extensive vineyard holdings so that by the tenth and eleventh centuries the wine country was well-established. Medieval scripts document the sale of vine-yards in villages or convents and abbeys near or along the road to Santiago. Monks from Cluny and elsewhere throughout Europe, as they passed through the region, carried with them further knowledge of viticulture and winemaking. And wines were made and drunk in liberal quantity, in the monasteries, abbeys and convents themselves, as well as by thirsty and eager pilgrims undertaking what was for many of them the greatest adven-ture of their lives.

Historical antecedents notwithstanding, the wines of medieval Rioja, though probably passably good for their time, bore little or no relation to the wines of the Rioja as we know them today. Indeed, the majority of vineyards, as elsewhere in Spain, were planted with white grapes. Haro – 'La Ciudad de Jarreros', the City of Jug-makers – was famous in the six-teenth century for its white wines above all, and documents note the over-whelming preponderance of the sale of white wines over reds. Even in this early era, however, the first association of wine growers was created in 1560 in order to guarantee the origin and quality of the wines of Rioja.

By the seventeenth century, the region had become renowned for its light red wines, traded to Spanish colonies in the Americas, and which came to be widely appreciated by the claret-loving British as early as the seventeenth and eighteenth centuries. The wines of Rioja, it seems, have long looked north and abroad for their commercial impetus, never south to the nation's capital.

In 1787, Don Manuel Esteban Quintano y Quintano, a native of Labistida, and later dean of the Santa Iglesia Metropolitana of Burgos, attempted to introduce enlightened French techniques of viticulture, vinification, ageing and transport of wines with the aim of improving and conserving the region's products so as to further sales, primarily in overseas markets. This was indeed a pressing need, for wines incapable of conservation clearly had little export potential. Though initially successful (in 1795 the ship *La Natividad* sailed from Santander loaded with 9760 litres of Rioja wine, eventually reaching Havana and Veracruz with the wines in perfect condition), Quintano's reforms were eventually quashed by narrow local interests and jealous municipal officials eager to maintain the status quo. His further efforts were interrupted by the outbreak of the Peninsular War.

In the mid-nineteenth century, the *Diputación Foral de Alava* attempted once more to introduce French methods of viticulture and vinification on its *La Granja Modela de la Diputación de Alava*, a model farming community. The officials contracted the services of an oenologist from the Médoc, Monsieur Jean Pineau, to initiate French practices in both vineyard and cellar. However, lack of resources and resistance to change were apparently too much for the Frenchman; frustrated, Pineau abandoned his efforts on the model farm, and in 1868 moved to Elciego where he was contracted by Don Camilo Hurtado de Amézaga, Marqués de Riscal, who granted him the freedom and ample funds to build the region's first modern French-style *bodega*.

Pineau's great innovation at the time was the introduction at Riscal of French systems of vinification, based on de-stemming and crushing the grapes before vatting and fermentation in large oak *tinas*. After the first or tumultuous fermentation, the wines underwent the secondary malolactic fermentation, usually in large vats, which was then followed by a traditional ageing discipline in 225-litre oak *barricas*, the standard cask size of Bordeaux. This method was in marked contrast to the local peasant custom of whole grape fermentation in open stone *lagos*, producing fruity wines for immediate, youthful consumption, but which were unsuitable for conservation.

These initial innovations were highly successful and were followed and developed elsewhere in the region. Bodegas Marqués de Murrieta was actually making and exporting wines some decades before its aristocratic rival

Riscal was even founded. Indeed, Don Luciano de Murrieta, after a brief apprenticeship in Bordeaux, brought French viticulture and vinification techniques to his estate, too, and undoubtedly it was such methods that led to the early fame and commercial success of the prestigious wines of 'Chateau Ygay' as they were already known by the end of the nineteenth century. Other producers followed this lead, and viticulture in the Rioja was thus firmly set on a quality-driven path that was to lead it in directions far and away from Spain's other wine regions, and which enabled it to reach the commanding position it maintains today.

The wines of Rioja received a further spectacular commercial boost when the French vineyards were struck down first by oidium (a particularly pervasive and damaging form of powdery mildew) then, in the 1880s, by the catastrophic outbreak of phylloxera, an epidemic which led to the wholesale destruction of virtually all the vineyards in France. Naturally, this disaster presented an opportunity for winegrowers from scores of other regions and countries to fill the shortfall of wine from Bordeaux, Burgundy and elsewhere. The French-style oak-aged wines of Rioja were considered especially suitable either for blending with claret or to be used as an outright substitute, and the region's proximity to France was a further advantage. Thus, a brisk trade soon developed, with French merchants settling in Haro, and with the creation there of new *bodegas* sited conveniently by the new railway line that led to Miranda del Ebro, Bilbao and eventually north to France. Indeed, some of the greatest names in the Rioja date from this period; in the *barrio de la estación* in Haro, for example, R. López de Heredia was founded in 1877; CVNE in 1879; La Rioja Alta in 1890; and Bodegas Bilbainas in 1901.

Phylloxera, of course, finally reached the Rioja by the turn of the century (virtually no vineyards in Europe escaped its ravages). Though the damage was profound, it was not catastrophic. The *Estación de Viticultura y Enología* in Haro, founded in 1892, was prepared and ready to arrest the spread of the disease within only a few years. The means of dealing with this pest had already been perfected elsewhere, and the growers were thus able to replant their vineyards with the indigenous local vines grafted on to phylloxera-resistant American rootstocks.

The Rioja wine industry continued to prosper and expand through the early part of the twentieth century as the fame of its smooth, oak-aged wines spread and found favour both nationally and internationally. The oak barrel was originally used primarily as a means of storage, a receptacle for spontaneous clarification and stabilization, and for transport. Of course, it was soon realized that the oak barrel did much more than merely serve as a container; it also had the unique propensity to improve the wines held therein by imparting the smoothness and sweet vanilla tannins present in the wood itself.

The reputation of the great *bodegas* of the Rioja thus came to be based upon their quite considerable expertise in the oak ageing of wines and the handling of quite immense quantities of *barricas*. Indeed, long after the French had themselves abandoned lengthy cask ageing in favour of shorter stays in barrel followed by more lengthy periods in bottle, the traditional and lengthy maturation of Rioja wines in oak *barricas* continued and continues even today. Hardly any other region in the entire world of wine holds proportionally such enormous stocks of wine in 225-litre barrels. There are

Racking

'Here in Rioja, we would consider it a fault if our wines had to be decanted because of heavy bottle sediment prior to drinking,' one *bodega* owner told me.

As red wine ages in the cask, it sheds a deposit of dead yeast cells, crystal tartrates, and other solid matter. To render the wine clear and to ensure that it does not pick up tainted flavours from the sediment, the wine must be racked, that is, transferred to clean barrels in order to remove it from its lees. This is one of the most fascinating tasks to be seen in a traditional Rioja *bodega*. At La Rioja Alta SA, for example, there are three full-time teams who do nothing but rack wine day in and day out. Considering that this traditional *bodega* has some 32,000 barrels, and that each is racked twice a year, one can understand the dimensions of the task.

To rack wines, the oak *barricas* are emptied usually by gravity into a clean barrel below. The *bodeguero* must quickly and deftly remove the *falsete* or bung from the front of the cask and insert a brass tap. The wine flows freely into a barrel below, while the *bodeguero* carefully monitors its clarity by holding a glassful up to the light of a candle. When it becomes the least bit cloudy, the tap is closed, and the barrels are sent off to be steam cleaned and disinfected. The remaining turbid wine, usually a few litres at least, may either be sent off to be distilled or it may be reserved. At La Rioja Alta, for example, it is collected in special vats, allowed to clear again, then drawn off and distributed free to the cellar workers, a generous ration of a *garrafa* (16 litres) each fortnight.

at present some 600,000 barrels of wine ageing in the Rioja, and the number is still growing. Add to this the fact that about 5–8% of such barrels are replaced each year, and this highlights the continued importance of wood-ageing wines in the Rioja.

Clearly, Rioja remains one of the most traditional of all wine regions. Many *bodegas* still have their own *tonelería* – cooperage – if no longer solely for the production of their own *barricas*, then at least for their continual repair and maintenance. The manual or semi-manual transfer of wine from vat to cask and cask to cask is carried out today as in the past, the *barricas*, after being cleaned, disinfected and re-filled, are rolled up wooden ladders to be piled as many as five high and chocked manually with blocks.

Yet tradition in Rioja is not followed slavishly simply for the sake of it, or to maintain a historic image at the expense of quality. For example, many *bodegas* still consider it necessary to use the traditional beaten egg white to clarify and fine their wines. At the region's most ultra-traditional *bodega*, R. López de Heredia, not only are the Gran Reserva wines fined with beaten egg white, they are then bottled by hand directly from the *barrica*. Such antiquated hand-care, and its consequent lack of cost-effectiveness, must be a financial director's nightmare. Yet this is done for a very specific reason, explained Don José Ossés, the company's Export Director. 'We want our old wines to emerge from the cellar as bright as diamonds. Beaten egg white is still the finest fining agent, but after the sediment has settled, we want to disturb as little of it as possible. For this reason, we bottle by hand direct from the *barrica*.'

Elsewhere, in another famous traditional *bodega*, Bodegas Muga, beaten egg white is also used, but primarily because Isaac Muga feels that it gives his wines a softer flavour, and rounds off the astringency that lengthy wood ageing can give. There is nothing old-fashioned about the prestigious and forward-thinking La Granja Remelluri estate. But here, too, beaten egg white is chosen, not only because it is a natural product in this environmen-tally-aware *bodega* but also, quite simply, because it is deemed to give the best results.

Rioja, with its century-old tradition of oak-aged wines, has rightly long enjoyed its prestigious position as Spain's premier quality table wine region. Today, in a wine world increasingly dominated by Cabernet Sauvignon and Chardonnay wines, Rioja stands proudly apart and is still unique. Cabernet is not allowed officially in the Rioja vineyard (though it is planted on a small-scale 'experimental' basis), for in Tempranillo, the Riojans believe that they have a grape of world class and distinctive character that can compete with any. In refusing to permit the introduction of 'foreign' grape varieties, moreover, the Riojans express their awareness of the need to maintain a clear identity which distinguishes their wines from those produced anywhere else in the world.

Maintaining its historical identity and tradition, however, should not denote that Rioja is living in the past. The last decade in particular has seen massive investment in the region by the best *bodegas* on a scale that is quite awesome. Marqués de Murrieta is one of the region's most traditional *bodegas*; under the new ownership of Vicente Cebrián Sagarriga, Conde de Creixell, there have been significant expansions and innovations in both the vineyard and the winery. The property currently has some 180 hectares of its own vineyards in production, but, through major earth-moving projects to reclaim otherwise unsuitable land, this will be extended by another 75 hectares in the course of the next decade. That should enable Murrieta to supply 100% of its own grapes (at present about 20% of grapes are bought in from a farm under the control and direction of Murrieta).

In the *bodega*, a modern new vinification plant with gleaming stainless steel vats has replaced the old oak *tinas* for the fermentation of the wines. However, to maintain Murrieta's unique style of long-lived wines, there are modern innovations based firmly on long-standing tradition. For example, to gain sufficient extract, colour and tannin for the production of wines capable of lengthy conservation, *bodegueros* in the Rioja have traditionally employed a practice known as '*bazuqueo*' whereby the *sombrero*, or dense mass of grape skins and pips in the fermentation vat, was kept moist by being broken up, stirred and lifted by hand with wooden shovels and spiked poles. This labour-intensive task has now been virtually abandoned in favour of *remontaje* (the process whereby grape must is taken from the bottom of the vat and pumped back and sprayed over the cap of skins). However, in Murrieta's new vinification plant, the age-old method of *bazuqueo* is achieved mechanically with remarkable specially-designed telescopic, articulated arms that can be extended into each vat to stir the mass before moving along on rails to the next one, a key process carried out in addition to *remontaje*.

Another example of modern innovation based on historical tradition can be seen in the remarkable new vinification plant of CVNE in Haro, one of the region's largest but most highly-respected traditional producers. When Don José Madrazo wanted to build a new vinification plant to replace his old epoxy-lined cement fermentation vats, he remembered how, even before the cement vats had been installed in the *bodega*, small *cubillos* of grapes

Barrel store in CVNE's Haro *bodega*.

used to be lifted by mechanical cranes to fill the old wooden *tinas*. This led him to develop a remarkable and unique system whereby the grapes, once de-stemmed and crushed, could be transferred to small 5000-kg rotary receptacles which then could be lifted and deposited precisely into any one of over 100 different new 25,000 kg stainless steel fermentation vats. This system, although inspired by earlier methods, is hugely innovative, for it clearly offers significant advantages in the precise control and selection of small quantities of grapes, particularly necessary for the pursuit of quality since CVNE's production demands mean that the company's grapes come from a variety of sources and sub-zones.

The region's co-operatives – there are about 30 – have similarly invested considerably within the last decade to improve their winemaking facilities and installations, as well as to provide crucial technical support in the vineyard to their winegrower members. The co-operatives have traditionally supplied much of the bulk wine to the great *bodegas* to be blended, matured and marketed by them, rather than elevating and commercializing the wine themselves (the excellent Santa Daria Cooperative in Cenicero is a notable exception). Today, as more and more *bodegas* are seeking to purchase grapes rather than wine, I wonder if the co-operatives will have to change their function and become more market aware?

Bodegas Berberana, a large company 50% owned jointly by seven co-operative wineries from throughout the region, is an example of how co-operative-made wines can be commercialized successfully. The wines of this immense group account for a staggering 12–15% of the total production of Rioja (second in volume only to Campo Viejo). Each of its member co-operatives (three in Rioja Baja and four in Rioja Alta) produces its own wines, and these are subsequently assembled and aged in the functional and immense central *bodega* in Cenicero. Yet the impressive range of Berberana wines, especially the Carta de Oro white and red wines and the top-quality Reservas and Gran Reservas, clearly demonstrates how fine such wines can be, even when produced on such an immense scale.

Elsewhere new and sometimes quite spectacular *bodegas* continue to be created, almost it seems overnight. In the last decade alone the number of *bodegas* in Rioja has doubled. One of the most impressive is the newly inaugurated Bodegas Campillo in Laguardia. This architecturally magnifi- cent edifice in the heart of the Rioja Alavesa was actually created to give a physical identity to a long-established brand of wines produced by the prestigious Bodegas Faustino Martínez. However, Bodegas Campillo, though wholly owned by Faustino Martínez, will function entirely indepen- dently; it has planted its own vineyards in the Rioja Alavesa, and aims to produce wines for the top end of the market from 100% Tempranillo grapes aged in a mixture of French and American oak casks. Other equally striking modern *bodegas* that stand as something of a sharp contrast to the tra- ditional cobwebbed image include Bodegas Ollara in Logroño and Bodegas Montecillo in Fuenmayor, among others.

These few examples give some idea of the energy and investment under way in Spain's oldest quality wine region. The aim throughout, clearly, is to maintain and improve the high standards of the existing wines of the Rioja, as well as to increase the prestige of the zone. There is far less emphasis here, on the other hand, on experimentation, innovation or the introduction of new styles or types of wines. Indeed, there is even a return to the traditional. For example, white Rioja, like red, used to undergo lengthy maturation in oak until the advent of cold-fermentation techniques led to the virtual abandonment of such classic wines. Admittedly, not all the wines of old were that great: many, apparently, were stale, oxidized and totally lacking in fruit or charm. When introduced, the new-style wines, produced mainly from the neutral Viura grape, were considered refreshingly crisp and modern in style, and they have proved hugely successful. However, it must be said that they are not overly distinctive or different from similar cold-fermented wines produced anywhere else in Spain. Traditional oak- aged white Rioja from the best producers – El Dorado de Murrieta and R. López de Heredia's Viña Tondonia Reservas – are unique and among the great white wines of the world, while the region's best-selling Crianza white wine, Monopole from CVNE, though less oaked than the two classic examples above, is particularly successful at combining the refreshing lemony fruit of the Viura with a well-rounded polish of new oak. These wines are so excellent – and so different from those produced virtually anywhere else in the world – that it is no wonder, in my opinion, that many *bodegas* are now reconsidering a return to the production of traditional oak-aged white Rioja.

Tour of the Wine Country

The wine region of the Rioja is a tale of two cities surrounded and connected by prestigious vineyards. Logroño is the region's capital, and an important commercial and business centre as well as a major wine town, while Haro is considerably smaller, more charming, busily awash with wine, and the true capital of the wine region. No wine-loving visitor to Rioja will wish to miss spending time in both.

Begin a tour in the region's capital, today a city of more than 110,000 inhabitants and a busy modern metropolis. The wide Ebro river passes languidly along the northern edge of the town, and is spanned by stone and iron bridges, the former dating from medieval times when it was part of the *Camino de Santiago*. The *Espolón* is Logroño's Trafalgar Square (the fountain is even ringed by lions), and the undoubted centre for locals and visitors alike. Shaded by leafy plane trees, and with ample benches, it is the place to come and sit and watch the city relax. To the south of the *Espolón* lies the modern city, with its wide avenues such as the Gran Vía, Avenida de Jorge Vigón, and the Avenida de la Republica Argentina all lined with sleek, fashionable shops, modern banks, and tall office buildings.

Head north from the *Espolón*, though, to explore the old *casco*, a maze of tiny streets and alleys within the bounds of the old walled city leading down to the river. This is a splendid old quarter simply to explore on foot, visiting important monuments such as the Imperial Church of Santa María del Palacio, founded in the eleventh century and a noteworthy landmark with its remarkable 44.5-metre-high pyramidal tower. The highly-decorated Cathedral of Santa María la Redonda, with its handsome baroque towers, is located in the heart of the old *barrio* on the pleasant Plaza del Mercado. The town's market no longer takes place here but has moved indoors to a nearby 4-storey building that is definitely worth a visit simply to view the abundance of superlative raw ingredients, produce and products of the Rioja: tiny carcases of *cordero lechal* (milk-fed lamb); dangling sausages and *chorizos*; a surprisingly varied selection of fish and dried *bacalao*; and of course the fresh fruits and vegetables for which the region is so famous.

The Espolón, Logroño.

Afterwards, repair around the corner to the nearby Calle Laurel, one of the great drinking streets in Spain. This small alley is literally lined with bars and *mesóns*, simple places serving a vast range of bar-top *banderillas*, tasty morsels and titbits speared on a toothpick to accompany good young Rioja wines by the tumbler. The Calle Laurel is virtually an institution of Logroño, and before lunch, after work hours, or at weekends, the bars are full of locals – businessmen, wine merchants, workers – who dash in for a '*chiquito*' – a small measure of wine – together with a nibble of this or that.

Logroño, while a regional, commercial and administrative centre, is undoubtedly an important wine town in its own right. The *Consejo Regulador de La Rioja* has its headquarters here, as does the *Grupo de Exportadores*, while there is no shortage of good specialist wine shops, and even the humblest *mesóns* offer extensive wine lists of local vintages. And of course, Logroño itself is the home to important and world-renowned wineries such as Bodegas Campo Viejo, Rioja's largest, the sleek and modern Bodegas Ollara, located on an industrial estate, and the historic Bodegas Franco-Españolas, while just outside town on the road to Calahorra lies the famous Marqués de Murrieta Castillo Ygay estate.

Logroño is centrally located for exploration of the Rioja wine country, and is the logical starting-point for tours of the Rioja Alta, Rioja Alavesa and Rioja Baja. If time is limited, the Rioja Baja is probably of less interest for the single-minded wine lover and wine tourist, for though Calahorra, Alfaro and Arnedo are interesting towns and worth visiting, the Rioja Alta and Rioja Alavesa provide more pleasant and interesting country for wine tour-

ing, and contain the greatest concentration of *bodegas*.

Unless you choose to take the unexciting *autovía* from Logroño to Haro, it is impossible to reach that destination without passing through the classic wine towns and *pueblos* of the Rioja. Haro can be reached either by following the southern bank of the Ebro through the heart of the Rioja Alta, or by heading north into the Rioja Alavesa via Laguardia and Labastida. Both routes are recommended, so the best option is either to make a circular journey, or to make separate forays into the wine country on different days.

La Rioja Alta

The Rioja Alta extends from Logroño to Haro, mainly along the southern slopes and banks of the Ebro river and its tributaries. The vineyard zone comprises some 77 municipalities with almost 15,000 hectares of vines in production. The soil is mainly rust-red ferruginous clay, with some calcareous clay and, nearer the rivers, alluvial silt and clay deposits with large, smooth-washed stones. The Rioja Alta is renowned above all for its sturdy, long-lived medium-body wines that have a great capacity for ageing. The principal wine towns of the Rioja Alta are Logroño itself, Haro, Fuenmayor and Cenicero.

The *Camino de Santiago* passes from Logroño south to Navarrete, Nájera and Santo Domingo de la Calzada before crossing the little Oja river (which gives its name to the region) and passing into the historic region of Old Castile. Navarrete, only 12 km from the regional capital, is a fine little wine town with some notable monuments, including the late Gothic parish Church of the Assumption. Navarrete was once a fortress town, its castle the most important in the region until the Catholic Kings had it destroyed. Its old centre has been declared of historic-artistic interest and there are plenty of handicraft shops where traditional pottery is made and sold. Bodegas Navajas, a family company located on the outskirts of the town, can be visited.

From Navarrete, return towards Logroño, then find the N232 that follows the Ebro to Haro. This leads through the heart of the Rioja Alta vineyard, and there are literally scores of famous *bodegas* located along the route.

Fuenmayor is a major wine centre of considerable importance; though today the town rather sprawls beyond its historic bounds, its old centre is still mainly intact. The traditional *ruta del vino* begins in Fuenmayor at what used to be the headquarters of the Royal Economic Society of Harvesters, founded in 1788 in the El Palacio building. Fuenmayor, like so

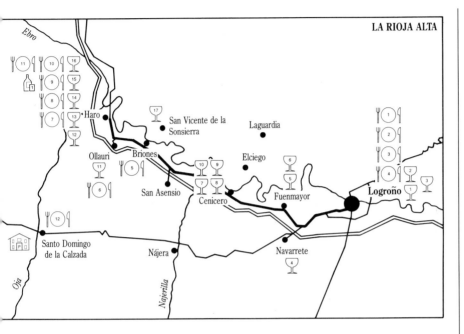

many of the towns of the Rioja, is noted for its wealthy mansions and noble houses, all decorated with impressive *escudos*, or coats-of-arms. In one such magnificent palace, the so-called Mesón, there is a casino. Fuenmayor is the home to a number of illustrious wine companies, including AGE Bodegas Unidas, Bodegas Lagunilla SA, Bodegas Lan SA, and the striking Bodegas Montecillo SA.

The wine route continues next to Cenicero, a former Roman town whose name means 'ash dump': the legionaries had a crematorium there. The town has retained its historic centre, and boasts some notable baroque mansions and monuments, such as its famous church tower, defended against the Carlist troops in 1834. Cenicero lies in the heart of the Rioja Alta wine country and is the home of Bodegas Berberana SA (second largest in the region), Unión Viti-Vinícola (Marqués de Cáceres), Bodegas Riojanas SA, and the Bodega Cooperativa Santa Daria.

From Cenicero, the excursion through the wine country can either head north to Elciego and Laguardia in the Rioja Alavesa (see below), or else continue to Haro on the N232 via typical wine towns such as San Asensio, Briones and Ollauri. Briones is a particularly atmospheric hilltop village, its medieval walls still mainly intact and its old centre well-preserved. Ollauri is a small, but proud old Riojan *pueblo* with some fine mansions.

LA RIOJA

The town itself is riddled underground with cellars, some tiny and private, others the property of large and well-known concerns such as Federico Paternina SA, Bodegas Beronia SA, and Bodegas Abalos SA (owned by Bodegas Berberana).

Haro, located 43 km west of Logroño, is much smaller than the region's capital, but it is the true centre of the wine trade. The *Estación de Viticultura y Enología* was founded in Haro as long ago as 1892, and there are some 11 *bodegas* located in or just outside this bustling provincial town. The town offers probably the best and most comfortable hotel in the region, and there are some excellent though basically simple local restaurants, as well as some fine specialist wine shops. In short, Haro has everything that the intrepid wine traveller seeks and every wine lover will wish to spend extended time here.

Many of the great *bodegas* of Haro are located just outside the hilltop town, across the river on the road to Vitoria in the area by the railway line known as the *barrio de la estación*. Indeed, it was the ease with which the wines of Haro could be transported to Bilbao and then on to France and other northern destinations that led to the creation of some of the century-old *bodegas* that are still producing some of the region's greatest wines today: R. López de Heredia, CVNE, La Rioja Alta SA, Bodegas Muga SA and Bodegas Bilbainas SA are all located in this *barrio*, great names producing great traditional wines, each with its own particular style and following. This concentration of *bodegas* provides visiting opportunities that are almost unrivalled elsewhere in Spain. Moreover, here more than anywhere else one is able to appreciate the essential contrast between the age-old and the ultra-modern which is the hallmark of Rioja today.

Haro was inhabited in Roman times, and its central position in the rich alluvial valley of the Ebro, crisscrossed by other tributaries such as the Tirón, the Glera and the little Oja, combined with the abundant vegetation and pasture land, has made the town an important market centre, a role it maintains even today.

But it is above all for wine that Haro is famous. Its position has brought prosperity, as evidenced by the many fine manorial houses dating from the sixteenth, seventeenth and eighteenth centuries, glowing a warm yellow in the afternoon sun, proudly decorated with their noble *escudos*. The town is dominated by the ornate baroque belltower of the church of Santo Tómas. Climb up to the church to view its remarkable interior columns and interlaced vaulting, then explore the maze of small streets leading down to the central Plaza de la Paz. This zone is known as '*La Herradura*' and it is noted above all for its scores of tiny corner bars, many apparently unnamed, but all serving good house Rioja to accompany a fine selection of bar-top *banderillas – setas a la plancha, calamares, tortilla, pimientos rellenos, chorizo, jamón, anchoas, patatas bravas, oreja frita, albóndigas* and much else.

From Haro, a side-trip should be made to Santo Domingo de la Calzada, a historic pilgrim town founded by Santo Domingo in the eleventh century. This bridge-builder saint erected a causeway over the little Oja for pilgrims to cross here on their way to Santiago. He later founded a hospice for the weary which was subsequently enlarged, and the town thus became one of the principal stops on the well-travelled road. The hospice has been converted into an atmospheric *parador*. The town's Romanesque-Byzantine cathedral should also be visited, if only for the sight of a bizarre pair of live chickens who live in a little side chapel therein. As miracles go, the story is worth recounting: apparently a young and pure-minded pilgrim passing through the town resisted the amorous advances of the innkeeper's raunchy daughter. Unaccustomed to being scorned, she falsely accused him of theft, for which the poor lad was hanged. However, through the miraculous intervention of the eponymous saint, he did not die: when this fact was reported to the local judge who was at that moment enjoying a pair of roasted fowl, he replied that this was nonsense and that the pilgrim was as dead as the chickens on his table. With that, the birds sprouted feathers, stood up and crowed, and promptly flew out of the window. Needless to say, the wronged pilgrim was cut down, and so was able to continue on his pure-minded way to Santiago.

LA RIOJA ALAVESA

The Rioja Alavesa is that part of the Rioja delimited vineyard which lies within the Basque province of Alava. The soil here, mainly extending across the northern flanks of the Ebro leading up to the foothills of the Sierra de Cantabria, is markedly different from that of the Rioja Alta, for in contrast to the ferruginous red clay of the Alta, that of the Alavesa is warm yellow in appearance, composed primarily of lime-rich marl and calcareous clay. There are more than 7000 hectares of vineyards under cultivation, stretching over 18 municipalities.

The Rioja Alavesa is noted above all for its charming and elegant wines, finer, more delicate than the wines of the Rioja Alta, though generally with a lower acidity that makes them on their own less suitable for lengthy conservation. The Rioja Alavesa is also famous for its *vinos de cosechero*, produced by traditional whole-grape fermentation, and vinified to be con-

LA RIOJA

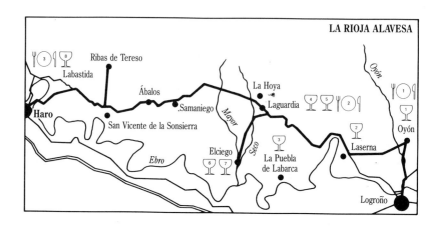

sumed within the year of production. Such wines, at odds in style and image with wood-aged Riojas, find particular favour on the Basque coast, their traditional market. The important wine centres in the Rioja Alavesa are Oyón, Laguardia and Elciego.

To tour the Rioja Alavesa, leave Logroño by the stone bridge over the Ebro, then briefly take the road to Pamplona (N111) before branching left to find the small but prosperous wine town of Oyón, home of prestigious and world-famous wine firms such as Bodegas Faustino Martínez SA, Bodegas Martínez Bujanda SA and Bodegas El Coto. Oyón, located on the pilgrim route to Santiago, was an important stopping-point, and the former seat of the Bishop of Navarra.

From Oyón, find the small L127 road across country to join the N232 that leads to Laguardia. On reaching the N232, turn right and shortly thereafter look out for signs to the Contino estate in the hamlet of Laserna. Contino is one of the region's few single-vineyard estate wineries, owned in part by CVNE. Its well-exposed 50 hectares of vines lie in a cup of hills extending down to the banks of the Ebro, and it is always one of the earliest sites for the beginning of the *vendimia* in the Rioja Alavesa.

Laguardia is the principal town of the Rioja Alavesa, still wholly medieval in character and hugely atmospheric, perched on its high ridge, its fortified ramparts guarding its old narrow streets, stone houses and impressive churches such as the late Gothic Santa María de los Reyes and the Church of San Juan. Laguardia is the centre for the Rioja Alavesa wine industry, and the home of the *Casa del Vino*, an official Basque wine institute located in a fine historic mansion (the writer Sameniego was born in this house) which serves to assist the winegrowers of the Rioja Alavesa with technologi-

...entos hanging out to dry from a stone townhouse in ...edieval town of Laguardia.

cal expertise, courses in viticulture and oenology, and investment. A further aim is to promote the wines of the Rioja Alavesa as distinct from those of the rest of the Rioja. The great *bodegas de crianza* may have little need of such assistance, so its efforts are concentrated more specifically towards the small individual *cosecheros* producing primarily wines to be drunk young with no oak ageing.

Large wine firms in or just outside Laguardia include Bodegas Alavesas SA, Bodegas Palacio SA and Bodegas Campillo SA, while Bodegas Artadi is a small co-operative of *cosecheros* producing excellent young *tintos jóvenes* by whole grape fermentation.

From Laguardia, make a detour on the small L1210 to Elciego, one of the most important wine communities in the Rioja. It was here, in 1868, that Jean Pineau designed the first winery in the Rioja utilizing French precepts of winemaking for the Marqués de Riscal; today, Vinos de los Herederos del Marqués de Riscal SA remains in the control of the family and produces some of the most respected wines of the region. In contrast to the great historic *bodegas* of Riscal, a more recent but none the less significant venture also located in Elciego is the important Bodegas Domecq SA, owned by the famous sherry firm and with extensive vineyard holdings. Bodegas Murua Entrena, Viña Salceda, and Bodegas Murua are also located in this small but important wine hamlet.

Continue the wine tour of the Alavesa by returning to Laguardia, and there follow the road north-west towards Haro. Just outside Laguardia, it is worth visiting the Iron Age settlement of La Hoya which dates from the thirteenth century before Christ. Further on, just before Samaniego, branch off right to climb into the hills to the so-called '*balcón de la Rioja*' which provides a particularly striking view of the vineyards and hills leading

LA RIOJA

down to the Ebro valley and the mightier *sierras* to the south.

After Samaniego, the route briefly leaves the political and vinous boundaries of the Rioja Alavesa to re-enter the Rioja Alta, but in fact the soil in vineyards around municipalities such as Abalos and San Vicente de la Sonsierra differs little from that of the adjoining Alavesa. San Vicente de la Sonsierra, fortified and imposing in its dominant position overlooking the steep gorge of the Ebro across to Briones, is a particularly atmospheric little wine town. Stop to purchase a bottle or two of *vino de cosechero* wherever you see a sign. Bodegas Sierra Cantabria SA is noteworthy for good young wines as well as for some tasty wood-aged Reservas.

The wine road re-enters the Basque Country; before reaching Labastida, branch off right on the road to Rivas de Tereso to visit La Granja Remelluri, another single-estate winery, its vineyards sited on the high slopes of the Sierra de Toloño. This is one of the most beautiful estates in the region, the fifteenth-century farmhouse having been lovingly restored by the Rodriguez family. Its steep hill vineyards provide the raw materials for an exceptional and distinctive top-quality estate wine. There is a small museum on the wine estate, and visitors are particularly warmly received.

Labastida is another atmospheric wine hamlet, its two churches, Nuestra Señora de la Asunción and the higher Ermita del Santo Cristo, remarkably large and imposing for such a small *pueblo*. Certainly, the impressive mansions of the town indicate a prosperity that has for centuries been based on the rich agricultural hinterland and vineyards in the midst of which it stands. Climb up to the hermitage for a fine view of the Rioja vineyard extending down to Haro. There are some cool shaded benches up here for the weary.

From Labastida, the wine route leads on to Haro.

LA RIOJA BAJA

The Rioja Baja extends south-east from Logroño to Alfaro, on lower-lying, hotter countryside along the flatter, wider valley of the Ebro basin. The soil is primarily rich alluvial silt, though there are also pockets of ferruginous clay. The climate of the Rioja Baja is Mediterranean in comparison to the cooler Atlantic influence that extends over the Rioja Alta and Alavesa. There is less precipitation and temperatures are considerably hotter. Vines are grown on some 22,000 hectares located in 37 municipalities, including 6 municipalities within the region of Navarra.

The Rioja Baja is probably best toured en route to Zaragoza or the Catalonian coast. Leave Logroño on the N232 (passing along the way the famous

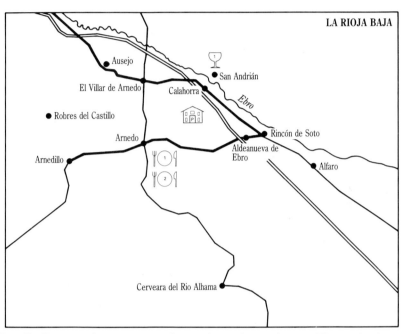

Castillo Ygay) and continue south-east for 30 km to Ausejo. This is the first important wine town in the Rioja Baja, a typical fortified hill town still dominated by its thirteenth-century castle. The old town centre is a maze of twisting, winding streets built around the conical hilltop, and it is still riddled with wine cellars and underground passages. In addition to wine, Ausejo is famous for its cultivated mushrooms.

Calahorra, 48 km from Logroño, is the second largest town in the region. This ancient episcopal seat was already an important township 200 years before Christ; known to the Romans as Calagurris, it was the birthplace of the Roman orator Marcus Fabius Quintilianus (35 A.D.) and the Latin Christian poet Marcus Aurelius Clemens Prudentius (348 A.D.). Razed by Hannibal and later by Pompey, the massive town walls that are still mainly intact today are evidence of its strategic importance through the Middle Ages. Calahorra was reconquered from the Moors in 1072. Today, the impressive Gothic cathedral dominates the old town. Calahorra has always served as a market centre for its extensive *vega*, a broad plain on which vineyards vie with plantations of other luscious fruits and market vegetables, especially the bright red *pimientos* that are such a favourite Riojan food.

LA RIOJA

South-east of Calahorra, at Rincón de Soto, another rich agricultural town, a detour can be made into the fertile Cidacos valley, through Aldeanueva de Ebro to Arnedo, a busy thriving town today most famous for its shoe industry, and, further up the valley, to Arnedillo, a quiet spa town in the foothills of the Sierra de la Demanda. The most important wine town in the Rioja Baja is Alfaro, located virtually on the region's border with Navarra. There was a Celtic-Iberian settlement here before the Roman occupation, but it was the Arabs who gave the town its present name, apparently because the Ebro was navigable even this far upriver where they sited a lighthouse. Today Alfaro is a busy and historic medieval town with notable seignorial mansions, as well as some important wine producers, including Bodegas José Palacios Remondo SA and Bodegas Campo Burgo SA.

The Rioja Baja stands rather apart from the élite wine zones of the Rioja Alta and Rioja Alavesa. In truth, it has long been considered something of the ugly sister of the Rioja, but this is not wholly fair. True, her wines are on the whole coarser and higher in alcohol, produced primarily from the Garnacha grape, not the thoroughbred Tempranillo. These wines, however, are essential components of blended Riojas, contributing above all backbone, structure and roundness. Moreover, good, plentiful, if somewhat powerful wines are produced in quantity in the Rioja Baja that are eminently drinkable in their own right. It is, as always, a question of priorities – whether to pick early to reduce potential alcohol for finer wines, or late for stronger wines more suitable for blending.

Bodegas: Stop to Taste; Stop to Buy

La Rioja Alta

1

BODEGAS MARQUÉS DE MURRIETA SA
CASTILLO DE YGAY
CTRA DE ZARAGOZA, KM 5
26080 LOGROÑO
LA RIOJA
TEL: (941) 25 81 00; FAX: (941) 25 16 06

WINES PRODUCED: El Dorado de Murrieta *blanco*; Marqués de Murrieta *tinto* Crianza Reserva, Gran Reserva; Castillo Ygay *blanco*

y tinto Gran Reserva.

VISITS: By appointment (groups no larger than 15 persons).

The historic aristocratic estate was founded by Don Luciano de Murrieta García Ortiz Lemoine, Marqués de Murrieta, in 1872 although this innovative South American businessman had experimented with French precepts as early as the 1840s, and even

The *Tonelería*

Today there are few if any wine regions in the world with a greater number of oak *barricas* in proportion to wine produced than the Rioja. Most *bodegas* purchase their barrels from specialist *tonelerías* such as Murúa of Logroño. The yard of this family business founded in 1920 always holds at least two years' stock of American oak, for the wood must be well seasoned before it can be used. Though at Murúa, much of the manual labour has been eased through the use of machines for sawing and planing, the production of a *barrica* is still a wholly individual and intuitive craft.

Each *barrica* consists of some 27–30 shaped staves 95 cm in length held together by 8 galvanized hoops. Once the first hoops have been placed to hold the *barrica* together at one end, the open staves must be heated and/or scorched (by direct fire, steam, or hot water) to make them flexible. They are then winched together with a rope or cable while more hoops are hammered down over the belly. The heads and bottoms of the barrel are finally added, each made from 5–7 boards, and the whole is made water-tight with the addition of strips of reed.

An oak barrel does much more than merely contain the wine. Therefore, a number of variables in its construction are significant. Foremost is the choice between American and French oak (American is still overwhelmingly preferred in Rioja); if French, then whether from the forests of the Limousin, Tronçais, Allier, or Vosges; other considerations may include whether the

staves have been sawn mechanically or split by hand; the degree of 'toasting' or scorching of the inside of the barrel is another factor that contributes to character and can affect the finished taste of the wine.

TONELERÍA MURÚA (TONELERÍA
    MECÁNICA RIOJANA SA)
CABO NOVAL 24
26006 LOGROÑO
LA RIOJA
TEL: (941) 25 25 99; FAX: (941) 23 79 49

American oak staves left outdoors to season for at least two years.

exported wines to Mexico and Cuba in 1852.

Today, the estate remains in aristocratic hands, under the private family ownership of Don Vicente Cebrián Sagarriga, Conde de Creixell. Though investment has been immense in the expansion and modernization of the *bodega*, as well as in new plantations and extension of the vineyard (there are now 180 ha. in production, but it is planned to increase this to 255 ha. over the next decade), Murrieta remains totally dedicated to its tradition, and to the unique style of aged Reservas and Gran Reservas for which it is so rightly famous. There are at present 13,200 *barricas* and this number will be increased by a further 4000; Murrieta thus holds the largest number in relation to wine released each year.

The wines of Murrieta are renowned especially for their structure, longevity and elegance. El Dorado de Murrieta is the new name for the traditional oak-aged white wine, so called to distinguish it from other light white Riojas to which it bears no resemblance. While the Marqués de Murrieta Reservas and Gran Reservas are always wines of great concentration and elegance, the Castillo Ygay wines are even more unique for their lengthy ageing in *barrica* prior to release, in some cases 25 years or more.

Marqués de Murrieta is one of the great flagship wine estates in Spain. There are plans for the expansion of visiting facilities, as well as an outlet for direct sales; at present all visits should be arranged as far in advance as possible. English, French spoken.

---

2 BODEGAS FRANCO-ESPAÑOLAS SA
CABO NOVAL 2
26006 LOGROÑO
LA RIOJA
TEL: (941) 25 13 00

WINES PRODUCED: Castil Corvo *blanco*; Rioja Diamante *blanco semi-dulce*; Viña Soledad *blanco* Gran Reserva; Viña Bordoón *tinto* Reserva; Rioja Royal Tête de Cuvée *tinto* Gran Reserva.
VISITS: By appointment.

Located just across Logroño's iron bridge, this historic *bodega* was founded in 1901 by Bordelais winegrowers escaping the plague of phylloxera. Though the name recalls its French origins, it is today wholly Spanish-owned and produces a well-respected range of traditional wines. The underground cellars in the old *bodega* are particularly impressive. French spoken.

---

3 BODEGAS CAMPO VIEJO DE SAVIN SA
GUSTAVO ADOLFO BÉCQUER 3
26006 LOGROÑO
LA RIOJA
TEL: (941) 23 80 00; FAX: (941) 23 81 11

WINES PRODUCED: Albor *blanco*; Campo Viejo *blanco, rosado*; Campo Viejo *tinto* Crianza, Reserva, Gran Reserva; Marqués de Villamagna *tinto* Gran Reserva.
VISITS: Mon–Fri 8h30–12h; 15h30–17h. Appointment advised though not essential. Telephone the Department of Public Relations. It is possible to pre-book typical Rioja meals in the *bodega* dining room for individuals or groups up to 80 persons.

Notwithstanding that this immense winery is Rioja's largest, its wines the market leader in Spain, Campo Viejo still manages to produce a range of quality wines that are consistently satisfying. The company was founded in 1959 and has 450 hectares of its own vineyards, though even this large amount supplies only a fraction of its needs. The *bodega* contains some 45,000 *barricas* and 5,600,000 bottles of wine ageing. Campo Viejo is the flagship winery of the Bodegas y Bebidas Group, Spain's largest drinks conglomerate.
English, French spoken.

---

4 BODEGAS NAVAJAS SL
BALGARANZ 2
NAVARRETE
LA RIOJA
TEL: (941) 44 01 40; FAX: (941) 44 06 57

WINES PRODUCED: Bodegas Navajas *blanco, rosado, tinto*; Bodegas Navajas *tinto* Crianza, Reserva.

VISITS: Mon–Fri 9–13h; 15–18h. Appointment necessary.
Relatively small family winery in Navarrete along the *Camino de Santiago* 10 km south-west from Logroño. *Bodega* is located below the old hilltop *casco* near the Guardia Civil installation.

---

5 BODEGAS MONTECILLO SA
CTRA FUENMAYOR–NAVARRETE, KM 2
26360 FUENMAYOR
LA RIOJA
TEL: (941) 44 01 25; FAX: (941) 44 06 63

WINES PRODUCED: Viña Cumbrero *blanco*; Viña Cumbrero

tinto Crianza; Montecillo *tinto* Reserva, Gran Reserva; Viña Monty *tinto* Gran Reserva.
VISITS: Mon–Fri 11–13h. Appointment necessary. Closed August.
This prestigious *bodega* located between Navarrete and Fuenmayor

is strikingly modern and belongs to the Osborne y Cía SA group of companies. Though Montecillo owns no vineyards of its own, it purchases only grapes, not wine, and vinifies them entirely in its own installations to produce a sleek modern range of wines with an emphasis on shorter ageing in new French and American oak, followed by lengthy bottle ageing.

---

6 AGE BODEGAS UNIDAS SA
BARRIO DE LA ESTACIÓN
26360 FUENMAYOR
LA RIOJA
TEL: (941) 29 35 00; FAX: (941) 29 35 01

WINES PRODUCED: Romeral *blanco, rosado, tinto*; Siglo *blanco, rosado, tinto*; Siglo Saco *tinto* Reserva; Marqués del Romeral *tinto* Gran Reserva.

VISITS: By appointment.
Another giant of the Rioja, most famous for its Siglo Saco wines, sold in the distinctive burlap-covered bottle. Despite this gimmick, the wines are well made and rarely disappoint. There are some 30,000 *barricas* here and a storage capacity for 3 million bottles.

---

7 GRUPO BODEGAS BERBERANA SA
CTRA ELCIEGO, S/N
26350 CENICERO
LA RIOJA
TEL: (941) 45 31 00; FAX: (941) 45 31 14

WINES PRODUCED: Preferido *blanco, rosado, tinto*; Carta de Plato *blanco, rosado, tinto*; Carta de Oro *blanco, rosado, tinto*; Berberana *tinto* Reserva, Gran Reserva.
VISITS: Daily, by appointment. Meals in the *bodega comedor* can be arranged for individuals and groups.
Berberana was founded over 100 years ago in the charming village of Ollauri, but today this immense winery is the property of a consortium of seven co-operative

wineries, financial investors and the Comunidad de La Rioja. Second only in scale of production to Campo Viejo, Berberana has access to grapes from 2600 growers who collectively work 5200 ha. of vineyards. This accounts for a remarkable 12–15% of the entire Rioja production.

The massive winery is functional not atmospheric, but the wines produced are of a remarkably high quality. Naturally there is less scope for creativity with the cheaper range of wines that account for the bulk of sales (70% of production is *sin crianza*), but the Berberana Reserva and Gran Reserva wines

are well-made oak-aged wines of
considerable distinction.
English, French, German spoken.

---

8 BODEGAS MARQUÉS DE CÁCERES
UNIÓN VITI-VINÍCOLA SA
CTRA DE LOGROÑO, S/N
26350 CENICERO
LA RIOJA
TEL: (941) 45 40 00; FAX: (941) 45 44 00

WINES PRODUCED: Marqués de
Cáceres *blanco, rosado, tinto*;
Marqués de Cáceres *tinto* Crianza,
Reserva and Gran Reserva.
VISITS: Mon–Fri 9–13h; 15–17h.
Appointment necessary.
The Forner family took refuge in
France in the aftermath of the
Spanish Civil War and were the
proprietors of Château Camensac in
the Haut-Médoc before returning to
Spain in the 1960s. Bodegas
Marqués de Cáceres was founded in
1970 by Henri Forner in
co-operation with local
winegrowers and the local
co-operative with the aim of
combining modern French
winemaking techniques with the
traditions of the Rioja.

Thus, this was one of the first
bodegas in the region to introduce
stainless steel vats for
temperature-controlled
fermentation to produce the then
'new-style' white Rioja (previously
white Rioja, like red, was always
fermented and aged in oak). So
successful was this innovation that
today there are far more 'new-style'
white wines than traditional.
Similarly, the Marqués de Cáceres
red wines are also somewhat
atypical, spending shorter periods in
new or nearly new oak, followed by
more time in bottle.
English, French spoken.

---

9 BODEGAS RIOJANAS SA
ESTACIÓN 1–21
26350 CENICERO
LA RIOJA
TEL: (941) 45 40 50; FAX: (941) 45 45 29

WINES PRODUCED: Canchales
blanco, tinto; Viña Albina *blanco
semi-dulce*; Puerta Vieja *blanco,
rosado, tinto*; Monte Real *blanco,
rosado* Crianza; Monte Real *tinto*
Crianza, Reserva, Gran Reserva;
Viña Albina *tinto* Reserva, Gran
Reserva.
VISITS: Mon–Fri 9–13h; 15–18h.
Appointment necessary.
Old typical *bodega* originally
founded in 1890 under French
technical advice and to a French
design (hence the 'château'-style
architecture). The company

remains family-owned, and is one of the few large-scale firms still utilizing in part the traditional methods of whole grape fermentation.

English, French spoken.

---

10 BODEGAS 'SANTA DARÍA'
COOPERATIVA VINÍCOLA DE
CENICERO
CTRA DE LOGROÑO, S/N
26350 CENICERO
LA RIOJA
TEL: (941) 45 41 10; FAX: (941) 45 46 18

WINES PRODUCED: Santa Daría *blanco, rosado, tinto*; Valdemontan *blanco, rosado, tinto*; Santa Daría *tinto* Crianza, Reserva.
VISITS: Daily, working hours. No appointment necessary.
Though there are more than 30 co-operative wineries in the Rioja, most have traditionally sold their members' grapes or finished wine to the large *bodegas de crianza* rather than elevating, bottling and marketing it themselves. Santa Daría is a highly-regarded exception. There are nearly 600 winegrowing *socios* who between them work about 1000 ha. of vineyards; the winery has modern installations and the know-how to make sound wines, as well as the initiative and get-up-and-go to sell them both nationally and internationally.

---

11 BODEGAS DE ABALOS SA
CALLE ALTA, S/N
26220 OLLAURI
LA RIOJA
TEL: (941) 33 80 02

WINES PRODUCED: Viñedos d'Avalos *blanco* Crianza; Viñedos d'Avalos *tinto* Crianza, Reserva, Gran Reserva.
VISITS: By appointment.
This lovely old wine town near Haro is literally riddled with deep underground cellars. Bodegas de Abalos is located in the original cellars of Bodegas Berberana, and still belongs to that large group. The newly inaugurated company will concentrate on the upper end of the market, producing only oak-aged Crianza, Reserva and Gran Reserva wines.

There is a small wine museum and private *comedor* which may be open to visitors provided it is arranged well in advance.

La Estación de Viticultura y Enología de Haro

The *Estación de Viticultura y Enología* in Haro was founded in 1902 and is one of the country's oldest research and oenological institutes. Its role today, as in the past, is continual research into and improvement of both the cultivation of grapes and the production of wines in Rioja. The *Estación* furthermore undertakes controls and tests to guarantee the continued quality of the wines of the region.

'Our aim here should not be to discover or develop new styles or types of wine, but to improve on what we already have,' explained Don Manuel Ruiz Hernández, the *Estación*'s eminent and authoritative Technical Director. 'It is far easier to be dynamic in new zones which lack history, tradition or an already defined identity for their wines. What we must attempt in Rioja is to maintain the integrity, prestige and identity that has been established here over more than 100 years. When our forefathers reclaimed the vineyard after phylloxera, they could have replanted with the classic French varieties then. We must ask ourselves why they chose instead to maintain their faith in Tempranillo and the other traditional varieties of the Rioja. We should no more consider planting our vineyards with Cabernet Sauvignon than should, for example, the Burgundians. Just as Cabernet Sauvignon is the great grape of Bordeaux, just as Pinot Noir is supreme in Burgundy, so is Tempranillo the great grape of Rioja. Our aim must be the continued improvement of our existing wines based on our long-established history and prestige which the consumer can distinguish from all others.'

In a wine world increasingly inundated with wines produced from the ubiquitous Cabernet Sauvignon and Chardonnay, this is a path that is to be wholeheartedly applauded.

The *Estación Enología* has an extensive and informative scientific museum of wine and winemaking in the Rioja which is open to the general public.

MUSEO DEL VINO
ESTACIÓN DE VITICULTURA Y ENOLOGÍA DE
  HARO
AVDA BRETÓN DE LOS HERREROS 4
26200 HARO
TEL: (941) 31 05 47; FAX: (941) 31 18 00

OPEN: Mon–Sat 10–14h.

LA RIOJA

12 COMPAÑIA VINÍCOLA DEL NORTE DE
ESPAÑA SA (CVNE)
AVDA COSTA DEL VINO 21
26200 HARO
LA RIOJA
TEL: (941) 31 02 76, 31 06 50;
FAX: (941) 31 28 19

WINES PRODUCED: CVNE *blanco,
rosado, clarete*; Monopole *blanco*;
CVNE *tinto* Reserva; Viña Real
tinto Crianza, Reserva, Gran
Reserva; Imperial *tinto* Reserva,
Gran Reserva.
VISITS: Mon–Fri 9–13h; 15–18h.
Founded in 1879, CVNE remains
one of the most respected and
traditional *bodegas* of Haro, still in
the hands of the original founders'
families. Located by the railway
line that revolutionized the
transport of wine in the last
century, CVNE today is a blend of
the traditional and the
super-modern. The new vinification
plant has been designed especially
to accommodate its own needs, and
though capable of working on an
extremely large scale, it provides
unrivalled control and selection
during every phase of the
vinification. The company today
owns 550 ha. of vineyards, providing
it with about half its requirements.

Monopole is a particularly
successful white Rioja,
cold-fermented and aged for a short
period in new or nearly new wood.
So successful is this wine, that it
accounts for as much as 90% of the
traditional oaked white Rioja
market. While CVNE *clarete* is a
pleasant light luncheon wine to
drink in the region, the wines that
have brought the company its
greatest fame are Viña Real and
Imperial, especially the Reserva
and Gran Reserva examples of each.
Viña Real is a Rioja Alavesa wine
produced in the company's
installation in Elciego that is noted
above all for its warm, rounded,
voluptuous fruit; it is always
bottled in a sloping-shouldered
Burgundy-style bottle. Imperial
Reservas and Gran Reservas are
somewhat grander, more austere
wines of great concentration and
elegance.
English, French, German spoken.

---

13 LA RIOJA ALTA SA
AVDA DE VIZCAYA, S/N
26200 HARO
LA RIOJA
TEL: (941) 31 03 46; FAX: (941) 31 28 54

WINES PRODUCED: Viña Ardanza
blanco Reserva; Viña Alberdi *tinto*
Crianza; Viña Arana *tinto* Reserva;
Viña Ardanza *tinto* Reserva;
Reserva 904; Reserva 890;
Centenary Gran Reserva 1890–
1990.
VISITS: Mon–Fri 9–14h; 15–
18h30. Appointment only necessary

for extended or special visits.

BODEGA SHOP: Open above hours. Wines can be tasted and purchased in pleasant surroundings, and there are also wine accessories, books and typical Riojan products on sale.

One of the great *bodegas* of the Rioja, founded in 1890 in the *barrio de la estación* of Haro and still owned by the founding families. Extensive expansions and modernization during the boom years of the last decades have been accomplished without compromise to this company's commitment above all to the great oak-aged wines for which it is so famous. For example, although La Rioja Alta holds over 32,000 *barricas* of wine, the average age of wine released for sale is 7–8 years; over 4 million bottles of wine are ageing in the bottle store.

Stainless steel fermentation vats have finally replaced the great old 20,000-litre wooden *tinas*, but apart from this concession to technology, the production and elevation of the wines is carried out today as in the past.

The wines of La Rioja Alta SA are well known in Britain and the US: especially favoured are the relatively young and fruity Viña Alberdi, the voluptuous and silky Viña Ardanza and the somewhat leaner Viña Arana. More austere and complex in style are the powerful 904 and 890 Gran Reservas.

The *bodega* dining room can be booked for private groups; however, as this is extremely popular, it is necessary to make arrangements as far in advance as possible. English, French spoken.

14

R. LÓPEZ DE HEREDIA VIÑA
    TONDONIA SA
AVDA DE VIZCAYA 3
26200 HARO
LA RIOJA
TEL: (941) 31 02 44; FAX: (941) 31 07 88

WINES PRODUCED: Viña Gravonia *blanco*; Viña Cubillo *tinto*; Viña Bosconia *tinto* Crianza, Reserva, Gran Reserva; Viña Tondonia *blanco y tinto* Crianza, Reserva Gran Reserva.
VISITS: By appointment.

Founded in 1877 by Don Rafael López de Heredia, this remarkable old *bodega*, with its striking red pagoda roof, is one of the landmarks of the Rioja. Indeed, here more than anywhere else in the region, the classic traditional methods remain, barely changed at all in over 100 years.

Don Rafael planted the famous Viña Tondonia vineyard in 1913, and it, together with Viña Cubillo, Viña Bosconia and Viña Zaconia

LA RIOJA

(140 hectares in total), provides the company with its finest grapes for the production of both oak-aged white and red wines of the highest quality. Such wines are produced entirely in the old artisan traditions of the Rioja, and a visit to this historic *bodega* is like going back in time. Both white and red wines are fermented in large oak *tinas*, then filtered coarsely through bundles of bound vine shoots. In the case of reds, after decanting, the mass of grape skins is pressed in small vertical presses of the type seen elsewhere only in museums. The wines then undergo their malolactic fermentations in large 700-litre *bocoys* before being transferred to oak *barricas* for a minimum of two years for all wines. Most wines spend considerably longer in wood than this company's minimum.

Viña Tondonia *blanco* is one of the classic white wines of the Rioja, matured for 6 years with at least 4 years in cask: buttery, toasty yet surprisingly fresh and full of crisp, citrusy acidity, we consider it one of the great white wines of the world. The company's flagship reds, Viña Tondonia and Viña Bosconia, are similarly both classics. Older Reservas and Gran Reservas emerge from lengthy sojourns in *barrica* still brilliantly alive and full of fruit; they are remarkably vivid and well-defined wines, all the more noteworthy since modernists claim that excessive wood ageing leads to tired wines lacking in interest. Clearly this company demonstrates that there is plenty of room for both the traditionalist and modernist schools in the Rioja today.

---

15 BODEGAS BILBAINAS SA
BARRIO DE LA ESTACIÓN, S/N
26200 HARO
LA RIOJA
ADMINISTRATIVE ADDRESS:
  PARTICULAR DEL NORTE 2, BILBAO
TEL: (94) 415 28 15, 416 57 18;
  FAX: (94) 415 00 59

WINES PRODUCED: Viña Paceta *blanco*; Imperator *tinto* Crianza; Viña Pomal *tinto* Crianza, Reserva, Gran Reserva; Viña Zaco *tinto* Crianza, Reserva; Gran Zaco *tinto*

Gran Reserva; Royal Carlton Cava. VISITS: By appointment at least 2–3 days in advance. HOURS FOR VISITS: Jan–April and Oct–Dec Mon–Fri 8–13h; 15–18h; May–Sept 8–15h. The *bodega* is closed 24–30 June and 20 August–15 September. Another famous old wine company, founded in Bilbao in 1901 where the headquarters remain today. The *bodega* is located opposite Haro's railway station, and has extensive underground cellars.

The company owns 250 ha. of vineyards. Viña Pomal and Viña Zaco are popular wines, well known in Britain since the company opened a London office as long ago as 1925.

Sparkling wines made by the classic method of secondary fermentation in the bottle have been produced since 1914.

English, French spoken.

16

BODEGAS MUGA SA
BARRIO DE LA ESTACIÓN, S/N
26200 HARO
LA RIOJA
TEL: (941) 31 04 98; 31 18 25;
    FAX: (941) 31 28 67

WINES PRODUCED: Muga *blanco*, *rosado*; Muga *tinto* Crianza; Prado Enea *tinto* Reserva, Gran Reserva; Conde de Haro 'Extra Brut' Cava.
VISITS: Mon–Fri 10–12h.
Appointment advised.
Bodegas Muga was founded in 1932 by Isaac Muga but for most of this century the company concentrated on the production of young unaged wines to sell to other *bodegas de crianza* or to bars and private customers. However, a new generation has since 1971 changed direction radically to concentrate instead on the production of classic

vinos de crianza according to the most traditional methods of the region. Today, for example, Muga remains one of the few *bodegas* where initial fermentation takes place exclusively in American and French oak vats. The *crianza* in 225-litre oak *barricas* made from both French and American oak is almost always considerably longer than the minimum requirements (24 months for Crianza wines; 30 months for Reservas; 48 months for Gran Reservas, followed by a minimum of 6, 12, and 36 months bottle age before release). The wines are still fined with beaten egg white. This is artisan winemaking at its most traditional. Prado Enea is a particularly powerful, complex classic.

French spoken.

17

BODEGAS SIERRA CANTABRIA SA
AMOREBIETA 3
26338 SAN VICENTE DE LA
    SONSIERRA
LA RIOJA
TEL: (941) 33 40 80; FAX: (941) 33 43 71

WINES PRODUCED: Sierra Cantabria *blanco*, *rosado*, *tinto*; Sierra Cantabria *tinto* Crianza, Reserva, Gran Reserva.
VISITS: Daily, working hours. Telephone to arrange a convenient time.

San Vicente is a lovely hill town high above the Ebro near Labastida, located geographically in the Rioja Alavesa but politically in the Rioja Alta. This is a sub-zone famous primarily for its *vinos de cosecheros*, young, intensely fruity wines produced by carbonic maceration which are the popular drinks in the bars of the region. Bodegas Sierra Cantabria has long produced such wines with grapes from the company's own 230 ha. of vineyards, as well as those purchased from local growers. However, this is a young, forward-looking company, undertaking serious research in the vineyard as well as in the *bodega*. The range of oak-aged reds is also excellent and should be sampled. French spoken.

La Rioja Alavesa

1

BODEGAS FAUSTINO MARTÍNEZ SA
CTRA DE LOGROÑO, S/N
01320 OYÓN
ALAVA
TEL: (941) 12 21 00; FAX: (941) 12 21 06

WINES PRODUCED: Faustino V *blanco, rosado, tinto*; Viña Faustino *tinto joven*; Faustino V *tinto* Reserva; Faustino I *tinto* Gran Reserva; Faustino Brut Reserva Cava.
VISITS: Mon–Fri 9–11h; 15–17h. Appointment necessary, at least one week in advance.
Long-established company founded in 1861, and still in the hands of the founder's family. Extensive vineyard holdings, mainly in the Rioja Alavesa provide Faustino Martínez with most of its grape requirements.

While noted above all for its traditional Faustino V Reserva and Faustino I Gran Reserva wines, the company is a keen and forward-looking innovator. It was one of the region's pioneers in the 1970s of the new-style cold-fermented white Rioja. Faustino V *blanco*, made from 100% Viura, remains today one of the benchmark wines of its type: fresh, delicately fruity, impeccably clean. In contrast to its great flagship oak-aged red wines, the company also produces Viña Faustino, a tasty *tinto joven* produced by whole grape fermentation, as well as a fine sparkling Brut Reserva Cava. English, French, German spoken.

———

Vinos de Cosechero

Though Rioja is best known for its great oak-aged reds produced according to French winemaking precepts, the old-fashioned traditional methods of whole grape fermentation are still widely practised in the region, especially in the sub-zone of the Rioja Alavesa. The old peasant fashion, still in use even today, is to harvest the grapes, then place the whole bunches, neither de-stemmed nor crushed, directly into open stone fermentation troughs known as *lagos*. The grapes undergo a primitive form of semi-carbonic maceration whereby the grapes ferment within their own skins until the interior build-up of pressure from carbonic gas causes them to swell and finally burst, so releasing their juice. As the process continues, different fractions of wine are drawn off. The first, known as *vino de lágrima*, is the juice that simply runs off from the weight of the grapes with no additional pressure. Next, the remaining mass of grapes, still primarily intact within their skins, is broken up by the naked foot, or turned with wooden shovels or pikes. The juice thus released is known as *vino medio* and is of good quality, though not as fine as the *vino de corazón* which comes from the first light pressing. Finally, a hard pressing to extract the remaining juice

Vino de cosechero can be purchased from numerous small producers throughout the region.

yields *vino de prensa*, which is coarse, harsh and usually undrinkable. The best fractions of wine are subsequently blended together to result in intensely fruity, colourful red wines with a characteristic peppery prickle in the throat which are famed for drinking young.

While such open stone *lagos* are still used today, more and more growers in the Alavesa are either modernizing their installations individually, or else grouping together into co-operatives of *cosecheros*. The installation of modern stainless steel fermentation tanks, however, does not necessitate a change in methods: the grapes are still fermented in whole bunches, and the wine is drawn off in fractions, blended and sold either in *garrafas*, or, more and more these days, in labelled bottles as *vino de cosechero* or *vino joven de Rioja Alavesa*.

2 VIÑEDOS DEL CONTINO
FINCA SAN GREGORIO
LASERNA-LAGUARDIA
ALAVA
TEL: (941) 10 02 01; FAX: (941) 12 11 14

WINE PRODUCED: Contino Reserva.
VISITS: Mon–Fri 9–13h; 15–19h. Telephone before coming.

The historic Contino estate, under a consortium of owners of which CVNE holds a controlling interest, has since 1979 produced a unique single-estate wine from grapes grown on the 50-ha. vineyard. The advantages of working on such a relatively small scale are evident: the grapes are transported from the vine to the *bodega* in minutes not hours, and with the latest technologies every phase of the vinification cycle can be followed with minute care. The wine is produced from a blend of Tempranillo (38 ha.), Mazuelo (7 ha.) and Graciano (5 ha.). The wines once assembled, age for a minimum of 2 years in new or nearly new French and American *barricas* followed by a minimum of 1 year in bottle prior to release. English spoken.

---

3 COOPERATIVA DE COSECHEROS
LAPUEBLA DE LABARCA (CoVila)
LAPUEBLA DE LABARCA
ALAVA
TEL: (941) 12 72 32

WINE PRODUCED: CoVila Rioja *blanco*; CoVila Rioja *tinto joven*.

VISITS: Mon–Fri 8–13h; 15–18h.

Lapuebla de Labarca is a poor, rambling *pueblo* in the Rioja Alavesa across the river from Fuenmayor with little to offer save the excellence of its young *vinos de cosecheros*.

CoVila is a co-operative of some 70 growers from the village who grouped together in 1988 to invest in a small but modern installation for the production of their own wines from their own grapes grown on 230 ha. of vineyards. Though the equipment is the most up-to-date, the techniques followed are traditional: the whole bunches of grapes, without being de-stemmed, are placed directly into the stainless steel fermentation vats which are closed but not sealed. The grapes ferment from within for 8–12 days. The malolactic fermentation occurs after the separation of the wine from its skins, then the best fractions of wine are assembled and selected to bottle. The classic method of whole grape fermentation produces intensely fruity and aromatic *tinto joven* with a characteristic peppery prickle in the back of the throat which is much loved especially throughout the Basque country.

4

BODEGAS CAMPILLO SA
CTRA DE LOGROÑO, S/N
01300 LAGUARDIA
ALAVA
TEL: (941) 10 08 26; FAX: (941) 10 08 37

WINES PRODUCED: Campillo *tinto* Crianza, Reserva, Gran Reserva.
VISITS: Mon–Fri working hours, by appointment. There is a tasting room for direct sales.
New and striking neo-classical *bodega* located below the medieval town of Laguardia. Campillo is an ultra-modern, up-market *bodega*, with the ambition of producing only Crianza, Reserva and Gran Reserva wines, primarily from its own 85 ha. of Tempranillo vineyards planted in the Rioja Alavesa.

Campillo is impressive, and it represents a new market-led approach to production and sales of wine in the region. For the *bodega* is the concrete manifestation of an already long-established (and highly respected) brand previously produced by Faustino Martínez in its *bodegas* at Oyón. At Campillo, the French and American *barricas* are already in place, as is the impressive and striking bottle store; yet, at the time of writing, the company has not yet produced any wine of its own, nor has the vinification plant even been completed. None the less, given the level of investment, the emphasis on image and prestige, and the historical pedigree and century-old expertise of Faustino Martínez, there is little doubt that in the future fine château-style estate wines will be produced here which will gain their own identity and following.
English, French, German spoken.

LA RIOJA

Casa del Vino

The *Casa del Vino* is the headquarters of an official organization set up under the auspices of the Regional County Council of Alava and the Department of Agriculture for the Basque Government to help winegrowers in the Alava province with technical aspects of viticulture and oenology, as well as to assist them with the promotion and marketing of their wines. As such, it is a great champion of the small individual *cosechero* winegrower in the Rioja Alavesa and in recent years has been active in helping such individuals to produce and market their own wines, rather than to sell either grapes or wines in bulk.

The *Casa del Vino* is located in a lovely stone mansion in the historic centre of Laguardia; behind these time-worn walls is a highly modern and up-to-date laboratory that assists winegrowers with detailed analyses. There is also a small wine museum open to the public, while any who would like to make contact with *cosecheros* can seek advice here.

CASA DEL VINO
PALACIO SAMANIEGO
PLAZUELA DE SAN JUAN
01300 LAGUARDIA
ALAVA

5 BODEGAS ARTADI COSECHEROS
ALAVESES S. COOP.
CTRA DE LOGROÑO, S/N
01300 LAGUARDIA
ALAVA
TEL: (941) 10 01 19

WINES PRODUCED: Artadi *vino joven de Rioja Alavesa blanco, rosado, tinto*; Viña de Gain *tinto* Crianza.
VISITS: Daily, working hours.

Artadi is located directly across the road from Campillo, but the two are worlds apart. Campillo is aiming to occupy the top end of the Rioja market in terms of the image and prestige of its oak-aged wines; Artadi, on the other hand, is a small co-operative of 10 *cosecheros* whose aim is to produce and market collectively *vinos jóvenes*, traditional Alavesa wines produced by whole grape fermentation to be enjoyed without fuss or pretension within their year of production. Such young wines must be tried when in the region, for they can be astoundingly good.

6 BODEGAS DOMECQ SA
CTRA VILLABUENA 9
01340 ELCIEGO
ALAVA
TEL: (941) 10 60 01; FAX: (941) 10 62 35

WINES PRODUCED: Marqués de
Arienzo *blanco*; Marqués de Arienzo
tinto Crianza, Reserva, Gran
Reserva.
VISITS: Mon–Fri 9–13h.
Appointment necessary.

Audiovisual room for visitors.
Bodegas Domecq, owned by the
great sherry producing group, was
founded in 1973 and has done much
pioneering work especially in the
vineyard. The company now has
over 500 ha. of vineyards, mainly
planted on wires. Its wines are well
known outside Spain under the
export label Domecq Domaine.
English spoken.

---

7 VINOS DE LOS HEREDEROS DEL
    MARQUÉS DE RISCAL SA
TORREA 1
01340 ELCIEGO
ALAVA
TEL: (941) 10 60 00; FAX: (941) 10 60 23

WINES PRODUCED: Marqués de
Riscal *tinto* Crianza, Reserva, Gran
Reserva.
VISITS: Mon–Fri 8–12h; 14h30–
16h30. Appointment advisable.
Closed month of August.
The history of the Rioja is
inextricably linked with Marqués de
Riscal, probably the region's oldest
commercial *bodega*, built to the
original French design under
supervision by Jean Pineau in 1868.
A visit to this historic *bodega* is
crucial to gain an understanding of
the development of the region and

its wines.
  Interestingly, when Pineau laid
out the original *bodega*, he also
oversaw the planting of a
considerable amount of Cabernet
Sauvignon alongside Tempranillo,
Graciano and Viura. Riscal has thus
always historically included some
Cabernet in its final assembled
blend. Riscal, at any rate, has a
lengthy history of innovation and of
going its own way. It was a bold
decision initially in 1860 to lay out
the winery along French precepts.
The company went its own way too
in the early 1970s when it
abandoned production of white Rioja
in favour of pioneering new white
wines in the then unknown wine
zone of Rueda.
English, French spoken.

LA RIOJA

8 LA GRANJA NUESTRA SEÑORA DE
REMELLURI
01330 LABASTIDA
ALAVA
TEL: (941) 33 12 74; FAX: (941) 33 14 41
ADMINISTRATIVE OFFICE: CALLE
SARASATE 3, CASA BERAUN, 20300
IRUN, GUIPÚZCOA
TEL: (943) 63 17 10; FAX: (943) 63 08 74

WINE PRODUCED: Remelluri
Reserva.
VISITS: By appointment, working
hours. Open for direct sales Mon–
Fri 11–13h; 16–18h; Sat 10–13h.
There is an informative wine
museum open to visitors.
One of the most beautiful wine
estates in Spain and a highly
regarded *finca* producing a
single-estate Reserva wine of the
highest class and elegance. La
Granja Remelluri is located in a
sheltered position below the Sierra
de Toloño overlooking the Ebro
valley, and there is a medieval
necropolis on the estate. Today the
Rodriguez family has restored this
historical vineyard and there are
now about 58 ha. of vines in
production, planted 600–650 metres
above sea level. The small winery
is extremely well-equipped and
up-to-date with modern
installations, and Telmo Rodriguez
is a young and forward-looking
winemaker of considerable skill.
Only the finest vats of wine from
each year are utilized for the final
blend; the rest is sold off in bulk if
necessary to maintain quality.
    The Granja is located 4 km
outside Labastida off the road to
Rivas de Tereso.
English, French spoken.

La Rioja Baja

1 BODEGAS MUERZA SA
PLAZA VERA Y MAGALLÓN 1
31570 SAN ADRIÁN
NAVARRA
TEL: (948) 22 72 83; FAX: (948) 22 99 99

WINES PRODUCED: Rioja Vega
blanco; Rioja Vega *tinto* Crianza,
Reserva, Gran Reserva.
VISITS: Mon–Fri 9–14h; 15–18h.
Appointment necessary.
There are fewer opportunities for
visiting producers in the southern
Rioja Baja, but this well-regarded
bodega, located in the tiny part of
the Rioja situated in the province
of Navarra, demonstrates that
wines from this overlooked zone
deserve to be taken seriously in
their own right.
English, French spoken.

Taking a break from grape picking on the Contino estate, near Logroño.

Single Estate Wines

Rioja, like Burgundy and Champagne, is historically a blended wine produced from grapes or wines not only from various vineyards, but indeed from different sub-zones and grape varieties, in the past even from different vintage years. This has been a great boon to both producer and consumer, for it has allowed Rioja to establish itself as consistently satisfying, year in and year out.

A new and welcome advance in recent years, however, is the development of the concept of the single-vineyard or château-bottled wine, produced entirely or almost entirely from grapes grown within an estate's own vineyard. The Contino estate, for example, was granted by the Catholic Kings to one Pedro de Samaniego in the sixteenth century in recognition of services rendered to the Crown as a bodyguard. Today the estate is considerably smaller than it once was, but it remains historically intact, a remarkably well-sited *finca* with 50 hectares of vines in production, located on a south-facing, steep bend of the Ebro not far from Laguardia. This sheltered and favourable microclimate results in grapes that are usually the earliest harvested in the Rioja Alavesa. No wonder they are able to produce Contino wines that are always powerful, well-structured and richly satisfying.

Another well-known single estate is La Granja Nuestra Señora de Remelluri. Like Contino, Remelluri is an estate with a historical basis: it was the farm for the Monasterio de Toloño, located high above, on a ridge of the Sierra de Toloño, an extension of the dominant Sierra de Cantabria. Jaime Rodriguez, a Basque businessman, purchased the farmhouse and 15 hectares of vineyards in 1968 and has since then painstakingly purchased additional plots in order to piece together the historical estate. High-altitude terraced vineyards, abandoned as uneconomical, have been

reclaimed not simply as part of the reconstruction process, but primarily because such vineyards, planted on rugged calcareous terrain, are capable of producing grapes that are finer, more aromatic and characterful than grapes grown on flatter, richer alluvial plains, even if the resulting yields are by comparison minuscule. The finely perfumed, elegant wines of Remelluri demonstrate the value of such an approach.

Today both Contino and Remelluri are making individual and remarkable wines, each a true expression of its respective microclimate, terrain, history and winemaking philosophies. The Marqués de Murrieta estate, though not yet wholly self-sufficient in grapes, aims to be so within this decade; other properties with future single-estate ambitions include Baron de Ley, Amézola de la Mora and Bodegas Campillo.

Restaurantes, Hoteles y Paradores

La Rioja Alta

1
HOTEL CARLTON RIOJA
GRAN VÍA DEL REY DON JUAN
   CARLOS 1, 5
26002 LOGROÑO
LA RIOJA
TEL: (941) 24 21 00; FAX: (941) 24 35 02

Logroño's best hotel is a modern 4-star situated in the heart of the city and has a well-regarded restaurant serving local foods, such as *chuletillas al sarmiento, pochas a la riojana, pimientos rellenos, bacalao a la riojana,* together with an extensive list of Riojas from virtually all the principal *bodegas.*
Hotel **Expensive**
Restaurant **Moderate**

2
RESTAURANTE LA MERCED
MARQUÉS DE SAN NICOLÁS 109
26002 LOGROÑO
LA RIOJA
TEL: (941) 22 11 66

Closed Sun eve.
The finest and most stylish restaurant in the region is located in the old part of town in the splendid mansion of the Marqués de Covarrubias. Here in an elegant setting, Lorenzo Cañas offers a stylish repertoire of dishes mainly based on traditional and seasonal foods of the region: *txangurro gratinado, lomo de merluza con salsa de pimientos, costillas de cordero lechal al horno.* Extensive

selection of the finest wines of Rioja, including well-kept old and rare vintages.
Expensive

---

3 RESTAURANTE CACHETERO
CALLE LAUREL 3
26002 LOGROÑO
LA RIOJA
TEL: (941) 22 84 63

Closed Sun.
Old favourite on this popular drinking street, a cut above some of its more basic eating houses. Has been satisfying people of Logroño for nearly a century with a well-loved formula of mainly local Riojan specialities together with some innovative dishes.
Moderate

---

4 CASA MATUTE
CALLE LAUREL 6
26002 LOGROÑO
LA RIOJA
TEL: (941) 22 00 15

Simple, basic home-cooked foods, served without fuss or pretension: *pochas a la riojana, bacalao al ajoarriero, pollo a la riojana, cuajada*. Decent house wine.
Inexpensive

---

5 MERENDERO LOS 4 ARCOS
CALLE BAJADA DEL VALLE 1
BRIONES
LA RIOJA

Small and typical, this popular eating house is virtually built into the old town walls of the hill-top *pueblo*. Menu is classic foods of the region: *patatas a la riojana, revuelto de ajos, chuletillas al sarmiento*, the latter cooked over an enormous fire in the dining room.
Inexpensive

---

6 MESÓN MERCHE
CALLE MAYOR 2
26220 OLLAURI
LA RIOJA
TEL: (941) 33 80 86

Closed Wed.
Pleasant, rustic wood-panelled dining room in this important wine town of the Rioja Alta, serving simple homecooked foods: *pochas*

LA RIOJA

con chorizo, menestra de verduras, chiperones en su tinta, cordero asado.
Inexpensive

---

7 HOTEL LOS AGUSTINOS
CALLE SAN AGUSTÍN 2
26200 HARO
LA RIOJA
TEL: (941) 31 13 08, 31 15·62;
    FAX: (941) 30 31 48

The historic San Agustín convent, founded in 1373, has recently been converted into a luxurious and well-appointed 4-star private hotel with 54 double rooms and probably makes the most comfortable base for exploring the Rioja wine country. The atmospheric dining room is noted for its fine Riojan cuisine – *patatas a la riojana, revuelto de ajos con bacalao, cordero asado, truchas riojana, melocotón en almibar* – together with an extensive selection of the wines of the zone.
Expensive

---

8 HOTEL ITURRIMURRI SL
CARRETERRA N232
26200 HARO
LA RIOJA
TEL: (941) 31 12 13; FAX: (941) 31 17 21

This simple 3-star motel, located just south of the town on the main road to Logroño, has expanded in recent years and now has much improved facilities, including a swimming pool and tennis court. The restaurant serves mainly regional as well as some international foods, accompanied by a good selection of wines of Rioja.
Moderate

---

9 RESTAURANTE BEETHOVEN I Y II
CALLE SANTO TOMÁS 3-5-8
26200 HARO
LA RIOJA
TEL: (941) 31 00 18, 31 11 81

Closed Mon eve, Tue.
There are now two separate establishments across the lane from each other: the original *restaurante/bar/mesón* is located in the old-style house (on the right looking up towards the church). It is more rustic and informal, a long-standing Haro institution noted above all for its splendid array of bar-top *tapas*. Beethoven II is a little smarter and more comfortable in atmosphere. But the

foods are the same in both: absolutely authentic and including local specialities such as *menestra de verduras, cocido de alubias y caparrones, sopa Beethoven, setas silvestres, caza, cordero lechal asado,* *rabo al vino, pescados y mariscos.* The wine list is extensive and particularly strong on Reservas and Gran Reservas from Haro, while the house wine is own-produced. **Moderate**

10

CASA TERETE
LUCRECIA ARANA 17
26200 HARO
LA RIOJA
TEL: (941) 31 00 23

Closed Sun eve, Mon.
Terete is a Haro landmark: a classic *horno de asar* open for business since 1867. Little has changed, we imagine, since that auspicious date: the wood-fired baker's oven is downstairs by the entrance, while upstairs you eat an unchanging menu off scrubbed wooden trestles: *alubias con chorizo, menestra de verduras, morcilla, chorizo,* followed by earthenware *cazuelas* of the most tender and succulent *cordero lechal asado.* These are the true, simple foods of the Rioja, to accompany an extensive selection of wines from virtually all the *bodegas* of Haro. **Inexpensive to Moderate**

11

LA KIKA
CALLE SANTO TOMÁS 9
26200 HARO
LA RIOJA
TEL: (941) 31 14 47

Open midday only, except weekends. Evenings by reservation. Closed Sun; September.
Notwithstanding that this tiny eating house has a kitchen no bigger than in most homes and only a half dozen or so tables, it is a firm favourite with the town's discriminating *bodegueros*, many of whom recommend it as the best restaurant in town for the true foods of the region served simply and without fuss. Menu changes with the seasons and market, but specialities include: *acelgas con patatas, bonito con tomate, lechecillas, cordero asado, torrijas.* Essential to book or to arrive early. Good *tinto joven* house wine. **Inexpensive**

---

12 MESÓN EL PEREGRINO
ZUMALACÁRREGUI 18
26250 SANTO DOMINGO DE LA
CALZADA
LA RIOJA
TEL: (941) 34 02 02

Closed Mon.
Basically simple but authentic
foods of the region in this much
visited pilgrim town.
Inexpensive to Moderate

Parador

P PARADOR NACIONAL DE SANTO
DOMINGO
PLAZA DEL SANTO 3
26250 SANTO DOMINGO DE LA
CALZADA
LA RIOJA
TEL: (941) 34 03 00; FAX: (941) 34 03 25

Atmospheric and historic *parador*
actually installed in the original
Hospital de Peregrinos founded by
Santo Domingo de la Calzada. Has
recently undergone extensive
renovation.
Moderate

La Rioja Alavesa

1 MESÓN LA CUEVA
CALLE CONCEPCIÓN 15
01320 OYÓN
ALAVA
TEL: (941) 11 00 22

Closed Sun eve, Mon.
Another old favourite, located just

4 km out of Logroño in this
important wine town, serving the
classic foods of the Rioja: *menestra
de verduras, merluza a la plancha*
and *lechazo asado* cooked in the
wood-fired *horno de asar*.
Moderate

---

2 HOSTAL MARIXA
SANCHO ABARCA 8
01300 LAGUARDIA
ALAVA
TEL: (941) 10 01 65; 10 02 02

Closed Jan.
This friendly hotel-restaurant with
10 rooms would make a good quiet
base for exploring the wine

country. The comfortable old dining
room has views on one side of the
town walls of Laguardia, on the
other of the vineyards of the Rioja
Alavesa. Restaurant serves both
traditional Basque and Riojan
foods: *merluza a la bilbaina, merluza
a la vasca, patatas con chorizo,
cabrito asado al horno*. House wine

comes from the local co-op, while there is a good small list of Reserva and Gran Reserva wines.
Moderate

---

3 EL BODEGÓN
FRONTÍN 31
01330 LABASTIDA
ALAVA
TEL: (941) 33 10 27

Labastida is a small but atmospheric and charming wine town, famed for its grand old mansions decorated with noble *escudos*. This simple restaurant is located in such a *caserón*, and serves simple but tasty foods: *pochas a la riojana, patatas con chorizo, chuletillas al sarmiento* and own-produced *vino de cosechero*.
Inexpensive

La Rioja Baja

1 HOTEL VICTORIA
PASEO DE LA CONSTITUCIÓN 97
26580 ARNEDO
LA RIOJA
TEL: (941) 38 01 00; FAX: (941) 38 10 50

Comfortable hotel located in typical wine town with restaurant serving local foods: *lomo con pimientos, patatas con chorizo, espárragos* accompanied by the wines of the zone.
Moderate

---

2 CASA SOPITAS
CARRERA 4
26580 ARNEDO
LA RIOJA
TEL: (941) 38 02 66

Closed Sun.
This famous old restaurant has recently been refurbished, but it retains its unique *bodega* atmosphere, and serves classic foods of the Rioja Baja: *espárragos, revuelto de ajos tiernos, pimientos rellenos, cordero asado* and a good selection of local wines.
Moderate

LA RIOJA

P

Parador

PARADOR NACIONAL DE CALAHORRA
PASEO MERCADAL, S/N
26500 CALAHORRA
LA RIOJA
TEL: (941) 13 03 58; FAX: (941) 13 51 39

Newly-constructed *parador* in the Roman town of Calahorra, and a good base for exploration of the

Rioja Baja. Restaurant is noted for its regional foods, especially based on vegetables for which the zone is famous: *menestra de verduras, espárragos, pimientos rellenos,* accompanied by wines of the Rioja.

Moderate

Tomar Unas Copas: Stop for a Drink; Stop for a Bite

The Rioja is a great region for drinking and eating, for the tradition of the *'chiquiteo'* is a long-established one. A *'chiquito'* is a small measure of wine, served by the tumbler in any number of bars throughout the region, accompanied always by a selection of bar-top *banderillas* or *tapas*.

In Logroño, head first for the Calle Laurel, a small alley literally lined with bars and *mesóns*, vying with one another to serve the best house wine and nibbles. Many bars specialize, such as Bar El Cid for its superb *setas a la plancha*, Bar Blanco y Negro for *anchoas*, or Bar Simpatia for *calamares fritas y patatas bravas*.

In Haro, the area to head for is the zone known as *'La Herradura'*, located in the old part of town between the church of Santo Tomás and the Plaza de la Paz. This is an area of corner bars, some little more than stand-up watering-holes. Yet all serve good wines by the glass as well as both hot and cold *tapas*. Our favourite here is the ever popular Bar Beethoven.

House wine in such bars is often *tinto joven*, purchased from *cosecheros* and poured from unlabelled bottles. It is considered *the* wine *par excellence* for the *'chiquiteo'*. Remember, though, that almost all bars also keep a selection of open wines from superior bottles on hand which are almost always worth paying the few extra *pesetas* for. Ask for a *'tinto especial'*.

1

BAR OÑATE
PLAZA DE LA PAZ
26200 HARO
LA RIOJA

Our favourite street hangout, the place to nurse a *café cortado*, or have a glass of wine and a nibble of *tortilla* in early evening, sitting outdoors watching the town go by.

Los Campings

LA PLAYA CAMPING
LOGROÑO
TEL: (941) 25 22 53

NAVARRETE CAMPING
NAVARRETE
TEL: (941) 44 01 69

Open all year.

HARO CAMPING
HARO
TEL: (941) 31 27 37

Open all year.
Family-run, swimming pool.

Vinos y Comestibles: Stop to Taste; Stop to Buy

PALACIO DEL VINO
AVENIDA DE BURGOS 136–142
26006 LOGROÑO
LA RIOJA
TEL: (941) 22 82 00, 22 82 36;
    FAX: (941) 20 13 84

This large and important 'wine warehouse' stocks wines from virtually all the main Rioja houses, and is able to sell them, so it claims, at the same prices as ex-*bodega*. Located on the Burgos road on the outskirts of town, this may be the best place to stock up on wines of the region to bring back home. Sales only by cases of 6 or 12 bottles. English spoken.

LA CATEDRAL DEL VINO
PORTALES 25
26002 LOGROÑO
LA RIOJA
TEL: (941) 25 41 44

In the old part of town near the cathedral, a good small wine shop with an excellent selection of Riojas, as well as some conserves and typical products.

JUAN GONZALEZ MUGA
CALLE CASTILLA 3
26200 HARO
LA RIOJA
TEL: (941) 31 14 25; FAX: (941) 30 33 60

Open seven days a week, mornings only.
Most traditional speciality wine shop in the zone with an extensive selection of more than 2000 wines,

LA RIOJA

as well as a variety of conserved vegetables and other typical products of the Rioja. English, French spoken.

SELECCIÓN VINOS DE RIOJA
ISABEL GUTIERREZ ORTIZ
PLAZA DE LA PAZ 5
26200 HARO
LA RIOJA
TEL: (941) 30 30 17

On Haro's main square, this stylish shop has a good selection of Riojas, as well as an excellent range of conserved vegetables and fruit. There is a 'wine bar' area where wines can be sampled, though this is not always open.

Las Botas: Wine Skins

BOTAS RIOJA
FÉLIX BARBERO BOTERÍA
SAGASTA 8
26002 LOGROÑO
LA RIOJA
TEL: (941) 24 86 33

Félix Barbero's family have been *boteros* for three generations. Come to the workshop by Logroño's old iron bridge for a selection of authentic hand-made wine skins.

BOTERÍA LAS TRES A
LA VENTANILLA 15
26200 HARO
LA RIOJA

Production and sale of high-quality wine skins.

¡Fiesta! Wine and Other Related Celebrations

mid-May	Fiesta de Santo Domingo de la Calzada	Santo Domingo de la Calzada
29 June	Batalla del Vino	Haro
early Sept	Fiesta de la Vendimia	Cenicero
19 Sept	Fiesta de San Mateo	Logroño

La Batalla del Vino

Haro's famous annual 'wine battle' is one of the country's more unusual wine festivals. Each year on the morning of 29 June, participants, known as *romeros*, make their way out of town to the hill hamlet of San Felices in the Riscos de Bilibio, dressed all in white, wearing red bandanas. Once there and after a blessing in the church, they emerge to a riotous wine battle, spraying or throwing wine at one another from any number of containers or receptacles: leather wine skins, wine-filled balloons, barrels, even sprayers used by growers to treat their vines. Needless to say, great quantities manage also to be consumed, so that by the time the *romeros* return (unsteadily) to Haro, their white clothing is stained a majestic shade of purple. The drinking continues throughout the day, fortified by great bowls of *caracoles* – snails stewed in tomatoes and wine, spiked liberally with hot chillis to encourage thirst. Then, so fortified, the youths of the town make their way in the afternoon to the Plaza de Toros to pit their wits against *vaquillas* – young fighting calves let loose in the public ring.

Y para saber más Additional Information

Dirección General de Turismo
Calle Villamediana 17
26002 Logroño
La Rioja
tel: (941) 29 11 00

Exposicion e Información
   Turistica
Carpa de El Espolón
26002 Logroño
La Rioja
tel: (941) 29 11 92
Permanent tourist exhibition and
   information centre set up in the
   central Espolón park.

Departamento de Cultura y
   Turismo
Delegacion Territorial de Alava
Gobierno Vasco
Calle San Prudencio 8
01005 Gasteiz-Vitoria
Alava
(For information on the Rioja
   Alavesa)

Consejo Regulador de Rioja
Jorge Vigón 51
26003 Logroño
La Rioja
tel: (941) 24 11 99; fax: (941)
   25 35 02

Grupo Exportadores de Vinos
   Rioja
Gran Vía 7
26003 Logroño
La Rioja
tel: (941) 25 75 55

GLOSSARY

Acero inoxidable Stainless steel, a material widely used in modern *bodegas* for fermentation deposits and storage vats. Stainless steel deposits allow greater control over the various phases of fermentation, particularly through the control of temperature.

Acido Acid.

Aguardiente Distilled spirit.

Aguardiente de orujo Spirit produced from distillation of mass of grape skins and pips left over after pressing and/or fermentation.

Aguja Slight carbonation, usually the result of uncompleted malolactic fermentation. **Vino de aguja** Young, fresh style of wine, usually relatively low in alcohol and with slight carbonic prickle.

Almendrado Bitter almond flavour.

Amagro Bitter.

Añada Year in which a wine is made.

Añejo Wine which has been subjected to an ageing process.

Arroba Measurement equivalent to 16 litres.

Arrope Sweet syrup made by boiling grape must to evaporate it.

Aspero Sour astringency.

Azufre Sulphur.

Barrica Oak cask. Term has come to be used particularly in relation to oak casks containing 225 litres, used for traditional wood ageing of wines.

Blanco White. **Vino blanco** White wine.

Bocoy Large oak or chestnut cask containing up to 600 litres utilized for the storage of wines. Does not usually impart wood flavours to the wine.

Bodega Wine establishment or firm; also, literally, the cellar where wines are made or stored. May also signify a wine shop.

Bomba 16-litre bulbous glass container utilized for 'sunning' wines outdoors for the production of certain *vinos rancios*.

Bota Leather wine skin; also a large oak cask, usually containing upwards of 500 litres.

Caldos Wines.

Capataz Cellar-master.

Cava Spanish *denominación* for natural sparkling wine produced to stringent guidelines utilizing the classic method of secondary fermentation and expulsion of the lees within the same bottle from grapes grown in defined wine zones of Catalunya, Aragón, Navarra, La Rioja, Alava and Valencia.

Clarete Light red or dark pink wine.

Comarca District or sub-zone.

Consejo Regulador Board of control for each *denominación de origen*, responsible primarily for supervizing the control of wines under its jurisdiction according to a specific set of rules and regulations.

Control de calidad Quality control, a constant supervision to ensure at all phases of production that a wine is developing as it should.

Cooperativa Wine co-operative.

Cosecha Harvest. **Cosechero** Wine grower.

Criadera Literally nursery. In Jerez, term signifies a series of butts from which wine is drawn to refresh a *solera* or another *criadera*.

Crianza Maturation of wine. Term is used generally to indicate any wine that has been submitted to wood ageing process (as opposed to wines that are *sin crianza* – unaged and produced to be consumed immediately).

Cru French word signifying growth or superior-quality wine, usually indicated as from a single vineyard. This term is increasingly used in Spain to describe single-estate wines.

Cuerpo Body.

Degustación Tasting, sampling.

Deposito Container for storage of wine.

Doble pasta Cutting or blending wine, produced through fermentation on double amount of grape skins for maximum extract of colour, tannin and alcohol.

Dulce Sweet.

Duro Hard.

Elaboración Winemaking and further phases of maturation.

Enología Oenology, the science of wine-making.

Estabilización Stabilization, achieved through a number of processes (filtration, centrifugation, sterile-bottling, pasteurization).

Etiqueta Label.

Fermentación alcoholica Alcoholic fermentation, the natural process, in winemaking, of converting grape sugars to alcohol through the biological interaction of yeasts.

Fermentación malolactica Malolactic fermentation, a natural bacterial process whereby tart malic acid is converted into softer lactic acid.

Flor Particular strain of surface yeast prevalent in sherry zone essential to the development of the character of *fino* wines.

Garrafa Large glass carboy, usually containing 16 litres. Usual method of purchasing bulk wines for home consumption in Spain itself.

Generoso; vino generoso Fortified wine; produced in many areas, including Jerez de la Frontera, Condado de Huelva, Rueda and Tarragona.

Girasol; girapaleta Catalan invention utilized in the production of Cava for the mechanical process of riddling to eliminate sediment after secondary fermentation in the bottle.

Granel, en The term *en granel* as applied to wine signifies sales in bulk not bottle. 'Bulk' may mean in quantities as large as container loads, or as small as 16-litre *garrafas*.

Gran Reserva Term generally utilized for Spain's greatest aged wines. Signifies that wines have undergone lengthy minimum ageing requirements in both wooden cask and bottle.

Granvas Sparkling wine produced by secondary fermentation in sealed stainless steel vats, then transferred to the bottle under pressure.

Hectárea Hectare, a land measurement of 10,000 square metres; equivalent to 2.47 acres.

Hectolitro Hectolitre, a liquid volume measurement of 100 litres, or about 22 gallons. A hectolitre of wine is equivalent roughly to a metric quintal (100 kg).

Holandas Alcoholic grape spirit.

Injerto Vine graft.

Joven Young. **Vino joven** Young wine, made for immediate consumption: usually relatively low in alcohol and preferably fermented at low temperature to preserve fruit and aroma.

Lagar, lago Signifies both wine press (usually old-fashioned, wooden screw-type) and the traditional open-topped fermentation trough.

Lágrima; mosto de lágrima Free-run juice, obtained without the application of mechanical pressure.

Vino de lágrima Wine obtained from this must.

Levadura Yeast.

Licoroso Strong; rich in alcohol.

Vino licoroso Wine, usually sweet, which has been fortified by the addition of grape alcohol.

Maceración Maceration, the process whereby the grape must is left in contact with its mass of grape skins and other solid matter to extract colour and tannin.

Maceración carbónica Carbonic maceration, a process of vinification whereby whole grapes are fermented intact in sealed vats under a blanket of carbon dioxide to result in light, intensely fruity wines usually meant to be consumed young.

Madera Wood. **Madera nueva** New wood, usually oak, which imparts intense and particular flavours.

Madura Mature.

Mistela Sweet partially fermented grape must arrested by the addition of grape alcohol; usually added to *vinos rancios* to sweeten them.

Mosto Fresh grape must that has not yet undergone fermentation.

Orujo Solid residue of grape skins and pips left over after pressing and/or fermentation; also fiery spirit produced through the distillation of this residue (similar to French *marc* and Italian *grappa*).

Oxidación Oxidation. A wine becomes oxidized through contact with air. **Oxidado** Wine which has oxidized.

Pago Vineyard or estate.

Pasa Raisin. **Uvas pasas** Grapes that have been left to dry and shrivel to concentrate sugar.

Prensa Press.

Remontaje The process during fermentation of pumping and spraying must from the bottom of the vat back up to the top to keep the *sombrero* of grape skins steeped in juice and to aid in extraction of colour and tannin.

Reserva Fine aged wine which has undergone minimum ageing according to specific criteria in both wooden cask and bottle.

Retrogusto Aftertaste.

Roble Oak; wood from trees belonging to the genus *Quercus ruber*. In Spain, the preferred wood for the ageing of wines is American white oak, though French oak from the Limousin and elsewhere is also used.

Rosado Rosé wine.

Sangría Drink made from red wine, fruit juice, sugar, fruit and brandy.

Sarmiento Vine shoot. In the wine regions, meats are often cooked over vine shoots (*al sarmiento*).

Seco Dry.

Socio Member, usually of a co-operative; grape-grower member who sells his crop to the co-operative to be made into wine.

Solera system System of dynamic ageing of wines whereby older wines are continually refreshed with younger wines. The *solera* itself is the final series of butts from which mature wines are extracted to be bottled and sold.

Tina Large fermentation vat (usually wood).

Tinaja Earthenware fermentation and storage deposit.

Tinto, vino tinto Red wine.

Típico, vino típico Wine that is typical of its region of production, which demonstrates the characteristics of its particular zone or *denominación*.

Trasiega Racking, the process of decanting wine off its lees or barrel sediment into a clean cask or other container.

Uva Grape.

Variedad Grape variety.

Vendimia Wine harvest.

Verde Green. **Vino verde** Wine with pronounced acidity (can be either red or white).

Vid Vine.

Viejo Old; aged.

Viña, viñedo Single vineyard. The name of a particular *viña*, however, does not necessarily signify a single vineyard wine.

Vino Wine.

Vino de mesa; vino de pasto Ordinary everyday table wine.

Vino rancio Traditional, aged,

maderized style of wine, usually fortified, often sweetened with *mistela*, and aged either in wooden casks or outdoors in loosely-stoppered glass jars.

Viticultura Viticulture.

Yema, mosto de yema Juice extracted generally from a light first pressing.

SELECT BIBLIOGRAPHY

Begg, Desmond, *Traveller's Wine Guide Spain* (London: Philip Clark, 1989)

Brown, Gordon, *Handbook of Fine Brandies* (London: Garamond, 1990)

Casas, Penelope, *The Foods and Wines of Spain* (Harmondsworth: Penguin Books, 1985)

Ellingham, Mark, and Fisher, John, *The Rough Guide to Spain* (Bromley: Harrap-Columbus, 1990)

España 1991 (Barcelona: Guía del Viajero, 1991)

Fodor's Spain (New York and London: Fodor's Travel Publications, 1991)

Gibson, Ian, *Fire in the Blood: The New Spain* (London: Faber & Faber and BBC Books, 1992)

Guía BMW Gastronomía y Turismo en España (Madrid: Club de Gourmets, 1991)

Guía de Vinos Gourmets (Madrid: Club de Gourmets, 1991)

Hernández, Manuel Ruiz, and Koch, Sigfrido, *One Hundred Years of Rioja Alta* (Haro: La Rioja Alta, 1990)

Jeffs, Julian, *Sherry* (London: Faber & Faber, 1982)

Johnson, Hugh, *The Story of Wine* (London: Mandarin Paperbacks, 1991)

La Rioja de Los Vinos y Las Bodegas (Madrid: Ediciones EUHA, 1989)

Larraina, Miguel González, *Viñas y Vinos de Alava* (Vitoria-Gasteiz: Diputación Foral de Alava, 1990)

Lord, Tony, *The New Wines of Spain* (London: Christopher Helm, 1988)

Metcalfe, Charles, and McWhirter, Kathryn, *The Wines of Spain and Portugal* (London: Salamander Books, 1988)

Mey, Wim, *Sherry* (Rhoon: Asjoburo, 1988)

Michelin España Portugal 1990 (Clermont-Ferrand: Michelin, 1990)

Michelin Spain (Clermont-Ferrand: Michelin, 1987)

Millon, Marc and Kim, *The Wine and Food of Europe: An Illustrated Guide* (Exeter: Webb & Bower, 1982)

—— *The Wine Roads of Europe* (London: Robert Nicholson, 1983)

Morris, Jan, *Spain* (Harmondsworth: Penguin Books, 1982)

Read, Jan, *Sherry and the Sherry Bodegas* (London: Sotheby's Publications, 1988)

—— *The Mitchell Beazley Pocket Guide to Spanish Wines* (London: Mitchell Beazley, 1988)

—— *The Wines of Spain* (London: Faber & Faber, 1986)

Read, Jan, Manjón, Maite, and Johnson, Hugh, *The Wine and Food of Spain* (London: Weidenfeld and Nicolson, 1987)

Sevilla, María José, *Life and Food in the Basque Country* (London: Weidenfeld and Nicolson, 1989)

Sordo, Enrique, *Cómo Conocer la Cocina Española* (Barcelona: Editorial Argos Vergara, 1980)

Torres, Miguel A., *Manual de los Vinos de Cataluña* (Madrid: Ediciones Penthalon, 1981)

Wheaton, Kathleen (ed.), *Spain* (Singapore: Apa Publications, 1989)

ACKNOWLEDGEMENTS

Many people have helped us considerably in the research, compilation and production of this book. Spain is fortunate to have such an active, enthusiastic and helpful Institute for Foreign Trade (ICEX-UK) which serves, among many other activities, to promote the country's wines and foods. We would particularly like to thank Jeremy Watson of *Wines from Spain*, María José Sevilla of *Foods from Spain*, and Graham Hines of *The Sherry Institute of Spain*.

As always, we have received a great deal of help and assistance from members of the British wine trade. I would particularly like to single out for special thanks John Hawes of Laymont & Shaw Ltd of Truro, and my good friend Tim Garland of Direct Wine Suppliers.

In Spain itself, we owe an enormous debt to the scores of wine producers who received us so kindly, gave us their time, supplied wines for tasting, and taught us much about not only the wines of Spain but also their regions, too. Indeed, they certainly made this project an extremely enjoyable one to research and we thank them again for all their help and generosity. Also in Spain, we owe particular thanks to Iñigo Cañedo of the Rioja Wine Exporters Group and to Don Bartolomé Vergara of the *Asociación de Criadores Exportadores de Vinos de Jerez* (ACES).

We would also like to thank Brittany Ferries for assistance with ferry crossings.

Finally, we would like to thank our editor John Boothe for his support and assistance over the past years.

INDEX

INDEX

INDEX